FOR THE PRESIDENT'S EYES ONLY

CHRISTOPHER ANDREW is Professor of Modern and Contemporary History at Cambridge University, a Fellow of the Royal Historical Society, former visiting Professor of National Security at Harvard University, and guest lecturer at numerous universities. He is the author of *Secret Service: The Making of the British Intelligence Community* and (with Oleg Gordievsky) of *KGB: The Inside Story*, the book that revealed the identity of the fifth man, as well as chair of the British Study Group on Intelligence and co-editor of *Intelligence and National Security*. Professor Andrew is also a frequent presenter of BBC TV and radio programmes on history and world affairs.

Further praise for *For the President's Eyes Only*:

'Christopher Andrew has written far and away the best study of how American presidents have used – and misused – secret intelligence. The evidence is solid, the argument persuasive. It should be required reading for presidents, national security advisors, and Congressional watchdogs.'

PROFESSOR WARREN KIMBALL, Rutgers University

'This is the most important book ever written about American intelligence. Andrew has done what hardly any other studies do: tell how the intelligence gathered by so many people at such risk and cost is actually used by the most powerful men in the world.'

DAVID KAHN, author of *The Codebreakers* and *Hitler's Spies*

'One of the world's most eminent scholars of intelligence has brought us a fascinating, deeply researched and authoritative account of the important and largely unknown relationship between American presidents and their intelligence services, throwing new light on American history and contemporary foreign policy.' MICHAEL BESCHLOSS, author of *The Crisis Years: Kennedy and Kruschev, 1960–1963*

D0267155

'An engrossing account of how presidents use intelligence . . . Andrew not only illuminates the history of intelligence, but implicitly answers a question much in doubt these days: did intelligence matter in the Cold War? Given that Aldrich Ames clearly didn't help the Soviet Union win the Cold War, many have wondered if the CIA *et al* were but a sideshow. Andrew offers numerous examples of just how pivotal intelligence was.'

ZACHARY KARABELL, *Boston Globe*

'The flavour of this book and its achievements cannot be adequately captured by way of a thumbnail summary. It has a great sweep and a first-class narrative engine. Read him on the Cuban missile crisis, for the drama of espionage at one of the Cold War's break points. *For the President's Eyes Only* stands as the best available history of US intelligence and a fascinating portrait of US presidents at work in the secret world.'

WESLEY WARK, *Toronto Globe and Mail*

'Highly readable . . . Christopher Andrew stuffs his account of the US Presidents and their spies with engaging anecdotes. And so he should. For all the gee-whiz technology of satellite photography and electronics intelligence, the human factor kept intruding.'

MARTIN WALKER *Literary Review*

'Lively and authoritative . . . Andrew has an eye for telling detail and a good sense of balance. He appreciates that the CIA is neither a magic wand nor a bunch of thugs, that intelligence is critical to wise foreign policy, and that presidents are all too human.'

EVAN THOMAS *Washington Post Book World*

'Admirably constructed and carefully researched. '

RONALD PAYNE *The Times*

'A finely detailed story of American presidents and their relationship to the world of espionage and intelligence . . . Andrew clearly knows his way around the dark corridors of the history of espionage . . . [and] has a sharp sense of the importance and impact of intelligence and a flair for creating a colorful historical tapestry.'

Kirkus

For the President's Eyes Only

Secret Intelligence and the American Presidency from Washington to Bush

CHRISTOPHER ANDREW

HarperCollins*Publishers*

HarperCollins*Publishers*
77-85 Fulham Palace Road,
Hammersmith, London W6 8JB

This paperback edition 1996
3 5 7 9 8 6 4 2

First published in Great Britain by
HarperCollins*Publishers* 1995

ISBN 0 00 638071 9

Set in Century Light

Printed and bound in Great Britain by
Caledonian International
Book Manufacturing Ltd, Glasgow

CONTENTS

ABBREVIATIONS AND ACRONYMS USED IN THE TEXT

ABM	antiballistic missile
ACIS	Arms Control Intelligence Staff
AEC	Atomic Energy Commission
AFSA	Armed Forces Security Agency
AFSAC	Armed Forces Security Agency Committee
AFSS	Air Force Security Service
APL	American Protective League
ASA	Army Security Agency
ASARS	Advanced Synthetic Aperture Radar System
BDA	battle damage assessment
BI	Bureau of Investigation (predecessor of FBI)
BSC	British Security Coordination
CIA	Central Intelligence Agency
CIC	Counter-Intelligence Corps
CIG	Central Intelligence Group
CINCPAC	Commander in Chief Pacific
COI	(Office of) Coordinator of Information
COMINT	intelligence derived from intercepted communications
CRP	Committee for the Re-election of the President (irreverently known as CREEP)
DCI	Director of Central Intelligence
DDI	Deputy Director for Intelligence (CIA)
DDO	Deputy Director for Operations (CIA)
DDP	Deputy Director for Plans (CIA)
DI	Directorate of Intelligence (CIA)
DIA	Defense Intelligence Agency
DNI	Director of Naval Intelligence
DST	Direction de la Surveillance du Territoire (French security service)
DO	Directorate of Operations (CIA)
ELINT	electronic intelligence
EO	Executive Order

Ex-Comm	Executive Committee (NSC)
FBI	Federal Bureau of Investigation
G-2	(i) U.S. Military Intelligence (ii) Assistant Chief of Staff for Intelligence, Army General Staff (iii) chief of intelligence in an army command
GC&CS	Government Code and Cypher School (predecessor of GCHQ)
GCHQ	Government Communications Head-Quarters (British SIGINT agency)
GRU	Soviet Military Intelligence
HUAC	House Un-American Activities Committee
HUMINT	human-source intelligence (espionage)
IAC	Intelligence Advisory Committee
ICBM	intercontinental ballistic missile
ICG	Intelligence Coordinating Group
IIC	Interdepartmental Intelligence Committee
IOB	Intelligence Oversight Board
IMF	International Monetary Fund
IMINT	imagery intelligence
INF	intermediate-range nuclear forces
JCS	Joint Chiefs of Staff
JIC	Joint Intelligence Committee
JSTARS	Joint Surveillance and Attack Radar System
KGB	Soviet intelligence and security service
KHAD	Afghan security service
MACV	U.S. Military Assistance Command Vietnam
MI1c	British foreign intelligence agency (predecessor of SIS)
MI5	British security service
MI6	alternative designation for SIS (UK)
MI-8	U.S. military SIGINT agency
MID	Military Intelligence Division
MIRV	multiple independently targetable reentry vehicle
MPLA	Popular Movement for the Liberation of Angola
MRBM	medium-range ballistic missile
NASA	National Aeronautics and Space Administration
NATO	North Atlantic Treaty Organization
NIA	National Intelligence Authority
NIC	National Intelligence Council
NIE	National Intelligence Estimate
NIO	National Intelligence Officer
NKVD	predecessor of KGB
NPIC	National Photographic Interpretation Center
NRO	National Reconnaissance Office

NSA	National Security Agency
NSAM	National Security Action Memorandum
NSC	National Security Council
NSCID	National Security Council Intelligence Directive
NSD	National Security Directive
NSDD	National Security Decision Directive
NSDM	National Security Decision Memorandum
NSPG	National Security Planning Group
NSR	National Security Review
NSSM	National Security Study Memorandum
NTM	National Technical Means
OB	order of battle
OCI	Office of Current Intelligence (CIA)
OMB	Office of Management and Budget
ONE	Office of National Estimates
ONI	Office of Naval Intelligence
OP-20-G	U.S. Navy SIGINT agency
OPC	Office of Policy Coordination
OPNAV	Naval Operations, Washington
ORE	Office of Reports and Estimates (CIA)
OSO	Office of Special Operations (CIA)
OSS	Office of Strategic Services
OTP	one-time pad
PA	principal agent
PDB	president's daily brief
PDF	Panama Defense Force
PFIAB	President's Foreign Intelligence Advisory Board
PHOTINT	photographic intelligence
PIU	Photographic Interpretation Unit (UK)
PLO	Palestine Liberation Organization
PRC	Policy Review Committee
PRG	Policy Review Group
R&A	Research and Analysis Branch (OSS)
RYAN	Raketno-Yadernoye Napadenie (Nuclear Missile Attack)
SALT	Strategic Arms Limitation Talks
SAM	surface-to-air missile
SCC	Special Coordination Committee
SDI	Strategic Defense Initiative
SI	Secret Intelligence Branch (OSS)
SIDS	Secondary Image Dissemination System
SIGINT	intelligence derived from interception and analysis of signals (includes COMINT, ELINT and TELINT)

SIS	Secret Intelligence Service (UK)
SIS	Signal Intelligence Service (U.S. Army)
SO	Special Operations Branch (OSS)
SOVA	Office of Soviet Analysis (CIA)
SPG	Special Procedures Group (CIA)
SPOTCOM	spot commentary
SSU	Strategic Services Unit
START	Strategic Arms Reduction Treaty
SNIE	Special National Intelligence Estimate
SOE	Special Operations Executive (UK)
TELINT	telemetry intelligence
UAR	United Arab Republic
UAV	unmanned aerial vehicle
USCIB	United States Communications Intelligence Board
VC	Viet Cong
WiN	Wolności Niepodległość (Freedom and Independence)
X-2	Counterintelligence Branch (OSS)

The President and Intelligence

The early history of secret intelligence in the United States is closely interwoven with the career of the first president. In 1983, two centuries after Britain recognized American independence, the head of the intelligence community, William Casey, told a Senate committee, "I claim that my first predecessor as Director of Central Intelligence was . . . George Washington, who appointed himself."[1] Washington, declared Ronald Reagan, also began the "proud tradition" of American codebreaking.[2] The victory of the United States in the Revolutionary War was hastened by a series of successful covert operations. The next thirty presidents, however, rarely showed much enthusiasm for intelligence. Not till the Cold War did any of Washington's successors rival his flair for intelligence and covert action.

Despite the experience of the Revolutionary War, the United States was the last major power to acquire either a professional foreign intelligence service or a codebreaking agency. Though wars and other crises intermittently involved nineteenth- and early twentieth-century presidents in intelligence activities, there was no American intelligence community until the Second World War. Before the 1940s, because of its relative isolation and self-sufficiency, the United States had less need of foreign intelligence than the great powers of Europe. During the one and a half centuries between Washington and the Second World War, however, a series of precedents were set that profoundly affected the later development of the intelligence community. The president responsible for the most important precedents was, perhaps surprisingly, Woodrow Wilson, better known as the champion of "open diplomacy." At the outbreak of the First World War in Europe, Wilson was deeply ignorant and suspicious of intelligence operations. Once the United States entered the war, however, the station chief of British intelligence in the United

States won Wilson's confidence to a greater degree than his own secretary of state. The origins of the "special relationship" with British intelligence are to be found in Wilson's presidency.

Wilson's assistant secretary of the navy, Franklin Roosevelt, was deeply impressed by what he believed was Britain's "wonderful intelligence service." No existing study of FDR's foreign policy grasps the importance of his admiration for British intelligence during the First World War in explaining his later willingness as president to begin collaboration with it well before Pearl Harbor. The United States remained the junior partner in the wartime Anglo-American intelligence alliance. During the first decade of the Cold War, however, America assumed the intelligence, as well as the military, leadership of the Western world.

Despite the vast increase in the production of classified information since the outbreak of the Second World War, secret intelligence accounts for only a fraction of the flood of information that pours into the White House every day. All postwar presidents, however, have been influenced—often more than they have realized—by what the intelligence community tells them. The first document that most have read each morning has been an overnight intelligence summary from the Central Intelligence Agency. Had Franklin Roosevelt and his successors retained the feeble and fragmented foreign intelligence systems of the First World War and the interwar years, the history of both the Second World War and the Cold War would have been quite different.

Since the 1950s the American intelligence community, despite its late beginnings, has been the most technically advanced in the world. The more sophisticated it has become, the higher presidential expectations have risen. According to Robert M. Gates, the director of central intelligence from 1991 to 1993:

> . . . Presidents expect that, for what they spend on intelligence, the product should be able to predict coups, upheavals, riots, intentions, military moves, and the like with accuracy. . . . Presidents and their national security teams usually are ill-informed about intelligence capabilities; therefore they often have unrealistic expectations of what intelligence can do for them, especially when they hear about the genuinely extraordinary capabilities of U.S. intelligence for collecting and processing information.[3]

All postwar presidents have used the CIA for covert action as well as for intelligence collection and analysis. Almost all have developed exaggerated notions of what it can—or should—achieve. Some of the lowest points in the modern history of the presidency—the Bay of Pigs, Watergate, Iran-Contra—have arisen from grotesque misjudgments about the role of covert action. The key to the main U.S. intelligence failures and successes is to be found as frequently in the Oval Office as in the performance of the intelligence agencies. It is sometimes more difficult to make effective use of good intelligence than to collect it in the first place.

How presidents use intelligence is largely a matter of temperament and experience. The chapters that follow seek to show the extent to which the fortunes of the intelligence community have been influenced by the personalities, as well as the policies, of the presidents they have served. In a high-tech world, the human factor has remained crucially important. The character of the president helps to determine not merely how much interest, but also what sort of interest, he takes in intelligence. Though Franklin Roosevelt paid far more attention to intelligence than most of his predecessors, it was a curiously lopsided attention. Even before Pearl Harbor, by far the most important intelligence available to him came from the codebreakers. Roosevelt's temperament, however, led him to take a much keener interest in spies and covert operations than in cryptanalysis. Had he shared Winston Churchill's passion for, and understanding of, signals intelligence (SIGINT),[4] the outcome of the Japanese attack on Pearl Harbor might have been very different. The far more successful use of SIGINT after Pearl Harbor helped to shorten the Second World War.

FDR's sudden death in April 1945 changed the history of the intelligence community. Had he lived, it is unlikely that he would have closed down the wartime foreign intelligence agency, OSS, before establishing a peacetime replacement. His successor, Harry Truman, did. As well as being generally less interested in intelligence than Roosevelt, Truman had a different set of intelligence priorities. Though Truman took some time to adjust to the idea of peacetime espionage, he was quickly impressed by the SIGINT successes that hastened victory over Germany and Japan. Truman's biographers fail to mention that in September 1945, in addition to abolishing OSS, he approved the continuation of peacetime SIGINT in collaboration with the British. This collaboration led to an unprecedented peacetime Anglo-American intelligence alliance that still remains the most special part of a perhaps fading special relationship.

The election of Dwight D. Eisenhower in 1952 was a landmark in intelligence history. While Truman had arrived in the White House almost totally ignorant of intelligence, Ike's experience as Allied commander in chief in Europe during the Second World War had given him a far better grasp of SIGINT and imagery intelligence (IMINT) than any previous president. The IMINT revolution of the 1950s, which was to change the history of the Cold War, owed much to Eisenhower's personal backing for the development of spy planes and satellites. The Second World War, however, had distorted Eisenhower's understanding of the peacetime role of human-source intelligence (HUMINT). Influenced by memories of wartime operations behind enemy lines and support for resistance movements, Eisenhower made covert action by the CIA a major part of his foreign policy. Though Truman had authorized more covert action than he later liked to admit, he would never have approved Eisenhower's secret schemes to overthrow regimes in Iran, Guatemala, Indonesia, Cuba, and elsewhere.

John F. Kennedy's brief presidency witnessed both the most spectacular American intelligence failure and the most striking intelligence success of the Cold War. His willingness to approve the Cuban operation that ended in fiasco at the Bay of Pigs in April 1961 was due, in part at least, to his inexperience with intelligence and covert action. Kennedy, however, learned quickly on the job. Only eighteen months later, skillful use of good intelligence by the president and his advisers helped to resolve the Cuban missile crisis—the single most dangerous moment since the Second World War. Kennedy's assassination a year later was a disaster for the CIA. His successor, Lyndon Johnson, absurdly suspected the agency of having plotted to make sure he lost the Democratic nomination to Kennedy in 1960. John McCone, a remarkably able director of central intelligence, eventually resigned because of his inability to gain the president's ear. Kennedy would surely not have been as slow as LBJ to come to terms with gloomy CIA estimates on the Vietnam War.

Despite Richard Nixon's flair for international relations and sophisticated understanding of some foreign intelligence, his election as president was another blow for the CIA. Like Johnson, he bizarrely believed that the agency had conspired to make him lose the 1960 election. Nixon was by nature a conspirator as well as a conspiracy theorist, for whom covert operations had an irresistible, and ultimately fatal, attraction. He became the first president to set up a White House covert action unit to operate against his political enemies. Gerald Ford lacked both Nixon's intellectual gifts and his persecution complex. His more balanced personality gave him a more balanced view of intelligence and the intelligence community.

Jimmy Carter's desire at the beginning of his presidency to return the nation to the paths of righteousness, combined with his exaggerated faith in advanced technology, made him inclined to believe that spies and covert action were becoming obsolete. Many months spent agonizing over the fate of American hostages in Teheran and growing disillusion with the Soviet Union produced a profound change in Carter's thinking. During his last year as president, covert action became a major instrument of his foreign policy.

Unlike Carter, Ronald Reagan arrived in the White House with high expectations of what covert action could achieve, confident that the CIA could begin the "rollback" of world communism. Covert action, however, was almost Reagan's undoing. White House involvement in clandestine operations brought the presidency, once again, to the brink of disaster. The strength of Reagan's convictions about the Evil Empire also made him slow to heed intelligence warnings that the Kremlin feared he might be planning a first strike against the Soviet Union.

The Great Communicator was sometimes seized with the desire to communicate intelligence. On several dramatic occasions he made unprecedented public use of hitherto top-secret SIGINT. Surprisingly, SIGINT still remains conspicuous by its absence from almost all biographies of postwar presidents and histories of American policy during the Cold War. George Bush, however, claimed that it was "a prime factor" in his foreign policy.

Bush was the first former director of central intelligence (with the arguable exception of Washington) to be elected president. Partly as a result, he had closer contact with the intelligence community, and probably a better grasp of what intelligence could and could not do, than any of his predecessors. But intelligence reports had to contend with Bush's sometimes conflicting personal impressions of Mikhail Gorbachev and other world leaders. Intelligence in the Oval Office usually has to compete with other forms of information. "Most presidents," argues Robert Gates, "often attach as much—if not more—credibility to the views of family, friends, and private contacts as they do to those of executive agencies"—including the intelligence community.[5]

For better, and sometimes for worse, however, intelligence and the intelligence community have transformed, and been transformed by, the presidency of the United States. What follows is the history of that dual transformation.

CHAPTER 1

From George Washington to the Twentieth Century

"First in war, first in peace, and first in the hearts of his countrymen," as Henry Lee famously described him, George Washington also ranks first in the early history of American intelligence. The pious images of the child who could not tell a lie, of the leader who scorned all double dealing, and of the hero who never used power "but for the benefit of his country" have tended to obscure Washington's lifelong fascination with espionage.

In 1753, aged only twenty-one, Washington was sent with an Indian scout on a mission from Virginia to the Ohio wilderness to discover whether the French were on English soil and, if so, to instruct them politely to withdraw. Part of his assignment was secret: to spy out the strength of French forts, garrisons, and communications. At dinner in the fort of Venanges (now Franklin), Washington drank little while the French officers "dos'd themselves pretty plentifully":

> The Wine . . . soon banished the restraint which at first appeared in their Conversation, & gave license to their Tongues to reveal their Sentiments more freely. They told me it was their absolute Design to take Possession of the Ohio, & by G— they wou'd do it. . . .[1]

Two years later, Washington fought at the side of General Edward Braddock during his crushing defeat by the French in the battle of Fort Duquesne (now Pittsburgh), a disaster due chiefly to British ignorance of the strength of enemy forces.[2] The lack of intelligence proved fatal to Braddock and nearly fatal to Washington; two horses were shot from under him, and he emerged from battle with four bullet holes in his coat. Had the enemy given chase instead of being distracted by captured jars of English rum, Washington would probably have perished.[3] His experience of the French and Indian Wars convinced him that "There is nothing more necessary than good Intelligence to frustrate a designing enemy, & nothing that requires greater pains to obtain."[4]

When he took command of the Continental Army at Cambridge, Massachusetts, on July 3, 1775, Washington was determined to be better informed than Braddock twenty years before. "Gaining Intelligence" about the British forces, he wrote, was one of his most "immediate and pressing Duties."[5] On July 15 he recorded in his accounts a payment for the curious sum of $333.33 to an unidentified agent whom he instructed to enter British-occupied Boston "to establish a secret correspondence for the purpose of conveying intelligence of the Enemys movements and designs."[6] Washington's correspondence with the officers of the Continental Army contains frequent requests for "the earliest Advises of every piece of Intelligence, which you shall judge of Importance."[7] He was also deeply concerned about British espionage. ". . . There is one evil that I dread," he wrote to Joseph Quincy, "& that is their Spies. . . . I think it a matter of some importance to prevent them from obtaining Intelligence of our Situation. . . ."[8]

The Continental Congress was quick to grasp the need for foreign intelligence during the Revolutionary War. On November 29, 1775, it created the Committee of Secret Correspondence, the distant ancestor of today's CIA, "for the sole purpose of Corresponding with our friends in Great Britain, Ireland and other parts of the world." Two weeks later the committee wrote to one of the first of its secret correspondents, Arthur Lee, a well-connected American-born lawyer resident in London:

> It would be agreeable to Congress *to know the disposition of foreign powers toward us,* and we hope this object will engage your attention. We need not hint that *great circumspection and impenetrable secrecy* are necessary. The Congress rely on your zeal and ability to serve them, and will readily compensate you for whatever trouble and expense a compliance with their desire may occasion. We remit you for the present £200.[9]

Military intelligence, however, played a far more important part in the Revolutionary War than foreign intelligence. Since the Continental Army possessed no organized intelligence service, Washington became his own spymaster, using intelligence from his numerous spies to maneuver his troops away from premature contact with the stronger

British forces. Washington avoided more battles than he fought. That goes far to explain why he won the war. His winning strategy was less to engage the enemy than to outlast him.[10]

The most famous, though possibly the least talented, of Washington's spies was the young Yale graduate Nathan Hale, captured by the British on Long Island during his first espionage mission. On September 22, 1776, Hale became the first American spy to be executed. According to a pious but plausible tradition, he declared just before he was hanged in Manhattan, near today's intersection of Third Avenue and Sixty-sixth Street, "I only regret that I have but one life to lose for my country." His British executioners, impressed by his bravery, may have recognized his now famous last words as the paraphrase of a line from the well-known tragedy *Cato* by the English writer Joseph Addison. Statues of Hale, hands trussed behind his back and a noose around his neck, stand today both on Yale's Old Campus and in front of CIA headquarters at Langley, Virginia.[11] Hale's fate must surely have been in Washington's mind when, in 1780, he refused a personal appeal from the captured English spy Major John André to be executed by firing squad rather than "die on the gibbet."[12]

Though Nathan Hale is the best remembered of Washington's spies, the most successful was probably the Culper spy ring set up by Hale's Yale contemporary, Major Benjamin Tallmadge, in August 1778 to gather intelligence on the British troops commanded by General Sir Henry Clinton, who had recently occupied New York City. Two years later Tallmadge played a major part in the detection of both Major André and the American traitor, Major General Benedict Arnold. Arnold tried unsuccessfully to persuade Tallmadge to defect. "As I know you to be a man of sense," Arnold wrote to him, "I am convinced you are by this time fully of opinion that the real interest and happiness of America consists of a reunion with Great Britain." Tallmadge told Washington he was "mortified that my patriotism could be even suspected by this consummate villain."[13]

Because all members of Washington's espionage networks were sworn to secrecy, most of their identities were not revealed until long after the Revolutionary War. Some are still unknown. Washington repeatedly insisted that the secrecy of intelligence operations was a condition of their success:

> The necessity of procuring good intelligence is apparent & need not be further urged—All that remains for me to add is, that you keep the whole matter as secret as possible. For upon Secrecy, success depends in most Enterprizes of the kind, & for want of it, they are generally defeated, however well planned. . . .[14]

Almost two centuries later, in the early years of the Cold War, visitors from the newly founded CIA to the headquarters of the British Secret Intelligence Service (better known as SIS or MI6) were sometimes surprised to find a copy of that letter hanging on the wall in the office of the chief.

Washington handed over the running of some of his agents to aides. But his fascination with intelligence frequently made him reluctant to delegate. He even found time to instruct his agents on tradecraft. Washington gave this advice, for example, on the use of invisible inks to a member of the Culper spy ring:

> He may write a familiar letter on domestic affairs, or on some little matters of business, to his friend at Setauket or elsewhere, interlining with the stain [invisible ink] his secret intelligence, or writing it on the opposite blank side of the letter. But that his friend may know how to distinguish these from letters addressed solely to himself, he may always leave such as contain secret information without date or place (dating it with the stain), or fold them up in a particular manner, which may be concerted between the parties. This last appears to be the best mark of the two, and may be the signal of their being designated for me. The first mentioned mode, however, . . . appears to me the one least liable to detection.[15]

Unsurprisingly, Washington sometimes found it difficult to keep track of all his intelligence operations. He wrote absentmindedly to one of his agents: "It runs in my head that I was to corrispond [sic] with you by a fictitious name, if so I have forgotten the name and must be reminded of it again."[16]

Washington's reluctance to delegate the running of his operations was reinforced by the lack of professional staff officers among the citizen soldiers of the Continental Army. Had he possessed a competent intelligence staff he would surely not have lacked the basic intelligence on battlefield terrain that led to his nearly disastrous defeat at Brandywine Creek in September 1777. The failure of the local militia to scout the English advance, combined with Washington's ignorance of the ford across the creek immediately to his north, led to the loss of between twelve hundred and thirteen hundred of his eleven thousand troops. During the terrible winter that followed in Valley Forge, Pennsylvania, Washington prepared fake documents in his own hand, full of references to nonexistent infantry and cavalry regiments, which were then passed on to the enemy by double agents. The British credited Washington with more than eight thousand troops he did not have and mistakenly concluded he was too strong to attack.[17] But for this successful deception operation, the Continental Army might not have survived the winter.

Over the Revolutionary War as a whole, Washington's grasp of military intelligence and deception comfortably exceeded that of his British opponents. In the summer of 1780 the Culper spy ring warned Washington that Clinton was planning a preemptive attack on the French forces of General Jean Rochambeau, who had just landed at Newport, Rhode Island, after two debilitating months at sea. Thus forewarned, Washington succeeded in planting bogus papers on British spies that described his (in reality, nonexistent) preparations for an offensive against New York. Clinton's troops were already on board ship, ready to leave for Newport, when the fraudulent intelligence reached him. Taken in by Washington's deception, the British commander called off what might well have been a successful attack before Rochambeau was ready to fight.[18]

Intelligence and deception operations also played an important part in the victorious campaign that led to the surrender of Lord Cornwallis's forces at Yorktown, Virginia, on October 19, 1781. Captured American dispatches in the early summer of 1781 had alerted Clinton to Washington's original plan for a combined Franco-American attack on New York. When Washington decided in mid-August to move south against Cornwallis instead, he arranged for fake dispatches, indicating that his objective remained New York, to fall into the hands of British spies. Once again Clinton was successfully deceived. Washington strengthened the deception by setting up a camp at Chatham, New Jersey, and assembling boats along the Jersey shore in apparent preparation for a crossing to Staten Island. Even when Clinton's spies discovered from the mistress of General Rochambeau's son that the French army was moving south, he at first refused to believe it.[19]

Once Washington had begun the siege of Yorktown, his most valuable intelligence came from British dispatches intercepted by his agents and decrypted by the Boston schoolteacher James Lovell, remembered today as the father of American cryptanalysis. On September 21, 1781, Lovell sent the British cipher to Washington to enable intercepted British messages to be decrypted as rapidly as possible. Two weeks before the British surrender Washington wrote to Lovell:

> I am much obliged by the Communication you have been pleased to make me in your Favr. of 21st ulta.
>
> My Secretary has taken a copy of the Cyphers, and by help of one of the Alphabets has been able to decypher one paragraph of a letter lately intercepted going from L[or]d Cornwallis to Sir H[enr]y Clinton.[20]

Though Yorktown settled the outcome of the war, skirmishing continued for almost a year. Peace was not concluded until 1783. The Yorktown campaign and the scattered fighting that followed left Washington with a fascination for codebreaking. Washington pored over decrypted enemy dispatches and agent reports, personally sifting and collating the intelligence they contained, recognizing that the whole picture was usually more important than any single item of intelligence, however sensational. After Lovell had sent him a number of decrypted British messages in March 1782, Washington wrote to him:

> I thank you for the trouble you have taken in forwarding the intelligence which was inclosed in your letter. . . . It is by comparing a variety of information, we are frequently enabled to investigate facts, which were so intricate or hidden, that no single clue could have led to the knowledge of them[. I]n this point of view, intelligence becomes interesting which but from its connection and collateral circumstances, would not be important.[21]

As this letter suggests, Washington was his own chief intelligence analyst as well as his own spymaster.

As president of the United States from 1789 to 1797, Washington took personal responsibility for foreign intelligence. In his first State of the Union message to Congress on January 8, 1790, he requested a "competent fund" to finance intelligence operations. Congress responded with an act of July 1, 1790, setting up the Contingent Fund of Foreign Intercourse, better known as the Secret Service Fund ("for spies, if the gentleman so pleases," as it was later acknowledged in the Senate). For the first year, the fund was $40,000; By the third year, it had risen to over $1 million, about 12 percent of the federal budget—a far higher proportion of the budget than the massive U.S. intelligence expenditure of the late twentieth century. The fund was used for a great variety of purposes, not all of them strictly related to intelligence, ranging from bribing foreign officials to ransoming American hostages in Algiers. Washington correctly foresaw that all his actions as first president of the United States would set precedents for his successors. Thus it was with his handling of the Secret Service Fund. Congress required him to certify what sums he had spent, but allowed him to conceal both the purposes and recipients of payments from the fund. A century and a half later the Central Intelligence Act of 1949 authorized the director of central intelligence to adopt similar accounting procedures.[22]

During his lifetime Washington's role as spymaster was little mentioned. But it provided the plot for the first major American novel, James

Fenimore Cooper's *The Spy*, published in 1821. The central character of the novel is Harvey Birch, a fictional English spy "possessed of a coolness and presence of mind that nothing appeared to disturb," who is finally unmasked as a patriotic American double agent working for Washington in the enemy camp. Clasped to Birch's dying breast is "a tin box, through which the fatal lead had gone." Inside the punctured box is a secret document whose contents, though not revealed until the last page, will have been guessed by attentive readers about two hundred pages earlier:

> Circumstances of political importance, which involve the lives and fortunes of many, have hitherto kept secret what this paper now reveals. Harvey Birch has for years been a faithful and unrequited servant of his country. Though man does not, may God reward him for his conduct!
>
> GEO. WASHINGTON

Though James Fenimore Cooper is best remembered nowadays for *The Last of the Mohicans* and *The Leatherstocking Tales*, it was *The Spy* that made his reputation, going through fifteen American, and many foreign, editions before his death in 1851.[23]

No nineteenth-century president came close to equaling Washington's flair for intelligence. The War of 1812, the so-called Second War of Independence, witnessed a series of intelligence debacles. In February 1812 President James Madison spent $50,000, then the entire annual budget of the much-reduced Secret Service Fund, purchasing documents from a disaffected British agent, John Henry, and an entrepreneurial French aristocrat, the Comte Édouard de Crillon. These documents, he believed, provided "formal proof" that his political opponents, the New England Federalists, were conspiring with the British to destroy the Union. On closer inspection, after Henry and de Crillon had left the country, the papers seemed somewhat less exciting. They showed only that Henry had been employed by the British "to obtain the most accurate information of the true state of affairs" in New England. Though authorized to put disaffected Federalists in touch with officials in Canada, he had not in fact done so. Madison was also disconcerted to discover that the Comte Édouard de Crillon was actually a confidence trickster named Paul Émile Soubiran. The papers, however, served their purpose. "We have made use of Henry's documents," Secretary of State James Monroe told the French minister, "as a last means of exciting the nation and Congress."[24]

Soon after the outbreak of war in 1812, the American commander, General William Hull, who had been ordered to invade Canada, lost the trunk containing his orders and muster roll. On discovering the contents of the trunk, the British commander, General Sir Isaac Brock, successfully fed Hull with disinformation that persuaded him that he was heavily outnumbered. Falling back on Detroit, Hull was surrounded by forces that, though he did not know it, were no larger than his own. A further bogus dispatch, reporting that five thousand Indians had joined forces with Brock, persuaded Hull to surrender.

Though American fortunes improved over the following year, in August 1814 the British succeeded in burning Washington. The secretary of war, John Armstrong, had convinced himself that the British would never attack the capital and made no serious preparations to defend it. Military intelligence was so poor that the threat to Washington was not realized until the enemy was only sixteen miles away at Upper Marlboro. The future president, James Monroe, saddled his horse, volunteered for service as a cavalry scout, and ventured perilously close to British lines. President Madison was given so little warning of the rapid British descent on Washington on August 24 that the First Lady barely had time to snatch Gilbert Stuart's famous portrait of George Washington from its frame and rescue the original draft of the Declaration of Independence before both were forced to flee. A group of British officers led by Admiral George Cockburn found the Madisons' table laid for dinner. "[W]e found a supper all ready," one of them reported, "which many of us speedily consumed . . . and drank some very good wine also." Cockburn then selected a few souvenirs, among them one of the president's hats and one of Dolley Madison's cushions, then left his soldiers to loot and burn the house. The coats of white paint used to cover the British scorch marks on the Executive Mansion later gave it a new name—the White House.[25]

Throughout the nineteenth century, as for much of the twentieth, Congress was usually content to leave intelligence matters to the president and his advisers. The first major challenge to presidential control came in a resolution of the House of Representatives in 1846, requesting President James K. Polk to produce records of Secret Service Fund expenditure during the previous administration. Polk told his cabinet "that my mind was convinced that it would be a most dangerous precedent to answer the call of the House by giving the information requested." The cabinet unanimously agreed, and Polk sent a message to the House, declining its request on the grounds of national security:

> In time of war or impending danger the situation of the country may make it necessary to employ individuals for the purpose of obtain-

ing information or rendering other important services who could never be so prevailed upon to act if they entertained the least apprehension that their names or their agency would in any contingency be divulged. . . . But this object might be altogether defeated by the intrigues of other powers if our purposes were to be made known by the exhibition of the original papers and vouchers to the accounting officers of the Treasury.[26]

Like previous nineteenth-century presidents, Polk sent individuals on occasional secret missions, but made no attempt to establish a permanent intelligence service. At the outbreak of the Mexican War of 1846 the American commander, General Zachary Taylor, had little information even on the Mexican terrain, let alone the strength and deployment of the Mexican army. The best intelligence available in the War Department was the journal written by Lieutenant Zebulon M. Pike during his travels through Texas and northern Mexico thirty years before. Taylor's crushing victories over the Mexicans won him the popular acclaim that later enabled him to win the 1848 presidential election. Dressed in farmer's clothes and a battered straw hat, seated sidesaddle on his aging and phlegmatic war-horse, "Whitey" Taylor embodied, in a mildly eccentric way, the virtues of "true grit." But his grasp of intelligence barely went beyond peering at the enemy through binoculars. During the Mexican War he rejected instructions from Secretary of War William Marcy to employ natives as scouts on the grounds that natives could not be trusted. Taylor also turned down a request from his deputy, General Winfield Scott, to use Mexican bandits for military intelligence work. Scott, however, persisted and gained approval from President Polk and Secretary Marcy to set up the Mexican Spy Company, consisting of the outlaw Manuel Domínguez and two hundred of his mostly criminal followers. While Scott was laying siege to Mexico City in 1847, Domínguez's agents succeeded in crossing enemy lines and bringing back intelligence on Mexican defenses. The Spy Company received a total of $16,566.50 for its services. Polk as well as Scott seems to have regarded the money as well spent.[27]

At the outbreak of the Civil War in 1861, both sides had to construct intelligence systems virtually from scratch. Despite the flamboyant spy stories and colorful romances generated by the war, secret agents probably provided less information than the press. General William T. Sherman regarded Northern journalists as one of the South's major assets: "I say in giving intelligence to the enemy, in sowing discord and discontents in an army, these men fulfil all the conditions of spies." When told that three Union journalists had been killed by an exploding shell, he replied savagely, "Good! Now we shall have news from hell before break-fast." "Napoleon himself," Sherman declared, "would have been defeated by a free press." Among the chief tasks of the Confederate Signal and Secret Service Bureau was to obtain Northern newspapers. Union censorship was erratic and ineffective; the rules laid down by the War Department confused both censors and journalists. Confederate newspapers provided less intelligence to the North chiefly because there were fewer of them. With only 5 percent of American paper mills, the South suffered from a constant shortage of newsprint. Both Sherman and General Ulysses S. Grant, however, attached great importance to the intelligence provided by the Confederate press.[28] So too did President Abraham Lincoln. When Southern press reports failed to reach the White House, he wanted to know why. Lincoln telegraphed Grant on March 2, 1865: "You have not sent contents of Richmond papers for Tuesday or Wednesday—Did you not receive them? If not, does it indicate anything?" Three hours later Grant replied reassuringly (though with defective spelling, probably supplied by the telegraphist): "Richmond papers are received daily. No bullitins were sent Teusday or Wednsday there was not an item of either good or bad news in them."[29]

Lincoln's first direct involvement in an intelligence operation came shortly before his inauguration as president. On the evening of February 21, 1861, while on his way to Washington, he was visited in his Philadelphia hotel room by Allan Pinkerton, head of one of the world's first private detective agencies. Pinkerton announced that he had discovered a plot to assassinate Lincoln as he changed trains in Baltimore en route to his inauguration. A Pinkerton detective claimed to have penetrated the conspiracy and to have been present at a secret meeting in a darkened room where the plotters drew lots for the privilege of killing the president-elect. According to the detective, the chief conspirator had arranged for no fewer than eight men to draw the assassin's lot, in the hope that each would believe "that upon him, his courage, strength and devotion, depended the cause of the South." Though skeptical of this doubtless embroidered tale, Lincoln was persuaded by a letter from William H. Seward, the secretary of state, and General Winfield Scott (general in chief of the United States Army) that there was indeed a plot to kill him at Baltimore. He agreed to change trains secretly, and spent a sleepless night traveling to Washington in a sleeping car berth reserved in the name of the invalid brother of Kate Warne, America's first professional female detective. News of Lincoln's furtive journey to his inauguration leaked to the press and gave rise to a series of satirical reports under titles such as "The Flight of Abraham." Stories circulated for the rest of his presidency that he had arrived in Washington disguised as an old woman, wearing a Scotch cap and shawl. Lincoln's reluctance to protect his own security at the end of the Civil War owed at least something to his memory of the ridicule to which he had been subjected four years earlier. The failed plot of 1861 thus contributed to his assassination in 1865.[30]

Though Lincoln took an active interest in both intelligence and counterintelligence work during the Civil War, he showed little aptitude for either. His immediate concern at the outbreak of war was with what he called "the enemy in the rear." The Confederacy, he wrongly believed, had long-prepared subversive plans to undermine the Union war effort:

> . . . Under cover of "Liberty of speech," "Liberty of the press" and *"habeas corpus"* they hoped to keep on foot amongst us a most efficient corps of spies, informers, supplyers, and aiders and abettors of their cause in a thousand ways.[31]

Lincoln promptly suspended the writ of habeas corpus, authorizing army commanders to respond to Confederate subversion by declaring martial law and trying civilians in military courts.[32]

On April 21 Pinkerton wrote to Lincoln from Chicago, offering his wartime services and enclosing a secret cipher to be used for correspondence with him. "In the present disturbed state of affairs," he told the president, "I dare not trust this in the mails so send by one of my force who was with me at Baltimore . . . " On the evening of May 2 he was received at the White House by Lincoln and Seward, his secretary of state.[33] According to Pinkerton's exaggerated account, the president informed him that "the authorities had for some time entertained the idea of organizing a secret service department of the government, with the view of ascertaining the social, political and patriotic status of the numerous suspected persons in and around the city." A few days later Pinkerton accepted alternative employment. Major General George B. McClellan made him his intelligence chief.[34] The departments of state, war, and the navy separately employed government agents, U.S. marshals, Pinkerton detectives, city police, and private informers to wage a chaotic campaign against subversion. Lincoln became concerned that enthusiasm for rooting out "the enemy in the rear" was going too far. "Unless the necessity for these arbitrary arrests is *manifest* and *urgent*," he declared, "I prefer they should cease."[35]

Espionage was equally uncoordinated. In July 1861 Lincoln personally recruited as a secret agent William Alvin Lloyd, a publisher of railroad and steamboat guides and maps of the Southern states. To continue his business, Lloyd needed a pass enabling him to cross Union lines. Lincoln agreed to provide it on condition that he work as a part-time spy in the Confederacy for a salary of $200 a month and expenses. Lloyd set off for the South with his espionage contract, signed by Lincoln, sewn into the lining of the dress of his wife's chambermaid. His early exploits included a comic-opera attempt to ingratiate himself with the Confederate provost marshal at Richmond by buying him a $1,200 dress uniform. Unsurprisingly, Lloyd was twice imprisoned on suspicion of espionage. Though none of his intelligence reports survive, it is unlikely that any had a significant impact on the conduct of the war. When Lloyd returned to Washington after Lincoln's assassination, the government agreed to refund his expenses but refused to pay the four years' salary owing to him. Following prolonged litigation the case eventually came before the Supreme Court. In 1876 the Court delivered a landmark judgment upholding the president's right to employ secret agents. While accepting that contracts with agents were binding, however, it denied the right of agents to sue the president for payment on the grounds that "The publicity produced by an action would itself be a breach of contract. . . . Both employer and agent must have understood that the lips of the other were to be forever sealed respecting the relation of either to the matter."[36]

Generals on both sides during the Civil War organized their own intelligence operations and hired their own spies and detectives. After the Union defeat in the first major battle of the war at Bull Run in July 1861, Lincoln summoned General McClellan to Washington to command the Army of the Potomac defending the capital. With him came his intelligence chief, Pinkerton, who wrote grandly of his plans for counterintelligence work in Washington:

> In operating my detective force I shall endeavor to test all suspected persons in various ways. I shall seek access to their houses, clubs, and places of resort, managing that among the members of my force shall be ostensible representatives of every grade of society, from the highest to the most menial. Some shall have the *entrée* to the gilded saloon of the suspected aristocratic traitors, and be their honored guests, while others will act in the capacity of valets, or domestics of various kinds, and try the efficacy of such relations with the household to gain evidence.[37]

Pinkerton had a number of well-publicized successes in rounding up enemy agents, among them the glamorous Rose Greenhow, who declared that her "delicacy was shocked and outraged" by his detectives' surveillance. "All the mysteries of my toilette," she complained, had been "laid bare to the public eye."[38]

Pinkerton's most important role was as McClellan's intelligence chief during his march to the gates of Richmond in the Peninsula campaign of 1862. More men and weapons of war were assembled on the Virginia Peninsula than in any other campaign of the Civil War. McClellan, however, constantly exaggerated the size of the Confederate forces. Instead of challenging what one observer described as McClellan's statistical "hallucinations," Pinkerton fell into the classic intelligence trap of telling the general what he expected to hear. His estimates of the forces defending Richmond grew steadily from one hundred thousand to almost two hundred thousand. In reality, they numbered about eighty-five thousand at their peak, as compared with the Union army of over one hundred thousand men. To Lincoln's intense frustration, McClellan constantly used his alleged "great inferiority in numbers" as an excuse for not attacking. Lincoln wrote to him in April that the country could not fail to note his "present hesitation to move on an entrenched enemy": "I beg to assure you that I have never written you, or spoken to you, in greater kindness of feeling than I do now. . . . *But you must act.*" Having led his army to within sight of Richmond in the spring of 1862, however, McClellan then began retreating in the face of an outnumbered and outgunned enemy that, he claimed, outnumbered him. Lincoln finally relieved him of his command in November, tired, he complained, of dealing with a general who fought like "a stationary engine." Pinkerton, whose faulty intelligence had reinforced McClellan's inertia, resigned soon afterward.[39]

Perhaps the most enduring intelligence myth of the Civil War is the belief that the United States Secret Service was founded during it. In reality, the Treasury Department agency of that name was not set up until after the war was over, and was not at first concerned with intelligence. The myth derives partly from Pinkerton's war memoirs, in which he grandly styled himself "Chief of the United States Secret Service." Pinkerton's pretensions, however, were exceeded by those of the former vigilante from the California goldfields, Lafayette C. Baker, who entitled his Civil War memoirs *The History of the United States Secret Service.* For eighteen months from the summer of 1861, Pinkerton's and Baker's rival "secret services" in Washington were in simultaneous operation.[40] Originally employed by General Winfield Scott to undertake espionage in Virginia, Baker next organized a counterespionage unit in Washington, which he named the National Detective Bureau, reporting first to Secretary of State Seward, then to Secretary of War Edwin M. Stanton. Baker moved beyond his counterespionage brief to lead a crusade against war profiteers, corrupt officials, prostitutes, gamblers, and deserters. He later claimed to have burned a consignment of pornography destined for

Union troops outside the White House, while Lincoln looked on approvingly from the window of the Oval Office. Baker admitted that he sometimes acted outside the law. But, he claimed, "However censurable, unjustifiable, or illegal my course may have been, my only desire was to serve the President and the Government." After one of his raids on Washington gambling houses, according to Baker:

> Mr. Lincoln sent for me, and I repaired to the White House to find him carelessly sitting in shirt-sleeves and slippers ready to receive me. He said:
> "Well Baker, what is the trouble between you and the gamblers?" I told my story. He laughed and said:
> "I used to play penny ante when I ran a flat boat out West, but for many years have not touched a card."
> I stated to him the havoc gambling was making with the Army. . . . He approved my course but reminded me of the difficulties in the way of reform.
> I replied: "I cannot fight the gamblers and Government both."
> The President replied: "You won't have to fight me."
> I added: "It is a fight, and all I ask is fair play: that the Government will let me alone, and I will break up this business."
> And, with this perfect understanding, we parted for the time.[41]

The understanding was less perfect than Baker claimed. Lincoln seems, nonetheless, to have tolerated at least some of Baker's irregularities.

When not in the White House, Lincoln was usually to be found next door in the War Department's telegraph office and cipher section, studying the stream of telegraphed orders and reports that gave him more detailed and up-to-date information on the war than any other source. The young telegrapher and cipher clerk David Homer Bates wrote later: "Outside the members of his cabinet and his private secretaries, none were brought into closer or more confidential relations with Lincoln than the cipher-operators. . . ." Bates and his two colleagues, Arthur B. Chandler and Charles A. Tinker, also introduced Lincoln to the mysteries of codebreaking. Aged only seventeen, twenty, and twenty-three, respectively, at the outbreak of war, the "Sacred Three," as they liked to style themselves, were probably the youngest group of cryptanalysts in American history. Among the codebreaking coups that particularly impressed the president was their success in decrypting ciphered correspondence in 1863 that revealed that plates for printing Rebel currency were being manufactured in New York. The Confederate secretary of the treasury enthused in one of the intercepted letters, "The engraving of the plates is superb." After the engraver had been tracked down in Lower Manhattan, the plates and several million newly printed Confederate dollars were seized by a U.S. marshal.[42]

In addition to showing some enthusiasm for SIGINT, Lincoln was the first president to acquire an interest in overhead reconnaissance, which was to lead, a century later, to the use of spy planes and spy satellites to collect imagery intelligence (IMINT). He was greatly impressed with a remarkable demonstration by a twenty-eight-year-old balloonist and self-styled professor, Thaddeus S. C. Lowe, on June 18, 1861. From five hundred feet above Washington, Lowe telegraphed a message to Lincoln down a cable linking the balloon to the ground:

TO THE PRESIDENT OF THE UNITED STATES:

THIS POINT OF OBSERVATION COMMANDS AN AREA NEARLY FIFTY MILES IN DIAMETER. THE CITY, WITH ITS GIRDLE OF ENCAMPMENTS, PRESENTS A SUPERB SCENE. I TAKE PLEASURE IN SENDING YOU THIS FIRST DISPATCH EVER TELEGRAPHED FROM AN AERIAL STATION, AND IN ACKNOWLEDGING INDEBTEDNESS TO YOUR ENCOURAGEMENT, FOR THE OPPORTUNITY OF DEMONSTRATING THE AVAILABILITY OF THE SCIENCE OF AERONAUTICS IN THE MILITARY SERVICE OF THE COUNTRY. YOURS RESPECTFULLY,

T. S. C. LOWE

The experiment achieved three firsts: the "first electrical communication from an aircraft to the ground, first such communication to a president of the United States, and first 'real-time' transmission of reconnaissance data from an airborne platform." With Lincoln's enthusiastic support, a balloon corps was founded two months later with Lowe as self-styled "chief aeronaut" in charge of seven balloons and nine balloonists. The corps's greatest success during the Peninsula campaign was in detecting a large concentration of Confederate troops preparing to attack before the battle of Fair Oaks, Virginia, on May 31. The early experiments in overhead reconnaissance, however, were to prove a false dawn. Though Lowe's balloonists made some military converts, they were heavily criticized because of the inability of the unwieldy balloon trains, with their cumbersome gas generators, to move at more than a snail's pace. The corps was disbanded in June 1863.[43]

Despite his interest in HUMINT, SIGINT, and IMINT, Lincoln, like most statesmen of his time, had little grasp of the formidable problems of intelligence coordination and analysis. In the absence of any centralized system of assessment or official distribution list, intelligence reports were liable to be directed unpredictably to any one or more of a great variety of recipients: the president, the secretary of war, the general in chief, the governors of threatened states, army and divisional commanders. Intelligence operations also suffered from the lack of central direction. During the Gettysburg campaign of 1863, the turning point of the Civil War, the major Union commands—the Army of the Potomac, the Department of the Susquehanna (Pennsylvania east of the Laurel Mountains), the Eighth Army Corps (or Middle Department) based at Baltimore, the Department of Washington, even the Military Railway Department—all ran their own independent intelligence systems.[44]

The best-run intelligence agency of the war was the Bureau of Military Intelligence, founded early in 1863 by the new commander of the Army of the Potomac, General "Fightin' Joe" Hooker. Under Hooker's intelligence chief, Colonel George H. Sharpe, the bureau collated information from all sources, ranging from spies to newspapers, and furnished regular and usually reliable assessments. Hooker, however, proved incapable of making effective use of the intelligence he received. Before and during the battle of Chancellorsville in May 1863, Sharpe provided detailed and accurate intelligence on the strength and deployment of the Confederate forces of General Robert E. Lee. "Instead of using this information," writes Jay Luvaas in his study of the battle, "Hooker seemed overwhelmed by it . . ." Sixty thousand Confederate troops defeated a Union Army of 130,000 men. Most historians of the Civil War consider Chancellorsville to be Lee's most brilliant victory.[45] After the battle, Hooker seemed to resent being given intelligence showing that he had been beaten by inferior forces. A detailed bureau assessment of Lee's forces on May 27 has been described by his biographer, Douglas Southall Freeman, as "correct in nearly every particular." The provost marshal general, Marsena Rudolph Patrick, noted in his diary:

> [Hooker] has treated our "Secret Service Department" [the Bureau of Military Information] which has furnished him with the most astonishingly correct information with indifference at first, and now with insult. . . . We get accurate information, but Hooker will not use it and insults all who differ from him in opinion. He has declared that the enemy are over 100,000 strong—it is his only salvation to make it appear that the enemy's forces are larger than his which is all false and he knows it. He knows that Lee is his master and is afraid to meet him in fair battle.

The fortunes of the bureau improved dramatically after Lincoln sacked Hooker on June 27 and replaced him as commander of the Army of the

Potomac with General George G. Meade. Before and during the battle of Gettysburg (July 1–3), Sharpe once again supplied accurate intelligence on Confederate strength and troop movements. Lee, by contrast, had less information on the Union forces than in any of his previous battles. "He was forced," writes Jay Luvaas, "to fight a battle without intelligence." That was one of the reasons for his defeat.[46]

The growing reputation of the Bureau of Military Information after Gettysburg led in March 1864 to Sharpe's appointment as intelligence officer to the new general in chief of the Union armies, Ulysses S. Grant. Henceforth the bureau served both Grant and Meade. The success of Grant's war of attrition over the next year, though due chiefly to his larger forces and the superior resources of the North, was assisted by good intelligence. Sharpe himself gave most of the credit for the bureau's successes in the months before Lee's surrender at Appomattox in April 1865 to an agent network in Richmond, apparently including clerks in the Confederate war and navy departments, run by Elizabeth Van Lew, a wealthy pro-abolitionist spinster. Financing the network out of her own pocket cost "Miss Lizzie" most of her fortune. After the war Grant tried and failed to persuade Congress to recompense her with a grant of $15,000. When he became president four years later he appointed Miss Van Lew postmaster of Richmond to provide her with an income.[47]

Lincoln's presidency ended in a tragedy made possible by outrageously bad security. On the evening of April 14, 1865, only five days after Lee's surrender, the actor John Wilkes Booth entered the president's box at Ford's Theater unchallenged and shot him at close range. Booth then jumped from the box to the stage and, despite fracturing his leg in the fall, escaped amid the pandemonium he had caused. As the manhunt got chaotically under way, a motley assortment of military and police squads swarmed across Virginia and Maryland, each hoping to claim the reward offered for the capture of Lincoln's assassin. Booth was eventually tracked down in a tobacco barn near Port Royal, Virginia, by a troop of New York cavalry, following a lead provided by Lafayette Baker and his National Detective Bureau. The barn was set ablaze, and Booth was shot as he tried to escape.

In recognition of his detective work, Baker was given a $3,750 reward and promoted to the rank of brigadier general. Some of his detectives were employed to protect Lincoln's vice-president and successor, Andrew Johnson. President Johnson entrusted Baker with various "strictly confidential" inquiries and with the surveillance of individuals who were believed to pose a potential threat to him.[48] On his own initiative, Baker also began to investigate the activities of the "pardon-brokers" who used their influence at the White House to obtain pardons that they sold to former Rebels. In November 1865 he reported to Johnson that his investigations had proved "conclusively that a System of Manipulation and Corruption are [*sic*] being practiced by persons holding Official positions under the Government in connection with the procuring of Pardons." The pardon-broker who most concerned Baker was a Mrs. Lucy Cobb, who, despite what he considered her "notorious bad character and Reputation," frequented the White House and engaged in "public boastings that she could procure pardons at all times quicker than any other person in Washington."[49] When Baker questioned Mrs. Cobb, she allegedly replied, "You have never seen my legs." According to Baker, "She then raised her clothes and showed me her fine legs some distance above her knees. . . ."[50] President Johnson, apparently an admirer of Mrs. Cobb, refused to take action against her. Instead, he dismissed Baker for conducting unauthorized investigations and "maintaining an espionage network at the White House."[51]

Conspiracy theories about Lincoln's assassination rumbled on throughout Johnson's presidency. As after the shooting of John F. Kennedy almost a century later, many Americans found it impossible to believe that the death of a president could have been masterminded by an individual as insignificant as John Wilkes Booth or Lee Harvey Oswald. Like his namesake after Kennedy's assassination, Johnson was himself attracted by some of the conspiracy theories. In the immediate aftermath of Lincoln's death, it was widely believed in Washington that the assassination must have been planned by the Confederate leadership. A proclamation by President Johnson on May 2, 1865, charged Confederate president Jefferson Davis, together with Confederate representatives in Canada, with having "incited, concerted and procured . . . the atrocious murder of the late President, Abraham Lincoln, and the attempted assassination of the Hon. William H. Seward, Secretary of State," and offered a reward of $100,000 for Davis's arrest. But Andrew Johnson himself, as the man whose career benefited most by Lincoln's death, came under suspicion from some conspiracy theorists (again like Lyndon Johnson a century later). Probably the most remarkable of President Johnson's accusers was Lafayette Baker. Johnson's battles with the Radical Republicans in Congress gave the embittered Baker a chance to revenge himself for his dismissal in 1865. In February 1867 he gave evidence to a subcommittee of the House Judiciary Committee, appointed to consider the impeachment of the president. Baker testified under oath that he had seen secret wartime correspondence between Johnson, Davis, and other Confederate leaders proving that Johnson had been a Rebel spy. Though unable to produce the correspondence, Baker gave the names of witnesses who had seen it. An investigation by the Capitol police convincingly demonstrated that the alleged witnesses, like the letters themselves, were figments of Baker's imagination. The subcommittee concluded that Baker had added "to his many previous outrages . . . that of wilful and deliberate perjury."[52] Baker's fraudulent testimony represents the only known attempt by a senior American intelligence officer to frame the president.

The conspiracy theories involving Johnson did not end with Baker's death in 1868. In 1961 two sensational cipher messages concerning Lincoln's assassination, allegedly written in 1868, were discovered by Civil War buff Ray A. Neff on the blank pages of an old military journal. When decrypted, the messages identified their author as Lafayette Baker and implicated Johnson, Stanton, eleven members of Congress, twelve army officers, three naval officers, the governor of a loyal state, and more than twenty others in the assassination plot. The volume in which the messages were found also contained Baker's signature, written in secret ink and certified as genuine by a handwriting expert. The allegations in the cipher messages have now been as thoroughly discredited as Baker's testimony to the subcommittee of the House Judiciary Committee.[53] There are two possible explanations for the allegations. If the handwriting expert is to be believed and Baker's signature is genuine, Baker set out just before his death to take a posthumous revenge on President Johnson and those who had discredited his testimony in 1867. Or, if the handwriting expert is in error, the cipher messages and other documents that emerged subsequently are the work of an unknown hoaxer.

After the Civil War, the Bureau of Military Information, which had become the first professional United States intelligence agency, evaluating as well as collecting all-source intelligence, had been rapidly wound up. One of the by-products of the war, however, was the foundation in 1865 of the first permanent federal intelligence agency, the Secret Service of the Treasury Department. Initially it had little to do with intelligence. Its first priority was to deal with the spate of forgeries that had followed the introduction of paper money in 1862. Since, however, it was the only federal law enforcement agency until the founding of the Justice Department's Bureau of Investigation (later the FBI) in 1908, it was intermittently employed for other purposes as well. After the Secret Service uncovered a plot to assassinate Grover Cleveland in 1894, it was used to protect the president, initially only on an ad hoc basis as threats came to light. In 1902, a year after the assassination of President William McKinley, it began the permanent round-the-clock protection that has continued ever since.[54]

For a generation after the Civil War the combination of mostly passive presidents and a general absence of major threats to United States security ensured that the development of American foreign intelligence proceeded both slowly and fitfully. Woodrow Wilson was later to say of Ulysses S. Grant, president from 1869 to 1877, that "He combined great gifts with great mediocrity." Though he had been a successful Civil War general, he made an indifferent president, presiding ineffectually over a corrupt administration and a business boom. Grant continued, however, to show some interest in secret agents. Soon after becoming president, he dispatched James Wickes Taylor to the area of the Red River rebellion in Canada, in the optimistic hope of finding support in the Selkirk region for annexation by the United States. None was discovered.[55]

The most important development of the 1880s was the creation of the first permanent naval and military intelligence departments. The War of the Pacific, in which Chile fought Bolivia and Peru from 1879 to 1882, introduced modern naval warfare to the Western Hemisphere. The discovery that Chile's fleet was larger than that of the United States, together with the possibility of European interference in Latin American affairs as a result of the war, spurred Congress to authorize the modernization of the antiquated U.S. Navy. President Chester A. Arthur ("Elegant Arthur"), though best remembered for his white gloves, the silk handkerchief in his top pocket, the flower in his buttonhole, and his general resemblance to a stuffed shirt, also had an interest in ships. He declaimed, soon after entering the White House in 1881: "I cannot too strongly urge upon you my conviction that every consideration of national safety, economy and honor imperatively demands a thorough rehabilitation of our Navy." In March 1882 the Office of Naval Intelligence (ONI), initially comprising four officers, was founded as part of the New Navy program, charged with "collecting and recording such naval information as may be useful to the Department in time of war, as well as of peace."[56] In October 1885 an even smaller Military Intelligence Division (MID), consisting of only one officer assisted by several civilian clerks, was established to collect "military data on our own and foreign services which would be available for the use of the War Department and the Army at large."[57]

Most naval and military officers found intelligence a tedious business. U.S. naval records contain many reports from shipboard intelligence officers that say simply: "I have to report that no intelligence report was sent in during the quarter, as nothing has occurred to furnish material for a report." ONI succeeded nonetheless in attracting some of the navy's brightest recruits. Of the fifteen essay prizes awarded by the Navy Institute between ONI's foundation in 1882 and the end of the century, ten went to past or present ONI officers.[58] ONI's most enthusiastic

presidential supporters during its first half-century were the two Roosevelts, Theodore and his fifth cousin Franklin, both of whom served as
assistant secretary of the navy with responsibilities that included naval
intelligence. Theodore Roosevelt's enthusiasm for ONI as assistant secretary in 1897–98 had much to do with the support that it provided for
his ambitious plans for naval expansion. ONI, like Roosevelt, was committed to the construction of a great U.S. battle fleet to dominate the
Western Hemisphere and project American power into the world
beyond. Roosevelt wrote in December 1897, "The Chief of the Office of
Naval Intelligence has got to be the man on whom we rely for initiating
strategic work."[59] ONI, with Roosevelt's active support, performed what
he called "invaluable work . . . in formulating and preparing plans of
action for the war with Spain." The Kimball Plan, completed by ONI in
June 1897, called for naval blockades of Cuba and Manila, both prominent features of American strategy when war began in April 1898.[60]
While President William McKinley went reluctantly to war, Roosevelt
was unable to contain his enthusiasm and resigned from the Navy
Department to fight in Cuba as lieutenant colonel of the Rough Riders,
the First Volunteer Cavalry Regiment.

The main intelligence problem at the outbreak of war was the difficulty in locating the Spanish naval squadron sent from Cadiz under the
command of Admiral Pascual Cervera y Topete. Uncertainty over
Cervera's whereabouts initially hamstrung American plans for an invasion of Cuba. The Spanish fleet was eventually located by an agent network of Cuban telegraph operators set up by Captain Martin L. Hellings
of the U.S. Volunteer Signal Corps. Hellings's intelligence was telegraphed
to Signal Corps headquarters in Washington, then passed on to an
improvised war room on the second floor of the White House. On May 19
McKinley received a report from Hellings that "The Spanish flagship
arrived Santiago-de-Cuba." The U.S. Navy was promptly ordered to
blockade Cervera in Santiago harbor, thus enabling American forces to
land unopposed in June. Among the victorious U.S. troops were Roosevelt and the Rough Riders, whose well-publicized storming of Kettle
Hill and San Juan Heights on July 1 made him a national hero. Victory
over Spain made the United States an imperial power. The United States
gained Puerto Rico and Guam free of charge, and paid $20 million to
"educate, uplift and Christianize" the Philippines. McKinley was the first
American president to become a world leader.[61]

Boosted by his reputation as a war hero, Roosevelt was elected governor of New York in November 1898, and vice-president of the United
States two years later. On McKinlev's assassination in September 1901,
six months after the beginning of his second term, TR became, at forty-

two, the youngest president in American history and the first to be known by his initials. Once in the White House, Roosevelt dominated the making of United States foreign policy as no president had done for a century. "The biggest matters," he later boasted, ". . . I managed without consultation with anyone, for when a matter is of capital importance, it is well to have it handled by one man only."[62]

In Latin America, TR showed a taste for covert action as well as his celebrated "big stick." He later claimed in his autobiography that "by far the most important action I took in foreign affairs" was to acquire the Panama Canal Zone.[63] In August 1903 the Colombian Senate refused to ratify a treaty on the construction of the Panama Canal and the cession of the Canal Zone (then part of Colombia) to the United States. The Indianapolis *Sentinel*, among others, divined the president's thoughts. "The simplest plan of coercing Colombia," it declared, "would be inciting a revolution in Panama . . . and supporting the insurrectionary government." Panamanian insurrectionists were left in no doubt that they could depend on Roosevelt's support. The White House's celebration of their victory proved slightly premature. On the morning of November 3, 1903, the acting secretary of state cabled the U.S. consul in Panama: "Uprising on isthmus reported. Keep Department promptly and fully informed." The freedom fighters, however, were running slightly behind schedule. The consul replied that afternoon: "No uprising yet. Reported will be in the night." Confirmation followed the same evening: "Uprising occurred tonight 6; no bloodshed. Government will be organized tonight." The admiral commanding the nearby Colombian fleet was bribed to steam away, and U.S. warships prevented the Colombian government from landing troops to reassert its authority. Three days later the Roosevelt administration recognized the new Republic of Panama, which on November 18 concluded a treaty leasing the Canal Zone in perpetuity to the United States.[64] TR claimed all the credit:

> I do not think that any feat of quite such far-reaching importance
> has been to the credit of our country in recent years; and this I can
> say absolutely was my own work, and could not have been accomplished save by me or by some man of my temperament.[65]

When asked by Roosevelt to prepare a legal justification for his actions, Attorney General Philander C. Knox is said to have replied, "Oh, Mr. President, do not let so great an achievement suffer from any taint of legality!" After the cabinet had discussed press denunciations of his actions in Panama, Roosevelt turned to his secretary of war, Elihu Root. "Well," he asked, "have I answered the charges? Have I defended myself?" "You certainly have, Mr. President," replied Root, "You have shown that you were accused of seduction and you have conclusively proved that you were guilty of rape."[66]

The acquisition of the Canal Zone involved none of the elaborate planning of later CIA covert actions. Roosevelt employed no intelligence agency to achieve his policy aims; he simply seized the opportunities offered him to provide covert encouragement to the coup leaders and then to prevent the Colombian government from reestablishing control over its own territory. But the Panamanian adventure nonetheless set an important precedent. The 1904 Roosevelt Corollary to the Monroe Doctrine, asserting the right of the United States to "the exercise of an international police power" in the Western Hemisphere in "flagrant cases of . . . wrongdoing or impotence," was to be the unspoken ideological underpinning for the CIA covert actions in Latin America approved by a series of presidents half a century later. "The fact is," wrote the CIA's deputy director for intelligence, Robert Gates, in 1984, "that the Western hemisphere is the sphere of influence of the United States."[67]

The achievement of which Roosevelt seemed most proud, at the end of his years in the White House, was to have built more battleships:

> During my tenure as President I have more than doubled the navy of the United States, and at this moment our battle fleet is doing what no other similar fleet of a like size has ever done—that is, circumnavigating the globe. . . .[68]

TR expected ONI to provide evidence of threats from foreign navies in order to justify his own ambitious building program. Half a century or more later, during the Cold War, presidents were sometimes accused of "politicizing" intelligence analysis. None did so more unashamedly than Roosevelt. There is little doubt that many ONI assessments were slanted to fit the president's policy needs. Naval intelligence officers rarely dared to challenge Roosevelt's obsession with battleships as the virility symbols of American naval power. At the outbreak of the First World War, the United States was to be desperately short of destroyers.[69]

Roosevelt was particularly anxious for ONI to document what he insisted was the growing naval menace from Japan. The U.S. naval attaché in Berlin reported a series of frequently unreliable rumors, among them the remarkable claim that Admiral Togo, the hero of the Russo-Japanese War, was touring Germany purchasing weapons with bags of Chinese gold. Such stories were grist to the president's mill. He was not pleased, however, by reports from the naval attaché in Tokyo that Japan was not in fact rebuilding its fleet after the war with Russia. Roosevelt seized instead on alarmist claims by military intelligence that Japan was gearing up for war as part of his justification for sending the "Great White Fleet" of the United States around the world to warn the Japanese not to become too "cocky."[70]

Roosevelt's interest in intelligence collection and assessment during his years at the White House went little beyond expecting it to demonstrate the need for more battleships and provide support for his other main policy aims. He failed to grasp the weaknesses of a foreign intelligence system based on a limited number of naval and military attachés collecting mostly unclassified information on other armed services, supplemented by the spasmodic use of frequently unreliable part-time agents. It seems never to have occurred to Roosevelt, still less to his undynamic successor, William H. Taft (the last president to keep a cow on the White House lawn), to consider setting up a specialized foreign intelligence service. Both were blissfully unaware that French and Russian codebreakers found no difficulty in breaking the primitive diplomatic ciphers employed by the State Department.[71] SIGINT, though it had fascinated Washington, was beyond most early twentieth-century American imaginations. Washington's grasp of intelligence had equaled that of any European leader of his time. On the eve of the First World War, by contrast, the intelligence system of the United States was more backward than that of any other major power. Most Americans, however, preferred it that way. Ever since John Winthrop set out to build "a city on a hill" in Puritan Massachusetts, Americans had believed that their country was guided by uniquely high ethical principles. They regarded peacetime espionage, if they thought of it at all, as a corrupt outgrowth of Old World diplomacy, alien to the open and upright American way. It took two world wars and a cold war to persuade them otherwise.

CHAPTER 2

The First World War and After: From Woodrow Wilson to Herbert Hoover

The United States, President Woodrow Wilson believed, had been chosen by Providence "to show the way to the nations of the world how they shall walk in the paths of liberty."[1] There was no place within his vision of the chosen nation for the building of an American intelligence community. The First World War was gradually to force covert operations on the president's reluctant attention. But in August 1914 he was still, like most Americans, an intelligence innocent. After the war, he publicly poked fun at his own prewar naïveté:

> Let me testify to this, my fellow citizens, I not only did not know it until we got into this war, but I did not believe it when I was told that it was true, that Germany was not the only country that maintained a secret service. Every country in Europe maintained it, because they had to be ready for Germany's spring upon them, and the only difference between the German secret service and the other secret services was that the German secret service found out more than the others did! (*Applause and laughter*) And therefore Germany sprang upon the other nations at unawares [*sic*], and they were not ready for it.[2]

No nation was less ready than the United States. Neither the Justice Department's Bureau of Investigation (the future FBI) nor the Treasury Department's Secret Service had much experience of counterespionage work. Each made matters worse by refusing to cooperate with the other. Both German and British intelligence agencies thus found it easier to operate in the neutral United States than in war-torn Europe. The twenty-one German spies operating in Britain in the summer of 1914 had been under surveillance for some time by the British Security Service (later known as MI5) and the Special Branch at London's Scotland Yard. All were immediately arrested on the outbreak of war. Subsequent German espionage in wartime Britain achieved nothing of significance; most enemy spies were rapidly rounded up. British intelligence similarly failed to establish any effective network in security-conscious wartime Germany.[3] Espionage in the United States was a far less risky business.

Immediately after the outbreak of war in Europe, Germany took the offensive in a secret war within the United States. "The German government," writes Wilson's biographer, Arthur S. Link, ". . . mounted a massive campaign on American soil of intrigue, espionage, and sabotage unprecedented in modern times by one allegedly friendly power against another."[4] The main objective of the campaign was to prevent American industry and finance from supplying Britain and its allies with the sinews of war. Because of Britain's dominance of the seas and financial reserves (supplemented by American loans), it was able to import far more than its enemies from the United States. American exports to Britain and France rose from $750 million in 1914 to $2.75 billion two years later; exports to Germany dwindled during the same period from $345 million to a mere $2 million.[5] Despite a number of short-term tactical successes, the German secret war in the New World ended in strategic defeat. Like the German sinking of the British liner *Lusitania* in May 1915 with the loss of 128 American lives, the gradual revelation of German covert operations in the United States proved a public relations disaster for the German cause. The disaster was skillfully exploited by British intelligence. Profiting from German bungling and American innocence, it gradually succeeded in winning the confidence not merely of the fragmented American intelligence community but also of President Wilson himself.

"The United States must be neutral in fact as well as in name during these days that are to try men's souls," Wilson told the American people in August 1914. "We must be impartial in thought as well as action, must put a curb on our sentiments as well as upon every transaction that might be construed as a preference of one party to the struggle before another."[6] Wilson was at first reluctant to publicize the evidence of German covert operations in the United States for fear of compromising his policy of neutrality. The first substantial evidence reached the White House in December 1914. Reports from the Bureau of Investigation revealed the involvement of the German ambassador, Count Johann

Heinrich von Bernstorff, in the wholesale forgery of American passports to enable German reservists in the United States to return to Germany via neutral ports. The president was less disturbed by the misbehavior of the German embassy, however, than by the unwelcome prospect of a public controversy with Germany. He wrote to the attorney general, T. W. Gregory:

> The . . . matter is evidently of the most sensational kind. I hope that you will have it looked into thoroughly, but that, at the same time, you will have all possible precautions taken that no hint of it may become public until it materializes into something upon which we have no choice but to act.[7]

Though a number of German citizens in the United States were convicted of counterfeiting passports, the German embassy was kept out of court proceedings on the private understanding that it would abstain from forgery in future.[8]

In May 1915, on Wilson's instructions, the Secret Service began investigating other suspected violations of American neutrality, some involving the German commercial attaché, Dr. Heinrich Albert. On July 23 Albert boarded a Sixth Avenue elevated train in New York, shadowed by Secret Service operative Frank Burke, who had his eye on the attaché's bulging briefcase. Burke could scarcely believe his luck when Albert got off at Fiftieth Street and absentmindedly left his bag behind. Seeing Burke make off with the briefcase, Albert gave chase. Burke hurriedly boarded another train and told the conductor he was being followed by a madman. According to Burke's report, "The wild-eyed appearance of the Doctor corroborated my statement and the conductor called to the motorman to pass the next corner without stopping so the nut could not get on."[9]

The next day the chief of the Secret Service, William J. Flynn, delivered the contents of the stolen briefcase to Wilson's son-in-law, William J. McAdoo, secretary of the treasury. Among them were documents detailing the planting of pro-German news stories in the American press, subsidies paid to German-American and Irish-American organizations and periodicals, the purchase with German money of a large munitions plant in Bridgeport, Connecticut (to prevent its production going to the Allies), and various secret schemes to influence United States opinion. McAdoo took these documents in some excitement to the president at his summer home in Cornish, New Hampshire. Wilson, however, saw them chiefly as a tiresome distraction from his efforts to preserve American neutrality. He left his confidant and chief adviser, Colonel Edward M.

House, Secretary of State Robert Lansing, and McAdoo to decide what to do with them. The three men jointly agreed to publish selected items from Albert's briefcase in the New York *World* on condition that the editor did not reveal his source. The documents provoked the expected press uproar. ". . . Woe to the newspaper or lecturer who takes the German side," declared the New York *Nation*. "'How much are you being paid by the Germans?' will be an inevitable question."[10]

Though not greatly exercised by passport forgery and the contents of Albert's briefcase, Wilson was much more concerned by German sabotage in the United States. The main initial organizers of wartime covert action on American soil were the military and naval attachés at the German embassy, Major Franz von Papen (later German chancellor and Adolf Hitler's vice-chancellor), and Captain Karl Boy-Ed. Apparently dissatisfied with the early results achieved by the attachés, the German admiralty dispatched the international banker and naval reserve officer, Franz von Rintelen, to step up the tempo of the secret war. Rintelen promised rapid results. "I'll buy up what I can and blow up what I can't," he told the admiralty. Within a few months he had set up a successful sabotage network, which used East Coast dockworkers and longshoremen to place time bombs on departing munitions ships.[11]

The first word of Rintelen's activities reached Wilson early in July 1915 in a remarkable letter from Miss Anne Seward, niece of Lincoln's secretary of state, who had met Rintelen in Germany before the war. She told the president that she had recently been shocked to encounter Rintelen in the United States, traveling under a false identity as, apparently, "a secret but intimate emissary from the Kaiser":

> . . . His utterances are distinctly offensive and his threats alarming. His national prominence in Germany and his high military rank coupled with his various aliases, his frequent changes of address give rise to uncomfortable suspicions.

Miss Seward was reluctant to put more details of this "sinister situation" on paper but offered to do so orally.[12] Wilson thanked her for having "performed a public duty in a very considerate and admirable way":

> . . . I shall take the liberty, if I may, of asking the Secretary of State to send someone who is entirely trustworthy . . . to see you, so that he may learn fully from you what you think, I believe rightly, we should look into.[13]

Miss Seward told Lansing's emissary that Rintelen had admitted being a German secret agent. Agents of the Bureau of Investigation who were put on Rintelen's tail reported that he was head of a powerful German underground that was fomenting strikes, disrupting the export of munitions, and trying to provoke conflict between the United States and Mexico. The investigation was assisted by Rintelen's apparently compulsive need to boast about his exploits. He told an undercover BI agent that he had personally given the order for the sinking of the *Lusitania*.[14] Rintelen's memoirs, in which he grandly styles himself the "Dark Invader," recapture some of the absurdity of his wartime braggadocio: "Singlehandedly I . . . ventured an attack against the forty-eight United States! . . . The word 'fear' did not and does not exist in my vocabulary . . ."[15]

Both Wilson and Lansing were anxious not to disturb American neutrality by disclosing the full extent of Rintelen's covert operations. Instead they hoped to deter further operations by revealing in press briefings that a major investigation was under way into alleged German intrigues.[16] Wilson, however, was shaken by Bureau of Investigation reports. He wrote to House on August 4, 1915, "I am sure that the country is honeycombed with German intrigue and infested with German spies. The evidences of these things are multiplying every day."[17] On August 24 Wilson gloomily told his wife-to-be, Edith Bolling Galt:

> The Colonel [House] evidently regards it as not incredible ([nor] do
> I, for that matter) that there might be an armed uprising of German
> sympathizers. Rumors of preparations for such a thing have fre-
> quently reached us. . . .[18]

Wilson was partly reassured by the news that the Dark Invader was now in a British prison. Early in August Rintelen had been recalled from the United States, probably after complaints from Papen and Boy-Ed. Carrying a forged Swiss passport, he crossed the Atlantic in the Dutch liner *Nordau*. British naval intelligence appears to have learned of Rintelen's recall from intercepted German messages. When the *Nordau* called at Ramsgate, Rintelen was arrested ("the darkest moment in my life!" he later claimed), interrogated personally by the director of naval intelligence, Captain (later Admiral Sir) Reginald "Blinker" Hall, and confessed to being a German naval officer.[19]

Blinker Hall (so called because of his facial twitch and habit of high-speed blinking) was the most successful intelligence chief of the First World War. As the war progressed, he made an indelible impression on the American ambassador in London, Dr. Walter Hines Page, who sent Wilson this astonishing eulogy of him:

Neither in fiction nor in fact can you find any such man to match
him. . . . The man is a clear case of genius. All other secret service
men are amateurs by comparison. . . . I shall never meet another
man like him; that were too much to expect.

For Hall can look through you and see the very muscular movements of your immortal soul while he is talking to you. Such eyes as
the man has! My Lord![20]

Hall's chief contact at the U.S. embassy was the second secretary,
Edward Bell, known as Eddie to his British friends and as Ned to Americans, who acted as unofficial liaison officer in London with the British
intelligence community. Skillfully, and at times unscrupulously, Hall used
the intelligence he obtained on German operations in the New World to
win the confidence not merely of Page and the U.S. embassy but ultimately of the president himself. He ranks as the founding father of what
later became the secret Anglo-American intelligence alliance.

In August 1915 Hall gave Bell details of his interrogation of Rintelen,
together with copies of some of Rintelen's papers dealing with operations in Mexico and the United States. Hall also handed over documents
captured from an American courier for the German and Austrian
embassies in Washington.[21] Among the most compromising was a handwritten proposal by the Austrian ambassador, Constantin Dumba, for
funding strikes in the American steel and munitions industries, subsequently published in the American press. Lansing reported to Wilson
after seeing Dumba, "He is evidently very much distressed because of
what has occurred, but I do not think he really repents of his action; he
only deplores the fact that he was found out." Though still anxious to
avoid public controversy, Wilson privately insisted on Dumba's recall.[22]

After Dumba had left Washington on September 24 it was the turn of
Papen and Boy-Ed. On November 22 the attorney general publicly
denounced what he implied were German-inspired "attacks upon lawful
American industries and commerce through incendiary fires and explosions in factories, threats to intimidate employees and other acts of violence." A week later Lansing told Wilson that there was now enough evidence to expel Papen and Boy-Ed:

I feel that we cannot wait much longer to act. . . . The increasing
public indignation in regard to these men and the general criticism
of the Government for allowing them to remain are not the chief
reasons for suggesting action in these cases, although I do not think
that such reasons should be ignored. We have been over-patient
with these people. . . .

The president agreed. "There need be no further delay in this matter," he told Lansing. "I would be obliged if you would act at once. . . ."[23] The expulsion of Papen and Boy-Ed was announced on December 3. Four days later, in his annual message to Congress, Wilson denounced in barely veiled language those who had served as their agents:

> There are citizens of the United States, I blush to admit, born under other flags . . . , who have poured the poison of disloyalty into the very arteries of our national life; who have sought to bring the authority and good name of the Government into contempt, to destroy our industries wherever they thought it effective for their vindictive purposes to strike at them, and to debase our politics to the uses of foreign intrigue.[24]

The British ambassador, Sir Cecil Spring Rice, reported exultantly to London:

> It is believed that the President, having written this passage, thought for some time of withdrawing it, but finally he determined to read it as it had stood originally. He has thus crossed the Rubicon. He has openly attacked the German-Americans who have openly attacked him.[25]

Further humiliation awaited Papen on his journey home. Though he had been given safe passage across the Atlantic, the British claimed the right to search his baggage when his ship called at Falmouth. Papen thought he had brought no compromising documents with him, but had forgotten to destroy the stubs from his checkbooks that recorded details of payments to agents responsible for sabotage in the United States and Canada. Once again, Hall forwarded the incriminating evidence to Bell at the United States embassy.[26]

Hall's attempts to influence American opinion suffered a temporary setback after the 1916 Easter Rising in Dublin. The self-styled provisional government of the Irish Republic, proclaimed on Easter Monday "in the name of God and of the dead generations," won little support and surrendered after six days of street fighting. But the 450 lives lost during the rising and the execution of its leaders shocked most Irish Catholics into supporting the nationalist demand for independence from Britain. American sympathy for Britain fell to its lowest point of the war. Hall tried to undo some of the damage to the British cause by secretly passing to the U.S. embassy lurid extracts from the diary of the Irish nationalist Sir Roger Casement, who had been captured shortly before the rising when he landed in Ireland from a German U-boat. The diary extracts contained records of Casement's numerous payments to male prostitutes, together with enthusiastic descriptions of "*huge*," "*enormous*" male genitalia, "much groaning and struggles and moans." Dr. Page, the U.S. ambassador, read half a page but declared himself unable to continue without becoming ill. Hall must certainly have hoped that Wilson would be as shocked as Page. He also offered exclusive extracts for publication to Ben Allen of the Associated Press, but Allen turned them down.[27]

German covert action ultimately did far more than British policy in Ireland to alienate American opinion. During 1916 German agents succeeded in planting bombs in munitions factories, warehouses, and cargo vessels. Their most spectacular exploit was the explosion at the huge freightyard on Black Tom Island in New York harbor in July 1916. Two million pounds of explosives, awaiting shipment to Russia, were destroyed. Thousands of plate-glass windows from Brooklyn and Manhattan skyscrapers cascaded into the streets; the blast shattered almost every window in Jersey City.

The success of German sabotage operations made glaringly obvious the weakness of American counterespionage. Both Lansing and Frank L. Polk, the State Department counselor responsible for intelligence, had a far better grasp than Wilson of the problems caused both by the inadequate resources of the Bureau of Investigation and the Secret Service, and by the bitter rivalry between them. In the summer of 1916 Lansing made Polk head of a new unit, later known as U-1, that sought to coordinate intelligence gathering by acting as "the 'Clearing House' or at least the depository of information gathered from various sources." The Bureau of Investigation and the Secret Service, Lansing later told the president, were "willing to report to the State Department but not each other."[28] Wilson could not bring himself either to tackle the problem of intelligence coordination personally or to delegate it to Lansing. The secretary of state's stuffy demeanor and bureaucratic habits increasingly grated on the president. As one of his critics complained, it seemed that Lansing "worked at being dull." Wilson acted largely as his own secretary of state and showed greater confidence in the inexperienced diplomacy of Colonel House than in the State Department and U.S. missions abroad.[29] Lansing's understanding of the problems of intelligence collection and assessment, however, greatly exceeded that of Wilson and House.

British intelligence was better informed than the Americans about German espionage and covert action in the United States. Hall's representative in Washington was the extrovert British naval attaché, Captain (later Admiral Sir) Guy Gaunt. Soon after the outbreak of war in Europe Gaunt breezily informed Spring Rice that henceforth he proposed to concentrate on covert operations:

> My idea was to strike out in the Intelligence-cum-propaganda line —independently, in case trouble arose. It might be advisable, I suggested to the Ambassador, that he should be able to say: "I didn't know what the fool was doing"—the fool being me.

Gaunt's main agent network was composed of Central European nationalists working under the Czech leader Emanuel V. Voska. Since most of the agents were past or present citizens of Germany's ally, the Austro-Hungarian Empire, they were often wrongly presumed by potential employers to be pro-German and were thus able to find jobs in German or German-American offices. Neither the Bureau of Investigation nor the Secret Service, at least in the early years of the war, possessed any comparable agent network.[30]

Gaunt's success attracted the envious attention of Commander (later Captain Sir) Mansfield Cumming, head of Britain's wartime foreign intelligence agency, MI1c. Like Hall, Cumming was a larger-than-life figure who, though unknown to the public, enjoyed becoming a legend in his own lifetime in the corridors of power. "C," as he liked to be known within Whitehall, brought enormous enthusiasm and a degree of eccentricity to the direction of British espionage, which he described as "capital sport." When his mobility was reduced by a wooden leg fitted after a car accident in 1914, he propelled himself around the War Office on a child's scooter, later replaced by an "autoped" purchased in the United States. Before the war, shortage of funds had forced Cumming to restrict his operations almost entirely to Germany.[31] Late in 1915 his larger wartime budget enabled him to open his first American station in New York.[32] The head of station, Sir William Wiseman, was only thirty. Despite his mustache, he appeared "the merest boy" to his American friends. He had, however, been a member of the boxing team at Cambridge University and held a baronetcy dating back to 1628. After an unsuccessful period as a journalist and playwright, Wiseman had embarked on a much more successful business career in North America. At the outbreak of war he had enlisted in the Duke of Cornwall's Light Infantry but was declared unfit for active service after being gassed at the battle of Ypres early in 1915, and joined MI1c.[33] Wiseman's deputy in New York, Norman Thwaites, was another British officer invalided out of the trenches. Thwaites had been partly educated in Germany, spoke fluent German, and was well connected in the German-American community. Before the war he had been private secretary to Joseph Pulitzer, later publisher of the New York *World* and founder of the Pulitzer prizes, then assistant foreign editor of the *World*. Thwaites was an old friend of Frank Polk, the intelligence coordinator at the State Department.[34]

The initial priorities of the MI1c station in New York were to counter German espionage and covert operations in North America and to keep under surveillance leading Irish and Indian nationalists.[35] Wiseman's most remarkable achievement, however, was to win the confidence first of Colonel House, then of President Wilson. At his first meeting with House on December 17, 1916, Wiseman impressed him as "the most important caller I have had for some time."[36] Knowing that Spring Rice's Republican sympathies and indiscreet wit had made him unpopular with Wilson, Wiseman set out to supplant the ambassador as the most influential British representative in the United States by boldly misrepresenting his true role. Seduced by Wiseman's charm and ancient baronetcy, House naïvely concluded that Wiseman was well qualified to become a direct channel of communication with the government of David Lloyd George that had come to power in Britain on December 7. House wrote to Wilson on January 26, 1917:

> [Wiseman] told me in the *gravest confidence*, a thing which I had already suspected and that is that he is in direct communication with the Foreign Office, and that the Ambassador and other members of the Embassy are not aware of it.
>
> I am happy beyond measure over this last conference with him, for I judge that he reflects the views of his government.[37]

In reality, so far from Wiseman being a spokesman for the British government, Lloyd George and most (perhaps all) of his ministers were as yet unaware of his existence. Wiseman was not, as he claimed, "in direct communication with the Foreign Office." Instead, he reported to Cumming, who passed on to the Foreign Office and other Whitehall ministries what intelligence he judged appropriate. Having won over House by a mixture of charm and deception, he then used House's confidence in him to persuade Whitehall that he could provide a direct link with the White House. A later SIS head of station in the United States, John Bruce Lockhart, who served in Washington during the early 1950s, believes that Wiseman's achievement during 1917 in gaining the confidence of the president gives him a "claim to be considered the most successful 'agent of influence' the British ever had."[38]

As well as deceiving Wilson about his role in the United States, Wiseman also directed an imaginative array of covert operations of which the president, had he known, would certainly have disapproved. Among the most imaginative was Thwaites's success, during a Long Island house party, in stealing a photograph showing Bernstorff, the German ambassador, with two young women in bathing suits. The photograph was innocent, but Thwaites swiftly grasped its publicity value. It was taken to New York, copied, and returned to the owner before she had noticed its absence. Thwaites then arranged for an enlarged copy of the apparently compromising photograph to be prominently displayed in the office of the Russian ambassador, thus exposing Bernstorff to ridicule among the Washington diplomatic corps. According to Thwaites, "Poor Bernstorff heard of it promptly and cursed the Muscovite, quite definitely of the opinion that some rascally secret servant in Russian pay had purloined the picture." When the photograph appeared in the press, Wilson too probably assumed that the source was the Russian embassy.[39]

Both Blinker Hall's and Mansfield Cumming's intelligence agencies made a remarkable impression on the president, in part by successfully exploiting his naïveté about intelligence operations. The single greatest intelligence coup of the war derived from the ability of Room 40, the secret SIGINT section of British naval intelligence, to intercept and decrypt German diplomatic and naval traffic. After the Germans' transatlantic cable was cut by the British at the outbreak of the war, the officially neutral but pro-German Swedes allowed them to use the Swedish cable to communicate with German diplomatic missions in the New World. When Britain protested in the summer of 1915, Sweden agreed to stop allowing Germany to use its cables, but in fact continued cabling German messages, disguised by reencipherment in Swedish ciphers, by a roundabout route from Stockholm via Buenos Aires to Washington. This circuitous itinerary also included Britain, and by the spring of 1916 Room 40 had detected the Swedish ruse. This time, however, Britain made no protest because of the opportunity offered by the "Swedish roundabout" to intercept German diplomatic traffic undetected. At the end of 1916 the Germans acquired a second and more direct communication link with North America. Bernstorff successfully argued that President Wilson's peace initiatives would make speedier progress if the German embassy in Washington could use the American transatlantic cable to communicate with Berlin. That cable too went via Britain, and Room 40 was "highly entertained" to discover German ciphers among the American diplomatic traffic that, unknown to Wilson, it routinely intercepted.[40]

British cryptanalysts were further entertained by the simplicity of U.S. codes and ciphers. The State Department had yet to emerge from a state of cryptographic innocence and employed ciphers that the head of the first American SIGINT agency, Herbert Yardley, later dismissed as hopelessly insecure. The president was even more naïve than State. Anxious to ensure the absolute secrecy of his own personal communications, Wilson and his wife spent "many hours of many nights" laboriously encoding and decoding messages in a supposedly unbreakable cipher to and from Colonel House during his confidential missions for the president to the capitals of Europe.[41] Herbert Yardley later claimed that, while a youthful code clerk in the State Department, he copied down a five-hundred-word message from House to Wilson:

> Imagine my amazement when I was able to solve the message in less than two hours. . . . Is it possible that a man sits in the White House, dreaming, picturing himself as a maker of history, an international statesman, a mediator of peace, and sends his agents out with schoolboy ciphers?[42]

Room 40 doubtless found the few hours required to decrypt the top-secret cables of the president of the United States unusually diverting. The great champion of open diplomacy was splendidly unaware of the degree to which he was practicing it himself.

Until the beginning of 1917 Hall concealed Room 40's success in breaking German codes from the Americans for fear of alerting them to the vulnerability of their own communications. On the morning of January 17, however, he suddenly found himself faced with a difficult dilemma. One of his leading cryptanalysts, Nigel de Grey, who had been working the night shift, dramatically inquired of Hall, "Do you want to bring the Americans into the war?"

"Yes, my boy," replied Hall. "Why?"

"I think I've got something here for you," said de Grey, and handed him an incomplete translation of an intercepted telegram from the German foreign minister, Arthur Zimmermann, to the Washington embassy for onward transmission to Mexico City. The Zimmermann telegram, as it became known, contained a German offer of alliance with Mexico if war broke out between Germany and the United States. Zimmermann promised "generous financial support and an undertaking on our part that Mexico is to reconquer the lost territory in Texas, New Mexico, and Arizona." Because of its importance, the telegram was transmitted from Berlin by both the "Swedish roundabout" and the American transatlantic cable. By a remarkable diplomatic impertinence, the United States had thus been hoodwinked into providing one of the channels through which Germany hoped to persuade Mexico to enter the war against it. Hall quickly recognized the potential risks as well as the advantages of publicizing the decrypt. If Washington realized that Britain had been tapping the U.S. transatlantic cable and intercepting American as well as German diplomatic traffic, the Zimmermann telegram might lead not to a triumph for Room 40 but to a spectacular intelligence disaster. Before the intercept could be used to enrage American opinion, therefore, Hall had to devise a method of disguising its origins.

For over two weeks Hall kept the secret of the Zimmermann telegram to himself and Room 40. At first he thought that Germany's announcement that it would begin unrestricted U-boat warfare on February 1 might possibly bring the United States into the war without the assistance of British intelligence. But it was not to be. On February 3 Wilson broke off diplomatic relations with Germany but declared his hope that the United States could still preserve its neutrality. Two days later Hall at last delivered the Zimmermann telegram to the Foreign Office. At his request, the British minister in Mexico succeeded in illicitly obtaining from the Mexico telegraph office a copy of the version of the telegram forwarded by the German embassy in Washington. It thus became possible to pretend to the Americans that Room 40 had obtained the telegram not from intercepting American and Swedish diplomatic communications but from an agent in Mexico City. On February 19 Hall showed Eddie Bell of the U.S. embassy a decrypted copy of the version of the telegram obtained in Mexico. Hall said later that he had rarely seen anyone "blow off steam in so forthright a manner": "Mexico to 'reconquer the lost territory'! Texas and Arizona? Why not Illinois and New York while they were about it?" But, asked Bell, might the telegram be a hoax? Was it to be given officially to the United States? That, said Hall, had still to be decided by the Foreign Office. He failed to tell Bell that he was still facing opposition from the permanent undersecretary, Lord Hardinge, who disliked the idea of admitting that the British government engaged in codebreaking even in wartime.

The foreign secretary, Arthur Balfour, overrode Hardinge's objections. "I think Captain Hall may be left to clinch this problem," he told him. "He knows the ropes better than anyone." Lengthy discussions followed at the U.S. embassy between Hall, Bell, and Page. The ambassador insisted that if the foreign secretary would personally present him with a copy of the telegram, the impact on the president would be greatly heightened. Balfour's patrician calm was rarely ruffled. But, when he received Page at the Foreign Office on Friday, February 23, he found it difficult to suppress his excitement. The moment when he handed over a copy of the decrypted Zimmermann telegram was, he said, "the most dramatic in all my life." For Page too it was an unforgettable moment. He spent most of the night drafting a lengthy telegram to the State Department. When Room 40 decrypted Page's telegram, probably with little delay, Hall must have been delighted at what he read.[43] Unaware that Hall had known the gist of Zimmermann's message for the last month, Page reported to Washington with unintentional inaccuracy:

> The receipt of this information has so greatly exercised the British Government that they have lost no time in communicating it to me to transmit to you, in order that our Government may be able without delay to make such disposition as may be necessary in view of the threatened invasion of our territory.[44]

Page's telegram arrived in Washington late on Saturday, February 24, but, as sometimes happened on weekends, was not deciphered until the following afternoon. Since Lansing was on a short vacation, the message was taken to the president by Polk, who was acting secretary of state as well as head of the intelligence unit. Wilson was as shocked and angry as Hall had hoped he would be. The Zimmermann telegram showed that at the very moment when Wilson had been negotiating in good faith with Germany on ways to bring the war to an end, Germany had simultaneously been trying to entice Mexico into attacking the United States. On reading the text, Wilson lost all faith in further negotiations with the German government.[45] But his handling of the telegram over the next few days shows how strange, and even bewildering, he found his first experience of SIGINT. Wilson's immediate instinct on the evening of February 25 was to publish the telegram at once. Polk persuaded him to wait until Lansing returned from his vacation. By the time the secretary of state arrived at the White House on the morning of Tuesday, February 27, the president had had second thoughts. He told Lansing he had been wondering how the Zimmermann telegram could actually have reached Bernstorff in Washington, and was now "a little uncertain as to its authenticity." Lansing reminded the president that the Germans had been allowed to communicate with their Washington embassy via the U.S. transatlantic cable and explained how the telegram had been sent first to Bernstorff, then forwarded by him to Mexico City. Wilson several times exclaimed, "Good Lord!" during Lansing's explanations, but was convinced by him. He also agreed that, before publicizing the telegram, he would need confirmation that Bernstorff had forwarded it to Mexico City. Later the same day Polk extracted a copy of Bernstorff's cipher telegram from a reluctant Western Union. On the afternoon of Wednesday, February 28, Wilson telephoned Lansing to say he had decided the telegram should be published in the following day's papers. The president agreed to Lansing's suggestion that it should be released through

Associated Press on the grounds that "this would avoid any charge of using the document improperly and would attract more attention than issuing it officially. . . . When we were asked about it we could say that we knew of it and knew that it was authentic."[46]

The publication of the Zimmermann telegram created an even greater sensation in the United States than the German invasion of Belgium or the sinking of the *Lusitania.* "No other event of the war," writes Arthur Link, ". . . so stunned the American people." Partly as a result of previous revelations of German covert action, most newspaper readers on the morning of Thursday, March 1, assumed that the telegram was authentic. Some German-American spokesmen, however, dismissed it as a forgery fabricated by British agents.[47] The State Department telegraphed Page on the evening of March 1 that, to disprove such charges:

> . . . IT WOULD BE OF THE GREATEST HELP IF THE BRITISH GOVERNMENT WOULD PERMIT YOU OR SOMEONE IN THE EMBASSY TO PERSONALLY DECODE THE ORIGINAL MESSAGE WHICH WE SECURED FROM THE TELEGRAPH OFFICE IN WASHINGTON . . . AND MAKE IT POSSIBLE FOR THE DEPARTMENT TO STATE THAT IT HAD SECURED THE ZIMMERMANN NOTE FROM OUR OWN PEOPLE.

The next day Page cabled Washington:

> BELL TOOK THE CIPHER TEXT OF THE GERMAN MESSAGE . . . TO THE ADMIRALTY AND THERE, HIMSELF, DECIPHERED IT FROM THE GERMAN CODE WHICH IS IN THE ADMIRALTY'S POSSESSION.[48]

In fact, Bell had merely looked on while the British cryptanalyst, Nigel de Grey, deciphered the telegram for him.[49] Room 40 also decrypted three other coded German cables sent to London by the State Department. Hall offered to decrypt promptly any further intercepted telegrams, but claimed speciously that there would be no point in providing Washington with a c)py of the German code book. Page reported innocently:

> I am told actual code would be of no use to us as it was never used straight, but with a great number of variations which are known to only one or two experts here. They cannot be spared.[50]

Wilson and the State Department appear to have accepted this pretext for Hall's refusal to share cryptanalytic secrets with the United States. The steps taken to prove the authenticity of the Zimmermann telegram turned out to be unnecessary. On March 3 Zimmermann unexpectedly confessed. "I cannot deny it," he admitted. "It is true." Lansing heard the news "with profound amazement and relief":

> By admitting the truth he blundered in a most astounding manner
> for a man engaged in international intrigues. Of course the message
> itself was a stupid piece of business, but admitting it was far
> worse.[51]

To Hall's delight, the American press generally gave credit for obtaining the Zimmermann telegram to U.S. secret agents rather than to British codebreakers. Hall had "no little fun" covering the tracks of Room 40 by deceiving American journalists in London. Much of the "fun" centered on a trunk of Swedish diplomatic documents on board the ship that had brought Bernstorff across the Atlantic after the breach of German-American diplomatic relations in February. Hall spread rumors that the trunk had contained some of Bernstorff's secret papers. He wrote gleefully to Guy Gaunt in Washington:

> [The journalists] are quite convinced that the American Secret Service abstracted the Zimmermann telegram from the trunk. . . . They
> tackled me yesterday about it, and I had to admit that all the evidence pointed to the seals having been broken before we opened
> the chest. It is a very safe line and I think we will stick to it.[52]

Wilson's address to a joint session of Congress on April 2, 1917, calling for a declaration of war on Germany, was one of the great speeches of American political history. It is best remembered for Wilson's vision of a postwar world "made safe for democracy" with peace "planted upon the tested foundations of political liberty." Americans, said the president, remained "the sincere friends of the German people . . . however hard it may be for them, for the time being, to believe that this is spoken from our hearts." They had been brought into the conflict by "Germany's irresponsible government which has thrown aside all considerations of humanity and is running amok." Among the evidence of "running amok" that Wilson cited were German intelligence operations:

> One of the things that has served to convince us that the Prussian
> autocracy was not and could never be our friend is that from the
> very outset of the present war it has filled our unsuspecting communities and even our offices of government with spies and set
> criminal intrigues everywhere afoot against our national unity of

counsel, our peace within and without, our industries and our commerce. Indeed it is now evident that its spies were here before the war began . . . That it means to stir up enemies at our very doors the intercepted note to the German Minister in Mexico City is eloquent evidence.[53]

Even without "the intercepted note," the United States would doubtless have declared war on Germany. But Room 40 had accelerated the decision to do so and had helped Americans to go to war as a united nation. On April 6 the United States formally declared war on Germany. That night Hall and de Grey celebrated with champagne.[54]

With the United States now in the war, Wiseman began organizing the first joint Anglo-American covert operation. Its aim, following the February Revolution in Russia that had overthrown the czarist regime, was a propaganda campaign, secretly financed by Britain and the United States, to help keep Russia in the war against Germany. The campaign had two parts: first, black propaganda "to expose present German intrigues and their undoubted [in fact imaginary] connection with the late reactionary [czarist] Government"; second, a more straightforward attempt "to persuade the Russians to attack the Germans with all their might and thus accomplish the overthrow of the Hohenzollern dynasty and autocracy in Berlin."[55] Wiseman gained funding for the operation by an ingenious piece of deception. He won American support by implying that his scheme already had Foreign Office backing, then used American backing to gain Foreign Office support. On May 26 Wiseman reported triumphantly to Cumming that the Americans were willing to leave the running of the operation to the British—in effect, to MI1c:

> The U.S. authorities are willing to facilitate this propaganda in every possible way, and join with the British Government in putting up the necessary funds; but, as they have no organization of their own through which to conduct such an operation, they would like the matter left entirely in my hands, on behalf of both the Governments.

Wiseman asked Cumming to see Balfour's private secretary, Sir Eric Drummond, "immediately and obtain his authorization." The proposed covert action would, he believed, "work in very well" with the operations of the MI1c station in Petrograd, headed by the future British foreign secretary, Sir Samuel Hoare.[56]

Wiseman did not mention his project to the British ambassador. He did, however, discuss it with House, Polk, and Lansing—all of whom gave their enthusiastic support. On June 15 Wilson authorized funding of $75,000 for what he naïvely believed was an Allied propaganda exercise rather than a covert operation run by British intelligence.[57] The next day Wiseman cabled Drummond to ask for the same amount from London. The Foreign Office, unlike Cumming, was not keen on the idea of a joint operation with the Americans, even if it was effectively run by MI1c. Wiseman won Balfour over by stressing Wilson's alleged interest in the operation and the intelligence on American policy that he expected to obtain if it went ahead:

> It is possible that by acting practically as a confidential agent for Remus [the U.S. administration] I might strengthen the understanding with Caesar [House] that in future he will keep us informed of steps taken by Remus in their foreign affairs which would ordinarily not be a matter of common knowledge to the Governments of the two countries.[58]

The Foreign Office agreed to contribute $75,000 to the Russian operation on the grounds that "the scheme seems to afford sound measures for checking German pacifist propaganda to Russia, and that [the] President is interested in it."[59]

To head the covert operation in Petrograd, Wiseman chose the celebrated playwright and novelist W. Somerset Maugham, who used his writing career to provide cover for his work as a wartime MI1c agent. Maugham was "staggered" by his new mission. "The long and short of it," he wrote later, "was that I should go to Russia and keep the Russians in the war." With Maugham, in a supporting role, went Gaunt's former agent, Emanuel Voska, with instructions to "organise the Czechs and Slovaks of the Empire to keep Russia in the war." As well as organizing pro-Allied propaganda in Petrograd, Maugham succeeded, through his former mistress, Sasha Kropotkin, in gaining an introduction to Alexander Kerensky, the head of the provisional government. With Sasha acting as hostess and interpreter, Maugham entertained Kerensky or members of his government once a week at the Medved, the best restaurant in Russia, paying for the finest caviar and vodka from the ample funds provided by the British and American governments. Wilson can scarcely have imagined that some of the $75,000 "propaganda" budget he had authorized was being used to fund such lavish entertainment. "I think Kerensky must have supposed that I was more important than I really was," wrote Maugham later, "for he came to Sasha's apartment on several occasions and, walking up and down the room, harangued me as though I were at a public meeting for two hours at a time."[60]

While Maugham was listening to Kerensky's monologues, Wiseman's stock continued to rise in Washington. His first meeting with the president took place at a diplomatic reception on June 26. According to Arthur Willert, the Washington correspondent of the London *Times*:

Instead of treating [Wiseman] to the perfunctory sentence or two usual to such introductions, the President talked to him for nearly half an hour, and then desisted only because he was pried loose by his entourage. Onlookers were astonished and mystified. Who was this unknown young man, obviously English, whom the President had singled out for his attentions?[61]

The next day House wrote to Wilson, "Sir William is and has been the real Ambassador over here for some time"—a remarkable tribute to the illusion that Wiseman had been able to create. By the attention that they paid to Wiseman, however, Wilson and House succeeded in turning the illusion into something approaching reality. Both were so taken with the MI1c head of station that they would have preferred him to replace Spring Rice as ambassador. "However," wrote House regretfully, "I suppose his youth would preclude consideration of his name."[62] Two weeks after their first meeting the president invited Wiseman to dinner at the White House. After dinner the two men retired into Wilson's study to discuss United States relations with Britain and its allies, and the proposed formation of an Allied Military Council to "determine what was needed in the way of supplies and money from America." The next day House noted in his diary, "Sir William is in the seventh heaven of pleasurable excitement." He wrote to Wilson, "I never saw anyone so pleased as Sir William was at being asked to dine with you. He speaks of it with emotion, and declar[e]s it to be the happiest event of his life."[63]

Wiseman's euphoria was understandable. No other foreign intelligence officer has ever succeeded in gaining such remarkable access to the president. The British press baron Lord Northcliffe, then in the United States as chairman of the British War Mission responsible for recruiting British citizens and obtaining American war supplies, was staggered to discover the extent of Wiseman's influence in the White House. Wiseman was, he reported, "the only person, English or American, who had access at any time to the President or Colonel House."[64] Meeting at Magnolia, Massachusetts, in House's luxurious summer home, Wiseman, Northcliffe, and House agreed on the need for a British financial mission, headed by Lord Reading, to visit Washington to negotiate American financial assistance for the British war effort. On August 1, armed with notes on his meeting with Wilson and letters of introduction from House and Northcliffe, Wiseman arrived in London. Over the next three weeks he won approval for the Reading mission from both the prime minister, Lloyd George, and the chancellor of the exchequer, Andrew Bonar Law. On September 12 Lord Reading landed in New York, accompanied by Wiseman and the young Treasury official John Maynard Keynes, later to become the most celebrated British economist of the twentieth century.[65]

With him on his return from London Wiseman brought for the personal attention of the president a series of diplomatic messages from Berlin to German missions in Latin America, transmitted by Swedish cables and decrypted by Room 40. These intercepts, he told House, contained the "most important disclosures since [the] Zimmermann note."[66] As well as revealing Sweden's breach of neutrality in transmitting German messages, they also contained a series of embarrassing comments by the German ambassador in Buenos Aires, Count Karl-Ludwig von Luxburg, who contemptuously described Argentinians as "Indians covered by a thin veneer" and dismissed the Argentinian foreign minister as "a notorious ass." Luxburg also recommended rejecting Argentina's request for Germany to stop sinking its shipping; an alternative solution, he suggested, was simply to "sink them without leaving any trace" of German involvement. Wilson approved the publication of the Luxburg cables in the American press, though the English origin of the intercepts was concealed. An outraged Argentina swiftly broke off diplomatic relations with Germany. The unfortunate Luxburg cabled Berlin: "Whether this a case of theft of documents or betrayal of a cipher, I am unable to say with certainty. I infer the latter."[67]

In addition to the decrypted German telegrams, Wiseman also conveyed to Washington a British request that Wilson send House as his personal representative to an Allied War Council in London.[68] When House arrived in Britain in November, accompanied by a group of experts known as the "House Party," Wiseman was at his side. House noted the astonishment in London at the position of influence Wiseman had acquired in the United States:

> I have given Wiseman an immense leverage by putting him in touch with the President and with the leaders of his own country. They do not quite understand why I have done this, but it is because of his ability, loyalty and trustworthiness. He has qualities which are rarely met with in one man.

House failed to grasp that Wiseman's success was due less to his "trustworthiness" than to his own and Wilson's naïveté about intelligence operations, which Wiseman had skillfully exploited. During a visit to Buckingham Palace, House told King George V that Wiseman was "one of the most efficient men of his age [he] had ever met."⁶⁹

While House and Wiseman were in London, Somerset Maugham's secret mission to Petrograd, jointly funded by Britain and the United States, was coming to a spectacular, though unsuccessful, conclusion. On the evening of October 31, 1917, Maugham was summoned by Kerensky and asked to take a secret message to Lloyd George, appealing for guns and ammunition. Without that help, said Kerensky, "I don't see how I can survive." Kerensky, however, was past saving. On November 7 his provisional government was overthrown by the Bolshevik Revolution. The first joint Anglo-American intelligence operation, whose budget was personally approved by Wilson, thus achieved nothing of political significance. It did, however, inspire two of the short stories in Maugham's *Ashenden Papers*, and thus made a notable contribution to one of the classics of spy fiction.⁷⁰

By the autumn of 1917 Wiseman's dealings with House and Wilson had become so time-consuming that they required a reorganization of the MI1c station in New York. Wiseman's liaison work with the White House, which he described as "of a personal and absorbing nature," was recognized by Cumming as his first priority. The day-to-day running of the MI1c station was taken over by his deputy, Thwaites, but Wiseman retained overall control of American operations. He wrote to Cumming in a memorandum on the reorganization:

> . . . I shall remain its [the station's] ex-Office chief under you; and . . . I shall thus have authority over Capt. Thwaites if it appears to me necessary to exercise it. . . . In addition to my political work and general supervision over Capt. Thwaites, I am to be permitted to maintain a small Secret Service organization, which will be directed and controlled by myself, principally for the purpose of obtaining information regarding IRISH and MEXICAN affairs.⁷¹

Wilson was almost certainly unaware that Wiseman, his main channel of communication to the British government, was simultaneously running covert operations on American soil.

Wiseman returned to the United States in January 1918 with a new and cumbersome title bestowed on him by Lloyd George: "liaison officer between the War Cabinet and any special representative they might send out to represent them in the United States." "This," Wiseman told Cumming, "is to cover up my real work which is to be Liaison Officer between H. [House] and the F.O. [Foreign Office]."⁷² Immediately on his return to the United States, Wiseman was summoned to the White

House for an hour's discussion with the president—"an unusual compliment," he believed, "considering how much he was occupied by the debate in the Senate." Wilson ended the meeting by telling Wiseman, "Give my love to House, and tell him we have had a 'bully' talk."[73] Wiseman was confident of his ability, at least on some issues, to influence the president, whom he referred to by the code name Adramyti in his cables to London. On February 19, for example, he cabled Drummond:

CERTAIN INFLUENCES NEAR ADRAMYTI ARE URGING HIM TO RECOGNISE OR
OTHERWISE SUPPORT BOLSHEVIKI GOVERNMENT [IN RUSSIA]. IF YOU WILL GIVE ME
YOUR VIEWS I COULD PROBABLY GET ADRAMYTI TO ADOPT THEM BEFORE HE
COMES TO ANY OTHER DECISION.[74]

Lord Reading, who succeeded the unpopular Spring Rice as ambassador early in 1918, never rivaled Wiseman's influence with Wilson and House.[75]

MI1c had thus built up a wholly remarkable position as by far the most successful intelligence agency in the United States. While Wiseman spent most of his time cultivating Wilson and House, the MI1c station in New York, managed by his deputy Thwaites, had established itself as the dominant partner in an informal alliance with most of the fragmented American intelligence community. The New York station boasted in March 1918:

As this office has been in existance [sic] longer than any of the other organizations of investigation and intelligence, it is naturally regarded as the best source of experienced information. There is complete cooperation between this office and

1. United States Military Intelligence
2. Naval Intelligence
3. U.S. Secret Service
4. New York Police Department
5. Police Intelligence
6. U.S. Customs House
7. The American Protective League and similar civic organizations.
8. U.S. Department of Justice, Bureau of Investigation.

. . . Everyone of them is in the habit of calling us up or visiting the office daily. They have access to our files under our supervision and we stand ready to give them all information in our possession. They, on the other hand, are equally ready to reciprocate, and the spirit of friendly cooperation makes the work extremely pleasant and, I venture to think, useful.

. . . With regard to "agents and enquiries," it might be possible to curtail our activities and leave such matters to the U.S. Intelligence Bureaux but the London office [MI1c headquarters] frequently send us questionnaires which in no way concern America. Also we have facilities of gaining information which the U.S. has not. For months Major Thwaites has been the only intelligence officer in New York who was able to read and speak German. He has spent many nights at Police headquarters, etc. examining captured enemy documents. None of the U.S. Bureaux employ Germans whereas this office has several most dependable German agents who are trusted acquaintances in enemy circles. This office supplied the addresses of all the persons apprehended this last week when the U.S. authorities were at a loss.[76]

Had Wilson realized that MI1c carried out operations on American soil that it considered "in no way concern[ed] America" and employed its own "dependable German agents" in the United States, his trust in Wiseman would surely have been destroyed. But Wilson did not know. Wiseman reported to Cumming two months before the Armistice that, though "Our cooperation with the many Intelligence branches of the U.S. Government has always been most cordial, and I believe of value," "The details of our organization they have never known and do not know to this day."[77]

MI1c's main problems in the United States were turf battles with other British intelligence agencies that seem to have passed unnoticed by either House or Wilson. Gaunt was unhappy to be upstaged by the more junior Wiseman, whom he later tried to belittle in his memoirs by claiming inaccurately that he "played only a very small part under me" in intelligence operations. In the spring of 1918 he returned to England, his wounded pride mollified by a knighthood (and, later, by an American Distinguished Service Medal).[78] The main challenge to the MI1c station in New York came from Cumming's great rival, Vernon Kell, head of the British Security Service, MI5. Claiming that the primary function of British intelligence operations in the United States was counterespionage, Kell made a nearly successful takeover bid for the MI1c station.[79] With Reading's support, Cumming and Wiseman beat off most of Kell's challenge. MI5 assumed responsibility only for visas and passport control of travelers from the United States to Britain. The feuding, however, continued. "The pity of the whole thing," Wiseman wrote to Cumming, "is that for some reason or other Kell seems determined to reject any sort of cooperation with us."[80]

Despite Wilson's interest in the intelligence provided by Hall and Wiseman, he paid little attention to the organization and functioning of his own intelligence agencies. Immediately after the declaration of war on Germany Lansing had tried to impress on the president "the very great importance" of "the coordination of the secret service work of this Government." Despite Polk's attempt to organize an intelligence "clearing house" in the State Department, Lansing reported that two serious problems remained: the divorce between foreign and domestic intelligence; and the "extreme jealousy" of the two domestic agencies, the Secret Service and the Bureau of Investigation. Lansing proposed solving these problems by putting all intelligence operations at home and abroad "under the general control of one efficient man." He ruled out the warring heads of the Secret Service and the Bureau of Investigation, William J. Flynn and A. Bruce Bielaski, as candidates for the new post of intelligence supremo. Apart from their mutual antagonism, neither possessed "the requisite knowledge of foreign affairs." "I am not courting additional responsibilities," Lansing told Wilson, "but I do feel that the central office of all sorts of secret information should be in the State Department. . . ."[81] The president did not. Wilson remained unwilling either to delegate the problem of intelligence coordination to his secretary of state or to tackle it himself. While he accepted the need to monitor German covert operations and domestic subversion of the war effort, the idea of a strengthened and coordinated American intelligence community seemed so clearly at odds with his postwar vision of a brave new world of open diplomacy that he could not bring himself to face up to the problems of wartime intelligence gathering. The consequence of entry into the First World War, combined with lack of presidential direction, was thus the rapid but uncoordinated growth of the fragmented American intelligence agencies.

Although the United States, unlike the other major combatants, continued to lack a specialized foreign espionage agency, the war produced a rapid expansion of the small prewar naval and military intelligence personnel. By the Armistice, the permanent staff of the Office of Naval Intelligence had been augmented by almost three thousand reservists and volunteers.[82] In August 1918 military intelligence was raised in status to become one of four divisions of the War Department General Staff; MID personnel increased from only 3 in 1916 to 1,441 in 1918.[83] The most significant innovation in wartime military intelligence was the founding of the United States' first specialized SIGINT agency. In June 1917 Herbert Yardley, the twenty-eight-year-old State Department code clerk who had allegedly disconcerted his superiors by breaking one of President Wilson's supposedly unbreakable codes, was commissioned as first lieutenant (later rising to major) and placed in charge of a new military intelligence code and cipher unit, MI-8. Over the next year MI-8 compiled new code and cipher systems for army use, translated foreign language messages in various forms of shorthand passed on by the censors, prepared chemical preparations to reveal messages written in secret inks, and deciphered intercepted communications that employed known codes and ciphers. But, reported Yardley at the end of the war, "it was not until the beginning of August, 1918, that the staff was enlarged sufficiently to permit of serious attack upon the large number of code messages in various [unknown] codes which had been accumulating in the files."[84] By the November Armistice, MI-8 employed 18 army officers, 24 civilian cryptographers, and 109 typists and stenographers.[85] Wilson gave no sign of interest in this turning point in the history of American intelligence. Possibly he was not informed. Perhaps he preferred not to know.

The primary target of U.S. wartime intelligence was the apparent threat of domestic subversion. The military intelligence "weekly summaries," which began in June 1917, were preoccupied by fear of disloyalty among foreign-born GIs, and quick to detect—frequently mistakenly—the hidden hand of German agents and socialist subversion. "At the bottom of the negro unrest," reported one weekly summary, "German influence is unquestionable." MID was also disturbed by trivia such as a report that "The National Bible Students' League is distributing Socialist Pamphlets."[86]

The main responsibility for domestic counterintelligence after the declaration of war was assumed by the Bureau of Investigation. Its four hundred agents, however, could not cope with the BI's enormous workload, which included surveillance of a million "enemy aliens," for the most part immigrants from Germany and Austria-Hungary not yet granted U.S. citizenship. Bielaski, the bureau director, accepted an offer of help from the unpaid volunteers of the American Protective League (APL), founded by an excitable Chicago advertising executive, Albert M. Briggs, to counter German espionage and sabotage. Military and naval intelligence also made use of APL members. As spy scares swept the nation, the league grew to become a quarter of a million strong—according to a supporter, "the largest company of detectives the world ever saw." Each volunteer was given a badge shaped like a police shield, bearing the legend "American Protective League, Secret Service Division." Though the 250,000 amateur detectives failed to find a single spy, they waged a zealous, sometimes illegal, often tragicomic campaign against real or imaginary opponents of the war, forcing those alleged to be disloyal to kiss the flag, and mounting "slacker raids" to root out draft dodgers. The Secret Service inevitably resented being thus upstaged by the BI and its APL volunteers.[87] Treasury Secretary McAdoo, who was responsible for the Secret Service, proposed ending the rivalry with the bureau by founding a new, centralized domestic intelligence agency.[88]

Wilson turned down McAdoo's proposal just as he had earlier rejected Lansing's, but failed to find an alternative solution. The president was uncomfortably aware of the increasingly chaotic confusion of "secret service" work, but found the whole subject too distasteful to give it his sustained attention. In July 1917 he wrote to Attorney General Gregory, who was responsible for the Bureau of Investigation:

> You may remember the other day I spoke jestingly at the Cabinet about my perplexity concerning the various counsels among the several departments having secret service with regard to a correlation of these services. Underneath the jest, of course, lay a very serious difficulty. . . .

Wilson asked Gregory, McAdoo, and Polk to work out "a plan for the coordination of these [secret] services into which we can all enter with spirit and effect."[89] But, as Lansing had warned him several months earlier, Gregory and McAdoo, who controlled the two main rival services, were at daggers drawn and unable to agree. Once again the president let the matter drop. It forced itself on his attention again in November 1917 as a result of the case of William Bayard Hale, who had come under suspicion after working for the German Information Bureau in New York. Hale alleged that a Secret Service agent had attempted to seduce his stenographer—"a young girl of good family" who "had become hysterical and afraid to leave his [Hale's] house":

> . . . Offers of all sorts had been made to her—of jewelry, government bonds, employment under the British government, double salary, threats of fine and imprisonment, threats of personal violence at the point of a revolver, and, worst of all, . . . attempts had been made through the medium of a procuress, to keep assignations for immoral purposes.

Wilson was so confused by the organization of domestic intelligence gathering that he passed the complaint on to Gregory for investigation, forgetting that the Secret Service was McAdoo's responsibility.[90] Gregory replied, probably with some relish, that a BI investigation had confirmed that the whole affair was the fault of the Secret Service.[91] McAdoo told Wilson that he was "really deeply distressed about the attitude of the

Attorney General concerning the Secret Service," which, he claimed, had been "generally scrupulously correct." The Hale case prompted further Cabinet discussion on November 16 about confusion between "the various secret agencies and the need for cooperation." Wilson admitted that "It made me feel derelict in not having sought a remedy . . . though I must say I am still in doubt as to what the best remedy is."[92]

For the remainder of his presidency, Wilson either remained in doubt or pushed the problem to one side. He continued, at least intermittently, to "feel derelict in not having sought a remedy." Growing protests against the abuses of the "slacker raids" led him, in September 1918, to ask for a report from the attorney general. Gregory admitted that "excess of zeal for the public good" had led to some breaches of the law, but insisted that "some such dragnet process is necessary unless thousands upon thousands of deserters and slackers are to remain at large":

> I believe also . . . that the great body of our people will cheerfully submit to the minor inconveniences which the execution of any such plan necessarily entails, to the end that this indictment of the Nation's honor, this drain on the nation's strength, may be removed.

By releasing the attorney general's report to the press, Wilson appeared to give presidential endorsement to Gregory's justification for the "slacker raids."[93]

The only intelligence officer capable of holding the president's attention continued to be Sir William Wiseman. During the last great crisis of the war, the German spring offensive of 1918 that for a time threatened to sweep all before it, both House and Wilson turned to Wiseman for an on-the-spot assessment of the situation in France and England. House noted in his diary on April 9: "It has been definitely arranged for Wiseman to go to Europe at once. Reading objected, but the President agrees with me that he should go, and . . . Reading was compelled to yield."[94]

On April 24 Wiseman cabled House from London, "I have now seen the British General Staff, Prime Minister, Balfour, Milner [Secretary of War] and others, who have given me freely all their information. . . ." House replied effusively, "It is a perfect joy to be in such intimate touch as we now are through you. Argus [House's code name for Wilson] and I not only deeply appreciate your cables, but feel that they make intelligent action possible."[95] Perhaps never again was an intelligence officer to be informed that the president of the United States found his reports "a perfect joy." Once back in the United States, Wiseman saw his main intelligence role as maintaining "close touch" with the Inquiry, a group of experts assembled by House on Wilson's instructions to study political and territorial problems likely to arise at the peace conference. He wrote to Reading in July:

> It must be quite clear to you that when in New York I occupy practically the position of political secretary to House. I think he shows me everything he gets, and together we discuss every question that arises.

Wiseman thus gained access to "much of the data which will be used by the American delegates at the Peace Conference."[96]

Wilson's enthusiasm for Wiseman's company even extended to his summer holidays. While spending a week's vacation at Magnolia in August, the president lunched on most days at House's summer home with Wiseman and House. Each evening Wiseman and House dined with the Wilsons. Though Wiseman, with his customary tact, waited to discuss the problems of war and peacemaking until these subjects were raised by the president, he was able to report to London in some detail Wilson's views on most "questions of the moment." The most important topic of the week was Wilson's plan for a new world order based on the League of Nations.[97] It is difficult to imagine Wilson choosing to spend so much of his vacation talking with any American intelligence officer or, indeed, with most members of his own administration. Arthur C. Murray of the Foreign Office Political Intelligence Department wrote to Wiseman after he returned from Magnolia, ". . . The importance of the hours that you spent with House and the President cannot, I feel sure, be exaggerated."[98] Wiseman boasted in September, "House and the President have come to regard me as perhaps their chief source of information."[99]

The only foreign intelligence from American sources whose impact on the president seems to have equaled that of the British intelligence supplied by Hall and Wiseman were documents obtained in February and March 1918 by Edgar Sisson, the Petrograd representative of the wartime U.S. propaganda agency, the Committee on Public Information. These sensational documents, Sisson reported, had been abstracted from the secret files of both the Bolshevik government and German intelligence. Wilson told Lord Reading on April 25 that he was eagerly awaiting the imminent arrival in Washington of Sisson and his documents that "were alleged to prove conclusively that Trotzsky and Lenine [*sic*] were in the pay of the German government."[100] Though the Sisson documents were, in reality, rather amateurish forgeries, Wilson accepted them as genuine. The State Department was not so sure. Polk put them away in his confidential file, probably intending never to allow them to see the light of day. Sisson and the head of the Committee on Public Information, George Creel, however, persuaded Wilson to publicize the documents to expose what they naïvely believed was the true nature of the Bolshevik regime. In September, against Lansing's advice, Wilson agreed to publish the documents both in the press and in an official U.S. government publication.[101] The Foreign Office, as well as the State Department, was appalled. Wiseman told House, "The English experts and authorities had gone over carefully the Sisson papers and had come to the definite conclusion that they were forgeries." To avoid embarrassing Wilson, however, Balfour offered "to have these papers published if he, the President wished it, in spite of the opinion of the British authorities that the papers were forgeries." Wilson was shaken but anxious not to lose face. Wiseman reported to London after seeing him:

> He very much regrets that U.S. authorities did not consult H.M.G. before the papers were published here, but as the case now stands he would be gratified if Mr Balfour would permit the publication in England.[102]

To counter the well-founded charges of forgery, Creel commissioned a report on the Sisson documents by two university professors who, to their subsequent embarrassment, declared them genuine. The forgeries were then handed for safekeeping to the president, who placed them in his personal White House files.[103]

Though Wiseman's access to the president remained remarkable, as the end of the war approached his optimism earlier in 1918 that he could bring Wilson closer to British views about the postwar settlement faded rapidly. He wrote in September:

> I must admit that our most practical difficulty is the attitude of the President himself. . . . His attitude lately has tended to become more arbitrary and aloof, and there are times when he seems to treat foreign governments hardly seriously. Col. House realizes this, and any influence that he has will be used to the uttermost to remedy it.[104]

Without Wiseman, Britain would have been far less well-informed about Wilson's policies, and the president's suspicions of British peace aims would have been significantly greater. But there remained a gulf that neither Wiseman nor anyone else could bridge between Wilson's vision of "peace without victory" and the less idealistic ambitions of the European victors.

On October 5, 1918, a new German government headed by Prince Max of Baden appealed directly to Wilson for an armistice over the heads of the European allies. Unsurprisingly, Britain and France resented the president's independent negotiations with the enemy. Fearful that Wilson might be seduced by the newly conciliatory Huns, Blinker Hall sent him a series of intercepts designed to demonstrate Germany's continuing duplicity. One decrypt, forwarded to the White House on October 14, which contained evidence of German double-dealing over the evacuation of conquered territory in Eastern Europe, clearly enraged the president. "Every word," he told Wiseman, "breathed the old Prussian trickery and deceit. It was difficult to see how we could trust such people." But he made it clear that even "Prussian trickery" would not deflect him from armistice negotiations: "Of course, . . . we can never trust them. . . . But we must not appear to be slamming the door on peace."[105]

At the end of October Wilson dispatched House to Europe to inform his allies of the armistice terms he had negotiated with Germany. With him, once again, went Wiseman. Hall now redoubled his efforts to convince Wilson of the error of his ways, apparently manufacturing intelligence calculated to demonstrate that the kaiser would not honor the Armistice terms. Hall reported on October 30 that he had "learned from an absolutely sure source that at a recent council in Berlin the German Emperor said: 'During peace negotiations or even after peace, my U-boats will find an opportunity to destroy the English fleet.'" Though asking "to be excused from divulging the source of this astonishing piece of information," Hall insisted that it was just as reliable as the German radio and cable intercepts. In reality, his claim was highly suspect. He had no source in Berlin capable of providing accurate reports of German war councils. Lansing, however, was "inclined to give full credence to this information" on the grounds that Hall's intelligence had been "most reliable in the past."[106] Wilson and House almost certainly agreed. But Hall's doctored intelligence did nothing to delay the conclusion of an armistice with Germany on November 11. (Its impact was in any case diminished when the kaiser was forced to abdicate two days before the armistice.) House cabled Wilson on November 5, "I doubt whether any other heads of government with whom we are dealing realize how far they are now committed to the American peace program." Hall, whose cryptanalysts doubtless decrypted House's telegram, cannot have been pleased. House added that Wiseman had been "splendidly helpful" in resolving differences with Lloyd George.[107] Major differences, however, remained. "England and France have not the same views that we have with regard to peace by any means," Wilson had written in the summer of 1917. "When the war is

over, we can force them to our way of thinking . . ."[108] That task was to
prove much more difficult than the president had supposed.

Wiseman tried tactfully but ineffectively to persuade Wilson to stay
away from the peace negotiations. He told House that British officials
"who admire the President, and want to see his authority maintained,
are unanimous in advising against his taking part in the Peace Conference. . . . He would be . . . likely to lose prestige and authority and be
drawn into a very difficult diplomatic situation, which he would have to
deal with under the worst possible conditions for himself."[109] Wilson paid
no attention. Full of missionary zeal, he set out from New York in
December to make the world "safe for democracy," becoming in the process the first president to set foot in the Old World during his term of
office. Wiseman attended the peace conference that opened in Paris in
January 1919 as a member of the British delegation. But his previous
importance as intermediary with, and adviser to, the president and
House was coming to an end. Wilson and Lloyd George, together with
their staffs and experts, were now in direct contact in Paris.

The U.S. Peace Commission, which Wilson headed at the peace conference, included a forty-strong team from the Inquiry, newly designated
the "Territorial, Economic and Military Intelligence Division," and a
group of twenty military intelligence officers, headed by the director of
military intelligence (DMI), General Marlborough Churchill. Intelligence
reports reached the commission from agents and staff members in many
parts of Europe. The weekly MID summaries concentrated on political
rather than military intelligence, to provide "guidance" for the peace
commissioners. The summaries were of indifferent quality. Though they
provided Wilson and the commissioners with useful news digests, they
also included elements of fantasy mixed with disinformation. MID pro-
pounded a conspiracy theory of German policy, claiming absurdly that
the Spartacist Rising in Germany early in 1919 had been stage-managed
by the Berlin government to provide an excuse to rebuild its army. Like
other Western intelligence agencies, MID was also sometimes taken in by
forged Soviet documents, among them what it described as "a very
pretty Bolshevist program drawn up by Lenin and his council," ordering
their agents abroad to "blow up arsenals, bridges, railroads, powder
magazines, [and] seize shipments of raw materials destined for factories."[110]

The MID provided Wilson with the first professional intelligence staff
in the history of the presidency. He paid scant attention to it—or, indeed,
to most of his advisers. Three of the five peace commissioners—Lansing,
General Tasker Bliss, and the toker Republican Henry Lane White—met
regularly to lament their ignorance, but saw little of the other two, Wilson

and House. Wilson's overriding aim was the creation of the League of Nations as the basis of a new world order. Once the League had been agreed on, he told House, "nearly all the serious difficulties will disappear."[111] The Covenant of the League, which Wilson read to a plenary session of the peace conference on February 14, looked forward to a brave new world of open diplomacy in which espionage would have no place. It bound League members not to conclude secret treaties or agreements, and to make military and naval intelligence collection virtually obsolete:

> The High Contracting Parties undertake in no way to conceal from each other the condition of such of their industries as are capable of being adapted for war-like purposes or the scale of their armaments and agree that there shall be full and frank interchange of information as to their military and naval programs.[112]

Returning immediately afterward for a month in the United States, Wilson told Americans that their country was "the hope of the world," taking the lead in sweeping away the underhanded practices of the old diplomacy: "I think I am stating the most wonderful fact in history . . . there is no nation in Europe that suspects the motives of the United States. . . ."[113]

Wilson's rhetoric, however, was at odds with the intelligence operations of his own Peace Commission. Both Lansing and General Churchill were anxious that the wartime SIGINT agency, MI-8, should continue operating in peacetime. On their joint initiative, the commission was supplied with a cipher bureau, headed by Major Herbert Yardley, which sought to decrypt some communications of other delegations as well as to protect the security of those of the United States.[114] How much Wilson knew about the bureau may never be known. Possibly he preferred not to know too much about its operations lest they disturb his vision of an "open diplomacy" that would put such practices behind it.

Though a gifted cryptanalyst, Yardley was still politically naïve and socially gauche. With no previous experience either of Europe or of high society, he found his "stacks of tea and dinner invitations" in Paris a heady experience. He boasted in his memoirs that "in typical American fashion it was the custom to blackball any French host or hostess who failed to serve champagne. No wonder the French dislike our manners!" Combining cryptanalysis with an unaccustomed social whirl, Yardley became prone to fantasy. He was convinced that some of the fashionable women he encountered over champagne were experienced seductresses employed by foreign secret services to penetrate the U.S. delegation.

One who caught his attention was "a certain woman—let us call her Madame X—. . . so famous for her beauty . . . in Paris in the employ of one of our Allies for the purpose of influencing the decisions of one of our Peace Commissioners." What most alarmed Yardley, however, was what he believed was a plot against the president. Even when writing his memoirs twelve years later, he failed to realize that he had been the victim of a hoax:

> . . . The reader may well appreciate the shock I received as I deciphered a telegram which reported an Entente plot to assassinate President Wilson, either by administering a slow poison or by giving him the influenza in ice. Our informant, in whom we had the greatest confidence, begged the authorities for God's sake to warn the President. I have no way of knowing whether this plot had any truth in fact, and if it had, whether it succeeded. But there are these undeniable facts: *President Wilson's first sign of illness occurred while he was in Paris, and he was seen to die a lingering death.*[115]

Yardley's fantasies failed to disturb the president. Wilson was preoccupied instead, after his return to Paris, by the unexpected difficulties of the peace negotiations. He had gravely underestimated both the opposition from isolationists in Congress, who would eventually succeed in preventing American membership in the League, and the demands of the European Allies for reparations from Germany. By the end of March Wilson had lost confidence even in House, whom he suspected of making unwarranted concessions to the Europeans.

Though Lansing and General Churchill had little influence on Wilson, they took the lead in ensuring the survival of the first peacetime United States SIGINT agency. On May 16 Churchill signed a memorandum, probably drafted by Yardley, recommending the maintenance "in time of peace as well as of war [of] an organization of skilled cryptographers sufficient in number to carry out the program of deciphering promptly all foreign code and cipher messages submitted to it, of solving new codes, of developing new methods and of training adequate personnel." The proposal was approved, in Lansing's absence, by the acting secretary of state Polk on May 17 and by the army chief of staff, General Peyton C. March, on May 20. By August 1919 a Cypher Bureau, better known as the Black Chamber, headed by Yardley and jointly funded by the departments of War and State, was operating at a secret address in New York. Its early priorities were the diplomatic traffic of Japan, Britain, and Germany (in that order). In May 1920 Yardley reported that the Black Chamber had broken four Japanese and two German codes.

(The section of Yardley's report dealing with the attack on British codes and ciphers is, remarkably, still classified.)[116]

The main intelligence target of Wilson's postwar presidency, however, was domestic rather than foreign: the threat, more imagined than real, of internal subversion. Revolutionary unrest in Europe combined with industrial disruption in the United States to create what became known as the "Big Red Scare." The scare began with a series of bombings in the spring of 1919. Wilson, still in Paris and preoccupied with the peace negotiations, left Gregory's successor as attorney general, A. Mitchell Palmer, to deal with the problem. Palmer was not initially alarmist, but after his own house had been bombed in June he secured $500,000 from Congress to wage war against subversion and appointed the former chief of the Secret Service, William J. Flynn, to head the rival Bureau of Investigation. Flynn, he announced, was the country's leading "anarchist chaser": "He knows all the men of that class. He can pretty nearly call them by name." Within the BI, Palmer set up a new Radical (later General Intelligence) Division under the youthful law school graduate J. Edgar Hoover. Though these changes did not end rivalry with the Secret Service, they clearly established the BI as the leader in the war against subversion. The Big Red Scare also began the meteoric rise of Hoover, who in 1924 was to become head of the Bureau of Investigation at the age of only twenty-eight.[117]

Wilson's main preoccupation, when he returned to the United States in July after signing the peace treaty with Germany, was his unsuccessful crusade to secure American membership in the League. But the president was also deeply concerned by the threat of revolutionary subversion. He declared during a speaking tour in September:

> If you had been across the sea with me, you would know the dread in the mind of every thoughtful man in Europe is that that [Russian] distemper will spread to their countries. . . . That poison is running through the veins of the world, and we have made the methods of communication throughout the world such that all the veins of the world are open and the poison can circulate. The wireless throws it upon the air. The cable whispers it beneath the sea. Men talk about it in little groups, men talk about it openly in great groups, not only in Europe, but here also in the United States. There are disciples of Lenin in our own midst. To be a disciple of Lenin means to be a disciple of night, chaos and disorder.[118]

Two weeks after delivering that apocalyptic warning, the president collapsed in the middle of his speaking tour. On October 2 he suffered a stroke. Medical evidence released in 1991 reveals that the stroke was so severe as to make it "impossible for him ever to achieve more than a minimal state of recovery."[119]

It was over six months before Wilson was well enough to attend a cabinet meeting. But the oft-repeated claims that his wife henceforth ran the government of the United States are unfounded. Though she acted as Wilson's amanuensis, her only major influence on policy was to help suppress accurate information about his health and to ensure that he continued as president for the remainder of his second term.[120] Mrs. Wilson also played a part in ending Wiseman's association with the White House. On early acquaintance the First Lady had succumbed to Wiseman's celebrated charm. In February 1919 she wrote him an effusive letter of thanks after he had smuggled her into the plenary session of the peace conference to hear the first reading of the Charter of the League of Nations: ". . . I shall always bless and thank you . . . & hope you got the 'thought wave' of appreciation I sent you."[121] Over the next few months, possibly influenced by what she learned of Wiseman's role as a "secret agent of the British Government," Mrs. Wilson's thought waves changed dramatically. She later claimed, quite inaccurately, that she "had never liked this plausible little man." On September 30, shortly after Wilson's breakdown and two days before his stroke, Wiseman called at the White House, bearing what he said was "important information for the President." Mrs. Wilson told him to come back later in the day. When Wiseman returned she told him that the president could not see him. "This," she wrote in her memoirs, "was the only instance that I recall having acted as an intermediary between my husband and another on an official matter, except when so directed by a physician."[122]

Wiseman's exclusion from the White House brought almost to an end the special relationship between the British and American intelligence communities built up during the war. Soon after the Armistice, his deputy, Norman Thwaites, had recommended awarding British decorations to, among others, the directors of military and naval Intelligence, and the chiefs of the Secret Service and the New York police, all of whom had "cooperated in the most energetic way" with the MI1c station.[123] The DMI, General Churchill, was one of a number of senior American intelligence officers who wished the collaboration to continue. When he heard of the possibility that Thwaites might be withdrawn after the Armistice, he asked London to ensure "the continuance of this [MI1c] office and of Maj. Thwaites personally."[124] In April 1919 Wiseman wrote to arrange a meeting with Churchill "in the hope that we may perfect a system of exchanging information with your Military Intelligence. I am just as convinced as you are that this is a sound and sensible thing to do in the interests of both our countries."[125]

The close wartime collaboration, however, was not to survive the peace conference. At the end of the war Cumming was forced to cut back and reorient his operations. The budget for the Secret Intelligence Service (SIS), the peacetime successor of MI1c, was cut by almost half in 1919 from £240,000 to £125,000.[126] Wiseman noted soon after the end of the war, "The Chief wants us to wind up our organization in New York, as it now exists, at the earliest possible moment." The Americans were not told, however, that a new and smaller SIS station was to be set up at a different New York location and its existence kept secret from them.[127] Though Cumming was happy to continue an Anglo-American exchange of intelligence on defeated Germany and revolutionary Russia, the United States now ranked as a major SIS target. Britain and the United States emerged from the war as naval rivals. The British General Staff were also concerned by the possibility of the United States making "preparations for chemical warfare," and informed Cumming that they were "particularly anxious to have information on this subject from America."[128]

While the wartime MI1c station in New York was being wound up during 1919, Wiseman's own influence was also declining. His close friendship with House lost most of its political significance when House fell out of favor with the president in the spring. After the loss of his entrée to the White House in September, Wiseman saw no future for himself in the peacetime SIS. Instead he embarked on a successful banking career in Wall Street, joining Kuhn, Loeb & Co. in 1921. He continued, however, to assist from time to time in SIS operations and to act as an unpaid intelligence source.[129] The informal Anglo-American intelligence alliance that he had established as MI1c head of station was to serve as an influential precedent for the more enduring special relationship later established during the Second World War.

Wilson's greatly diminished energies after his stroke were devoted first and foremost to foreign affairs. For several months he engaged in an irrational vendetta against Lansing, whom he suspected of going behind his back at the Paris Peace Conference and of trying to usurp presidential power. In February 1920 Wilson dismissed Lansing and replaced him as secretary of state with New York lawyer Bainbridge Colby. For the remainder of his presidency Wilson steadfastly rejected numerous pleas from his advisers to accept some compromise on the terms of the peace treaty with Germany to secure Senate acceptance of American membership of the League of Nations.[130]

While an enfeebled but intransigent president remained preoccupied with foreign policy, Palmer, his attorney general, conducted a vigorous offensive against the Red Menace, with some assistance from Wilson's secretary, Joseph Tumulty, and little interference from Wilson himself.

The intelligence provided by the Bureau of Investigation persuaded an increasingly excitable Palmer that "the Government was in jeopardy" from an organized Communist conspiracy:

> My information showed that Communism in this country was an organization of thousands of aliens who were direct allies of Trotzky. Aliens of the same misshapen cast of mind and indecencies of character, and it showed that they were making the same glittering promises of lawlessness, of criminal autocracy to Americans, that they had made to the Russian peasants. How the Department of Justice [Bureau of Investigation] discovered upwards of 60,000 of these organized agitators of the Trotzky doctrine in the United States, is the confidential information upon which the Government is now sweeping the nation clean of such filth.[131]

The "alien filth" were rounded up in what became known as the "Palmer Raids." The first raid, in New York on November 7, 1919, directed against the Union of Russian Workers, led to 650 arrests; 43 of those arrested were later deported. On January 2, 1920, there was a much larger series of raids against Communist and Communist Labor parties in over thirty cities across the United States. Many of the four thousand people arrested later turned out to have little if any connection with either party: one indication of the dubious quality of some of the intelligence that so excited the attorney general.[132]

Wilson seems to have had little idea of the extent of the Palmer Raids until April 14, when he attended his first cabinet meeting since his stroke. Though the president put up a brave front, members of the cabinet were shocked by his appearance. One arm did not function; his jaw sagged on one side; his voice was weak and strained. To Palmer, "he looked like a very old man and acted like one."[133] The cabinet meeting turned into what Navy Secretary Josephus Daniels called "a red-hot debate," which began with a lurid account by Palmer of the Bolshevik influences allegedly responsible for labor disturbances. Palmer was then challenged by the labor secretary, who argued that the attorney general's call for more deportations would only make matters worse. The president's doctor and Mrs. Wilson then appeared anxiously in the doorway, clearly impatient for the meeting to end. Wilson's final comment, addressed to the attorney general, was to warn him in a thin, weak voice, "Palmer, do not let this country see red!" According to Daniels, "It was a much needed admonition for Palmer was seeing red behind every bush and every demand for an increase in wages."[134] But the president lacked the energy to curb Palmer's war against subversion.

During the second half of April J. Edgar Hoover issued almost daily bulletins warning that the long-awaited Communist revolution would break out on May Day. The entire New York police force was put on alert. Troops were called out in other cities. But there was no revolution. Palmer's reputation never recovered. The absence of May Day revolutionaries ruined his hopes of gaining the Democratic nomination to succeed Wilson in the 1920 presidential election.[135] The Big Red Scare had nonetheless marked a turning point in American security policy. For the first time a federal intelligence agency, at least initially with the approval of the president, had waged a major peacetime campaign against subversion.

Probably the last intelligence issue to which Wilson briefly gave his attention during the sad, final months of his presidency were the forged Sisson documents that he had naïvely published shortly after the Armistice. In August 1920 the head of the State Department Russian Division asked the White House for the loan of the originals that Wilson had kept in his possession. Tumulty, the president's secretary, replied:

I have brought to the attention of the President your desire for the return of the Sisson papers, and he has asked me to tell you that just now he has not time to lay his hand on these papers, but when he does he will make the proper disposition of them.

George Creel, former head of the Committee on Public Information, also tried to prise the papers out of Wilson's possession, but without success. He wrote to Sisson in December:

The situation is hopeless. The President will not let anybody go into his files and insists that he will look up the documents himself. I have put the matter in the hands of Mrs. Wilson and will keep up the search.

After Wilson left the White House, it was wrongly believed that he had taken the Sisson papers with him. They were not seen again for over thirty years. Then, in December 1952, while another Democratic president, Harry Truman, was packing his bags at the end of eight years in office, the documents were discovered at the back of a presidential safe. They were removed to the National Archives, where they now reside.[136]

The return to "normalcy" under Wilson's genially complacent and immensely popular Republican successor, Warren Gamaliel Harding (president from 1921 to 1923), continued the rundown of foreign intelligence that had begun after the peace conference. Appropriations for

MID contingency funds fell from $2.5 million in 1919 to $225,000 in 1922. MID headquarters personnel were cut back from 1,441 at the time of the Armistice to 90 by 1922.[137] Late in 1921 shortage of staff forced MID to abandon its weekly intelligence summaries, begun in June 1917, and move to a fortnightly schedule. The summaries also became noticeably thinner. Those for 1918 to 1921 filled five volumes a year; from 1922 to 1927 MID produced only one volume a year.[138] Drastic though the rundown was, however, both MID and ONI remained more active than before the war.

The most dramatic foreign intelligence success of the 1920s came during Harding's first year as president. It was achieved by the cryptanalysts of the Black Chamber during the Washington Conference on the Limitation of Armaments, the first major international gathering to meet in the nation's capital, which began four months of deliberations in November 1921. The record of their success in Herbert Yardley's memoirs is characteristically untainted by modesty:

> The Black Chamber, bolted, hidden, guarded, sees all, hears all. Though the blinds are drawn and the windows heavily curtained, its far-seeing eyes penetrate the secret conference chambers at Washington, Tokio [sic], London, Paris, Geneva, Rome. Its sensitive ears catch the faintest whisperings in the foreign capitals of the world.[139]

Though never approaching the omniscience suggested by Yardley's hyperbole, the Black Chamber was strikingly successful in decrypting Japanese diplomatic traffic. Initially Harding's secretary of state, Charles Evans Hughes, was alarmed by the aggressive rhetoric contained in Japanese intercepts. In May 1921 he told the British ambassador that the intercepts suggested "that Japan intends to seize Eastern Siberia" and asked Britain to "take action to persuade [the] Japanese Government to desist from attempting to carry out their projects."[140] During the Washington Conference, Yardley's cryptanalysts were able to decrypt most, if not all, of the telegrams exchanged between Tokyo and the Japanese delegation. Relayed by a daily courier service from the Black Chamber in New York, the decrypts gave the American delegation in Washington a remarkable negotiating advantage. The American negotiators called for a 10:6 naval ratio between the United States and Japan. The Japanese insisted that they would not go below 10:7. Then, on November 28, 1921, the Black Chamber decrypted a message from Tokyo that Yardley claimed was "the most important and far reaching telegram that ever passed through its doors." Tokyo instructed its delegation to "redouble your efforts" to obtain the 10:7 ratio. "In case of unavoidable necessity," it was authorized to accept 10:6.5. Since it was "necessary to avoid any clash with Great Britain and America, particularly America," however, even a 10:6 ratio would, in the last resort, have to be accepted. The U.S. delegation knew henceforth that it had only to stand firm to achieve the ratio that it wanted. "Stud poker," commented Yardley, "is not a very difficult game after you see your opponent's hole card." Finally, on December 10, Tokyo cabled its delegation, ". . . There is nothing to do but accept the ratio proposed by the United States. . . ."[141]

"Christmas in the Black Chamber," wrote Yardley, "was brightened by handsome presents to all of us from officials in the State and War Departments, which were accompanied by personal regards and assurances that our long hours of drudgery during the conference were appreciated by those in authority."[142] On this occasion, Yardley probably did not exaggerate. Other records reveal that he received a curiously calculated Christmas bonus of $998 to distribute among his staff. The award to Yardley of the Distinguished Service Medal in 1923 was, almost certainly, primarily in recognition of his achievements during the Washington Conference.[143]

Yardley does not, however, record any sign of interest in the Black Chamber's work by President Harding. Had there been any, Yardley would surely have mentioned it. Ironically, Harding commended the Washington treaties to the Senate as examples of open diplomacy. This may not have been a conscious deception by the president. Once he had opened the conference, he handed over the chairmanship to Hughes. Thereafter he did not follow the complex negotiations attentively. On December 20, 1921, for example, Harding told a press conference that the treaties did not cover the Japanese main islands, thus providing the leading news story on the following day in the *New York Times* and other papers. Hughes hurried to the White House to remind the president that he had already explained that the islands were indeed covered. "Hughes," replied Harding, "I don't want to appear a dub!" The two men laughed. Harding then issued a retraction. The president probably did not see the daily dossier of Japanese decrypts supplied during the conference by the Black Chamber. How much Hughes told him about their contents may never be known.[144]

By enabling most major foreign ministries to read at least some of their rivals' communications, the SIGINT agencies developed during the war contributed, albeit in an incomplete and curious way, to the introduction of the postwar "open diplomacy" called for by President Wilson and the enthusiasts of the League of Nations. Despite its success with Japanese and some Latin American traffic, however, the Black Chamber lagged behind its main European rivals. It broke no British, French, or

German ciphers after 1921, and never succeeded in decrypting any Soviet diplomatic traffic.[145] The interwar British SIGINT agency, the Government Code and Cypher School (GC&CS), by contrast, had considerable success throughout the 1920s with American, French, and Japanese diplomatic traffic, and—until 1927—with Soviet traffic also.[146]

Though some intelligence, especially about the Soviet Union and the Communist International, continued to be exchanged between Britain and the United States, wartime collaboration had given way to peacetime suspicion. Both the Bureau of Investigation and the MID discovered the existence in New York of the new peacetime SIS station that Cumming had tried to keep secret, but wrongly concluded that it was operating on the same scale and with the same success as in Wiseman's day. J. Edgar Hoover was particularly alarmist. Some of the United States' leading subversives, he believed, were probably British agents. Among them, he reported in February 1921, were the black leader Marcus Garvey, "the main instigator and active leader of approximately 80% of the Negro agitation in this country at the present time"; the Irish labor leader James Larkin, "in the employ of the British Secret Service, specializing on [sic] Sinn Fein activities in this country"; and Louis C. Fraina, "one of the highest authorities on international communism in the world today and certainly the ablest writer on the subject who has been active in the United States," who had "departed for Russia where he is today in the intimate confidence of the Soviet authorities."[147] Hoover's early reports on British intelligence seem to have contained as much fantasy as fact.

Fantasy also figured prominently in the life of the head of the United States' first SIGINT agency. After the strain of the Washington Conference, Herbert Yardley suffered a temporary breakdown. When he returned to work he was plagued by fantasies of seduction by beautiful female agents of the kind that had so disturbed him during the Paris Peace Conference. Unable to tolerate the rigors of Prohibition, Yardley stopped off after work each day at a speakeasy in the Manhattan West Forties. There he encountered a "gorgeous creature" with "golden hair which curved in an intriguing manner about her ears," but who "showed a bit too much of her legs as she nestled in the deep cushions." "Very beautiful legs, too," Yardley reflected, "at the end of the third cocktail." On further reflection, he became convinced that she had been sent to spy on him and thus discover the closely guarded cryptanalytic secrets of the Black Chamber. According to his own account of their encounter, Yardley decided to get the "lovely creature" drunk, then took her back to her apartment in the East Eighties. While she slept on a couch in a drunken stupor, he searched her dressing table and found a note that appeared to provide proof of her secret mission: "See mutual friend at first opportunity. Important you get us information at once." Yardley quietly let himself out of her apartment.[148] Since he was left to run the Black Chamber more or less as he pleased, his mostly harmless fantasies of sex and espionage seem to have attracted little or no attention from the administrations he served.

Elihu Root said of Harding's vice-president and successor, Calvin Coolidge (president from 1923 to 1929), "He did not have an international hair on his head." Coolidge's *Autobiography* contains no mention of foreign policy, still less of foreign intelligence. The least active and most taciturn of twentieth-century presidents, "Silent Cal" claimed, no doubt with some exaggeration, that he kept himself fit by "avoiding big problems" and working only four hours a day. Even more than Harding, Coolidge left foreign affairs to his secretaries of state: Hughes until 1925, Frank B. Kellogg thereafter. There is only one recorded example of Coolidge's reaction to a decrypt from the Black Chamber. The reference occurs solely in Yardley's memoirs. But, since it is incidental to the main point Yardley wishes to make and contains none of the elaboration or boasts that characterize his less reliable recollections, it is probably to be believed. The decrypt revealed corruption involving a foreign ambassador and a U.S. government official. When shown the document by the secretary of state, Coolidge allegedly replied, with his usual economy of expression, "Yes, the Attorney General showed that to me a few moments ago. He just left." Yardley, by his own account, was immediately summoned to the State Department. The chief cause of the excitement, however, was not the contents of the decrypted telegram but the fact that the Justice Department had obtained a copy. Yardley said that the intercept had been sent to the attorney general because "this looked to me like a Justice Department case." "The activity of an Ambassador," he was firmly told, "is never a Department of Justice case."[149]

The Coolidge presidency marked a period of decline for the Black Chamber. Yardley's main problem was less the difficulty of foreign codes and ciphers than a shortage of intercepts on which to work. The cable companies were reluctant to supply copies of telegrams passing over their lines, and the flow of radio intercepts from the Army Signal Corps dwindled to a trickle. The Black Chamber also had to contend with legal restrictions imposed by the Radio Communications Acts. According to a secret in-house history:

The effect of the Act of 1912 was to hamper, and that of the Act of 1927 to forbid, the interception of radio traffic of any kind, either in peace or time of war, though this could hardly have been the intention of Congress in enacting these two laws.

In 1927 the Black Chamber received a total of 428 Japanese intercepts in over ten different code and cipher systems, but because a shortage of telegrams prevented cryptanalysis of some of the systems, it was able to decrypt only 150. During the decade after its foundation in 1919, the Black Chamber produced a total of about 10,000 decrypts, 1,600 of them during the Washington Conference.[150]

After a gradual decline during the Coolidge presidency, the Black Chamber ground to an abrupt halt under his successor, Herbert C. Hoover. Following Hoover's inauguration in March 1929, Henry Stimson became secretary of State. In view of Stimson's well-advertised insistence on high moral standards in public affairs, his officials decided not to bring the existence of the Black Chamber to his attention until he had had some weeks to acclimate himself to the lower moral tone of day-to-day diplomacy. In May the State Department finally decided, with some trepidation, to place a few Japanese intercepts on Stimson's desk. According to the confidential account of the sequel later compiled by the great codebreaker, William F. Friedman:

> His reaction was violent and his action drastic. Upon learning how the material was obtained, he characterized the activity as highly unethical and declared that it would cease *immediately*, so far as the State Department was concerned. To put teeth into his decision he gave instructions that the necessary funds of the State Department would be withdrawn *at once*.[151]

Stimson's own account in his diary, though less dramatic, agrees with Friedman's. On seeing the decrypts on his desk, he immediately summoned his friend, Joseph P. Cotton, a New York lawyer whom he had made his undersecretary:

> . . . We both agreed that it was a highly unethical thing for this Government to do to be reading the messages coming to our ambassadorial guests from other countries. So then and there . . . I discontinued these payments [to the Black Chamber] and that put an end to the continuing of this group of experts who subsequently disbanded.[152]

It was only with difficulty that Stimson was persuaded to allow the Black Chamber two months to close down and hand its files to the Army Signal

Corps, and to give the six sacked cryptographers, none with pension rights, a gratuity of three months' salary.[153]

Even after he decided to close the Black Chamber down, Stimson remained curiously ignorant about its past activities. He did not discover its success in decrypting Japanese telegrams during the Washington Conference until Yardley published his memoirs in 1931. Stimson was staggered by Yardley's revelations. "I cannot believe this is true . . . ," he wrote in his diary. He was still uncertain how much Hughes and Kellogg had known about what the Black Chamber was up to, and declined to respond to press questions about Yardley's book because—he told his diary—it might damage his predecessors' reputations.[154]

Hoover seems to have had no regrets about the closure of the Black Chamber. Yardley told Friedman (though he did not mention it in his memoirs) that "the fundamental objection" to the Black Chamber "arose from President Hoover rather than from . . . Secretary Stimson." An in-house history of interwar U.S. SIGINT later concluded that the problem of responsibility for its closure, as between Hoover and Stimson, "remains obscure."[155]

Hoover's scruples about intruding on the privacy of foreign diplomats did not extend to some of his political opponents. As the United States slid into depression after the Wall Street crash, he became increasingly sensitive to the mounting criticism of him. Stimson wrote in his diary:

> . . . I do wish [the President] could shield himself against listening to so much rumor and criticism. If he would only walk out his own way and not worry over what his enemies say, it would make matters so much easier. That is the point about which I am most concerned.[156]

Hoover's private secretary, Lawrence Richey, kept a "black list" of the president's enemies. Among those put under surveillance was the future head of the wartime OSS, William J. Donovan, whom Hoover had failed to nominate as attorney general after apparently promising that he would. Hoover seems to have preferred not to use Bureau of Investigation agents for political surveillance, possibly in order not to leave embarrassing information on bureau files. Richey, however, had many contacts in the surveillance business acquired during his own long association with the Secret Service. That association began at the age of only thirteen after he saw a gang of counterfeiters at work through a basement window. At sixteen he became a full-time Secret Service operative. At twenty-one he was appointed bodyguard to President Theodore Roosevelt. Richey first met Hoover during the First World War and worked for him for the next forty-two years as his chief personal assistant. He was also a member of the same Masonic lodge as J. Edgar Hoover. Richey had, it has been claimed, "a special gift for turning up embarrassing tidbits about political opponents."[157]

In the spring of 1930 President Hoover received a confidential report, probably from Richey, claiming that the Democratic party offices in New York had assembled a dossier of damaging information that they proposed to use to destroy his reputation. Determined to gain access to the dossier, Hoover approached his former private secretary, Lewis Lichtenstein Strauss, now a Wall Street banker and a partner in the same firm as Sir William Wiseman, Kuhn, Loeb & Co., Strauss in turn made contact with a naval intelligence officer, Lieutenant Commander Glenn Howell, who recorded in his log:

> Strauss told me that the President is anxious to know what the contents of the mysterious documents are, and Strauss is authorized by the President to use the services of any one of our various government secret services.

Howell already had experience of covert operations that included breaking and entering the offices of the Communist party and the Japanese consul. But he was unhappy at undertaking an operation prompted by purely political considerations rather than reasons of national security. "I am going to tackle it, of course," he noted in his log, "but it's a devilish awkward job and I may very readily find myself in a hell's brew of trouble." To assist him, Howell recruited a former police inspector, Robert J. Peterkin. Together the two men broke into the Democratic party office, where the compromising file on Hoover was supposed to be kept. To their surprise, they found it empty. They then tracked down the former tenant, a Democrat publicist named James J. O'Brien. "We shadowed him for ɩ bit," wrote Howell in his log, "and then came to the conclusion that no President of the United States need be afraid of a ham-and-egger like O'Brien." Howell's report was relayed by Strauss to Richey, who passed it to the president. Hoover sent back a message to Howell "to tell me to call off my watch and to consider the case closed."[158]

The abortive operation remained secret. Forty-two years later a similarly unsuccessful and somewhat farcical break-in to Democratic party offices by intelligence personnel, conducted on behalf of Herbert Hoover's eighth cousin, once removed, Richard M. Nixon (like Hoover brought up as a Quaker), but far less successfully covered up, generated the most serious crisis in the history of the twentieth-century presidency.

CHAPTER 3

Franklin D. Roosevelt:
The Path to Pearl Harbor

Franklin Roosevelt presided over both the worst intelligence failure and the greatest intelligence success in American history. On December 7, 1941, the inability of the disorganized and under-resourced U.S. intelligence community to detect the movements of the Japanese fleet made possible the devastating surprise attack on Pearl Harbor. Over the next few years, however, Allied codebreaking and intelligence coups hastened victory in both Europe and the Pacific. Roosevelt bears some personal responsibility both for the disaster that brought the United States into the Second World War and for the successes that shortened it.

Roosevelt's first experience of codes and ciphers went back to the beginning of the century. While a student at Harvard, he became the first future president since Jefferson to construct his own secret cipher. Jefferson's cipher, probably invented during his term as Washington's secretary of state, was characteristically ingenious.[1] Roosevelt's was much simpler. Vowels were turned into numerals; AEIOU became 12345. Consonants were replaced by symbols, usually formed from fragments of the letters they represented. ("And," for example, became 1\Ɔ). There were no gaps to indicate the beginning and end of individual words. Though a cryptanalyst would have cracked the cipher in minutes, it was probably good enough to defeat casual inspection by curious friends and relatives. Roosevelt used the cipher to record briefly in his diary the most emotional moments of his early manhood.[2]

"Once upon a time when I was in Cambridge," he later wrote to a friend, "I had serious thoughts of marrying a Boston girl and settling down in the Back Bay to spend the rest of my days. . . . It was a narrow escape." The "Boston girl" was the beautiful Alice Sohier, not yet sixteen when Roosevelt first met her as a Harvard freshman.[3] A cipher passage in his diary for July 8, 1902, at the end of his sophomore year, records: ALICE CONFIDES IN HER DOCTOR. Roosevelt wrote the next day, also in cipher: WORRIED OVER ALICE ALL NIGHT.[4] What Alice Sohier confided, and why Roosevelt spent an uncharacteristically sleepless night, can now only be guessed at. But it is possible that Alice was worried by a sexual encounter (not necessarily, given her innocence, going as far as intercourse) with the young FDR. Half a century later she would say only, "In a day and age when well brought-up young men were expected to keep their hands off the persons of young ladies from respectable families, Franklin had to be slapped—*hard*."[5] The next reference to her in Roosevelt's diary comes in an unciphered entry of October 8: "See Alice Sohier off on the 'Commonwealth' for Europe."[6] That, it seems, was the end of the romance. Roosevelt's diary also briefly records his courtship of his cousin Eleanor. He wrote in cipher on July 7, 1903, almost a year to the day after he had spent a sleepless night worrying about Alice Sohier: E. IS AN ANGEL. On November 22, 1903, another ciphered entry records: AFTER LUNCH I HAVE A NEVER TO BE FORGOTTEN WALK TO THE RIVER WITH MY DARLING.[7] During that walk, Eleanor accepted his proposal of marriage. They were married on March 17, 1905; the president, cousin Theodore Roosevelt, gave the bride away.[8]

During his early political career Roosevelt showed greater interest in intelligence than any president-to-be since Washington in the Revolutionary War. But it was a curiously lopsided interest. Despite his early use of a secret cipher, he was fascinated by HUMINT but relatively indifferent to SIGINT. His first experience of intelligence work came as assistant secretary of the navy in the Wilson administration from 1913 to 1920. All his life he had a passion for the sea. At the age of five he illustrated his first letter with an elaborate drawing of a sailboat. As a sixteen-year-old at Groton, he singlehandedly sailed a yawl from New York to Eastport, Maine. During his time at Harvard, his wealthy father bought him first the forty-foot *Half Moon*, then the eighteen-ton auxiliary cruiser *Half Moon II*.[9] As assistant secretary of the navy, Roosevelt was fond of contrasting his own proactive style with the allegedly deskbound inertia of the secretary, Josephus Daniels. In 1920 he made the preposterous claim that, to prepare the U.S. Navy for war without the knowledge of Daniels and President Wilson, "I committed enough illegal acts to put me in jail for 999 years." In reality, all FDR's supposedly illegal expenditure had been cleared in advance with the secretary. Though Roosevelt successfully kept himself in the public eye, most of the decisions were made by the less publicity-conscious Daniels.[10]

The main area for which Roosevelt had direct responsibility as assistant secretary was the Office of Naval Intelligence. Initially ONI found his enthusiasm for its work somewhat disconcerting. In January 1916 the director of naval intelligence, Captain James Harrison Oliver, complained that the assistant secretary was recruiting his own espionage network and interfering in intelligence operations. Roosevelt got on far better with Captain Roger Welles, who succeeded Oliver as DNI shortly after the United States entered the First World War in April 1917. Welles seems to have been happy to appoint as naval intelligence officers a number of the assistant secretary's socialite friends: among them his golf partner, Alexander Brown Legare, founder of the Chevy Chase Hunt Club; the leading polo player, Lawrence Waterbury, husband of FDR's sister-in-law; and Roosevelt's Harvard classmate, Steuart Davis, commander of FDR's Volunteer Patrol Squadron, which became the nucleus of the Naval Reserve.[11]

The discoveries of German secret agents and sabotage operations in the United States, culminating in the Black Tom explosion in New York harbor in July 1916, increased Roosevelt's fascination with covert operations.[12] His grasp of the potential threat from enemy agents after U.S. entry into the war, however, owed at least as much to his reading of spy novels as to a cool assessment of the risks. In April 1917 he instructed ONI to inquire into the improbable danger that German-Americans in New Hampshire might purchase an aircraft to bomb Portsmouth Navy Yard.[13] He also sent ONI a series of "disturbing reports" on allegedly suspicious behavior by German-Americans forwarded by alarmist friends whom he described as "a pretty good source." FDR demanded prompt investigation.[14] ONI responded with reports such as that in May 1917 on the Krantz Manufacturing Company of Brooklyn, where agent investigation revealed "the following facts":

> The employees are almost German to a man. Every official has a German appearance and pro-German influence is very strong. The German officials keep their business activities very quiet and always converse in German.

Some ONI reports were as alarmist as those forwarded by Roosevelt's friends and relations. A memorandum to FDR on May 17 claimed that the Philadelphia firm of Schutte and Koerting had for some years past been "installing defective apparatus in the U.S. Navy," and that "these defects have been carefully concealed."[15]

Roosevelt began to speculate, and later to fantasize, that he had been marked out for assassination by German secret agents. He subsequently told a deeply improbable tale of how, in the spring of 1917:

. . . the Secret Service found in the safe of the German Consul in New York, a document headed: "To be eliminated." The first name on the list was that of Frank Polk [intelligence coordinator at the State Department]; mine was the second followed by eight or ten others. As a result the Secret Service asked us both to carry revolvers as we both habitually walked to and from our offices. I was given the revolver and the shoulder holster.

Roosevelt claimed that after a few days he stopped wearing the revolver and kept it in a desk drawer instead.[16] In 1929 he told an equally unlikely tale of how a bomb had been sent to him during the war at the assistant secretary's office, but had been discovered before it went off.[17]

After the United States entry into the war, the DNI, Captain Welles, rashly boasted to Roosevelt that ONI would soon surpass the feats of the legendary Blinker Hall and the British NID.[18] Admiral William S. Sims, who was sent to London in April 1917 to command U.S. naval forces in the European theater, did not share Welles's confidence. To Welles's annoyance, he insisted that reports from U.S. naval attachés in Europe be sent to him for checking against Hall's superior intelligence before being forwarded to Washington. Hall briefed Sims daily on the intelligence derived from German naval decrypts, but did not tell him the full story. In particular, he concealed from Sims the existence of the diplomatic section of his SIGINT unit and Room 40's success in decrypting American traffic, including, no doubt, that between Sims and Washington.[19]

Roosevelt's own meeting with Blinker Hall, during a visit to London in the summer of 1918, made a profound impression on him that still colored his attitude toward British intelligence at the beginning of the Second World War. "Their intelligence unit is much more developed than ours," he wrote after his visit, "and this is because it is a much more integral part of their Office of Operations."[20] What struck Roosevelt most was the apparently phenomenal success of the admiralty's secret agents. Still anxious to conceal how much of his intelligence was obtained from SIGINT rather than from espionage, Hall arranged an elaborate charade designed to deceive the impressionable assistant secretary. As the two men discussed German troop movements, Hall, probably blinking furiously as he did at moments of excitement, said suddenly to Roosevelt: "I am going to ask that youngster at the other end of the room to come over here. I will not introduce him by name. I want you to ask him where he was twenty-four hours ago." When Roosevelt put the question, the young man replied, "I was in Kiel, sir." The assistant secretary was as astonished as the DNI had intended. Hall then explained that British spies crossed the German-Danish border each night, went by boat to Sylt, and thence by flying boat to Harwich. Roosevelt was amazed and deeply impressed. He went to his grave never realizing that he had been taken in by one of Blinker's deceptions.[21]

Like President Wilson, Roosevelt was also deceived at the end of the war by some of the forged Soviet documents circulated after the October Revolution in an attempt to discredit the Bolshevik regime. Among the most absurd was a "Decree on the Socialization of Women" that declared:

> All women according to this Decree are exempted from private ownership and are declared the property of the whole nation. . . . Men citizens have the right to use one woman not oftener than three times a week for three hours.

Roosevelt was suitably scandalized. He told a women's luncheon group that the League of Nations offered the best defense against this evil doctrine.[22] Similar nonsense continued to arrive on the assistant secretary's desk for the remainder of his term of office, some of it from allegedly "reliable" military as well as naval intelligence sources. Rear Admiral Albert P. Niblack, who had succeeded Welles as DNI, reported in December 1919:

> A Nation-wide Terrorists' campaign is being hatched on the Pacific and Atlantic Coasts by Germans, Russian and Mexican Terrorists. . . . The main planning is being done in Mexico City by old-time German anarchists who escaped from Chicago during the Haymarket riots. No definite date has yet been set. The Terror will surpass anything that ever happened in this country and the brains of the plot are already on the Pacific Coast, but it may be January or February before anything will be attempted, but the real directing is being done from Mexico City and the Mexicans who enter this country as railroad laborers are the message carriers.[23]

FDR's direct involvement in secret service work led to the most serious personal crisis of his early political career. The crisis began with a homosexual scandal at the Newport naval base. In April 1919 eighteen sailors were charged with various sexual offenses; fourteen were later court-martialed. Niblack told the assistant secretary that allegations of sexual perversion were not the business of naval intelligence. Roosevelt unwisely paid no attention. On May 1 Lieutenant Erastus Mead Hudson of the Navy Medical Corps, who had led the investigation, and Chief

Machinist Mate Ervin Arnold, a former detective who claimed to be able "to detect a sexual pervert by watching . . . his walk, manner and bearing," were summoned to the assistant secretary's office. Four days later FDR sent Niblack a confidential memorandum, asking him to employ Hudson and Arnold "for work in connection with suppressing these practices. . . . It is requested that this be the only written communication in regard to this affair, as it is thought wise to keep this matter wholly secret." Niblack refused on the grounds that the whole affair was no concern of ONI. Roosevelt then decided to attach the investigation directly to his own office. He instructed Lieutenant Hudson:

> You are hereby designated as Commanding Officer of a group of enlisted (or enrolled) men and women who have been assigned or may be assigned certain confidential special duties as agents of the Assistant Secretary of the Navy. This group, or unit, will bear the name: "Section A—Office of the Assistant Secretary," or simply: "Section A-OASN."

Roosevelt ordered Hudson and Arnold to be given naval intelligence identity cards. Section A-OASN was financed out of his own contingent naval fund; all its orders and correspondence went through Roosevelt's confidential stenographer. In all, the section recruited forty-one enlisted men—ten aged only sixteen to nineteen—to take part in its investigations. Roosevelt's later claims that he knew "absolutely nothing" about the methods used in the investigation, which included sexual entrapment, fail to carry complete conviction. He personally signed at least twenty orders relating to it, including instructions to Arnold concerning "duty of such a nature that he does not have written orders."[24]

Section A-OASN's investigation led to the arrest of sixteen Newport civilians, including Father Samuel Kent, chaplain at the naval base. At his trial in August 1919 two sailors working for the section testified that they had been instructed to go "to the limit" sexually to gain evidence against the chaplain. Father Kent was acquitted, and a hunt began for the naval officers who had authorized sexual entrapment. After Kent was again found not guilty at a federal trial early in 1920, a naval court of inquiry was set up under Admiral Herbert O. Dunn. Though Roosevelt still denied all knowledge of the methods employed by Section A-OASN, the Newport scandal continued to hang over him after he resigned as assistant secretary of the navy in August to stand unsuccessfully as the Democratic vice-presidential candidate in the November election. In March 1921 the Dunn court of inquiry expressed "the opinion that it was unfortunate and ill-advised that Franklin D. Roosevelt, Assistant Secretary of the Navy, either directed or permitted the use of enlisted personnel to investigate perversion." Far more damaging was the report of the Senate Naval Subcommittee in July 1921. Its Republican majority concluded that Section A-OASN men "had allowed lewd and immoral acts to be performed upon them," and "thoroughly condemned" his actions as "immoral and an abuse of the authority of his office." The *New York Times* reported the subcommittee findings under the banner headlines: LAY NAVY SCANDAL TO F. D. ROOSEVELT . . . DETAILS ARE UNPRINTABLE.

Roosevelt declared himself the innocent victim of Republican mudslinging. While he probably did not know many of the details of Section A-OASN's work, it seems likely that he knew more than he admitted. He had, however, insisted from the start that "written communication" be avoided to keep the handling of the case "wholly secret." Roosevelt's behavior during the Newport scandal looks suspiciously like an early example of the doctrine of plausible denial used by later presidents to distance themselves from intelligence operations for which they were unwilling to take responsibility.

The fallout from Roosevelt's direct involvement in the intelligence investigation of the Newport scandal was far more painful than defeat in a presidential election he had not expected to win. But it was quickly overtaken by a much greater personal tragedy. A week after the Senate subcommittee report, he contracted the polio virus that was to leave him a cripple, unable to use his legs. Polio marked the watershed of FDR's career. His suffering and the courage with which he slowly surmounted it turned him from a precociously successful but slightly shallow politician into an inspirational leader, able in the depths of the Depression to bring hope to the American people. Elected president by a landslide majority in November 1932, Roosevelt almost did not live to give his famous inaugural address on March 4, 1933, proclaiming his "firm belief that the only thing we have to fear is fear itself." At a rally in Miami on February 15 the Secret Service failed to prevent an attempt to shoot him. The bullet intended for the president fatally wounded the mayor of Chicago, who was standing next to him.[25] Another bullet that injured a policeman is exhibited today at the Franklin D. Roosevelt Library in Hyde Park, New York.

Foreign intelligence was plainly a low priority during the frenetic first Hundred Days that launched the New Deal and created an alphabet soup of new federal agencies. Roosevelt found time, however, to renew contact with ONI and to begin cultivating his own private sources of information.[26] The Washington journalist John Franklin Carter (Jay Franklin), later head of a wartime intelligence unit in the White House, began providing him with confidential reports on his own administration.[27]

The most important of Roosevelt's diplomatic sources was probably William C. Bullitt, a man of great wealth, intellectual energy, and egocentric brilliance who had traveled widely around Europe since the First World War without finding adequate employment for his considerable talents. FDR's use of Bullitt as a secret agent during the interval between his election and his inauguration almost ended in disaster. On November 19, 1932, Bullitt left for Europe on a mission of inquiry into the prospects for repayment of American loans and for Franco-German reconciliation. For legal reasons, the mission was surrounded by great secrecy. The Logan Act provided for a fine of $5,000 and up to three years' imprisonment for any U.S. citizen conducting negotiations on government business with foreign governments without the official authorization that Roosevelt was not yet in a position to give. Bullitt thus sought to preserve the fiction that his trip was purely private. His reports used a code in which his brother's given name, Orville, meant debt, and his own, Bill, meant debt repayment. They were sent to a New York lawyer for forwarding to FDR. One of Bullitt's first cables from London began:

CONVERSATION WITH PHILIP [RAMSAY MACDONALD, THE PRIME MINISTER] THIS MORNING SO INTIMATE THAT I CONSIDER IT UNWISE TO CABLE STOP OSWALD [NEVILLE CHAMBERLAIN, CHANCELLOR OF THE EXCHEQUER] AND OTHERS OPPOSE BILL [DEBT REPAYMENT] STOP

During a follow-up trip to Europe early in 1933, however, Bullitt's secret leaked out. On January 24 a news agency wire, headed ROOSEVELT "SECRET AGENT" IS REPORTED IN LONDON, reported that British officials were mystified by the request "from an important quarter that Bullitt's mission must not be made known in the Washington State Department." Bullitt made a hasty exit. He wrote privately to MacDonald to explain that, in view of Republican calls for his prosecution under the Logan Act, "I am deeply sorry that I cannot say good-bye to you before leaving for home." Bullitt's reports to FDR are chiefly memorable now for one spectacular misjudgment. He wrote at the end of 1932, "Hitler is finished—not as an agitator or as a leader of an aggressive minority, but as a possible dictator." On January 30, 1933, Hitler became chancellor of Germany.[28]

In November 1933, after the establishment of diplomatic relations with the Soviet Union, Roosevelt appointed Bullitt as the first U.S. ambassador to Moscow. In 1936 Bullitt moved on to Paris. He was one of a number of American envoys who maintained a personal correspondence with the president that bypassed the State Department. As during his years as assistant secretary of the navy, FDR also began cultivating his own intelligence sources. Among the most prominent was the multi-millionaire publisher and property developer Vincent Astor. In 1927 Astor had set up an informal intelligence group known as "The Room" that met monthly in New York City in an apartment at 34 East 62nd Street with a mail drop and an unlisted telephone number. Prominent members of The Room included FDR's cousin, Kermit Roosevelt, son of President Theodore Roosevelt; banker Winthrop W. Aldrich; Judge Frederic Kernochan; philanthropist William Rhinelander Stewart; the assistant secretary of air F. Trubee Davison; and David Bruce, who later served in London both as wartime chief of the OSS and as postwar ambassador.[29]

By the time FDR became president, Astor was one of his closest friends. Roosevelt spent his last holiday before his inauguration aboard Astor's luxury motor yacht, the *Nourmahal*; he wrote to his mother while on the cruise, "Vincent is a dear and perfect host."[30] During his first term as president FDR took annual holidays of up to two weeks on board the *Nourmahal*. Accompanying Astor and the president on their vacations were several other members of The Room, among them Kermit Roosevelt, Kernochan, and Stewart. The eccentric male bonding and well-lubricated hilarity aboard the *Nourmahal* was itemized in bogus bills that Astor sent his guests after every voyage. In September 1934 each was charged $187.50 for "Expenses incurred for Alcoholic Stimulants and repeated Correctives (NOTE: The Chief Steward reports that consumption of the above Stores was so Vast as to overwhelm his accounting system)," with a further $1.90 for "Chipping Mother-of-Pearl Surfaces of Bell Contacts, through Impatient Punching of the above, to hasten the arrival of Correctives." Charges were also levied for "General Abuse and Battering of [backgammon] Tables, etc, through Exhibitions of Nasty Temper, etc," "Inept and Stupid Handling of Dials and Knobs on [radio], thereby causing Havoc," and "Expensive and Wasteful Use of Launches with attendant Fuel Expenditures, for purposes of Frumping, and Allied Activities ashore."[31] Roosevelt loved every moment of both the voyages and the somewhat adolescent shipboard humor. He wrote to Astor, "When we purchase Flores from the Portugee [*sic*] Republic, . . . I think you as principal owner should assume the title of Khan or possibly Satrap."[32] He included in his collection of "Amusing Things" a card sent by Astor showing a naked woman concealed in a picture of "A Dirty Dog."[33]

No written record was kept of Roosevelt's dealings with Astor and The Room. Some tantalizing glimpses, however, survive in the Roosevelt papers. In addition to receiving a bizarre mixture of jokes, gossip, and intelligence from members of The Room, FDR also encouraged Astor to go on unofficial intelligence-gathering voyages. During his first term the *Nourmahal* went on a number of cruises in the Caribbean and along the Pacific and Atlantic coasts of Latin America, investigating Japanese and other activities. In 1938 Astor went on a more ambitious voyage to gather intelligence from some of the Japanese Pacific islands. Early in 1938 he acknowledged receipt of the president's "instructions" for the trip. "They could not be more clear," Astor wrote. Though the instructions themselves do not survive, his letter of acknowledgment makes clear that they concerned a voyage to "the Marshall Islands and possible trouble."[34] Astor was confident, he told the president, that he would "do a usefull [sic] job in a way that the Regular Service never could." Among the secret assignments that he discussed with the DNI, Admiral Ralston S. Holmes, was the use of *Nourmahal*'s direction finder to locate Japanese radio stations. Astor arranged for the *Nourmahal* to be put on radio watch by the U.S. Navy as soon as he transmitted the coded signal "Many Happy Returns of the Day" to his New York office. If he feared "real trouble," he would send a coded "Automobile" message to Samoa and Hawaii: "Appreciate offer of car. Am in Lat[itude]—Lon[gitude]—so date of arrival uncertain." "Believe me," Astor assured the president, "I will never send 'Automobile' unless completely up against it . . . . If only you were *not* President I would try to see to it that you *had* to come!" Astor was pleased with the intelligence he collected. On his way home, he sent Roosevelt a summary report from Honolulu, in view of "the remote possibility of trouble" with the Japanese during the remainder of his voyage. Eniwetok, he reported, was Japan's "principal naval base in the Marshall Islands," with Bikini "probably their second string base." Wotje contained both a new Japanese airfield and a submarine base.

Roosevelt's and Astor's attitudes to espionage before the outbreak of the Second World War in Europe were reminiscent of those of the gentlemen amateur agents of late-Victorian and Edwardian Britain. "For anyone who is tired of life," wrote the founder of the Boy Scout movement, Sir Robert Baden-Powell, "the thrilling life of a spy should be the very finest recuperator." Commander Mansfield Cumming, head of the foreign section of the Edwardian Secret Service Bureau, described espionage as "capital sport."[35] Roosevelt and Astor agreed. "I don't want to make you jealous," Astor wrote to the president before the *Nourmahal* left on its 1938 intelligence-gathering mission, "but aren't you a bit envious of my trip?"[36] Despite the unprecedented number of new federal agencies founded during the New Deal, it did not yet occur to Roosevelt that the United States might also require a professional foreign intelligence service.

Besides Astor, the unofficial prewar intelligence source most valued by Roosevelt was probably the war hero and wealthy New York lawyer William J. Donovan, who had links with The Room though he may not have been a regular member of it. Donovan and Roosevelt had been contemporaries and, according to Roosevelt, friends at Columbia Law School. Despite being a prominent Republican opposed to the New Deal, Donovan was one of twenty-one members of the law school class of 1907 to attend President-elect Roosevelt's fifty-first birthday party at Warm Springs, Georgia, in January 1933.[37] Though FDR was later to make him coordinator of information (intelligence) in 1941 and head of the Office of Strategic Services (OSS) in 1942, it has been generally assumed that he did not use Donovan in an intelligence role until after the outbreak of the Second World War. There is evidence, however, that Donovan began a series of transatlantic intelligence missions with the president's blessing, and perhaps at his request, as early as 1935. In December of that year Donovan paid a private visit to the Italian dictator Benito Mussolini, whom Roosevelt still vainly hoped would block the expansion of Nazi Germany. At a meeting in Mussolini's absurdly grandiose study at the Palazzo Venezia in Rome, Il Duce authorized Donovan to tour the East African battlefront where the Italian army was engaged in the brutal conquest of Ethiopia. "We are not afraid to have an impartial observer see everything," boasted Mussolini. In January 1936 Donovan traveled the entire length of the Ethiopian war front, flying by Caproni bomber from one airfield to another, and spent three hours conferring with the Italian commander, Marshal Pietro Badoglio. He was impressed by what he thought he saw. Unlike the Italian troops in the First World War, of whom he had formed a low opinion, the new army of Fascist Italy struck him as well organized and with high morale; he even judged it to be on excellent terms with the Ethiopians in conquered areas. Donovan, however, had been misled by a well-orchestrated Italian deception. Evidence of the use of mustard gas had been successfully concealed from him. He had been transported by air so that he should not realize how unsafe many of the roads remained, and had been deceived by a visit to a Potemkin village populated by compliant, conquered natives. Though Badoglio was to be victorious in May, his forces narrowly escaped disaster less than two weeks after Donovan had toured the front. As Mussolini had hoped, however, Donovan returned to the United States impressed by the apparent strength of Fascist resolve. At a private meeting with the president at Hyde Park in February, he emphasized both the effectiveness of the Italian armed forces and the determination of the Italian people, under Mussolini's leadership, not to yield to international pressure to stop the war. His report may have contributed to

Roosevelt's decision not to seek the imposition of an American oil embargo against Italy.[38]

FDR's contacts with Astor's Room and with Donovan reflected the confusion of his prewar foreign policy-making. Instead of relying on an orderly system of assessment, he preferred to base his judgments on impressions drawn from a wide range of official and unofficial sources. Henry Stimson, who became his secretary of war in 1940, confided to his diary:

> Conferences with the President are difficult matters. His mind does not easily follow a consecutive chain of thought but he is full of stories and incidents and hops about in his discussions from suggestion to suggestion and it is very much like chasing a vagrant beam of moonshine around a vacant room.[39]

Though it sometimes remains as difficult for the historian as for Stimson to reconstruct the elusive sequence of thought that guided FDR's prewar foreign policy, it is clear that intelligence from both unofficial and official sources influenced some of his most important decisions. One striking example was the White House conference called by the president on November 14, 1938, to determine American air power requirements: the first major step toward U.S. rearmament. Roosevelt believed that Hitler's superiority in the air helped to explain both his aggressiveness and the capitulation to his demands by Britain and France at the Munich conference six weeks earlier. The White House conference, which he chaired, concluded that to defend the Western Hemisphere the United States required ten thousand planes. This estimate was based on wildly inaccurate intelligence from a mixture of unofficial and official sources that had combined in Roosevelt's brain to produce a conveniently round figure.[40]

Among the most influential of the unofficial sources was the celebrated, vain, and gullible American aviator Colonel Charles A. Lindbergh, whose admiration for Hitler as "undoubtedly a great man" had persuaded the Germans to permit him to make three tours of inspection of the Luftwaffe, and even to fly some of their planes. Lindbergh's alarmist views of German strength in the air were pressed on the president by, among others, his ambassadors in London and Paris, Joseph P. Kennedy and William C. Bullitt. According to a report from Lindbergh that reached Roosevelt during the Munich crisis:

> The rate of progress of German military aviation is without parallel. I feel certain that German air strength is greater than that of all other European countries combined. . . . Germany has such a pre-

ponderance of war planes that she can bomb any city in Euro
with comparatively little resistance. England and France are far to
weak in the air to protect themselves.[41]

On September 28, 1938, Bullitt sent an urgent personal message to the
president containing "secrets of the highest importance" from French
military intelligence for his *"most private eye"* only. If the Munich crisis
ended in war, "the French would have six hundred battle planes"; over
the following two weeks the British would make available another 240.
By contrast:

> To the certain knowledge of the French Military Intelligence, the
> Germans have ready for battle at this moment six thousand five
> hundred planes of the very latest types. . . . The Italians have of the
> very latest types eight hundred pursuit planes and twelve hundred
> bombers.

In addition, both Germany and Italy were said to possess "large quantities" of older planes. If war came, "The [French] Minister for Air felt that
the destruction in Paris would pass all imagination. He said that he had
sent his wife and child to Brittany already. . . ."[42]

The president shuffled these and other woefully inaccurate figures
around in his head and somehow arrived at a figure for annual German aircraft production capacity of twelve thousand planes (almost 50 percent
higher, he calculated, than the combined capacity of Britain and France).
Acting, in effect, as his own intelligence analyst, he presented these mis-
calculated figures to the White House conference on November 14, 1938.[43]
In reality, at the time of the Munich crisis the Luftwaffe possessed only
2,928 planes of all kinds (including transport and trainers), of which
only 1,669 were serviceable—markedly fewer than the combined total
of the British, French, and Czechoslovaks. British air intelligence,
whose assessments were either unknown to, or ignored by, Washington,
arrived at remarkably accurate figures for frontline aircraft: 2,909 German, 1,550 British, 1,349 French, 628 Czechoslovak, and 198 Belgian.[44]
Though even the British statistics exaggerated the number of combat-
ready planes in the Luftwaffe, the claims of massive German aerial
superiority that preoccupied Roosevelt during the Munich crisis were
clearly mythical.

Prewar counterintelligence was almost as confused as foreign intelligence collection, though the president was less inclined to dabble in it
himself. The first major case affecting internal security to attract Roosevelt's attention did so as the result of a complaint from the German

ambassador to FDR's newly appointed secretary of state, Cordell Hull, on March 28, 1933, that he had received a letter "wherein the assassination of the Chancellor of the Reich, Mr. Adolf Hitler, is threatened." An FBI investigation failed to track down the author of the letter, but uncovered instead what J. Edgar Hoover claimed were subversive activities by pro-Nazi organizations. In May 1934 Roosevelt instructed Hoover, the chief of the Secret Service, and the commissioner of immigration and naturalization to cooperate in the investigation of Nazi and Fascist organizations.[45] Another round ensued in the traditional turf battles between Secret Service and FBI, which eventually ended in victory for the FBI.

On August 24, 1936, Hoover was summoned to the Oval Office to discuss "the question of subversive activities in the United States, particularly Fascism and Communism." According to a memorandum by Hoover (the only surviving record of the meeting):

> The President stated that he had been considerably concerned about the movements of the Communists and of Fascism in the United States and that while the Secret Service of the Treasury Department had assured him that they had informants in every Communist group, he believed that if it was true it was solely for the purpose of getting any information upon plots upon his life, whereas what he was interested in was obtaining a broad picture of the general movement and its activities as may affect the economic and political life of the country as a whole.

Hoover briefed the president on various, mostly Communist, activities monitored by the FBI. The bureau, he announced, had discovered instructions from the Communist International to American Communists, telling them to vote for Roosevelt rather than for his Republican opponent, Alf Landon, in the 1936 presidential election. Hoover complained that neither the FBI nor any other federal agency possessed the authority to acquire the "general intelligence information" that Roosevelt wanted. However, he suggested a legal loophole that would allow the bureau to do so:

> I told him that the appropriation of the Federal Bureau of Investigation contains a provision that it might investigate any matters referred to it by the department of State and that if the State Department should ask for us to conduct such an investigation we could do so under our present authority in the appropriation already granted.[46]

Roosevelt seized on the loophole offered to him. According to Hoover, he said that he would place a handwritten memo in his safe, saying that he had instructed the secretary of state, Cordell Hull, to request the "general intelligence" he wished the FBI to provide.[47]

The next day, August 25, 1936, the director of the FBI returned to the White House to discuss Communist and Fascist subversion with both Roosevelt and Hull. According to Hoover, who, once again, made the only surviving record of the meeting:

> The President pointed out that both of these movements were international in scope and that Communism particularly was directed from Moscow, and that there had been certain indications that [Konstantin] Oumansky, [later Soviet ambassador] attached to the Russian Soviet Embassy, was a leading figure in some of the activities in this country, so consequently, it was a matter that fell within the scope of foreign affairs over which the State Department would have a right to request an inquiry to be made.

Hoover later claimed that Hull had told him, "Go ahead and investigate the hell out of these cocksuckers!" In his official record of the meeting he noted, less vividly, that Hull had authorized a general investigation of "the subversive activities in this country, including communism and fascism." Hoover undertook to proceed with this investigation "in a most discreet and confidential manner," and to coordinate FBI inquiries with MID, ONI, and State.[48]

Though he stepped up FBI surveillance of Communist activities within the labor movement, Hoover, like Roosevelt, failed to grasp the threat of Soviet intelligence penetration within the Washington bureaucracy, where a growing agent network had been operating since the early 1930s. The initial motivation of the Washington moles was much the same as that of their counterparts in London: the lure of a secret war against international fascism and of an idealized myth-image of the Soviet worker-peasant state free from Western class exploitation. Julian Wadleigh, a Soviet agent who penetrated the State Department in 1936, said later:

> When the Communist International represented the only world force effectively resisting Nazi Germany and the other aggressor powers, I had offered my services to the Soviet underground in Washington as one small contribution to help stem the fascist tide.[49]

Hoover and Roosevelt, however, still had outdated images of the front-line Soviet agent as a labor agitator rather than a bright young Washington bureaucrat. For the rest of his life, Roosevelt never took seriously the possibility that his own administration might be penetrated.

With the experience of the First World War behind him, FDR found the threat from German agents easier to understand. The most important prewar espionage case resulted from a tipoff by MI5 in London that led to the arrest in February 1938 of Guenther Gustave Rumrich, a German-American army deserter. Rumrich had run an agent network, codenamed Crown, that had successfully collected large amounts of military intelligence. The case exposed the sometimes comic confusion of U.S. counterespionage as the FBI, MID, State Department security officers, the postal authorities, and the New York police tripped over each other's investigations. Leon G. Turrou, the FBI special agent in charge of Rumrich's interrogation, was so poorly briefed that he confused the Gestapo (the German secret police) with the Abwehr (German military intelligence), whose head, Admiral Wilhelm Canaris, he wrongly identified as "Colonel Busch." Assisted by the interagency confusion, fourteen of the eighteen people indicted succeeded in making their escape. Hoover and the prosecuting attorney blamed each other. The judge, to Hoover's fury, blamed the FBI.[50] At a press conference in October, Roosevelt sounded almost as confused as the counterespionage system over which he presided:

> . . . We have got to the point of studying what the best kind of [counterespionage] machinery is that we can set up. One of our problems today, quite frankly, is that we have too many organizations that are not sufficiently tied together. As we all know, we have the Military Intelligence, G-2, the Office of Naval Intelligence, and the FBI and several organizations in the Treasury Department. . . .

A reporter asked, "Which one of these organizations is primarily responsible?" FDR replied, "They all are, within limits."

The president sought to extricate himself from the confusion by claiming that his administration was giving the problem "very, very deep study."[51] Attorney General Homer S. Cummings recommended increased appropriations of $35,000 each for MID and ONI, and a further $300,000 for the FBI. Roosevelt decided instead on $50,000 for MID and ONI, and $150,000 for the FBI. In December 1938 he announced confidently—and prematurely—that counterespionage was now fully coordinated.[52] Though Hoover accepted the principle of collaboration with MID and ONI, he instructed his special agents in February 1939 that "all complaints relating to espionage, counter-espionage, and sabotage cases should be referred to the Bureau, should be considered within the primary jurisdiction of the Bureau, and should, of course, receive preferred and expeditious attention."[53]

There was an immediate outcry from the state and treasury departments. According to Hoover, Assistant Secretary of State George S. Messersmith called a conference of representatives from the departments of state, war, navy, treasury, justice, and the post office—but not the FBI.[54] Hoover complained to the new attorney general, Frank Murphy, that other agencies were trying to "literally chisel" their way into the counterespionage territory of the FBI: "We don't want to let it slip away from us." Messersmith later gave a different version of events. Roosevelt, he claimed, had asked him to bring together the heads of all the overlapping intelligence agencies. All had been invited to dinner and an after-dinner business meeting at his Georgetown home, but Hoover had failed to turn up. Roosevelt personally insisted that Hoover attend subsequent meetings called by Messersmith. On June 26, 1939, the president instructed the directors of the FBI, MID, and ONI "to function as a committee to coordinate their activities." Hoover was, as usual, the main victor in the bureaucratic infighting that followed.[55]

On September 6, following the beginning of the Second World War in Europe, Roosevelt announced that the FBI would "take charge of investigative work in matters relating to espionage, sabotage, and violations of neutrality regulations":

> To this end I request all police officers, sheriffs and all other law enforcement officers in the United States promptly to turn over to the nearest representative of the Federal Bureau of Investigation any information obtained by them relating to espionage, counterespionage, sabotage, subversive activities and violations of the neutrality laws.

Roosevelt's reference to subversion, which he never defined, introduced an enduring element of vagueness into the FBI's responsibilities. The president had chiefly in mind the German covert operations of the First World War. At a press conference on September 8, though he did not identify Germany by name, he emphasized the need "to protect this country against . . . some of the things that happened over here in 1914 and 1915 and 1916 and the beginning of 1917, before we got into the war."[56] Following FDR's directive of June 26 the directors of the FBI, MID, and ONI formed a chairmanless Interdepartmental Intelligence Committee (IIC). Messersmith and, from 1940, his successor as assistant secretary of state, Adolf A. Berle Jr., attended meetings of the IIC to keep a watching brief for both the State Department and the president.[57]

The main gap in the U.S. intelligence community at the outbreak of war remained the lack of a professional foreign intelligence service. MID's foreign intelligence branch had fewer than seventy personnel in the late 1930s, less than at any point since 1916. General George C. Marshall later acknowledged that "prior to entering the war we had little more than what a military attaché could learn at a dinner, more or less, over the coffee cups. . . ." While ONI in 1939 believed itself in better shape than MID, the DNI, Rear Admiral Walter S. Anderson, admitted in 1939 that "a real undercover foreign intelligence service, equipped and able to carry on espionage, counterespionage, etc. does not exist."[58]

Though Roosevelt did not yet see the need for a professional "undercover foreign intelligence service," Vincent Astor's Room acquired an increased sense of self-importance. The prewar Room, while pandering to FDR's liking for his own secret sources, had been little more than an exclusive social club providing confidential gossip from around the world and opportunities for mildly adventurous intelligence-gathering vacations. With the outbreak of war in Europe, The Room adopted a new cover name, "The Club," and became far more active, though no less boisterous, than before. "Things are going really well up our alley," Astor assured the president. The Club, he told him, was consuming "a considerable amount of Saki and some caviar," and was about to open a "Long Island clubhouse," equipped with "a good supply of Pilsner beer."[59] Thus lubricated by its usual impressive intake of alcohol, The Club performed two intelligence functions of some significance. It enabled Roosevelt to obtain intelligence from telegraph companies and banks without exposing his administration to charges of breaking federal law, and to begin intelligence liaison with the British without infringing U.S. neutrality.

As director of the Western Union Telegraph Company, Astor was able to order the covert interception of telegrams on his own authority. The Club also monitored radio transmissions in the New York area in the hope of detecting messages sent and received by foreign spies. Since its operations were intended to be unavowable by the president, there is no written record of his instructions to it. But it is clear that there were instructions nonetheless. Astor reported to Roosevelt on October 20, 1939, that "in accordance with your wishes . . . a continuous watch on radio observation was established. . . . We will be glad to undertake such a program on an extensive scale if it seems desirable."[60]

Among other Club members in key positions was Winthrop Aldrich, chairman of the board of Chase National Bank, whose accounts included that of the Soviet Amtorg Corporation, which was used to channel money for Soviet intelligence operations in the United States. Soon after The Club's formation, Astor informed the president that he was "starting to work on the banks, using the Chase as the Guinea Pig": "Espionage and Sabotage need money, and that has to pass through the banks at one stage or another. What we need is to have them *volunteer* information, and not merely to allow themselves to be tapped, when asked." Roosevelt was plainly disturbed by the detailed records that he received from The Club, showing Amtorg's expenditure of over $2 million a week (mostly on metals and machinery). In February 1940 he forwarded some of the Amtorg records supplied by The Club to the treasury secretary with a note asking, "Can nothing be done to cut this down?"[61] In April Astor reported that the Japanese ambassador had told Winthrop Aldrich that his government was "exceedingly interested in the Chase Bank organizing & sending to Japan a commission, under the bank's guidance, for the purpose of studying present economic conditions in Japan." Astor suggested that the commission might be used to gather intelligence.[62]

Using his and The Club's extensive family and social connections on the other side of the Atlantic, Astor made contact soon after the outbreak of war with Sir James Paget, the head of the New York station of the British Secret Intelligence Service (SIS, also known as MI6), and his deputy, Walter Bell. Astor reported to Roosevelt:

> . . . I asked [Paget] for unofficial British [intelligence] cooperation, but made it clear that we, for obvious reasons, could not return the compliment in the sense of turning over to them any of our confidential information. This somewhat one-sided arrangement was gladly accepted. This was natural, inasmuch as any success that we might have in discouraging sabotage, etc., would be to his advantage.

Astor's now forgotten meeting with Paget was to mark the first step in the creation of a remarkable Anglo-American intelligence alliance. In February 1940, however, Messersmith was outraged to learn that Paget and Bell had been supplying intelligence direct to both Astor and Hoover, and bypassing the State Department. At his insistence the SIS station was ordered henceforth to communicate exclusively with State. Following Messersmith's replacement as assistant secretary shortly afterward by Adolf Berle, State agreed, in principle, to allow SIS to resume its previous contacts with Astor and Hoover.[63]

In the spring of 1940 Paget was succeeded as head of station by William Stephenson, a wealthy Canadian businessman who had worked part-time for SIS during the 1930s. "Little Bill" Stephenson was a close friend of Astor and probably had long-standing links with The Room.

Like his First World War predecessor, Sir William Wiseman, he was also an ex-amateur boxer, whose rapid punching had, he claimed, won him the nickname "Captain Machine Gun." His friend Gene Tunney, the world champion boxer, arranged for him to meet Hoover soon after his arrival. Though relations between Stephenson and Hoover later soured, initially—according to Tunney—they hit it off "extremely well." A year later, Astor told Roosevelt, liaison between SIS and the FBI was still "working perfectly." Stephenson's engaging personality, business contacts, and fondness for dry martinis cemented many friendships in the United States. During his early months as SIS head of station in New York, Stephenson stayed, at Astor's insistence (and possibly also at his expense), in the St. Regis Hotel, which Astor quaintly described as his "broken-down boarding house."[64]

While at the St. Regis, Stephenson met William Donovan for the first time. Over the next two years the friendship between Little Bill and Wild Bill helped to forge, with Churchill's active encouragement and Roosevelt's blessing, a full-blown intelligence alliance. Soon after the outbreak of war in Europe Donovan's close friend, Frank Knox, self-made Republican millionaire and publisher of the Chicago Daily News, told him that Roosevelt was contemplating a coalition cabinet in which Donovan might be asked to serve as secretary of war. In the event, it was another nine months before FDR reshuffled his administration. When he did so, in June 1940, Knox joined the cabinet as secretary of the navy. The post of secretary of war went not to Donovan but to another prominent Republican, Henry Stimson.[65] One of Knox's first actions as secretary of the navy was to urge Roosevelt to send Donovan on a mission to study Britain's capacity to stave off defeat and to assess the threat posed by the German Fifth Column.[66] The president, almost certainly, required little persuasion. The sheer speed of Germany's six-week conquest of France and the Low Countries in May and June 1940 was mistakenly ascribed, in part, to the assistance of a large Fifth Column working behind the lines. After the surrender of the Dutch on May 15 the British War Cabinet was presented with an alarmist report from the British envoy in The Hague asserting that in Britain, as in Holland, "Every German or Austrian servant, however superficially charming and devoted, is a real and grave menace. . . ." There was, he claimed, a Fifth Column waiting in Britain for the order to embark on a massive sabotage campaign.[67] Memories of the Black Tom explosion in 1916 must have ensured that such warnings struck a chord with Roosevelt.

According to a later account by Donovan, he was summoned to the Oval Office on July 3, 1940, and asked by the president to investigate Britain's handling of the Fifth Column menace. Donovan crossed the

Atlantic at a turning point in Anglo-American relations. Contacts between the Roosevelt administration and the government of Neville Chamberlain had been cool. Disillusioned by the apparent strength of American isolationism, Chamberlain expected little help against Hitler from the United States. By contrast, his successor, Winston Churchill, who took office as prime minister of a coalition government on May 10, 1940, bombarded FDR with impassioned pleas for American assistance. Faced with an appeal for the loan of fifty mothballed U.S. destroyers to help protect British sea-lanes and repel a German invasion, Roosevelt hesitated. The British ambassador in Washington, Lord Lothian, gloomily reported "a wave of pessimism passing over this country to the effect that Great Britain must inevitably be defeated, and that there is no use in the United States doing anything more to help it and thereby getting entangled in Europe." "There is some evidence," he warned, "that it is beginning to affect the President. . . ." Among those most pessimistic about Britain's chances of survival was the U.S. ambassador in London, Joseph Kennedy, father of the future president.[68]

Donovan's visit to Britain, though it enraged Kennedy, helped to tilt the balance of opinion in Washington.[69] Stephenson, convinced that Donovan had the ear of the president, insisted that he be shown the red carpet, indeed a whole series of red carpets. Donovan was received by Churchill, granted an audience with King George VI, and taken to secret meetings with Stewart Menzies, chief of SIS, and most of Britain's intelligence chiefs. He confided to Admiral John Godfrey, the DNI, that he had been warned that the British would prove difficult, patronizing, and secretive. But the British were on their best behavior, and Donovan found them "quite the opposite."[70] After his return to Washington in August, Stephenson cabled SIS headquarters: "Donovan believes you will have within a few days very favorable news, and thinks he has restored confidence as to Britain's determination and ability to resist." The "very favorable news" was the destroyers deal of September 2, by which Britain received the mothballed destroyers it had requested in return for leasing to the United States naval and air bases in the Caribbean and the Western Atlantic: the forerunner of the Lend-Lease Act of March 1941, which made the United States the "arsenal of democracy" eight months before the American entry into the war.[71]

Donovan also urged on Roosevelt "full intelligence collaboration" with the British.[72] The president had already approved a recommendation from Stimson and Knox to accept a British proposal on sharing "technical secrets."[73] He now agreed to the principle of intelligence sharing as well, a decision that reflected both the influence of Donovan and other advisers, and his own admiration for the achievements of Britain's "wonderful intelligence service" in the First World War. At a meeting in London on August 31 between the British chiefs of staff and the American Military Observer Mission, the U.S. Army representative, Brigadier General George V. Strong (later G-2), reported that "it had recently been arranged in principle between the British and United States Governments that periodic exchange of information would be desirable," and said that "the time had come for a free exchange of intelligence."[74] To conduct the exchange Stephenson set up the offices of the newly founded British Security Coordination (BSC) on the thirty-fifth and thirty-sixth floors of the International Building in Rockefeller Center on Fifth Avenue, New York. For much of the war BSC included liaison officers from MI5 and the Special Operations Executive (SOE) as well as SIS. In a later, romanticized account of his career produced after the war, Stephenson was styled "the man called Intrepid." In reality, Intrepid was not the code name of Stephenson but the cable address of BSC, publicly registered with Western Union.[75]

On December 1, 1940, Roosevelt asked Donovan to undertake another mission of inquiry to Britain and the Mediterranean, where the war seemed to be entering a crucial phase. Donovan was accompanied by Stephenson on his flight across the Atlantic, a trip financed from SIS funds. Stephenson believed that by winning Donovan's confidence and helping him become Roosevelt's intelligence chief, he would surpass even the triumphs of his First World War predecessor, Sir William Wiseman. The permanent undersecretary at the Foreign Office, Sir Alexander Cadogan, reported to the foreign secretary:

> "C" [Stewart Menzies] tells me that Mr Stephenson, who travelled over with Colonel Donovan, has impressed upon him that the latter really exercises a vast degree of influence in the administration. He has Colonel Knox in his pocket and, as Mr Stephenson puts it, has more influence with the President than Colonel House had with Mr Wilson. Mr Stephenson believes that if the Prime Minister were to be completely frank with Colonel Donovan, the latter would contribute very largely to our obtaining all that we want of the United States.[76]

Churchill took Stephenson's advice. On December 16, two days after Donovan's arrival in London, the prime minister invited him to lunch at 10 Downing Street and ordered him to be given "every facility" during his tour of the Mediterranean and the Middle East. Commanders in the field and intelligence stations were told that Donovan had "great influence with the President" and had been "taken fully into our confidence." No effort was spared to secure Donovan's goodwill. On the Sunderland flying boat in which he departed Plymouth Sound for the Mediterranean, Lord Louis Mountbatten supplied a hamper to celebrate Donovan's fifty-eighth birthday that made no concessions to wartime rationing. Inside were a thermos flask of hot turtle soup, fresh lobster, cold pheasant, Stilton cheese, Bath Olivers, and three bottles of Moselle. On Mountbatten's orders, the meal was served during the flight by an immaculately dressed orderly in a white mess jacket. The rest of the journey was less relaxing. Donovan visited the Middle East Intelligence Centre in Cairo, toured SIS stations and SOE training schools in several countries, met the leading British commanders, and was received by a series of local monarchs and dignitaries. Churchill cabled Roosevelt to thank him for "the magnificent work" done by Donovan during his tour: "He has carried with him throughout an animating, heart-warming flame."[77] The main purpose of this purple Churchillian prose was to underscore Donovan's qualifications for the post of wartime foreign intelligence chief that both the prime minister and SIS hoped the president would create for him.

At a meeting of his cabinet on April 4, 1941, Roosevelt returned to the problem of intelligence coordination that he had so far failed to solve. The president was clearly impressed with the way the British dealt with the problem but muddled about how they did it. "Disputes," he told the cabinet, "were settled in Great Britain by a gentleman known as 'Mr. X,' whose identity was kept a complete secret"; he suggested "a similar solution for our country in case we got into war."[78] FDR seems to have confused the chief of the Secret Service (Stewart Menzies), known as "C," whose identity was secret, and Lord Swinton, head of the Security Executive, set up by Churchill in May 1940 to sort out the "overlaps and underlaps" in British counterespionage and countersubversion.[79] After the cabinet meeting, however, both ONI and MID were afraid that Roosevelt intended to appoint Donovan as an American "C." General Sherman Miles, assistant chief of staff for intelligence, wrote to Marshall on April 8:

> In great confidence O.N.I. tells me that there is considerable reason to believe that there is a movement afoot, fostered by Col. Donovan, to establish a super agency controlling *all* intelligence. This would mean that such an agency, no doubt under Col. Donovan, would collect, collate and possibly evaluate all military intelligence that we now gather from foreign countries. From the point of view of the War Department, such a move would appear to be very disadvantageous, if not calamitous.[80]

Though Donovan's star was in the ascendant, however, there still seemed an outside chance that the new intelligence post, when Roosevelt decided what it was to consist of, might go instead to his old friend Vincent Astor. In March, without consulting Stimson and Knox, he gave Astor the new job of intelligence coordinator in the New York area, thus conferring semi-official status on the activities of The Club.[81] Though Stephenson continued to do all he could to advance Donovan's cause, he thought it prudent to cultivate Astor as well. Among the highly classified intelligence that he gave to Astor for forwarding to FDR were summaries of the contents of a great variety of diplomatic bags in transit to Europe, surreptitiously opened by the British in Bermuda and Trinidad. Stephenson swore Astor to secrecy. "I have given my word never to tell anyone,—with always you excepted," Astor wrote to Roosevelt. "The fear of the British is, that if the facts become known, the writers would exercise greater caution, or send their letters via a different route": a statement of the obvious that reflected Astor's amateur status in an increasingly professional intelligence world. Only one selection of the material from intercepted diplomatic bags forwarded by Stephenson via Astor to the president survives. It includes brief extracts from Brazilian, Chilean, French, Japanese, Romanian, and Spanish diplomatic dispatches. Among them is a prophetic account by the French financial attaché in Washington, Hervé Alphand (later French ambassador), which described existing deficiencies in U.S. aircraft, tank, and artillery production, but concluded that there would soon be a dramatic change in public opinion, followed by a massive movement of American arms across the Atlantic: "We will be making a great mistake if we think the sad example of our country is going to be followed by American democracy."[82]

The primary British intelligence objective in the United States during the spring and summer of 1941 was to create an Anglo-American intelligence alliance with Donovan as U.S. intelligence coordinator. On May 25, 1941, the British DNI, Admiral Godfrey, arrived in the United States to lend weight to the campaign, unsubtly indicating his own preferences by staying initially in Donovan's New York apartment. With him he brought Commander Ian Fleming of British naval intelligence, later to achieve fame as the creator of James Bond. Fleming spent some time with Donovan, composing a memorandum on "how to create an American secret service," which, after the war, he was to claim immodestly had been "the cornerstone of the future OSS."[83] Godfrey was dismayed by what he considered the poor quality and organizational confusion of U.S. intelligence. He reported to London:

Even the more senior U.S. Navy, Military and State Department officials are credulous and prefer their intelligence to be highly coloured. For instance, the Navy Department's estimate of the size of the German U-boat fleet is higher than our own by approximately one third, while the War Department's estimates of the first line strength and first line reserves of the German Air Force are higher than ours by 250%.

This predilection for sensationalism hinders the reasoned evaluation of intelligence reports. For instance, in April, 1941, both War and Navy Departments accepted a report from the U.S. Embassy in Rome that there were more than 20 German Divisions in Libya. This report was believed for some time in spite of the known shortage of Axis shipping in the Mediterranean, and in spite of the inadequate port facilities at Tripoli and Benghazi, of which the U.S. authorities were fully informed. There is no U.S. Secret Intelligence Service. Americans are inclined to refer to their "S.I.S.," but by this they mean the small and uncoordinated force of "Special Agents" who travel abroad on behalf of one or another of the Governmental Departments. These "Agents" are, for the most part, amateurs without special qualifications and without training in Observation. They have no special means of communication or other facilities and they seldom have clearer brief than "to go and have a look."[84]

After a fortnight in Washington, Godfrey felt he was "up against a brick wall." His visits to ONI, MID, and the FBI convinced him that "collaboration hardly existed." "These three departments showed the utmost goodwill towards me and Ian Fleming but very little towards each other." After taking advice from Stephenson and Wiseman in New York, Godfrey decided that he must talk directly to Roosevelt. With the assistance of Wiseman's friend, Arthur Hays Sulzberger, publisher of the *New York Times*, he gained a dinner invitation at the White House and the promise of an hour's discussion with the president afterward. Godfrey arrived for dinner at 7:30 P.M., having been warned by Wiseman that Roosevelt "would almost certainly pull my leg and make some provocative remark about the British, or Imperialism, and that I must on no account allow myself to get cross (or 'mad' as the Americans say)." The leg-pulling came early in the evening. FDR asked his guest how he had traveled to the United States. When Godfrey replied that he had come via Bermuda, the president responded, "Oh yes, those West Indies Islands. We're going to show you how to look after them, and not only you but the Portuguese and Dutch. Every nigger will have his two acres and a sugar patch." Godfrey privately considered this "rough stuff and rather brash," but kept his notoriously short fuse unlit and—in the national interest—"mustered up the semblance of a laugh."

For an hour after dinner, Godfrey had to sit through what he found "a rather creepy crawly film" about snake worship in Laos, but was then rewarded with one and a quarter hours' conversation with the president in the Oval Office. Roosevelt began by recalling his own visit to London in 1918 and his admiration for Godfrey's predecessor, Blinker Hall. "Of course," he added, "Hall had a wonderful intelligence service but I don't suppose it's much good now." Once again, the usually irascible DNI controlled his temper and failed to rise to the bait. Roosevelt then went on to recount some of the mythical exploits of British spies crossing the German border every night with which Hall had regaled him during the First World War. Amazed to discover that the president was still unaware that he had been the victim of a British intelligence deception a quarter of a century earlier, Godfrey prudently forbore to enlighten him. When Godfrey had a chance to "get a word in edgeways," he pressed the case for greater cohesion in the U.S. intelligence community, with "one intelligence security boss, not three or four."[85] FDR responded with more reminiscences. Godfrey listened once again with uncharacteristic patience, then reemphasized the need for a "Coordinator of Intelligence" and praised Donovan's qualifications for the job.[86]

Actively encouraged by Stephenson and Godfrey, Donovan put the same case to Roosevelt in more detail. In a memorandum of June 10 he proposed the creation of the post of "Coordinator of Strategic Information who would be responsible directly to the President" and oversee a new "central intelligence organization that would itself collect either directly or through existing departments of government, at home and abroad, pertinent information concerning potential enemies."[87] On June 18 Donovan saw the president in the Oval Office. Roosevelt approved his proposal and offered him the job of coordinator of information (COI). Donovan accepted on three conditions:

1. That I would report only to him [FDR]
2. That his secret funds would be available
3. That all the departments of the government would be
   instructed to give me what I wanted.

The third condition woefully overestimated the likely level of cooperation from the Washington bureaucracy, but accurately reflected the optimism with which Donovan embarked on his new career as COI. Shortly after he left the White House, he passed on the good news to Stephenson, who triumphantly cabled SIS headquarters in London:

DONOVAN SAW PRESIDENT TODAY AND AFTER LONG DISCUSSION WHEREIN ALL POINTS WERE AGREED, HE ACCEPTED APPOINTMENT. . . . DONOVAN ACCUSES ME OF HAVING "INTRIGUED AND DRIVEN" HIM INTO APPOINTMENT. YOU CAN IMAGINE HOW RELIEVED I AM AFTER THREE MONTHS OF BATTLE AND JOCKEYING FOR POSITION IN

WASHINGTON THAT OUR MAN IS IN A POSITION OF SUCH IMPORTANCE TO OUR
EFFORTS.

A remarkable memorandum by Churchill's intelligence aide, Major
Desmond Morton, vividly conveys both the rejoicing in Whitehall and the
exaggerated expectation that henceforth Stephenson's influence on Roosevelt would surpass even that of Wiseman on Wilson a quarter of a century earlier:

> [A] most secret fact of which the Prime Minister is aware but not all
> the other persons concerned, is that to all intents and purposes U.S.
> Security is being run for them at the President's request by the
> British. A British officer [Stephenson] sits in Washington with Mr.
> Edgar Hoover and General [*sic*] Bill Donovan for this purpose and
> reports regularly to the President. It is of course essential that this
> fact should not be known in view of the furious uproar it would
> cause if known to the Isolationists.[88]

Some years after the Second World War, Stephenson fantasized that
he had indeed become Roosevelt's trusted confidant and acted as
Churchill's secret emissary to him, sometimes bearing information "so
shattering in its implications that nothing could be placed on the record
without the risk of political chain reaction." He claimed that Roosevelt
had told him, "I'm your biggest undercover agent!" Though Stephenson
vouched for the "authenticity" of these and other fantasies on the publication of the best-selling biography *A Man Called Intrepid* in 1974, he
later changed his mind. "I never at any time claimed to provide a secret
liaison between the British Prime Minister and the American President,"
he declared in 1982.[89] In reality, however, Stephenson first made that
fraudulent claim in 1940. He made it then to persuade Hoover to allow
him to send coded messages to London by FBI radio.[90] Years later he
began to believe his own claims. Deception turned into self-deception.

Stripped of the myths that he later propagated about his wartime
career, Stephenson's achievements still remain remarkable. From his
friendship with Donovan and his early contacts with Hoover and the FBI
sprang a full-blown Anglo-American human intelligence (HUMINT)
alliance that went far beyond the intelligence collaboration of the First
World War. Though Donovan was not, of course, the compliant
Anglophile tool suggested by Major Morton, he was strongly influenced
by British advice both as coordinator of information and when setting up
the Office of Strategic Services (OSS) in the summer of 1942. As well as
receiving a knighthood when the war was over, Stephenson became the

first non-American to receive the U.S. Medal for Merit, the nation's highest civilian decoration. The citation eulogized his "assistance and counsel of great value at every step" in the creation of American wartime intelligence and special operations. "Bill Stephenson," said Donovan, "taught us all we ever knew about foreign intelligence."[91] Never before had one power had so much influence on the development of the intelligence community of another independent state.

During 1941 and the early months of 1942, however, Stephenson took enormous risks that might well have ended in disaster. Convinced that Blinker Hall's brilliantly stage-managed revelation of German intrigues in Mexico early in 1917 had played a critical role in bringing the United States into the First World War, Stephenson planned to use similar intelligence on Nazi conspiracies in Latin America to persuade Roosevelt to enter the Second World War. Since there were no real Nazi conspiracies of sufficient importance, he decided to invent them. Among the BSC forgeries with which he deceived the president was a fabricated letter from Major Elias Belmonte, the Bolivian military attaché in Berlin, describing a plot to establish a Nazi dictatorship in Bolivia. Roosevelt used the letter in a broadcast "fireside chat" on September 11 to denounce Hitler's designs on Latin America.[92] The attempt "to subvert the government of Bolivia" was, he claimed, evidence of Hitler's attempts to secure "footholds and bridgeheads in the New World, to be used as soon as he has gained control of the oceans." He went on to cite other Nazi plots in Uruguay, Argentina, and Colombia, the last "within easy range of the Panama Canal." "Conspiracy," he declared, "has followed conspiracy." But, boasted the president, Hitler's every move was being closely watched: "His intrigues, his machinations, his sabotage in this New World are all known to the Government of the United States."[93]

The State Department and the FBI were, however, less easily taken in than the president. Soon after Roosevelt's fireside chat, both privately complained to the British embassy that "British intelligence had given us documents that they had forged." Berle accurately deduced the purpose of the forgeries. "British intelligence," he wrote, "probably has been giving attention to creating as many 'incidents' as possible to affect public opinion here."[94] Probably reassured by Donovan (who had also been taken in by Stephenson), Roosevelt remained convinced that the document was genuine.

Despite the now evident risks involved, BSC continued to produce forgeries designed to inflame American opinion against imaginary Nazi conspiracies in Latin America. In October Stephenson sent the president, probably via Donovan, a forged map that, he claimed, had been obtained by British agents from a German diplomatic courier in

Argentina.[95] Roosevelt made the map the centerpiece of his "Navy and Total Defense Day Address" on October 27, 1941:

> . . . I have in my possession a secret map, made in Germany by Hitler's government—by planners of the New World Order. . . . The geographical experts of Berlin have ruthlessly obliterated all the existing boundary lines; they have divided South America into five vassal states, bringing the whole continent under their domination. And they have also so arranged it that the territory of these new puppet states includes the Republic of Panama and our great life-line—the Panama Canal. This map, my friends, makes clear the Nazi design not only against South America but against the United States as well.

Roosevelt went on to denounce another imaginary Nazi master plan, also probably supplied by BSC:

> Your government has, in its possession, another document, made in Germany by Hitler's government. . . . It is a plan to abolish all existing religions—Catholic, Protestant, Mohammedan, Hindu, Buddhist and Jewish alike. . . . The cross and all other symbols of religion are to be forbidden. The clergy are to be forever liquidated. . . .[96]

The centerpiece of Roosevelt's most outspoken attack on Nazi Germany before Pearl Harbor and Hitler's declaration of war on the United States was thus bogus intelligence foisted on him by Sir William Stephenson.[97]

The history of the disaster at Pearl Harbor is bedeviled by endlessly recycled conspiracy theories that mistakenly assert that Roosevelt (or Churchill, or both of them) had advance warning from SIGINT of the Japanese attack but kept the information secret to ensure that the United States was forced into the Second World War. Not only was Roosevelt not involved in any conspiracy before Pearl Harbor, but the chaotic handling of SIGINT over which he presided would probably have made a well-organized conspiracy unworkable even in the inconceivable event that he wished to arrange one. No existing account of Roosevelt's policy before Pearl Harbor quite does justice to the staggering ineptitude with which the best foreign intelligence in American history was handled before the Japanese attack. Among the most inept was the president himself.

The best intelligence of the Second World War in both Europe and the Pacific came not from espionage, which had long interested Roosevelt, but from codebreaking, which had not. Churchill, by contrast, had a long-standing passion for SIGINT. As first lord of the admiralty in 1914, he had presided over the rebirth of British codebreaking in Room 40. Ten years later he claimed to have read every decrypt supplied to Whitehall by Room 40's interwar successor:

> I have studied this information over a longer period and more atten-
> tively than probably any other minister has done. . . . I attach more
> importance to [the decrypts] as a means of forming a true judge-
> ment of public policy in these spheres, than to any other source of
> knowledge at the disposal of the state.

By a remarkable coincidence, Churchill became prime minister in May 1940 just as Bletchley Park, the British Second World War SIGINT agency, made the first major break in the hitherto unbreakable German Enigma machine cipher and the best intelligence in British history began to come on stream. Churchill followed the development of Ultra, the high-grade signals intelligence produced by Bletchley Park, with passionate attention. At first he demanded to see all the decrypts produced by the cryptanalysts. When persuaded that there were now too many intercepts for him to study them all, he consented to have a buff-colored box containing the most interesting of them supplied to him each day, sometimes delivered personally by Stewart Menzies, who as chief of the Secret Service also had overall responsibility for Bletchley Park.[98] Churchill called the intercepts "my golden eggs" and the cryptanalysts who produced them "the geese who laid the golden eggs and never cack-led." Bletchley Park knew that it could count on the prime minister's personal support. When it needed more resources in October 1941 its four leading cryptanalysts appealed directly to him. Churchill responded at once with the order: "ACTION THIS DAY. Make sure they have all they want on extreme priority and report to me that this has been done."[99]

Roosevelt, however, was slow to grasp the potential importance of SIGINT and showed no personal interest in the problems of producing it. A secret postwar report on cryptanalysis concluded that the two main prewar problems had been "lack of unified control" and "extremely lim-ited funding." For much of the 1930s the military Signal Intelligence Ser-vice (SIS) and the Navy Code and Signal Section, which shared responsi-bility for SIGINT after the closure of the Black Chamber in 1929, were not on speaking terms. Each sought independently to crack the same diplomatic codes and ciphers to "gain credit for itself as the agency by which the information obtained was made available to the Government."[100] By 1936 SIS had succeeded in cracking the main Japanese diplomatic cipher, to which it gave the code name Red. Red decrypts were probably the first SIGINT to be seen by Roosevelt as president. Early in 1937, for the first time in American history, SIGINT began to be regularly delivered to the White House, initially at the rate of about one decrypt a day. The first major revelation of the Red intercepts was probably the disclosure in March 1937 that Italy was considering joining the German-Japanese Anti-Comintern Pact. It was another six months before similar information reached the State Department from American diplomats abroad. Red decrypts also provided part of the text of the treaty.[101] Roosevelt, however, was more interested in the less reliable but superficially more exciting intelligence supplied by Astor's Room and Donovan. The cryptanalysts, unlike the amateur agents, received no sign of the president's interest in their work.

During 1938 Red decrypts revealed that a new Japanese cipher machine was under construction. On March 20, 1939, the first diplomatic messages were intercepted in a new machine cipher, code-named Purple by SIS. Over the next three months the Red machine was gradually phased out and replaced by the new system. The head of SIS, the redoubtable William F. Friedman, later established a reputation as "the man who broke Purple." But though he supervised the team, headed by the former schoolteacher Frank B. Rowlett, which led the eighteen-month attack on Purple, Friedman played no direct part in its solution. Since the appointment of Major General Joseph Mauborgne as the army's chief signal officer in October 1937, relations with the Naval Code and Signal Section, now renamed OP-20-G, had somewhat improved. Though chiefly occupied with work on Japanese naval codes, OP-20-G cooperated with SIS in the attack on Purple for about four months before it abandoned the attempt. Purple was finally broken on the afternoon of September 20, 1940. Unable to contain his excitement, the usually soft-spoken Rowlett jumped up and down, exclaiming, "That's it!" His principal assistant, Robert O. Ferner, also abandoned his customary reserve and shouted, "Hooray!" Junior cryptanalyst Albert W. Small was less out-spoken, but ran around the room with his hands clasped in triumph above his head. The victorious codebreakers then jointly celebrated the greatest success thus far in the history of United States intelligence by sending out for bottles of Coca-Cola. They drank them and returned to work.[102] Mauborgne began referring to Rowlett and his fellow cryptanalysts as "magicians." The name stuck and Magic became a code word for the Japanese decrypts (or, sometimes, for high-grade SIGINT in general).[103]

It was ironic that the secretary of war when the military codebreakers broke Purple should be Henry Stimson, who as secretary of state eleven years earlier had closed down the Black Chamber.[104] Stimson later explained that in 1929, at a time of international "good will," he had felt obliged to deal "as a gentleman" with the representatives of foreign powers.[105] In 1940 he did so no longer. He noted excitedly in his diary the "wonderful progress" made by SIS, but added, "I cannot even in my diary go into some of the things that they have done."[106] There is no evidence of any similar excitement in the Oval Office. Purple, however, was broken at a critical time. Only a week later Japan began stationing troops in northern French Indochina and signed the Tripartite Pact establishing the Berlin-Rome-Tokyo Axis.

Once Purple had been broken, OP-20-G began to cooperate with SIS in the laborious work of decrypting the daily changes in the machine cipher settings. Interservice rivalry, however, led to an absurdly bureaucratic formula intended to prevent either of the SIGINT agencies gaining an advantage over the other. According to a postwar report:

> It was agreed after lengthy negotiations that the Army and the Navy would exchange all diplomatic traffic from their intercept facilities, and that both services would work on this traffic. But in order to avoid as much duplication of effort as possible it was agreed that the Army would receive all traffic of days with an even date and the Navy all traffic of days with an odd date. This arrangement was [intended] . . . to give both services equal opportunities for training, "credit" and so on.[107]

Roosevelt either did not care or did not know about this bizarre arrangement that continued to cause serious complications in the production of Magic until after Pearl Harbor.

Interservice rivalry also added to the problems of SIGINT collaboration with the British. When General Strong had proposed "a free exchange of intelligence" to the British chiefs of staff on August 31, he had included SIGINT.[108] Probably influenced by memories of the Zimmermann telegram and the success of British codebreakers in the First World War, Stimson was also a keen supporter of cryptanalytic collaboration. The navy, however, was strongly opposed. The lead in overcoming naval opposition was taken not by Roosevelt but by Stimson, who wrote optimistically in his diary on October 23:

> The British are here and are ready to sell [tell?] us all they had learned during the war on the subject of field codes and other code

methods of the Germans. The Army, which has made great progress in that matter, is willing to exchange information but the Navy has been stubborn against it, so I asked [Knox][109] if he would meet me today with his people and go over it and see if we couldn't get on a basis by which we could exchange this information with the British, subject only to letting the President know about it, and possibly Mr. Hull.[110]

Hull gave his consent the next day, and Stimson sent a message to Roosevelt through his military aide, General Edwin "Pa" Watson, seeking his agreement. Soon afterward Watson "brought back the word that the President was perfectly satisfied to rest upon the judgment of Knox and myself in the matter and approved what we proposed to do."[111] While FDR took an active interest in HUMINT and the establishment of the COI, he was content to delegate all matters concerned with SIGINT (by far the most important intelligence he possessed) to others.

Stimson proved overoptimistic, however, about the willingness of the British to reveal "all they had learned" about German codes and ciphers. The fact that Bletchley Park had broken the Luftwaffe variant of the Enigma machine cipher was one of the most closely guarded secrets in British history, unknown even to a majority of Churchill's ministers. Both the prime minister and his leading cryptanalysts understandably feared that the secret might be unsafe in the United States. But they also had one quite different reason for limiting the cryptanalytic exchange with the United States. The British continued, as they had done intermittently since the First World War, to decrypt American diplomatic cables. The selection of intercepts produced for Churchill each day occasionally included one from the United States—not a secret he was prepared to share with Roosevelt.[112] In the early stages of Anglo-American SIGINT collaboration, it was thus the Americans who proved more forthcoming. In February 1941 SIS cryptanalysts delivered a copy of the Purple cipher machine to Bletchley Park and explained its working method. The British provided some intelligence in return, but they did not reveal the existence of the top-secret electromechanical devices KNOWN AS "Bombes" that eventually enabled them to break all the versions of the German Enigma.[113]

By the beginning of 1941 Stimson was increasingly concerned by Roosevelt's apparent lack of interest in Magic. He made an appointment with the president on January 2, hoping to impress on him the importance of the intelligence that Magic provided not merely on Japanese policy but also, through the decrypted telegrams of the Japanese ambassador in Berlin, on German policy as well. Stimson arrived at 10:30 A.M. to find FDR working in bed:

First I told him that he should read certain of the important [Magic] reports which had come in from Berlin giving the summary which the Japanese ambassador there had made of the situation and others like it. He hadn't read them. They were extremely interesting. I told him they reported a very serious situation which was coming on. They reported that Germany was calm and confident in spite of the British successes in the Mediterranean; that she had her troops in good condition and that she probably was going to make an attack upon Great Britain and attempt to end the war this year.[114]

Probably at Stimson's initiative, discussions followed on ways of ensuring that important decrypts were regularly brought to Roosevelt's attention. The compromise arrived at after further interservice wrangling was almost as eccentric as the odd/even date navy/army arrangement for the production of Magic. It was agreed that Magic should be supplied to the president by his naval aide in even-numbered months and by his military aide in odd months.[115] But there was no arrangement for providing FDR with SIGINT either on Sundays or on weekday evenings.[116] It is difficult to imagine Churchill tolerating these bizarre procedures for a single day.

The main value of Magic for both the president and those of his advisers with access to it was that it exposed the gulf between Japan's policy declarations and its undeclared aims. On February 14, for example, Roosevelt received a visit from the new Japanese ambassador, Admiral Kichisaburo Nomura, whom he had known since the First World War. The president said that they were old friends and could talk candidly. Nomura agreed and assured Roosevelt of his determination to preserve the peace. On reading the decrypt of the instructions sent to Nomura by the Japanese foreign minister, Yosuka Matsuoka, however, FDR commented that they seemed to be "the product of a mind which is deeply disturbed and unable to think quietly and logically."[117]

By the summer of 1941 the curious odd/even month Magic delivery system to the president had begun to break down. The immediate cause of its collapse was the carelessness of Roosevelt's genial long-serving military aide, General Watson, who had the responsibility for supplying Magic during odd army months. Pa Watson was the court jester of the Roosevelt White House. When FDR commented on his liking for after-shave and inquired, "Do all generals smell this nice?" or made other jokes at his expense, Watson never forgot to laugh appreciatively. G-2 was less happy about Pa's notions of security. Probably in May, a Magic summary went missing. A prolonged search of the White House eventually discovered it in Watson's wastepaper basket. At almost the same moment Magic appeared to reveal a major breach of SIGINT security.[118]

On May 6 a Purple decrypt disclosed that the Japanese ambassador in Berlin had been warned by an "absolutely reliable source" that the Americans had broken the Japanese diplomatic code. The "absolutely reliable source" was probably German cryptanalysis. A coding error at the British embassy in Washington had led to the transmission of Magic material to London in a cipher officially designated only for "telegrams of a less confidential nature," which had probably been broken by the Germans. On May 20 Ambassador Nomura reported to Tokyo, "I have discovered that the United States is reading some of our codes though I do not know which ones." Though Tokyo rashly concluded that Purple was still secure, there is some indication that it became more cautious about including secret information in diplomatic telegrams.[119] The combined result of Pa Watson's carelessness and the discovery of Japanese suspicions was tighter SIGINT security. During June, a navy month, the president received Magic decrypts from his new naval aide, Captain John R. Beardall. But in July military intelligence declined (with possibly a few exceptions) to supply SIGINT to the White House because, it later admitted, of "lack of confidence in General Watson's idea of security." The G-2, General Sherman Miles, decided that since Magic dealt almost solely with diplomatic business, it was henceforth up to the State Department to keep the president informed. Though dissatisfied by the interruption in the supply of decrypts, Roosevelt curiously did not insist that it be resumed. Instead, even though July was an army month, he several times asked Beardall for news about the latest Magic revelations. OP-20-G allowed Beardall to read the decrypts to keep the president informed, but, to comply with the odd/even months agreement with SIS, did not allow him to take them to the White House.[120]

The Magic reported, but not shown, to the president by Beardall during July was of unusual importance. It provided clear warning of Japanese preparations for the occupation of French Indochina on July 21. The military intelligence estimates supplied to Roosevelt, however, were curiously inept. Despite the evidence of Magic, there was no mention of the possibility of a Japanese occupation until July 11. Even then the warning was remarkably vague: "Should the [Japanese] choice be the southward advance, it will probably consist of a containment of Hong Kong and the Philippine Islands while attacking British Malaya via Thailand and Indo-China." On July 17 G-2 gave details of the Japanese ultimatum to the government of Vichy France, but rashly concluded that a Japanese cabinet reshuffle meant that "Vichy will be given a breathing spell and the expedition to Indo-China may be deferred or even abandoned." Next day, with further details of the new Tokyo government available, G-2 jumped to the opposite conclusion: "It may be that added impulse will be given to Japan's Southward Advance." Despite the price-less advantage of the Magic decrypts, military intelligence probably had a weaker grasp of Japanese policy than the *New York Times*. The United States responded to the occupation of Indochina by imposing an oil and cotton embargo on Japan. Magic made clear the anger of the Japanese reaction. Tokyo informed Nomura on July 31, "There is more reason than ever before for us to arm ourselves to the teeth for all-out war."[121] War was now inevitable. "The United States would not accept a Japanese-dominated East Asia. Japan would not accept anything less."[122]

During the summer of 1941 growing Anglo-American naval coopera-tion in the North Atlantic increased Churchill's willingness to share Ultra intelligence from decrypted German signals with the United States. In June Bletchley Park broke the naval version of the German Enigma machine cipher. Churchill pressed his reluctant intelligence chief, Stew-art Menzies, who remained doubtful of American security, to give Wash-ington the contents of decrypts that referred to U.S. naval units. After a U-boat attacked the U.S. destroyer *Greer* on September 4 Roosevelt authorized American warships to escort British and Canadian convoys three-quarters of the way across the Atlantic. The U.S. Navy was by this time already routing convoys with the help of Ultra intelligence on U-boat positions supplied by the Admiralty.[123]

Though Roosevelt had probably been made aware of the British suc-cess in decrypting German naval signals by the fall of 1941, he is unlikely to have seen any German decrypts. Magic, meanwhile, continued to grow in importance. During the second half of 1941 the supply of Japanese decrypts was running at about fifty a day.[124] Apart from the press, Magic was by now almost the only significant source of informa-tion on Japanese policy that Roosevelt possessed. The ambassador in Tokyo, Joseph C. Grew, told the State Department:

> Please remember that in Japan we are generally groping in the dark
> and that now, more than ever, it is exceedingly difficult to ascertain
> what is going on behind the scenes, especially since few of our for-
> mer Japanese contacts dare come to the Embassy or meet us else-
> where. Many have been warned by the police to avoid us.[125]

Despite its increasing importance, however, Magic continued to reach the president erratically. During August (a navy month) the supply was normal. In September (an army month) it dried up once again. As in July, Beardall was allowed to brief Roosevelt on the contents of the lat-est decrypts but not to show them to him for fear of offending G-2. By the latter part of the month FDR's patience was, unsurprisingly, wearing thin. He told Beardall he wished to see the decrypts themselves. Beardall asked the chief naval intelligence translator, Lieutenant Commander Alwin D. Kramer. Kramer approached Colonel Rufus S. Bratton, head of the G-2 Far Eastern Section. Faced with a direct request from the commander in chief, G-2 grudgingly allowed the navy to trespass on an army month.[126]

During October, a navy month, Beardall continued to supply the president with Magic. With the fall of the Konoye cabinet on October 16 and the installation the next day of the bellicose government of General Hideki Tojo (later executed as a war criminal), SIGINT became still more important. At the beginning of November, another army month, however, the flow of Magic to the White House incredibly dried up once again. This time Roosevelt had finally had enough. Although briefed by Beardall and Hull on the contents of the latest decrypts, he demanded to see the original Magic. When Beardall reminded him that November was an army month, Roosevelt told him "to bring it anyway." Hurried interservice consultations followed. General Miles offered to resume the supply of Magic during army months. By now, however, the president was no longer willing to tolerate the nonsense of army and navy months. After conferring, Miles, Watson, and Beardall agreed that, at the president's request, the decrypts should henceforth be channeled to him through his naval aide. The even greater nonsense of odd and even navy and army days for the production of Magic, however, remained intact.[127]

On November 5 a Japanese imperial conference made the decision to prepare a surprise attack on the U.S. Pacific Fleet at Pearl Harbor in Hawaii on December 8, Tokyo time (December 7 in the United States). The decision was not mentioned in Japanese diplomatic messages. But Magic did make clear that Japan was moving toward a rupture of relations with the United States and that the risk of war was growing. The first major indication of the tougher line being adopted by the Tojo government came in an intercepted telegram to its Washington embassy on November 5, decrypted the same day, that declared it "absolutely necessary" to settle the dispute with the United States not later than November 25. It was probably the news of this decrypt that finally persuaded FDR to insist henceforth on uninterrupted access to Magic. In a further decrypt of November 15 the new foreign minister, Shigenori Togo, reaffirmed that the November 25 deadline was "absolutely immoveable." In fact, another intercepted telegram extended the "immoveable" deadline on November 25 until November 29, but it did so in language that was more ominous than ever: "This time we mean it, that deadline absolutely cannot be changed. After that things are automatically going to happen."[128]

Roosevelt had little doubt what these "things" would be. At noon on November 25 Stimson, Knox, Hull, Marshall, and Admiral Harold R. "Betty" Stark, chief of naval operations, arrived at the White House, expecting to discuss the annual defense budget. Instead, the president opened the meeting with a warning that "we were likely to be attacked perhaps next Monday [December 1] for the Japs are notorious for making an attack without warning. . . ." But the idea of a surprise attack on the Pacific Fleet did not occur to him. "The question was," he said, "how we should maneuver them into the position of firing the first shot without allowing too much danger to ourselves." On the evening of November 25 Stimson sent Roosevelt by courier an intelligence report on impending Japanese troop movements south from Shanghai. When Stimson asked for his reaction the next day, the president "jumped into the air, so to speak, and said he hadn't seen it." Stimson sent a second copy by special messenger, together with a later report that the troop movements were "already underway." A note by Pa Watson records that the original report was discovered "in the inside pocket of a very distinguished gentleman"—almost certainly the president himself. According to Stimson, Roosevelt "fairly blew up" when told that Japanese troops were on the move, claiming that it was "evidence of bad faith on the part of the Japs" while they were still negotiating an end to the crisis with the United States.[129]

While intelligence was coming in on November 26 about the departure of a Japanese expeditionary force from Shanghai, Hull was presenting the Japanese envoys, Admiral Nomura and Saburo Kurusu, with what were to be the final American terms for a settlement of the crisis. Japan must give up the territory it had occupied in China and Indochina, end recognition of the Chinese puppet government at Nanking, and withdraw from the Axis with Germany and Italy. Nomura's pessimistic account of the meeting with Hull was not decrypted until two days later. But Kurusu's report by phone to the Japanese foreign ministry shortly before 8 P.M. EST on November 26, using a voice code, was decrypted the same evening. "I have made all efforts," he told Tokyo, "but they *will* not yield. . . . I believe it is of no avail." "The situation in Tokyo," he was informed, "is extremely critical."[130]

November 27, wrote Stimson in his diary, was "a very long, tense day," with intelligence coming in that the Japanese expeditionary force was headed for Indochina. Its ultimate targets were believed to include the Philippines, Burma, the Burma Road, and the Dutch East Indies. Japan's most likely aim, Stimson believed, was an invasion of Thailand to establish a base for an eventual attack on Singapore.[131] OPNAV (Naval Operations in Washington) telegraphed a "war warning" to the commanders in chief of the Asiatic and Pacific fleets.[132] While Stimson, Knox, and OPNAV were trying to work out where the Japanese intended to strike, Roosevelt was receiving Nomura and Korusu for what was to be the last time. According to the envoys' decrypted report to Tokyo, FDR warned them that he had intelligence on the Japanese expeditionary force moving southward from Shanghai. Tokyo doubtless welcomed the news that the president's attention was focused on Southeast Asia rather than on Hawaii. Roosevelt had no intelligence at all on the task force, including six aircraft carriers and two battleships, that on November 26 had secretly steamed out of Hittokapu Bay, headed for Pearl Harbor with instructions to deal the U.S. Pacific Fleet "a mortal blow."[133]

The continued flow of intelligence on the movements of the Japanese expeditionary force in Southeast Asia appeared to Stimson to present so many "dangerous possibilities" that he insisted on seeing Roosevelt before he got up on the morning of November 28, even though the president was due to meet his "war cabinet" (Stimson, Knox, Hull, Marshall, and Stark) at noon. Stimson left him with a report on the latest intelligence and told him he "ought to read it before the War Cabinet meeting." The president duly did so, and impressed Stimson with his grasp of its significance. At the noon meeting Roosevelt reviewed the various possible targets for a Japanese attack mentioned in the report (essentially those listed by Stimson on the previous day) and suggested one further possibility: a Japanese invasion of the Kra Isthmus, followed by an attack on Rangoon to cut the Burma Road at its starting point. Stimson thought this "very likely." There was no discussion, however, of a possible threat to Hawaii.[134] Nor was such a possibility mentioned in the military intelligence assessment produced that day on the Japanese threat over the next four months.[135]

But if U.S. intelligence failed to detect the first target of the Japanese attack, it provided clear evidence that war was on the way. On November 26 and 28 the cryptanalysts decrypted in two parts the celebrated "Winds Messages" sent by Tokyo to its foreign embassies on November 19, containing the coded signals that would indicate the intention to break off diplomatic relations with the United States, Britain, and the Soviet Union. For the United States, it would be "East Wind Rain"; for Britain, "West Wind Clear"; and for the USSR, "North Wind Cloudy." As soon as the embassies concerned received these signals, they were to destroy all code books and secret papers.[136]

On Tuesday, November 25, Roosevelt had surprised his war cabinet with a warning that a Japanese surprise attack might come as early as Monday, December 1. On Friday, November 28, he surprised them again by leaving for a short holiday in Warm Springs, Georgia. Probably soon after the president had left, Magic provided the clearest evidence yet that, while preparing for war, Tokyo was attempting to lull Washington into a false sense of security. Togo informed the Washington embassy in a decrypted telegram that all chance of an agreement had disappeared:

> However, I do not wish you to give the impression that the negotiations are broken off. Merely say to them [the Americans] that you are awaiting instructions and that, although the opinions of your Government are not yet clear to you, to your own way of thinking the Imperial Government has always made just claims and has borne great sacrifices for the sake of peace in the Pacific.[137]

Stimson summed up the intelligence on Japan received during the weekend of November 29–30 as "just about the same as it was—critical."[138] On November 29 OPNAV issued a warning of "hostile action possible at any moment." On November 30 it warned the commander in chief of the Asiatic fleet of "indications that Japan is about to attack points on Kra Isthmus by an overseas expedition."[139] These warnings seem to have persuaded Roosevelt to cut short his holiday in Warm Springs and return to the White House. In Stimson's view, "He should never have gone. . . ."[140]

Soon after Roosevelt's return to Washington on Monday, December 1, the cryptanalysts decrypted a telegram from Tokyo to the Japanese ambassador in Berlin, containing a message for Hitler and his foreign minister, Count Joachim von Ribbentrop:

> . . . Say very secretly to them that there is extreme danger that war may suddenly break out between the Anglo-Saxon nations and Japan through some clash of arms and add that the time of the breaking out of this war may come quicker than anyone dreams. . . .[141]

No previous intercept seems to have made quite such an impression on the president. After reading it, he handed it back, as usual, to Beardall. Then, a day or so later, apparently for the first time, he asked for a copy to keep, which was duly provided by OP-20-G (December 1 was a navy day).[142] Tokyo's secret message to Hitler probably helped to persuade the president to make one last appeal to the Japanese emperor. So did another message that, probably unknown to his war cabinet, Roosevelt found waiting for him at Union Station when he returned to Washington on the morning of December 1. The sender was his friend, Dr. E. Stanley Jones, a well-known Methodist minister, who enclosed a secret request from a diplomat at the Japanese embassy, Hidenari Terasaki, asking the president to appeal directly to the emperor. If the emperor could be persuaded to intervene in the cause of peace, urged Dr. Jones, his political and military leaders would obey his orders.[143]

At a White House conference on December 2 with Stimson, Knox, and Sumner Welles (substituting for Hull), Roosevelt announced that he was seriously considering an appeal to the emperor. "All the rest of us," noted Stimson, "are rather against it."[144] The next day Dr. Jones slipped secretly through the East Gate of the White House, bringing with him a further appeal from Terasaki to the president. Jones emphasized to Roosevelt the risks that Terasaki was taking in the cause of peace, and asked him "never [to] refer to Mr. Terasaki in connection with the message." "You tell that young Japanese he is a brave man," replied the president. "No one will ever learn of his part in this from me. His secret is safe."[145] Roosevelt would doubtless have felt less warmly about Terasaki had he consulted the FBI, naval, or (probably) military intelligence about him. He would then have discovered that Terasaki was head of Japanese espionage in the Western Hemisphere. Unaware of Terasaki's real role in the Japanese embassy, however, Roosevelt drew the mistaken conclusion that his approach indicated that "the Japanese were running around like a lot of wet hens." The president was probably somewhat embarrassed two days later when the decrypt of a telegram from Nomura to Tokyo revealed that Terasaki's claim to be taking a private initiative whose revelation would put him and his family in danger was a complete sham. "Terasaki," reported Nomura, "had Stanley Jones, with whom he is on the most intimate terms, call upon Roosevelt." A further decrypted telegram to Tokyo, sent by Kurusu, praised Terasaki's role in "the intelligence set-up," and begged "as a personal favor" that he be allowed to continue his work in Washington.[146]

Further evidence of impending conflict was contained in instructions from Tokyo to a number of its foreign missions on December 1 and 2 to destroy codes and cipher machines. The message to the Washington embassy (which instructed it to retain one Purple machine for the time being) was decrypted on December 3 and probably shown to the president by Beardall on December 4.[147] Hitherto, FDR's naval aide had usually handed him his daily Magic without comment. On this occasion, as Beardall quaintly put it, "I took the liberty of inviting [his] special attention." "Mr. President," he declared, "this is a very significant dispatch." Roosevelt read it attentively, then asked, "Well, when do you think it will happen?" Beardall understood him to be asking "when war is going to break out, when we are going to be attacked, or something." "Most anytime," he replied. This brief dialogue is the first recorded discussion of the contents of a Magic intercept between the president and his naval aide.[148]

At a meeting of the war cabinet on Friday, December 5, Knox

announced, "We have very secret information that mustn't go outside this room that the Japanese fleet is out. They're out of the harbor. They're out at sea." But he was referring to fleet movements off Japan, not to the undetected carrier force now less than two days from Pearl Harbor. Attention was still focused on discovering the likely targets of Japanese aggression in Southeast Asia.[149] The next day intelligence reports from British patrols reported that "large Japanese forces were moving up into the Gulf of Siam." The British were uncertain whether their destination was Indochina, the Kra Isthmus, or Malaya.[150]

Intelligence during the day and a half before the attack on Pearl Harbor was dominated by four Magic decrypts of telegrams from Tokyo to the Washington embassy whose production was complicated by the continuing absurdity of the odd/even navy/army day cryptanalytic compromise. The first, which has become known as the "pilot" message, announced that the situation was now "extremely delicate," and that a fourteen-part reply to the final U.S. terms of November 26 would follow shortly. This message was intercepted by the navy's West Coast listening station near Seattle at 7:20 A.M. EST on Saturday, December 6, and forwarded by teleprinter to the Navy Department in Washington. Since December 6 was an army day, the navy sent the message to be decrypted by the military SIS, which received it at 12:05 P.M. The first thirteen parts of the fourteen-part message announced by the "pilot" were intercepted in slightly jumbled order between 8:05 and 11:52 A.M., and sent by teleprinter to Washington at intervals from 11:45 A.M. to 2:51 P.M. (The fourteenth part did not arrive until the following day.)[151] Having received from the navy the most important intercepts in its history, SIS now found itself in a deeply embarrassing position. Its civilian translators and other staff went off duty for the weekend at midday on Saturday, and there was no provision for overtime.[152] SIS was thus forced to return the intercepts to the navy and ask OP-20-G to deal with them. Ironically, when the Japanese reply rejecting the American terms was decrypted, it was discovered to be in the English language. While OP-20-G spent the afternoon decrypting most of the reply, SIS succeeded in arranging its first evening shift to help deal with overnight messages. SIS cryptanalysts also decrypted two of the thirteen parts, though all the typing was done by the navy.[153] Once the typing was complete, Lieutenant Commander Alwin D. Kramer, the tense and overworked chief translator in naval intelligence, spent some time checking its accuracy and ensuring that the thirteen parts were assembled in correct order.[154]

While work continued on the thirteen parts of the Japanese reply, the president finished drafting his final appeal to Emperor Hirohito "to restore traditional amity and prevent further death and destruction in

the world." The message was cabled to the Tokyo embassy at 9 P.M.[155]
Half an hour later Kramer arrived at the White House with the thirteen
parts of the Japanese message in a locked pouch. This was the first
Magic decrypt judged sufficiently important to be given to Roosevelt
outside normal office hours. Beardall's assistant, Lieutenant Lester R.
Schulz, who had begun work at the White House only the previous day,
was waiting to take it to the president. Roosevelt had been warned,
probably by Beardall, to expect its arrival. Schulz found him in his study,
seated at his desk, talking to his confidant and adviser, Harry Hopkins.
The president studied the decrypt for about ten minutes. Schulz later
testified that Roosevelt "then turned toward Mr. Hopkins and said in
substance—I am not sure of the exact words but in substance—'This
means war.'" It was too bad, observed Hopkins, that the United States
could not strike the first blow. "No, we can't do that," replied the president. "We are a democracy and a peaceful people." According to Schulz:

> During this discussion there was no mention of Pearl Harbor. The only
> geographical name I recall was Indo-China. The time at which the war
> might begin was not discussed, but from the manner of the discussion
> there was no indication that tomorrow was necessarily the day.[156]

The fourteenth and final part of the Japanese rejection of American
terms was intercepted at 2:38 A.M. on Sunday, December 7, a navy day.
It was followed at 4:37 A.M. by the "time of delivery" message—the third
of the four main Magic decrypts that immediately preceded the Japanese
attack—instructing Nomura to deliver the Japanese reply at 1 P.M. local
time. Finally, at 5:07 A.M. the navy intercepted a message ordering the
destruction of the remaining codes, ciphers, and secret documents in the
Washington embassy. All three messages intercepted in the early hours of
December 7 were decrypted by OP-20-G, but, to save time, SIS civilian
staff working on their first night shift assisted in the translation.[157]

Kramer delivered the final part of the fourteen-part message to the
White House at about 9:45 A.M. Beardall, who had come to work on a
Sunday for the first time since becoming naval aide, took the message to
Roosevelt in his bedroom. The president said "Good morning," read the
decrypt, told Beardall, "It looks like the Japanese are going to break off
negotiations," then returned the document to him. There was nothing in
Roosevelt's manner, Beardall later testified, to indicate that he antici-
pated war within a matter of hours. This brief exchange was, according to
Beardall, only the second conversation he had had with the president on
Far Eastern affairs.[158] Roosevelt spent the next two hours with his personal physician, Rear Admiral Ross M. McIntyre. According to McIntyre,

the president thought the Japanese might "take advantage of Great Britain's extremity and strike at Singapore or some other point in the Far East, but an attack on any American possession did not enter his thought."[159] At about 11 A.M. Kramer left the intercepts of the "time of delivery" and code-destruction messages for Beardall at the White House. But, not expecting another morning delivery, Beardall had taken the final part of the fourteen-part message to the Navy Department and did not return to the White House until after lunch.[160] So it appears that the president did not receive the two further Magic decrypts until after the news of the Japanese attack.

Since 10:30 A.M. Stimson and Knox had been meeting in Hull's office to discuss the latest intelligence. Stimson noted in his diary, "Hull is very certain that the Japanese are planning some deviltry and we are all wondering where the blow will strike."[161] At noon, following the instructions in the "time of delivery" message, Nomura called Hull to ask for a one o'clock meeting. Shortly afterward he was forced to ask for a postponement. As on a number of previous occasions the Japanese embassy was taking longer to decode and type messages from Tokyo than the American cryptanalysts. The 1 P.M. meeting ordered by Tokyo had been intended to avoid charges that Japan had attacked without warning. The delay caused by the embassy code clerks meant that, when Nomura and Kurusu arrived at the State Department at 2:05 P.M., the attack had already taken place.[162] News of the attack reached Roosevelt in a phone call from Knox at about 1:40 P.M. while he was lunching in his study with Hopkins, chatting "about things far removed from war." Hopkins's immediate reaction was that "there must be some mistake . . . that surely Japan would not attack in Honolulu." Roosevelt shook his head. This was "just the kind of unexpected thing the Japanese would do."[163] By 3 P.M. Roosevelt's advisers had begun to gather at the White House. Most of the news of the attack came in a series of telephone messages from Admiral Stark, his voice registering stunned disbelief. It fell to the president's secretary, Grace Tully, "to take these fragmentary and shocking reports from him by shorthand, type them up and relay them to the Boss." Because of the hubbub around her, she was forced to retreat to Roosevelt's bedroom and use the phone there.[164] When the cabinet met that evening, the president could hardly bring himself to describe what had happened. According to his labor secretary, Frances Perkins:

His pride in the Navy was so terrific that he was having actual physical difficulty in getting out the words that put him on record as knowing that the Navy was caught unawares, that bombs dropped on ships that were not in fighting shape and not prepared to move, but were just tied up.[165]

Eighteen ships, including eight battleships, had been sunk or seriously damaged. Almost two hundred aircraft had been destroyed on the ground; 2,403 people had been killed. It was the worst naval disaster in American history.

Magic had revealed that on November 29 Ribbentrop promised the Japanese ambassador in Berlin: "Should Japan become engaged in a war against the United States, Germany, of course, would join the war immediately. . . . The Fuehrer is determined on that point."[166] But, in the absence of any centralized system of intelligence assessment, Roosevelt's advisers in the immediate aftermath of Pearl Harbor gave him bewilderingly different interpretations of the intentions of the Axis powers. Stimson insisted, quite wrongly, "We know from the intercepts and other evidence that Germany had pushed Japan into this."[167] Adolf Berle, perhaps confused by his reading of Italian intercepts, argued, also wrongly, that SIGINT made "plain" that the Japanese had the enthusiastic backing of the Italians but not yet of the Germans.[168] There was further confusion in Washington over who had access to Magic and who did not. Stark labored under the delusion that Admiral Husband Kimmel, commander in chief of the Pacific Fleet at Pearl Harbor, was regularly supplied with Magic. In fact, he had received only a few fragments since July. Military intelligence similarly believed, also mistakenly, that the army commander at Pearl Harbor, General Walter Short, was on the Magic circulation list. Kimmel and Short later became the chief scapegoats for the disaster.[169]

The confusion of Magic assessment and circulation before Pearl Harbor was ultimately the responsibility of the president himself. When putting Donovan in charge of intelligence coordination in June 1941 he had failed to include SIGINT in his responsibilities, despite the fact that it provided by far the most important intelligence. Until November, Roosevelt had tolerated a remarkable level of confusion in the distribution of Magic even to himself. In Britain, by contrast, Churchill took an active personal interest in both the coordination of intelligence assessment (including SIGINT) through the JIC system and in its orderly and secure application to the war effort.

The best-known study of the intelligence failure before Pearl Harbor remains the prize-winning study by Roberta Wohlstetter published in 1962. The disaster, she argues, was the result of a failure not of intelligence collection but of intelligence analysis. The system, she maintains, failed to distinguish the crucial intelligence "signals" that pointed to an attack on Pearl Harbor from the mass of confusing background "noise." "In short," she concludes, "we failed to anticipate Pearl Harbor not for a want of the relevant materials, but because of a plethora of irrelevant ones."[170] Brilliantly argued though the Wohlstetter thesis is, more recent research indicates that it is mistaken. The primary problem was precisely "a want of the relevant materials." Not a single Japanese decrypt available in Washington pointed to an attack on Pearl Harbor. Since no Japanese mission abroad was given advance notice of the attack, Magic made no mention of it. Japanese intercepts reporting ship movements between August 1 and December 6 included only twenty references to Pearl Harbor as compared with fifty-nine to the Philippines and twenty-three to the Panama Canal.[171]

But if the diplomatic cables failed to point to an attack on Pearl Harbor, Japanese naval traffic did. Though thousands of naval signals were intercepted during the last six months of 1941, however, the great majority could not be decrypted. While the cryptanalysts had made progress in solving the basic Japanese naval code, known to OP-20-G as JN25, the attack on the variant, JN25b, introduced in December 1940, had so far failed. A detailed study by the postwar SIGINT agency, NSA, later concluded that the failure to break JN25b was due solely to a shortage of resources. For most of 1939, 1940, and 1941, usually two and never more than five cryptanalysts were assigned to work on all Japanese naval code and cipher systems. Not till late in 1941 was the number working on JN25 and JN25b raised to eight. "If the Japanese navy messages had enjoyed a higher priority and [had been] assigned more analytic resources," writes the NSA historian, Frederick D. Parker, "could the U.S. Navy have predicted the Japanese attack on Pearl Harbor? Most emphatically yes!" When the unsolved intercepted messages of late 1941 were decrypted as part of a secret postwar study, they were found to reveal many of the preparations for Pearl Harbor. There were numerous indications in the intercepts by mid-November of planning for a surprise attack by a naval task force including six aircraft carriers on an enemy fleet at anchor somewhere in the North Pacific. There were references also to the modification of large numbers of torpedoes for an attack in shallow waters. (Pearl Harbor was believed in Washington to be too shallow for a conventional torpedo attack.) Though the Japanese strike force observed radio silence during its long voyage, clues as to its destination multiplied in the intercepted (but undecrypted) naval signals. Weather messages addressed to the "Strike Force" contained forecasts for the North Pacific route. A radio message of December 1 reported that one of the tankers in‛ended to refuel the strike force was steaming to a position en route for Hawaii. The order on December 2, "Climb Mount Nitaka December 8, Repeat December 8" would have revealed, if decrypted, that the attack was planned for December 8, Japanese time (December 7 in Hawaii).[172]

American successes in breaking Japanese naval ciphers after Pearl Harbor confirm the conclusion of the NSA study that, had their importance been recognized and an adequate number of cryptanalysts set to work on them, JN25b could have been broken in time to reveal preparations for the surprise attack on December 7, 1941. The low priority given to the attack on JN25b was due, in part, to the myopia of the Navy Department that had failed to grasp the importance of SIGINT in naval warfare. But it also reflected the shortsightedness of a president who, despite his passion for the navy, his long-standing enthusiasm for intelligence, and his firsthand experience of the value of Japanese diplomatic intercepts, showed little interest in Japanese naval signals. Given the brevity of his comments to his naval aide about Magic, it seems unlikely that he ever asked Beardall what progress was being made in the attack on naval ciphers. It is inconceivable that Churchill would have shown a similar indifference. During the weeks before Pearl Harbor, Churchill frequently telephoned Bletchley Park himself for the latest intelligence. One of the leading Japanese cryptanalysts, Captain Malcolm Kennedy, wrote in his diary on December 6:

> The All Highest (. . . Churchill) is all over himself at the moment for latest information and indications re Japan's intentions and rings up at all hours of day and night, except for the 4 hours in each 24 (2 to 6 A.M.) when he sleeps.

Captain Kennedy, like Churchill, first learned of the attack on Pearl Harbor the next day not from SIGINT but from the BBC:

> A message rec[eived] just before leaving the office this evening had indicated that the outbreak of war was probably only a matter of hours, but the news on the 9 P.M. wireless, that Japan had opened hostilities with an air raid on Pearl Harbour, more than 3000 miles out in the Pacific, came as a complete surprise.[173]

The "complete surprise" of both Roosevelt and Churchill reflected a failure of imagination as well as of intelligence. It did not occur to either the president or the prime minister that the "little yellow men," as Churchill sometimes spoke of them and Roosevelt thought of them, were capable of such an astonishing feat of arms. When General Douglas MacArthur first heard the news of the attack by carrier-borne aircraft on Pearl Harbor, he insisted that the pilots must have been white mercenaries.[174] Had the Japanese been taken more seriously as potential opponents, had they been considered the racial equals of Americans, intelligence on their navy would have been accorded a higher priority in the White House as well as in the Navy Department.

CHAPTER 4

Roosevelt at War
(1941-1945)

The initiative in the long-overdue reorganization of SIGINT after Pearl Harbor came not from the president but from the secretary of war. On January 19, 1942, Stimson recruited the New York lawyer Alfred McCormack (later Colonel McCormack) "to make order in 'Magic.'"[1] At almost the same moment, the absurd arrangement that had given military and naval cryptanalysts responsibility for producing Magic decrypts on alternate days was abandoned. 0P-20-G agreed, no doubt reluctantly, that SIS should henceforth have sole responsibility for working on diplomatic traffic.[2] Together with Colonel (later Brigadier General) Carter C. Clarke, McCormack carried out a review of SIGINT procedures at every stage from interception to analysis that led to the centralization of the whole process under the control of the Special Branch (originally the Special Service Branch) of Military Intelligence.[3] An interdepartmental agreement of June 30, 1942, formally gave responsibility for diplomatic and military SIGINT to the army, for naval SIGINT to the navy, and for clandestine radio communications to the FBI and the Coast Guard.[4]

To soften the blow to naval pride, diplomatic SIGINT, though produced by the army, continued illogically to be supplied to the president by his naval rather than his military aide. Magic intercepts were delivered to Captain John McCrea, who succeeded Beardall as naval aide in January 1942, by army courier. McCrea normally took Magic and important naval documents to the president twice a day. When he arrived in the morning, Roosevelt was usually either working in bed or shaving in the bathroom. If the president was still in bed, McCrea would give him the papers to read. If he was in the bathroom, McCrea would close the toilet cover, sit on it, and, in these incongruous surroundings, read aloud top-secret intelligence to the president. When McCrea came on his afternoon visit, Roosevelt was most frequently to be found in the map room (which became the White House war room), where he would read the documents selected for his attention by his naval aide. If not in the map room, the president would probably be nearby in his doctor's office, having his withered legs massaged or his sinuses packed, and McCrea would read the afternoon Magic to him. When McCrea left the White House in 1943, Magic was delivered to the president by his successor as naval aide, Rear Admiral Wilson Brown; Brown's assistant, Commander John A. Tyree; or a young member of the map room staff, Lieutenant Commander William C. Mott. One or another of them briefed Roosevelt twice a day. Usually FDR was content with intelligence digests; sometimes he asked to read individual intercepts.[5]

The SIGINT delivered or read to Roosevelt in bed, in the bathroom, in the map room, and in the doctor's office was the most remarkable intelligence yet received by a president of the United States. Within six months of Pearl Harbor, it had helped to turn the tide of the Pacific war. By the spring of 1942 cryptanalysts in the Pearl Harbor SIGINT unit, code-named Hypo (later known as FRUPac), had made enough progress in decrypting the latest variant of JN25 to reveal the plan by Admiral Isoruku Yamamoto to attack Port Moresby in New Guinea. Though the battle of the Coral Sea (May 8–9, 1942) ended without clear victory for either side, it effectively stopped the Japanese advance toward Australia. Exactly what SIGINT during and after the battle particularly caught the president's eye will never be known, but it must surely have included the after-action damage report of the Japanese Fourth Fleet at Rabaul, of which Hypo produced the following (slightly confused) decrypt:

> Our losses: SHOHO [light carrier], sunk (hit by 7 torpedoes and 13 bombs), 22 aviation personnel made forced landings; 80 of these were injured, 16 seriously, 64 minor; others went down with the ship. SHOKAKU [heavy carrier] . . . hits, 3 and 8; damage to gasoline storage, engine rooms, etc. [some blanks here]; 94 killed, including 5 officers; 96 seriously injured—number of minor injuries.[6]

A few weeks later Hypo achieved one of the great cryptanalytical coups of the war by revealing Yamamoto's plan to capture Midway Island, in the middle of the North Pacific, as a base from which to repel any future American advance toward Japan. Yamamoto calculated that the capture of Midway would lure out the U.S. Pacific Fleet to be destroyed by his own superior forces, thus opening the way to a Japanese attack on Hawaii. The intelligence on the strength and deployment of the Japanese fleet provided by the cryptanalysts was so detailed that it initially inspired some skepticism in Washington,. The army chief of staff, General George C. Marshall, later admitted:

. . . We were very much disturbed because one Japanese unit gave Midway as its post office address, and that seemed a little bit too thick, so when the ships actually appeared it was a great relief, because if we had been deceived, and our limited number of vessels were there, and the Japanese approached at some other point, they would have had no opposition whatsoever.[7]

Roosevelt must surely have shared Marshall's sense of relief. Forewarned of the enemy battle plan, the commander in chief of the U.S. Pacific Fleet, Admiral Chester W. Nimitz, positioned his three aircraft carriers 350 miles northeast of Midway, from where, on the morning of June 4, he was able to launch a surprise attack on the larger Japanese fleet. Midway, Nimitz said later, "was essentially a victory of intelligence. In attempting surprise, the Japanese were themselves surprised." With the loss of four of the six aircraft carriers that had carried out the attack on Pearl Harbor, Yamamoto was forced back on the defensive. Two months later the U.S. Army landed at Guadalcanal in the Solomon Islands, thus taking the first step in its long and bloody "island-hopping" advance toward the Philippines and Japan. After Midway there were no decrypted Japanese damage assessments for the president to read of the kind that had been available to him after the Coral Sea battle, for on the eve of the battle the Japanese fleet adopted a new variant of JN25 that took Hypo some weeks to break. By early 1943, however, naval cryptanalysts had mastered the JN25 system so thoroughly that they were able to decrypt all its variants almost without interruption for the remainder of the war.[8]

Perhaps Roosevelt's most dramatic personal initiative in the use of Magic was taken at the prompting of Marshall. In August 1942 FDR passed on to Stalin the contents of intercepts showing that Japan had decided not to attack the Soviet Union. Though he did not tell Stalin the source of his information, the president told him it was "definitely authentic."[9] (Having heard the same information from his own cryptanalysts, Stalin probably believed him.)[10] Roosevelt was usually content to leave SIGINT to his military and naval chiefs to make what use of it they judged appropriate. McCrea later recalled that, when shown an intercept of particular importance, Roosevelt would sometimes say, "Make sure nie King [Admiral Ernest J. King, chief of naval operations] sees that!" After the war, however, neither McCrea nor Mott nor Tyree could recollect a single occasion on which an intercept led the president to order any military or naval action.[11] By contrast, Roosevelt bombarded McCrea during 1942 with detailed questions about naval personnel, ships, and equipment, such as "the present location and use of all patrol craft" of six different types put into service since the beginning of 1941, "the progress of tank lighter equipment," and appointments of commanders of 110-foot submarines and 173-foot submarine chasers ("Regular or Reserve Officers? What rank?").[12] The SIGINT delivered to the president does not seem to have provoked a comparable range of questions.

Churchill's commanders, by contrast, sometimes complained—justifiably—that he was too quick to urge them to take action after a dramatic decrypt had fired his imagination. German intercepts revealing Field Marshal Erwin Rommel's repeated demands for more men, tanks, aircraft, and supplies in North Africa initially misled him into believing that the German Afrika Corps was weaker than it was. He wrongly blamed Generals Archibald Wavell and Claude Auchinleck, both of whom he sacked, for being too slow to exploit Rommel's supposed weakness.[13] But Churchill's strengths as a consumer and organizer of wartime intelligence were much greater than his weaknesses. No previous British statesman and no other war leader equaled his flair for it.[14]

Despite its enormous importance to the war effort, SIGINT failed to capture the president's imagination. Roosevelt continued to find spies and secret operations more appealing than codebreaking. As in the days of Astor's Room, however, there continued to be an element of almost adolescent fantasy in FDR's approach to covert operations during the Second World War. On February 9, 1942, he sent Donovan a scheme drawn up by a Mr. Adams of Irwin, Pennsylvania (who, the president insisted, was "*not* a nut"), for a "surprise" bat attack on Japan. Mr. Adams was convinced that the Japanese were terrified of bats and proposed "frightening, demoralizing and exciting the prejudices of the people of the Japanese Empire" by dropping large quantities of bats on them. Though Roosevelt admitted that the plan appeared eccentric, he urged Donovan to look into it. Bat-dropping experiments, involving the COI (later the OSS), the American Museum of Natural History, and the Army Air Corps, continued for some time but were abandoned when the bats froze to death in the high-altitude aircraft intended to launch the bat attack against the terrified Japanese.[15]

Though Roosevelt left the reorganization of SIGINT wholly to others, he took a personal interest in the development of the first specialized U.S. foreign intelligence agency. As coordinator of information, Donovan reported directly to Roosevelt and was financed by him in unvouchered funds.[16] During the last six months of 1941 Donovan had easy access to the White House. The president was attracted by his energetic, free-wheeling style, and seemed pleased when his son James joined Donovan's organization.[17] The turf battles among Washington's fragmented intelligence community, which intensified after Pearl Harbor, gradually diminished Roosevelt's enthusiasm for the COI. On December 9, 1941, probably at Donovan's suggestion, the president instructed him to look into the coordination of strategic intelligence in the United States, Canada, and the rest of the Western Hemisphere. Hoover immediately protested, and Roosevelt backtracked. A further presidential directive received by Donovan on December 29 reaffirmed the authority of the FBI to operate its Special Intelligence Service in Canada and Latin America, and directed other agencies to clear "any intelligence work" in the Western Hemisphere with the bureau. Never good at resolving demarcation disputes within his administration, Roosevelt was exasperated by the interdepartmental wrangling that followed. Donovan tried to persuade him to issue a new directive authorizing the COI, after consultation with the secretary of state, to set up offices in Ottawa and other parts of the Western Hemisphere, and instructing Cordell Hull to "exercise his good offices in setting up a joint committee" consisting of State, COI, Stephenson's BSC, and the Canadian Department of External Affairs. Roosevelt refused. "You have got to work this out yourself with the Attorney General and Berle to the satisfaction of all three," he told Donovan. Both Berle and Attorney General Francis Biddle, however, sided with Hoover.[18]

During the months after Pearl Harbor, Roosevelt became preoccupied with the danger of Japanese subversion within the United States. Memories of German sabotage in North America during the First World War and the exaggerated belief on both sides of the Atlantic in the role played by Nazi subversion in Hitler's Blitzkrieg victories in Europe encouraged unfounded fears of a large and dangerous Fifth Column among Japanese-Americans. In the immediate aftermath of Pearl Harbor, the FBI interned 942 Japanese aliens. Hoover, however, argued against calls for the evacuation of the 110,000 Japanese-Americans (70,000 of them U.S. citizens by birth) living on the West Coast:

> The necessity for mass evacuation is based primarily upon public and political pressure rather than on factual data. Public hysteria and, in some instances, the comments of the press and radio announcers have resulted in a tremendous amount of pressure being brought to bear on Governor [Culbert] Olson [of California]

and Earl Warren, Attorney-General of the State, and on the military authorities.

Roosevelt disregarded Hoover's advice. He listened instead to alarmist voices from California, among them that of the general commanding West Defense Command, John L. De Witt, who insisted that, despite their peaceable appearance, Japanese-Americans were "organized and ready for concerted action." De Witt drew sinister conclusions from his own lack of evidence. "The very fact that no sabotage has taken place to date," he perversely argued, "is a disturbing and confirming indication that such action will be taken." The president was surprisingly impressed by De Witt's lack of logic. On February 19 he signed Executive Order 9066, which paved the way for the mass internment of Japanese-Americans on the West Coast, who were branded as disloyal and deprived of their liberty without trial or right of redress.[19]

Donovan's most difficult problems early in 1942 as he tried to gear the COI to the war effort derived from the continued feuding within the Washington intelligence community. A year earlier Donovan's close links with Stephenson and BSC had helped him win Roosevelt's support for the creation of the COI. By 1942, however, Stephenson had become embroiled in the Washington turf battles. Adolf Berle in the State Department complained, "Though it is not possible to say so, Bill Donovan gets a good many of his ideas from the British. . . ."[20] Berle had already complained about Stephenson's use of forged Nazi documents to deceive the president before Pearl Harbor[21] and claimed that "a British espionage service functioning here . . . might at any time be turned not to espionage on the enemy, but to operations within the United States."[22] Early in 1942 Berle and Donovan had "no end of a row" over BSC.[23] The McKellar Bill, passed by Congress on January 28, transferred registration of all foreign agencies in the United States from the State Department to the Justice Department, and subjected them to greater scrutiny. Stephenson, who saw it as a threat to his somewhat freewheeling operations, immediately protested. Donovan jumped to Stephenson's defense and asked Roosevelt to veto the bill. Berle urged the president not to do so:

> I do not see that any of us can safely take the position that we should grant blanket immunity for any foreign spy system, no matter whose it is. Logically, why have it? If our interests diverge, it is adverse; if they are the same, our own people ought to be able to do the job with such assistance as they may want.
> Hoover and Biddle are fully informed.[24]

At this point Stephenson seriously overplayed his hand. Seeing Berle as a dangerous opponent both of BSC and of Anglo-American intelligence collaboration, he set out to discredit him. On February 13 Hoover's aide, Edward A. Tamm, informed Berle that Denis Paine of BSC had been trying to "get the dirt" on him to feed it to the press and force his removal from the State Department. The FBI had waited until they had "conclusive proof" of Paine's operation, then called in Stephenson. According to a memo by Berle:

> They told him that they wanted Paine out of the country by six o'clock "or else," in which case they would arrest him promptly and go right to it. Stevenson [*sic*—Berle habitually misspelled Stephenson's name] had said first, weakly, that Paine had been a long time in the United States; to which they replied that that made it worse; he ought to know better; and Stevenson had then professed surprise and horror that any of his men should do such a thing, and had finally put Paine on the plane for Montreal, and that was that.
>
> It developed that the only dirt they had dug up so far was a column about having twin bath tubs in our house.[25]

On February 26 Hoover, Biddle, Berle, and the directors of military and naval intelligence met to discuss BSC and its attempt to discredit Berle. All were uncertain how the British had succeeded in creating "a large intelligence secret service activity in this country," but thought it might have been the result of "an informal agreement between Churchill and the President before the war." They condemned Stephenson's use of "unscrupulous informants" and "irresponsible" undercover agents, and agreed that Biddle should inform the president.[26]

On March 5 Berle, Biddle, and Hoover met the British ambassador, Lord Halifax, and his deputy, Sir Ronald Campbell. Biddle began by saying bluntly that Roosevelt and his cabinet were unhappy about BSC operations in the United States. They believed that it should limit its activities to liaison work and that Stephenson should be replaced. Clearly surprised by this attack on BSC, Halifax read a statement from Stephenson claiming that "everything he did was submitted to, passed upon by, and approved by Mr. J. Hoover." Hoover denied this; though he claimed to have "pleasant personal relations" with Stephenson, he said the FBI did not find it possible to have "close working relations" with him. Once again, the British ambassador seemed taken aback. According to Berle:

> Lord Halifax said that his "mental structure" was altered on learning that there was not a close working relationship between Mr.

Hoover and Mr. Stephenson. He had assumed these two agencies were working perfectly together. Specifically, referring to the incident of Paine, he had understood that [Stephenson] had discovered Paine's activities and had promptly called him down and requested him to leave the country. He had not understood that the F.B.I. had intervened in the matter.[27]

At this critical moment Stephenson's survival depended on the continued strong support of Donovan and his own immense personal charm. As even Berle said later, "It was impossible not to like Bill Stephenson."[28] At a further meeting with Berle and Biddle on March 10 Lord Halifax insisted that "British Intelligence here had done nothing except with the direct authority and cooperation of the American officials." Under questioning, it emerged that by "American officials," Halifax meant Donovan and his organization. With Donovan's help, Stephenson survived, but he had lost Roosevelt's confidence. Biddle told Halifax that the president was seriously concerned by the way BSC was operating. By falsely claiming to be acting as a secret channel of communication between Roosevelt and Churchill, Stephenson had persuaded the FBI to let him use its radio network to send cipher traffic to London. According to Berle:

> [Halifax] said he had inquired of Ste[ph]enson whether these cipher messages going forward were kept secret because they reflected a correspondence between the president and Mr. Churchill; Ste[ph]enson denied that he had ever made any such statement. The Attorney General thereupon pulled out a report by Mr. Hoover, dated last July, in which Ste[ph]enson had given this reason as an excuse for not permitting any American official to know the code.[29]

Stephenson's selective postwar memory suppressed all recollection of how close he had come to disrupting the Anglo-American intelligence alliance that he had helped to create. The reality of his remarkable but checkered career as head of BSC was replaced by the heroic myth of "the man called Intrepid."

Stephenson's bungled attempt to dispose of Berle and his damaged reputation in the White House weakened the position of his main American supporter, Donovan, in the turf battles of early wartime Washington. By the spring of 1942 the president seems finally to have realized that before Pearl Harbor he had been taken in by BSC forgeries that Donovan had assured him were genuine. Continued wrangling over the future of the COI increased Roosevelt's irritation with Donovan. He told Berle in April that "he was thinking of putting [Donovan] on some nice, quiet isolated island, where he could have a scrap with some Japs every morning before breakfast. Then he thought the Colonel would be out of trouble and be entirely happy."[30] On June 13, while Donovan was away in London, Roosevelt finally decided on the replacement of the COI. A presidential order made Donovan head of the newly created Office of Strategic Services (OSS), which was instructed to "collect and analyze strategic information" and "plan and operate . . . special services." Instead of reporting directly to the president as before, however, Donovan was placed under the "direction and supervision" of the Joint Chiefs of Staff. The Foreign Information Service, formerly part of COI, was removed from his control and handed over to the newly established Office of War Information. The establishment of OSS did not end the internecine warfare within the intelligence community. A year later General George Strong, head of G-2, denounced OSS and its "ambitious and imaginative Director" for being "constantly at war with other Government agencies" and seeking to reduce G-2 and ONI "to the status of reporting agencies and research bureaus for the O.S.S."[31]

In the spring of 1943 Strong incurred the personal wrath of the president. Late in March G-2's Counter-Intelligence Corps (CIC) bugged Eleanor Roosevelt's hotel room at the Blackstone Hotel, Chicago, while she was meeting the former Communist fellow-traveler, Sergeant Joe Lash (later her biographer). Mrs. Roosevelt learned of the bugging from hotel employees, said nothing to Lash, but complained to Marshall as soon as she returned to Washington. Marshall responded by closing CIC down altogether and roasting "a lot of butts." Rumors about Eleanor Roosevelt, however, continued to circulate within G-2. Some senior military intelligence officers, apparently confusing tapes of Lash making love to his mistress in a hotel bedroom with tapes of his meeting with the First Lady in the same hotel, told the FBI that the recordings "indicated quite clearly that Mrs. Roosevelt and Lash engaged in sexual intercourse."[32] The scandal over CIC was only one of a series of military intelligence failings that concerned Stimson. He noted in November 1943 that he had been discussing the reform of G-2 with Marshall and others but had made little progress.[33] Knox was equally unhappy with naval intelligence. A devastating report on ONI early in 1943 by the Chicago management consultant Rawleigh Warner almost led to its disbandment in its existing form.[34] Only the SIGINT components of the service intelligence agencies inspired much confidence in the secretaries of war and the navy. "Knox and I agreed," wrote Stimson, "that our two intelligence services are pretty bum."[35]

The problems of naval and military intelligence reflected the larger administrative disarray of wartime intelligence. OSS calculated that there were ten major intelligence units, each with subdivisions, and thirty police and law enforcement agencies with some responsibility for intelligence collection. Numerous committees and joint agencies added to the confusion.[36] The Joint Intelligence Committee (JIC), established late in 1941, played a much smaller part in coordinating the work of the intelligence community than its British counterpart, on which it was modeled. On May 17, 1940, only a week after Churchill became prime minister, the British JIC had been instructed to take the initiative whenever it saw fit, "at any time of day or night" (a phrase repeated twice in its revised terms of reference), to send reports to the prime minister, the war cabinet, and the chiefs of staff. The Foreign Office, service departments, and intelligence agencies were no longer allowed to bypass the JIC and submit their own independent assessments. Early in 1941 the Joint Intelligence Staff (JIS) was set up as a subcommittee of the JIC, charged with coordinating, assessing, and disseminating strategic intelligence. Behind the growing coordination of the British intelligence community itself and the integration of intelligence with the British war effort, it is possible to detect the powerful influence of the prime minister.[37] Roosevelt's influence on the diffuse U.S. intelligence community was very much weaker. When the British JIC visited Washington in September 1944, "with a view to discussing the coordination of Far Eastern intelligence," it found the members of the American JIC at odds with each other. According to a British note:

> The American J.I.C. . . . stated that while they were glad to discuss Far Eastern matters in individual talks between the U.S. and British Directors of Intelligence for each Service, they were not prepared for a combined three service discussion on the matter.[38]

Roosevelt made a small but significant contribution of his own to the organizational confusion of wartime intelligence. Throughout the war he maintained at the White House a small personal intelligence unit under the journalist John Franklin Carter, alias Jay Franklin. The White House unit may well deserve the booby prize for providing, against stiff competition, the most absurd U.S. intelligence report of the war. In January 1942 Carter sent Roosevelt a "Secret Memorandum on U.S.S.R." obtained "under conditions of extraordinary secrecy from a man who is believed to have accurate and swift means of communications with Moscow." The memorandum reported that Stalin had a secret strategy board wholly composed of foreigners: "3 Americans, 1 German (brother of man who arrested Hitler in Munich Putsch), 1 British General (hated by Chamberlain), and a Frenchman named Collet (brother of General

Collet in Syrian campaign)." One of the Americans was alleged to be
directing Stalin's Siberian strategy and preparing an air attack on Japan
with eighty-three hundred planes hidden in underground hangars at
Vladivostok that would result in "the burning of Japan and the islands
from one end to the other."[39]

Carter may never again have scaled quite such heights of absurdity,
but there were times when he came close—in October 1942, for example, when he reported an alleged plot between two of Roosevelt's bêtes
noires, General Charles de Gaulle, leader of the Free French, and the
union leader John L. Lewis, to seize control of the U.S. government.[40]
Carter's biggest and longest-lasting operation, in cooperation with OSS,
was to prepare biographies of ten thousand leading Nazis. He made the
mistake, however, of using as his chief consultant Hitler's former crony
and Nazi press officer, the plausible but unreliable Ernst "Putzi" Hanfs-
taengl, whom Roosevelt had known at Harvard.[41] Carter said later of his
wartime intelligence work: "It was a picturesque and wildly funny affair
at times. Very fantastically amusing things happened as they always do
in an off-beat operation and I think we all had fun."[42] Donovan was closer
to the mark when he described Carter as still "in the 'horse and buggy'
stage of intelligence thinking."[43] Roosevelt's use of Carter's eccentric unit
provides graphic illustration of the continuing element of fantasy in his
understanding of intelligence.

As head of OSS, Donovan lacked the easy access to the president
that he had enjoyed during his first six months as COI. OSS reports and
intelligence assessments had to compete with the rest of the paper
mountain that daily accumulated in the wartime White House. Donovan
regularly selected reports that he asked the president's secretary, Grace
Tully, to bring to his attention.[44] The analysts whom Donovan assembled
in the Research and Analysis (R&A) Section of OSS compared in intellectual quality with any section of the Washington bureaucracy. Its head,
the celebrated Harvard historian William L. Langer, recruited a more
remarkable group of distinguished scholars than could have been assembled by any one American university. Eventually the analysts were
almost two thousand strong with an astounding range of expertise. But
they were denied access to the best intelligence of the war, Ultra and
Magic, and their work suffered accordingly. Ray S. Cline, later deputy
director for intelligence (DDI) in the CIA, had had access to SIGINT
when working in naval intelligence. But when he moved to R&A, he discovered that "Neither the JIC Weekly Summary nor any component of
OSS ever used signals intelligence in their reporting."[45]

How many of the R&A assessments and reports on OSS foreign operations from its Special Intelligence (SI) and Special Operations (SO)

branches attracted the president's attention remains a mystery. Some OSS operations, however, certainly captured Roosevelt's imagination. The first was its role in preparing Operation Torch, the Anglo-American invasion of French Northwest Africa, in November 1942. Robert D. Murphy of the State Department was sent to take secret charge of political negotiations with French leaders in North Africa. Colonel William Eddy, OSS station chief in Tangiers, was made responsible for intelligence collection and covert operations. "The North African expedition," wrote Murphy later, "appealed to [Roosevelt's] sense of adventure. . . ." The president could not resist the temptation to become personally involved in the secret preparations. He summoned Murphy to see him on September 4, appointed him "personal representative of the President" during the period up to the landings, briefed him on the plans for Torch, and told him to say nothing to anyone in the State Department. When Murphy objected that this might put him in an awkward position with Secretary Hull, Roosevelt replied, "Don't worry about Cordell. I will take care of him. I'll tell him our plans a day or so before the landings."

Most of the population of French North Africa, according to Murphy, was "complacently neutral. Far from wanting to be liberated, they just wanted to be left alone." But OSS made contact with secret sympathizers (though it exaggerated their numbers and importance) in the French armed forces, police, and administration.[46] Beginning on November 8 over one hundred thousand Allied troops went ashore at intervals along an almost two-thousand-mile stretch of North African coastline. On many beaches they were met by friendly guides recruited by OSS. An OSS agent removed the fuses from demolition charges in the tunnel connecting the Algerian naval base of Mers el Kebir with Oran. According to OSS, "The tunnel was vital to Allied movement and it was estimated that it would have required three months to rebuild."[47] Not everything, however, went according to plan. In Morocco the initial landings took place on the wrong beaches and met stiff resistance. General Dwight D. Eisenhower, the Allied commander, reported to the combined chiefs: "The actual state of existing sentiment does not repeat not agree even remotely with some of our prior calculations."[48] Largely because the landings had taken the enemy by surprise, however, they suffered only a fraction of the casualties that had been expected. At a cabinet meeting on November 15, a week after Torch began, Roosevelt was in high spirits, claiming credit for devising the operation.[49] Torch put OSS on the map. In the first American offensive of the war in the European and Mediterranean theater, OSS had demonstrated to both the president and his high command that covert action as well as intelligence collection had a role in military operations.

Roosevelt's most important personal contribution to the development of the wartime intelligence community, apart from the creation of OSS, was to approve intelligence collaboration with Britain on an unprecedented scale. After Pearl Harbor, Churchill's remaining reservations about sharing SIGINT with Roosevelt disappeared. On important decrypts the prime minister would sometimes add the notation: "Make sure that President Roosevelt sees this at my desire."[50] When General Dwight D. Eisenhower arrived in Britain as commander in chief of U.S. forces in June 1942, Churchill briefed him personally on Ultra.[51] Roosevelt was less personally involved than Churchill in the making of the intelligence alliance. He was content to be kept generally informed and apparently was unconcerned by the details. In July 1942 the president appears to have asked the army chief of staff, General George C. Marshall, how collaboration between MID Special Branch and the British was proceeding. Marshall in turn inquired of his British opposite number, General Sir John Dill, as well as of the Special Branch, then sent Roosevelt a brief memorandum that reported simply: "We find that an interchange of cryptanalytic information has been in progress for over a year and appears to be satisfactory to both services."[52]

Marshall's memorandum was somewhat misleading as well as bland. In June 1942 one Army Special Branch cryptanalyst and two from OP-20-G had begun work at Bletchley Park, headquarters of the interservice British SIGINT agency, but it took another nine months to establish full Anglo-American cryptanalytic collaboration.[53] Despite its success with the Luftwaffe and the main naval versions of the German Enigma machine cipher, Bletchley Park suffered a serious setback in February 1942 with the introduction of a new U-boat variant of Enigma, which took ten months to crack.[54] The breaking of that cipher at the end of the year must certainly have been discussed by Roosevelt and Churchill when they met at Casablanca in January 1943, but no record of their discussion of it survives. Churchill arrived full of enthusiasm, as usual, for Ultra's contribution to the Allied war effort. Though the prime minister received SIGINT summaries twice a day during the conference, he was never satisfied with the amount he received at Casablanca. "Volume should be increased at least five-fold and important messages sent textually," he telegraphed London.[55] Roosevelt's supply of SIGINT at Casablanca, of which only half a dozen examples survive, did not compare with Churchill's. Nor did his enthusiasm for it.

The breaking of U-boat Enigma late in 1942 opened a new era in naval SIGINT collaboration between Britain and the United States. On December 27 the "Secret Room," a submarine tracking room on the British model able to exploit the newly available U-boat decrypts, began operating in the Main Navy Building in Washington.[56] The twenty-three-year-old Harry Hinsley (later the official historian of British wartime intelligence), recruited by Bletchley Park at the outbreak of war while still an undergraduate at Cambridge University, visited OP-20-G to settle details of its collaboration with Bletchley's Naval Section. It was agreed that both agencies would exchange all U-boat signals intercepted on either side of the Atlantic, and that whichever agency broke the daily cipher key first would send it to the other. From early in 1943 British and American cryptanalysis of naval Enigma was carried out according to a single program coordinated by Bletchley Park.[57] Communication via direct signal links between the U-boat tracking rooms in London, Washington, and (from May 1943) Ottawa became so close that, according to the British official history, for the remainder of the war "they operated virtually as a single organization."[58] Roosevelt, who took an interest in all changes in naval organization, was doubtless kept informed of the work of the tracking rooms by his naval aide. During the battle of the Atlantic, the longest and most complex battle in the history of naval warfare, which reached its climax in the spring of 1943, Ultra made a major, possibly decisive, contribution to the Allied victory.[59]

After the beginning of Operation Torch in November 1942 Eisenhower began receiving Ultra from Bletchley via his British chief intelligence officer. However, Bletchley failed to send copies of Eisenhower's Ultra to Washington. The G-2 in Washington, General Strong, had been one of the earliest advocates of SIGINT collaboration with the British.[60] Now he complained that he was being deliberately bypassed. A later American analysis concluded:

> . . . As one examines the early records, the picture that emerges is of G-2 and British authorities walking around and eyeing each other like two mongrels who have just met. Presumably and quite naturally the ministries in London were reluctant to risk Source's [Ultra's] neck by sharing his precious information with an unproved and shadowy group in Washington. G-2 was from Missouri and wished to be quite certain that he had access to all the material Source was turning up.[61]

The conflict was resolved in the spring of 1943 by the signing of the BRUSA SIGINT agreement and by an exchange of missions between the Special Branch and Bletchley Park. The term BRUSA was devised by Harry Hinsley, who had been sent to Washington by Bletchley to conduct negotiations with the Special Branch. The Americans, he had noticed, "loved acronyms," but he initially worried—needlessly, as it turned out—

that putting Britain ahead of the United States in the acronym he had devised might cause problems. His only major difficulty was in coping with continued interservice rivalries between the American military and naval SIGINT agencies. OP-20-G and the Special Branch were far more suspicious of each other than of the British. As Hinsley recalls, "The Navy didn't like me talking to the Army. But I wasn't allowed to tell the Navy any details [of BRUSA] because the Army would have been furious." Hinsley did, however, assure OP-20-G that the BRUSA agreement was not "anything like as intimate" as its own less formal working arrangement with Bletchley. Whereas naval cryptanalysts on both sides of the Atlantic were decrypting the same German naval messages and exchanging keys daily, the military cryptanalysts agreed instead on a division of labor.[62]

Over half a century later, parts of the BRUSA agreement still remain classified—one of a number of indications of its unusual importance. The essence of the accord, however, is summarized in its first three clauses:

1. Both the U.S. and British agree to exchange completely all information concerning the detection, identification and interception of signals from, and the solution of codes and ciphers used by, the Military and Airforces of the Axis powers, including secret services (Abwehr).

2. The U.S. will assume as a main responsibility the reading of Japanese Military and Air Codes and ciphers.

3. The British will assume as a main responsibility the reading of German and Italian Military and Air Codes and ciphers.[63]

At the end of the war the head of Hut 3 at Bletchley Park (the section processing German military and air force decrypts) praised "the friendship and close cooperation that have throughout so clearly marked the integration of American and British personnel." The only substantial problem of SIGINT liaison that the BRUSA agreement and the working arrangement on naval cryptanalysis failed to resolve was the continuing friction between OP-20-G and the Special Branch. Writing after the war, the head of the Special Branch mission at Bletchley Park, Telford Taylor, regretted that it had not also represented naval interests. The problems of American interservice intelligence rivalry, he concluded, "have not been solved by this war. A solution is not impossible and is greatly to be desired."[64]

While the BRUSA agreement was being negotiated, Roosevelt authorized one remarkably risky use of SIGINT in the Pacific war. On April 14, 1943, a decrypted Japanese signal revealed that four days later Yamamoto would be visiting locations in the Northern Solomons in a plane escorted by six fighters, and gave the precise times of his arrival and departure. Nimitz telegraphed Admiral William F. "Bull" Halsey, commander South Pacific: "If forces you command have capability shoot down Yamamoto and staff you are hereby authorized initiate preliminary planning."

Before giving final approval, however, Nimitz sought the authorization of both Knox and the president. No record survives of Roosevelt's reasons for giving his consent. Presumably, he accepted his advisers' argument that the potential damage to Japanese morale and to the Japanese direction of the war outweighed the risk that they might deduce their ciphers had been broken. It was a dubious argument. Less than a year earlier the secret had almost been given away. Immediately after Midway the Chicago *Tribune* had published the front-page headline NAVY HAD WORD OF JAP PLAN TO STRIKE AT SEA. Congressman Elmer J. Holland denounced the *Tribune* on the floor of the House, but made matters worse by declaring, "Somehow our Navy had secured and broken the secret code of the Japanese Navy." The broadcaster Walter Winchell twice revealed over the air that the navy had advance knowledge of the movements of the Japanese fleet. Remarkably, the Japanese failed to draw the obvious conclusion. The willingness of Roosevelt and his advisers, after so narrow an escape in the summer of 1942, to take the risk a second time in April 1943 of alerting the Japanese to the compromise of their ciphers for the sake of killing a single Japanese commander, however talented, suggests a curious order of priorities. Yamamoto's mid-air assassination would have been poor compensation for the loss of Japanese SIGINT.

Early on April 18 eighteen Army Air Force P-38 fighters took off from Henderson Field on Guadalcanal, flew low over the ocean to evade Japanese radar, intercepted Yamamoto's plane, and shot it down over the southern tip of Bougainville Island. As after the victory at Midway, SIGINT security proved dangerously lax. According to Captain Jasper Holmes of Hypo:

> It became an item of widespread interservice gossip that the dramatic interception of Yamamoto's plane had been contrived through broken Japanese codes. It was a miracle that the story did not break in American newspapers.

Roosevelt and Nimitz, however, had greater good fortune than they deserved. Once again the Japanese failed to deduce that the interception of Yamamoto's plane resulted from the decryption of their signals. The Japanese war effort undoubtedly suffered as a result of Yamamoto's death. His successor, Admiral Mineichi Koga, lacked both his intellect and his charisma.[65]

Roosevelt seems never to have grasped that SIGINT provided him with the best intelligence in the history of warfare. Even when the flow of Magic was at its peak, FDR still dreamed unrealistically of penetrating Japan with agent networks. In November 1943 the president summoned Stimson and Knox to the White House "to see whether we couldn't get any better information out of Japan." "He was," Stimson noted in his diary, "dissatisfied with the fact that we were getting practically nothing from the inside of Japan. . . ."—a staggering statement given both the quality and quantity of Japanese SIGINT that reached him daily. After hearing the president's complaint, Stimson saw his G-2, General Strong, who "admitted that we had no spies in Japan and were not getting anything that way."[66]

Though Roosevelt did not grasp the full significance of the BRUSA agreement, his willingness to embark on intelligence collaboration with Britain was of crucial importance not simply for the Second World War but also for the postwar world. BRUSA formed the basis of an enduring Anglo-American SIGINT alliance, later extended to include Canada and Australasia, which will probably survive into the twenty-first century.[67] Wartime intelligence collaboration, embodied in a series of formal accords and informal understandings, went far beyond SIGINT. The founding of OSS in 1942 was accompanied by an agreement with SIS and SOE on spheres of influence. SOE was given the major responsibility for most of Europe, but OSS was accorded the leading role in North Africa, Finland, and eventually Bulgaria, Romania, and northern Norway.[68] OSS relations with SOE and SIS, though not always smooth, were, according to the British official history, "always close and eventually harmonious."[69] X-2, the counterintelligence branch of OSS, founded in 1943 partly in response to British pressure, rapidly developed a relationship with MI5 that compared in intimacy with that established by the Special Branch with Bletchley Park. An X-2 officer was given a desk in the office of the head of MI5's Double Agent section and followed in all its operational detail the astonishing "Double Cross" system that fed disinformation to the Germans through a network of turned Abwehr agents. X-2 expressed amazement at the closeness of its cooperation with the British:

For even an Ally to be admitted to a full access to all secret files and to a knowledge of their sources; to information on most secret methods and procedures; and to a knowledge of personnel and the system of organization and of operations—in short to the innermost arcana, in this case, of perhaps the world's most experienced and

efficient, and therefore most carefully safeguarded, security systems—was beyond precedent or expectation. Yet the British did it.
The implications of this fact are staggering—and completely inex-
plicable in terms of merely cheap exchange of mutual advantages.
The advantages were enormously heavy on the American side.[70]

By D-Day, June 6, 1944, there had also been a complete merger of
British and American strategic photo reconnaissance from bases in the
United Kingdom.[71] Roosevelt was briefed personally on the development
of what later became known as imagery intelligence by his son Elliott,
who in 1942 became commander of an army air force photographic unit
that took part in Operation Torch. Elliott went on numerous reconnaissance missions, sometimes taking the photographs himself. In 1943 he
was given command of Allied aerial photography over a large area of the
Mediterranean. He was later awarded the Distinguished Flying Cross and
promoted to brigadier general.[72]

Operation Overlord, the Allied invasion of occupied Europe in the
summer of 1944, made better use of intelligence than any other great
offensive in the previous history of land or amphibious warfare. Without
command of both sea and air, the D-Day landings on the Normandy
beaches would have been unthinkable. On the ground, however, the
seven divisions of the initial Allied assault faced fifty-nine German divisions in occupied France. Overlord's success thus depended on the ability of a huge deception operation, code-named Fortitude, to fool the
Germans into believing that the Normandy landings were only a feint
and the main attack would come in the Pas de Calais. Fortitude in turn
depended not merely on the Double Cross system but also on Ultra,
which revealed how the deception was working. It worked astonishingly
well. The Germans estimated the Allied divisions assembled in Britain at
almost double their real strength.

Overlord was a triumph of Allied intelligence as well as military collaboration. The three-man Jedburgh teams (named for the Scottish town
where they were trained) who parachuted into France to liaise with the
French Resistance mostly consisted of one officer each from SOE and
OSS and a French operative.[73] Roosevelt, however, had long distrusted
General Charles de Gaulle, the head of the French provisional government. When the two men met at Casablanca early in 1943, Secret Service men hid behind the curtains and doors—all, according to Hopkins,
"armed to the teeth with perhaps a dozen tommy guns among the
group."[74] OSS reports were partly responsible for convincing the president that de Gaulle could be replaced. After the D-Day landings began
the liberation of occupied France in June, however, Donovan reported

that, though many in the Resistance had reservations about de Gaulle "as a political figure," almost all regarded him as the "main symbol of resistance." Following secret conversations with de Gaulle, Donovan flew back to Washington on June 14 and helped to persuade a reluctant Roosevelt to receive de Gaulle at the White House early in July.[75] The visit was not a success, and was made worse by a curious lapse of presidential security. Roosevelt wrote to a friend soon after his meeting with de Gaulle, "I think he is essentially an egotist." A photocopy of the letter soon found its way to de Gaulle, who writes loftily in his memoirs, "I shall never know whether Franklin Roosevelt thought that Charles de Gaulle's egoism in matters concerning France was on behalf of France or of himself." There is little doubt, however, that he interpreted it as a personal insult.[76]

OSS believed that its best intelligence from Germany during the final stages of the war in Europe came via the future DCI, Allen W. Dulles, then stationed at Bern in Switzerland. Dulles's most productive source was a German foreign ministry official Fritz Kolbe (code-named Wood), who traveled periodically to Bern as courier. Beginning in August 1943 Kolbe gave Dulles top-secret German documents "by the pound." The sheer volume of Wood's material initially raised fears that it might be part of an elaborate German deception. Donovan did not send a first selection of the documents to the president until January 10, 1944, and he did so then with a note of caution:

> We have secured through secret intelligence channels a series of what purport to be authentic reports, transmitted by consular, military and intelligence sources to their headquarters. The source and material are being checked as to probable authenticity both here and in London.

Comparison with Ultra intercepts gradually resolved most doubts about Wood's material (code-named the Boston series). Until the spring of 1944 Dulles forwarded the documents with little or no comment.[77] On April 12, however, he cabled to Washington an exuberant commentary on Kolbe's latest delivery. Donovan told the president that Dulles had previously been "by no means optimistic with regard to the possibility of an early German internal collapse," but had now changed his mind. Dulles's vivid description of the crumbling of the Third Reich made a powerful impression on Roosevelt's chief of staff, Admiral William D. Leahy—and, in all probability, on the president himself:

> In some 400 pages, dealing with the internal maneuverings of German diplomatic policy for the past two months, a picture of immi-

nent doom and final downfall is presented. Into a tormented General Headquarters and a half-dead Foreign Office stream the lamentations of a score of diplomatic posts. . . .

The final death-bed contortions of a putrefied Nazi diplomacy are pictured in these telegrams. The reader is carried from one extreme of emotion to the other, from tears to laughter, as he examines these messages and sees the cruelty exhibited by the Germans in their final swan-song of brutality toward the people so irrevocably and pitifully enmeshed by the Gestapo after half a decade of futile struggles, and yet at the same time also sees the absurdity of the dilemma which now confronts this diplomacy both within and without the Festung Europa [Fortress Europe].[78]

Vividly though the Wood documents described the death throes of the Third Reich, by far the most important intelligence on Germany continued to come from Ultra. The close alliance of the Anglo-American intelligence communities could not, however, ensure that Roosevelt, Churchill, and their high commands would give equal weight to Ultra intelligence. Overlord, perhaps the high point of Anglo-American collaboration, was swiftly followed by a serious dispute over Allied strategy. Late in June 1944 Ultra revealed that the Germans felt themselves particularly vulnerable in northern Italy. Churchill and his chiefs of staff were anxious for a major new Italian offensive. The Americans insisted on going ahead instead with plans for landings in the south of France (Operation Anvil). Churchill unsuccessfully sought a meeting with FDR to try to convince him personally of the vital importance of the German decrypts. In a final attempt to win Roosevelt over, he instructed Sir Stewart Menzies, chief of SIS, to prepare an intelligence assessment to send directly to the president. Roosevelt's mind, however, was already made up for him by his chiefs of staff. Churchill told him that the decision to proceed with Anvil at the expense of a major Italian offensive was "in my humble and respectful opinion, the first major strategic and political error for which we two have been responsible."[79]

In the Pacific, as in Europe, SIGINT shortened the Second World War. The army chief of staff, General Marshall wrote in September 1944:

Operations in the Pacific are largely guided by the information we obtain of Japanese deployments. We know their strength in various garrisons, the rations and other stores continuing [*sic*] available to them, and what is of vast importance, we check their fleet movements and the movements of their convoys. The heavy losses reported from time to time which they sustain by reason of our submarine action largely results from the fact that we know the sailing dates and routes of their convoys and can notify our submarines to lay in wait at the proper point.[80]

Roosevelt did not share Marshall's enthusiasm. Marshall wrote to him, almost reproachfully, in February 1944, "I have learned that you seldom see the Army summaries of 'Magic' material." He tried to persuade the president to pay greater attention to SIGINT by telling him that improvements had been made "in the very necessary process of separating the wheat from the chaff and correlating the items with past information":

> The recent discovery of the Japanese Army machine code has added a tremendous amount of such material and will continue to give us a great deal from day to day. The problem is how to avoid being buried under the mass of information, and I think the present arrangement satisfactorily meets that difficulty. I am attaching two of the current booklets [Magic summaries] which I hope you will glance through in order to familiarize yourself with the manner in which the information is presented. I should like to send these booklets each day direct to the White House and have them delivered to you by Admiral Brown [FDR's naval aide].[81]

Marshall may have slightly underestimated the attention paid by Roosevelt to the SIGINT supplied to him by his naval aides of the previous two years, McCrea and Brown. But his letter is a certain indication that the president rarely mentioned decrypts at meetings with him.

In September 1944, while Roosevelt was campaigning for a record fourth term in the White House, his handling of SIGINT very nearly became an election issue. His Republican opponent, Thomas E. Dewey, governor of New York, was told by an army officer hostile to Roosevelt that Japanese codes had been broken before Pearl Harbor. But for an unprecedented personal intervention in the campaign by Marshall, Dewey might well have used that information to accuse the president of criminal negligence in failing to act on the warning given him by Japanese decrypts. Without consulting Roosevelt or any member of the administration, Marshall decided to appeal to Dewey's patriotism. On September 25 in Tulsa, Oklahoma, Colonel Carter Clarke of the Army Special Branch, wearing a newly pressed civilian suit, handed Dewey a top-secret letter from Marshall. Dewey opened the envelope and remarked, according to Clarke, "Well, Top Secret—that's really top, isn't it?" He then read the first two paragraphs:

My Dear Governor:

I am writing to you without the knowledge of any other person except Admiral King (who concurs) because we are approaching a grave dilemma in the political reactions of Congress regarding Pearl Harbor. What I have to tell you below is of such a highly secret nature that I feel compelled to ask you either to accept it on the basis of your not communicating its contents to any other person and returning this letter or not reading any further and returning the letter to the bearer.

Dewey stopped reading. He told Clarke that Roosevelt must be behind the letter:

Marshall does not do things like that. Now if this letter merely tells me that we were reading Japanese codes before Pearl Harbor and that at least two of them are still in current use, there is no point in my reading the letter because I already know that.

Dewey handed the letter back and said that Roosevelt deserved to be impeached. He consented, however, to meet Clarke again in Albany on September 28.

On this occasion, it was agreed that Dewey could discuss with a trusted adviser, Elliott V. Bell, the contents of a revised letter from Marshall that Clarke brought with him, and that Clarke would answer whatever technical questions they wished to put to him. Marshall's second letter began with an assurance that "neither the Secretary of War nor the president has any intimation whatsoever that such a letter has been addressed to you." As Clarke was taking the letter from the envelope, however, Bell said disparagingly, "Colonel, hundreds of people know all about the Midway affair and how most of our other successes in the Pacific have been due to our reading Jap naval codes. Everyone who has ever been out there knows about it and talks freely about it." Before Dewey had even finished reading Marshall's account of the vital importance of SIGINT in the Pacific war, he exclaimed, "Well, I'll be damned if I believe the Japs are still using those two codes." Clarke assured him that they were, and that "one of them was our life blood in intelligence." Dewey was also puzzled by the conclusion of Marshall's letter:

The conduct of General Eisenhower's campaign and of all operations in the Pacific are closely related in conception and timing to the information we secretly obtain through these intercepted codes. They contribute greatly to the victory and tremendously to the saving in American lives, both in the conduct of the current operations and in looking towards the early termination of the war.

"What in hell do Jap codes have to do with Eisenhower?" asked Dewey. Clarke then told him of the breaking of the German Enigma cipher.[82]

Dewey's two conversations with Clarke strongly suggest that he had intended to denounce Roosevelt for disregarding a clear intelligence warning of the Japanese attack on Pearl Harbor. But for Marshall's intervention, FDR's use of SIGINT would probably have emerged as the most controversial issue in his last electoral campaign. Five months after Roosevelt's reelection for a record fourth term Dewey and Marshall met for the first time at his funeral. Soon afterward Marshall invited Dewey to the Pentagon, where he briefed him on the codebreakers' contribution to victory.[83]

Roosevelt's sudden death on April 12, 1945, left the postwar fate of the intelligence community, which had expanded so rapidly since the outbreak of war, unresolved. Since the autumn of 1944 Donovan had been campaigning for the establishment of a peacetime intelligence system based, he told Roosevelt, on "the establishment of a central authority reporting directly to you, with responsibility to frame intelligence objectives and to collect and coordinate the intelligence material required by the Executive Branch in planning and carrying out national policy and strategy."[84] Opposition to the scheme was led by the service intelligence chiefs and the FBI, who suspected Donovan of empire building at their expense. Roosevelt showed himself, once again, reluctant to take sides in the new round of turf battles within the intelligence community.

As Donovan pondered the future role of U.S. peacetime intelligence, his mind, unlike the president's, was already turning to intelligence operations against the Soviet Union. Though Donovan did not know it, the Russians were well supplied with agents in both the United States and Britain, some of them in OSS. Neither the Americans nor the British, by contrast, had a single agent of any significance in Moscow. In November 1944, however, Donovan made one breakthrough of great potential importance by purchasing from the Finns a partially charred, captured code book of the NKVD (predecessor of the KGB). He did so without informing Hull's successor as secretary of state, Edward Stettinius, who apparently continued to believe that gentlemen should not read their allies' mail. Though Donovan informed the president that he had purchased code books from the Finns, he seems not to have told him that they were Soviet codes. Alarm bells quickly began ringing at the NKVD stations in Washington and New York. The NKVD courier, Elizabeth Bentley, said later that she was warned by one of the agent networks in Washington that "the Americans were on the verge of breaking the Soviet code." Stettinius also discovered that Donovan had purchased the NKVD code book. Two days before Christmas 1944 he protested in person to the president. According to Stettinius, Roosevelt instructed him "to see that the Russians were informed on this matter at once" and to report to the White House "exactly what has been done."[85]

To Donovan's chagrin, he was forced to comply. He made an unconvincing attempt to persuade the head of NKVD foreign intelligence, General Pavel Mikhailovich Fitin, that he had acted as "a loyal ally," obtaining the Soviet code book from the Finns only to prevent it from falling into hostile hands:

> General Donovan would like General Fitin to know that we have made no study of this material and he, therefore, cannot positively state its value but has acted on the assumption that this is a matter of real importance to the Russian Government.

It was indeed. Fitin sent Donovan his "sincere thanks" for his assistance in what he described as "this very essential business." At his request, the charred code book was handed over personally to the Soviet ambassador in Washington.[86] Fitin was not, of course, deceived by Donovan's high-minded display of loyal cooperation, though he must have been surprised by the naïveté of Roosevelt and Stettinius. The NKVD would never have considered returning captured U.S. codes. Donovan, however, concealed from the president what Fitin doubtless suspected: that, when returning the original NKVD code book, he kept a copy. Several years later that copy was to prove of crucial importance in identifying wartime Soviet agents in both the United States and Britain.[87]

Shortly after returning the NKVD code book to the Russians, Donovan began sending Roosevelt OSS reports from Rome (code-named Vessel) on secret Vatican discussions with the Japanese concerning the possibility of a negotiated peace. Since the president had been warned by his chiefs of staff that an invasion of the Japanese homeland might cost a million U.S. casualties, evidence of weakening Japanese resolve was of the highest importance. According to a Vessel report of January 17:

> On 10 January the Japanese Emperor attended a secret council meeting during which someone dared to speak about peace feelers. The Emperor was informed that certain Japanese individuals have

been attempting to interest [the Pope] in mediating the Pacific War. The Emperor did not express any disapproval of these efforts.

Other reports included transcripts of alleged discussions between the Vatican's acting secretary of state, Cardinal Montini (the future Pope Paul VI), and the Japanese minister to the Holy See, who was quoted as saying that "it is urgent His Holiness come to our assistance before the Big Three meet to discuss Japan [at Yalta], and [that] this mediation be in full swing at the time." Roosevelt's secretary, Grace Tully, told Donovan, "The President finds this material most interesting and reads every one carefully." By early February, however, Roosevelt must have changed his mind—not least because of the reports' inaccurate statements about him. According to a Vessel report of February 2, "A very important White House spokesman advised the Apostolic Delegate to Washington that he could tell the Holy See that President Roosevelt will take account of all the Pope's communications, especially concerning Poland and spheres of influence, at the 'Big Three' conference." Roosevelt knew that report to be wholly untrue. OSS was probably informed accordingly. Early in March Donovan, to his considerable embarrassment, was forced to acknowledge that the Vessel reports were complete fabrications.

In addition to the unpublicized humiliation of the Vessel case, Donovan also had to contend with a hostile press campaign. On February 9 the Washington *Times-Herald*, the New York *Daily News* and the Chicago *Tribune* denounced his still-classified proposal for a postwar intelligence system as a plan for a "super Gestapo agency" that would spy on "good neighbors throughout the world," "pry into the lives of citizens at home," and use "secret funds for spy work along the lines of bribing and luxury living described in the novels of E. Phillips Oppenheim." The author of all three articles was a Washington journalist close to J. Edgar Hoover, whom Donovan suspected of inspiring the press campaign. It is equally possible that the culprit came from military intelligence. Donovan complained to the president that the press attack was "'an inside job' or at least, it was abetted by someone on the inside."[88]

Donovan's ambitious plan for postwar intelligence reorganization had failed to capture the president's imagination. FDR gave him no support during the press campaign against his proposed "super Gestapo agency." Burdened by declining health and overwork during the closing stages of the conquest of Germany, Roosevelt let matters drift. He remained committed, however, to some reform of the postwar intelligence community. "At the end of this war," he had said in January 1945, "there simply must be a consolidation of Foreign Intelligence between

State and War and the Navy."[89] On April 5, only a week before his death, Roosevelt sent Donovan a memorandum drafted for him by one of his advisers:

> Apropos of your memorandum of November 18, 1944, relative to the establishment of a central intelligence agency, I should appreciate your calling together the chiefs of the foreign intelligence and internal security units in the various executive agencies, so that a consensus of opinion can be secured.[90]

Given Roosevelt's haphazard approach to interdepartmental coordination, it is unlikely, had he lived, that he would have acted swiftly and decisively to create a central intelligence agency. But it is difficult to believe either that he would simply have closed down OSS after victory over Japan or that he would have excluded Donovan from any role in the postwar intelligence community. His successor, Harry Truman, did both.

CHAPTER 5

Harry S. Truman
(1945-1953)

On April 12, 1945, Harry Truman became, at the age of sixty, the oldest vice-president to become president until the election of George Bush in 1989. "Boys," he told reporters the next day, "if you ever pray, pray for me now. I don't know whether you fellows ever had a load of hay fall on you, but when they told me yesterday what happened, I felt like the moon, the stars, and all the planets had fallen on me."[1] During his three months as Roosevelt's last vice-president, Truman had been kept in ignorance by the White House of most affairs of state. Of all the areas of government, intelligence was probably the one about which he knew least. In November 1952, as his own presidency was drawing to a close, Truman was careful to assure CIA staff that his successor, Dwight D. Eisenhower, would not arrive in the White House as poorly briefed as he had been. "I am giving this President—this new President," he declared, "more information than any other President ever had when he went into office."[2]

Though Truman began work in the Oval Office after breakfast on April 13, 1945, he and Bess Truman did not move into the White House until May 7, the eve of V-E (Victory in Europe) Day. Twenty army trucks were required to move the Roosevelts' possessions out, only one to move the Trumans' in.[3] By the time he took up residence, the new president had been "indoctrinated" into the two greatest secrets of modern warfare: the atomic bomb and Ultra. At the end of his first cabinet meeting on the evening of April 12, only a few hours after Roosevelt's death, Stimson stayed behind and talked briefly to Truman "about an immense project that was under way—a project looking to the development of a new explosive of almost unbelievable destructive power." Truman was so stunned by the events of the day that the briefing about the bomb did not at first sink in. Only when he was given more details the next day did he begin to grasp "the awful power that might soon be placed in our hands." Even then, Truman was probably not fully convinced. Leahy, who stayed on as chief of staff, told him, "This is the biggest fool thing we have ever done. The bomb will never go off, and I speak as an expert in explosives."[4]

As chairman of the wartime Senate Committee to Investigate the National Defense Program, Truman had long been aware that an important top-secret project was under way, but, at Stimson's request, had agreed not to investigate what he later discovered were atomic plants. Stimson noted in his diary that the Truman committee was "as mild as milk."[5] When Truman was briefed on the Manhattan Project to develop the atomic bomb during his first days in the Oval Office, he described it as "a miracle" that the secret had been successfully preserved from Congress.[6] His last doubts about the Manhattan Project seem to have dissolved on April 25 when Stimson brought the project director, Major General Leslie Groves, to brief him. They left the president a detailed memorandum that contained the heart-stopping sentence: "Within four months we shall in all probability have completed the most terrible weapon ever known in human history, one bomb of which could destroy a whole city."[7] Truman told the next member of his staff to enter the Oval Office, "I am going to have to make a decision which no man in history has ever had to make. I'll make the decision, but it is terrifying to think about what I will have to decide."[8] Though awed by his office and the scale of the decisions that awaited him, Truman was equal to them. Stimson, initially uncertain whether the new president could cope, was quickly won over by his no-nonsense manner. It was, he told his diary, "a wonderful relief . . . to see the promptness and snappiness with which Truman took up each matter and decided it."[9]

Truman's initiation into the Ultra secret came a few days later than his briefing on the atomic bomb—partly because his military aide, Colonel (later Brigadier General) Harry H. Vaughan, an extrovert poker-playing crony from Missouri and a former comrade-in-arms of the president during the First World War, was not at first trusted with SIGINT. Outside his new White House office, Vaughan hung the relaxed notice: ENJOY YOURSELF—IT'S LATER THAN YOU THINK. His door was always open. When there were minor mixups, Truman's staff would joke, "Cherchez le Vaughan." Vaughan seemed happy to join in the laughter.[10] There was understandable anxiety at the thought of briefing him on the biggest intelligence secret of the war. The White House map room log for

April 17 records, "Only Ad[miral] Brown and Col. [Richard] Park [FDR's naval and military aides] see the Army ULTRA material delivered to the Map Room if anyone should inquire." The log for the same day also notes the arrival of a message marked, "For President's Eyes Only," which map room staff were instructed to place in Truman's folder, "but under no circumstances to open."[11] The message was from General Marshall and contained an introduction to Ultra, together with two SIGINT summaries. Marshall informed Truman that the intelligence on Germany came from "a purely British source, which incidentally involves some 30,000 people, and we have bound ourselves to confine its circulation to a specific and very limited group of people. Therefore I request that this be 'For Your Eyes Only.'"[12]

Truman regarded Marshall as "the greatest living American."[13] But, as with his first briefing on the atomic bomb, he seems not to have grasped immediately the full significance of Marshall's explanation of Ultra. Truman did not pay his first visit to the map room, which housed SIGINT and other top-secret material, until he had been president for a week. On the afternoon of April 19 he went with Vaughan on a tour of inspection and was shown how the positions of the Japanese fleet were plotted twice a day with the assistance of SIGINT. Truman seemed more interested, however, in the position of the USS *Missouri*, named for his home state, and in the movements in Germany of the 35th Division, in which he had served during the First World War, and of his nephew's division, the 44th.[14] As he received further briefings on Ultra from Marshall and from his naval and military aides (henceforth cleared for SIGINT), however, he began to grasp the dramatic contribution of SIGINT in shortening the war against both Germany and Japan. Marshall doubtless repeated to Truman what he had told Dewey during the election campaign, that Ultra was vital both to Eisenhower as Allied commander in chief in Europe and to "all operations in the Pacific."[15] Truman later described in his memoirs his amazement at discovering the secrets of the Manhattan Project. But Ultra remained so highly classified for the rest of his life that he was never able to put on record his reaction to it—an omission not so far rectified by his biographers. In August 1945 Truman issued an executive order prohibiting public release, "except with the specific approval of the President in each case," of any "information regarding the past or present status, technique or procedure, degree of success attained, or specific results of any cryptanalytic unit acting under the authority of the U.S. Government or any Department thereof."[16]

SIGINT gave Truman a dramatic insight into the last days of the Third Reich and, more importantly, into the final four months of the

Pacific war. Among the first decrypts shown to him (possibly in summary form) was a report to Tokyo from the Japanese Vice Admiral Hiroaki Abe in Berlin on his attempts to arrange the transfer of German naval forces to the Far East to assist the Japanese war effort when they became unable to operate in Europe. On April 17 Ribbentrop told Abe that though his proposal would be put to the Führer, Hitler would almost certainly be too busy to see him. "Even I," said Ribbentrop, "have not seen him for over a month." On April 19 Abe cabled Tokyo that Hitler had agreed to give the Japanese proposal further consideration in the "unlikely" event of Germany being unable to continue the fight in Europe. The next day, however, Admiral Karl Dönitz told Abe that Germany's shortage of fuel would make it impossible to transfer more than, at most, two or three large U-boats to Japan. After Hitler's suicide on April 30 secret messages from Tokyo, decrypted in Washington, instructed Japanese missions abroad to emphasize Japan's "infallible preparedness, . . . despite the defeat of her ally," to repulse any Allied attack.[17]

At the end of April the head of Bletchley Park, Sir Edward Travis; his assistant Harry Hinsley; and Commander Clive Loehnis of the Admiralty Operational Intelligence Centre arrived in Washington with proposals for the peacetime continuation of Anglo-American SIGINT collaboration.[18] They began separate talks with the army, navy, and state departments, then held a series of meetings with representatives of all three. By comparison with his last visit to negotiate the BRUSA agreement two years earlier, Hinsley felt that interservice tension "wasn't so bad this time. They'd sunk some of their differences and they knew what each other was doing." The Anglo-American negotiations agreed on the principle of, and a broad framework for, postwar collaboration.[19] Marshall and King were already persuaded of the need for an Anglo-American attack on Soviet codes and ciphers.[20] The proposal for peacetime SIGINT collaboration does not seem to have been put to Truman, however, until after victory over Japan.

On July 13, while Truman was traveling to Potsdam for his first meeting with Stalin and Churchill, intercepted Japanese telegrams revealed that Tokyo was seeking Soviet mediation in an attempt to persuade Washington to moderate its demand for unconditional surrender. Tokyo was unaware that Stalin had secretly promised his Western allies to declare war on Japan three months after the defeat of Germany. On July 15, however, Naotake Sato, the Japanese ambassador in Moscow, told Tokyo that its request for Soviet mediation betrayed a "lack of reality." Sato telegraphed on July 24 that Japan was "entirely alone and friendless," and had no option but to surrender on any terms available.

Tokyo, however, replied that unconditional surrender was out of the question and that Japan must fight on.[21]

A few hours after Truman arrived in Potsdam on July 16, he learned that the first atomic bomb had been successfully tested in the New Mexican desert. When Japan rejected the Big Three's "Potsdam Declaration," calling on it to surrender, he had little hesitation in approving the use of the bomb. The conquest of Okinawa, a narrow Japanese island only sixty miles long, had required almost three months and forty thousand American casualties. Truman's conviction that the invasion of the Japanese main islands would be far bloodier was strengthened by intelligence reports that Allied forces would have to confront at least seventy Japanese divisions and home defense forces of over eight million men.[22] Before Truman gave the final go-ahead on July 31 for the bombing of Hiroshima, however, he must surely have reflected that, had Germany still been in the war, it rather than Japan would probably have been the first target for the atomic bomb. And, given what Marshall and others had told him about Ultra's dramatic role in hastening Germany's defeat, he may also have concluded that SIGINT had saved Europe from becoming the birthplace of nuclear warfare.

Truman was returning to the United States from Europe aboard the USS *Augusta* when he heard the news of the destruction of Hiroshima on August 6. His first reaction was a sense of relief that the bomb had worked rather than of foreboding that the nuclear age had dawned. "This is the greatest thing in history," he told the crew of the *Augusta*.[23] Over the next week Magic allowed the president to follow what SIGINT summaries called "Japan's surrender maneuvers" as its warlords struggled to avoid the humiliation of unconditional surrender.[24] According to George Elsey, one of the map room staff who dealt with SIGINT, the Magic intercepts reporting Japanese peace moves were shown to the president almost as soon as they were decrypted.[25]

Immediately after Hiroshima, Magic revealed a further Japanese attempt to seek Soviet mediation. On August 7 Tokyo instructed Ambassador Sato in Moscow to use "still greater efforts to get a reply from them in haste." Sato replied that the Soviet foreign minister, Vyacheslav Molotov, had agreed to meet him next day. At the meeting, however, instead of discussing mediation, Molotov handed Sato a formal declaration of war that came into effect on August 9, the day on which a second atomic bomb obliterated Nagasaki. Magic did not disclose that at a meeting of Japan's six-man Supreme War Council on August 9 three members supported Foreign Minister Shigenori Togo's proposal to surrender, provided Emperor Hirohito's position was safeguarded, while three wanted to continue the war. "Would it not be wondrous for this whole nation to be destroyed like a beautiful flower?" asked the war minister. Nor did Magic disclose the emperor's decision in the early hours of August 10 that "We must bear the unbearable," followed by the war council's acceptance of Togo's proposal.[26] SIGINT did, however, reveal the sequel. At 8:47 A.M. (Japanese time) on August 10, Tokyo sent cables to the Japanese legations in the neutral capitals of Berne and Stockholm for onward transmission to the Allied governments, agreeing to surrender provided the "prerogatives" of the emperor were preserved. Truman learned of the Japanese decision from Magic even before he received official notification.

The reply to the Japanese message, drafted by Truman's secretary of state, James F. Byrnes, and approved by the Allies, declared:

> From the moment of surrender, the authority of the Emperor and the Japanese Government to rule the State shall be subject to the Supreme Commander of the Allied powers who will take such steps as he deems proper to effectuate the surrender terms.

SIGINT revealed the outraged reactions of a number of Japanese warlords. The commander of the China Expeditionary Force protested in one decrypted message, "Such a disgrace as the surrender of several million troops without fighting is not paralleled in the world's military history." A Magic summary concluded:

> With regards to leaders of the Army and Navy, there seems little doubt that many of the former and some of the latter, though knowing that the war was lost, would have followed blindly the code that (as one of them said) "required them to die for the Emperor but not to live for him." It is . . . probable that others who voiced equally vehement protests against capitulation did so merely to satisfy their professional pride.[27]

Though outwardly composed, Truman waited with bated breath on Sunday, August 12, and Monday, August 13, for the Japanese reply to the message on surrender terms drafted by Byrnes. SIGINT summaries on August 13 reported worrying signs of "a probable attempt for an all-out banzai [suicide] attack" by the Japanese.[28] On the morning of Tuesday, August 14, newsmen in Berne reported that the Japanese legation had received a lengthy message from Tokyo. "That," Truman believed, "should be the answer we were waiting for."[29] The cryptanalysts, however, quickly dashed the president's hopes. A Magic summary described the Japanese message as "one of the finest pieces of irony of the war." It said not a word about the surrender terms. Instead, it demanded the exemplary punishment of the U.S. submarine commander responsible for sinking the Japanese hospital ship *Awa Maru*, and attached an itemized claim for damages totaling 227,286,000 yen, together with a demand for prompt payment by the United States. (A sarcastic note on the Magic summary observed that no claim was made for the munitions being carried by the hospital ship.)[30]

While the Japanese Foreign Ministry was cabling its indignant claim for damages, the emperor summoned an imperial council, called on his ministers to "bow to our wishes and accept the Allied reply forthwith," and announced his intention to make an unprecedented broadcast to the nation. The news reached the White House on the afternoon of August 14. "At three o'clock," Truman wrote later in his memoirs, "Byrnes informed me that he had just learned that a code message was then being received in Berne from Tokyo." Though Truman could not say so in his memoirs, the first confirmation that Japan had accepted the Allies' surrender terms probably came from Magic. At 6 P.M. Japan's formal acceptance of the terms was delivered by the Swiss chargé d'affaires in Washington to Byrnes, who immediately took it to the White House. At 7 P.M. Truman read the Japanese message to newspaper correspondents gathered in the Oval Office, then went outside to acknowledge the cheers of the crowd, and made what he described as "a V sign in the manner of Churchill." As the crowds continued to grow and the noise of automobile horns echoed across Washington, the president returned to the north portico of the White House and made a short speech through a loudspeaker. "This is the day," he declared, "when Fascism and police government cease in the world."[31]

The contrast with Hirohito's address to the Japanese people the next day could scarcely have been greater. The dignity of the divine emperor would not allow him to speak live over the air. Instead, Japanese Radio broadcast a message recorded by Hirohito in a court dialect incomprehensible to most of his subjects. Truman probably first read the text of the speech in Magic decrypts of Japanese diplomatic circulars. "My subjects," the emperor loftily concluded, "let us carry forward the glory of our national structure and let us not lag behind in the progress of the world. Submit ye to Our Will!" A decrypt of a message from the navy minister to the Japanese fleet revealed the emperor's decisive role at the imperial council on August 14. "We who were present," said the navy minister, "fully realized the extent of his determination and could not hold back the tears which welled up."[32] The war minister committed *seppuku*, ritual suicide. His example was followed by a number of generals and admirals, and by the plotters of an unsuccessful coup who wished to continue the war.

Truman's speech at the moment of victory on the ending of "police government" reflected not merely his hatred of fascism but also a confused suspicion of peacetime intelligence agencies, which he was apt to liken to "Gestapos." SIGINT, however, bothered him much less than HUMINT. Though he understood little about the technical mysteries of Ultra and Magic, Marshall's briefings and his own experience of SIGINT during the most dramatic months of his life persuaded him of its importance. Truman took an entirely different view of the OSS. If he did not already associate Donovan's plan for postwar intelligence reorganization with the vague idea of an American "Gestapo" before the press attacks of February 1945, he undoubtedly did so afterward. That confused association of ideas was powerfully reinforced by a hostile report on OSS prepared by Colonel Richard Park, who had become Roosevelt's military aide after the sudden death of Pa Watson in February 1945. Park presented his report to Truman shortly before leaving the White House at the end of April. Some sections of OSS, Park concluded, "can and should be salvaged. It has performed some excellent sabotage and rescue work. Its Research and Analysis section has done an outstanding job." Overall, however, Park's verdict was a damning one:

> Poor organization, lack of training and selection of many incompetent personnel has resulted in many badly conceived, overlapping and unauthorized activities with resulting embarrassment to the State Department and interference with other secret intelligence agencies of this government. General MacArthur even refuses to allow the O.S.S. to operate in his theater. . . . If the O.S.S. is investigated after the war it may easily prove to have been the most expensive and wasteful agency of the government.

Among alleged examples of waste, Park cited a program run by four highly paid doctors at the Congressional Country Club in Virginia to study the "psychopathic" effects of heavy alcohol consumption; information from "reliable banking sources" that OSS in Turkey was spending $20,000 to $30,000 a month on "parties and entertainment'; a report that an OSS party in Bombay had been "a real orgy" ("source reports that no work was performed at the office for the following three days"); and the failure of schemes costing millions of dollars to produce improved weapons and communication systems. Park dismissed out of hand Donovan's plan for postwar intelligence reorganization: "There have been suggestions that this proposal was motivated by his personal ambitions. It has all the earmarks of a Gestapo scheme."[33]

If Truman read and believed only part of Park's report, the fate of

OSS must have been effectively sealed by the end of his first month in office. The fact that MacArthur refused to allow OSS to operate in much of the Pacific meant that Donovan had no successes to report during the final stages of the war against Japan comparable with the heroic exploits that had assisted the D-Day landings a year earlier. Donovan succeeded in seeing Truman for a total of only about half an hour. On April 30 he asked for a meeting with the president to discuss Roosevelt's request that he consult the rest of the intelligence community "to consider a plan for a Central Intelligence Agency."[34] Truman saw him for a quarter of an hour on the morning of May 14, noting sarcastically afterward that Donovan had explained "how important the Secret Service [sic] is and how much he could do to run the government on an even basis."[35] A renewed press campaign in May, almost certainly fueled by the leaking of the Park report, accused OSS of being "scarcely more than an arm of the British Intelligence Service," planning for war with Russia, and using its secret funds for purchases "ranging from whiskey to real estate and radio stations." *Newsweek* claimed that when Truman's Committee to Investigate the National Defense Program had been dissuaded from investigating OSS funds on the grounds that it would interfere with wartime operations, he had vowed to "see to it that the practices were aired after V-E Day." If true, the story may help to explain some of Truman's evident personal dislike of Donovan. Truman saw Donovan briefly on June 16 (their last meeting before the end of the Pacific war), on the eve of Donovan's departure for the Nuremberg war crimes trials, for which OSS provided some of the evidence.[36] Donovan had not quite given up attempting to impress the president with OSS's achievements. During Donovan's absence in Europe, his deputy sent Truman a memorandum that began optimistically, "I believe you will be interested in a review of OSS operations in Switzerland." He went on to describe the setting up of agent networks leading from Switzerland into France, Germany, Austria, and Italy; intelligence obtained on the attempt on Hitler's life in July 1944; the development of the V-1 and V-2 rockets and the midget tank; the classified German documents obtained by the Wood operation; support for partisans in France, Italy, and Austria; and the OSS role as intermediary in the surrender of the German armies in Northern Italy.[37] Truman gave no sign of being impressed.

Truman was also unhappy with the wartime growth in FBI powers, complaining to his aides that Hoover, like Donovan, seemed to want "to set up a gestapo." The budget bureau director, Harold D. Smith, told Truman in May 1945 that he thought it "not altogether appropriate" for the FBI "to be spending federal funds merely to satisfy curiosity concerning the sex life of Washington bureaucrats and members of

Congress." "The President," he noted, "seemed to agree heartily." Truman was also unhappy about FBI activities in Latin America. They would, he told Smith, make it difficult "to complain very much when they send their intelligence people in the United States." According to Smith, the president repeated "with considerable vigor that he was 'very much against building up a gestapo.'"[38]

Though suspicious of Hoover, however, Truman also depended on him for intelligence about disgruntled liberal Democrats and White House staff whom he suspected of leaks to the media. Hoover submitted his first report on disaffected liberals as early as April 23. Truman's military aide, Colonel Vaughan, told Hoover that the president had read it "with much interest": "Future communications along that line would be of considerable interest whenever in your opinion they are necessary." Among the first to have his phone tapped under the Truman administration was Edward Pritchard, an aide to one of the president's political advisers. On May 8 the FBI recorded a conversation between Pritchard and Supreme Court Justice Felix Frankfurter, during which they discussed leaking stories to the celebrated columnist Drew Pearson. A White House aide told the FBI:

> . . . Upon reading the technical log [wiretap transcript] the President commented that in some ways it was comical (meaning that a Justice would engage in such juvenile conversations), whereas with reference to the major portion of it he stated that it is "the damnedest thing I have read."[39]

During the first few weeks of the Truman administration Hoover thus successfully deployed two forms of intelligence that, though usually of little importance, seduced in varying degree every president under whom he served: inside information on the foibles (or worse) of public figures and evidence of leaks by White House staff.

Truman preferred to keep Hoover himself at arm's length. He allegedly rebuffed one early overture from the director of the FBI by informing his emissary, "Anytime I need the services of the FBI, I will ask for it through my Attorney General."[40] Hoover came to feel personally slighted by the president. According to Drew Pearson, "He hated Truman and almost everyone around him."[41] Hoover was also outraged by a highly critical study of the bureau published in 1950 by the president's close friend, Max Lowenthal. Truman felt far less passionately than Lowenthal. He would listen patiently to Lowenthal's diatribes against Hoover and the FBI, then, as soon as his friend had left, laugh and say, "Oh, Max is that way."[42]

Though Truman wished to cut back FBI operations at the end of the war, it did not occur to him to abolish the bureau. OSS was in a much weaker position. Unlike the bureau and the service intelligence organizations, it had been founded as a wartime agency and lacked the support in either the White House or Congress necessary to ensure its postwar survival. By the end of the Pacific war, Donovan had accepted the demise of the OSS as inevitable. On August 25 he informed the budget director that "the liquidation of OSS" should be complete by the end of the year, and urged on him "the necessity of designating an agency to take over its functions and assets." Simultaneously Donovan sent Truman a "Statement of Principles which I believe should govern the establishment of a central intelligence agency." The statement was perhaps the most succinct and persuasive case thus far put to any president for the establishment of a centralized, peacetime intelligence system in the United States:

> The formulation of national policy both in its political and military aspects is influenced and determined by knowledge (or ignorance) of the aims, capabilities, intentions and policies of other nations.
>
> All major powers except the United States have had for a long time past permanent worldwide intelligence services, reporting directly to the highest echelons of their Governments. Prior to the present war, the United States had no foreign secret intelligence service. It never has had and does not now have a coordinated intelligence system.

Donovan proposed that each department of government should have its own "intelligence bureau" to serve its individual needs; that a "national foreign intelligence agency" should collate intelligence from these bureaus bearing on the national interest and collect further intelligence as required; and that the new agency should be "administered under Presidential direction." He asked Truman for a meeting to discuss his proposals before he returned to the Nuremberg war crimes trials two weeks later.[13] The president failed to respond.

Donovan did not give up. He inspired a major press campaign celebrating OSS exploits under headlines such as 4,000 STRANDED FLIERS RESCUED BY OSS UNDERGROUND RAILWAY and CAPITAL AX FALLING ON OUR PRICELESS SECRET SPY SYSTEM. Simultaneously Donovan continued his private attempts to persuade Truman to keep OSS's "secret spy system" as part of the postwar intelligence community by emphasizing the (in fact, illusory) threat from a continuing Nazi intelligence network. On September 4, for example, he wrote to the president, "From Spain we learn through our representatives that every effort is being made in that country by German representatives to maintain a German espionage organization."[44] During the final weeks of OSS's life, Donovan also sought to persuade Truman of the importance of its liaison with the British Secret Intelligence Service (SIS), and of the danger of losing access to British intelligence. In August 1945 SIS supplied seventy-six intelligence reports to the OSS mission in London. OSS was enthusiastic about their quality. SIS reports on Greece were rated "excellent," those from Italy and Siam "of special interest," those from Austria "of considerable interest," and one from Yugoslavia "most interesting." The last OSS report from London in September 1945 concluded, "There has been a marked step-up in the importance as well as an expansion in coverage in the reports received from Broadway [SIS headquarters] in the course of our normal exchange."[45] Donovan also emphasized the potential importance of intelligence collaboration with Nationalist China. He reported to Truman on September 4 after a discussion with the Chinese ambassador:

> It was clear that he wanted our help in watching the situation in Korea and Manchuria. He suggested a working arrangement intelligence wise—with a postwar [U.S.] intelligence agency maintaining liaison with them in China and exchanging information with them on the Far Eastern area.[46]

Truman's mind was already made up against the establishment of a postwar foreign intelligence agency. The flood of material that he received from Donovan, and failed to acknowledge, seems, however, to have increased his embarrassment at closing down OSS. Executive Order 9621, which wound up OSS, was drafted by Donald Stone, assistant to Budget Director Harold Smith, without his consulting Donovan, the Joint Chiefs of Staff, or the rest of the intelligence community. Truman signed it on September 20, together with a formal letter, also drafted by Stone, thanking Donovan for his wartime services. Smith tried to persuade the president that he should at least receive Donovan at the White House to thank him personally. Truman, however, could not bring himself to do so. Smith thereupon ordered Stone to hand the executive order and the letter of thanks to Donovan himself. "'The President doesn't want to do it and I don't want to do it," he told Stone, "but . . . I'm ordering you to do it." "When I delivered the documents," Stone later recalled, "Donovan took it with a kind of stoic grace. He knew it was coming, but he gave no outward indication of the personal hurt he felt by the manner in which he was informed."[47] Executive Order 9621 gave the R&A section of OSS to the State Department and transferred the espionage and counterespionage elements to the army as a new Strategic Services Unit (SSU). Neither group received much of a welcome. Though State was allocated 1,655 OSS personnel, it sought funds for only 800 to 900 of them. The director of the SSU, General John Magruder, resigned in January 1946 in protest at military indifference to his unit.[48]

Some of Truman's biographers record his decision to close down OSS on September 20. None, however, mentions that just over a week earlier he had made the even more important decision to secure the peacetime future of SIGINT. Marshall and King agreed on the need to continue wartime SIGINT collaboration, and in particular to join with the British in a cryptanalytic attack on Soviet codes and ciphers. Though no record survives of what they told the president, their views almost certainly echoed those of Colonel McCormack, the main architect of SIGINT reorganization after Pearl Harbor:

> My personal opinion is that there is no field of intelligence in which it is so essential that [the] British and ourselves work closely together. . . . The Russians themselves go after intelligence by any means and from any source that may be available. If I had the responsibility for talking to a Russian G-2, I would not hesitate to tell him that information about his country, army, air forces, etc., are important to the rest of the world, and that we intend to work on it as hard as possible.[49]

On September 4, as part of the postwar reorganization of army SIGINT, all military communications and cryptanalysis were brought under the control of a newly created Army Security Agency (ASA). On September 12 Henry Stimson (who was shortly to retire as secretary of war), James Forrestal (who had succeeded Knox as secretary of the navy), and Dean Acheson (acting secretary of state in the absence of Byrnes), jointly submitted to Truman a top-secret memorandum (still only partly declassified) reminding him of "the outstanding contributions to the success of the Allied forces in defeating Germany and Japan" made by Allied cryptanalysts:

> Not only were many military and naval victories of the Allies made possible by learning the plans and intentions of the enemy, but also much important diplomatic and economic information, otherwise unobtainable, was furnished to cognizant authorities.
>   . . . In view of the disturbed conditions of the world and the necessity of keeping informed of technical developments and possible hostile intentions of foreign nations, [*two lines censored*] it

is recommended that you authorize continuation of collaboration between the United States and the United Kingdom in the field of communications intelligence.[50]

One of the still-classified passages in this fifty-year-old memorandum probably refers to the importance of Allied collaboration in breaking Soviet ciphers.

Truman acted promptly on the recommendation submitted to him. On September 12 he signed a top-secret one-sentence memorandum, which became the cornerstone for an unprecedented—and still unique—peacetime intelligence alliance:

The Secretary of War and the Secretary of the Navy are hereby authorized to direct the Chief of Staff, U.S. Army and the Commander in Chief, U.S. Fleet, and Chief of Naval Operations to continue collaboration in the field of communication intelligence between the United States Army and Navy and the British, and to extend, modify or discontinue this collaboration, as determined to be in the best interests of the United States.[51]

Four days later, on September 16, the Combined (Anglo-American) chiefs of staff ordered that "All temptation to divulge the Ultra Secret must be resisted. The present and future best interests of our countries demand it." Ultra was expected to continue providing intelligence on the defeated enemy powers and on the underground resistance that it was feared might emerge in Germany and Japan. The main reason, however, for preserving the Ultra secret was to avoid putting "our future enemies on their guard" by revealing past SIGINT successes.[52] Unknown to Truman and his advisers, these successes had already been revealed to Moscow by its moles in London and Washington.[53]

Truman's memorandum of September 12, 1945, made possible the creation of a global SIGINT network including Canada and Australasia as well as the United States and the British Empire. A few weeks later, Travis, Hinsley, and Group Captain Eric Jones (later director-general of the postwar British SIGINT agency, GCHQ, from 1952 to 1960) visited Washington to continue negotiations on peacetime collaboration.[54] They established the principle that an agreement should be drawn up for collaboration "on a national basis" between Britain and the United States, and not, as in the case of the wartime accords, on a "departmental basis" involving separate agreements with the army and navy. The British delegation then traveled to Ottawa to discuss Canadian participation in the postwar SIGINT alliance.[55] Commander Edward "Teddy" Poulden went on a similar mission from Bletchley Park to Australia; he later became head of the postwar Australian SIGINT agency, the Defence Signals Bureau.[56]

A top-secret Anglo-American SIGINT conference to settle the details of collaboration met in London for most of February and March 1946. The British were given authority by Ottawa and Canberra to negotiate on their behalf. Attended by top brass from both sides of the Atlantic, the conference was chaired by Sir Stewart Menzies, chief of the Secret Intelligence Service, who also had overall responsibility for British SIG-INT. When particular negotiating difficulties arose, Menzies adopted the technique of taking those concerned to lunch at the Ritz Hotel, followed by talks in his office in the more accommodating atmosphere usually engendered by the lunch. The conference produced a still-classified agreement of about twenty-five pages, which seemed at the time to have settled all outstanding details of SIGINT collaboration between the United States and the British Commonwealth.[57]

The March 1946 agreement was not, in fact, the final text of the peacetime Anglo-American SIGINT accord. Further negotiations (all still classified) followed at intervals for the next two years to deal with problems that included Commonwealth reorganization after Indian independence and the start of the Cold War. The final text, the UKUSA agreement, whose existence has never been officially acknowledged, was not signed until June 1948.[58] But the postwar Anglo-American SIGINT alliance was already firmly in place in March 1946. During the Truman administration, as during the war, the alliance between British and American SIGINT agencies functioned more smoothly than intelligence collaboration between the United States armed services. Though the UKUSA agreement was made possible by Truman's decision to approve postwar SIGINT collaboration, it is unlikely that he took more than a passing interest in its negotiation.

Because of his inexperience in foreign policy, Truman leaned heavily at first on his secretary of state, Byrnes. It was to Byrnes that he turned on September 20, the day that he abolished OSS, for guidance on foreign intelligence:

> I particularly desire that you take the lead in developing a comprehensive and coordinated foreign intelligence program for all Federal agencies concerned with that type of activity. This should be done through the creation of an interdepartmental group, heading up under the State Department, which would formulate plans for my approval.[59]

The Byrnes directive, like the executive order closing down OSS and the letter to Donovan, was drafted for Truman by the Budget Bureau. As he signed it, the president remarked that he had "in mind a different kind of intelligence service from what this country had in the past."[60] He was clearly confused about what he wanted. Truman's main priority was probably for a more orderly system of providing him with intelligence reports; he later complained in his memoirs about the confusion that prevailed when he became president. But he remained anxious to avoid "under any guise or for any reason" anything that resembled his vague notion of "a Gestapo."[61]

Byrnes had neither the interest in, nor the understanding of, intelligence to take the lead for which Truman had hoped. Many of his officials were, in any case, deeply suspicious of the idea of a centralized intelligence system that might poach on State Department territory.[62] The Byrnes directive thus provoked a new round of turf battles. The army, the navy, the State Department, and the FBI were agreed only in a common desire to protect their departmental prerogatives from outside interference. By the end of 1945 the confusion was worse than that which Truman had inherited from Roosevelt. The map room, which had acted as the main coordinating center for intelligence distribution in the wartime White House, was dismantled soon after the surrender of Japan. Truman also began to resent Byrnes's habit of conducting foreign policy with little reference to the White House.[63]

The eventual outcome of the bureaucratic wrangling over the future of peacetime intelligence was a compromise plan, embodied in a presidential directive of January 22, 1946, establishing a National Intelligence Authority (NIA) composed of the secretaries of state, war, and the navy, with Leahy representing the president. The NIA was to "plan, develop and coordinate . . . all Federal intelligence activities." Truman's directive also established the post of director of central intelligence (DCI), who was to attend the NIA as a nonvoting member and direct the work of a new Central Intelligence Group (CIG), a small analytical agency set up to collate and process intelligence collected by the rest of the intelligence community. The chief architect of this reorganization, Rear Admiral Sidney W. Souers, agreed to Truman's request that he become the first DCI on condition that he serve for no longer than six months.[64] Relieved to have found at last an apparent solution to the thorny problem of intelligence reorganization, Truman celebrated the occasion with a notably eccentric White House lunch. The president solemnly presented his guests with black cloaks, black hats, and wooden daggers, then called Leahy forward and stuck a large black mustache on his upper lip. Souers, Truman announced, was to become "Director of Centralized Snooping."[65]

As this comic ritual indicates, Truman still did not take the idea of

American peacetime espionage entirely seriously. What he hoped for from the CIG was help in coping with the daily deluge of sometimes contradictory cables, dispatches, and reports on the complex problems of the outside world. His lack of experience in international affairs increased his frustration at the problems of making sense of the paper mountain on his desk. He told Souers that what he needed was "a digest every day, a summary of the dispatches flowing from the various departments, either from State to our ambassadors or from the Navy and War departments to their forces abroad, wherever such messages might have some influence on our foreign policy." A blazing row followed between Souers and Byrnes. Souers asked for State Department cables to incorporate in the daily digest. Byrnes refused, on the grounds that it was his responsibility alone to inform the president of the cables' contents. Truman, however, sided with Souers, and Byrnes was forced to hand the cables over.[66] Thus was born the so-called daily summary: forerunner of the president's daily brief, which, since the 1960s, has usually been one of the first documents seen by the president each day. According to one of its early assistant editors, R. Jack Smith (later CIA deputy director for intelligence), "It seemed almost that the only CIG activity President Truman deemed important was the daily summary." Its first editor was the former radio newsman, Merritt Ruddock, who impressed Smith with his "boundless zest and unremitting playfulness . . . in the midst of an organizational chaos that made the operation resemble that of a circus wild-animal trainer working without benefit of cage, chair or whip." The frequent battles between analysts over what to include in the daily summary usually revolved around the question, "Is this important enough to be brought to President Truman's attention?" CIG was told that Truman frequently asked, "Where's my newspaper?" but never learned what particularly he wished to read in it.[67] Unlike the later presidents' daily briefs, the summaries did not make "estimates" or forecasts. These, Smith noted, were "contrary to the President's request."[68]

On June 10, 1946, Souers was succeeded as DCI, on his own recommendation, by the strikingly handsome forty-seven-year-old war hero, Army Air Force Lieutenant General Hoyt S. Vandenberg, later named by Marilyn Monroe as one of the three men she would most like to be marooned with on a desert island.[69] Within the CIG, Vandenberg was given the nickname "Sparkplug." He was visibly anxious to make his mark quickly and use the post of DCI as a stepping-stone in his air force career. On July 16 the well-known columnist Arthur Krock published an article entitled "The President's Secret 'Newspaper,'" based on secret briefings by Vandenberg and Truman's special counsel, Clark Clifford (formerly his naval aide). Krock began dramatically:

At eight fifteen every weekday morning a typewritten sheet or two is handed to the President which, in the opinion of his intimate staff, makes him the best-informed Chief Executive in history on foreign affairs. The paper is an integration of topmost secret reports made to the State, War and Navy Departments by their several intelligence groups throughout the world and is prepared by a central staff headed by Lieut. Gen. Hoyt S. Vandenberg.[70]

Clifford's assistant, George M. Elsey, formerly a member of the map room staff, privately considered the article a skillful piece of news management by Vandenberg but "a very great exaggeration. The morning summary is not an 'evaluated' job at all; it is just a synopsis of army, navy & state dispatches."[71] In one important respect the CIG lagged behind the wartime map room, which had had access to Ultra and Magic. For security reasons, CIG and early CIA daily summaries were not allowed to incorporate SIGINT. Only the most senior officials were allowed to inspect intercepts in secure rooms. The analysts preparing the daily summary had no direct access to SIGINT, though they were sometimes informed if the contents of the summary were at variance with the evidence of the intercepts. On his first day as assistant editor, R. Jack Smith observed a SIGINT analyst approach Ruddock, the editor, whisper something rapidly in his ear, and then depart. Smith said he had failed to catch a single word. "You know something?" Ruddock replied. "I didn't either!"[72] The armed services also refused to provide what they regarded as operational documents for inclusion in the daily summary. Smith complained in 1950:

> Under this guise, they have withheld from CIA such sensitive materials as General MacArthur's reports from Tokyo, General Clay's reports from Berlin, Admiral Struble's reports from the Seventh Fleet, Admiral Badger's reports from Tsingtao, General Van Fleet's reports from Athens, etc. CIA does not receive reports made to the Joint Chiefs, many of which, because of their origin and their subject, must be worthy of the President's attention.[73]

Just as Truman found it hard to accept the idea of American peacetime espionage, so he also had difficulty in facing up to the fact of Soviet agent penetration of the United States. In November 1945 the former NKVD courier Elizabeth Bentley began revealing to the FBI her extensive knowledge of intelligence operations in Washington and New York. Her defection led the FBI to investigate seriously for the first time Whittaker Chambers's earlier evidence of prewar Soviet espionage. Further intelligence was provided by a Soviet cipher clerk, Igor Guzenko, who had defected in Ottawa in September. Though the corroboration necessary to secure the conviction of most of the agents identified by Bentley and Chambers was lacking, Moscow continued to fear for several years that the FBI would uncover sufficient evidence for a major spy trial. Of those named by Bentley and Chambers, however, only Alger Hiss was ever prosecuted; in 1950 he was sentenced to five years' imprisonment for perjury.[74]

On November 8, 1945, Hoover began sending Truman a series of reports that "a number of persons employed by the Government" had been passing information to Soviet intelligence. The most senior member of the Truman administration named by Hoover was Harry Dexter White, assistant to Secretary of the Treasury Fred M. Vinson. Hoover repeated the charges against White on November 27. Truman seems simply to have passed the reports to Vinson and to have given them no further thought when Vinson failed to take them seriously. On January 23, 1946, at Vinson's recommendation but to the outrage of Hoover, Truman nominated White as first executive director of the International Monetary Fund. Hoover responded on February 4 with a twenty-eight-page review of the case against White, based on evidence from thirty allegedly reliable sources. Truman had paid so little attention to the previous reports on White that this was the first report he could later recall receiving. On February 6 the Senate confirmed White's nomination to the International Monetary Fund. Byrnes, who had been sent a copy of Hoover's report of February 4, suggested three possible courses of action to Truman: that he ask a senator to move the reconsideration of the nomination; that he withhold the presidential commission from White; or that he summon White and confront him with Hoover's report. Truman turned down all three. He seems to have given the matter no further thought. When White resigned from the IMF a year later, the president sent him a courteous farewell letter. White died in 1948, soon after being publicly identified by Elizabeth Bentley as a former Soviet spy.[75]

In the summer of 1946 Truman gave way to pressure from the Justice Department to authorize wiretapping and bugging of "persons suspected of subversive activities against the Government of the United States, including suspected spies." On July 17 Attorney General Tom Clark (later privately condemned by Truman as "My biggest mistake . . . about the dumbest man I think I've ever run across") sent him a memorandum, drafted by Hoover, reminding him that Roosevelt had approved electronic surveillance in 1940:

It seems to me that in the present troubled period in international affairs, accompanied as it is by an increase in subversive activity

here at home, it is as necessary as it was in 1940 to take the
investigative measures referred to in President Roosevelt's memorandum.

Truman wrote, "I concur" at the foot of the memorandum, believing that
he was simply continuing a practice authorized by his predecessor. In
fact he was extending it. When quoting Roosevelt's memorandum,
Hoover had deliberately omitted the final sentence instructing the FBI
to limit electronic surveillance "insofar as possible to aliens." Truman's
authorization contained no such restriction.[76]

In 1947 the Cold War began in earnest. On March 12 Truman
appeared before a joint session of Congress, asked for $400 million to
help save Greece and Turkey from the Communist threat, and pronounced what became known as the Truman Doctrine: "I believe that it
must be the policy of the United States to support free peoples who are
resisting attempted subjugation by armed minorities or by outside pressures." "Containment" of the Soviet threat became for the next forty
years the basis of American foreign policy. On March 21 Truman issued
Executive Order 9835, establishing an "Employee Loyalty Program" for
more than two million federal workers: an unprecedented peacetime
attempt to give the United States "maximum protection . . . against infiltration of disloyal persons into the ranks of its employees." "I am not
worried about the Communist Party taking over the government of the
United States," Truman declared, "but I am against a person, whose
loyalty is not to the government of the United States, holding a government job." To avoid adding dramatically to Hoover's power, Truman
asked Congress to allocate two-thirds of the budget for the loyalty
investigations to the Civil Service Commission and only one-third to
the FBI. Congress, however, reversed the proportions and gave two-
thirds to Hoover. After conducting an unsuccessful rearguard action,
Truman reluctantly agreed in November that all loyalty investigations
should be conducted by the bureau. According to Clark Clifford, the
president thought the threat of Communist infiltration of the administration was "a lot of baloney. But political pressures were such that he
had to recognize it."[77]

The onset of the Cold War also led to the transformation of the CIG.
In July 1946, less than a month after becoming DCI, Vandenberg had
proposed legislation to establish an independent central intelligence
agency, unfettered by the control exercised over the CIG by the departments of state, war, and the navy. George Elsey noted on July 17 after a
White House meeting attended by him, Clifford, and two senior members of the CIG:

After lengthy discussion, it was agreed by all present that the original concept of the Central Intelligence Group should now be altered; experience had shown that it would be ineffective if it remained only a small planning staff and that it must now become a legally established, fairly sizeable, operating agency.[78]

Truman agreed. According to Clifford, "he felt he had given the CIG concept a fair test and that it had failed."[79] Fifteen months after becoming president, Truman at last accepted, without enthusiasm, the case for a foreign espionage agency. His first priority, however, was to persuade the armed services to agree to the creation of a single Department of Defense. "We must never fight another war the way we fought the last two," he told Clifford. "I have the feeling that, if the Army and the Navy had fought our enemies as hard as they fought each other, the war would have ended much earlier." Truman was determined not to compromise the complicated negotiations to establish the Department of Defense by a premature effort to centralize foreign intelligence.[80]

Vandenberg, however, was equally determined to press ahead. While Clifford was still considering the wording of future legislation, he succeeded in giving the CIG an operational role by founding the Office of Special Operations (OSO) to collect foreign intelligence.[81] A proposal for the establishment of a central intelligence agency was included in early drafts of Truman's State of the Union message of January 1947, but was withdrawn at the last moment.[82] When Vandenberg protested the omission, Clifford told him in a stormy meeting that "the war between the Army and the Navy" had to be settled first.[83] On February 26, 1947, with interservice warfare now reduced to minor skirmishes, a bill was sent to Congress that, with some amendments, became law on July 26 as the National Security Act. "For the first time in the history of the nation," Truman wrote proudly in his memoirs, "an over-all military establishment was created."[84] Though the army, navy, and newly established U.S. Air Force retained executive departments with their own secretaries, they were brought together under the umbrella of a new Department of Defense.

The act also created the National Security Council (NSC), intended by Truman as "the place in the government where military, diplomatic, and resources problems could be studied and continually appraised." Truman persuaded Souers, "as a personal favor," to return from private business to become the NSC's first executive secretary.[85] The act also established, under NSC "direction," the Central Intelligence Agency (CIA), "for the purpose of coordinating the intelligence activities of the several Government departments and agencies in the interest of national security." The director of the CIA held the additional title of director of central intelligence (DCI) with, in principle but never fully in practice, authority over the rest of the foreign intelligence community.

In May 1947 Vandenberg left CIG to return to the Army Air Force. On the foundation of the independent U.S. Air Force four months later, he became, at the age of only forty-eight, the second youngest American ever to reach the rank of full general. Only Ulysses S. Grant had been more rapidly promoted. Vandenberg's far less dynamic successor as DCI, Rear Admiral Roscoe H. Hillenkoetter, was the first, and probably the weakest, director of the CIA. "Hilly" had not wanted the job that was thrust upon him. He lacked both the drive and the political clout required to discharge the DCI's responsibility to coordinate intelligence analysis and the intelligence community. "In the hierarchical maze of official Washington," writes R. Jack Smith, "his authority scarcely extended beyond the front door."[86] Few, if any, of the officials who saw Truman even half as frequently as Hillenkoetter made so little impression on him. Hilly was frequently Truman's first caller of the day, bringing with him the president's daily summary. During these almost daily meetings, however, Hilly acted as little more than messenger. He is the only DCI of the Truman presidency not mentioned by name in Truman's memoirs. When Hillenkoetter delivered the summary, he was accompanied first by Leahy, then from 1949 by Leahy's successor as chief of staff, Admiral Souers, who was given the additional title of special assistant to the president for intelligence.[87] Hilly's influence on Truman did not compare with that of either Leahy or Souers. The president seems to have regarded him as a friendly and modest lightweight with much to be modest about. A note prepared for Truman at the end of Hillenkoetter's term as DCI singled out as his most striking "personal attributes":

1. Extreme modesty and self-effacing devotion to duty.
2. Friendliness and good will in his dealings with other members of the team [of] which he was a member.
3. Patience and forbearance in the face of difficult but unavoidable problems arising from his task of coordinating the national intelligence effort.

When Hilly, to his relief, returned to sea in October 1950, Truman wrote him a cheery and appropriately banal letter of farewell, which concluded, "So I say to you as you return to active service with the Navy: Well done."[88] It is inconceivable that Eisenhower, or any other president who attached a higher value to intelligence than Truman, would have been content to be served for three years by such a nondescript, though genial, DCI.

"I never had any thought when I set up the CIA," claimed Truman in retirement, "that it would be injected into peacetime cloak and dagger operations."[89] It is hard to imagine Truman authorizing the landing in the Bay of Pigs or the other operations to dispose of Fidel Castro approved by his successors. But it is equally difficult to take at face value his later attempts to disclaim all responsibility for covert action. The original role assigned to the CIA by the National Security Act included, in addition to intelligence collection and analysis, "such other functions and duties related to intelligence affecting the national security as the National Security Council may from time to time direct." Clark Clifford later testified that this studiously vague formula was intended to include covert operations, albeit of "limited scope and purpose": "We did not mention them by name because we felt it would be injurious to our national interest to advertise the fact that we might engage in such activities."[90] When Truman later tried to deny any responsibility for "peacetime cloak and dagger operations," Allen Dulles (DCI from 1953 to 1961) privately reminded him of his own "very important part" in its origins.[91] Dulles wrote to the agency general counsel:

I . . . reviewed with Mr. Truman the part he had had in supplementing the overt Truman Doctrine affecting Greece and Turkey with the procedures largely implemented by CIA to meet the creeping subversion of communism, which could not be met by open intervention, [or] military aid, under the Truman plan. I reviewed the various covert steps which had been taken under his authority in suppressing the Huk rebellion in the Philippines, of the problems we had faced during the Italian elections in 1948, and outlined in some detail the various points raised in the memorandum furnished me by Cord Meyer [on other covert action]. Mr. Truman followed all this with keen interest, interjected reminiscences of his own, recalled vividly the whole Italian election problem, as well as the Huk situation. . . . At no time did Mr. Truman express other than complete agreement with the viewpoint I expressed. . . .[92]

The earliest covert action authorized by Truman, for which he later tried to evade any personal responsibility, was prompted by fear of a Communist victory in the Italian elections of April 1948. The first numbered document issued by the National Security Council, NSC 1/1 of November 14, 1947, warned, "The Italian Government, ideologically inclined toward Western democracy, is weak and is being subjected to continuous attack by a strong Communist Party." The NSC recommended, in addition to public support for the beleaguered Italian government, a program to "Actively combat Communist propaganda in Italy by an effective U.S. information program and by all other practicable means, including the use of unvouchered funds." Truman approved NSC 1/1 on November 24. He also directed, on the recommendation of the NSC, that Marshall, who had succeeded Byrnes as secretary of state at the beginning of the year, coordinate "psychological warfare" against the Communists in Italy.[93] Marshall, however, feared that his "Marshall Plan" for the economic regeneration of postwar Europe would be gravely compromised if the State Department were discovered to be involved in covert action. To meet his objections, Truman signed NSC 4/A on December 14, giving responsibility for psychological warfare to the CIA. A week later, the agency set up the Special Procedures Group (SPG), which laundered over $10 million from captured Axis funds for use in the Italian election campaign.[94] Hillenkoetter accepted his new covert action responsibilities with great reluctance but, as usual, without complaint.[95]

Some of the SPG's laundered millions were secretly handed over to the Italian prime minister, Alcide de Gasperi, to help finance the campaign of his Christian Democratic party. Other millions went on media campaigns to spread black propaganda against the Communists and extol the virtues of their opponents. Truman took a personal interest in both overt and covert attempts to support the Christian Democrats and defeat the Communists. One evening he summoned the secretary of agriculture, Clinton P. Anderson, and told him to "get more wheat to Italy." Anderson immediately diverted several shiploads then en route for Latin America. Once unloaded at Italian ports, the redirected wheat was distributed in cars and trucks festooned with the stars and stripes by Christian Democrat politicians—many of them, according to Anderson, "in American pay." Despite equally active Soviet involvement in the elections, the Christian Democrats won 307 of the 574 seats.[96] Truman sent Hillenkoetter his personal congratulations.[97]

The actual influence of CIA "psychological warfare" on the outcome of the Italian elections remains impossible to estimate. The apparent success of covert action against the Communists, however, led to its rapid expansion. In May 1948 George Kennan, head of the State Department planning staff and the leading apostle of containment, proposed the creation of a permanent covert action group able to engage in far more than psychological warfare.[98] A month later, "taking cognizance of the vicious covert activities of the USSR, its satellite countries and Communist groups to discredit and defeat the aims and activities of the United States and other western powers," Truman signed NSC 10/2, ordering the creation within the CIA of an office to plan and engage in:

propaganda; economic warfare; preventive direct action, including sabotage, anti-sabotage, demolition and evacuation measures; subversion against hostile states, including assistance to underground resistance movements, guerillas and refugee liberation groups, and support of indigenous anti-communist elements in threatened countries of the free world.

NSC 10/2 also formally adopted the principle of "plausible deniability." Contrary to the maxim prominently displayed on Truman's desk, the buck—as far as covert action was concerned—was not to reach the Oval Office. Covert operations, Truman ordered, were to be "so planned and executed that any U.S. Government responsibility for them is not evident to unauthorized persons and that if uncovered the U.S. Government can plausibly disclaim any responsibility for them."[99] So far from being, as he later claimed, entirely opposed to "peacetime cloak and dagger operations," Truman was the first president to found a peacetime covert action agency. In August 1948 he approved NSC 20, authorizing guerrilla operations behind the Iron Curtain using Soviet émigrés recruited in the West. The preface to NSC 20, drafted by Kennan, claimed optimistically that, though "it is not our peacetime aim to overthrow the Soviet Government," covert action could create "circumstances and situations" that would make it difficult for the "present Soviet leaders . . . to retain their power in Russia."[100]

The founding of a covert action section within the CIA, soon given the blandly misleading title Office of Policy Coordination (OPC), caused immediate administrative confusion, due in about equal measure to the traditional Washington turf battles and to Hillenkoetter's lack of authority. The director of OPC, Frank Wisner, former OSS station chief in Romania, was appointed not by the DCI but by the secretary of state, and took instructions from the State Department and the Department of Defense. Administratively, OPC remained entirely distinct within the CIA both from the intelligence collectors of the Office of Special Operations (OSO) and from the analysts of the Office of Reports and Estimates (ORE).[101] In the autumn of 1948 Truman appointed a three-man committee, chaired by Allen Dulles, to investigate the CIA. Its report to the NSC on January 1, 1949, contained a devastating criticism of Hillenkoetter's leadership:

The principal defect of the Central Intelligence Agency is that its direction, administrative organization and performance do not show sufficient appreciation of the Agency's assigned functions, particularly in the fields of intelligence coordination and the production of intelligence estimates. The result has been that the Central Intelligence Agency has tended to become just one more intelligence agency producing intelligence in competition with older established agencies of the Government departments. Since it is the task of the Director to see that the Agency carries out its assigned functions, the failure to do so is necessarily a reflection of inadequacies of direction.[102]

The "inadequacies of direction," however, were as much Truman's as Hillenkoetter's. Hilly was heavily outgunned on the NSC by the secretaries of both state and defense. Without the strong support of the president, he could not hope to fulfill the task of intelligence coordination required of the DCI.

During the summer of 1948 the dramatic rift between the Soviet Union and Marshal Tito's Communist regime in Yugoslavia seemed to offer new opportunities for covert action to weaken the Soviet bloc. The image of a monolithic Communist empire was so firmly rooted in Washington that Tito's breach with Moscow took both the CIA and the State Department by surprise.[103] At first there was speculation that the breach was purely temporary; some even argued that it was a ruse to deceive the West. Within a few months, however, few doubted the reality of Stalin's quarrel with Tito. Franklin Lindsay of OPC, a former OSS officer who had been head of the wartime U.S. military mission to Tito, made secret contact with the Yugoslav representative to the United Nations, Ales Bebler, whom he had known as a partisan leader during the war. Secret discussions continued in 1949 between Lindsay; Vladimir Velebit, deputy Yugoslav foreign minister; and Robert Joyce of the State Department, on ways in which the United States could help Tito withstand the Soviet invasion that he feared was imminent. The open delivery of American arms, Tito believed, might give Stalin a pretext to attack. Truman therefore approved five secret shipments of arms to Yugoslavia. Thereafter Tito felt strong enough to accept open military and economic aid from the United States, which was to total more than a billion dollars over the next decade.[104]

Truman had few illusions about Tito himself. In December 1949 he signed NSC 58/2, which concluded:

> The best we can hope from Tito is crafty self-interest in playing both sides, similar to that practiced by Franco in his relations with the Axis and the Allies during the last year of the war. Uncongenial as such a relationship may be, it is far less inimical to us and other nations of good will than a Yugoslavia cemented into the Soviet monolith.

Truman also approved a long-term program of covert action designed to encourage the emergence of further Titos in Eastern Europe by spreading "communist heresy among the satellite states":

> . . . The United States should attempt, by methods short of war, to disrupt the Soviet-satellite relationship and bring about the gradual reduction and eventual elimination of preponderant soviet power in Eastern Europe.

In the short term, however, the NSC recognized that no other Soviet satellite was likely to follow the Yugoslav example.[105]

For much of his presidency, Truman remained confused about the nature and extent of the Communist threat within the United States. The problem for the president at the time, as for historians since, was to distinguish the reality of Soviet espionage from the anti-Communist paranoia generated by the Cold War. It is now clear that both the actual expansion of Soviet espionage in the United States during the Second World War and the mythical expansion of postwar Communist subversion were on a remarkable scale. The unscrupulous exploitation of the Red Menace during the presidential and congressional election campaigns of 1948 increased the difficulties of distinguishing myth from reality. Truman did not trust what he believed were the alarmist reports on Soviet espionage provided by Hoover and the FBI. Hoover, however, had so successfully established himself as a national institution that the president could not bring himself to take the political risks of replacing him. Truman reacted with understandable anger to Republican attempts to use the evidence of Soviet espionage to suggest that his administration was prey to Communist subversion. That anger, like his suspicion of Hoover, clouded his judgment.

In August 1948, at the beginning of a presidential campaign that most pundits confidently expected Truman to lose, the former NKVD couriers, Whittaker Chambers and Elizabeth Bentley, testified to the House Committee on Un-American Activities (HUAC) that the Roosevelt administration had been infiltrated by Communists, among them Alger Hiss, who still had high-ranking Democratic friends. Truman smelled a Republican rat. At a press conference on August 5 he unwisely allowed a reporter to put words into his mouth. "Mr. President," he was asked, "do you think that the Capitol Hill spy scare is a 'red herring' to divert public attention from inflation?" Truman gave the reporter the headline he had been hoping for. "Yes, I do," he replied.[106] Secretly unhappy at the excessive zeal of the loyalty program, Truman showed little interest in raking over the confused and controversial past history of Soviet penetration of Washington. Significantly, in over twelve hundred pages of presidential memoirs, he made no mention of Hiss, White, and their principal accusers, Bentley and Chambers. Nor did he make any reference to the Rosenbergs and the atom spies.

Truman's confused and reluctant response to the problems of Soviet espionage and Communist subversion did him little damage during his unexpectedly victorious election campaign. Senator Joseph McCarthy had not yet discovered the Red Menace as a means of advancing his disreputable career. Truman's opponent, Dewey, confident of victory, also avoided Red-baiting. With some help from the Democrats, anti-Communist fire was concentrated instead on the third-party candidate, Henry A. Wallace, who had actually been endorsed by the Communists. Soon after Truman's election victory, however, the public controversy over Soviet espionage flared up again. At a HUAC hearing on November 17, Chambers produced about seventy pages of documents, four of them in Hiss's handwriting, that appeared to provide evidence of prewar Soviet espionage. Chambers then revealed that he had hidden away other espionage documents. On December 2 he led two HUAC investigators to a pumpkin patch on his Maryland farm, removed the top from one of the pumpkins, and extracted two strips of developed film and three canisters containing undeveloped reels. The discovery of the "Pumpkin Papers" made headline news across the nation. Hoover was outraged not to have been given advance warning, and composed a curious haiku-like protest note:

> What are the facts?
> Was there any pumpkin
> involved at all?
> H

Truman remained unrepentant after the discovery of the Pumpkin Papers. When asked at a press conference a week later whether he still considered the HUAC investigation "a red herring," he replied, "I do." The statute of limitations made it impossible to charge Hiss with espionage. But on December 15, 1948, he was indicted by a grand jury on two counts of perjury for denying passing documents to Chambers, among them some of the Pumpkin Papers. Justice Department officials were forced to hold a press conference to deny charges that the Truman administration had tried to prevent Hiss's indictment. At least one HUAC member, Representative Richard M. Nixon, grasped the potential political advantages to be extracted from Truman's apparent indifference to

Soviet-inspired subversion. "Rather than the herring on the hook," said Nixon, "I think that Mr. Truman is on the hook."[107]

Truman knew, at the beginning of his second term, that within a few years the American nuclear monopoly would be at an end, and that the Soviet Union would have the atomic bomb. Intelligence reports, however, underestimated the speed of Soviet atomic development. Hillenkoetter informed him in July 1948:

> On the basis of the information in our possession, it is estimated that the earliest date by which it is remotely possible that the USSR may have completed its first atomic bomb is mid-1950, but the most probable date is believed to be mid-1953.[108]

Within a few months a Long Range Detection Program had been established to monitor air samples over the North Pacific for signs of Soviet atomic tests. For over a year nothing was discovered. Dean Acheson, who succeeded Marshall as secretary of state at the beginning of Truman's second term, reported in July 1949 that "the best intelligence estimates available indicated that the Soviets might have a bomb by mid-1951."[105] On September 3 a WB-29 weather reconnaissance aircraft of the Long Range Detection Program flying at eighteen thousand feet over the North Atlantic picked up abnormally high levels of radiation on a litmus paper. Over the next week the U.S. Air Force and the Royal Air Force together tracked the radioactivity as it was blown by high-altitude winds over North America and across the Atlantic toward the United Kingdom. The mounting evidence pointing to the successful explosion of a Soviet atomic bomb between August 26 and 29 was reported regularly to Truman in his daily summary. He later claimed in his memoirs that, after an expert committee had reviewed the scientific intelligence gathered by the Long Range Detection Program, "There was no room for doubt." In reality, Truman was at first skeptical of the highly technical intelligence assessments submitted to him. His doubts, however, seem to have been resolved after a meeting on September 21 with the former DCI, General Hoyt Vandenberg, who as air force chief of staff was responsible for running the detection program.[110] Against the advice of Acheson and other advisers, Truman courageously decided to make the intelligence finding public. He announced on the morning of September 23:

> I believe the American people, to the fullest extent consistent with national security, are entitled to be informed of all developments in the field of atomic energy. That is my reason for making public the

following information. We have evidence that within recent weeks an atomic explosion occurred in the USSR.[111]

The shock caused by the Soviet Union's sudden emergence as a nuclear superpower was heightened by the triumph of Communism in the most populous state on earth. On September 21, 1949, Mao Zedong proclaimed the establishment of the People's Republic of China.

Almost simultaneously ASA, the army SIGINT agency, began providing dramatic secret evidence that the Soviet atomic program had been accelerated by wartime espionage in the United States. The crucial breakthrough was made by Meredith Gardner, a brilliant though introverted ASA cryptanalyst, who had belatedly identified a breach of cipher security in NKVD cables sent in 1944–45. During the last year of the war the sheer volume of intelligence telegraphed to the "Center" (NKVD, later KGB, headquarters) in Moscow by NKVD cipher clerks in the United States had led to the use of "one-time pads"of cipher additives more than once, thus making vulnerable a normally unbreakable cipher system. During 1948, with the help of a copy of the NKVD code book purchased by Donovan from the Finns four years earlier as well as the plain-text versions of some of the ciphered NKVD messages obtained by the FBI, Gardner began to decrypt some fragments of the cables of 1944–45. Initially his progress was painfully slow. Over the next few years, however, several thousand Soviet telegrams (code-named Venona) were decrypted in whole or part. In September 1949 Gardner solved an NKVD message containing intelligence from the Manhattan Project. According to Robert Lamphere, an FBI counterespionage specialist studying the Venona decrypts, ". . . It became immediately obvious to me that the Russians had indeed stolen crucial research from us, and had undoubtedly used it to build their bomb." By the time Truman announced that the Soviet Union possessed the atomic bomb, Lamphere had identified the author of a top-secret scientific report summarized in the decrypted NKVD cable as Klaus Fuchs, a British scientist who had worked on the Manhattan Project.[112]

Fuchs's interrogation began in Britain in December, but was complicated by the need to conceal from him the existence of the Soviet decrypts that had led to his discovery. On January 24, 1951, however, he began to confess. The next day, in New York, Alger Hiss was sentenced to five years' imprisonment for perjury in denying espionage charges before a grand jury. Nixon promptly attacked the Truman administration for dereliction of duty in failing to investigate Hiss's involvement in a Communist conspiracy. "Then," wrote Acheson later, "a bomb exploded in London." Truman had been aware for the past four months that the "bomb" was likely to detonate, but its explosion could scarcely have been worse-timed. On February 2 Fuchs was formally charged in London, and the menace of Soviet atomic espionage burst onto the front pages of the American press. Senator Homer E. Capehart declared that there were other spies like Fuchs, "and there will continue to be as long as we have a president who refers to such matters as 'red herrings' . . ." Thus began what Acheson called "The Attack of the Primitives."[113]

The leading "Primitive" was the hitherto little-known Wisconsin Senator, Joseph R. McCarthy. On February 9, in Wheeling, West Virginia, he flourished a paper that, he falsely claimed, contained a list of 205 Communists in the State Department who were "shaping its policy." By the time he returned to Washington, McCarthy had somewhat pruned his imaginary list. In a telegram to Truman on February 11 he declared, "I have in my possession the names of 57 Communists who are in the State Department at present." McCarthy demanded that Truman hand over to Congress full reports by the Loyalty Security Board on all those in the State Department with "communistic connections": "Failure on your part will label the Democrats of being the bedfellow of international Communism." "There was," Truman told a press conference on February 16, "not a word of truth in what the Senator said."[114]

The president had good reason to claim six weeks later that "the greatest asset that the Kremlin has is Senator McCarthy." McCarthy did far more for the Soviet cause than any agent of influence the KGB ever had. His self-serving crusade against the Red Menace and wild, if newsworthy, exaggerations made liberal opinion around the world skeptical of the reality of the Soviet intelligence offensive against what Moscow Center privately called its "main adversary," the United States. Nothing Truman could have done would have prevented the emergence of McCarthyism. As late as January 1954 opinion polls found 50 percent of Americans with a favorable view of McCarthy and only 29 percent opposed to him. McCarthy won mass support because he succeeded in tapping a popular chord. To many Americans the idea of "an enemy within," given plausibility by the convictions of Hiss and Fuchs, helped to explain why, despite its immense power, the United States seemed unable to stem the onward march of world Communism, the Soviet acquisition of atomic weapons, and the "fall" of China. Yet Truman did not handle McCarthyism well. On the one hand, he promoted a loyalty program that claimed a number of innocent victims in its purge of potential subversives. On the other hand, he sometimes seemed publicly skeptical of the reality, or at least the significance, of Soviet intelligence operations against the United States. Truman's unwillingness to say anything at all in his lengthy memoirs about the major espionage cases that figure in all histories of his presidency bears witness to his continuing confusion about them. He tended to focus on the exploitation of them by his political opponents rather than on the underlying reality of the Soviet intelligence offensive. A decade after his retirement Truman said in response to an interviewer's question about Hiss, "They didn't come up with any proof. That's the way I felt about it at the time anyway."[115] It is not certain that this was Truman's opinion in January 1950. Richard Nixon claimed to have learned from reliable White House sources that Truman told one of his aides:

> Of course, Hiss is guilty. But that damn committee [HUAC] isn't interested in that. All it cares about is politics, and as long as they try to make politics out of this communist issue, I am going to label their activities for what they are—a 'red herring.'[116]

Nixon's evidence is partisan, but not wholly implausible.

McCarthyism could have been even worse. Despite briefings by Hoover, Nixon, and others, McCarthy's understanding of both Communism and intelligence operations remained superficial. He once amazed his briefers by claiming never to have heard of Earl Browder, former head of the U.S. Communist party.[117] Had he paid more attention to the Pearl Harbor investigations, McCarthy might have asked himself if the administration had failed to heed the warnings of a Soviet Magic about the espionage offensive against the United States. McCarthy, however, failed to discover, or even to suspect the existence of, the Venona secret. By the time McCarthyism began, the NKVD decrypts were steadily producing clues, some clear, others cryptic, to the identities of wartime Soviet agents in the United States.[118] Even if SIGINT had not been regarded as too secret to use in legal proceedings, the NKVD decrypts would not have constituted adequate evidence in a court of law. But they would have furnished McCarthy with plentiful, powerful, and confusing ammunition. The Truman administration's inevitable reluctance to produce Venona, had McCarthy discovered its existence, could easily have been presented as part of another White House cover-up. It is unlikely that McCarthy, like Dewey, would have been constrained by considerations of the national interest in his use of SIGINT to attack a Democratic administration.

Ironically, neither McCarthy nor Nixon ever discovered one of the espionage cases that would have caused most embarrassment to the Truman administration. In 1946 the MGB (forerunner of the KGB) had recruited a cipher clerk named William Weisband working in ASA. Two years later he betrayed the Venona secret to his Soviet controller. Weis-

Above: The first U.S. intelligence chief, George Washington, states the case for an American intelligence service in a letter to Col. Elias Dayton, July 26, 1777:

The necessity of procuring good Intelligence is apparent & need not be further urged—All that remains for me to add is, that you keep the whole matter as secret as possible. For upon Secrecy, Success depends in most Enterprizes of the kind, and for want of it, they are generally defeated, however well planned & promising a favourable issue.

At right: Almost two centuries later, President Kennedy thanks DCI Allen Dulles for sending him a copy of Washington's letter; JFK had asked for a copy after seeing the original displayed in a CIA exhibition.

(Both letters courtesy of the Walter Pforzheimer Collection on Intelligence Service, Washington, D.C.)

THE WHITE HOUSE
WASHINGTON

February 10, 1961

Dear Allen:

I want to thank you for sending to me a photostat of General Washington's letter to Colonel Dayton.

I hope you will extend to Mr. Pforzheimer my thanks for the letter and the permission he has granted for its use. It is both a fine memento of my visit with you and a continuing reminder of the role of intelligence in national policy.

With every good wish,

Sincerely,

Honorable Allen W. Dulles
Director
Central Intelligence Agency
Washington 25, D. C.

Left: As British intelligence chief in the United States from 1916 to 1919, Sir William Wiseman gained better access to President Wilson than most of Wilson's cabinet. *Below:* Unknown to Wilson, before the United States entered the war, Wiseman supervised a number of covert operations designed to discredit the Germans: among them the publication of this apparently compromising photo of the German ambassador, Count von Bernstorff. *(Both courtesy of Rhodri Jeffreys-Jones)*

Right: As head of British Security Coordination during the Second World War, Sir William Stephenson played a major part in creating the Anglo-American special intelligence relationship. In 1941, however, he planted a number of anti-German forgeries on an unsuspecting President Roosevelt in the hope of hastening American entry into the war.

Below: Among them was this bogus map of German designs in South America, which FDR used as the basis of a major speech. *(Both courtesy of William H. Stevenson)*

From OSS to CIA.

Left: Gen. William "Wild Bill" Donovan, chosen by President Roosevelt as coordinator of information in 1941 and as head of the Office of Strategic Services in 1942.

Below: The OSS memorial and Donovan's statue in the lobby of today's CIA headquarters. *(Both courtesy of the Central Intelligence Agency)*

IN HONOR OF THOSE MEMBERS
OF THE OFFICE OF STRATEGIC SERVICES
WHO GAVE THEIR LIVES IN THE SERVICE OF THEIR COUNTRY

MAJOR GENERAL
WILLIAM J. DONOVAN

DIRECTOR
OFFICE OF STRATEGIC SERVICES
FORERUNNER OF THE
CENTRAL INTELLIGENCE AGENCY

Right: Seal of the CIA, with President Harry S. Truman's signature. *(Courtesy of the Walter Pforzheimer Collection on Intelligence Service, Washington, D.C.)*

Left: Truman and Gen. Walter Bedell "Beetle" Smith (Director of Central Intelligence, 1950–53) survey the globe in the Oval Office. *(Courtesy of the CIA Center for the Study of Intelligence)*

Dwight D. Eisenhower and IMINT (imagery intelligence).

Left: Elliott Roosevelt, son of FDR, briefs Ike on aerial reconnaissance photos in North Africa during Operation Torch (late 1942). *(Courtesy of Dwight D. Eisenhower Presidential Library)*

Below: Eisenhower displays U-2 photography in public for the first time during a TV broadcast after the shootdown of a U-2 over Russia in 1960. *(Courtesy of the National Park Service and the Dwight D. Eisenhower Presidential Library)*

Richard Bissell *(second from left)*, CIA Deputy Director for Plans
responsible for overseeing the highly successful U-2 program and the
disastrous Bay of Pigs operation, receives the National Security
Medal from President Kennedy in April 1962. On the left is the outgoing
DCI, Allen Dulles; on the right, his successor, John McCone.
(Courtesy of the Central Intelligence Agency)

Left: Soviet Colonel Oleg Penkovsky, probably the most important Western spy of the Cold War; President Kennedy was kept regularly informed about his activities. *(Courtesy of the Central Intelligence Agency)*

Below: At the suggestion of his brother Robert, Kennedy unwisely used the KGB officer Georgi Bolshakov *(second from right)* as a backchannel to Moscow. JFK later concluded that he had been "deceived" by Bolshakov. *(Courtesy of UPI/Bettman)*

band's treachery was discovered in 1950. Though he was sentenced to a year's imprisonment for failing to answer a summons to appear before a grand jury, he was never prosecuted for espionage. The decision not to prosecute seems to have been made, at least in part, to avoid the embarrassment of a trial that, even if held mostly *in camera*, would have risked revealing one of the most closely guarded U.S. intelligence secrets. Weisband, however, was not the only Western agent to reveal the Venona secret to the MGB. In October 1949 Kim Philby, later identified as one of the most successful of all Soviet agents, arrived in Washington as British SIS liaison officer with the CIA. The cryptanalyst Meredith Gardner later mournfully recalled how Philby had stood looking over his shoulder, smoking a pipe and admiring the progress he was making with the NKVD decrypts.[119]

On January 31, 1950, Truman directed his secretaries of state and defense to conduct a wide-ranging "re-examination of our objectives in peace and war." The result of that review was the now celebrated NSC 68 of April 7, drafted by a team of State and Defense officials headed by Paul Nitze, an investment banker who had succeeded Kennan as head of the State Department's Policy Planning Staff.[120] NSC 68 interpreted the Cold War as an elemental struggle between the forces of Western light and Eastern darkness, between freedom and slavery:

> The existence and persistence of the idea of freedom is a permanent and continuous threat to the foundation of the slave society; and it therefore regards as intolerable the long continued existence of freedom in the world.

The dawn of the atomic age meant that the forces of darkness were closer than they had ever been before to possessing the power to put out the light:

> . . . The Soviet Union, unlike previous aspirants to hegemony, is animated by a new fanatic faith, antithetical to our own, and seeks to impose its own authority over the rest of the world. . . . Any substantial further extension of the area under the domination of the Kremlin would raise the possibility that no coalition adequate to confront the Kremlin with greater strength could be assembled. . . . Thus unwillingly our free society finds itself mortally challenged by the Soviet system.

NSC 68 restated the doctrine of "containment" of Soviet expansion that had governed Truman's policy toward the Soviet Union since 1947.

Though its rhetoric grated on liberal sensitivities when it was declassified a quarter of a century later, much of its sweeping denunciation of the Soviet system in its Stalinist phase was fully justified. No responsible policy toward the Soviet Union could evade the fact that Stalin's Russia had condemned tens of millions of its own citizens to a brutal gulag from which many never returned, and had imposed tyrannical regimes on the peoples of Eastern Europe.

NSC 68 was, nonetheless, a dangerous document. What made it dangerous was its alarmist and simplistic insistence on a Soviet plot to rule the world, and its failure to take seriously Soviet fears, whether well-founded or not, of the threat from the West. The Kremlin did not, as Nitze and his co-authors claimed on no adequate evidence, possess a master plan "for the complete subversion or forcible destruction of the machinery of government and structure of society in the countries of the non-Soviet world and their replacement by an apparatus and structure subservient to and controlled from the Kremlin." NSC 68 failed to distinguish between the Kremlin's faith in the long-term triumph of Communism and an actual plan for world domination. This failure was due largely to unacknowledged ignorance. No American intelligence analyst in 1950 could be certain that Stalin did not possess some secret plan for major aggression. Equally, there was no reliable evidence that he did. The authors of NSC 68 refused to face up to the fact that they lacked sufficient hard information to determine what Stalin's ultimate foreign policy objectives were. Given the closed nature of Stalinist society, that information could only have come from secret intelligence. Though NSC 68 called for "the improvement and intensification of intelligence activities," it did not analyze their existing deficiencies. The U.S. intelligence community had not a single agent capable of providing a serious insight into Soviet policy, no ability to penetrate current high-grade Soviet cipher systems, and no aerial reconnaissance of more than the fringes of the Soviet Union. There was thus a staggering discrepancy between the quality of the intelligence available to Truman on Germany and Japan during the final phases of the Second World War, and that supplied to him on the Soviet Union during the early phases of the Cold War. The one major insight on the nature of the Soviet adversary supplied to him by the intelligence community thus far had been based on scientific analysis of the radioactive dust blown by the winds far beyond Soviet borders.

NSC 68's main prescription for "containing" Soviet expansion was a massive increase in the arms budget, "building up our military strength in order that it may not have to be used." The loss of the United States' atomic monopoly increased the need for it to be able to resist Soviet aggression with conventional forces. But, argued the authors of NSC 68, "containment" should not be purely defensive. It should seek "by all means short of war to . . . induce a retraction of the Kremlin's power and influence and . . . foster the seeds of self-destruction within the Soviet system. . . ." NSC 68 thus foresaw a major role for covert action within the Soviet bloc. Though it did not spell out this role in detail, it called for "intensification of . . . operations by covert means in the fields of economic warfare and political and psychological warfare."

Faith in the potential of covert action behind the Iron Curtain derived in part from optimistic forecasts by the OPC director, Frank Wisner, to the State and Defense departments, who were jointly responsible for the production of NSC 68. During 1949 OPC made contact with an anti-Communist underground in Poland that called itself Wolnośći Niepodległość (Freedom and Independence), or WiN for short. Beginning in 1950 Wisner began supplying WiN with arms, radio transmitters, and gold coins by parachute. WiN, in return, provided dramatic accounts of resistance to the Communist regime that went unreported in the Polish press. Wisner allegedly claimed, after reading a particularly optimistic series of reports, that WiN needed only antitank weapons "to drive the Red Army out of Warsaw." Other operations in which Wisner placed high hopes included assistance to anti-Communist partisans in the Ukraine and Albania. All were doubtless reported to Truman in the still-classified president's daily summary. Wisner's high hopes, however, were progressively dashed. Throughout the Soviet bloc, Communist security and armed forces were too powerful for resistance movements to stand any realistic chance of success, even with OPC support. WiN was eventually revealed as a deception operation, run from the outset by the UB, the Polish security service. A mocking two-hour broadcast on Polish radio in 1952 revealed that a million dollars of OPC money intended for WiN had gone to the UB instead. Genuine partisan movements supported by Wisner elsewhere in the Soviet bloc were invariably penetrated by local security services. OPC's operations were further undermined by the knowledge of them obtained by Kim Philby while SIS liaison officer in Washington from 1949 to 1951.[121]

Truman's main concern when NSC 68 was presented to him in the spring of 1950 was not the likely intensification of covert action in the Soviet bloc, which he now accepted as an unfortunate fact of life in the Cold War, but the massive increase that it called for in the military budget. The president was uncharacteristically indecisive, asking the NSC for further information, especially on probable costs.[122] But in speeches and press conferences during May and June he gave no sign of planning a major budget increase. His mind was made up for him by the start of the Korean War.[123]

Though the North Korean invasion of the South in the early hours of June 25 (the afternoon of June 24 in Washington) posed a less direct threat to American security than Pearl Harbor, it was as big an intelligence surprise. Acheson was reading in bed on the evening of Saturday, June 24, after an afternoon spent gardening at his nineteenth-century Maryland farmhouse when he received a call on the white telephone that connected him with the State Department via the White House switchboard. The North Koreans, he was told, were advancing across the 38th Parallel, but it was still unclear whether they intended a full-scale invasion. Truman was sitting in the library of his home at Independence, Missouri, when Acheson telephoned him with the news soon after 10 P.M. Missouri time. The president suggested flying back to Washington immediately, but Acheson urged him to wait until the following day, when the situation would be clearer. Acheson's next call came at 11 A.M. on Sunday, June 25, shortly after Truman had returned from a visit to his brother's farm. The president's daughter, Margaret, picked up the phone. "Daddy," she said, "it's Dean Acheson, and he says it's important." Acheson said it was now clear the North Koreans were engaged in a full-scale invasion. Truman, by his own account, replied, "Dean, we've got to stop the sons of bitches no matter what."[124]

While Truman was on the three-hour flight back from Independence, the United Nations Security Council in New York, boycotted by the Soviet representative, condemned the North Korean aggression by a vote of 9–0. Acheson, meanwhile, shut himself in his room at the State Department, banned both callers and messages, and tried to think. "Thought," he later admitted, "would suggest too orderly a process. It was rather to let various possibilities, like glass fragments in a kaleidoscope, form a series of patterns of action and then draw conclusions from them." Over the past few months, both State and Defense had considered the possibility of a Soviet attack at a variety of locations in Europe and the Middle East. The most likely flash points were considered to be Berlin, Turkey, Greece, and Iran, in all of which, it was believed, the Soviet Union would have an initial military advantage. Korea was thought too near U.S. bases in Japan and too far from those of the Soviet Union to strike Stalin as a tempting target. The idea that the initiative might be taken by the North Korean dictator, Kim Il Sung, occurred to no one.[125] Soviet documents make clear, however, that Kim had been seeking Moscow's support for an invasion of the South since March 1949. He eventually persuaded Stalin that the invasion would trigger a popular uprising in the South, and that victory would be achieved before the Americans could intervene.[126]

Only four days before the war began, Dean Rusk, assistant secretary of state with responsibility for the Far East, told a congressional committee that there was no evidence of an impending conflict in Korea. According to Rusk's memoirs:

> After the attack occurred, some of our intelligence people, already bitten by Pearl Harbor, thumbed back through thousands of tidbits of information and found maybe six or seven items that seemed to point toward the invasion. They wanted to be able to say, "We warned you." That was just damn nonsense.[127]

Though dismissed by Rusk as "just damn nonsense," the claims made by CIA analysts to have provided some warning of the threat to South Korea were not entirely without foundation. The agency *had* taken seriously the possibility of an attack on the South early in the following year, but as late as June 14 had ranked Korea only fifth in order of "explosiveness."[128] That ranking was too low to dent the skepticism of State and Defense.

At the heart of the intelligence failure before the Korean War were defects in the handling of SIGINT strikingly similar to those before Pearl Harbor. Despite a series of investigations and reports on the causes of the intelligence failure at Pearl Harbor, both Truman and most of his advisers had failed to grasp the damage done by the confused organization of prewar cryptanalysis. Truman had been introduced to SIGINT in the closing stages of a war during which it had achieved spectacular and unprecedented successes. After V-J Day, the wonders of Ultra and Magic rapidly gave way to what a top-secret SIGINT investigation, chaired by the lawyer George A. Brownell, described in 1952 as decrypts "of far lower grade." American cryptanalysts and their allies in the UKUSA alliance had the technical capacity, though not sufficient resources and manpower, to break the cipher systems used by a majority of UN members. Both the military and naval SIGINT agencies suffered what Brownell called "drastic cutbacks in personnel and funds" after the end of the war. Save for the Venona decrypts dating back to 1944–45, the high-grade code and cipher systems of the Soviet Union remained invulnerable. According to Brownell, "A sense of frustration and anticlimax was felt by all those who remained in the business. An ebbing of morale . . . set in very soon after V-J Day."[129]

As the Korean War was to demonstrate, however, SIGINT remained vital to United States national security. Had Truman grasped its potential significance for the Cold War as well as the Second World War, he would scarcely have allowed the interservice rivalry that had bedeviled prewar cryptanalysis to return in a more complex form. The president was personally committed to the creation of a unified Department of Defense as a means of containing the wrangling between armed services that, he sometimes complained, had delayed victory over Germany and Japan.[130] It took the Korean War, however, to focus the president's attention on the need to resolve SIGINT rivalries also.

After V-J Day the prewar battles between military and naval cryptanalysts rapidly revived. Faced with the dramatic postwar decline in naval signals, the navy tried to reclaim its pre–Pearl Harbor share of diplomatic traffic. ASA, the military SIGINT unit, refused to surrender its monopoly simply—so it claimed—for the sake of "giving the Navy something to do." Eventually it grudgingly agreed to a (still-classified) compromise, which failed, however, to prevent a series of bitter army-navy demarcation disputes. The creation of an independent air force caused further complications. At Vandenberg's insistence, it was given its own independent SIGINT unit.[131] In August 1948 a committee chaired by Rear Admiral Earl F. Stone, director of naval communications, was ordered to resolve the confusion. It failed. After further wrangling a new Armed Forces Security Agency (AFSA) was set up in 1949 to coordinate SIGINT operations by the three armed services. AFSA was overseen, but not controlled, by a ten-man Armed Forces Security Agency Committee (AFSAC). Composed of three members from each of the armed services under the chairmanship of the AFSA director, AFSAC was instructed to "determine and coordinate joint cryptologic military requirements." Arguably, it only made the existing confusion worse. According to the Brownell report:

> In place of the two COMINT [communication intelligence] organizations (Army and Navy) that existed during the war, we now have four. . . . AFSA has no authority over the service units, which in turn are independent of each other.[132]

SIGINT targeting—the choice of priorities for signals interception and cryptanalysis—was supposed to be coordinated by the United States Communications Intelligence Board (USCIB), established in July 1948 to represent the six SIGINT consumers: the three armed services, the State Department, the CIA, and the FBI. The chairmanship of the board rotated between the various bodies represented on it. Despite Hillenkoetter's responsibility as DCI for the coordination of the national intelligence effort, he was thus denied the personal authority required to coordinate HUMINT and SIGINT operations. Since USCIB decisions had to be reached unanimously, it was largely ineffective.[133] Most of the SIGINT faction-fighting of the late 1940s passed the president by. Like Roosevelt before Pearl Harbor, Truman seems to have regarded SIGINT management as an esoteric technicality that did not demand his personal intervention.

A later CIA study concluded that SIGINT became "a critically important source of information" during the Korean War.[134] It failed, however, to provide advance warning of the North Korean invasion for two reasons. First, as before Pearl Harbor, the SIGINT agencies were weakened by administrative confusion and inadequate resources. Secondly, and partly as a result, North Korea was not specifically targeted until the invasion began.[135] According to the Brownell report, during the seven months before the invasion, "the various intelligence agencies were becoming increasingly concerned . . . about the possibility of a Soviet move against South Korea, and yet this concern was never directly communicated to AFSA through the mechanism of the USCIB Intelligence requirements lists." The minutes of the monthly meeting of the USCIB Watch Committee on April 12, 1950, record that:

> A report relayed by CinCFE [General MacArthur] stated that the North Korean Peoples' Army will invade South Korea in June of 1950. Representatives of the Department of the Army undertook to ask for further information on this subject.

By the time the invasion began two and a half months later, military intelligence had still not provided the promised information. At the meeting of the Watch Committee on June 15 the chairman (on this occasion the CIA representative) listed Korea as the fifth most dangerous of "potential sources of conflict with the USSR . . . in the near future (six months to a year)." North Korea, however, still did not become a priority SIGINT target.[136] Had it been targeted, it is difficult to believe—given the success of SIGINT operations after the outbreak of war—that there would not have been some warning of the massing of over ninety thousand North Korean troops and 150 T-34 tanks at "jump-off points" north of the 38th Parallel before the invasion began.

The outbreak of the Korean War accelerated Hillenkoetter's overdue departure from the CIA. In May 1950, after long delay, Truman had personally selected General Walter Bedell Smith as Hilly's successor. Nicknamed "Beetle," Smith had a small black beetle embossed on his personal stationery. He had impressed Truman with his reputation as both soldier and diplomat. As Eisenhower's wartime chief of staff, Smith was reputed to have been the organizer of victory in the European theater. As ambassador in Moscow from 1946 to 1949 he had dealt personally with Stalin. Smith had a powerful personality and a legendary temper. Irascible impatience was part of his management style. "I have a more even disposition than anyone else," he boasted. "Always terrible." He liked to tell erring subordinates, "Every officer is entitled to make *one* mistake. *You* have just made yours."[137] Truman must have been confident when selecting Beetle as the next DCI that he would not tolerate the indignities heaped on Hilly by the Washington bureaucracy.

Smith was initially unenthusiastic about taking charge of the CIA. When Truman selected him as the next DCI in May 1950 he was undergoing major stomach surgery in the Walter Reed Hospital. As soon as it was clear that the operation had been successful, Truman ordered Smith to accept the job of DCI. Beetle obeyed the orders of the commander in chief and was confirmed by the Senate on August 28.[138] By the time Smith was formally sworn in as DCI on October 7 the tide of the Korean War seemed to have turned in favor of the United Nations forces commanded by General Douglas MacArthur. On September 15 MacArthur turned defense into attack with a brilliantly executed amphibious landing at Inchon, the port of Seoul, two hundred miles behind the front line of the North Korean forces. Early in October, with UN troops beginning to advance across the 38th Parallel into North Korea, Truman decided to meet MacArthur on Wake Island. On the early evening of October 10, only twenty-four hours before his departure from Washington, the president informed his new DCI that he wished to take with him intelligence estimates on six subjects: the threat of full-scale Chinese intervention in Korea; the danger of direct Soviet intervention; the likelihood of a Chinese Communist invasion of Formosa; the danger of a Chinese invasion of Indochina; the threat from Communist insurgency in the Philippines; and the general problem of Soviet and Chinese intentions and capabilities in the Far East.[139]

Beetle proved equal to the challenge. Almost as soon as he received the president's request, he personally telephoned five members of the Intelligence Advisory Committee (IAC), representing the State Department, the service intelligence agencies, and the Joint Chiefs of Staff, and summoned them to a 7 P.M. meeting in his office. One member, who objected to being disturbed at dinner, was, according to a CIA historian, "straightened out in the language of a drill sergeant addressing a lackadaisical recruit." The meeting set up six ad hoc committees to prepare overnight the six intelligence assessments asked for by the president, their work coordinated by a senior agency analyst. At the last moment Truman requested a seventh intelligence estimate, on the likelihood of a Soviet decision to start a Third World War. That estimate was provided from a report already on file. All seven assessments were delivered to the president before he left Washington on the evening of October 11. Smith continued to stamp his authority on the intelligence community in a way that would have been inconceivable during Hillenkoetter's three years as DCI. At his first formal meeting with the IAC on October 20 he announced the foundation of a new Office of National Estimates (ONE) to produce major intelligence assessments based on collaboration among all sections of the intelligence community. By the end of November ONE had a staff of about twenty, headed by the Harvard historian William Langer, who had directed the research and analysis branch of OSS. Interdepartmental rivalries did not suddenly disappear. But, according to an eyewitness, "No one wanted General Smith to hear that he or his agency was hindering the production of estimates."[140]

Truman's brief meeting with MacArthur at dawn on October 17 at Wake Island left him in an optimistic mood. "General MacArthur," he wrote, "was at the Airport with his shirt unbuttoned, wearing a greasy ham and eggs cap that evidently had been in use for twenty years. He greeted the President cordially. . . ." Contrary to claims made after MacArthur's dismissal six months later, the two men seemed, at their first meeting, to hit it off. Dean Rusk, who accompanied Truman, noted that "MacArthur showed complete respect for the President." He was also completely confident of victory, assuring Truman that "the Chinese Commies would not attack, that we had won the war and that we could send a Division to Europe in January 1951." Before he took off from the Wake Island airstrip, Truman told reporters, "I've never had a more satisfactory conference since I've been President."[141]

It was not long before the president changed his mind. After his return from Wake Island, MacArthur, taking some liberties with the orders given to him, continued his advance into the northern parts of North Korea. Late in October UN forces began to encounter small units of Chinese "volunteers." After a brief period of alarm, MacArthur's confidence returned. He planned a final offensive that would take his forces rapidly to the Chinese border and end the war. The offensive began on November 24. The next day three hundred thousand Chinese troops counterattacked and sent the UN forces reeling backward. The surprise in Washington was as great as after the North Korean invasion of the South five months earlier. "We were all wrong," writes Dean Rusk. "Not a single major element of the intelligence community warned about Chinese intervention." In fact, as Rusk acknowledges, though the significance of the information was not grasped, "Our intelligence did detect some movement of Chinese troops. . . ."[142] The most important intelligence came from SIGINT.[143]

The SIGINT warning went unheeded for two main reasons. First, the Chinese—like the Japanese before Pearl Harbor—were seriously underestimated. Truman, like most of his advisers, clung to the simplistic view that Beijing took its orders from Moscow. The Chinese, he told the skeptical British prime minister, Clement Attlee, were "complete satellites." At the president's request, Acheson spelled out the same erroneous view in greater detail for the benefit of the British:

> . . . The central enemy is not the Chinese but the Soviet Union. All the inspiration for the present action comes from there. The Chinese Communists were not looking at the matter as Chinese but as Communists who are subservient to Moscow.[144]

This was also Bedell Smith's firm conviction. CIA estimates asserted, without qualification, that the Soviet Union was engaged in an "experiment in war-by-proxy."[145] The North Korean invasion had caused such surprise in Washington because it was not anticipated that the *Soviet Union* might pick Korea as the battleground; it occurred to no one that the initiative might have come from Kim Il Sung. Similarly, the Chinese offensive on November 25 caught Washington off-guard because it was not anticipated that the *Russians* would decide to thrust three hundred thousand Chinese troops into the conflict. Intelligence assessment was once again distorted by false assumptions about total Soviet control of the entire Communist world that the White House did not question. Attlee's sensible suggestion that in Asia it was possible to "scratch a communist and find a nationalist" was brushed aside.[146]

The SIGINT warning before the Chinese offensive was also confused. The rapid expansion of SIGINT activities after the outbreak of war had produced another bout of interservice rivalry. ASA operations in Korea were controlled by its Pacific headquarters, ASAPAC. Those of its main rival, the Air Force Security Service (AFSS) were directed from Brooks Field in Texas. The Brownell committee later condemned the "duplication of effort" and "wasteful and inefficient practices" of the rival agencies. AFSA's attempts to reduce the confusion led to further disputes. As the Brownell committee noted:

> The tricky nature of order-of-battle intelligence and of tactical military intelligence (particularly when, as in Korea, we rely heavily on such intelligence) places an enormous premium on close working cooperation between the intelligence analysts, traffic analysts, and cryptanalysts.[147]

That "close cooperation" was visibly lacking. According to a CIA study, in the course of the war, "the responsible military authorities were themselves disgusted by the infighting . . . and by the inefficiencies inherent in the existing set-up."[148] MacArthur's attitude toward SIGINT added to the problems. During the Second World War he had been capable of brushing even Ultra aside when it failed to endorse his own strategic vision. During preparations for the expected invasion of Japan in the summer of 1945 he had told Marshall bluntly that he did not believe Ultra estimates of the Japanese forces waiting to confront him.[149] While planning his "final" Korean offensive of November 24, 1950, MacArthur seems similarly to have disregarded the much more fragmentary SIGINT evidence of an impending Chinese attack.

For several months after the Chinese onslaught Truman lived with the nightmare that the world might be on the brink of global atomic warfare. The CIA warned on December 2:

> Intelligence is inconclusive as to whether or not the Soviet intention is to precipitate a global war now. . . . Even if they do not intend to precipitate a global war, they must estimate that a broadening of the Korean war into a general war between the United States and China would be advantageous to the USSR. . . . Further direct or indirect Soviet aggression in Europe and Asia is likely, regardless of the outcome of the Korean situation.[150]

A National Intelligence Estimate (NIE) on December 11 concluded that the threat of Soviet aggression was most acute in Germany (especially Berlin), Indochina, Yugoslavia, and Iran.[151] On December 16 Truman declared a national emergency: "The increasing menace of the forces of communist aggression requires that the national defense of the United States be strengthened as quickly as possible."[152]

The crisis in Korea strengthened Bedell Smith's influence on the president. Truman had limited confidence in the judgment of the Joint Chiefs of Staff, whose chairman, General Omar N. Bradley, struck him as rather weak and indecisive (never a charge leveled at Beetle). Smith was careful, when giving his intelligence briefings to the NSC on Thursday mornings, not to second-guess Bradley's briefings on the Korean military situation. Every Friday morning, however, he went to the Oval Office to brief the president, taking with him a detailed order-of-battle map of Korea that he tried to make more precise than that shown by Bradley on the previous day. Truman and Smith had both, in their different spheres, risen through the ranks against the odds and shared a common suspicion of the West Pointers who dominated the high command. Beetle's view of the war carried more weight with the president than Bradley's. Truman used the DCI's Friday morning briefings as a means of checking the JCS assessments of the Korean War. Smith would regularly phone the White House when an urgent issue arose on other days, call for his car, and rush off to see the president unaccompanied. Few members of the administration had such easy access to Truman. Each Friday Smith left the president with a black looseleaf volume inscribed "The President" in gold lettering, containing a selection of the latest intelligence assessments. Within the agency Truman had a reputation as "a dutiful and diligent reader" of all the intelligence submitted to him. CIA officials noticed that, despite Smith's notoriously short fuse, he was usually in jovial mood when he returned from his Friday meetings with the president. It was at Truman's personal insistence that, in August 1951, Smith was made a four-star general—apparently despite the opposition of Bradley.[153]

Even with the support of the president, however, Beetle was unable to win some of his battles with the Joint Chiefs of Staff. Smith argued passionately that he could not properly estimate enemy intentions without adequate information on the U.S. forces that the enemy was facing. The JCS, however, stuck rigidly to the illogical position that such information was no concern of the DCI. They instructed that JCS papers and military operational cables were not to be transmitted to the CIA. In January 1951, at a time when he was deeply concerned by the danger of global atomic war, Truman asked Smith for an estimate of "the prospects for the creation of an adequate Western European defense." Because of the JCS refusal to provide the necessary information, Smith was unable to produce the estimate. A CIA study notes acerbically: "Thus it was demonstrated that not even the President of the United States could obtain a combined assessment of intelligence and operational information." An attempt to prepare an NIE on "the probability of a Communist attack on Japan during 1951" had similarly to be abandoned because of a lack of information on U.S. forces in and near Japan that would necessarily have been a major factor in Soviet calculations. Smith noted in frustration at the end of the Truman presidency, "As Western strength increases, estimates of Soviet military capabilities are increasingly meaningless without cognizance of Western capabilities to resist."[154]

Smith succeeded, however, where Hillenkoetter had failed, in gaining control over covert action. His first act on becoming DCI was to bring the OPC under his own personal authority. He initially decided, probably unwisely, not to merge OPC and OSO, who were responsible respectively for covert action and clandestine intelligence collection. Instead he brought in Allen Dulles to fill the new, misleadingly titled post of deputy director for plans, with responsibility for both organizations. The problems resulting from the fact that OPC and OSO were sometimes conducting different operations in the same location eventually led Smith to combine the two as the Directorate of Plans in August 1952.[155] The Korean War led to a spectacular increase in covert action. OPC's personnel grew from 302 in 1949 to 2,812 (plus 3,142 overseas contract agents), operating from forty-seven foreign stations, in 1952. Its budget skyrocketed during the same period from $4.7 million to $82 million. As the Korean battlefront stabilized in mid-1951, OPC moved increasingly into guerrilla warfare. Between April and December 1951 it trained and dispatched forty-four groups of Korean guerrillas behind enemy lines to harass Communist communication and supply lines from China.[156] It remains difficult to assess how much they achieved.

Smith briefed Truman personally on covert action and intelligence operations at their Friday morning meetings.[157] During 1951 he was able to report a steady growth in the number of agents operating in North Korea reporting to the CIA station in Seoul. One agent report that he probably brought to the president's attention gave details and troop strengths of every North Korean and Chinese unit on the battlefront. The army G-2 at Far East HQ described it as "one of the outstanding intelligence reports of the War." By early 1952 agent numbers in the North had risen to almost fifteen hundred. Then came disillusion. The new thirty-two-year-old head of station, John L. Hart, was dismayed by what he discovered on his arrival in Seoul. Of the almost two hundred Americans in the station, none was fluent in Korean. The agent networks in the North were mostly handled by Korean "principal agents" (PAs in agency jargon), who quickly aroused Hart's suspicions. He ordered a three-month investigation, at the end of which all the PAs were put through polygraph tests. The results were devastating. Hart discovered that most of the intelligence supplied by the CIA's much-vaunted "assets" in the North was bogus. Worse still, much of it was fabricated by the enemy. It emerged that the Seoul station's "agents" paid regular visits to "reception centers" run by North Korean and Chinese troops, at which they were debriefed on the latest happenings in the South, then supplied with spurious information on Communist military units—much of it, like the celebrated report giving details of all enemy units, deliberately misleading. Hart suggested that the CIA scrap its operations in the North. An emissary from the DCI arrived in Seoul to tell him to continue:

> General Smith wanted me to know, he said, that the CIA, being a
> new organization whose reputation had not yet been established,
> simply could not admit to other branches of Government—least of

all to the highly-competitive U.S. military intelligence services—its inability to collect intelligence on North Korea.

It seems unlikely that Truman was ever fully informed of the HUMINT debacle in Korea. As Hart discovered, the agents employed by military intelligence were as unreliable as those of the CIA. When instructed by Smith to continue operations in North Korea, Hart started again virtually from scratch. The Seoul station recruited agents living in the South who came originally from the North and had the right accents and knowledge of the areas in which they were to operate. They were then investigated, trained, given polygraph tests, supplied with radios, and parachuted into North Korea. During Hart's three years in Seoul from 1952 to 1955, none succeeded in maintaining radio contact for more than a brief period. All were believed to have been caught and executed.[158]

"SIGINT," recalls John Hart, "was almost the only intelligence worth having in Korea."[159] After the Chinese offensive of November 25, 1950, it came at last into its own. Dr. Louis Tordella, then of AFSA, later a long-serving deputy director of NSA, considered it "terribly important" in monitoring the Chinese advance.[160] General Matthew B. Ridgway, who took command of the U.S. Eighth Army in Korea on December 26, showed greater awareness of the importance of SIGINT than MacArthur, whom he was to succeed as commander in chief in April. By early 1951 SIGINT had alerted Ridgway to the concentration of Chinese forces in central Korea north of the mountain town of Wanju. At his request, U.S. air strikes were concentrated in that area. SIGINT also provided warning of the next Chinese offensive that began in mid-February. On March 15 Ridgway retook Seoul, which was never to be lost again. By then SIGINT had also provided evidence that Soviet pilots were flying MIG-15s in combat missions over Korea. At the end of March SIGINT operations by the 1st Radio Squadron Mobile resulted in what was later described as one of "the most important contributions to Air Force intelligence in its history." Though still classified, the operation appears to have revealed the presence of two hundred Soviet bombers stationed in northeastern China. SIGINT successes also improved the quality of aerial reconnaissance. Until the beginning of 1951 photographic interpreters were denied access to SIGINT and captured documents. In February, however, a Joint Photographic Center was established with access to all-source intelligence.[161] The Korean War also witnessed the first use of aerial color photography to trace enemy troop movements by revealing changes in the color of grass over which men and vehicles had moved. Another innovation of the war was the panoramic camera that provided horizon-to-horizon aerial pictures of the terrain below.[162] Truman's reaction to the examples he was shown of these advances in imagery intelligence is not recorded.

In addition to producing the best intelligence on the Korean War, SIGINT continued to provide disconcerting insights into Soviet espionage in the United States. The Venona decrypts supplied some of the clues that led to the detection of the atom spies, Julius and Ethel Rosenberg. In April 1951 the Rosenbergs became the first—and only—Soviet agents in the West to be sentenced to death. Two years and two months later, after an unsuccessful series of appeals, they were to die, one after the other, in the electric chair at New York's Sing Sing Prison. At almost the moment when the Rosenbergs were sentenced, another Venona decrypt revealed the identity of a Soviet agent code-named Homer, mentioned in a number of earlier intercepts. Homer was the British diplomat Donald Maclean, who had been stationed in Washington from 1944 to 1948, and in 1947 had become joint secretary of the Combined Policy Committee, which coordinated Anglo-American-Canadian nuclear policy. In a drunken episode in a London club, he once described himself as "the English Hiss." On May 25, 1951, shortly before he was due to be interrogated by MI5, the British Security Service, Maclean fled to Moscow. With him went another Soviet agent in the Foreign Office, Guy Burgess, who since August 1950 had been second secretary at the British embassy in Washington, staying with Philby and his wife at their home on Nebraska Avenue. Philby had expected Maclean to defect, but was horrified at the unexpected news that Burgess had gone with him. He drove into the Virginia countryside and buried in a wood the photographic equipment with which he had copied documents for Moscow Center—an action he had mentally rehearsed many times since coming to Washington as SIS liaison officer two years earlier.

Some of Philby's CIA colleagues could not at first believe that he could have been a Soviet mole. James Angleton, the future head of CIA counterintelligence, still thought of him as a likely future chief of SIS. Beetle Smith, however, was not taken in. He quickly told SIS that Philby was no longer acceptable as its liaison officer. At his regular Friday morning meeting with Truman on June 1, 1951, Smith doubtless informed him of the suspicion that had fallen on Philby. Though no record survives of what he told the president, it is probable that Smith also provided then and later damage assessments resulting from the defection of Burgess and Maclean. When Angleton and others who had trusted Philby eventually realized his treachery, the shock of betrayal was all the greater. The most enduring damage done by Philby and the other leading Cambridge moles, whom the KGB christened the "Magnificent Five," was to help lead a minority of intelligence officers on both sides of the Atlantic into a wilderness of mirrors, searching in vain for the chimera of a still vaster but imaginary Soviet deception.[163]

By the time the Korean battlefront stabilized into a military stalemate in the summer of 1951, SIGINT, supported by aerial reconnaissance, provided a reliable means of monitoring the deployment of enemy forces. It continued to do so during the two years of tortuous negotiations that preceded the signing of the armistice in July 1953. The vital importance of SIGINT, however, only served to strengthen Smith's frustration at his own lack of authority over it, despite his responsibility as DCI for coordinating the work of the intelligence community. He was outraged too by the continuing lack of cooperation between military and air force SIGINT units in Korea as well as by the inability of AFSA to impose its inadequate authority on the service agencies. By the later months of 1951 he was privately threatening that, unless State and Defense agreed to a major SIGINT overhaul, he would set about it himself.[164] On paper, Beetle was somewhat more restrained. In a memorandum of December 10, 1951, he emphasized "the unique value" of SIGINT and declared himself "gravely concerned as to the security and effectiveness with which the Communications Intelligence activities of the Government are being conducted." By the time Smith drafted this memorandum, he had—almost certainly—already won Truman's support for a major SIGINT overhaul by impressing on him, probably for the first time, the damage done by the existing system. The president formally approved the DCI's memorandum on December 13.[165] At a meeting chaired by Truman the same day in the Oval Office, attended by Smith, Bradley, representatives of State and Defense, and the executive secretary of the NSC, James S. Lay Jr., the terms were agreed for a high-level investigation into the running of SIGINT.[166] On December 28 a committee to conduct the investigation was appointed, headed by George A. Brownell and containing senior representatives of State, Defense, and the CIA.[167]

The Brownell committee submitted its report on 13 June 1952. Its unusual rapidity (by Washington standards) was due largely to the insistence of Smith, Acheson, and Robert A. Lovett (secretary of defense since September 1951) on a speedy solution, to the support of the president, and to a somewhat shamefaced awareness by the service intelligence agencies of the damage done by their infighting.[168] The report emphasized the "vital importance" of SIGINT to the national defense and detailed the confusion and inadequacy of its existing management:

The Director of AFSA is obliged to spend much of his energy on cajolery, negotiation and compromise in an atmosphere of interservice competition. He has no degree of control, except by making use of such techniques, over the three COMINT units operated by the three Services. In fact, he is under the control of the three Service units, through their representation on AFSAC. His only appeal is to the same three services sitting as the Joint Chiefs of Staff.

The Brownell committee recommended giving AFSA effective authority over the service agencies, abolishing AFSAC, and giving a strengthened USCIB, chaired by the DCI, greater power to oversee the coordination of SIGINT with other intelligence activities.[169] On October 24 Truman signed a top-secret eight-page presidential memorandum entitled "Communications Intelligence Activities," putting into effect the main recommendations of the committee, with one significant addition. In keeping with its enhanced authority, AFSA was renamed the National Security Agency (NSA).[170]

Whereas CIA was brought into being by an act of Congress, NSA was thus founded by a secret presidential signature. The date of its foundation, November 4, 1952, was deliberately chosen to keep it out of the news. All other events that day were overshadowed by the election of the Republican candidate, Dwight D. Eisenhower, to succeed Truman as president of the United States. Before long, both the new agency's budget and its personnel outstripped those of the CIA. NSA possessed the largest bank of computers in the world. For more than two decades, however, even its existence was unknown to the vast mass of the American people. Those in the know in Washington joked that NSA stood for "No Such Agency."[171]

Intelligence did not hold the fascination for Truman that it had sometimes had for his predecessor, Roosevelt. Nor did his understanding of it ever rival that of his successor, Eisenhower. Yet it was the Truman presidency, more than any other, that shaped the modern United States intelligence community (a phrase first used in 1952). In 1945 Truman authorized postwar Anglo-American SIGINT collaboration, the cornerstone of the world's most remarkable peacetime intelligence alliance. In 1946 he ordered the inauguration of the daily summary, forerunner of the president's daily brief, the first document seen each day by most of his successors. In 1947 Truman promoted the National Security Act, which founded the CIA. In 1948 he authorized the beginning, and during his second term the rapid expansion, of peacetime covert action by U.S. intelligence agencies. And in 1952, as one of his final acts as president, he founded NSA.

During his twenty-year retirement Truman sometimes seemed amazed, even somewhat appalled, at the size and power of the intelligence community he had brought into being. He wrote, inaccurately, to the managing editor of *Look* magazine in 1964 that he had never intended CIA to do more than get "all the available information to the president. It was not intended to operate as an international agency engaged in strange activities." NSA was so secret that Truman did not mention it at all. He would probably have been pleased that his biographers have shown a similar disinclination to dwell on his responsibility for the creation of the biggest peacetime intelligence community in the history of Western civilization.

CHAPTER 6

Dwight D. Eisenhower
(1953-1961)

Eisenhower was the first president since Washington already well informed about intelligence when he took the oath of office. Ike had been convinced of its importance both by the shock of Pearl Harbor and by his own experience as wartime commander. The outbreak of the Korean War reinforced the lesson of Pearl Harbor. According to his adviser for science and technology, James R. Killian, the possibility of another surprise attack "haunted Eisenhower throughout his Presidency."[1]

Ike learned firsthand during the Second World War the value of SIG-INT. Soon after his arrival in Britain in June 1942 as commander of American military forces, he was briefed personally on Ultra by Churchill, one of its greatest enthusiasts, after dinner at Chequers, the country home of British prime ministers. Eisenhower had won his command partly because he impressed Marshall with his openness to new ideas. He was an early convert to Ultra.[2] Not so his deputy, General Mark Clark. When the chief of SIS, General Sir Stewart Menzies, who was also responsible for Bletchley Park, and Group Captain F. W. Winterbotham, a senior British intelligence officer, called to brief Clark, they found him "restless from the start." According to Winterbotham, "after a quarter of an hour he excused himself and his officers on the grounds that he had something else to do." Menzies was "considerably upset" with Clark. He had no doubt, however, about Eisenhower's grasp of Ultra's importance.[3] Ike told Menzies at the end of the war that Ultra had been "of priceless value to me":

> It has simplified my task as commander enormously. It has saved thousands of British and American lives and, in no small way, con-

tributed to the speed with which the enemy was routed and eventually forced to surrender.

I should be very grateful, therefore, if you would express to each and everyone of those engaged in this work from me personally my heartfelt admiration and sincere thanks for their very decisive contribution to the Allied war effort.[4]

As Eisenhower's tribute to British cryptanalysts suggests, he was a committed supporter of Anglo-American intelligence collaboration. On becoming supreme commander of Allied forces in Europe at the end of 1943, he asked to keep the British general, Kenneth W. D. Strong, who had served with him in North Africa, as his chief intelligence officer. Ike was so determined to secure Strong's services that when his request was turned down by the chief of the imperial General Staff, General Sir Alan Brooke, he appealed directly to Churchill, who agreed. Unlike the intelligence officers of Ike's British comrade-in-arms, Field Marshal Bernard Montgomery, Strong had direct and unrestricted access to Eisenhower and his chief of staff, and the right to sack on the spot any intelligence officer, American or British, whom he believed was not up to the job. "The best time in a man's life," Strong enthused, "is when he gets to like Americans." Ike complained to Strong about the lack of training for, and low status of, U.S. military intelligence. On Eisenhower's instructions, Strong set up a training school for American intelligence officers. Of all the intelligence operations with which he was concerned in war and peace, Eisenhower later looked back with perhaps greatest pleasure on Fortitude, the great web of Anglo-American deception spun before and during the Normandy landings. "My God," he would say, grinning his famous grin and slapping his thigh, "we really fooled them, didn't we!" As Ike told the story, he reminded his biographer, Stephen Ambrose, of Tom Sawyer pulling a fast one on Aunt Polly.[5]

During the Second World War Eisenhower also acquired a passion for imagery intelligence (IMINT) that lasted for the rest of his life. He later recalled that his real initiation into IMINT came during a visit soon after his arrival in London to the Air Ministry's Photographic Interpretation Unit (PIU), which he was surprised to find staffed mainly by "a group of girls"—in fact, members of the Women's Auxiliary Air Force. (One of the PIU's founders had concluded, chauvinistically, that the job suited women, because "Looking through magnifying glasses at minute objects in a photograph required the patience of Job and the skill of a good darner of socks.") Ike was amazed at what the photographic interpreters were able to reveal:

It was the first time I realized what a science it had become. . . . Having gotten a taste for it, every once in a while I'd say to someone, "You don't have to bring me all the pictures you're taking, because thousands of them are of no value, but bring me some of your good ones."

His curiosity for what could be observed from the air was so great that almost a month after D-Day, on Independence Day 1944, to the alarm of his staff, he asked the Ninth Air Force commander, thirty-seven-year-old General Pete Quesada, to fly him over German-occupied France jammed in the rear seat of a Mustang P-51. "I couldn't have gotten out of there with a shoe horn," Ike recalled. "We came back and I said, 'Pete, it's absolutely impossible. You can't see anything but hedges from where we were with the naked eye. If we find anything at all, it's got to be with some kind of photography.'" Though deeply impressed by the skill of the photographic interpreters, Eisenhower admitted that he was baffled by their expertise: "If they could point out to me what I was supposed to see, then I'd see it, but to . . . find it for myself was always difficult."[6]

Though the Second World War taught Eisenhower the value of SIGINT and IMINT, it left him with a distorted understanding of HUMINT. He saw the role of human intelligence agencies less in terms of intelligence collection than as a means of continuing in peacetime the wartime covert operations carried out behind enemy lines by OSS, SOE, partisans, and resistance movements. Covert action was a central part of Eisenhower's Cold War strategy. That priority quickly showed itself in his choice of DCI. Beetle Smith had been Ike's wartime chief of staff, but was far less enthusiastic about covert action, which he feared was usurping the primary mission of the CIA to collect and interpret intelligence. His most violent rows as DCI were with the deputy director, Allen Dulles, and the DDP, Frank Wisner, who were anxious to expand rather than contract covert operations. Dulles's genial and confident manner was unruffled by Smith's formidable temper. "The General was in fine form this morning, wasn't he?" he would joke out of the DCI's earshot after witnessing one of his explosions. To Smith's immense chagrin, Ike chose Allen Dulles to succeed him as DCI and made him undersecretary to Dulles's brother John Foster Dulles, the new secretary of state. Because of his recurrent attacks of gout, Allen Dulles was the only member of the new administration who had permission to wear carpet slippers in the Oval Office.[7] Foster lacked Allen's clubability. "Dull, Duller, Dulles" ran one Washington joke. The secretary of state's sanctimonious public manner repelled even some of those who shared his hard-line views on the Soviet bloc. Beetle, who had rejoiced at Ike's election, said

dly when he learned he was to leave the CIA for the State
ment, "And I thought that it was going to be great!" He predicted
that once Allen Dulles was DCI, his passion for covert action would get
out of hand. "In short," according to a CIA in-house history, "Bedell
Smith anticipated a fiasco like the Bay of Pigs, although that did not happen until eight years later."[8]

Eisenhower changed the motto on the massive rosewood desk in the
Oval Office. For Truman's "The Buck Stops Here," he substituted
"*Suaviter in modo, fortiter in re*" (Gently in manner, strong in deed).
Throughout his two terms in office, Ike enjoyed an extraordinary level of
public support, averaging a 64 percent approval rating in the monthly
Gallup polls. His cheerful, reassuring public presence seemed to place
him above the petty machinations of party politics. But Eisenhower was
a master of what political scientist Fred Greenstein has called "hidden-
hand leadership." Behind the ready smile and the relaxed manner lay
iron resolution. He left the public role of the uncompromising Cold War
warrior to Foster Dulles while he himself tried to radiate goodwill as well
as firmness. It was Eisenhower, not Dulles, however, who made foreign
policy.[9] Covert action was an essential part of that policy, offering an
apparently effective alternative to the unacceptable risks and costs of
open military intervention. The most covert part of Eisenhower's covert
actions was his own responsibility for them. Though he discussed them
in private with the Dulles brothers, he was usually careful to ensure that,
in case anything went wrong, no compromising documents remained in
the Oval Office. Despite his evasion of public responsibility, Eisenhower's
use of covert action was based on principle. He believed there was no
other way of fighting the Cold War effectively against a ruthless enemy.
"I have come to the conclusion," he wrote privately, "that some of our
traditional ideas of international sportsmanship are scarcely applicable
in the morass in which the world now founders."[10]

Allen Dulles said later that 1953 and 1954 were his best years in the
CIA. As one agency official put it, he had "the American flag flying at his
back and the President behind him."[11] The first major covert action of
the Eisenhower presidency took place in Iran. The initiative came from
the British. In April 1951 the shah of Iran, Mohammad Reza Pahlavi,
yielding to public pressure, had appointed Dr. Mohammad Mossadeq as
his prime minister. Acheson wrote of Mossadeq in his memoirs: "We
were, perhaps, slow in realizing that he was essentially a rich, reactionary, feudal-minded Persian inspired by a fanatical hatred of the
British and a desire to expel them and all their works from the country
regardless of cost." Mossadeq's personal eccentricities—which included
conducting negotiations in his pajamas and weeping in public—added to

the West's suspicion of him.[12] In May 1951 he nationalized the oil industry, to the outrage of the British government, which owned 50 percent of the stock in the Anglo-Iranian Oil Company. When British efforts to regain some degree of control over the Iranian oil industry failed, Mossadeq's removal became, to quote a Foreign Office memorandum, "objective number one." Plans by SIS for an operation unsubtly code-named Boot captured the adventurous imagination of Winston Churchill on his return to office in November 1951. SIS, however, believed it needed the collaboration of the CIA, not least to finance the extensive bribery that Boot envisaged. It quickly became clear that, despite the sympathy for the operation shown by Allen Dulles (then DDP), Truman would never give his approval. Covert action in Iran during the Truman administration was limited to operations designed to diminish Soviet and Communist influence.[13] Following Eisenhower's election victory, however, SIS once again began to canvass Operation Boot in Washington. Monty Woodhouse, the SIS emissary, prudently decided "to emphasize the Communist threat to Iran rather than the need to recover control of the oil industry":

> I argued that even if a settlement of the oil could be negotiated with [Mossadeq], which was doubtful, he was still incapable of resisting a coup by the Tudeh [Communist] Party, if it were backed by Soviet support.[14]

That argument impressed Eisenhower as well as the Dulles brothers. Anthony Eden, Churchill's foreign secretary, found Ike "obsessed by the fear of a Communist Iran."[15] The head of CIA operations in the Middle East, Kermit Roosevelt (grandson of Theodore), was quickly converted to the basic framework of Operation Boot. Since Britain and Iran had broken diplomatic relations, it was far easier for Americans to travel to Teheran. SIS therefore agreed that the operation (renamed Ajax by the CIA) should be led by Roosevelt, and that SIS assets in Iran should be put at his disposal. Detailed planning by CIA and SIS began in March 1953. In April it was agreed that Mossadeq's successor should be the royalist General Fazlullah Zahedi. The twenty-two-page plan for Operation Ajax, jointly prepared by CIA and SIS, was finally approved on June 25 at a meeting in the State Department. Though some of the diplomats had reservations, there was no mistaking the enthusiasm of Allen and Foster Dulles. According to Roosevelt, Foster remarked, holding the plan for Operation Ajax, "So this is how we get rid of that madman Mossadeq!"[16]

On July 19 Roosevelt crossed the Iraqi border into Iran. His first assignment was to persuade a nervous shah to play his part in the coup by dismissing Mossadeq and appointing General Zahedi in his place. At the joint request of SIS and CIA, the shah's sister, Princess Ashraf, who had settled in Switzerland, flew to Teheran to try to persuade her brother but failed to gain a private audience with him. The American former head of the Iranian gendarmerie, Brigadier General Norman Schwarzkopf (father of the Allied commander in the Gulf War of 1991), was also sent to see the shah but left him unconvinced. Roosevelt decided that, contrary to his original plan, he would have to see the shah himself. To win him over, he enlisted the support of the president, who played an unprecedented personal part in overcoming the shah's final hesitations. Just before midnight on August 1 Roosevelt was driven through the gates of the Imperial Palace in Teheran, crouching on the car floor and covered by a blanket. Once inside, he told the shah that Eisenhower would secretly demonstrate his support for the operation by including an apparently innocuous coded phrase in a speech he was shortly to deliver in San Francisco. Roosevelt also claimed that Churchill had personally arranged for the BBC World Service announcer on the following night, instead of saying "It is now midnight," to use the phrase, "It is now"—pause—"exactly midnight."

With the shah's support secured, Roosevelt was able to begin implementing the coup. The shah signed decrees dismissing Mossadeq and appointing Zahedi as prime minister. Operation Ajax got off to a shaky start. Mossadeq arrested the army officer who tried to serve the decree dismissing him. On August 16, 1953, the shah fled the country in panic. Roosevelt was forced to drive Zahedi, lying on a car floor and covered with "another one of those invaluable blankets," to refuge in a safe house. Roosevelt claims that Tudeh mobs, "with strong Russian encouragement," took to the streets, chanting antiroyalist slogans.[17] Other CIA officers, however, have since revealed that the demonstration began with a fake Tudeh crowd organized by the CIA, designed to produce fears of a Communist coup and provoke a royalist backlash. The bogus demonstrators were soon joined by genuine Tudeh supporters, unaware of the CIA deception. Together they proceeded to tear down statues of the shah and his father.[18] On August 19 Roosevelt orchestrated the royalist backlash. CIA and SIS agents, well supplied with mostly American funds, mobilized support and street mobs.[19] The demonstrations that followed were bizarre as well as effective. According to an observer:

. . . With the army standing close guard around the uneasy capital, a grotesque procession made its way along the street leading to the heart of Tehran. There were tumblers turning handsprings, weight-lifters twirling iron bars and wrestlers flexing their biceps. As spectators grew in number, the bizarre assortment of performers began shouting pro-Shah slogans in unison. The crowd took up the chant. . . .[20]

After nine hours of fighting, in which over three hundred people were killed, troops loyal to Mossadeq were defeated and his house was stormed. Mossadeq escaped over the rooftops but, still in his pajamas, surrendered the next day to the new prime minister, General Zahedi. On hearing in Rome of the less than spontaneous uprising by his loyal subjects, the shah is said to have remarked, "I knew it! I knew it! They love me!" On August 22 His Imperial Majesty returned in triumph to Teheran. According to Roosevelt, the shah told him, "I owe my throne to God, my people, my army—and to you!" He reached into his inside pocket and presented Roosevelt with a large gold cigarette case.

The picturesque detail of the coup only heightened Eisenhower's and Churchill's satisfaction at its success. Both probably felt, like the SIS officer Monty Woodhouse, that for the first time the well-tried Communist technique of "spontaneous" demonstrations had been used against them. On his way back to Washington, Roosevelt stopped in London and called at 10 Downing Street to brief Churchill in person. He found the prime minister propped up in bed, recovering from a stroke but eager to hear the "exciting story" that Roosevelt had to tell. "Young man," said Churchill when the story was told, "if I had been but a few years younger I would have loved nothing better than to have served under your command in this great venture."[21] Roosevelt found an equally enthusiastic audience in the White House. Eisenhower, who took the doctrine of plausible deniability seriously, later claimed in his memoirs that the report on the events in Teheran prepared for him by Roosevelt was written by "an American in Iran, unidentified to me." In fact, on September 4, in the White House, Roosevelt repeated the briefing he had given Churchill to Eisenhower; the Dulles brothers; the secretary of defense, Charles E. Wilson; and the chairman of the Joint Chiefs of Staff, Admiral Arthur Radford. Roosevelt noted that, as John Foster Dulles listened to the briefing, "he seemed to be purring like a giant cat." Ike too seemed spellbound. "I listened to [Roosevelt's] detailed report," he wrote in his diary, "and it seemed more like a dime novel than a historical fact."[22] On September 23 the president personally awarded the National Security Medal to Roosevelt in a secret White House ceremony. A note in Eisenhower's diary records that "the entire file" relating to the award was retained by Allen Dulles.[23] It has still to be declassified.

Ajax, however, had been a less spectacular success than Eisenhower supposed. Once the shah recovered his nerve, the support of most of the army put him in a far stronger position than the eccentric Mossadeq. The future DDI, Ray Cline, fairly concluded that the operation "did not prove that CIA could topple governments and place rulers in power; it was a unique case of supplying just the right bit of marginal assistance in the right way at the right time."[24] Amid the euphoria that followed Ajax, however, neither Eisenhower nor Allen Dulles grasped the limited nature of the operation's success. The overthrow of Mossadeq strengthened the president's faith in covert action as a secret weapon in the Cold War. The next major target of CIA covert action was President Jacobo Arbenz Guzmán of Guatemala, who aroused the growing hostility of the Eisenhower administration by his dealings with Guatemalan Communists, his expropriation of the holdings of the U.S. United Fruit Company in February 1953, and his arms purchases from the Soviet bloc in May 1954.

Among several alarmist but influential reports on Guatemala during the early months of the Eisenhower presidency was one by the Latin American expert, Adolf Berle, who reported on March 31, 1953:

> Guatemala presents a genuine penetration of Central America by Kremlin Communists. While the President, Arbenz, claims not to be a Communist, he is estimated to be an opportunist and his government is, for practical purposes, dominated by Communists, both Guatemalan and from other parts of the hemisphere. . . . The situation results from the careful advance planning done by the Russian Ambassador, [Konstantin] Oumansky, during his lifetime and carried forward by his successors.

Berle's report and several subsequent assessments by the CIA were greatly exaggerated. Though a land reformer who had accepted Communists as minor partners in his ruling coalition, Arbenz was neither a Communist fellow-traveler nor a potential Castro. Party members played a part in his land reform agency, but they were excluded from his cabinet, from the national police force, and from most departments of government. Nor was there any Soviet master plan inaugurated by Oumansky to turn Guatemala into a Communist state. Berle, like Eisenhower, made a false analogy between the experience of states in Eastern Europe, where Communists had exploited initial participation in coalition governments to establish one-party regimes, and the situation in Guatemala, where the preconditions for a Communist coup did not exist.

Berle took it as axiomatic that "the United States cannot tolerate a Kremlin-controlled Communist government in this hemisphere." Once Arbenz had been misidentified as the harbinger of Communist control, the only question that remained was not whether, but how, to remove him. Berle excluded the possibility of direct American armed intervention "because of the immense complications which it would raise all over the hemisphere." The problem about intervention by Guatemala's neighbors, though Berle hoped to persuade them to undertake what he vaguely termed "moral intervention for political defense," was that it would involve the Nicaraguan regime of Anastasio Somoza, which had become "almost a symbol of corruption." The final possibility was for a Guatemalan opposition group to remove Arbenz with American support. Berle was uncertain whether such a group could be found.[25] Allen Dulles was confident that it could. Probably soon after the successful conclusion of Ajax, Eisenhower authorized planning to begin for Operation PB Success (PB was CIA code for Guatemala).

Planning continued for almost a year, known only to the president, the Dulles brothers, and a restricted circle of top officials in the CIA, White House, and State Department. The CIA marked its communications to Eisenhower and Foster Dulles "Top Secret Ita," a superclassification that restricted access to recipients of the documents; most were later burned. Eisenhower periodically discussed the progress of PB Success with the Dulles brothers over Sunday brunch at their sister Eleanor's. The Guatemalan chosen to lead the coup, Colonel Carlos Castillo Armas, had achieved the status of a folk hero. After being wounded in an unsuccessful rising against Arbenz's predecessor in 1950, he had been pronounced dead, had miraculously recovered shortly before his burial, and had subsequently escaped from prison, allegedly by digging a tunnel with his bare hands. In December 1953 Castillo Armas announced that he would shortly be returning to Guatemala at the head of a "National Liberation Movement." Supplied by the CIA with a base in Honduras, ample funds, and mercenaries from various parts of Latin America, he spent the next six months making leisurely preparations for the liberation.[26]

Early on the morning of June 18, 1954, Allen Dulles phoned the White House with the news that Operation PB Success had begun. "Officially," noted Eisenhower's press secretary, Jim Hagerty, "we don't know anything about it."[27] As in Teheran almost a year before, the coup combined conspiracy with farce. Headlines in the *New York Times* announced next day:

REVOLT LAUNCHED IN GUATEMALA
LAND-AIR-SEA INVASION REPORTED
RISINGS UNDERWAY IN KEY CITIES

The reality was far less dramatic. On June 18 Castillo Armas led a straggling band of 150 men six miles across the Honduran border into Guatemala, set up camp at the shrine of the Church of the Black Christ, demanded Arbenz's unconditional surrender, and awaited his reply.[28] The CIA was dismayed by the inertia of its protégé. Two days after the incursion, Allen Dulles informed the president:

> As of 20 June the outcome of the efforts to overthrow the regime of President Arbenz of Guatemala remains very much in doubt. The controlling factor in the situation is still considered to be the position of the Guatemalan armed forces.

Most accounts of PB Success tend to assume that its success was inevitable. At the time, however, there were serious fears within the agency that it would end in fiasco. Allen Dulles acknowledged that, despite the resources lavished on him by the CIA, Castillo Armas did not lead a serious fighting force. The fate of PB Success thus depended on the "psychological impact" of the invasion, and its ability "to create and maintain for a short time the *impression* of very substantial military strength." Dulles told Eisenhower that the two main methods being employed to create this improbable illusion were a massive media disinformation campaign jointly orchestrated by the CIA, State Department, and United States Information Agency, and a small air force nominally under Castillo Armas's command with pilots hired by the CIA:

> . . . It will be seen how important are the aspects of deception and timing. If the effort does not succeed in arousing the other latent forces of resistance within the next period of approximately twenty-four hours [i.e., by the evening of June 21] it will probably begin to lose strength.[29]

The most successful part of the deception operation was the psychological impact created when Castillo Armas's "air force" buzzed Guatemala City. Arbenz was so impressed that he ordered a blackout of all major cities. The Voice of Liberation Radio, set up by the CIA, won a major propaganda victory by broadcasting a carefully stage-managed interview with a pilot who had defected. Fearing further defections, Arbenz grounded his entire air force.[30] Within a few days, however, Castillo Armas's air offensive was in danger of petering out. Early on June 22 Allen Dulles told Eisenhower that two of his three bombers had been lost. That afternoon there was a crisis meeting in the Oval Office, attended by the Dulles brothers and Henry F. Holland, assistant secretary of state for inter-American affairs. Holland strenuously opposed further assistance to Castillo Armas on the grounds both of its illegality and the potential damage to United States relations with the rest of Latin America. The first argument at least had little impact on Eisenhower. "Mr. President," said Allen Dulles afterward, "when I saw Henry walking into your office with three large law books under his arm, I knew he had lost his case already." The mood of the meeting, however, was somber. Eisenhower asked Allen Dulles, "What do you think Castillo's chances would be without the aircraft?" "About zero," was the reply. "Suppose we supply the aircraft," the president continued. "What would be the chances then?" "About 20 percent," replied Dulles. Eisenhower was less pessimistic than his DCI: ". . . I knew from experience the importance of even a small amount of air support. In any event, our proper course of action—indeed, my duty—was clear to me. We would replace the airplanes."[31]

On June 25 Foster Dulles gloomily predicted that if Castillo Armas failed, Arbenz would emerge as a popular hero, and deliver "a great blow to the U.S. prestige." Eisenhower, however, proved right about "the psychological impact" of bombing civilian targets. On June 27 the chief of the Guatemalan armed forces, Colonel Carlos Enrique Diaz, met the U.S. ambassador, John E. Peurifoy, in Guatemala City. Diaz was in a state of shock and gave an exaggerated account of the devastation caused by air attacks on Guatemalan towns and cities. According to Peurifoy's report to the State Department:

> Diaz began by describing the horrible situation created by aerial bombardment of Chiquimila and Zacapa. He said towns were virtually wiped out; that in Zacapa dead lay unburied in streets and buzzards were having feast on them; civil population had fled. The army could cope with Castillo Armas' ground forces, but not his aviation.

For this death and destruction, albeit on a smaller scale than Diaz alleged, Eisenhower was directly responsible. It was a disreputable moment in his distinguished career. Peurifoy seemed to enjoy Diaz's humiliation. When Diaz observed, reasonably enough, that Castillo Armas could not have acquired his air force without American help, Peurifoy threatened to walk out if he insisted on making such outrageous (and well-founded) allegations. Diaz meekly insisted that "he was not accusing U.S.," and asked what terms the United States required to use its good offices to end the fighting—in other words, to call off Castillo Armas's air attacks. According to Peurifoy:

Constantly emphasizing I could speak only as individual and not for U.S. Government, I said there was only one important problem between our governments: That of communism. Colonel Diaz said he knew that and was prepared [to] guarantee in name of army that Communist Party would be outlawed and its leaders exiled.

Diaz agreed to lead a coup against Arbenz. Peurifoy then said he would recommend a cease-fire as soon as Diaz had taken over the presidency. Later the same day, June 27, the ambassador reported to Washington that Arbenz had agreed "to leave office gracefully." Peurifoy was not satisfied, however, that Arbenz resigned gracefully enough:

I told Colonel Diaz that I was amazed and astounded at fact that he had permitted Arbenz in delivering his valedictory to charge [quite correctly] that U.S. was responsible for supplying aviators to forces attacking Guatemala. . . . I told him that, this being his first act, I did not see how we could work together toward bringing about a peace. I suggested that perhaps he might wish to designate Colonel [Elfego Hernán] Monzón [Aguirra, one of Arbenz's ministers], well-known for his anti-Communist feelings, as President.

Faced with Peurifoy's further menaces, Diaz accepted the additional humiliation of stepping down as president in favor of Monzón. When Monzón said he "did not feel himself strong enough [to] assume the presidency alone," Peurifoy insisted that Castillo Armas become president without further delay. Diaz told him that "Castillo Armas could never govern Guatemala after [the] massacres his forces caused; he might have had some supporters in [the] army before, but no longer." After more pressure by Peurifoy, however, the junta gave way and accepted Castillo Armas as its president.[32] Peurifoy was confident of Eisenhower's personal support. "I was authorized to crack some heads together," he said later.[33] A celebratory verse by Mrs. Peurifoy appeared in *Time* magazine on July 26:

> *Sing a song of quetzals, pockets full of peace!*
> *The junta's in the palace, they've taken out a lease.*
> *The Commies are in hiding, just across the street;*
> *To the embassy of Mexico they beat a quick retreat.*
> *And pistol-packing Peurifoy looks mighty optimistic*
> *For the land of Guatemala is no longer Communistic.*

Eisenhower showed no sign of embarrassment at the bullying of a banana republic. David Atlee Phillips, responsible for black propaganda during PB Success, and some of his CIA colleagues were summoned to the White House to give a victory briefing. "How many men did Castillo Armas lose?" asked the president. When told only one had been lost, he replied, "Incredible!" It apparently did not occur to Eisenhower to inquire how many Guatemalans had been killed by the CIA air force. After the briefing, Ike was all smiles. His final handshake was with Allen Dulles. "Thanks, Allen, and thanks to all of you," he said. "You've averted a Soviet beachhead in our hemisphere."[34] On October 31 Castillo Armas arrived for a two-week victory tour of the United States that included a ticker-tape welcome in New York, a twenty-one-gun salute in Washington, and honorary degrees from Fordham and Columbia universities. Though recovering from a heart attack, Eisenhower congratulated him in person from his bed in Fitzsimons Army Hospital.[35] In January 1955, when Ike gave his first televised press conference, he listed the defeat of Communism in Iran and Guatemala as one of the proudest achievements of his first two years in office.[36] The role of the CIA in overthrowing Arbenz was by now an open secret. When Lyman Kirkpatrick, the CIA inspector general, toured Latin America in 1955, he found resentment of the agency's role in Guatemala everywhere he went.[37] Eisenhower, however, seemed untroubled by it.

On July 26, 1954, a month after the Guatemalan coup, Eisenhower commissioned a secret review of covert operations from a four-man study group headed by retired Air Force Lieutenant General James H. Doolittle. The "Report of the Special Study Group on Covert Activities" reached the president on September 30. It gave a chilling endorsement to the case for covert action:

> It is now clear that we are facing an implacable enemy whose avowed objective is world domination by whatever means and at whatever cost. There are no rules in such a game. Hitherto acceptable norms of human conduct do not apply. If the United States is to survive, long-standing American concepts of "fair play" must be reconsidered. We must develop effective espionage and counter-espionage services and must learn to subvert, sabotage and destroy our enemies by more clever, more sophisticated and more effective methods than those used against us.[38]

These were the president's views as well as Doolittle's. But the report also contained criticism of CIA management of covert action. On October 19 Eisenhower spent the afternoon with Doolittle and his study group. The president made a vigorous defense of his DCI:

We must remember that here is one of the most peculiar types of operation any government can have, and it probably takes a strange kind of genius to run it. . . . I'm not going to be able to change Allen. I have two alternatives, either to get rid of him and appoint someone who will assert more authority or keep him with his limitations. I'd rather have Allen as my chief intelligence officer with his limitations than anyone else I know.[39]

Eisenhower successfully resisted a resolution by Senator Mike Mansfield for a "Joint Congressional Oversight Committee for the American Clandestine Service." ". . . This kind of a bill," Ike said privately, "would be passed over my dead body."[40] Probably remembering the anxious moments in PB Success, however, Eisenhower sought to improve planning procedures for covert action. Two 1955 NSC policy directives (NSC 5412/1 and NSC 5412/2) established the 5412 Committee, a group of "designated representatives" of the president and the secretaries of state and defense to review and approve proposed operations.[41] The initiative remained with the CIA; Eisenhower continued to be kept personally informed of covert actions by Allen Dulles.

Though Eisenhower placed exaggerated reliance on covert action, he was under few illusions about the quality of CIA intelligence on its main target, the Soviet Union. At an NSC meeting chaired by the president on March 31, 1953, Allen Dulles had "freely admitted shortcomings of a serious nature" in Soviet intelligence collection. The CIA had no significant agent networks on Russian soil. By 1954 the parachuting of radio-equipped agents onto Soviet territory had virtually ceased because of their lack of success. The interrogation of returning German POWs provided useful intelligence on the factories in which some of them had worked, but neither they nor the Soviet emigrés who also passed on information were adequate compensation for the lack of agents. "We must remain highly critical of our intelligence effort," Allen Dulles told the NSC, "but we must not be defeatist in the face of the difficulties of securing adequate information."[42]

Among the steps to improve intelligence collection in the Soviet Union taken by Allen Dulles, with the support of his brother and the president, was the opening of CIA's first Moscow station. During the Truman administration, the State Department had vetoed a CIA presence in the Moscow embassy. Under Eisenhower the veto was lifted. But Charles "Chip" Bohlen, the new U.S. ambassador in Moscow, seems not to have been told the full story. To strengthen his cover, the first head of station, Edward Ellis Smith, who arrived in Moscow in the spring of 1954, had formally resigned from the CIA and joined the State Department's Office of Security. Bohlen was allegedly informed that Smith was being posted to Moscow as regional security officer. Smith was not a success. Early in 1956 he was seduced by his Russian maid, who, predictably, was in the service of the KGB. When the KGB, equally predictably, tried to blackmail Smith with photographs of his sexual liaison with his maid, he decided to confide in the ambassador. Bohlen was unsympathetic. Smith later discovered that, while the ambassador was on leave in Washington in April 1956, he told Eisenhower, during a round of golf, "CIA placed a man in my embassy without telling me, and he got involved with a Russian girl and they took pictures of them in the nude!" Eisenhower allegedly interrupted his round to place an immediate phone call to Foster Dulles.[43] The seduction rate in the Moscow embassy during the mid-1950s was remarkably high. No less than twelve embassy personnel admitted to Bohlen that the KGB had tried to blackmail them into becoming agents by secretly photographing them during sex with KGB "swallows." Bohlen later claimed, doubtless with some exaggeration, "All of these people were out of the country in twenty-four hours."[44] It is unlikely that all those seduced by "swallows" confessed to the ambassador.

During Eisenhower's first term, the CIA had less success against the Soviet target in Moscow than in Vienna and Berlin, whose reputations as centers of espionage by both East and West were enhanced by the fictional exploits of Graham Greene's Harry Lime and John le Carré's George Smiley. CIA's first major penetration of Soviet intelligence took place in Vienna. On the morning of New Year's Day, 1953, the U.S. vice-consul in Vienna, then occupied by the wartime Allies, was handed an envelope by a stranger dressed in civilian clothes who then walked rapidly away. Inside the envelope, the vice-consul found a note written in Russian:

I am a Soviet officer. I wish to meet with an American officer with the object of offering certain services. Time: 1800 hours. Date: 1 January 1953. Place: Plankengasse, Vienna 1. Failing this meeting, I will be at the same place, same time, on successive Saturdays.

The writer of the letter later proved to be Major Pyotr Semyonovich Popov of the GRU (Soviet military intelligence), who, it was later learned, had made several previous unsuccessful approaches to Americans in Vienna. Though not yet thirty, Popov was already marked for promotion to the rank of lieutenant colonel. The first contact with him in Plankengasse was kept brief to avoid attracting attention in a public place. Subsequent meetings took place in CIA safe houses. At the first of these meetings, Popov explained that he had both a family and "an affair to straighten out"; he needed money to support his mistress. Once given the money he had asked for, Popov added, "The only thing is, treat me like a human being!" His handlers were convinced that "Pyotr was not only seeking money, he wanted a sense of real worth. And that reassurance, unavailable from his harsh Soviet superiors, was what the Americans would henceforth give him." Popov was able to consult most of the files in Soviet military headquarters in Vienna. According to a study by a CIA officer with unrestricted access to the still-classified Popov files, of the documents he provided, "a considerable number were directly relevant to the subject uppermost in the minds of the Western leaders . . . the possibility of war with Russia."

For five years until his detection in 1958 Popov was the CIA's most important agent. In 1954 he was posted back to Moscow and then, from 1955, stationed in East Berlin. Because of the importance of the case, Eisenhower was briefed personally on it by Allen Dulles, and shown samples of his documents. As a sign of his personal appreciation, Dulles sent Popov a gift of specially made gold cuff links engraved with a sword (as a sign of bravery) and the helmet of the goddess Athena (to denote wisdom). Never having heard of Athena, Popov was grateful but some-what confused. The cuff links, however, also served a practical purpose. On one occasion a CIA emissary identified himself to Popov by display-ing an identical set showing a sword and Athena's helmet.[45] Popov's reports and the public pronouncements of Soviet leaders after Stalin's sudden death in March 1953 gradually helped to soften the CIA's assess-ment of the Soviet menace. Allen Dulles wrote in November 1954:

> While we continue to estimate that the Soviet leaders ultimately envisage "(a) the elimination of every world power center capable of competing with the USSR, (b) the spread of Communism to all parts of the world, and (c) Soviet domination of the other Commu-nist regimes," we have increasing evidence that the top Soviet lead-ership realize that this is a long-term objective and may be gen-uinely desirous of a considerable period of "coexistence," that is a period of some years in which tensions and risks of war are reduced.[46]

As well as running agents against Soviet targets in Vienna and Berlin, the CIA also tapped Soviet telephones in both cities. The original inspira-tion came from the British SIS. In 1949 SIS had begun Operation Silver in Vienna, secretly tunneling seventy feet from the cellar of a suburban house to tap the telephone cables used by Soviet military headquarters.

From 1951 Silver became a joint operation with the CIA. Its success led to plans for an even more ambitious Operation Gold in Berlin, personally approved by Eisenhower. A joint SIS/CIA conference in London in the spring of 1954 agreed on the construction of a five-hundred-meter tunnel running from the American sector of West Berlin into the East to tap landlines leading to the Soviet military and intelligence headquarters at Karlshorst. Most of the cost—estimated at from $4 million to $6 million—was borne by the United States. Operation Gold encountered formidable technical problems; the president was doubtless informed that, to quote a CIA report, "No one had ever tunneled under clandestine conditions with the expectation of hitting a target two inches in diameter and 18 inches below a main German Soviet highway." There were, inevitably, also some unanticipated problems. On one occasion during the winter months, heaters in the tunnel began melting snow on the ground immediately above it; the heaters were quickly turned off and refrigeration units hurried in.

During the fourteen months from February 1955, when the tunnel became operational, until April 1956, when the Soviet authorities staged an "accidental" discovery of it, the size of the intelligence take was phenomenal. Planeloads of tapes were flown out of Berlin each week to be studied by fifty CIA Russian- and German-speaking personnel working in cramped conditions in a prefabricated hut on the Washington Mall. It took two and a half years after the tunnel was abandoned to finish processing the telephone intercepts obtained from it. Only later did the CIA discover that the KGB had been informed from the outset of the building of the Berlin tunnel by George Blake, a Soviet mole in SIS who had taken part in the planning conference with the CIA. But the KGB wrongly believed that Soviet cipher messages intercepted in the tunnel were just as invulnerable to American attack as those sent by radio. It was unaware that Soviet cipher machines gave off faint echoes of the unciphered clear-text messages that could often be picked up on the cables tapped by Operation Gold. None of the intercepted messages has yet been declassified. According to Ray S. Cline, later DDI (deputy director for intelligence), the Berlin tunnel provided CIA analysts with a wealth of valuable military, scientific, and economic intelligence. The material was probably chiefly important for what it did not say. Like Popov, Operation Gold provided no evidence of major aggressive designs by the Soviet Union. Coexistence rather than world conquest appeared to be the keynote of Soviet foreign policy in the post-Stalin era.[47]

Despite the temporary success in penetrating Soviet cipher communications in Berlin, Eisenhower was aware from the outset of his presidency that the cryptanalytic offensive against the USSR could never become a Cold War Ultra. Unlike the Enigma cipher machine used by Nazi Germany, the OTP (one-time pad) employed for high-grade Soviet communications was unbreakable if security procedures were followed correctly. Ciphered Soviet diplomatic and military radio communications did not carry the faint plain-text echoes detected on the cables in the Berlin tunnel. The Brownell committee had concluded in June 1952:

> Because our enemies are today much better informed, perhaps because of our own disclosures of the importance of communications intelligence to this Government, we may never see a return of the great successes and victories attributable to COMINT during the course of World War II.

The committee was also disturbed by the problems of recruiting SIGINT personnel. "The COMINT agencies today," it believed, "are in poor position to compete for the people they need." ASA, the largest of the service agencies, had "only ten or fifteen top flight cryptanalysts left." Though SIGINT faced far greater problems during the Cold War than during the Second World War, however, the committee's report was not a counsel of despair:

> . . . The art is one of such importance to the defense of our country in the foreseeable future that we must maintain our efforts aggressively and efficiently. . . .
>
> It is the opinion of the experts that there is a reasonable chance of success, provided a greater and more efficient effort is made. This means the employment of a larger number of highly skilled personnel, and the expenditure of additional funds for machines. It also would require the development . . . , under civilian direction, of a strong research and development.[48]

Eisenhower took to heart the Brownell committee's recommendations. Founded on the day of his election, NSA received unprecedented resources during his two terms as president. By 1956 it had almost nine thousand employees, with as many more again working under NSA direction in the service cryptologic agencies. In 1957 a new NSA headquarters building, begun three years earlier, was completed at a cost of $35 million at Fort Meade, midway between Washington and Baltimore. The basement of the 1.4-million-square-foot main building contained the biggest and most sophisticated computer complex in the world. Though Eisenhower understood little of computer science, he was determined that the United States should have the most advanced SIGINT technol-

ogy. In 1957 he authorized Project Lightning, the world's largest govern-
ment-supported computer research program. Spread over five years
with a budget of $25 million, involving Sperry Rand, IBM, RCA, Philco,
General Electric, MIT, the University of Kansas, and Ohio State, the project surpassed its goal of extending circuitry capability by 1,000 percent.
Fort Meade became a major center of scientific and technological
research. The enormous resources poured into NSA during the Eisenhower presidency changed the balance of power in the English-speaking
intelligence network. In the wartime SIGINT alliance Britain had been
the senior partner. But a system of communication intelligence based on
huge banks of computers and intercept stations around the world was
simply too expensive for postwar Britain to take the lead. America's
wealth and technology gave it, for the first time, the intelligence as well
as the military leadership of the Western world. By 1956 NSA had set up
ten COMINT Communications Relay Centers (CCRCs): in Alaska,
Hawaii, Japan, Morocco, Okinawa, the Philippines, Taiwan, Turkey, the
United Kingdom, and West Germany. Each CCRC was operated by one of
the service SIGINT agencies and was responsible for coordinating
COMINT collection in its region; the center at Permasans in West Germany, probably the busiest of the ten, oversaw the work of thirty-one
SIGINT stations. NSA headquarters at Fort Meade was directly responsible for coordinating SIGINT in the continental United States, and for
communication with the British GCHQ at Cheltenham and the Canadian
SIGINT agency, CBNRC, at Ottawa.[49] Together with its British, Canadian,
and Australasian allies, NSA thus controlled a growing network of listening posts around the periphery of the Soviet Union and Communist
China.

NSA relied on old-fashioned burglary as well as on state-of-the-art
technology. Most major modern cryptanalytic coups have required information about the ciphers under attack to assist the codebreakers. As
postwar cryptography became steadily more sophisticated, so American
cryptanalysts, like their main allies and opponents, became increasingly
dependent on the penetration of foreign embassies (usually a less difficult target than foreign ministries abroad) to obtain intelligence on
cipher systems. Though Truman and his secretaries of state were not
prepared to authorize covert operations against Washington embassies,
Eisenhower and Foster Dulles had no such inhibitions. The embassy
penetrations begun during the Eisenhower administration had one or
more of three purposes: the theft or copying of embassy cipher material,
the suborning of cipher clerks, and the planting of bugs in embassy communication rooms.[50] Embassy break-ins were among the FBI's so-called
black bag jobs, each personally approved by Hoover or his associate

director, Clyde Tolson, and marked "Do Not File." An FBI memorandum of April 1954 described the techniques involved. Each black bag job began with a "survey" during which it was "necessary to develop confidential sources at the apartment or building involved." Usually two or three FBI agents took part in the break-in itself, usually at night. One had the responsibility for photographing embassy documents, another for ensuring that they were correctly replaced. On average, each break-in produced about five hundred photographic exposures. During the operation an FBI supervisor outside the embassy remained in touch by walkie-talkie with the agents inside. A further eight to ten FBI agents were needed to keep under surveillance exits and entrances to the embassy and any personnel likely to disturb the intruders.[51] The doctrine of plausible deniability ensures that there is no trace of any black bag operation against a Washington embassy in the declassified sections of the Eisenhower papers. There can be no doubt, however, that the president was informed.

NSA's greatest successes were, unsurprisingly, achieved against Third World countries whose ciphers and embassies were less secure than those of the Soviet bloc. The Third World traffic of greatest interest to Eisenhower and the State Department in the pre-Castro era was that of the Middle East. As a result of the UKUSA treaty, NSA was able to benefit from British as well as American penetration of foreign embassies. In the spring of 1956 Peter Wright of MI5 entered the Egyptian embassy in London, disguised as a telephone engineer, ostensibly to repair the telephone system, and succeeded in placing bugs that revealed the settings on the embassy's Hagelin cipher machines.[52] In September 1956 the British foreign secretary, Selwyn Lloyd, sent a top-secret letter to congratulate the director of GCHQ on the "volume" and "excellence" of the decrypts "relating to all the countries in the Middle East area. I am writing to let you know how valuable we have found this material and how much I appreciate the hard work and skill involved in its production."[53] The decrypts that so impressed Lloyd were the product of a joint NSA/GCHQ operation and were equally available to the Dulles brothers. Even the Suez crisis, which temporarily disrupted much else in the special relationship between the United States and Great Britain, did not affect the SIGINT exchange.[54] Nor did the volume of Middle Eastern decrypts diminish afterward. Victor Norris Hamilton, who was employed by NSA as a Middle Eastern "research analyst" from 1957 to 1959, later revealed after defecting to Moscow that during this period NSA was able to decrypt cipher systems used by Egypt, Syria, Turkey, Iran, Lebanon, Jordan, Saudi Arabia, and Yemen. In collaboration with GCHQ, NSA—according to Hamilton—decrypted Egypt's cables to its European embassies as well as to Washington and its UN delegation:

For example, I had in my desk all the deciphered communications between Cairo and the U.A.R. [Egyptian] embassy in Moscow relating to the visit of the U.A.R. government mission to the U.S.S.R. in 1958 for the purpose of purchasing petroleum in the Soviet Union.[55]

Within Europe, NSA's main successes, again in collaboration with GCHQ, were probably against France and Italy. French communication security (COMSEC) was frequently dreadful—and something of an embarrassment to its main NATO allies. In 1954 the KGB defectors Vladimir and Evdokia Petrov revealed that the French diplomatic documents available to Moscow Center were so numerous that the translators found difficulty in keeping up with the supply.[56] During the Suez crisis French diplomatic traffic seems to have been unreadable. But in 1960 a combined MI5/GCHQ operation succeeded in bugging the French embassy in London and obtaining clear-text versions of its cipher traffic.[57] When these and other intercepts become available to historians sometime during the twenty-first century, they will doubtless lead to some interesting reassessments of the foreign policy of the Eisenhower presidency.

NSA, however, had no significant success with current Soviet diplomatic traffic, although retrospective revelations from Venona intercepts of 1944-45 continued to provide further evidence of past Soviet espionage. When the new attorney general, Herbert Brownell, privately told Eisenhower in 1953, "We've got much more against [Harry Dexter] White than against Hiss," one of the four sources that he mentioned was probably Venona.[58] Though unable to penetrate high-grade Soviet cipher systems, the SIGINT stations of the UKUSA alliance around the periphery of the Soviet Union intercepted vast amounts of lower-grade voice and cipher communications. Most were individually insignificant. One of the eavesdroppers stationed at a base in West Germany, for example, recalls many tedious hours spent listening to Soviet fighter pilots communicating unimportant details to ground control or complaining about their automatic wing deicers and other malfunctioning pieces of equipment. Individually, such scraps of information were mostly insignificant. Collectively, they gave an interesting insight into the state of the Soviet air force.[59]

Despite its inability to break high-grade Soviet cipher systems, NSA achieved two major successes against the Soviet target during the Eisenhower presidency. The first was made possible by the construction of an NSA radar station near Samsoun in Turkey by General Electric. Though widely used for air defense since the Second World War, radar detection had never previously been used for intelligence purposes. The project was initially opposed by the Pentagon, but in 1954 the air force assistant secretary, Trevor Gardner, who pressed the case for developing technical intelligence systems capable of monitoring Soviet missile development, won the support of both the president and the air force. The Samsoun facility became operational in the summer of 1955, just in time to track the first Soviet IRBM launches from the testing ground at Kapustin Yar. The development of telemetry intelligence (TELINT, a variety of SIGINT), the analysis of the signals transmitted by the missiles, provided detailed information on their performance. In 1957 *Aviation Week* published a report on the work of the Samsoun base in monitoring Soviet missile development. Eisenhower's outraged response bears witness to the importance he attached to the intelligence collected at Samsoun. The publisher, Donald C. McGraw of McGraw-Hill in New York, was personally informed by a White House emissary "that in the judgment of the President the publication of this article constituted a serious breach of security and that the President wanted Mr. McGraw personally to know of the gravity with which he viewed the event." A chastened McGraw assured the president that in the future all articles relating to national security would be personally reviewed by a senior editor of *Aviation Week.*[60]

The second major SIGINT success against the Soviet target was the discovery of major gaps in the USSR's air defense system. NSA devised a risky program of airborne "ferret" missions to skirt and penetrate Soviet airspace with the aim of triggering Soviet radar signals for analysis by its ELINT (electronic intelligence) analysts. The most remarkable ELINT revelation, according to Eisenhower's staff secretary, General Andrew Goodpaster, was that "Over a large part of northern Siberia, up toward the pole, there were not [any] radars." This, according to an intelligence official concerned with the ferret missions, was "one of the great secrets of the Cold War": "We could have launched a strategic-bomber attack across the polar icecap and the Russians would never have known." In 1957 Eisenhower approved the top-secret Moonbounce project to build a huge satellite dish to capture Soviet radar signals bouncing off the moon. In the late 1950s Moonbounce detected the first Soviet P-14 "Tall King" radars constructed in northern Siberia as the centerpiece of an early warning system intended to perform the same function as the North American DEW (Distant Early Warning) line. NSA ELINT operations continued, however, to find serious deficiencies in the Soviet air defense network.[61]

The most important intelligence innovation of the Eisenhower presidency, as well as the one that owed most to his personal initiative, was in aerial reconnaissance. On becoming president, Ike was quick to complain about the lack of imagery intelligence (IMINT) from the Soviet Union. The ferret missions, despite taking risks that led, on average, to the loss of two planes a year during the 1950s, were usually able to penetrate only the fringes of Soviet airspace.[62] Eisenhower made frequent references to the postwar findings of the U.S. Strategic Bombing Survey that emphasized the accuracy and the importance of aerial photography in both the European and Pacific theaters.[63] The lack of any intelligence warning of the Soviet test of a hydrogen bomb in August 1953, only nine months after the first American explosion of a thermonuclear device, deepened Eisenhower's sense of frustration. In private, he showed an impatience he was careful to conceal in public. "Our relative position in intelligence, compared to the Soviets," he complained, "could scarcely have been worse. The Soviets enjoyed practically unimpeded access to information of a kind in which we were almost wholly lacking." Details of some American nuclear establishments were available in print; accurate, small-scale maps of the whole country were freely available in local bookstores and gas stations. The only way to gain similar information about the Soviet Union, Eisenhower believed, was by aerial reconnaissance.[64] The May Day parade in Moscow in 1954 made matters worse by unveiling the new Soviet Bison heavy bomber. "The number," reported Allen Dulles, "far exceeded what was thought to be available." The Soviet Union, it appeared, now had both thermonuclear weapons and a rapidly growing intercontinental bomber force capable of carrying them to the United States. Allen Dulles later admitted that the intelligence community had been deceived by the May Day parade and other Soviet displays into producing exaggerated estimates of Bison production. Analysts eventually realized that the same squadron must have been flying around in circles, reappearing every few minutes over Red Square.[65]

In July 1954, at Eisenhower's request, a task force headed by Dr. James R. Killian, president of the Massachusetts Institute of Technology, began studying ways of preventing surprise attack. Its first objective was "increasing our capacity to get more positive intelligence about the enemy's intentions and capabilities." Eisenhower personally assured Killian that he was "very keenly interested" in the task force's progress.[66] During its meetings, the Killian committee was given details of plans for a new high-altitude reconnaissance plane (later christened the U-2) that had been turned down by the air force. One of the key members of the committee was the future Nobel laureate, Dr. Edwin H. Land, inventor of the Polaroid camera, who quickly grasped the combined potential of the U-2 and new advances in aerial photography. On November 5 Land sent Allen Dulles a memorandum urging the CIA to become a "pioneer in scientific techniques for collecting intelligence" and seize "the present opportunity for aerial photography."[67] On the day before Thanksgiving, Allen Dulles, Killian, Land, and the Harvard physicist Edward Purcell (like Land, a Nobel laureate), went to the Oval Office for a secret meeting with the president. No minutes were kept. Usually Eisenhower liked to sleep on major decisions. The U-2 program for aerial reconnaissance over the Soviet Union, however, caught his imagination immediately.[68] He gave his consent on the spot, but recognized the risks. "Well, boys," he said, "I believe the country needs this information, and I'm going to approve it. But I'll tell you one thing. Some day one of these machines is going to be caught, and then we'll have a storm."[69]

On December 9 the CIA signed a construction contract with Lockheed. Eisenhower insisted that the U-2 project be kept top secret. "Any leak of information either at home or abroad," he warned, "could compel abandonment of the entire idea." Within the White House he limited knowledge of the U-2 to Goodpaster, his staff secretary and closest confidant.[70] The CIA project manager for the U-2, Richard Bissell, who was summoned to the Oval Office half an hour after Eisenhower had given his approval, shared his concern for secrecy. A former economics professor at Yale and MIT noted for his iconoclastic views, Bissell believed that "There are an awful lot of things that are much better done in private." Eisenhower described the U-2 as closer in design to a powered glider than to a conventional airplane. It was built in a Lockheed hangar in California known as the Skunk Works because no one unconnected with the project was allowed to go near it.[71] Bissell proved a remarkable project manager. The U-2 flew its first test flight in July 1955, only seven months after the contract was signed with Lockheed.[72]

The success of the U-2 program, completed by Bissell at $3 million below budget,[73] led Eisenhower to take a dramatic personal initiative soon after the plane's maiden flight. On Thursday, July 21, during a four-power summit in Geneva, Ike made his famous "Open Skies" proposal that the United States and the Soviet Union allow each other the right of overhead reconnaissance and aerial photography, and make available "a complete blueprint" of their military establishments. Though details of the proposal had been worked out by his advisers, the initiative was the president's. Eisenhower records in his memoirs that, as he finished his speech, "the loudest clap of thunder I have ever heard roared into the room, and the conference was plunged into Stygian darkness." The Soviet delegation seemed momentarily stunned. After the British and French prime ministers had supported the Open Skies proposal, the Soviet prime minister, Nikolai Bulganin, declared that the idea had real merit and would be studied sympathetically. But it was the party secretary, Nikita Khrushchev, not Bulganin, who called the tune. Over cocktails after the conference session closed, Khrushchev told Eisenhower that his scheme was "nothing more than a bald espionage plot against the Soviet Union."[74] Though rejected in 1955, the Open Skies proposal set an important precedent. Overhead reconnaissance by the U-2's successor, the spy satellite, later became an essential part of all United States–Soviet arms control agreements.

The high-level test flights of the U-2 in American airspace seemed to confirm all the claims made for its performance. Though U.S. radar stations in its flight path were warned to expect strange aircraft, they either failed to pick it up at all or tracked it imperfectly. Eisenhower was stunned by the new technology of aerial photography that it employed. In a photograph of San Diego taken from seventy thousand feet he was able to count the automobiles on the street and detect the lines separating spaces on parking lots. Eisenhower concluded that since Soviet radar would clearly find it difficult to track the U-2 and fighter planes could not operate at altitudes over fifty thousand feet, it would be possible to take similar photographs of the Soviet Union "with reasonable safety." But the president was misinformed about the likely consequences of an accident or of a successful Soviet attack on the U-2. Because of the plane's fragile construction, he was assured that "if things should go wrong," it would virtually disintegrate. The Russians would be unable to capture any intact equipment—or a live pilot. "This was a cruel assumption," wrote Eisenhower in his memoirs, "but I was assured that the young pilots undertaking these missions were doing so with their eyes wide open and motivated by a high degree of patriotism, a swashbuckling bravado, and certain material inducements."[75] The pilots themselves were told a rather different story. They were equipped with both parachutes and cyanide and told that it was up to them to decide, if they had to bail out, whether they preferred to be taken prisoner or to commit suicide. Secretly Bissell calculated that no pilot stood any real chance of survival if a U-2 crashed.[76]

Eisenhower personally reviewed and approved every U-2 mission. After each flight he was briefed in the Oval Office by the CIA's head of photographic intelligence, Arthur C. "Art" Lundahl, renowned within the agency for his ability to explain complicated technical problems to the layman. The first U-2 mission, on July 4, 1956, covered targets in the Leningrad area and long-range bomber bases in the western Soviet Union. Lundahl brought to the White House greatly enlarged photographs that he displayed on forty-inch by sixty-inch briefing boards. He pointed to the nuclear weapons loading pits at all the airfields overflown by the U-2. Ike pored over the photographs with a magnifying glass, marveled at the detail that they revealed, listened attentively to

Lundahl's technical explanations, and asked if the Russians had tried to intercept the mission. Lundahl put up on the briefing boards photographs of MIG fighters trying desperately to reach the U-2, then falling back as their engines cut out at high altitude. Eisenhower, he recalled, was "warm with satisfaction" at the end of the briefing. The second U-2 mission on July 5, only twenty-four hours after the first, photographed Moscow and targets in the southern Ukraine, twice crossing the two rings of surface-to-air missile sites that defended the capital. On this occasion, Lundahl told the president, Soviet air defenses had not even detected the intruder.[77] The initial range of the U-2s was twenty-two hundred miles, later increased to three thousand. Though assigned specific targets, pilots were encouraged to deviate from their flight paths if they saw other sites of particular interest. The U-2s also carried NSA payloads that recorded emissions from Soviet radar, microwave, and ground communications.[78]

Lundahl quickly established himself as one of the president's favorite briefers. At other intelligence briefings, Ike would frequently ask, "How does this compare with the U-2 information?"[79] The first major achievement of the U-2 and CIA's photographic interpreters, Eisenhower believed, was gradually to expose the myth of the "bomber gap."[80] In 1955 alarmist air force intelligence estimates had claimed that by the end of the decade the Soviet Long-Range Air Force would be more powerful than the U.S. Strategic Air Command. Production of Bear bombers during late 1956 was estimated at twenty-five per month; by 1959 or 1960, it was predicted that the Soviet air force would also possess a fleet of six hundred to eight hundred Bison bombers. Largely as a result of the evidence provided by the U-2s, these alarmist calculations were steadily scaled down during 1957 and 1958. By 1959 the Soviet air force possessed a combined total of fewer than two hundred Bisons and Bears.[81]

During the Suez crisis in the autumn of 1956 the U-2 also became a major source of intelligence on the United States' closest allies. At the root of what became the most serious rift in Anglo-American relations since the Second World War was the obsession of Churchill's successor as prime minister, Sir Anthony Eden, with the threat to British interests and oil supplies in the Middle East posed by Egyptian leader General Gamal Abdel Nasser. On March 15 Eden sent Eisenhower a top-secret assessment of Egyptian policy, based on intelligence "of whose authenticity we are entirely confident," claiming that a secret conference of the Egyptian leadership had decided on covert action to overthrow the pro-Western ruling families of Iraq, Jordan, and Libya, establish "purely Arab republics in Tunisia, Algeria and Morocco," "isolate Saudi Arabia as the only remaining Monarchy in the Eastern Arabian States and then to remove King Saud." Nasser's ultimate aim was alleged to be a union of Arab republics dominated by Egypt. Eisenhower too regarded Nasser as a menace and a potential Soviet bridgehead in the Middle East. He replied to Eden's note, "Assuming that the information therein contained is completely authentic, it seems to me to give a clue of how we—your Government and ours—might operate with the greatest chance of frustrating Soviet designs in the region." Ike approved Operation Omega, designed to avoid "any open break which would throw Nasser irrevocably into a Soviet satellite status," but to use both diplomacy and covert action to thwart his ambitions in the Arab world. "We should make sure we concert the overall plan with the British—i.e. with Eden and Lloyd," he instructed. In place of Nasser, Eisenhower wanted "to build up some other individual as a prospective leader of the Arab world." "My own choice," he noted unrealistically, ". . . is King Saud."[82] Eden was more impatient. "Nasser must be got rid of," he told the head of the Middle Eastern section in the Foreign Office. "It is either him or us, don't forget that."[83]

At least for a time, Eden seems to have been attracted by the possibility of a covert operation to assassinate Nasser. Eisenhower was not. At the end of March CIA officials were sent to London to confer with SIS on plans for covert action in the Middle East. They had instructions to discourage any proposal to go ahead with the assassination plan. At a meeting with the CIA delegation, the deputy director of SIS, George Young, accepted that Nasser could not be overthrown immediately, but proposed organizing a coup in Syria, which he claimed was about to become a Soviet satellite. In May Wilbur C. Eveland, one of the CIA officials at the meeting, was sent to Syria to conduct a "probing operation." According to Eveland, "To forestall the SIS plan to eliminate the Egyptian president, the CIA had, apparently, compromised with an offer to consider joining in a Syrian coup."[84] In July Eisenhower gave his approval to the Syrian operation, code-named Straggle. The leader of the conservative Syrian Populist party, Michail Bey Ilyan, who had been chosen to lead the coup, told the CIA, "It will take money—much of it and soon—to [take] care [of] the press, the 'street,' key army officers, and others." He asked Eveland for "a half-million and at least thirty days" to prepare the coup. Six weeks later Eveland transferred a suitcase containing the money into the trunk of a Chrysler limousine parked on a Syrian mountain road. Ilyan, to his annoyance, "puffed complacently in the backseat on a long cigar."[85]

After Nasser's decision to nationalize the Suez Canal Company on July 26 Eden could no longer be placated by covert action in Syria. A third of the ships using the canal were British; most of Britain's oil supply passed through it. Barely able to contain his rage, Eden cabled Eisenhower the next day that, despite the search for a diplomatic solution, "my colleagues and I are convinced that we must be ready, in the last resort, to use force to bring Nasser to his senses."[86] From this point on, British and American policies rapidly diverged. Eisenhower believed, rightly, that any attempt to revert to old-style gunboat diplomacy would alienate world opinion, produce an anti-Western backlash throughout the Arab world, and play into the hands of the Soviet Union in the Middle East. Early in August he sent Foster Dulles to London to persuade Eden to call a conference of canal users. By spinning out negotiations Ike hoped to wean Britain and France away from the use of force. During September, as the negotiations gradually ran into the ground, Eisenhower tried another tactic, seeking to persuade Eden to opt for covert action to overthrow Nasser rather than open military intervention. Eden wrote to Harold Macmillan, then chancellor of the exchequer, in a top-secret memorandum on September 23:

> The Americans' main contention is that we can bring Nasser down by degrees rather on the Mossadeq lines. Of course if this is possible we should warmly welcome it and I am all for making every effort provided the results show themselves without delay.[87]

When he received this message, Macmillan was in Washington for a meeting with the IMF. On September 25 he was smuggled into the White House by a side door for a secret meeting with the president. Ike seemed full of energy; he showed his guest the narrow fairway in the White House garden that he used as a driving range, taking aim toward a distant lamp post. Macmillan found it "really an exhilarating experience to see 'Ike' again, and have such a good talk with him." Eisenhower reaffirmed his support for covert action. "On Suez," Macmillan wrote in his diary, "he was sure that we must get Nasser down. The only thing was how to do it."[88]

In his desire to smooth over the rift in the special relationship, Eisenhower failed to make clear that he was thinking in terms of the gradual destabilization of the Nasser regime rather than a coup such as that which had disposed of Mossadeq three years earlier. When the CIA devised a plan "to topple Nasser" quickly, the president commented:

> An action of this kind could not be taken when there is as much active hostility as at present for a thing like this. . . . A time free from heated stress holding the world's attention as at present would have to be chosen.[89]

Eisenhower correctly grasped that Cairo in 1956 had little in common with Teheran in 1953. Nasser, unlike Mossadeq, was the popular hero of the Arab world. However well the CIA hid its involvement in a coup against him, the United States was bound to be a prime suspect in the eyes of the Arab world.

Eden, however, was set on Nasser's rapid overthrow. Though SIS drew up plans for replacing Nasser by an "alternative" government, Eden concluded that covert action, by itself, would be insufficient.[90] Removing Nasser, he believed, would require military intervention. On October 14 Eden sent Eisenhower affectionate greetings on his sixty-fifth birthday. "Our friendship," he told the president, "remains one of my greatest rewards. Public life makes one value such a relationship more than ever in these anxious times."[91] The prime minister, however, was simultaneously embarking on an act of calculated deception that has no parallel in the history of the special relationship. While Ike was opening his birthday presents, Eden was receiving a visit at Chequers from a representative of the French prime minister, Guy Mollet, accompanied by General Maurice Challe. The French emissaries produced a secret plan for the Israelis to launch an attack on Egypt across the Sinai desert, thus giving Britain and France a pretext to call on both sides to withdraw from the threatened Suez Canal. When Nasser refused, as he was bound to do, British and French forces would intervene, ostensibly to separate the two belligerents, in fact to return the canal to Anglo-French control. Eden was delighted by this outrageous proposal, which was formally agreed in a meeting of British, French, and Israeli representatives at Sèvres on the outskirts of Paris on October 24. The meeting was surrounded by extraordinary secrecy. According to the French version, the British foreign secretary, Selwyn Lloyd, arrived wearing a false mustache; the British later claimed that the mustache was a French invention. All those present "swore that none would in the lifetime of the others reveal what they had discussed." The Americans were kept in the dark. Eden and Macmillan, however, entirely misread Eisenhower's likely reaction to the Suez operation. Ike's support for the principle (if not the early implementation) of covert action to bring Nasser down, together with his apparent commitment to the special relationship, persuaded them that he would not seek to halt Anglo-French intervention even if he disapproved of it. Eden's press secretary, William Clark, records Macmillan as prophesying confidently and inaccurately, "I don't think there is going to be any trouble from Ike—he and I understand each other—he's not going to make any real trouble if we have to do something drastic."[92]

The CIA discovered the existence of the secret Anglo-Franco-Israeli negotiations but not what was being discussed.[93] NSA reported a "vast increase in diplomatic traffic between France and Israel," but was apparently unable to decrypt it.[94] Eisenhower ordered the use of U-2s to monitor the British, French, and Israeli military buildup in the Middle East. "I don't like to do this to my friends," said the president, "but I will G-2 [spy on] them if I have to."[95] He noted on October 15 that "our high-flying reconnaissance planes have shown that Israel has obtained some 60 of the French Mystère pursuit planes, when there had been reported the transfer of only 24."[96] The U-2s also monitored a steady flow of British troops and aircraft to Cyprus.[97] Britain and Israel, however, successfully confused American assessment of the arms buildup by disinformation suggesting that Israel's intended target was not Egypt but Jordan.[98] The extent of Eisenhower's confusion as he tried to make sense of the Middle East is well displayed by his "memorandum for the record" of October 15:

> It seems to be taken internationally as a foregone conclusion that Jordan is breaking up, and of course all the surrounding countries will be anxious to get their share of the wreckage, including Israel. In fact there is some suspicion that the recent savage blows of the Israel border armies against the strong points within Jordanian territory are intended to hasten this process of dissolution.
>
> On the other side of the picture, there is some indication that Britain is really serious in her announced intention of honoring her Pact with Jordan, which requires her to help defend Jordan in the case of outside invasion.
>
> Should this occur, we would have Britain in the curious position of helping to defend one of the Arab countries, while at the same time she is engaged in a quarrel—which sometimes threatens to break out into war—with Egypt over the Suez question.[99]

Foster Dulles concluded, correctly, that the British and French were "deliberately keeping us in the dark." He told his brother on October 18 that he lacked "any clear picture" of what they were up to. Allen replied optimistically that he felt "fairly well" informed of their intentions in Egypt.[100] He was wrong. Like Eisenhower, he seems to have believed that the main danger was of an Israeli attack on Jordan that, in the ensuing confusion, would give Britain and France a pretext to occupy the Suez Canal.

Eisenhower later described the next three weeks as the most crowded and demanding of his entire presidency. As the November 6 presidential election drew near, "All hell broke loose."[101] While the Suez crisis was moving toward its dismal climax, some of the "captive peoples" of Eastern Europe were beginning to rattle their chains. Following earlier unrest in Poland, a student demonstration in Budapest on October 23 brought a quarter of a million people out onto the streets, calling for free elections and the withdrawal of Soviet troops. As street fighting began, steelworkers brought a massive statue of Stalin crashing to the ground. The CIA was taken by surprise. A National Intelligence Estimate in the previous year had forecast flatly: "Popular resistance of an organized and active kind is unlikely to appear in any of the Satellites during the period of this estimate [1955–60]."[102] In the early hours of October 24 Cord Meyer, the CIA official responsible for the agency-controlled Radio Free Europe and Radio Liberty, was awakened by a phone call from Allen Dulles. "All hell has broken loose in Budapest," Dulles told him. "You'd better get into the office as soon as you can." Meyer and other senior officials spent the rest of the night in the CIA watch office, piecing together from fragmentary reports a dawn briefing for the president.[103]

In the same briefing Eisenhower was informed of a telegram received from London at 4:27 A.M., reporting that Sir Walter Monckton, who was resigning as British minister of defense, ostensibly on health grounds, had confidentially told the U.S. ambassador, Winthrop Aldrich, that the real reason was his opposition to the use of force to resolve the Suez crisis. At 11:30 A.M. Ike discussed with Foster Dulles the possibility of inviting Eden and Mollet to Washington in late November for a further attempt to seek a negotiated settlement. During the course of the day dramatic news continued to come in erratically from Hungary as Soviet tanks entered Budapest to crush the "counter-revolutionary uprising." As it did so, Eisenhower tried to focus his mind for a previously scheduled afternoon broadcast, in which he was due to answer questions on nuclear weapons, inflation, and the economy.[104]

The next day, October 25, after his early morning briefings, the president left by train to spend the rest of the day campaigning in New York City. He was met by large and enthusiastic crowds chanting "I like Ike!" "It was," Ike told himself, "a good time to be liked," but his mind was on Eastern Europe and the Middle East.[105] During the day, as reports came in of five thousand deaths in Budapest, Eisenhower issued a statement denouncing Soviet aggression and hailing the "renewed expression of the intense desire for freedom long held by the Hungarian people." That evening a teletype message from the Budapest legation, transmitted by an operator lying on the floor to avoid stray bullets, reported that the reformist Communist Imre Nagy had taken over as prime minister and that large crowds outside the legation were singing the Hungarian anthem, calling on the Russians to leave, and appealing for American help.[106]

Back in Washington the next day, October 26, Eisenhower presided at 9 A.M. over the 201st meeting of the National Security Council. Events continued to move with a speed made more bewildering by incomplete and sometimes faulty intelligence. Allen Dulles began the meeting by reporting "rumors flying around that the King of Jordan had been assassinated." His brother Foster found this inaccurate report "very worrisome":

> There was grave danger that Jordan would presently disintegrate. If this happened, the result might be a war between the Israelis and the Arabs, not to mention wars between the Arab states themselves, notably Iraq and Egypt.

A range of other possible disasters was considered. At the end of the meeting, however, Allen Dulles announced that the king had not, after all, been assassinated.[107] Despite the false alarms and real perils in the Middle East, "the compelling news," in Eisenhower's view, "continued to be Hungary." The president concluded the meeting at 10:40 A.M. in an almost apocalyptic mood:

> In view of the serious deterioration of their position in the satellites, might [the Soviet Union] not be tempted to resort to very extreme measures and even to precipitate global war? This was a situation which must be watched with the utmost care. After all, observed the President, Hitler had known well, from the first of February 1945, that he was licked. Yet he had carried on to the very last and pulled down Europe with him in his defeat. The Soviets might even develop some desperate mood such as this.

After the NSC meeting, Eisenhower instructed both Allen Dulles and Admiral Arthur W. Radford, chairman of the Joint Chiefs of Staff, to be "on special alert."[108] With his mind still on a possible apocalypse, Ike then received a delegation from the Pennsylvania Council of Republican Women, who presented him with a scroll welcoming his and Mamie's decision to set up a home in Gettysburg. "Though the heavens fall," Eisenhower reflected ruefully, "a President's planned schedules must be kept, or public interest might well turn into alarm." That afternoon Ike recorded a message of sympathy to drought-stricken Texas farmers. But he remained haunted throughout the day by the fear that the use of Russian troops to stamp out rebellion in the Soviet bloc might escalate into a third world war.[109]

After Eisenhower's early intelligence briefings on Saturday, October 27, he seemed to welcome the distractions of receiving the youngest Eagle

Scout in scouting history in the Oval Office and of being photographed with seven Michigan Minutemen. Forgetting for the moment the history of the Minutemen, Ike told himself that at least these engagements "had nothing to do with fighting and blood." During the rest of the morning, however, further disturbing intelligence came in from Hungary, where the revolt was spreading, and from the Middle East, where there was worrying evidence of the Israeli arms buildup. At 12:25 P.M. Eisenhower sent a personal message to the Israeli prime minister, David Ben Gurion, telling him, "I must frankly express my concern at reports of heavy mobilization on your side." Immediately after lunch the president entered Walter Reed Hospital for a prearranged twenty-six-hour medical checkup. That evening Foster Dulles gave a speech, as usual approved by Eisenhower beforehand, denouncing "Soviet imperialism" for imposing "an unnatural tyranny" on Eastern Europe. "The captive peoples," he declared, "should never have reason to doubt that they have in us a sincere and dedicated friend who shares their aspirations."[110]

The intelligence briefings that the president received in Walter Reed on the morning of Sunday, October 28, continued to be somber. They included "new evidence of heavy Israeli mobilization," traffic analysis by NSA of a large volume of diplomatic radio traffic between Paris and Tel Aviv (which Eisenhower thought highly significant), and U-2 photographs that showed that in the previous forty-eight hours the British had doubled their bomber strength on Cyprus. At 3:30 P.M., before leaving the hospital, Eisenhower sent a second, urgent personal appeal to Ben Gurion to do nothing "which would endanger the peace in the Middle East."[111] He sent no similar appeal to Eden, chiefly because the U.S. intelligence community, unused to targeting its closest ally, had only partially penetrated the deception operation designed to conceal British collusion with France and Israel. That operation, organized at the highest level, was still continuing. While Eisenhower was undergoing his medical checkup, Selwyn Lloyd assured Winthrop Aldrich with what struck the U.S. ambassador as "feeling and, I believe evident conviction" that:

[A] major Israeli attack either on Jordan or Egypt at this time would put Britain in [an] impossible situation. . . . He [was] unwilling [to] believe the Israelis would launch a full-scale attack upon Egypt despite the temptation to do so, in present circumstances. He also said categorically his recent conversations with [the] French give him no reason to believe [the] French were stimulating such an Israeli venture. . . . Lloyd's major concern is [the] threat [of] further large scale attacks on Jordan.

If Washington was slow to grasp the extent of British collusion with France and Israel, it was in part at least because U.S. officials and their president found difficulty in grasping that apparently upright British gentlemen whom they had known for years could be such shameless and accomplished liars when talking to their friends. Some of the gentlemen, however, had qualms of conscience. While Lloyd was expertly deceiving Aldrich on October 28, the chairman of the JIC, Sir Patrick Dean, was dropping a broad hint to the CIA liaison officer in London, Chester Cooper, that "You and I are in much trouble, and it isn't because of Hungary."[112] Eisenhower, however, still did not believe the British would allow themselves to be "dragged into" an invasion of Egypt.[113]

After his early intelligence briefings on Monday, October 29, Eisenhower felt slightly reassured. The situation in both Israel and Hungary was, he concluded, "a little better this morning than last evening."[114] At 8:20 A.M. he left Washington by plane to campaign in Miami and Jacksonville, Florida, and Richmond, Virginia. In the course of the morning the Dulles brothers discussed growing intelligence indicating that the "French Government, perhaps with British knowledge, is concerting closely with Israelis to provoke action which would lead to Israeli war against Egypt with probable participation by French and British." Their conclusions were passed on to the president via the communication facilities on his aircraft, the *Columbine*. The Israeli attack later in the day surprised Eisenhower by its direction even more than its suddenness. The Israelis advanced not into Jordan, as he had expected, but into Egypt. In the course of the night the Israeli spearhead reached a point in the Sinai desert only twenty-five miles east of the Suez. News of the attack reached Eisenhower just as the *Columbine* was touching down in Richmond for the last of his three campaign stops. True to his usual unruffled public manner, Ike went ahead with his scheduled engagement, but by 7 P.M. he was back in Washington for a crisis meeting with his chief advisers.[115]

Intelligence on the Suez operation was still poor. When the evening meeting began, Allen Dulles was not certain whether the Israelis had launched a full-scale invasion; he suggested "that the Israelis might still be planning to withdraw—that the operations thus far have been in the nature of probing action." Admiral Radford swiftly countered that "the operation has gone too far to pull back." Eisenhower was outraged at the deception practiced on him by the British. "We should," he insisted, "let them know at once . . . that we recognize that much is on their side in the dispute with the Egyptians, but that nothing justifies double-crossing us." No one, however, yet grasped the full extent of British collusion with France and Israel. Foster Dulles "thought there was still a bare chance to 'unhook' the British from the French . . . and that it ought to be undertaken." After the meeting Eisenhower summoned the British chargé d'affaires, J. E. Coulson, to the White House and confronted him with some of the intelligence pointing to French collusion with Israel, notably the supply of Mystère fighters revealed by the U-2 and NSA reports on the volume of diplomatic traffic between Paris and Tel Aviv. The president made no reference to British collusion, but insisted that Britain and the United States "redeem [their] word about supporting any victim of aggression."[116]

The Israeli invasion caused plans for Operation Straggle in Syria to be aborted, just as it was about to go ahead. The prospective coup leader, Michail Bey Ilyan, fled across the Syrian border into Lebanon. Attempts by his CIA paymaster, Wilbur Eveland, to persuade him that the agency had been unaware of plans for the Israeli attack fell on deaf ears. Eveland himself was shattered. "Hadn't the CIA been created just to be sure we'd never be caught napping again . . . ?" he asked himself. "But, unlike what had happened at Pearl Harbor, this time it was our allies who'd deceived us."[117]

At his morning briefings the next day, October 30, Eisenhower was disturbed by the lack of intelligence on British and French intentions after the Israeli attack. "We were," he complained, "in the dark about what they planned to do." Ike was so much in the dark that he speculated that "the hand of Churchill," rather than of Eden, might be behind the British Suez adventure, since it was "in the mid-Victorian style." At a meeting with his advisers shortly after 10 A.M. the president read a news report that had just come in that British and French forces were about to land at Suez. The report was wrong (though prophetic), but it was briefly taken seriously. Foster Dulles predicted that the British and French would have control of the canal by the afternoon. Eisenhower also read a message, drafted before the news report came in, that he was about to send to Eden. "It seems to me of first importance," he told Eden, "that the UK and U.S. quickly and clearly lay out their present views and intentions before each other"—in other words, that Britain come clean about what it was up to. Ike particularly wanted to know what was going on between Britain and France. He confronted Eden, as he had confronted the British chargé d'affaires the previous evening, with some of the intelligence pointing to Franco-Israeli collusion—in particular the secret supply of French arms and aircraft and the fact that, the day before the Israeli invasion, SIGINT revealed "that the volume of communication traffic between Paris and Tel Aviv jumped enormously; alerting us to the probability that France and Israel were concerting detailed plans of some kind."[118]

Eisenhower's message reached London just as Eden had begun speaking to the House of Commons. In accordance with the plan secretly agreed at Sèvres, the prime minister announced that Britain and France were issuing Egypt and Israel with an ultimatum demanding that, within twelve hours, both sides withdraw ten miles from the Suez Canal and permit Anglo-French occupation of key points along it. Israel, whose main forces were in any case over fifty miles from the canal, agreed. Egypt, as expected, did not. When news of the ultimatum reached Eisenhower, it is reported that "the White House crackled with barrack-room language the kind of which had not been heard since the days of General Grant."[119] The president rang Eden but was connected to his press secretary, William Clark, by mistake. "Anthony," Ike told Clark, believing him to be the prime minister, "you must have gone out of your mind!"[120]

Wednesday, October 31, marked the high-water mark of the Hungarian revolt. The previous afternoon Imre Nagy, the new prime minister, had announced the abolition of one-party rule and the formation of a coalition government including non-Communist ministers. The Soviet leadership pretended to accept these changes. An official declaration from Moscow on October 31 admitted "violations and mistakes which infringed the principles of equality in relations between socialist states," and promised "to withdraw Soviet Army units from Budapest as soon as this is recognized as necessary by the Hungarian Government."[121] Despite their deep distrust of the Kremlin, both the Dulles brothers surprisingly accepted the declaration at close to its face value. Foster concluded exultantly that the world was witnessing "the beginning of the collapse of the Soviet Empire."[122] Allen, equally euphoric, mistakenly assured the president that the declaration was "one of the most significant to come out of the Soviet Union since the end of World War Two." "Yes," replied Eisenhower more prudently, "if it is genuine."[123] In a broadcast address he welcomed the "historic events" in Hungary but rejected Foster Dulles's suggestion that he also refer to "irresistible forces of liberation unleashed in Eastern Europe."[124]

During the early hours of October 31 British and French forces began bombing Egyptian airfields. A U-2 was on a mission over the Cairo area just before the bombardment began; it returned twenty minutes later to photograph bomb damage at Cairo Military Airport.[125] The next day Art Lundahl displayed photographs of the airport before and after the attack on large briefing boards in the Oval Office. Eisenhower compared the two sets of pictures, then commented admiringly, "Twenty-minute reconnaissance. Now that's something to shoot for!"[126]

The last NSC meeting before the presidential election convened in the White House cabinet room at 9 A.M. on November 1. Allen Dulles began with an exultant intelligence briefing on Hungary:

> In a sense, what had occurred there was a miracle. Events had belied all our past views that a popular revolt in the face of modern weapons was an utter impossibility. Nevertheless, the impossible had happened, and because of the power of public opinion, armed force could not effectively be used.[127]

In the space of less than two weeks, the DCI had moved from believing that a popular rebellion against Soviet control in Eastern Europe was virtually impossible to concluding that the success of the Hungarian revolt was an accomplished fact. On the president's instructions, there was no further discussion of the Hungarian revolt after Allen Dulles's briefing. Instead, the rest of the NSC meeting was devoted to the crisis in the Middle East. Foster Dulles concluded a lengthy survey of "diplomatic developments" by saying:

> It is nothing less than tragic that at this very time, when we are on the point of winning an immense and long-hoped-for victory over Soviet colonialism in Eastern Europe, we should be forced to choose between following in the footsteps of Anglo-French colonialism in Asia and Africa, or splitting our course away from their course.

Eisenhower insisted that the United States was bound to take the second option: "How could we possibly support Britain and France if in doing so we lose the whole Arab world?" His main anxiety concerned the new opportunities for the Soviet Union in the Middle East created by the Suez crisis. U.S. intelligence coverage of Egypt was unusually good. NSA was able to decrypt large amounts of Egyptian diplomatic traffic; the CIA had assets inside Nasser's administration; the U-2s provided remarkable imagery. But Ike still feared that intelligence might not have revealed the magnitude of Soviet penetration of Egypt. The extent of his fears was demonstrated by a remarkable question that he put to Admiral Radford toward the end of the NSC meeting. He asked "whether it was at all possible that the Russians could have 'slipped' the Egyptians a half dozen atomic bombs." Radford said it was unlikely.[128]

That evening, in Philadelphia, Eisenhower gave his final platform speech of the presidential campaign, then canceled the remaining rallies on his schedule. While the president was telling his Philadelphia audience, "We cannot—in the world, any more than in our own nation—subscribe to one law for the weak, another for the strong," the United Nations General Assembly began debating an American resolution, introduced by Foster Dulles, calling for a cease-fire in the Middle East and requiring all UN members to abstain from the use of force. The resolution was approved in the early hours of November 2 by a vote of 64–5, with 6 abstentions. Only Australia and New Zealand sided with Britain, France, and Israel. The United States had taken an unprecedented public stand against its closest allies.

"Only a star-gazer," Ike gloomily told a close friend, "could tell how the whole thing is going to come out." But he admitted that it did not "make sleeping any easier"—not merely because of the "terrible mistake" made by the British and French but also "because of the opportunities that we have handed to the Russians."[129] The president continued to be preoccupied by the threat of overt or covert Soviet attempts to broaden the Middle Eastern conflict. A JCS assessment on November 3 concluded:

> By use of propaganda, agents and local Communist parties the Soviets can cause extensive anti-Western rioting, sabotage and general disorder throughout the area, particularly at Western oil installations. To direct and assist in such operations the Soviets could introduce small numbers of professional agents and saboteurs. The Soviets also could attempt to encourage or engineer coups in Syria and Jordan with the object of establishing governments willing to attack Israel in order to broaden hostilities. Such attempts are considered likely.[130]

Though Eisenhower opposed the Suez invasion, he said later that if Britain and France had "done it quickly, we would have accepted it."[131] When the Anglo-French air attacks began on the evening of October 31 Allen Dulles had expected the operation to be over quickly. The following morning he told Foster that Nasser was "pretty well on the ropes" and might be "toppling" in the face of "overwhelming force."[132] But Nasser did not topple, and the aerial bombardment was not immediately followed by an invasion. On November 3 Robert Amory, the DDI, telephoned the CIA liaison officer in London, Chester Cooper, and instructed him to tell the British "to comply with the God-damn cease-fire or go ahead with the God-damn invasion. Either way, we'll back them up if they do it fast. What we can't stand is their God-damn hesitation, waltzing while Hungary is burning."[133]

Hungary was not yet burning, but there were ominous signs of preparations for a new Soviet invasion. On November 2 Nagy complained to both Moscow and the United Nations that Russian troops were again moving into Hungary. Before dawn on November 4 the Red army began its assault. Two hundred thousand troops and four thousand tanks moved into Budapest "to help the Hungarian people crush the black forces of reaction and counter-revolution." As Eisenhower privately recognized, "We could do nothing."[134] The crushing of the Hungarian revolt finally exposed the impossibility of using either covert or overt means to help the "captive peoples" regain their freedom.

At dawn on November 5, just over twenty-four hours after the Soviet assault on Budapest, British and French paratroopers finally began landing in the Suez Canal Zone. Eisenhower's main immediate anxiety was "that the Russians would take actions through and in Syria." He instructed Allen Dulles to "keep a very close eye on this situation." Ike told his advisers that he was seriously concerned "that the Soviets, seeing their position and their policy failing so badly in the satellites, are ready to take any wild adventure." The Kremlin, he believed, was "furious and scared." Eisenhower's memories of the last days of Adolf Hitler had convinced him that "there is nothing more dangerous than a dictatorship in this state of mind":

. . . We better be damn sure that every Intelligence point and every outpost of our Armed Forces is absolutely right on their toes. . . . If those fellows start something, we may have to hit them, and if necessary, with *everything* in the bucket.[135]

Tuesday, November 6, was Election Day. At 8:37 A.M. Allen Dulles arrived in the Oval Office with new intelligence, probably from an NSA decrypt of Egyptian diplomatic traffic, "indicating that the Soviets told the Egyptians that they will 'do something' in the Middle East hostilities." The president ordered immediate U-2 reconnaissance of Syrian airfields. "If reconnaissance discloses Soviet Air Forces on Syrian bases," he told Dulles, ". . . there would be reason for the British and French to destroy them. . . ." But, to avoid provoking a "scared and furious" Kremlin, he ordered that for the moment U-2 missions should not cross the border from Syria into Russia.[136] There was a possibility, he feared, that the Soviet Union would launch a direct attack on Britain and France. If that happened, "we would of course be in a major war."[137]

Still preoccupied by the threat of a third world war, Eisenhower drove with his wife the eighty miles from the White House to Gettysburg to vote for himself. Ike's famous grin to the cameras concealed the vision of the apocalypse running through his mind. Returning to Washington by helicopter at noon, the president found Goodpaster waiting with worrying "intelligence reports received during the morning of jet aircraft of unknown nationality overflying Turkey." (The reports seem to have been a false alarm; later intelligence failed to provide any confirmation.) At a White House meeting with Radford and his military advisers, Eisenhower ordered a military alert to be "put into effect by degree—not all at once, in order to avoid creating a stir." It might soon be wise, he believed, for the armed services to cancel leave—"an action impossible to conceal which would let the Russians know—without being provocative—that we could not be taken by surprise."[138]

Election Day also marked the beginning of the end of the Suez crisis. Eden, Lloyd, and a minority of the British cabinet wanted to continue military operations at least until Suez had been taken. Macmillan and a majority of ministers, however, believed that Britain could not afford to go on. The crisis had begun a heavy run on the pound and a dramatic fall in British gold reserves. When Macmillan telephoned Washington, he was told that the price of American support for an IMF loan to prop up the pound was a cease-fire by midnight on November 6.[139] The Eden government was thus forced into a humiliating climbdown, without achieving either control of the canal or the overthrow of Nasser. While Eisenhower was meeting Radford and his military advisers to order a military alert, Eden announced that Britain would agree to a cease-fire at midnight.[140] Eisenhower's main reaction was one of relief that the fighting in the Middle East had stopped before the Soviet Union had been able to intervene. He telephoned Eden as soon as he heard the news. "We have given our whole thought to Hungary and the Middle East," the president told him. "I don't give a damn how the election goes. I guess it will be all right."[141] And so it was. In the early hours of Wednesday, November 7, Eisenhower found himself standing in front of a crowd of cheering Republicans, hailing a landslide victory.[142]

Though Eisenhower, like Allen Dulles, remained deeply suspicious of Soviet designs on the Middle East, he expressed "satisfaction" at the result of U-2 missions that showed no sign of Soviet units on Syrian airfields. During the review of the Suez crisis at the first postelection NSC meeting on November 8, "The President remarked with a sigh that he wished we could have a complete history of this cabal in which the British and the French were involved." The sheer incompetence of the Suez military operation led Eisenhower to believe that earlier intelligence reports had exaggerated the extent of British collusion with France and Israel. He told Foster Dulles that he knew from personal experience that the British were "meticulous military planners." If they had planned the whole operation with the French and Israelis, he was sure the landings would have taken place within hours after their ultimatum of October 30 expired:

. . . He now believed that the British had not been in on the Israeli-French planning until the very last days when they had no choice but to come into the operation. He had felt when the British originally denied collusion with the French and the Israelis that they were misleading us, but he had now come to the conclusion that they were telling the truth.[143]

Ike realized he was wrong on November 16 after Christian Pineau, the French foreign minister, confided in Allen Dulles. "On October 16," said Pineau, "Eden had come over from London and the plan had been worked out among the three of them and that was that."[144] The intelligence assessment of the Anglo-Franco-Israeli "cabal," requested by Eisenhower, was finished on December 5. Some significant facts remained undiscovered; there was no mention, for example, of the first French approach to Eden on October 14. But, in general, it reconstructed accurately the main chronology of collusion, and anticipated some of the major revelations of accounts published twenty years later. It demonstrated, beyond a doubt, that Eisenhower had been wrong to conclude, after the cease-fire, that Eden had, after all, been "telling the truth":

It is . . . disingenuous to believe that the British were unwitting tools of the French and Israeli principals and that they stumbled onto the scene at a late date without knowing what they were doing. Eden and Lloyd knew what they were getting themselves into, although they have not fully admitted it. Pineau has spoken for them and his evidence is conclusive.[145]

The greatest short-term intelligence damage done by the Suez crisis was the suspension of U-2 missions over the Soviet Union, which Eisenhower considered too provocative at a time when he believed the Kremlin was "both furious and scared."[146] On December 18, 1956, still anxious to avoid another East-West confrontation, the president ordered the cessation of any reconnaissance flights over any part of the Soviet bloc. By the New Year, however, he was increasingly concerned by the risks of *not* using U-2s to monitor Soviet missile development.[147] An intelligence estimate in November 1956 had predicted that "the Soviets would be capable of launching an earth satellite any time after November 1957."[148] Early in 1957 the U-2 missions resumed. Eisenhower continued to approve each flight personally. He also played some part in selecting the reconnaissance targets. As Bissell laid out large maps of the Soviet Union on the massive desk in the Oval Office and pointed out the flight path, Ike would sometimes tell him to avoid the risk of overflying heavily inhabited areas unless they were priority targets. "I want you to leave out that leg and go from straight that way," Eisenhower would say, "I want you to go from B to D, because it looks to me like you might be getting a little exposed over here."[149]

Early in 1957 a U-2 pilot flying over Turkestan saw in the distance the Tyura Tam missile test center, whose existence had previously not even been suspected. Within a week CIA photo interpreters had brought to the White House a cardboard model of the whole site, including railway sidings and feeder roads.[150] A National Intelligence Estimate (NIE) of March 12, 1957, predicted that the first Soviet ICBM might become operational in 1960 or 1961.[151] On August 1 Allen Dulles told the NSC that there was "no evidence of anything new or dramatic in the Soviet missile program." He sounded less optimistic after the successful test-firing of a Soviet ICBM on August 27. The DCI informed the NSC on September 12 that it might be necessary to revise the March forecast, and added: "We consider this question to be one of the highest possible priority."[152] Soon afterward a U-2 mission detected preparations at the Tyura Tam range for the launch of either a satellite or an ICBM. On October 4 the Soviet success in putting into orbit the first man-made satellite, the 184-pound *Sputnik 1*, created a global sensation. Allen Dulles told the NSC on October 10 that the speed with which *Sputnik 1* had been launched was due partly to the fact that, unlike the United States, "the Soviets had joined together their ICBM and earth satellite programs." NSA, he reported, had not yet determined whether the satellite's regular "bleep," which for a time became the world's most widely broadcast sound, was relaying information to Soviet ground control. Eisenhower had been expecting the *Sputnik* launch, but was taken aback by its weight. He interrupted the DCI's briefing to question whether a decimal point had been misplaced. The NSC was unimpressed by the president's query.[153] Its minutes record "no inclination in the Council to question the estimated weight as given by Mr. Dulles." What most surprised the president, however, was the "wave of near-hysteria" that swept the nation. The United States, it was widely claimed, had suffered a scientific Pearl Harbor that left it exposed to Soviet missile attack. The governor of Michigan, G. Mennen Williams, expressed his inner anguish in verse:

> Oh Little Sputnik, flying high
> With made-in Moscow beep.
> You tell the world it's a Commie sky,
> And Uncle Sam's asleep.[154]

An NIE of November 4 brought forward to 1959 the predicted date by which the Soviet Union would have up to ten operational ICBMs.[155] The classified information available to the president on U.S. weapons programs, combined with intelligence on the Soviet Union provided by the U-2, left him rightly convinced of the general superiority of American military technology. In a series of broadcasts on science and defense, Eisenhower insisted that "the over-all military strength of the Free World is distinctly greater than that of the Communist countries." But, as he later acknowledged in his memoirs, "I was hampered, of course, by the fact that I could not reveal secrets which in themselves would have reassured our people." Chief among these secrets was the capacity of the U-2 to overfly Soviet airfields and missile sites. At a meeting in the Oval Office with Goodpaster and the Dulles brothers, Foster asked the president, "Should we disclose . . . that the United States has the capability of photographing the Soviet Union from very high altitudes without interference?" Eisenhower refused.[156]

Lack of access to imagery intelligence from the U-2 missions also distorted the conclusions of the committee chaired by H. Rowan Gaither Jr., of the Ford Foundation, which had been commissioned by the president to study "security in the broadest possible sense of survival in the atomic age." At a meeting in the Oval Office on November 6 Gaither presented a frightening picture of an increasing Soviet threat that might "become critical in 1959 or early 1960." He urged Eisenhower to raise defense appropriations by over a quarter. Three members of his group were so alarmed by the growing Soviet menace that they favored a preventive war while there was still time. Leaks from the report marked the opening salvo in a "missile gap" controversy that rumbled on for the remainder of Eisenhower's presidency. According to a sensationalist report in the *Washington Post*:

> The still-top-secret Gaither Report portrays a United States in the gravest danger in its history. It pictures the Nation moving in frightening course to the status of a second-class power. It shows an America exposed to an almost immediate threat from the missile-bristling Soviet Union. It finds America's long-term prospect one of cataclysmic peril in the face of rocketing Soviet military might and of a powerful, growing Soviet economy and technology. . . .[157]

Though the president was more polite in public, he told his advisers in private "that this experience had proved, he thought definitively, the unwisdom of calling in outside groups."[158]

On November 7, 1957, Eisenhower announced the appointment of

Dr. James R. Killian, president of the Massachusetts Institute of Technology, as his special assistant for science and technology. Killian's main tasks were to advise on "the use of science and technology in relation to national security" and to improve the flow to the president of scientific intelligence, in particular on "the relative progress of Soviet and U.S. science and technology." "Only when Jefferson was his own science adviser and Vannevar Bush was advising Franklin Roosevelt during World War II," Killian later claimed, "was science so influential in top government councils as it became in Eisenhower's second term." Killian quickly acquired the right to attend the NSC as well as access to CIA and other intelligence. He reported on missile development to the president on December 28:

> Although it is probably true that we are at present behind the Soviets, we are in this position largely because we started much later and not because of inferior technology. Our technological progress in the missile field, in fact, has been impressive.
>
> The so-called failures of flight test vehicles, to which much publicity has been given, are normal and unavoidable occurrences in the development of complex mechanisms, many functions of which can be tested only in flight.

Together with other experts, Killian briefed Eisenhower again on February 4, 1958. They reported that the Soviet Union was probably about one year ahead in missile propulsion, a year behind in warhead development, and somewhat behind in guidance systems.[159]

The main priority of U-2 missions over the Soviet Union until they were abruptly halted in May 1960 was to seek out and monitor ICBM production and deployment sites as well as atomic energy facilities. Besides the one launchpad at the main test center at Tyura Tam, ICBMs were discovered at only one other site, at Plesetsk. Enlarged photographs, drawings, and models of Soviet military sites derived from U-2 imagery enabled Killian and his successor as the president's scientific adviser, George Kistiakowsky, to reassure Eisenhower that the United States was ahead of the Soviet Union in both weapons development and the deployment of strategic weapons. "It is no exaggeration to say," Eisenhower wrote in his memoirs, "that . . . there was rarely a day when I failed to give earnest study to reports of our progress and to estimates of Soviet capabilities." Intelligence on "what the Soviets *did not* have" was as important as information on what they did. The U-2, he claimed, "provided proof that the horrors of the alleged 'bomber gap' and the later 'missile gap' were nothing more than imaginative creations of irresponsibility."[160]

Though Eisenhower attached enormous importance to U-2 missions, he was anxious to limit the provocation to the Kremlin. For that reason he was frequently unwilling to authorize as many flights as Bissell wanted, and intermittently suspended them altogether. To increase the number of missions flown, Bissell proposed turning the U-2 program into a joint project with the British. Remembering the successful wartime Anglo-American merger of photo reconnaissance of occupied Europe from British bases, Eisenhower gave his consent. So did the British prime minister, Harold Macmillan, who had succeeded Eden in January 1957 and was anxious to rebuild the special relationship. Royal Air Force pilots were sent for secret training at Watertown Strip, a hundred miles northwest of Las Vegas. Henceforth, Macmillan, as well as Eisenhower, was able to authorize U-2 flights over the Soviet Union; he did so for the first time on August 24, 1958. Since Macmillan regularly saw the imagery intelligence collected by the U-2s, Eisenhower decided also to brief Konrad Adenauer, chancellor of West Germany, from which many missions were also flown. Adenauer usually listened to briefings impassively. But when Art Lundahl showed him some of the briefing boards of U-2 photographs regularly displayed in the Oval Office, the chancellor shook his head in disbelief, exclaiming *"Fabelhaft! Fabelhaft!"* ("Fabulous! Fabulous!")[161]

The confidence in the American lead over the Soviet Union in delivery systems that Ike derived from U-2 imagery enabled him to withstand formidable pressure from the military-industrial complex and its supporters on the Hill for massive increases in arms expenditure. The U-2 thus saved the American taxpayer tens of billions of dollars and spared the world a major escalation in the nuclear arms race. But Eisenhower failed to win a convincing public victory against those who denounced the fictitious "missile gap" because he felt unable to produce the secret evidence that would have demolished most of their arguments. Those outside the small U-2 circle could scarcely have imagined, without seeing the unprecedented imagery skillfully interpreted by Lundahl's analysts, the astonishing precision and detail of the intelligence it provided. The president was determined that no word of it should leak out. When a story hinting at American knowledge of the Tyura Tam launch site leaked to the *New York Times*, he "exploded" into one of the private rages that he carefully shielded from public view.[162]

The U-2 missions over the Soviet Union ended with a dramatic shoot-down on May Day, 1960. With a four-power summit conference in Paris scheduled for June, Eisenhower had been reluctant to authorize flights for several months beforehand. "If one of these aircraft were lost when we are engaged in apparently sincere deliberations," he presciently told his advisers, "it could be put on display in Moscow and ruin the President's effectiveness."[163] Ike authorized a U-2 flight on April 9 chiefly to look for evidence of new missile site construction. None was found. He was persuaded to approve one final mission before the summit. As usual, Eisenhower studied the flight plan on a large map spread out on his desk in the Oval Office. The U-2 was to take off from Peshawar in Pakistan, pass over Stalingrad, the Tyura Tam missile test center, the nuclear plants in the Urals, an ICBM base under construction at Yurya, the only operational ICBM site at Plesetsk, the Severodvinsk submarine shipyard, and the Murmansk naval bases, then land at Bodo in Norway.[164] The flight path was planned to avoid recently deployed batteries of SA-2 Guideline surface-to-air missiles. But neither Eisenhower nor the CIA realized how close previous missions had come to disaster. They had been saved chiefly by the administrative incompetence of the Soviet Air Defense Command. According to General Georgi Mikhailov, then serving on the command staff in Moscow, "One time the rockets were ready but the fuel wasn't. Another time, everything was ready, but the commanding officer was on leave and nobody knew what to do without him." Each time Khrushchev's wrath descended on the Air Defense Command.[165] On Sunday, May 1, however, while Khrushchev was reviewing the May Day parade in Moscow from the stand above Lenin's mausoleum, the commander in chief of the Soviet Defense Forces whispered in his ear that a U-2 had been shot down in the Urals.[166]

Ike heard the news not long after Khrushchev. On the afternoon of May 1 Goodpaster telephoned him to report that "one of our reconnaissance planes" was "overdue and probably lost." The president guessed immediately that a U-2 had disappeared over the Soviet Union. Early next morning Goodpaster entered the Oval Office. "Mr. President," he began, ". . . the [U-2] pilot reported an engine flameout from a position about thirteen hundred miles inside Russia and has not been heard from since. With the amount of fuel he had on board, there is not a chance of his still being aloft." Both men took it for granted that the pilot, Gary Powers, was dead. They had been assured that if a U-2 went down, it would be destroyed either in the air or on impact, so that proof of espionage would be lacking. Self-destruct mechanisms were built into the aircraft. Eisenhower approved a cover story, issued on May 3 by the National Aeronautics and Space Administration, that "A NASA U-2 research plane, being flown in Turkey on a joint NASA-USAF Air Weather Service mission, apparently went down in the Lake Van, Turkey, area at about 9:00 A.M. (3:00 A.M. E.D.T.), Sunday, May 1."[167] Khrushchev, who had never previously made a public protest about the U-2 flights, announced ominously to diplomats at a Moscow reception on May 4 that at the opening session of the Supreme Soviet the next day, he would have something "stupendous" to say.[168]

Reports of Khrushchev's speech came in as the NSC was meeting on May 5. For the first two hours of his marathon address, celebrating a dreary catalog of alleged Soviet successes, there was no "stupendous" announcement. Khrushchev's tone changed, however, as he turned to world affairs and the threat from "aggressive forces" in the imperialist West. "Comrade Deputies!" he announced, suddenly raising his voice, "On the instructions of the Soviet government, I must report to you on aggressive actions against the Soviet Union in the past few weeks by the United States of America." On May Day a U.S. "aggressor" plane had been shot down deep in Soviet territory. Deafening applause followed, punctuated by cries of "Shame to the aggressor!"[169]

Eisenhower asked Allen Dulles and other senior advisers to stay behind after the NSC meeting to discuss Khrushchev's speech. The president initially favored making no immediate response, but was persuaded to embroider further the original cover story. The State Department issued a statement referring to the U-2 reported lost over Turkey: "It is entirely possible that having failure in the oxygen equipment, which could result in the pilot losing consciousness, the plane continued on automatic pilot for a considerable distance and accidentally violated Soviet airspace." While the statement was being issued, however, the Soviet deputy foreign minister, Jacob Malik, was telling guests at a diplomatic reception in Moscow attended by the U.S. ambassador that the U-2 pilot had survived and was being questioned by the Soviet authorities.[170]

Eisenhower and his advisers had fallen into the trap set by Khrushchev. "Comrades, I must let you in on a secret," Khrushchev told the Supreme Soviet on Saturday, May 7: "When I made my report two days ago, I deliberately refrained from mentioning that we have the remnants of the plane—and we also have the pilot, who is quite alive and kicking!" After even more thunderous applause than on May 5, Khrushchev continued, "We did this quite deliberately, because if we had given out the whole story, the Americans would have thought up yet another fable. . . . Now when they learn the pilot is still alive, they will have to think up something else. *And they will!*" Powers, Khrushchev announced, would be put on trial. But he seemed to distance Eisenhower from the warmongers of the Pentagon and the CIA: "I am quite willing to grant that the President knew nothing about the fact that such a plane was sent into the Soviet Union. . . ."[171]

Eisenhower was spending the weekend at his Gettysburg farmhouse. The news of Khrushchev's speech was brought to him by his son John, Goodpaster's assistant. Ike's first reaction on hearing confirmation that

Powers was alive was that the news was "*unbelievable*."[172] Years later, John Eisenhower was still angry at the predicament in which the CIA had placed his father. "The CIA promised us that the Russians would never get a U-2 pilot alive. And then they gave the S.O.B. a parachute!"[173] Both Bissell and Allen Dulles had never expected that Powers would be able to use his parachute. Only a remarkable—and unpredictable—combination of circumstances enabled him to do so. Had a Russian missile hit the fragile U-2, Powers would almost certainly not have survived. But the SA-2 exploded behind the plane, throwing it out of control but not destroying it. Though neither Eisenhower nor the CIA knew it at the time, the Russians fired a second missile that hit not the U-2 but a Soviet MIG-19 tracking Powers.[174] While the Russian pilot was killed, Powers was able to release the canopy over his cockpit and struggle free. By his own later account, he was thrown clear before he could hit the destructor switches that would have destroyed the U-2.[175]

After Khrushchev's speech on May 7 plausible denial of the U-2 spy missions was no longer possible. Eisenhower was left with the option either of implausible denial of presidential responsibility or of making the first admission of presidential authorization for peacetime espionage. On the unwise advice of Christian Herter (who had succeeded the terminally ill Foster Dulles as secretary of state a year earlier), Eisenhower opted for implausible denial. The State Department announced soon after 6 P.M. on May 7:

> As a result of the inquiry authorized by the President, it has been established that insofar as the authorities in Washington are concerned, there was no authorization for any such flight as described by Mr. Khrushchev.
>
> Nevertheless, it appears that in endeavoring to obtain information now concealed behind the Iron Curtain, a flight over the Soviet Union was probably taken by an unarmed civilian U-2 plane.

Eisenhower quickly realized that denial of his own responsibility had only made matters worse. The St. Louis *Post-Dispatch* asked the next day, "Do our intelligence operatives enjoy so much freewheeling authority that they can touch off an incident of grave international import by low-level decisions unchecked by responsible policy-making power?"[176]

The president spent Mother's Day, Sunday, May 8, at Gettysburg, brooding over how much of the record to set straight, and how to do it. After morning church he telephoned Herter and told him to issue a new statement. Eisenhower was still unwilling to take public responsibility for the May Day flight or any other specific mission, but believed he must admit having authorized a program of reconnaissance flights over the past four years to protect the nation from surprise attack. On the morning of Monday, May 9, he entered the Oval Office visibly depressed by the confused mishandling of the whole U-2 affair and by the extent of the Soviet propaganda victory. "I would like to resign," he said gloomily to his secretary. By the afternoon his mood was not quite so somber. He told the NSC, when it convened in the cabinet room at 2:35 P.M.: "Well, we're just going to have to take a lot of beating on this—and I'm the one, rightly, who's going to have to take it." That afternoon Eisenhower authorized the CIA to give a classified briefing in the Senate on the achievements of the U-2 missions.[177] As Art Lundahl entered the Capitol chamber with Allen Dulles, he judged the mood of many senators to be "angry or combative." When Lundahl showed them a series of spectacular briefing boards of Soviet missile and other sites, he quickly won them over. At the end of his half-hour briefing, he received a standing ovation. Dulles was so taken aback that his lighted pipe fell from his mouth into his lap. As Lundahl acknowledged the senators' applause, he noticed that the DCI's tweed jacket had begun to smolder.[178]

Had Eisenhower been prepared to declassify Lundahl's briefing, he could have transformed public perceptions of the U-2 affair both in the United States and in the outside world. It would have been difficult to dispute either the United States' need for accurate information about the Soviet nuclear strike force or the impossibility of obtaining it without use of aerial reconnaissance. Having kept access to U-2 imagery tightly restricted for so long, however, Eisenhower found it psychologically difficult to make it publicly available. He also feared that, if he did so, he would escalate the crisis with the Soviet Union on the eve of the Paris summit. Instead, the succession of misleading and contradictory American public statements about the U-2 succeeded in giving a measure of plausibility to Khrushchev's preposterous display of outraged innocence at a time when the Soviet Union possessed the largest foreign espionage network in peacetime history.

While Lundahl was receiving a private ovation in the Capitol chamber, the State Department was issuing another misleading account of the U-2 affair. It admitted that, to provide the information needed to prevent surprise attack, the president had authorized "aerial surveillance by unarmed civilian aircraft," but denied that he had authorized "specific missions." James Reston reported from Washington to the *New York Times*:

This was a sad and perplexed capital tonight, caught in a swirl of charges of clumsy administration, bad judgement and bad faith. It was depressed and humiliated by the United States having been caught spying over the Soviet Union and trying to cover up its activities in a series of misleading official statements.[179]

After a predictably bad press on May 10 Eisenhower made a final attempt to clear the air before leaving for the Paris summit. At a press conference on May 11 he made an opening statement that represents a forgotten landmark in presidential history: the first public explanation by a president of "the need for intelligence gathering activities" in peacetime:

No one wants another Pearl Harbor. This means that we must have knowledge of military forces and preparations around the world, especially those capable of massive surprise attacks.

Secrecy in the Soviet Union makes this essential. In most of the world no large-scale attack could be prepared in secret, but in the Soviet Union there is a fetish of secrecy and concealment. This is a major cause of international tension and uneasiness today. . . .

. . . Ever since the beginning of my administration I have issued directives to gather, in every feasible way, the information required to protect the United States and the free world against surprise attack and to enable them to make effective preparations for defense.

Intelligence work, said Eisenhower, was "a distasteful but vital necessity." It would be far better to obtain openly the information needed to guard against surprise attack. At the Paris summit he proposed to revive his 1955 Open Skies proposal.[180]

The next day, May 12, the CIA Office of Current Intelligence sent the president its forecast of what to expect in Paris. It noted Khrushchev's "present mood of arrogant confidence mixed with resentment toward the United States," but believed he retained a "deep personal commitment" to the summit. Llewellyn Thompson, the U.S. ambassador in Moscow, thought differently. "All signs," he reported, "now appear to point to Khrushchev's intention of trying to extort maximum propaganda advantage from the Summit rather than attempt a serious negotiation."[181]

Thompson was right. On arriving in Paris on the morning of May 15, Eisenhower discovered that Khrushchev had made three demands. Before the summit could go ahead, the president must apologize for the U-2 flights, guarantee that there would be no more such flights, and "pass severe judgment" on those responsible. Eisenhower refused, as he was bound to do. Khrushchev lost his temper. De Gaulle observed that

Soviet satellites were daily passing over France. The summit was over before it began.[182]

On May 25 Eisenhower went on national television to explain "the remarkable events last week in Paris, and their meaning to our future." The broadcast gave him another opportunity to demonstrate what the U-2 missions had achieved, to show viewers the importance of imagery intelligence of the Soviet Union, and in the process to demolish most of the assertions of the "missile gap" scaremongers. CIA photographic analysts prepared a spectacular series of briefing boards comparing missile sites, long-range bomber airfields, nuclear installations, and other military facilities in the Soviet Union and the United States. Eisenhower's assistant for TV presentations, Robert Montgomery, famous as both film actor and producer, had planned a dramatic presentation in which, as the president spoke, the cameras would focus on the aerial photographs displayed around the walls of the Oval Office. Ike, however, vetoed the program plan on the grounds that U-2 photographs of the Soviet Union would make relations with the Kremlin even worse. Instead, he agreed to show only a single briefing board of an American airfield to demonstrate what his Open Skies proposal could achieve. Pointing to the board on an easel in the Oval Office, he told viewers:

> This is a photograph of the North Island Naval [Air] Station in San Diego, California. It was taken from an altitude of more than 70 thousand feet. You may not perhaps be able to see them on your television screens, but the white lines in the parking strips are clearly discernible from 13 miles up. Those lines are just six inches wide.
>
> Obviously most of the details necessary for a military evaluation of the airfield and its aircraft are clearly distinguishable.
>
> I show you this photograph as an example of what could be accomplished through United Nations aerial surveillance.[183]

By failing to show viewers similar U-2 photographs of Russian airfields, Eisenhower missed a golden opportunity to demonstrate how successfully the Soviet nuclear strike force had been monitored.

On August 18 the successful launch of U.S. *Discoverer XIV* space satellite from Vandenberg Air Force Base in California began a new era in imagery intelligence. The eighty-four-pound reentry capsule, recovered the next day in mid-air over Alaska by a C-119 Flying Boxcar, is now on display at the National Air and Space Museum in Washington, D.C. Inside was a twenty-pound roll of film. According to Dino Brugioni, one of the CIA photographic interpreters who worked on it, "we gained more than 1 million square miles of coverage of the Soviet Union—more coverage in one capsule than the combined four years of U-2 coverage."[184] Though the resolution was initially inferior to that of the U-2, satellite photography showed the first four operational Soviet ICBMs in place at Plesetsk. This and later *Discoverer* missions during the final months of the Eisenhower presidency found no other long-range missiles anywhere in the Soviet Union.[185]

The *New York Times* reported the successful recovery of the *Discoverer XIV* capsule, though not its photographic intelligence, on August 20. On the same front page was the news that Gary Powers, the downed U-2 pilot, had been sentenced to ten years' imprisonment after an elaborate show trial in Moscow. Five days later Eisenhower approved the creation of a new agency, the National Reconnaissance Office (NRO), to manage satellite reconnaissance programs for the entire intelligence community. For the next generation NRO was to be the most secret of all U.S. intelligence agencies. Its existence was not discovered by the media until 1973, and not officially acknowledged until September 1992.[186]

The shooting down of Gary Powers's U-2 marked only a temporary setback in one of the most successful intelligence operations of the twentieth century. The imagery revolution of the 1950s owed much to Eisenhower's own personal enthusiasm for it. His simultaneous support for the expansion of covert action, however, was to lead to an intelligence disaster. The first major danger signal came in Indonesia. The target of the covert action was President Achmed Sukarno, who in February 1957 had taken quasi-dictatorial powers with the support of the one-million-strong Communist party. In November 1957 Eisenhower authorized a much larger-scale version of the paramilitary Guatemalan operation to assist rebel Indonesian colonels to overthrow Sukarno. In addition to providing the colonels with arms, the CIA made a pornographic film starring a Sukarno look-alike, hoping to discredit the president among his followers; it had no observable effect other than, apparently, to titillate Sukarno. In February 1958, while Sukarno was on a state visit to Japan, the colonels declared the island of Sumatra independent. Most of the Indonesian army, however, remained loyal to the president. While Eisenhower publicly insisted that his policy in the conflict was "one of careful neutrality and proper deportment all the way through," the CIA tried vainly to turn the tide in favor of the colonels with a rebel air force financed from agency funds and flown by agency pilots. The air operation ended in fiasco on Sunday, May 18, when one of the pilots, Allen Lawrence Pope, was shot down after accidentally bombing a church and killing most of the congregation. When told that, contrary to his instructions, Pope had kept evidence of his identity on board his B-26, Eisenhower must surely have exploded in private fury. The whole operation had to be aborted and an ignominious attempt made to placate Sukarno, who shrewdly calculated that he had more to gain by avoiding public denunciation of CIA covert action than by adding to Eisenhower's embarrassment. Thirty-seven thousand tons of rice and a million dollars' worth of arms were swiftly dispatched to Indonesia, ostensibly as part of a U.S. foreign aid program. Ray Cline, then head of station in Taiwan and one of those involved in supporting the Indonesian colonels, later summed up the main lesson of the operation:

> The weak point in covert paramilitary action is that a single misfortune that reveals CIA's connection makes it necessary for the United States either to abandon the cause completely or convert to a policy of overt military intervention.[187]

Failure to learn that lesson was to lead to public humiliation at the Bay of Pigs in Cuba three years later. The main target of CIA covert action during Eisenhower's last year as president was Fidel Castro, who on New Year's Day, 1959, entered Havana in triumph after toppling the corrupt dictatorship of Fulgencio Batista. By the autumn Eisenhower had concluded that there was no prospect of "a reasonable modus vivendi" with Castro. "Our intelligence," he told Harold Macmillan, "increasingly indicated that the Communists began permeating Cuba's life and government." Action against Castro, Eisenhower was convinced, must be covert: "We could simply not afford to appear the bully."[188]

In December 1959 J. C. King, head of the CIA's Western Hemisphere Division, recommended to Allen Dulles that "thorough consideration be given to the elimination of Fidel Castro." That recommendation was to lead a few months later to the beginning of the now infamous CIA assassination plots against the Cuban leader. The DCI showed no immediate enthusiasm, however, for killing Castro. He told the 5412 Committee on January 13, 1960, that "over the long run the U.S. will not be able to tolerate the Castro regime," but suggested only "covert contingency planning to accomplish the fall of the Castro government"—not the "quick elimination of Castro." At this stage the president was more impatient than his DCI. When Dulles proposed using saboteurs to put a Cuban sugar refinery out of action, Eisenhower told him to come up with something stronger.[189] On February 17 the 5412 Committee discussed a further proposal for covert action in Cuba. No record of its discussion survives. But a note by the president's national security adviser, Gordon Gray, kept secret for more than thirty years, records Eisenhower's reaction to the 5412 Committee proposal:

· . . . He said first he wondered why we were thinking of something on such a narrow basis. He said that he wondered why we weren't trying to identify assets for this and other things as well across the board including even possibly things that might be drastic.

Allen Dulles still showed little enthusiasm for "drastic action." Gray told the president that Dulles "didn't know whether he had the capacity of going ahead." In keeping with the doctrine of plausible presidential deniability, Gray's note is studiously vague about what "drastic" covert action consisted of. It is, however, probably the first indication that Eisenhower was prepared to consider assassination.[190] This was one of the options considered by the Cuban operations task force, headed by Richard Bissell, set up in response to the president's demand for "drastic" action.[191] On March 17 Eisenhower approved Bissell's four-point "Program of Covert Action Against the Cuban Regime": "the creation of a responsible, appealing and unified Cuban opposition to the Castro regime," based outside Cuba; "a powerful propaganda offensive"; "the creation of a covert intelligence and action organization within Cuba"; and "the development of an adequate paramilitary force outside of Cuba." "The great problem," Eisenhower told his advisers, "is leakage and breach of security. Everyone must be prepared to swear he has not heard of it. . . . Our hand should not show in anything that is done."[192]

As well as seeking to implement his four-point plan, Bissell worked during the spring and summer of 1960 on a series of assassination plots. Unlike the KGB, the CIA had as yet no team of trained assassins. Bissell therefore proposed to subcontract. His preferred hitmen were the Mafia, whom he reasonably regarded as the United States' most professional killers. The Mafia had its own reasons for wanting to dispose of Castro, who had wrecked its lucrative gambling and vice operations in Havana, and Bissell believed "there was very little chance that anything the syndicate would try to do would be traced back to the CIA." Contact was made with Johnny Rosselli, former lieutenant of Al Capone, and Salvatore "Sam" Giancana, one of the FBI's ten-most-wanted criminals. Neither was attracted by Bissell's Hollywood-inspired vision of a gangland killing in which Castro would be mowed down in a hail of bullets. Giancana suggested an undetectable poison instead. On Bissell's instructions, the CIA Office of Medical Service prepared a botulinum toxin pill that "did the job" when it was tried on monkeys. Poisoning, however, was not really the Mafia's style, and the pills disappeared somewhere in Cuba without ever reaching Castro. Fascinated by now with the possibilities of poisons, Bissell and his task force devised other bizarre, though imaginative, schemes. A box of Castro's favorite cigars was treated with a deadly toxin. Another box was impregnated with a chemical designed to destroy Fidel's credibility by making him hallucinate in public. A further scheme proposed the use of thallium salts that would cause Castro to lose his beard and, it was hoped, destroy his macho image. None of the poison plots came even close to success.[193]

Eisenhower loyalists have found it difficult to accept that the president could have authorized such murderous farces. Ike probably did not know—or want to know—the details of how Castro was to be disposed of. These he was prepared to leave to Bissell in the mistaken belief that the remarkable talents Bissell had displayed in the U-2 program also extended to assassination. The hypothesis that the attempts to kill Castro were made without the president's knowledge and against his wishes is barely conceivable. Though most of Eisenhower's instincts were humane and generous, the Guatemalan operation had shown in 1954 that he had few qualms about limited numbers of deaths in banana republics if they were necessary to resist the onward march of Communism. Nor was Castro the only foreign leader Ike was prepared to have assassinated. Just as Eisenhower had regarded the 5412 Committee's February proposals for dealing with Castro as too feeble, so he was equally critical of its initial plans for covert actions against the pro-Soviet prime minister of the former Belgian Congo, Patrice Lumumba. When the committee met to discuss action against Lumumba on August 25, Gordon Gray reported that the president "had expressed extremely strong feelings on the necessity for very straightforward action in this situation, and he wondered whether the plans as outlined were sufficient to accomplish this." Thus admonished, the committee "finally agreed that planning for the Congo would not necessarily rule out 'consideration' of any particular kind of activity that might contribute to getting rid of Lumumba."[194] Allen Dulles told Eisenhower that Lumumba was insane; later reports alleged that he was also "a dope fiend." On September 21 the DCI reported to an NSC meeting, chaired by the president, that "Lumumba was not yet disposed of and remained a grave danger as long as he was not disposed of."[195] Still fascinated by the use of poisons in covert action, Bissell instructed a CIA scientist to prepare biological toxins designed to assassinate or incapacitate an unnamed "African leader." The CIA, however, proved no more successful at poisoning Lumumba than Castro. In December Lumumba was captured (and later murdered) by General Joseph Mobutu, who had seized power in a military coup.[196]

Eisenhower was far more anxious to dispose of Castro than Lumumba. The president's greatest fear during his final year in office was that the Communist bridgehead in Cuba would infect the rest of Latin America. He told Harold Macmillan in August 1960 that if Castro survived for another year, "most of the Governments in this Hemisphere . . . run the risk of being overtaken by revolution. . . ."[197] Macmillan was struck by the similarity between his own belief four years earlier in the urgency of overthrowing Nasser and Eisenhower's conviction now that there was no time to lose in disposing of Castro. "He is your Nasser," Macmillan told the president, ". . . I feel sure Castro has to be got rid of, but it is a tricky operation for you to contrive and I only hope you will succeed."[198] Just as Eisenhower had feared in 1956 that a British attempt to overthrow Nasser would outrage Arab public opinion, so Macmillan was worried that American action to topple Castro would have similar consequences in Latin America. The prime minister wrote to the president in July 1960:

> . . . Everything I hear of the state of feeling in other Latin American countries confirms the importance of avoiding any action which might create the impression that the United States was actively intervening in Cuba and arouse all sorts of latent suspicious.[199]

Ignoring the lessons of Guatemala and Indonesia, Eisenhower clung to the illusion that American sponsorship of a paramilitary operation to overthrow the Castro regime could be kept secret. During the summer of 1960 Bissell made little progress with his assassination plots. On August 18, however, both he and Allen Dulles gave the president an optimistic report on preparations for paramilitary operations. Dulles announced the creation of "a unified Cuban opposition" in exile, though he admitted that, as yet, "there is no real leader and all the individuals are prima donnas." Training of a five-hundred-strong Cuban invasion force in Guatemala was due to be completed by early November. A small air force of B-26s with Cuban air crews was also being assembled. Bissell was even more optimistic. Relying on what proved to be hopelessly unrealistic assessments of the potential of the anti-Castro underground inside Cuba, he told Eisenhower:

> . . . It is possible that the initial paramilitary operations could be successful without any outside help. . . . The plan would be to supply the local groups by air and also to infiltrate certain Cubans to stiffen local resistance. . . . There had been identified no less than eleven groups or alleged groups in Cuba with potential. We are in the process of sending radio communications to them at this time.

Eisenhower emphasized the importance of not beginning operations prematurely but approved a large (still classified) budget for Cuban covert action:

. . . He would go along so long as the Joint Chiefs, Defense, State and the CIA think we have a good chance of being successful. He wouldn't care much about this kind of cost; indeed, he said he would defend this kind of action against all comers. . . .[200]

By November Bissell was less optimistic. Most of the guerrillas landed to "stiffen local resistance" had been picked up, and it was now clear that there was "no true organized underground in Cuba." "If there was to be any chance of success," Bissell believed, "we would have to place main reliance on the landing force, and only minor reliance on any guerilla force."[201] The State Department warned that preparations for the landing were by now known "all over Latin America."

Remarkably, Eisenhower still believed that CIA involvement could be kept secret. According to the minutes of a meeting with his advisers in the Oval Office on November 29, "The President said that even if the operation were known, the main thing was not to let the U.S. hand show. As long as we pursued that course he was not too concerned."[202] On December 8 the 5412 Committee discussed plans for "an amphibious landing on the Cuban coast of 600–750 men equipped with weapons of extraordinarily heavy fire power," and supported by air strikes. Though the committee was told that "the existence of the U.S.-backed force of Cubans in training was well known throughout Latin America," it encouraged the CIA to continue preparations for the landing.[203]

On January 10, 1961, the *New York Times* published an article on the training of anti-Castro guerrillas, complete with map, which, as Eisenhower later admitted, "told most of the story." He gave instructions that there should be no official comment.[204] But in his final State of the Union speech two days later, Ike gave a remarkably public hint that Castro would go the way of Mossadeq and Arbenz at the beginning of his presidency: "Although, unhappily, Communist penetration of Cuba is real and poses a serious threat, Communist dominated regimes have been deposed in Guatemala and Iran."[205] Since CIA involvement in the overthrow of Arbenz was now an open secret, few in Latin America listening to Eisenhower's address could have doubted that plans were afoot to use the agency to topple Castro. At the end as at the start of his administration, covert action remained a major instrument of Eisenhower's foreign policy.

Eisenhower bequeathed to his successor an intelligence disaster in the making on the coast of Cuba. But he also left a more enduring and ultimately more important intelligence legacy: a system of overhead reconnaissance by spy plane and satellite that helped to stabilize the Cold War. It is difficult to believe that imagery intelligence could have made such rapid progress under Truman or any other president who lacked Eisenhower's enormous enthusiasm for it. A few days before he left office, Eisenhower signed NSCID-8, establishing the National Photographic Interpretation Center (NPIC), under CIA administration, with Art Lundahl as its director. It has remained ever since the world leader in interpreting imagery intelligence. At Ike's special request he was regularly updated after he left the White House on the progress of IMINT. His last briefing, eight years after his retirement, took place in Walter Reed Hospital on February 13, 1969. The "Eisenhower Package," as it had become known within the agency, was personally delivered by Lundahl and the DCI, Richard Helms. Lundahl found Eisenhower "just absolutely flabbergasted about the improvements achieved in the systems. . . . When we finished, he shook hands with us, saying that it had been very exhilarating and most enjoyable." Ike died six weeks later, on March 28, 1969.[206]

CHAPTER 7

John F. Kennedy
(1961-1963)

In the aftermath of the debacle at the Bay of Pigs in April 1961, Kennedy despairingly asked his special counsel, Theodore Sorensen, "How could I have been so stupid, to let them go ahead?"[1] The plan to topple Castro by a "Cuban brigade" of his exiled opponents secretly organized by the CIA, which the new president inherited from his predecessor, was based on wishful thinking. The first great illusion, given the scale of the enterprise, was to suppose that *covert* action was possible at all.[2] The second was to believe that any invasion force drawn from the Cuban opposition could possibly be strong enough to overthrow the Castro regime, given both Castro's own popularity and the strength of his armed forces and security services. Only overt military intervention by the United States could have succeeded—and Kennedy made it clear from the outset that he would never consent to that.

A new administration with the fresh and critical minds assembled in the Kennedy Camelot might have been expected to see through the wishful thinking behind the Cuban operation. That they did not do so was due in part to their ignorance of peacetime intelligence. One of the study aids in use today at the John F. Kennedy School of Government at Harvard University is a twenty-page condensed history of "The CIA to 1961."[3] Students who digest these twenty pages know more about the CIA than Kennedy did when he won the presidential election. Unlike Kennedy School students nowadays, neither the president nor his advisers grasped until it was too late the extent of the divorce between the CIA's directorates of Plans (Operations) and Intelligence. In the planning of the Bay of Pigs, Operations deliberately failed to consult Intelligence.

In 1941–42 Kennedy had served briefly in naval intelligence and had found it deeply tedious. According to his father, he became "disgusted with desk jobs" and applied successfully for a transfer to active service.[4] Though JFK knew little about intelligence before he became president, he was fascinated by guerrilla warfare and paramilitary operations. The Russians, he believed, had become experts in subversive warfare. The United States must therefore beat them at their own game. In 1958 Kennedy defined the new threat facing the free world as "Sputnik diplomacy, limited brush-fire wars, indirect non-overt aggression, intimidation and subversion, internal revolution." He read the works of Mao Zedong and Che Guevara, amusing his wife, Jackie, during weekends at their Virginia retreat at Glen Ora by composing maxims modeled on Mao's "Guerillas must move among the people as fish swim in the sea."[5] The idea, if not the actual plan, for toppling Castro by a paramilitary operation appealed to the president-elect. Kennedy found cloaks and daggers rather intriguing. He had a well-publicized, but probably genuine, liking for James Bond novels, and had dined with their author, Ian Fleming. The Bond adventure *From Russia with Love* appeared in a list of his ten favorite books.[6]

Soon after Kennedy's election victory, Eisenhower set out to remedy his ignorance of the intelligence community. He briefed Kennedy personally on the intelligence-sharing agreements with Britain, Canada, and Australasia, and listened while Art Lundahl and Richard Bissell, two of the most gifted and persuasive briefers in American history, described in detail the remarkable progress made by imagery intelligence since the mid-1950s. Ike triumphantly told the president-elect, "The enemy has no aerial photographic systems like ours!"[7] The sudden revelation of the extraordinary intelligence on the Soviet Union provided by overhead reconnaissance made an indelible impression on Kennedy. During the election campaign he had attacked the Eisenhower administration for allowing "a missile gap" to develop between the United States and the Soviet Union. IMINT showed that the gap did not exist. Robert M. McNamara, Kennedy's secretary of defense, estimated that he spent up to 20 percent of his first month in office examining intelligence estimates and satellite photographs of Soviet missiles. On February 6 he told the Pentagon press corps that, if there was a missile gap, "it is in our favor." McNamara had intended his remarks to be off the record. When the story made headline news the following day, he offered to resign. Kennedy told McNamara to stay on but to allow the missile gap controversy to die away.[8]

Lundahl's relationship with Kennedy became as close and confident as it had been with Eisenhower. Instead of displaying his large photographic briefing boards on easels, as he had done for Ike, Lundahl would spread them out on a coffee table in the Oval Office. Kennedy would leave his desk, sit in the famous rocking chair that had been specially designed to ease his back pain, and study them through a magnifying glass. Lundahl later became the only photographic analyst ever to be awarded, among his many honors, both the National Security Medal and an honorary British knighthood.[9]

Kennedy initially regarded Richard Bissell, the CIA's deputy director of plans (operations), as "probably one of the four or five brightest guys" in an administration crowded with youthful talent.[10] A member of the transition team told the president-elect, "There must be someone you really trust inside the intelligence community. . . . Who is that?" Kennedy replied, "Dick Bissell."[11] The Harvard historian Arthur M. Schlesinger Jr., a youthful veteran of OSS whom Kennedy made his special assistant, admired Bissell's "unsurpassed talent for lucid analysis and fluent exposition." The CIA as a whole initially impressed the president more favorably than the State Department. One of his first appointments was to renominate Allen Dulles as DCI. "Years in the intelligence business had no doubt given [Dulles] a capacity for ruthlessness," wrote Schlesinger later, "but he was urbane, courtly and honorable, almost wholly devoid of the intellectual rigidity and personal self-righteousness of his brother."[12] Though Schlesinger criticized "the autonomy with which the agency has been permitted to operate," he told the president that he was impressed by many of its staff:

> During the fifties it began in some areas to outstrip the State Department in the quality of its personnel. Partly because the CIA paid higher salaries and even more perhaps because Allen Dulles gave his people courageous protection against McCarthyite attacks, CIA was able to attract and hold a large number of able and independent-minded men.[13]

Kennedy looked on the State Department—"the Beast of Foggy Bottom"—as part of what he believed was the cumbersome bureaucracy of the Eisenhower era. "If I need some material fast or an idea fast," he was reported as saying, "CIA is the place I have to go. The State Department is four or five days to answer a simple yes or no."[14]

SIGINT, unlike IMINT, failed to capture Kennedy's imagination. His view of it may possibly have been colored by memories of tedious hours spent enciphering and deciphering low-grade naval signals during his wartime service in naval intelligence;[15] had he had access to Magic, he might have formed a different view. More important in explaining Kennedy's relative lack of interest in SIGINT when he became president was the fact that the information it provided on the Soviet Union was much less striking than that produced by overhead reconnaissance. Not until more than a month after his inauguration did NSA receive a request from the White House for a written briefing on its current performance and future prospects. The deputy director, Dr. Louis Tordella, sent a memorandum of about thirty-five pages in reply. During Kennedy's thousand-day presidency, NSA made several attempts to persuade him to visit its headquarters at Fort Meade, but always without success.[16] Just as CIA had about twice the budget of State, however, so NSA had twice the budget of CIA.[17]

On November 18, 1960, Kennedy received his first briefing as president-elect on the Cuban operation during a visit by Dulles and Bissell to his father's home at Palm Beach. On November 29 Dulles and Bissell returned to brief him again.[18] Kennedy later told Sorensen that he had had "grave doubts" about the operation—but he also admitted that he had been "astonished by its magnitude and daring," just as he had been by the IMINT operations.[19] In any case, he raised no objection to what at this stage he still saw as a contingency plan to which he was not yet committed. Kennedy's generally favorable initial impression of the CIA, his confidence in Bissell in particular, and his admiration for the wondrous progress of imagery intelligence under Bissell's leadership helped to blind him to the disastrous limitations of the covert operations being run by Bissell's Plans Directorate in Cuba. No covert operation could have had a more eloquent advocate. ". . . We all listened transfixed," wrote Schlesinger, ". . . fascinated by the workings of this superbly clear, organized and articulate intelligence, while Bissell, pointer in hand, would explain how the invasion would work or discourse on the relative merits of alternative landing sites." Kennedy said later that he could not understand "how men like Dulles and Bissell, so intelligent and so experienced, could have been so wrong."[20]

Another part of the explanation for Kennedy's failure to realize the folly of the Cuban operation until it was too late was that he simply lacked the time to think through the detailed plans. His main preoccupations during the transition were the twelve hundred jobs that he had to fill in his administration and preparations for what was to be the most crowded legislative program in American history.[21] Even after he took office, neither the president nor his key advisers were ever able to give plans for the operation their sustained attention for more than forty-five minutes at a time until the invasion had begun.[22] Bissell and his chief lieutenants, by contrast, increasingly thought of little else. All were so committed to its success that they banished from their mind all thought of turning back.

At a meeting of the NSC on January 28 Dulles reported that Cuba was "now for practical purposes a Communist-controlled state," and that both Castro's military power and "popular opposition to his regime" were growing rapidly. After long discussion, Kennedy authorized the CIA to go ahead with its plans for "increased propaganda, increased political action and increased sabotage," and ordered a Defense Department review of "CIA proposals for the active deployment of anti-Castro Cuban forces on Cuban territory."[23] At the next meeting of the NSC on February 1 Kennedy pressed ahead with his plans to improve American capacity for "special warfare," instructing his secretary of defense, Robert McNamara, to prepare, with CIA and State, "a doctrine for improved counter-insurgency operations."[24]

On February 6 the president asked his special assistant for national security affairs, McGeorge Bundy, to discover whether plans for the Cuban operation had yet been coordinated between Bissell, Defense, and State.[25] Bundy reported two days later that, though State took "a much cooler view," "Defense and CIA now feel quite enthusiastic about the invasion."[26] Dulles's enthusiasm was such that he had mentally rewritten the history of the overthrow of Arbenz in 1954 and banished from his mind the doubts that had assailed him at the time. He told Kennedy in the Oval Office: "I stood right here at Ike's desk and told him I was certain our Guatemalan operation would succeed, and, Mr. President, the prospects for this plan are even better than they were for that one."[27] Kennedy and his advisers all supposed that Dulles's and Bissell's optimistic assessments of the Cuban operation had "the Agency's full authority behind them."[28] They were unaware that both the DCI and the Plans Directorate had done their best to keep the whole operation secret from the Intelligence Directorate. The DDI, Robert Amory, later complained:

> . . . I was never in on any of the consultations either inside the Agency or otherwise. . . . At least on paper I knew more about amphibious warfare than anyone else in the Agency. I had made twenty-six assault landings in the South Pacific, Southwest Pacific and so on—and of about the same size, many of them, as the Bay of Pigs. Whereas the Marine they had advising them had made one in his whole goddam life, and that was Iwo Jima, which was three divisions abreast.[29]

Kennedy believed that he retained "the right to stop this thing up to 24 hours before the landing."[30] The reality was, however, that the longer preparations continued, the greater the momentum they acquired and the more difficult it became to call off the operation. On March 11 Bissell presented a paper entitled "Proposed Operation Against Cuba" to a meeting of the NSC in the cabinet room. He recommended an amphibious/airborne assault in force on the Cuban coastal town of Trinidad that, he confidently predicted, would demoralize Castro's militia and lead to widespread rebellion. Dulles skillfully emphasized the risks not of going ahead with the landing but of calling off the invasion and disbanding the Cuban opposition brigade being trained by the CIA in Guatemala:

> Don't forget we have a disposal problem. If we have to take these men out of Guatemala, we will have to transfer them to the United States, and we can't have them wandering around the country telling everyone what they have been doing.

Kennedy did not contest that argument but was worried that the Trinidad plan was too "spectacular" and instructed the CIA to devise another plan for a "quiet" landing, preferably at night at a different location. What neither the president nor the NSC seemed able to grasp was that no "quiet" option existed. The only realistic alternatives were to accept that United States involvement in the operation could not be concealed or to call the whole thing off. Since the realistic options were both unacceptable, Kennedy settled for an unrealistic alternative. On March 16 he gave his approval in principle to planning for Operation Zapata, a "quiet" landing in the Bay of Pigs.[31]

On March 29, two days before Good Friday, Bissell gave a progress report on Zapata in the cabinet room. In Palm Beach, over the Easter weekend, Kennedy played golf, went to church, swam in the ocean, watched films each night at his father's house, and pondered the invasion of Cuba and other affairs of state. By the time he returned to Washington on Tuesday, April 4, he was committed to Zapata. He made clear to Bundy that he "really wanted to do this. . . . He had made up his mind and *told* us. He didn't *ask* us." At a secret meeting that evening with Bissell and his chief advisers, Kennedy told them he was still concerned that the operation might be "too noisy," but admitted that if Zapata were abandoned, the anti-Castro forces might prove noisier still: "If we decided now to call the whole thing off, I don't know if we could go down there and take the guns away from them."[32] None of his advisers disagreed.

Robert McNamara, the secretary of defense, was also in favor of Zapata. Dean Rusk, the secretary of state, was skeptical, but, as he later admitted, "I never expressed my doubts explicitly in the planning sessions." The Joint Chiefs of Staff supported the operation, but Rusk believed "they never looked at the plan as professional soldiers. They figured that since the whole show was a CIA operation, they would just approve it and wash their hands of it." By far the most important influences on Kennedy were Dulles and Bissell. According to Rusk, "very little" of what they said "was put on paper."[33] In particular, no record survives of what the president was told about plans to assassinate Castro. As preparations for Zapata went ahead, the CIA gave the leading mafioso, Johnny Rosselli, botulinum toxin pills to pass to assassins stalking the Cuban leader. In keeping with the doctrine of plausible deniability, the agency left no smoking gun to link the assassination plot with the White House. But it is difficult to believe that the president was not informed the plot was under way, even if he was not told (and probably did not wish to know) all the details. Kennedy inherited from Eisenhower a system designed to ensure that major covert operations did not proceed without presidential approval. The plot to kill Castro was not a momentary aberration by a handful of agency deviants. In January 1961 Bissell instructed the veteran station chief, William Harvey, to set up a "standby capability" for "Executive Action," a euphemism for the killing of foreign leaders.[34] According to JFK's friend, Senator George Smathers, Kennedy told him while they were walking the White House grounds in March 1961 that he had been "given to believe" by the CIA that Castro would no longer be alive by the time the invaders landed in the Bay of Pigs. "He was certain it could be accomplished—I remember that—it would be no problem," Smathers recalled. Bissell later admitted that he had been hopeful "that Castro would be dead before the landing." He also believed that Dulles had told the president. "If Kennedy knew that the CIA's murderers were loose in Cuba and ready to strike," argues Michael Beschloss, "this would help explain his approval of an invasion plan that otherwise seems so implausible."[35] The Mafia's assassins, however, never came close to success.

Zapata began at dawn on Saturday, April 15, with an air strike against Cuban airfields by eight B-26s flown by Cuban exiles. Despite claims to the contrary by the pilots, the attack left most of Castro's air force intact. The CIA cover story that the air raid had been launched by defectors from Castro's air force began to fall apart when one of the B-26s made an emergency landing at Key West.[36] As part of the unsuccessful attempt to distance the CIA from Zapata, Dulles spent the weekend fulfilling a speaking engagement in Puerto Rico. Before he left, the DDI, Robert Amory, who was to be Sunday duty officer, told him, "Whether you know it or not, I know what's going on. Now what should I do if anything comes up?" Dulles replied sharply, "You have nothing to do with that at all." The deputy DCI, General Charles P. Cabell, would do what was necessary. Amory later recalled that on the morning of Sunday, April 16, "I came in and opened the cables from Uruguay and Nigeria and so on and so forth, and went home and played five sets of tennis. I said, "Screw 'em!'"[37]

Kennedy, meanwhile, was spending the weekend in his Virginia retreat at Glen Ora, in order not to arouse press suspicions by staying at the White House. At midday on Sunday he gave the go-ahead for landings in the Bay of Pigs on the following day. During the afternoon Rusk and Adlai Stevenson, the UN ambassador, both hotly insisted that there should be no further air strike against Cuba since it would be clear that Washington was responsible. Though conscious of the increased risk to the expeditionary force without air support, Kennedy agreed. After he had finished speaking to Rusk over the phone, he sat in silence for a moment, then began to pace the room. Those with him at Glen Ora had rarely seen him so depressed. For the first time in his presidency, he had a premonition of impending disaster. That evening Bissell and General Cabell called on Rusk at the State Department and tried to persuade him that a second air strike was essential. Rusk listened carefully, phoned the president, gave what Cabell thought was a very fair account of their arguments, but ended by saying he was still opposed to a further air raid. Then the secretary of state turned toward his visitors. "Well, the President agrees with me," he said, "but would you, General Cabell, like to speak to the President?" Cabell said there was no point.

Soon after 4 A.M. on Monday morning, April 17, Cabell had second thoughts. He woke Rusk in his apartment at the Sheraton Park Hotel and asked for fighter cover from the aircraft carrier *Essex* while ships landed the Cuban brigade and withdrew to international waters. Rusk telephoned Glen Ora, woke the president, and handed the phone to Cabell for him to put his case directly. Kennedy listened, then asked to speak to Rusk. After a brief conversation, Rusk hung up and told Cabell that the president had turned down his request. By now the landing in the Bay of Pigs was under way. It was poorly planned and badly executed. The invasion flotilla crashed into coral reefs that NPIC photographic interpreters, in an uncharacteristic error, had mistaken for seaweed. The first landing party ran into a Cuban patrol. At dawn attacks by Castro's air force began. The fourteen hundred men of the Cuban brigade stood no chance against Castro's army.[38]

David Atlee Phillips, who worked in the CIA war room, remembered the next two days as "a slow motion nightmare."[39] Kennedy called them "two full days of hell . . . the most excruciating period of my life."[40] Important signal equipment had gone down in one of the landing ships, and news from the beachhead reached the White House erratically. Portable radios got wet as they were carried ashore and failed to function properly. Part of Kennedy's ordeal, as he agonized about the fate of the Cuban brigade, was the need to keep up appearances in public. On the evening of Tuesday, April 18, dressed in white tie and tails, he received guests at the annual White House reception for members of Congress. At 10:15 P.M., as a marine band in red dress uniforms played "Mr. Wonderful," a smiling president and First Lady started the dancing in the East Room. Just before midnight, still in white tie and tails, Kennedy adjourned to the cabinet room for an emergency meeting with his chief advisers. The three hours of discussion that followed showed how many of the illusions that had led to the tragedy still survived. Unable to accept that Zapata was doomed, Bissell argued that the operation could still be saved if the president would authorize the use of jets from the *Essex*. He was supported by Admiral Arleigh Burke of the Joint Chiefs, who also suggested bringing in a destroyer.

"Burke," said Kennedy sharply, "I don't want the United States involved in this."

"Hell, Mr. President," replied Burke, "but we *are* involved!"

Finally Kennedy agreed to a pointless compromise. Six unmarked jets from the *Essex* were to fly for one hour over the beachhead to protect ammunition supply flights from Nicaragua, but were not to open fire unless attacked. At best, the jets might have postponed slightly the brigade's inevitable defeat. In fact, they arrived at the wrong time and made no difference at all. The fighting came to an end on Wednesday afternoon. The brigade commander radioed, "I have nothing left to fight with. . . . Am headed for the swamp." He cursed, and the radio went dead. A total of 114 members of the brigade were killed; 1,189 were captured by Castro's forces.[41]

Kennedy's finest moment in the greatest debacle of his presidency was his acceptance of his own responsibility. He told reporters at a press conference on April 21, "There's an old saying that victory has a hundred fathers and defeat is an orphan." What mattered was that "I am the responsible officer of government."[42] Privately, he admitted that his own ignorance of intelligence and covert action had made him too uncritical of Dulles's and Bissell's advice:

If someone comes in to tell me this or that about the minimum wage bill, I have no hesitation in overruling them. But you always assume that the military and intelligence people have some secret skill not available to ordinary mortals.[43]

Kennedy's relations with the DCI and DDP remained friendly. He told Bissell:

> If this were the British government, I would resign, and you, being a senior civil servant, would remain. But it isn't. In our government, you and Allen have to go, and I have to remain.

The president added that there was no rush. Bissell and Dulles were not to suffer the humiliation of overnight dismissal.[44] Henceforth, however, Kennedy placed less trust in the intelligence professionals and more in the opinions of his main personal advisers. Neither his brother Robert nor Theodore Sorensen had taken part in the meetings in the cabinet room that discussed plans for Zapata. Both were by his side in the future crises of his presidency. Kennedy began regular morning meetings for his National Security Council staff and other presidential foreign policy advisers. At "Mac" Bundy's suggestion, he ordered the creation of a White House situation room, located in Roosevelt's wartime map room, to act as a clearinghouse for intelligence, diplomatic, military, and naval information.[45]

As part of the agency's attempt to recover the president's confidence after the Bay of Pigs, the Directorate of Intelligence devised an upgraded version of the CIA daily summary, which had begun during the Truman presidency. Entitled "The President's Intelligence Checklist," and marked "For the President Only—Top Secret," it was delivered to the White House each morning shortly after 8 o'clock by a senior analyst who stood by to answer questions arising from it. Unlike the daily summary, the checklist included ultrasensitive CIA operational reports and was tailored to Kennedy's own tastes and interests. Written in a crisp, direct style, it quickly became part of the president's favorite reading. According to R. Jack Smith, one of the checklist editors:

> President Kennedy . . . entered enthusiastically into an exchange of comments with its producers, sometimes praising an account, sometimes criticizing a comment, once objecting to "boondocks" as not an accepted word. For current intelligence people, this was heaven on earth! A president who read your material thoughtfully and told you what he liked and did not like![46]

As well as dealing with the big issues of the day, the editors also included a sprinkling of some of the world's most highly classified gossip about foreign leaders. Among items that seem to have caught Kennedy's eye was a report that a Latin American leader had had his wife's lover murdered and a transcript showing what the Bavarian leader Franz-Josef Strauss "talks like when drunk."[47]

During the month after the Bay of Pigs, Kennedy's main foreign policy concern shifted from Cuba to preparations for a summit meeting with Khrushchev in Vienna in early June. He hoped to achieve both a test ban accord and a working relationship with the Soviet leader. Khrushchev, however, was in a belligerent mood. He had once told Rusk, in a characteristically colorful simile, that Berlin was the testicles of the West, which he could squeeze at will. In Vienna, Khrushchev demanded the abolition of the three-power status of West Berlin and a German peace treaty by the end of the year. "I want peace," he told Kennedy as he thumped the table. "But if you want war, that is your problem." His demand for a settlement not later than December was "firm and irrevocable." "If that is true," replied the president grimly, "it's going to be a cold winter." The two superpowers seemed set for the most dangerous confrontation since the Korean War. Kennedy afterward told James Reston:

> I think [Khrushchev] did it because of the Bay of Pigs. I think he
> thought anyone who was so young and inexperienced as to get into
> that mess could be taken, and anyone who got into it and didn't see
> it through had no guts. So he just beat the hell out of me.[48]

The Berlin crisis dominated Kennedy's summer. The intelligence that made the greatest impression on him during the crisis came from probably the most important Western penetration agent of the Cold War, Colonel Oleg Penkovsky, deputy head of the foreign section of the GRU (Soviet military intelligence). Run jointly by CIA and the British SIS, Penkovsky provided important insights into both Khrushchev's policy and the state of the Soviet armed forces. Twenty agency and ten British translators were needed to cope with the large number of secret military documents that he photographed with a Minox camera. During a visit to London with a Soviet delegation in April, Penkovsky was secretly debriefed at the Mount Royal Hotel, near Marble Arch, by a team of CIA and SIS officers. He astonished his Anglo-American handlers by telling them, ". . . The great desire which I have carried in my soul . . . is to swear my fealty to my Queen, Elizabeth II, and to the President of the United States, Mr. Kennedy, whom I am serving as their soldier." He asked for the queen and Kennedy to be informed.

Allen Dulles gave the president his first briefing on Penkovsky on July 13. Among the items that Dulles brought to the White House was Penkovsky's account of a meeting with Chief Marshal Sergei Varentsov, who had told him:

Firmness in politics is necessary, in particular on the German question, and the West will retreat before this firmness. The Soviet government knows that signing this treaty means a certain risk and danger, but they are not worried, because they know that the FRG [West Germany] still is not ready for war and needs two or three years more. The U.S., Britain, and France, because of this, will not start a big war and will retreat. We also do not want a big war, but we want to force the West to begin to negotiate with the GDR [East Germany]. . . . These first negotiations with the GDR will amount to the first recognition of the GDR, and this is important for history.

Penkovsky added a note insisting that, "The firmness of Khrushchev must be met with firmness. . . . He is not prepared for a big war, and is waging a war of nerves." Kennedy told Dulles that he wished to be kept personally informed of Penkovsky's progress. He incorporated some of Penkovsky's suggestions in a tough speech on July 25, which Sorensen described as "more somber than any previous presidential speech in the age of mutual nuclear capabilities." "West Berlin," declared the president, "has become the great testing place of Western courage and will, a focal point where our solemn commitments . . . and Soviet ambitions now meet in basic confrontation."

On July 18 Penkovsky returned to London with a Soviet delegation for a three-week visit, during which he was several times secretly debriefed at a safe apartment in Kensington. On the evening of his arrival, he reported that Varentsov had told him, "We are definitely embarking on a risky action." When his Anglo-American case officers asked him, "Is the Soviet Union ready for nuclear war?" Penkovsky replied, "They are not ready. Khrushchev's statements about this are all bluff, but he is preparing as fast as possible. Our officers do not want an atomic war." At a meeting in the safe apartment on July 28 Penkovsky was handed a copy of Kennedy's speech of July 25. "This," he was told by one of his CIA case officers, "is so you will know that your information is definitely reaching our leaders. . . . I can point out that in a number of the President's statements, exactly those thoughts which you expressed were mentioned by the President." Penkovsky beamed. He was also elated to be photographed in the uniform of both a U.S. and a British colonel. Be'ore leaving London, Penkovsky spent a night with a prostitute selected for him by SIS. He took with him, on his return to Moscow, presents for Varentsov's sixtieth birthday provided by SIS and CIA, among them a bottle of old cognac with a forged label indicating that it was the same age as the marshal.[49]

On August 9 Dulles handed Kennedy a Soviet transcript of the

Vienna summit and a copy of a secret Central Committee resolution approving Khrushchev's handling of it, both supplied by Penkovsky. The president noted that the Soviet version emphasized Khrushchev's tough talk and downplayed American resolve. That same day in Moscow, Penkovsky learned of secret plans to begin the construction of the Berlin Wall four days later to end free access for East Germans to West Berlin. But, partly because of the U.S. ambassador's reluctance to allow his embassy to become involved in a major espionage operation, Penkovsky was unable to warn CIA or SIS before construction began. As a result, Kennedy was taken by surprise.[50]

When the building of the Berlin Wall began, the president was spending the weekend at Hyannisport. After Sunday Mass on August 13 he changed into a polo shirt and white ducks, and boarded the *Marlin* to sail to Great Island for lunch. As the boat was leaving harbor, it was called back. Waiting for Kennedy at the dock was a yellow teletype "triple-priority" message from Washington, bearing the unexpected news from Berlin. "How come we didn't know anything about this?" demanded Kennedy. He telephoned Rusk with the same question: "What the hell is this? How long have you known? Was there any warning in the last few days?" The president's Berlin task force, set up on his return from the Vienna summit, went into continuous session. At first, no one was quite sure what the Russians were up to. One possibility that was seriously considered was that they had decided to drive the West out of Berlin. Kennedy himself put the chances of nuclear warfare at about one in five. It took four days before the task force could even agree on the wording of a protest note to Moscow.[51]

On August 22 the British businessman Greville Wynne, who was acting as an SIS courier, arrived in Moscow. The next day Penkovsky handed him six rolls of film of secret documents, which included the detailed specifications for the construction of the Berlin Wall.[52] On August 28, before Penkovsky's latest intelligence had reached the White House, NSA picked up signals for a new round of Soviet nuclear tests that began on September 1. "Fucked again!" said Kennedy. During the Vienna summit, Khrushchev had assured him that the Soviet Union would not be the first to break the voluntary moratorium on testing that had been in force since 1958.[53]

Penkovsky's next meetings with his Anglo-American controllers took place in Paris, where he arrived on September 20 to visit the Soviet trade fair. That evening in a safe apartment in the sixteenth arrondissement, he told them how much Varentsov had enjoyed the sixtieth-birthday presents supplied by CIA and SIS. During the birthday party, after they had drunk the cognac with the forged sixty-year-old label, the Soviet defense minister, Marshal Rodion Malinovsky, had declared: ". . . The situation is difficult. Our enemies are not giving in to us, although it is true that they have swallowed a pill [the Berlin Wall]. We handled this one well, but how will it be in future?"

Penkovsky then issued a dire warning of his own, which was duly recorded on his case officers' tape recorder:

> . . . Khrushchev is preparing nine armies in and adjacent to the immediate German theater, and now he has ordered a tenth army to that area. . . . His first purpose is to frighten us [the United States and Britain]. However, if the Communist world expresses complete approval at the Party Congress in October, and he also feels that world opinion is with him, he may strike us. He wants to take advantage of any indecision on the part of the Free World, and he actually may attack the leaders, which are the United States and England. He does not have all available means for carrying through such a strike to the final conclusion. The military people know this but they act meekly before Khrushchev. If he orders the beginning of hostilities they will comply.

Penkovsky's warning caused deep anxiety in Washington. At his next debriefing in the Paris safe apartment, he was faced with a series of supplementary questions. Who had told him that Khrushchev was prepared to strike? Penkovsky replied that he had been told this both by Varentsov and by two of his aides: "In addition I have heard the same thing in the General Staff from those who are in a position to know and with whom I have friendly relations." But Penkovsky continued to insist that it was necessary to stand up to Khrushchev: "If you retreat from Berlin, things will be quiet for a year and a half. Then Khrushchev will start crowing again that we have achieved a victory, that Kennedy was afraid to face him." Penkovsky was reminded that he had said previously that Khrushchev lacked the means to follow through with an attack on the West. What precisely did he lack? Penkovsky put at the top of the list the shortage of atomic warheads. There were also insufficient trained personnel and problems with guidance systems.

As well as helping to persuade Kennedy to maintain a tough stance on Berlin, Penkovsky also led the president and his advisers through the secret debate on nuclear strategy taking place within the Soviet Union, providing a wealth of intelligence ranging from information on missile site construction to details of the latest round of Soviet tests. The CIA produced two series of highly classified reports on Penkovsky's intelligence, the most important of which were shown to the president. The

Ironbark series was devoted to the documents supplied by him; Chickadee covered his oral debriefings. On October 15 Penkovsky flew back from Paris to Moscow. His CIA and SIS controllers were never to see him again, but at intervals for another ten months he passed films of classified documents to the wife of an SIS officer in Moscow and to Greville Wynne. Two days after Penkovsky's return from Paris, Khrushchev backed down. In a six-and-a-half-hour speech to the opening session of the Twenty-second Congress of the Communist party, he boasted that "the Soviet Union is stronger and more powerful than ever," but then withdrew the deadline for a German treaty: "We have the impression that the Western powers are displaying a certain understanding of the situation and that they are inclined to seek a solution for the German problem and for the West Berlin issue on a mutually acceptable basis."[54] The Berlin problem remained, noted Rusk, but "the Berlin crisis was over."[55]

The successful running of Penkovsky during the Berlin crisis enabled Dulles to step down as DCI in November 1961 with the sense that, at least in the Oval Office, the agency's reputation had been partly restored after the debacle of the Bay of Pigs. Shortly before he left, the CIA moved into its present headquarters at Langley, Virginia, whose large white marble lobby contains a bas-relief of Dulles. Kennedy's first choice as the next DCI was his brother Robert, but he quickly realized that such an appointment would make impossible plausible denial of White House involvement in covert operations. Instead, perhaps intent on securing conservative support for controversial policies, he appointed the Republican John A. McCone, a former businessman and chairman of the Atomic Energy Commission. McCone's interests, unlike Dulles's, were chiefly in intelligence analysis. Ray Cline, whom he made DDI, believed that "he absorbed more from complex briefings than any senior official I have ever worked with." Sherman Kent, head of the Board of National Estimate, took to asking agency officials the color of McCone's eyes. The answer was usually some variant of "ice-cold blue." In fact, McCone's eyes were dark brown. "But," replied one of those who gave the wrong answer, "his mind and persona were steely blue-eyed."[56]

The president retained a greater faith in covert action than his new DCI. The humiliation of the Bay of Pigs had not shaken Kennedy's determination to topple Castro. On the contrary, it made him determined to find more effective—and more secret—ways of doing it. In June 1961, after a review of U.S. paramilitary capabilities, "with special attention to the lessons which can be learned from the recent events in Cuba," he replaced Eisenhower's 5412 Committee with a more powerful Special Group (5412). The new group, consisting of the DCI, the chairman of the Joint Chiefs, and undersecretaries from State and Defense, chaired by Mac Bundy, was instructed to "assume the review of important covert operations" and "undertake the development and recommendations of Cold War plans and programs for those countries or areas specifically assigned to it by the President."[57] Even the State Department representative, U. Alexis Johnson, known as "Dr. No" because he raised more objections than his colleagues, considered it "one of the most successful and tightly held groups in Washington." Kennedy, he observed, took "a great deal of interest" in the Special Group.[58] During the first two years of the administration a total of 550 "covert action projects" were approved, ranging from secret funding for friendly foreign politicians to paramilitary warfare—more per year than under Eisenhower.[59] From the outset, the group's chief priority was operations "to undermine the Castro regime," all of them promptly reported to the president.[60] In January 1962 a Special Group (Counterinsurgency) was established, including the members of Special Group (5412), but chaired by the president's military adviser, General Maxwell Taylor, who called it "a sort of Joint Chiefs of Staff . . . for all agencies involved in counterinsurgency."[61]

To monitor the performance of the intelligence community as a whole, Kennedy revived and upgraded a board of consultants founded by Eisenhower in 1956, renaming it the President's Foreign Intelligence Advisory Board (PFIAB). Chaired initially by James Killian (succeeded in 1963 by Clark Clifford), the board met twenty-five times between May and November 1961, more than in the five years of its previous incarnation. During his presidency, Kennedy had at least twelve lengthy sessions with the PFIAB to review a wide range of intelligence issues, and regularly sought advice from individual members. In 1963 he privately described it as the most useful of all his advisory boards. In all, the PFIAB submitted 170 formal recommendations (most still classified); Kennedy approved 125, rejected 2, and deferred action on the rest. The board's first major preoccupation in the wake of the Bay of Pigs was the reorganization of the diffuse defense intelligence system, which gained added importance as a result of Kennedy's decision to transfer paramilitary operations from CIA to Defense. It approved the creation on October 1, 1961, of the Defense Intelligence Agency (DIA), which was intended to coordinate and extend the work of the rival service intelligence departments. McNamara confidently predicted that the new agency would bring about "more effective management of all Department of Defense intelligence activities, and the elimination of duplicating intelligence facilities, organization, and tasks." He was to be disappointed. "DIA was born old," one official said later. "McNamara just gathered the drones and put them all in one building."[62]

After the foundation of the DIA, the PFIAB devoted most of its attention to the rapidly expanding IMINT and SIGINT programs run by the NRO and the NSA. Its most influential members were two brilliant scientists: William Baker, the president of Bell Labs, and Edwin Land, the inventor of the Polaroid camera. "The tutelage of Drs. Baker and Land," wrote Clifford, "turned all of us into missionaries for intelligence collection by 'technical means': that is, electronic, photographic, and satellite espionage." Baker and Land brought to a meeting of PFIAB some of the first ultrahigh-resolution satellite photographs. "We were awed and amazed," Clifford recalls, "as we gazed for the first time upon photographs taken of a tennis court from one hundred miles above the ground, with resolution so clear that one could clearly see a tennis ball lying on the court!" IMINT and SIGINT collection, however, seemed in danger of becoming a victim of its own success. The intelligence explosion generated by NRO and NSA threatened to swamp the analysts who had to deal with it. Lundahl explained to Kennedy that even the U-2 camera could photograph an area about 125 nautical miles wide and 3,000 miles long on ten thousand feet of film. "Imagine," he told the president, "a group of photo interpreters on their hands and knees scanning a roll of film that extended from the White House to the Capitol and back." Kennedy regularly asked Lundahl to repeat the analogy at briefings of his advisers. NSA's problems were even greater than NPIC's. ELINT collection by satellite, ground stations, ships, and aircraft expanded so rapidly that, even with the world's largest and most advanced banks of computers and more personnel than any other Western intelligence agency, NSA could barely cope with it. Boxcars full of highly classified tapes lined up on the railway tracks outside Fort Meade.[63]

NRO and NSA were, nonetheless, vital to Kennedy's security policy. Without good technical intelligence, allegations of a missile gap, fueled by Khrushchev's misleading boasts of Soviet superiority, would inevitably have resurfaced, and Penkovsky's realistic assessments of Soviet nuclear capability would have been greeted with skepticism. In September 1961 a new National Intelligence Estimate (NIE), drawing on both Penkovsky and technical intelligence, reduced the estimate of Soviet nuclear strength to less than thirty-five missiles.[64] Kennedy agonized over whether to make public the facts of Soviet nuclear inferiority. Publicity would encourage the Russians to accelerate their ICBM program. But the experience of the Berlin crisis, strengthened by Penkovsky's insistence on the need to stand up to Khrushchev, persuaded the president that avoiding publicity carried greater risks. " . . . Khrushchev's several ultimatums on Berlin," concluded Roger Hilsman, head of the State

Department Bureau of Intelligence and Research, "indicated that, if he were allowed to continue to assume that we still believed in the missile gap, he would very probably bring the world close to war." McNamara's deputy, Roswell Gilpatric, was chosen to set the record straight on the grounds that he was sufficiently senior for his words to carry weight but would not appear as threatening as the president or McNamara.[65] On October 21, four days after Khrushchev's opening address to the party congress, Gilpatric made an uncompromising public assertion of American nuclear superiority: "In short, we have a second strike capability which is at least as extensive as what the Soviets can deliver by striking first. Therefore, we are confident that the Soviets will not provoke a major nuclear conflict." To drive the message home in private, Kennedy authorized classified briefings to be given to NATO allies whose administrations were believed to be penetrated by Soviet agents.[66]

Clark Clifford, like perhaps a majority of the PFIAB, believed "the era of cloak-and-dagger operations had more or less run its course."[67] Kennedy did not. Cloaks and daggers remained at the heart of his strategy for dealing with Castro. In the aftermath of the Bay of Pigs, he dispatched his brother Robert, who had taken no part in the preparations for Zapata, to determine what reforms were necessary at the CIA. But the major shake-up, which senior officials feared as they watched the abrasive attorney general delve, in his shirtsleeves, into the inner workings of the agency, did not happen. Instead, as one of them observed, Robert Kennedy "fell in love with . . . the concept of covert operations."[68] "The Cuban matter is being allowed to slide," he complained on June 1. "Mostly because nobody really has the answer to Castro." There was in fact an answer, but it was one that neither the president nor his brother was prepared even to consider. Senator William Fulbright had told Kennedy before the Bay of Pigs, "The Castro regime is a thorn in the flesh; but it is not a dagger in the heart."[69] A rational American policy to Cuba would have been based on containment, not on attempts to overthrow or destabilize its government whose main effect was to enhance the international standing of Fidel Castro and to lower that of the United States. But rationality had little place in Kennedy's Cuban policy. Even McNamara, the renowned "human computer" who was fond of warning that "You can't substitute emotion for reason," later admitted, "We were hysterical about Castro. . . ."[70] Penkovsky strengthened Kennedy's determination to be rid of the Cuban leader. "The fact that you still tolerate Castro in Cuba," he warned on September 22, was taken by Khrushchev as a sign of weakness.[71]

Robert Kennedy summarized his plans for covert action in Cuba in a short and aggressive note on November 4:

My idea is to stir things up on island with espionage, sabotage, general disorder, run & operated by Cubans themselves with every group but Batistaites & Communists. Do not know if we will be successful in overthrowing Castro but we have nothing to lose in my estimate.

That was also his brother's estimate. At the end of November the president launched Operation Mongoose with a top-secret order "to use our available assets . . . to help Cuba overthrow the Communist regime." The head of operations was the counterinsurgency specialist, General Edward Lansdale, reporting to a new Special Group (Augmented) with much the same membership as the other groups but under the effective direction of Robert Kennedy. Mongoose, said the attorney general in January 1962, was "top priority . . . all else is secondary." He ordered that "no time, money, effort—or manpower . . . be spared." The operations themselves were entrusted to a newly founded CIA Task Force W, whose Miami headquarters became the largest CIA station in the world with four hundred American staff, two thousand Cuban agents, its own navy and air force, and an annual budget of over $50 million.

Robert Kennedy was constantly pushing the agency to devise new ways of undermining the Castro regime. The pressure, according to Richard Helms, "was pretty intense. . . . Nutty schemes were born of the pressure. . . . No doubt about it, it was white heat." Among the nuttiest was a scheme for a U.S. submarine to shoot star shells into the night sky off Havana in an attempt to convince Roman Catholics in the capital that the Second Coming of Jesus Christ was at hand. Despite its manifest brutalities and absurdities, Mongoose was not some bizarre fringe activity by a government agency that barely captured the attention of a busy president. On the contrary, at the beginning of 1962, it was his chief—and most expensive—foreign policy initiative. Mongoose included a series of plans to assassinate Castro, all of which mercifully degenerated into farce. Some, like the proposal to place an exploding seashell on the seafloor where Castro went snorkeling, probably did not progress beyond the drawing board. The most practicable scheme devised during 1962 was probably for one of Fidel's mistresses to slip two poison capsules into his drink. While waiting for an opportunity, she hid them in a jar of cold cream. When she came to retrieve them, they had melted. It is doubtful in any case whether she would actually have used them.[72]

Kennedy loyalists, like Eisenhower loyalists, find it difficult to believe that the president could have approved of the attempts on Castro's life. Though no smoking gun survives, it is barely conceivable that the CIA would have gone ahead without the blessing of the president.

U. Alexis Johnson, the Special Group member least enthusiastic about covert action, insists that "there was never, to my knowledge, any foundation for charges of free wheeling by the CIA."[73] Both Helms, the DDP, and Cline, the DDI, conclude that the inspiration for the assassination plots came from the White House. ". . . The assassination of Castro by a Cuban," writes Cline, "might have been viewed as not very different in the benefits that would have accrued from the assassination of Hitler in 1944."[74] There is no mistaking the courage of the president, the inspirational qualities of his leadership, and the idealism of the New Frontier. But there was also a dark side to Camelot, which showed itself in the intermittent shabbiness of the president's private life and in the brutality of his Cuban policy. His speechwriter, Richard Goodwin, became convinced that "there was an inner hardness, often volatile anger beneath the outwardly amiable, thoughtful, carefully controlled demeanor of John Kennedy."[75]

In addition to overseeing Mongoose and acting as a goad on the CIA, Robert Kennedy performed two other important intelligence functions for the president. First, as attorney general, he was responsible for the FBI. Until he put a stop to it, FBI tour guides would tell visitors, "Mr. Hoover became the director of the bureau in 1924, the year before the attorney general was born." In 1952–1953 Robert Kennedy had spent six months as assistant counsel to Senator Joseph McCarthy, who he believed at the time "seemed to be the only one who was doing anything about . . . a serious security threat to the United States." But in January 1961 he dismissed Hoover's claim that the American Communist party was "a greater menace to the internal security of our nation today than it ever has been since it was first founded in this country in 1919." As Arthur Schlesinger has noted, Robert Kennedy now saw Communism as a threat *to*, but not *in*, the United States. "It is such nonsense to have to waste time prosecuting the Communist Party," he told a journalist. "It couldn't be more feeble and less of a threat, and besides its membership consists largely of FBI agents." Though there were few open clashes between them, the attorney general and the director of the FBI loathed each other. Ethel Kennedy, Robert's wife, once put a note on which she had written "Chief Parker in Los Angeles for Director" into the FBI suggestions box. (Parker was one of Hoover's bêtes noires.) Both John and Robert Kennedy were impressed, and at least mildly intimidated, by the amount of compromising information that Hoover had gathered in his files on public figures. "Boy, the dirt he has on those senators!" the president commented. Hoover discreetly made clear to both brothers that he had "dirt" on them as well, mostly relating to their promiscuous lifestyles. "Every month or so," Robert Kennedy later recalled, "he'd send somebody up or a memo . . . to give information on somebody I knew or on members of my family or allegations in connection with myself, so it would be clear whether it was right or wrong that he was on top of all these things and received all of this information."[76]

Hoover's dirt on the president went back to the Second World War, when Kennedy had had an affair with a suspected German spy, Inga Arvad, while working in naval intelligence. As representative and senator, Kennedy made several unsuccessful attempts to recover FBI tape recordings from bugged hotel rooms in which he and Ms. Arvad, according to a bureau report, had "engag[ed] in sexual intercourse on numerous occasions." On July 14, 1960, the day after Kennedy won the Democratic presidential nomination, Hoover moved the 628-page Kennedy-Arvad file into his office. Kennedy's knowledge of the embarrassing FBI tapes probably helps to explain his deference to Hoover before he became president. Though Hoover had declined an invitation to Kennedy's wedding in 1953, the Cape Cod resident agent reported to the director that, during the reception, "Senator Kennedy complimented you and the agents of the Bureau on the splendid job done and volunteered that he was anxious and willing at all times to 'support Mr. Hoover and the FBI. . . .'" On August 4, 1960, three months before the election, Kennedy announced that "he would, of course, retain Mr. Hoover and planned no major changes within the agency."[77]

Kennedy took the decision to "retain Mr. Hoover," however, less because he felt intimidated than because it was still difficult to imagine the FBI without him. After more than thirty-five years as director, Hoover had become a national institution. Clark Clifford disliked him, but thought he was "the only choice . . . we had at the time."[78] Kennedy's phenomenal libido, unimpaired by the cares of office, ensured that his file in Hoover's office continued to grow. "He was really unbelievable—absolutely incredible in that regard," his friend Senator George Smathers said later, "and he got more so the longer he was married." Of the president's numerous sexual liaisons, the one that occupied most space in Hoover's files was probably that with the beautiful Beverly Hills actress and painter, Judith Campbell. Though Kennedy knew that she was also the mistress of the Chicago mobster Sam Giancana, Ms. Campbell was a frequent clandestine visitor to the White House; the telephone log records seventy calls between her and the West Wing in 1961 and 1962. Whether or not, as Campbell claims, she took sealed envelopes back and forth between Kennedy and Giancana (which, she suggests improbably, may have been "helping Jack orchestrate the attempted assassination of Fidel Castro"), the affair clearly posed a security risk. Hoover finally took it up directly with Kennedy at a private White House lunch on

March 22, 1962. It must have been a humiliating moment for the president. Campbell's visits to the White House ceased shortly afterward. "Hoover was God," wrote Campbell bitterly, "and the special agents were his avenging angels." She later attempted to commit suicide.[79]

There was a third strand to Robert Kennedy's intelligence role within his brother's administration. In addition to acting as goad to the CIA and overseer of the FBI, he provided the president with what he believed was a "back channel" to the Kremlin through the Soviet intelligence officer Georgi Bolshakov, who operated in Washington under journalistic cover. After Bolshakov gained an introduction to the attorney general through an American journalist in May 1961, the two men began fortnightly meetings.[80] Bolshakov succeeded in persuading Robert Kennedy that, between them, they could short-circuit the ponderous protocol of official diplomacy, "speak straightly and frankly without resorting to the politickers' stock-in-trade propaganda stunts," and set up a direct channel of communication linking the president and Khrushchev.[81] Bolshakov cleverly presented himself in a manner calculated to make a particular appeal to Robert Kennedy. According to the attorney general's assistant, James Symington, Bolshakov "seemed to find satisfaction in being kidded. With self-deprecating nods, smiles, and circus English he enjoyed Bob's predilection for harmless buffoons, and had almost unlimited access to the inner sanctum." Forgetting that he was dealing with an experienced, professional intelligence officer who had been instructed to cultivate him, Robert Kennedy became convinced that "an authentic friendship grew" between him and Bolshakov.[82] He regarded Bolshakov as "Khrushchev's representative":

> Any time that he had some message to give to the President (or Khrushchev had) or when the President had some message to give to Khrushchev, we went through Georgi Bolshakov. . . . I met with him about all kinds of things.[83]

According to Bolshakov, "both sides made the most" of the back channel he provided.[84] The two sides, however, put it to rather different uses. Its primary purpose for the KGB was as a means of deceiving the president.[85] The supposed back channel to the Kremlin showed the talented and abrasive attorney general at his naïve and arrogant worst. He ignored warnings from both the FBI and the CIA that Bolshakov was a KGB officer. Symington saw through Bolshakov's "insinuating jocularity," resented his "almost unlimited access to the inner sanctum," and feared his boss was "playing a dangerous game." Rusk, Bundy, and Llewellyn

Thompson were all unhappy about Robert Kennedy's meetings with Bolshakov. None, however, realized just how frequent they were or much of what transpired during them. Only the president was kept fully informed of his brother's amateur diplomacy. Robert Kennedy later admitted:

> I unfortunately—stupidly, never—I didn't write many of the things down. I just delivered the messages verbally to my brother and he'd act on them. And I think sometimes he'd tell the State Department and sometimes perhaps he didn't.[86]

In using Bolshakov, Soviet intelligence was employing a technique it had used successfully before. Robert Kennedy's back channel through Bolshakov bears some resemblance to Harry Hopkins's contacts with the NKVD illegal Iskhak Akhmerov twenty years earlier. Like Bolshakov, Akhmerov, who operated in the United States under various aliases, had claimed to offer a secret direct route to the Kremlin that circumvented the cumbrous procedures of orthodox diplomacy, telling Hopkins that he brought confidential messages from Stalin on the vital importance of Soviet-American cooperation both in the war and in postwar reconstruction. The meetings with Akhmerov seem to have contributed to Hopkins's extraordinary admiration for Stalin and to his fear for the future "if anything should happen" to him. Hopkins's pressure for the removal of American official critics of Stalin (chief among them the U.S. ambassador in Moscow, Laurence Steinhardt; the military attaché Ivan Yeaton; and the head of State's Soviet desk, Loy Henderson), all of whom he saw as obstacles to Soviet-American cooperation, later enabled Akhmerov to make the unjustified boast that he had run Hopkins as an agent.[87]

Robert Kennedy did not suffer from Hopkins's illusions about the Soviet Union, but he showed a rather similar naïveté in regarding a Soviet intelligence officer as a reliable back channel to the Kremlin. Before the Vienna summit Bolshakov fed him and the president what has been fairly described as "bald disinformation" about Khrushchev's willingness to compromise on nuclear testing. The Kennedys failed to realize they had been deceived, concluding instead that Khrushchev had had a last-minute change of heart. After the construction of the Berlin Wall, of which Bolshakov had given no inkling, Robert Kennedy later claimed that he had temporarily broken off meetings with him, but had resumed them "three or four months later."[88] Bolshakov's account does not mention this interruption in their meetings. He claims simply that "the Khrushchev-Kennedy dialogue" conducted through the back channel "gained in frankness and directness from message to message."[89] The most important part of Bolshakov's intelligence assignment came in the summer and autumn of 1962. His mission then was to reassure the Kennedys that the Kremlin had no intention of installing nuclear missiles in Cuba until the installation of the missiles was a fait accompli.

Documents declassified in the early 1990s make clear that, even without the Soviet missiles, there would have been a Cuban crisis in the autumn of 1962. The plan for Operation Mongoose envisaged "open revolt by the Cuban people to overthrow the Communist regime" in October—the month of the missile crisis. On July 25 General Lansdale made a progress report to the Special Group (5412 Augmented). He announced that, by the end of the month, eleven "teams" would have been infiltrated into Cuba by the CIA. Despite setbacks, "our best hope is that we will have viable teams in all the potential resistance areas by early October":

> There are enough able bodied and properly motivated Cubans inside Cuba and in exile to do the job. There is widespread disaffection in Cuba, with strong indications that economic distress and demoralization of population is causing real concern and strain for the regime's control officials. Firm U.S. intention to help free Cuba is the key factor in assessing the Cubans themselves as an operational asset for Operation Mongoose.

If the United States showed the will in other words, Mongoose could succeed.[90] This nonsense was not far removed from the self-delusion that had led to disaster at the Bay of Pigs fifteen months before. The assumptions behind the operation were contradicted by an NIE on August 1 that acknowledged that the Cuban economy was "in deep trouble" and that "disaffection is increasing," but concluded:

> The Cuban armed forces are well able to intimidate the general population and to suppress any popular insurrection likely to develop in present circumstances. They are probably capable of containing and controlling any threat to the regime through guerrilla action and of repelling any invasion short of a direct U.S. military invasion in strength.[91]

In spite of this warning of impending disaster, Mongoose went ahead with Robert Kennedy as its chief supporter and overseer within the administration, regularly invoking the president's authority for his insistence on more rapid progress.

In his memoir of the missile crisis, Robert Kennedy claimed, quite inaccurately, "No official within the government had ever suggested to President Kennedy that the Russian buildup in Cuba would include missiles." Even more outrageously, he told an interviewer it was a "fact" that the DCI "wasn't really concerned about it himself."[92] In reality, McCone first raised the possibility that recent Soviet imports to Cuba included MRBMs (medium-range ballistic missiles) at a meeting to review Mongoose on August 10. He mentioned it again to the Special Group (5412 Augmented) on August 21. The other members were more concerned by the broader threat of Cuba's emergence as a Soviet satellite. The minutes record "general agreement that the situation was critical and that the most dynamic action was indicated":

> McNamara expressed strong feelings that we should take every possible aggressive action in the fields of intelligence, sabotage and guerrilla warfare, utilizing Cubans[,] and do such other things as might be indicated to divide the Castro regime. . . . The Attorney General queried the meeting as to what other aggressive steps could be taken. . . .

McCone, who had little direct involvement in Mongoose, which he had delegated to Helms, was less optimistic than Robert Kennedy about the prospects for covert action in Cuba. "Efforts to date with agent teams," he reported, "had been disappointing." "Sabotage activities" would probably produce "more failures than successes." Following the meeting, McCone drew up a "proposed plan of action for Cuba" that emphasized the dangers of a Communist Cuba serving as "a bridgehead for Soviet subversive activities in Central and South America," "a possible location for MRBMs," a base for SIGINT operations against the United States, and a site for electronic warfare (ECM) against the American space and missile programs. Covert action would be insufficient to deal with a menace on this scale. "Therefore," he wrote, "a more aggressive action is indicated than any heretofore considered. . . ." It would need to include the "commitment of sufficient armed forces to occupy the country, destroy the regime, free the people, and establish in Cuba a peaceful country which will be a member of the community of American states." McCone, unlike Robert Kennedy, now recognized that Mongoose by itself was scarcely more likely to overthrow Castro than the landing at the Bay of Pigs.[93]

McCone briefed the president on Cuba on both August 22 and 23. On the first occasion General Taylor, who was to become chairman of the Joint Chiefs on October 1, was also present. Most of the record of the meeting remains classified.[94] During August, however, the Pentagon announced plans for Exercise Philbriglex-62, a mock invasion of the island of Vieques to overthrow a leader named Ortsac (Castro spelled backwards).[95] At the meeting with the president on August 23 (also attended by Rusk, McNamara, Gilpatric, Taylor, and Bundy), McCone again raised the possibility of MRBMs on Cuba. According to the minutes:

> [The] President raised question of what we could do against Soviet missile sites on Cuba. Could we take them out by air or would a ground offensive be necessary or alternatively could they be destroyed by a substantial guerrilla effort[?]

Kennedy's question betrays a certain naïveté about guerrilla operations in general and about their prospects in Cuba in particular. After the meeting McCone had a private, and still mostly classified, conversation with Robert Kennedy. He ended it by saying, "Cuba is the key to all of Latin America; if Cuba succeeds, we can expect most of Latin America to fall."[96] On that at least, McCone and the Kennedys were probably agreed.

Most agency officials had failed to realize that the ice-cold DCI was a romantic at heart. He had been overwhelmed with grief after the death of his beloved first wife, Rosemary, in December 1961, but a few months later fell passionately in love again. On the evening of August 23 McCone left Washington for a month's leave, which began with preparations for his marriage to Theiline Piggott and continued with their honeymoon at Cap Ferrat in the South of France. He left in charge his deputy, General Marshall "Pat" Carter, a genial figure with a reputation as a practical joker. Carter had inserted a rubber hand into a crack in the wall between his office and McCone's to give the impression that the DCI was trying to escape. Briefers who continued too long in Carter's office were likely to find themselves prodded either by a large rubber foot or by a telescopic pointer that the deputy DCI referred to as his "goosing stick."[97]

McCone had a disturbed honeymoon, his mind constantly returning to the possibility that offensive missile bases were being installed in Cuba. For some months Cuban refugees, defectors, and agents had sent numerous reports of missile sightings. Almost all turned out to be SAM (surface-to-air) and defensive cruise missiles.[98] Increasingly, however, McCone feared that many of the SAMs were intended to defend MRBM or IRBM sites. Instead of leaving Cap Ferrat, the DCI sent Carter a series of what became known as the "honeymoon cables," explaining his anxieties. On August 25 McCone urged his deputy to press for low-level RF-101 flights over possible missile sites. In fact, because of the risks, there were no low-level flights for almost two months. But on August 29 a U-2 "flew over most of the island and photographed much of it," returning with photographs of eight SAM sites under construction. Kennedy was given the "readout" of the U-2 mission on the morning of August 31 and was shocked by it. At 1 P.M. he telephoned General Carter, asked how many people had been given access to the intelligence, and told him "he wished it put back in the box and nailed tight," while he decided what to do with it. On September 4 the president announced publicly that a missile defense system had been installed in Cuba.[99] "The gravest issues would arise," he said, if offensive missiles were introduced. The Soviet ambassador, Anatoli Dobrynin, gave Robert Kennedy an immediate personal pledge from Khrushchev, confirming assurances from Bolshakov, that this would not happen; there would be "no ground-to-ground missiles or offensive missiles placed in Cuba."[100]

Late on September 6 Carter, Cline, Lundahl, and a representative from DIA arrived in the Oval Office to brief Kennedy, McNamara, Rusk, and Bundy on the discovery of a cruise missile site on the Cuban coast at Banes, apparently designed to defend possible landing beaches. The president had never heard of cruise missiles. He was confused and worried by the briefing he was given, and bad-tempered after it.

"How far will this thing shoot?" he asked.

"We think from twenty to forty nautical miles," replied Cline.

Kennedy thought the answer vague and was unhappy with technical explanations for its imprecision.

"Can it hit our ships at sea?" he continued.

Cline said it could if a ship came in range.

"That would make it an offensive weapon, wouldn't it?" the president demanded.

Cline repeated that the missile seemed designed for coastal defense, but admitted that it could be "dual purpose."

"Do we have something like that?" Kennedy asked.

McNamara said no.

"Why in the hell don't we?" asked Kennedy. "How long have we known about this weapon?"

McNamara did not know. Cline guessed. "For several years," he suggested. Carter explained that this was an interim report. The president got up out of his rocking chair and glared at Carter. ". . . I don't want half-assed information," he said. "Go back and do your homework." When Carter returned to Langley, an aide asked him how the briefing had gone. "The President," he succinctly explained, "was pissed."[101] The "homework" demanded by Kennedy produced a CIA report on September 13 that admitted that "none of the known Soviet cruise missile systems precisely fit the facility at Banes," but concluded that "all available evidence" pointed to "a short-range 25–30 nautical miles missile system."[102]

In the "honeymoon cables" from the South of France, McCone continued to press for frequent aerial reconnaissance of Cuba. In fact, after a U-2 mission on September 5, there was no further overflight until September 17, followed by an additional delay until September 26. Though there was some dispute over responsibility for the delays after the missile crisis was over, the main culprit was probably bad weather. On September 10 a program of four flights was approved for the remainder of the month but was frustrated by heavy cloud cover; the mission on September 17 yielded "no useable photography." But there was concern too at the vulnerability of the U-2s to the SAMs. "In back of our minds," Carter cabled to McCone, "is growing danger to the birds." After a U-2 strayed over Sakhalin on August 30 and a Chinese Nationalist U-2 was lost over the Chinese mainland on September 8 there was also strong pressure to avoid further "incidents." Bundy and Rusk insisted that the U-2s avoid SAM sites in Cuba and take the "shortest possible" routes over the island.[103]

The accumulating evidence of the extent and cost of the defensive missile systems being installed in Cuba increased McCone's suspicions that they were the prelude to something more sinister. Though he decided not to abandon his increasingly disturbed honeymoon, he cabled on September 10:

APPEARS TO ME QUITE POSSIBLE MEASURES NOW BEING TAKEN ARE FOR PURPOSE OF ENSURING SECRECY OF SOME OFFENSIVE CAPABILITY SUCH AS MRBM'S TO BE INSTALLED BY SOVIETS AFTER PRESENT PHASE COMPLETED AND COUNTRY SECURED FROM OVER-FLIGHTS.[104]

But McCone's own analysts and DDI disagreed. Carter cabled to the DCI on September 18 that a new SNIE "discusses in detail possibility of introduction of MRBMs into Cuba, but judges this to be unlikely because of risk of U.S. intervention. . . ."[105] On the same day, however, the CIA circulated to the rest of the intelligence community a report from a Cuban agent that "very secret and important work is in progress, believed to be connected with missiles" in an area "heavily guarded by Soviets." McCone's return to Washington on September 23 coincided with the first positive evidence of MRBMs on Cuba. A CIA report on September 21 described the sighting of a convoy in Havana carrying "long canvas-covered objects" that had the appearance of MRBMs. On September 27 the same convoy was reported to be approaching San Cristobal. By the beginning of October CIA and DIA analysts had pinpointed the San

Cristobal area as "a suspect MRBM site" and requested "photographic confirmation."[106]

It was to be another fortnight, however, before confirmation was obtained by a U-2 mission. McCone complained on October 4 that "decisions to restrict U-2 flights had placed the United States Intelligence Community in a position where it could not report with assurance the development of offensive capabilities in Cuba." Bundy told him he was "satisfied that no offensive capability would be installed in Cuba because of its world-wide effects"; to McCone he "therefore seemed relaxed over the fact that the Intelligence Community cannot produce hard information on this important subject."[107] For the time being it was Bundy's view, rather than McCone's, that prevailed with the president.

During September the CIA lost contact with its most important Soviet agent of the Cold War. On July 20 Kennedy had been warned that Oleg Penkovsky was believed to be "under suspicion" and "possible surveillance" by the KGB. At a diplomatic reception in Moscow on August 27 Penkosky delivered what was to be his last Minox film of classified documents at a brief meeting with a CIA officer in the men's room. With the photographs was a letter saying that he was "in good spirits" but warning that "The 'neighbours' [KGB] continue to study me. For some reason they have latched on to me." Penkovsky turned up again at an American embassy reception on September 5 and at a British film show the next day, but had no new material to hand over. On September 10 his SIS and CIA case officers jointly prepared a letter telling him, "You should only do such photography as you consider safe and possible. . . . All your friends think of you all the time and sympathize with the difficulties you have." Penkovsky was told that Soviet arms deliveries to Cuba were now a major intelligence priority:

> . . . We are very much interested at this time in receiving concrete information as to military measures being undertaken by the USSR to convert Cuba into an offensive military base. In particular we would like to know if Cuba is to be provided with surface to surface missiles.

The letter, however, was never to be delivered. It was expected that Penkovsky would turn up at a diplomatic party on either September 13 or September 15. In fact, he attended neither. His case officers hoped against hope that he was on his annual leave, but they feared the worst.[108]

At the beginning of October the White House was still more preoccupied by the attempt to overthrow Castro than by the prospect of

Soviet MRBMs ninety miles from Florida. On October 4 Robert Kennedy convened a meeting of the Special Group (5412 Augmented) to discuss the progress of Operation Mongoose. He was in an angry mood. The president, he said, was dissatisfied with the fact that "nothing was moving forward," and, in particular, with the "lack of action in the sabotage field." McCone replied that the "lack of forward motion" was "due principally to 'hesitancy' in government circles to engage in any activities which would involve attribution to the United States." According to McCone's official record of the meeting, "A[ttorney] G[eneral] took sharp exception," and "There followed a sharp exchange." In other words, Robert Kennedy lost his temper and there was a blazing row. The meeting, however, ended with agreement on the need for "more dynamic action." It was accepted that the original plan for Mongoose "was now outmoded," that "actions which could be attributed to indigenous Cubans would not be very important or effective," and that the United States must become more directly involved. As a result, "a very considerable amount of attribution and 'noise' must be expected." General Lansdale was instructed to give particular priority to sabotage operations, including "mining harbors."[109] To Bundy the issues were now clear: "that we should either make a judgment that we would have to go in militarily [which seemed to him intolerable] or alternatively we would have to live with Castro and his Cuba and adjust our policies accordingly."[110] The president made it clear that he would not contemplate the second option. He told McCone on October 11, "We'll have to do something drastic about Cuba." Kennedy did not say, and probably did not know, precisely what he had in mind. But he added that he was "looking forward" to an "operational plan" due to be presented to him by the JCS in the following week.[111]

Kennedy's plans "to do something drastic about Cuba" were dramatically interrupted by the missile crisis. On October 14 a U-2 at last succeeded in photographing the suspected MRBM site at San Cristobal. The following afternoon NPIC photographic interpreters discovered the first hard evidence of the presence of MRBMs. For the CIA leadership, the discovery came at a difficult moment. McCone's stepson was fatally injured in a California auto race on October 14, forcing the DCI to leave for the West Coast next day. In his absence Carter and Cline hosted a conference on intelligence methods attended by senior British, Canadian, and Australasian intelligence officers, which opened at Langley on the morning of October 15. When Cline returned to his office at 5:30 P.M., he found a delegation of photographic and military intelligence analysts waiting to see him. "They were all agreed that they had just identified a missile base for missiles of a range upwards of 350 miles," noted

Cline. "I reviewed their evidence and was obliged to concur." At 6:15 P.M. Cline took Carter aside during a conference reception in the Executive Dining Room and told him the news. At 9:30 P.M. NPIC reported to Cline that it had identified "offensive missile systems probably in the 700-mile and possibly in the 1,000 mile range." Cline told them to prepare a written report and "stand by for action early the next morning." Then, at about 10 P.M., he telephoned Mac Bundy.[112] Kennedy had gone to bed early, tired after a strenuous weekend campaigning for the midterm elections and in considerable pain from his back. Bundy did not wake him. He knew that a detailed briefing would not be ready until the following morning and decided to allow the president a good night's sleep to prepare him for the ordeal that awaited him.[113]

At 8:30 A.M. on Tuesday, October 16, Bundy asked Cline to come to his office. Cline brought with him a brief memorandum and a map showing those parts of the United States within range of the MRBMs.[114] Bundy then took the intelligence to the president, who was having breakfast in his dressing gown. Kennedy's first reaction, after being convinced that the evidence of MRBMs was conclusive, was to insist that, one way or another, they would have to be removed.[115] While Bundy was seeing the president, Cline was briefing Robert Kennedy. "His initial comment," noted Cline, "was one four-letter word, off the record."[116] At 11:50 A.M. the president met with his top officials in the cabinet room. As sometimes happened, Caroline Kennedy, then almost five years old, seems to have been hiding beneath the cabinet table. There was a brief, light-hearted conversation between father and daughter that eased the tension at the start of one of the most anxious meetings in White House history. Though there was laughter as Caroline skipped cheerfully out of the room, those present around the table were reminded that the fate of future generations as well as their own might depend on the decisions they made.[117] Over the next few days they must all have pondered in their different ways not merely some of the most dramatic intelligence of the century but the meaning of life itself.

The main briefing in the cabinet room was given by Art Lundahl, who pointed out the MRBM launch site at San Cristobal and two nearby military encampments on briefing boards that he displayed on an easel near the fireplace. Lundahl then placed the boards on the conference table in front of the president and handed him a large magnifying glass so that he could see the missile trailers and erectors. The final briefing was given by Sidney N. Graybeal, a missiles expert from the CIA Office of Scientific Intelligence (OSI). "How long before it can be fired?" asked Kennedy. Graybeal replied that he did not know. He added, in response to a question from McNamara, that the nuclear warheads had yet to be located. McNamara then turned to Lundahl.

> McNamara: [The site] is not defensed, I believe at the moment?
> Lundahl: Not yet, sir.
> McNamara: This is important as it relates to whether these [missiles], today, are ready to fire, Mr. President. It seems almost impossible to me that they would be ready to fire with nuclear warheads on the site without even a fence around it. . . .
> Graybeal: Yes, sir, we do not believe they are ready to fire.

The meeting moved on to consider the options available. At this stage, Kennedy seemed to take it for granted that there would have to be an air strike against the missile sites. The main question in his mind was what further military action would be required and what the risks associated with it were:

> We're certainly going to do number one; we're going to take out these, uh, missiles. Uh, the questions will be whether [we move on to] what I would describe as number two, which would be a general airstrike. That we're not ready to say, but we should be in general preparation for it. The third is the, is the, uh, the general invasion.[118]

The hesitation with which Kennedy pronounced the final option, repeating the definite article three times, perhaps betrayed his inner tension at the possible escalation of the crisis. Those at the meeting, however, remembered him as cool and controlled, though deeply angry at the duplicity of Khrushchev and the Soviet officials who had tried to deceive him. According to Lundahl:

> The president never panicked, never shuddered, his hands never shook. He was crisp and businesslike and speedy in his remarks and he issued them with clarity and dispatch, as though he were dispatching a train or a set of instructions to an office group.[119]

Kennedy's calmness under fire was one of his most remarkable qualities. "That alone—keeping his cool," Rusk believed, "was JFK's greatest contribution in the crisis."[120]

"Intelligence," said the DDP, Richard Helms, later, "bought [Kennedy] the time he needed." The early warning of the installation of Soviet missile sites on Cuba gave the president and his advisers a week in which to consider in secret their response to the most dangerous crisis of the Cold War. The American media will probably ensure that in any future crisis there will be no such prolonged opportunity for calm deliberation. The group assembled in the cabinet room on October 16 remained in session for the next twelve days until the missile crisis was resolved, often without the president and with his brother as its unofficial leader; thereafter it continued to meet almost daily for another six weeks. Originally code-named Elite, it was renamed on October 22 the Executive Committee of the National Security Council (Ex-Comm for short). "It was no reflection on them," wrote Robert Kennedy later, "that none was consistent in his opinion from the very beginning to the very end." During the afternoon and evening of the October 16 the idea of a limited blockade of Cuba as a way of cutting off the flow of Soviet armaments began to be canvassed as an alternative to an air strike to destroy the missile bases. By the following day McNamara had become the blockade's strongest advocate. This limited pressure, he argued, could be increased if it proved ineffective. McNamara was supported by Robert Kennedy, later portrayed by Arthur Schlesinger as "a dove from the start."[121]

Robert Kennedy's account of the crisis, however, conceals the fact that he favored, at first, a two-track policy. Along with the blockade, he wanted an intensification of attempts to destabilize the Cuban regime and overthrow Castro. On the morning of October 16, shortly before Ex-Comm's first meeting, the Special Group (5412 Augmented) had met to consider a new CIA plan presented by General Carter to expand and accelerate sabotage operations. At 2:30 that afternoon Robert Kennedy convened a meeting in his office to berate Lansdale and representatives of the agencies involved in Mongoose (CIA, State, the Joint Chiefs of Staff, and the U.S. Information Agency) for their lack of progress. He was, he said, expressing "the general dissatisfaction of the President." Despite improvements in intelligence collection over the past year, "other actions had failed to influence significantly the course of events in Cuba." Kennedy then declared that, to ensure rapid progress, "he was going to give Operation Mongoose more personal attention." He announced that henceforth he would chair brief meetings every morning at 9:30, beginning the next day, to check on the progress of the operation. Carter's new sabotage plan was, he said, a step in the right direction. Helms, the DDP, said that the CIA would "get on with the new action program and . . . execute it aggressively." He noted that, before closing the meeting, the attorney general "made reference to the change in atmosphere in the United States Government during the last twenty-four hours, and asked some questions about the percentage of Cubans whom we thought would fight for the regime if the country were invaded." Pressure from the White House to intesify sabotage operations in Cuba continued throughout the missile crisis. Mercifully, the operations achieved little. Had they succeeded, they would have made peaceful resolution of the crisis even more difficult.[122]

At 9:30 A.M. on Wednesday, October 17, Robert Kennedy began the new series of Mongoose meetings. At the same moment, McCone, who had returned to Washington the previous evening, arrived at the White House to review with the president and Bundy arrangements for intelligence collection on Cuba. A total of six U-2 missions were to be flown that day, and it was expected that they would find more missile sites. For the remainder of the crisis, Kennedy was briefed at least once a day on the latest aerial photographs.[123] IMINT was supplemented by two other major intelligence sources. The first was a massive SIGINT collection program run by NSA, all details of which still remain classified, ranging from analysis of Cuban diplomatic traffic to ELINT operations against the missile bases by U-2s and U.S. ships off the Cuban coast.[124] On at least one occasion Kennedy personally ordered one of the ELINT ships to go further out to sea for fear that it might be attacked.[125] Though Penkovsky was by now in a Moscow prison being interrogated by the KGB, his intelligence remained of the highest importance. Without the information he had supplied on Soviet missile procedures and site construction, NPIC analysts would have been unable to interpret a significant part of what the photographs revealed. Dino Brugioni of NPIC considered what Penkovsky had provided "one of the most productive intelligence operations in history," which was "of special value" during the missile crisis.[126] The "Evaluations of the Soviet Missile Threat in Cuba" supplied to the president and Ex-Comm during the crisis carried the code name Ironbark, indicating that they depended in part on intelligence supplied by Penkovsky.[127]

Part of Kennedy's ordeal for the remainder of the week was that he had to spend much of his time campaigning for the midterm elections, as well as carrying out routine meetings with foreign visitors and others, in order to keep the secret of the developing crisis until he was ready to reveal it in public. Ex-Comm members also gathered as inconspicuously as possible, usually in a windowless conference room at the State Department, in order not to attract media attention. At 8 P.M. on Thursday, October 18, the intelligence analysts reported that they had located at least sixteen launchpads for MRBMs with a range of just over one thousand nautical miles and eight for IRBMs with a range of twenty-two hundred nautical miles. "The magnitude of the total Soviet missile force being deployed," they concluded, "indicates that the USSR intends to develop Cuba into a prime strategic base, rather than as a strategic show of strength."[128] After lengthy discussions at Ex-Comm that evening, McCone accurately forecast that the probable outcome of their deliberations, despite minority support for military action (mainly from the military), would be "a limited blockade designed to prevent the importation into Cuba of additional arms"; he correctly anticipated also that, following prior notification to (but not consultation with) United States allies, there would be a public announcement of the blockade by the president and the publication of photographic intelligence on the missile bases. McCone noted, "More extreme steps such as limited air strike, comprehensive air strike, or military invasion" had not been ruled out, but for the time being a majority considered them "unwise."[129]

Once the missile sites had been identified, there remained the problem of discovering when they would become operational. An intelligence evaluation completed at 8 P.M. on Friday, October 19, concluded, "The pattern of missile deployment appears calculated to achieve quick operational status and then to complete site construction." Eight of the missile launchers, it said, "must be considered operational now." It also announced the probable identification of a nuclear warhead storage site under construction.[130] The news reached Kennedy while he was campaigning in Chicago. Bundy left a message telling the president that the situation "was so hairy I think he'll want to come home." Kennedy called his wife, Jacqueline, at Glen Ora, and asked her to return to the White House with the children so that they could be together if there was a sudden emergency. "If we were only thinking about ourselves, it would be easy," he told an aide, "but I keep thinking about the children whose lives would be wiped out."[131]

Kennedy returned to Washington the following morning, Saturday, October 20, claiming to be suffering from a cold. At 2:30 P.M. he chaired an expanded meeting of Ex-Comm, held in the Yellow Oval Room rather than the cabinet room to avoid attracting press attention. The Yellow Room had recently been redecorated by Jacqueline Kennedy and was filled with priceless antiques provided by private donors. Lundahl, who arrived to give the intelligence briefings with McCone and Cline, described it as looking like pictures he had seen in *Better Homes and Gardens*. Cline began the meeting in these ornate surroundings with an overview of the current state of the missile sites. "In summary," he concluded, "we believe the evidence indicates the probability that eight MRBM missiles can be fired from Cuba today." Cline was followed by Lundahl, who displayed the latest U-2 photographs on his briefing boards. "During the past week," he announced, "we were able to achieve coverage of over 95 percent of the island and we are convinced that because of the terrain in the remaining 5 percent, no additional threat will be found there." As soon as he had finished, the president crossed the room, told Lundahl, "I want you to extend to your organization my gratitude for a job very well done," and shook his hand.[132]

Despite impassioned opposition from Adlai Stevenson, his ambassador at the UN and the chief opponent of the use of force, Kennedy declared his intention to announce a limited naval blockade of Cuba (or "quarantine," as he preferred to call it) in a televised speech as soon as the leading allies of the United States had been informed. He ordered the news to be delivered personally by senior emissaries to the British prime minister Harold Macmillan, the French president Charles de Gaulle, the West German chancellor Konrad Adenauer, and the Canadian prime minister John Diefenbaker. With the emissaries went senior CIA officials to give intelligence briefings and display some of the aerial photographs. Late on Sunday, October 21, Air Force One, the president's personal plane, landed at Greenham Common, a U.S. Air Force base north of London. Chester L. Cooper of the CIA, who had formerly been stationed in London, stepped off to be welcomed by the American ambassador and OSS veteran David K. E. Bruce. Air Force One then took off for the continent, carrying those who were to brief de Gaulle and Adenauer. Cooper reminded the ambassador that he had been instructed to travel with an armed escort. According to Cooper, "Bruce pulled up his jacket and pointed to the pistol that he was carrying. He was the armed escort." At about noon the next day, Monday, October 22, Bruce and Cooper briefed Macmillan at 10 Downing Street. Because of the Anglo-American intelligence liaison, the prime minister was already informed about the Cuban missile bases, but he had yet to see the photographs. Cooper later recalled, "He looked at them for a while and then said, more to himself than to us, pointing to the missile sites, 'Now the Americans will realize what we here in England have lived through for the past many years.'" Then remembering that his remarks would be reported to the president, Macmillan hurriedly corrected himself. He had not meant to appear unsympathetic and "would, of course, provide the United States with whatever assistance and support that was necessary." Macmillan added a plea that the photographs be made public to avoid charges that they were "a bit of fakery."[133]

De Gaulle was briefed soon afterward at the Elysée by Dean Acheson, the former secretary of state, and Sherman Kent of the CIA. "Are you here to consult with or to inform me?" asked de Gaulle. "I am here to inform you," replied Acheson. Despite the slightly frosty start, Kent felt "delighted at the great interest de Gaulle showed in these photographs" and impressed by his expertise; the French president had no difficulty in identifying the configuration of some MIG-19s and an IL-28 bomber.[134] When told that the photographs had been taken from a height of fourteen miles, de Gaulle exclaimed, *"C'est formidable! C'est formidable!"* He assured Acheson that Kennedy could count on his support. "It's exactly what I would have done," he added.[135] U.S. ambassador Walter C. Dowling and R. Jack Smith of the CIA, who were given the task of briefing Adenauer in Bonn, found him more jovial than de Gaulle and equally supportive. "Are you sure your name is Smith?" inquired the chancellor suspiciously at the beginning of the briefing. He studied the photographs spread out on a large mahogany coffee table and asked a few questions designed to demonstrate his technical knowledge. Were the missiles "cold" or "hot" (cryogenic or noncryogenic)? he inquired. "You may tell your President," he concluded, "that I will support him in meeting this challenge."[136] In Ottawa Prime Minister Diefenbaker told U.S. ambassador Livingston T. Merchant and William A. Tidwell of the CIA that "the evidence was overwhelming." He complimented them on the quality of the intelligence and promised the president his support.[137] Kennedy must have been pleased with the outcome of the four top-secret missions to foreign capitals. No previous president had made such dramatic use of peacetime intelligence for the purposes of Allied diplomacy.

Soon after noon on Monday, October 22, White House press secretary Pierre Salinger, requested thirty minutes of network time that evening for a broadcast by the president on a "matter of highest national urgency." At 3 P.M., after a swim and lunch with his family, Kennedy chaired a meeting of the NSC in the cabinet room.[138] Partly for the benefit of those who were not members of Ex-Comm, McCone began by reviewing the findings of the seventeen U-2 missions flown since October 14. The final tally was six MRBM bases with a total of twenty-four launcher positions and three IRBM bases with twelve launchpads. Sixteen of the MRBM launchers were believed to be "in full operational readiness"; the remainder were expected to be so within a week. The IRBM sites seemed likely to be fully operational before the end of the year.[139] The Joint Chiefs of Staff were given the chance to explain their opposition to naval "quarantine" and to put the case for an air strike, but, said General Taylor later, "the JCS tigers turned out to be pussycats." Soon after 4 P.M. Kennedy met his cabinet, who, as a group, took little part in the major decisions of his administration. He told McCone and Lundahl they need not attend. Instead, the president briefed the cabinet himself; he said later that its members seemed dumbfounded by

the news of the missile bases and asked few questions. At 5 P.M., flanked
by McNamara and Rusk, he met the congressional leadership in the cabinet room. At his request, McCone, Cline, and Lundahl attended to provide intelligence briefings.[140] Kennedy then announced his decision to
order a blockade. Senator Richard B. Russell demanded military action
instead. According to McCone, "He did not specifically say by surprise
attack; however he did not advocate warning." Senator William J. Fulbright, usually a dove rather than a hawk, supported Russell: ". . . It
would be far better to launch an attack and take out the bases from
Cuba."[141] "The trouble is," said Kennedy later, "that when you get a
group of senators together, they are always dominated by the man who
takes the boldest and strongest line. . . . After Russell spoke, no one
wanted to take issue with him."[142]

At 7 P.M. the president broadcast to the American people from the
Oval Office:

> Good evening, my fellow citizens: This Government, as promised,
> has maintained the closest surveillance of the Soviet military build-
> up on the island of Cuba. Within the past week, unmistakable evi-
> dence has established the fact that a series of offensive missile sites
> is now in preparation on that imprisoned island. The purpose of
> these bases can be none other than to provide a nuclear strike
> capacity against the Western Hemisphere.

For the millions who watched and heard the president, it was the most
shocking speech of the Cold War. In only twenty seconds Kennedy had
raised the specter of thermonuclear war on American soil. His repeated
charges of "deliberate deception" against the Soviet government underlined the gravity of the crisis. Kennedy made no specific reference to the
U-2 missions or to any other form of intelligence gathering, but promised
"continued and increased close surveillance." After announcing "a strict
quarantine on all offensive military equipment under shipment to Cuba"
and other defensive measures, Kennedy issued a thinly veiled call to the
Cuban people to rise in rebellion against leaders who were "puppets and
agents of an international conspiracy":

> Many times in the past, the Cuban people have risen to throw out
> tyrants who destroyed their liberty. And I have no doubt that most
> Cubans today look forward to the time when they will be truly free. . . .

Kennedy expected a long, drawn-out crisis. He warned the American
people, "Many months of sacrifice and self-discipline lie ahead." At the

end of those months, he hoped not merely for the removal of the missiles but also for the overthrow of Castro.[143] Listening to his brother's broadcast reminded Robert Kennedy how badly both of them had been personally deceived by Soviet spokesmen and by the KGB officer Georgi Bolshakov in particular. He refused to see Bolshakov again. But after the broadcast he telephoned his friend Charles Bartlett and told him, "Get ahold of Georgi and tell him how he betrayed us and how we're very disappointed."[144]

Instead of the months of international tension and nuclear danger expected by Kennedy and his advisers, the acute stage of the crisis was resolved within a week. But the next five days were to be the most dangerous of the Cold War. Rusk woke up soon after 6 A.M. on the morning of Tuesday, October 23, with the sun streaming through his bedroom window, mildly surprised to find himself still there and happy to conclude that Khrushchev had not responded to the president's speech with a nuclear first strike. "This was serious business," he thought, "but perhaps it wouldn't be fatal."[145] At a 10 A.M. meeting of Ex-Comm, McCone reported that construction work was carrying on at the Cuban missile sites. It was to continue for the remainder of the week.[146] In the course of the day, at Kennedy's request, McCone saw Senator Russell and other leading congressional critics who had attended the meeting on October 22, and used intelligence briefings to try to win them over. He reported significant success. Russell, he told the president, had moved from opposition to "reserved approval." McCone emphasized to the senator that, if the Soviet Union failed to heed Kennedy's warning, military action would follow in Cuba "at a time of our own choosing and by means of our own determination."[147]

At the 6 P.M. meeting of Ex-Comm McCone reported on NSA monitoring during the day of Warsaw Pact military traffic. This, he announced ominously, showed "an increased level of Soviet military communications."[148] Ex-Comm also considered and approved the draft "quarantine" order, "Interdiction of the Delivery of Offensive Missiles to Cuba," due to come into force at dawn the next day.[149] The president signed it after the meeting in front of photographers in the Oval Office. With a keen sense of the importance of the occasion, he wrote—most unusually—his full name, John Fitzgerald Kennedy, added the exact time, 7:06 P.M., as well as the date, and kept the pen his secretary had provided. At a 7:30 P.M. press conference, McNamara was stunned to discover from reporters that some of the aerial photographs of the missile sites had been shown on British television by the BBC. The advice of the IMINT specialists had been that the photographs should not be released in order to conceal from the Russians the technical advances in overhead reconnaissance. McNamara was unaware that Kennedy had given way to pressure from Macmillan to release the photographs to overcome public skepticism in Britain about the reality of the bases.[150] Chester Cooper of the CIA, still in London after briefing Macmillan on the previous day, had been given permission by the White House staff to give the photographs to the BBC.[151] Thus it was that the most highly classified U.S. imagery intelligence ever to be released was seen first by British rather than American viewers. Kennedy seems to have assumed that the photographs would be released simultaneously on both sides of the Atlantic, and was taken by surprise when they were published first in London.[152]

Just before the Ex-Comm meeting at 10 A.M. on Wednesday, October 24, the president told his brother, "It looks really mean, doesn't it? But then, really there was no other choice." The meeting that followed was to be one of the two tensest moments in the missile crisis. McNamara reported that two Soviet ships, the *Gagarin* and the *Komiles*, were within a few miles of the five-hundred-mile quarantine line around Cuba. It was expected that at least one of them would be stopped and boarded by 11 o'clock. Then came news that a Russian submarine had moved between the two ships.[153] Robert Kennedy looked at his brother across the table:

> His eyes were tense, almost grey. . . . Was the world on the brink of a holocaust and had we done something wrong? Isn't there some way we can avoid having our first exchange be with a Russian submarine—almost anything but that, he said. . . . [154]

Then at 10:25 A.M. McCone read a message from the NSA Navy Field Operational Intelligence Section: "Mr. President, we have a preliminary report which seems to indicate that some of the Russian ships have stopped dead in the water." At 10:32 A.M. the DCI was handed another note. "The report is accurate, Mr. President," he announced. "Six ships previously on their way to Cuba at the edge of the quarantine line have stopped or have turned back toward the Soviet Union." Kennedy instructed that no Soviet vessel was to be intercepted for at least an hour "while clarifying information was sought." During that time reports from navy reconnaissance and surface units began to confirm the results of NSA direction finding.[155] "We're eyeball to eyeball," said Rusk, "and I think the other fellow just blinked." He was outraged when his remark was leaked to the press. It was, he said later, "the only leak in my eight years as secretary that could have been calamitous."[156]

Immediately after the morning Ex-Comm meeting, there was a settling of accounts with Bolshakov. Sorensen said later, "President Kennedy had come to rely on the Bolshakov channel for direct private information from Khrushchev, and he felt personally deceived. He *was* personally deceived." At Robert Kennedy's request, Charles Bartlett took Bolshakov to lunch at the Washington National Press Club and confronted him with twenty U-2 photographs of the missile bases still marked "For the President's Eyes Only" in the top right-hand corner. "What would you say to that, Georgi?" asked Bartlett. "I bet you know for certain that you have your missiles in Cuba." Bolshakov, by his own account, replied: "I have never seen such photographs and have no idea of what they show. Baseball fields perhaps?" He then pulled a notebook from his pocket and read out notes of his meeting with Khrushchev in September, containing assurances that no offensive missiles would be stationed in Cuba. More menacingly, he warned that Soviet ships would be "coming through the blockade." That evening Bartlett dined at the White House with the president, the First Lady, Robert and Ethel Kennedy, and a small group of other guests. Coming and going during the dinner, Bundy reported that Soviet ships were still staying away from the quarantine line. Kennedy warned against premature celebration: ". . . We still have twenty chances out of a hundred to be at war with Russia." At 10:50 P.M., after the dinner party was over, Kennedy had a cabled letter from Khrushchev read to him over the phone. "We shall not be simply observers of the pirate-like actions of American ships on the high seas," Khrushchev declared. "We will be forced to take measures that we deem necessary and adequate to protect our rights." The president telephoned Bartlett: "You'll be interested to know I got a cable from our friend, and he said those ships are coming through. They are coming through tomorrow."[157]

The intelligence that came in during the night, most of it SIGINT, was more reassuring. McCone reported to Ex-Comm at 10 A.M. on Thursday, October 25:

> As of 0600 EDT at least 14 of the 22 Soviet ships which were known to be en route to Cuba had turned back. Five of the remaining eight are tankers. Two of the dry cargo ships not known to have reversed course may be carrying non-military cargo. . . . Changes in course appear to have been executed [at] midday on 23 October, before the president signed the procedure establishing the quarantine. We still see no signs of any crash procedure in measures to increase the readiness of Soviet armed forces.

In the course of the meeting, it became clear from further intelligence reports that the only Soviet ship likely to pass through the quarantine line in the course of the day was the tanker *Bucharest*. Kennedy instructed that no attempt be made to intercept it.[158]

That afternoon, on the president's instructions, imagery intelligence was used to win a major propaganda victory at the United Nations. During a debate in the Security Council, the Soviet representative, Valerian Zorin, poured scorn on "the falsified evidence of the United States Intelligence Agency." Kennedy, who was watching the debate on television, sent word to Adlai Stevenson to "stick him"—to produce the photographic evidence. Stevenson did so, with great panache. He began by asking:

> Do you, Ambassador Zorin, deny that the USSR has placed and is placing medium and intermediate-range missiles and sites in Cuba? Yes or no? Don't wait for the translation. Yes or no?

When Zorin prevaricated, Stevenson ordered some of the photographs taken by the U-2s over Cuba to be displayed on easels in the council chamber. He showed the transformation of San Cristobal from "peaceful countryside" to an MRBM launch site, then documented the construction of an IRBM site at Guanajay. Zorin responded lamely, ". . . Mr. Stevenson, we shall not look at your photographs." His reply merely served to confirm American charges of Soviet deception. "I never knew Adlai had it in him!" said Kennedy as he watched his triumph on television. Not since the Zimmermann telegram had secret intelligence been publicly used in the United States with such dramatic effect.[159]

Though the fear that the naval blockade might unleash nuclear warfare between the superpowers had receded, the fundamental problem of the missile bases remained. IMINT showed no let-up in construction work. At Ex-Comm's 10 A.M. meeting on Friday, October 26:

> The President directed that we dramatize the fact that the missile buildup in Cuba is continuing. He authorized daylight reconnaissance measures but decided to delay night flights. . . . The President said work on the missile sites has to cease. . . . [160]

Contingency planning thus continued for both an air attack on the missile bases and a full-scale invasion of Cuba. McCone informed Ex-Comm of a CIA plan to infiltrate ten teams of agents into Cuba by submarine to gather intelligence on the bases and "other points of interest" to the invasion planners. He reported that this had led to friction with Lansdale, who was reluctant to divert covert action on Cuba from the primary aim of Operation Mongoose "to take Cuba from Castro and turn it over to the Cuban people." Kennedy declared his continuing support for Mongoose, even suggesting that "the Lansdale organization . . . might serve as a Subcommittee" of Ex-Comm. A "Mongoose meeting" that afternoon produced further friction between McCone and Lansdale, who complained that he was not being kept informed of invasion planning. It was agreed that "The infiltration of agents is to be held up, pending a determination by the Department of Defense . . . as to just what military information is desired and determination by State . . . as to just what political information is desired."[161]

While interdepartmental wrangling continued over covert action inside Cuba, the first signs appeared of a possible solution to the crisis. With Bolshakov now discredited as a secret back channel to the White House, Khrushchev decided to use instead the KGB resident (station chief) in Washington, Aleksandr Semyonovich Feklisov, who used the alias Fomin. At 1:30 P.M. on October 26, Feklisov called the ABC television diplomatic correspondent, John Scali, whom he knew had good access to the White House. Feklisov sounded agitated. He asked Scali to meet him in ten minutes at the Occidental Restaurant on Pennsylvania Avenue. At the Occidental, Feklisov said he had an important message to pass on. In return for the removal of the Soviet missiles, would the United States be willing to issue a public pledge not to invade Cuba? "Would you," he asked Scali, "check with your high State Department sources?" Scali contacted Rusk, who took him to the Oval Office. Kennedy asked him to see Feklisov again, "but don't use my name. . . . Tell him you've gotten a favorable response from the highest authority in the government." At 7:35 P.M. Scali met Feklisov in the coffee shop of the Statler Hilton and told him that he had it on the highest authority that the United States saw "real possibilities" in his proposal but that time was "very urgent."[162]

By that time, however, Kennedy had heard directly from Khrushchev himself. At 6 P.M. a long and rambling message from Moscow began to rattle off the teletype. Khrushchev implied, but did not quite state, that he would accept the bargain proposed by the KGB resident in Washington:

> I propose: we, for our part, will declare that our ships bound for Cuba are not carrying any armaments. You will declare that the United States will not invade Cuba with its troops and will not support any other forces which might intend to invade Cuba. Then the necessity for the presence of our military specialists in Cuba will be obviated.

The president and his advisers all believed that the message bore Khrushchev's personal stamp. Though its contents were on balance reassuring, recalled Rusk later, "its distraught and emotional tone bothered us, because it seemed the old fellow might be losing his cool in the Kremlin."[163]

Robert Kennedy arrived for the 10 A.M. meeting of Ex-Comm on Saturday, October 27, "with some sense of foreboding." He had just received a report from J. Edgar Hoover that Soviet diplomats and intelligence personnel in New York were apparently destroying all˙sensitive documents in order to prepare for war.[164] The meeting began with a discussion of plans to stop a Soviet tanker at the quarantine line and details of the day's aerial reconnaissance missions over Cuba. Then Kennedy interrupted the discussion to read a news story coming over the wire: "Premier Khrushchev told President Kennedy yesterday he would withdraw offensive missiles from Cuba if the United States withdrew its rockets from Turkey." Initially, Kennedy was unclear whether this was a garbled version of the private communication of the previous day or a new public message that changed the terms of the offer. As the wire story continued, he realized that it was a new proposal. No intelligence was available to explain why the new message had been sent. While the president was out of the room, however, Ex-Comm reached what Bundy told him was "an informal consensus" that "last night's message was Khrushchev and this one is his own hard-nosed people overruling him. . . . They didn't like what he said to you last night." After animated debate over how to respond to the latest message, it was agreed that the president should ignore it and reply instead to Khrushchev's offer of the previous day—or rather to the version of it put by Feklisov to Scali. Robert Kennedy later claimed the credit for devising this bargaining ploy. In fact, the Ex-Comm transcript shows that it was first proposed by Bundy.[165]

While the reply was being drafted, Scali was called to the State Department and asked to contact the KGB resident Feklisov again. Acting on instructions, he met him that afternoon and accused him of engaging in a "stinking double-cross," merely playing for time while the Cuban missile sites became operational. When Feklisov raised the Turkish-Cuban exchange proposed in Khrushchev's latest message, Scali angrily denounced it and said that it would soon be too late. American troops were already making preparations for the invasion of Cuba. Feklisov seemed genuinely shaken and insisted that his proposal of the previous day had been sincere; he promised to contact Moscow.[166] For the first time the initiative in the back channel had passed from East to West. At a critical moment the White House was able to use it to put pressure on the Kremlin. As Scali warned Feklisov, preparations for a major offensive against Cuba were under way. At the afternoon meeting of Ex-Comm General Taylor passed on the recommendation of the Joint Chiefs that it begin "no later than Monday morning the 29th unless there is irrefutable evidence in the meantime that offensive weapons are being dismantled and rendered inoperable."[167]

Before Kennedy's official reply to Khrushchev had been dispatched, there was a dangerous escalation in the crisis. During the afternoon session of Ex-Comm, news came in that a U-2 had disappeared over Cuba. SIGINT showed that it had been shot down by a SAM missile.[168] When the possibility of a shoot-down had been discussed four days earlier, Ex-Comm had agreed that "the recommendation will be for immediate retaliation upon the most likely surface-to-air site involved in this action."[169] Kennedy's immediate response to the news of the shoot-down was to suggest even tougher action. "How can we put a U-2 fellow over there tomorrow unless we take out all the sites?" he asked. "I don't think we can," replied McNamara. Faced with the dangers of escalation, however, the president changed his mind. After sending his reply to Khrushchev, he concluded, "I think we ought to wait till tomorrow afternoon, to see whether we get any answer."[170]

Kennedy's reply accepted the proposal put by Feklisov and, less directly, by Khrushchev on the previous day:

1. You would agree to remove these weapons systems from Cuba under appropriate United Nations observation and supervision. . . .
2. We, on our part, would agree . . . (a) to remove promptly the quarantine measures now in effect, and (b) to give assurances against an invasion of Cuba.

Robert Kennedy asked the Soviet ambassador, Dobrynin, to come to his office, and handed him the message at 7:45 P.M. According to a memo he dictated after the meeting, he told Dobrynin that "we had to have a commitment by at least tomorrow that those bases would be removed. This was not an ultimatum, I said, but just a statement of fact." He added that the president was also willing to remove American missiles from Turkey—"But it cannot be made part of a package and published. . . .'" According to the Soviet version of the meeting, Robert Kennedy said that "the Pentagon was exerting strong pressure on his brother" to take military action without further delay. That evening, though the president continued to pin his hopes on a favorable response from Khrushchev, he was "not optimistic." He ordered to active duty the twenty-four troop-carrier squadrons of the Air Force Reserve that would be needed for an invasion of Cuba. "The expectation," according to his brother, "was a military confrontation by Tuesday and possibly tomorrow. . . ."[171]

The morning of Sunday, October 28, in Washington dawned bright and clear. At about 9 A.M., during breakfast in the White House mess, Bundy began receiving the text of Khrushchev's reply to the previous evening's message as it was broadcast over Moscow Radio. It was clear by the end of the fifth sentence that the crisis was over:

> . . . The Soviet government, in addition to earlier instructions on the cessation of further work at building sites for the weapons, has issued a new order on the dismantling of the weapons which you describe as "offensive," and their crating and return to the Soviet Union.

"It was my happy task," wrote Bundy later, "to give this news to the president over the telephone. He was pleased."[172] That Sunday morning, however, Ex-Comm was in no mood for understatement. McCone heard the news as he left Mass. "I could," he said, "hardly believe my ears." As the members of Ex-Comm gathered in the cabinet room shortly before 11 A.M., they asked themselves before the president arrived what would have happened if Kennedy had opted for an air strike rather than a blockade, or if they had been denied what Sorensen called "the combined genius and courage that produced the U-2 photographs and their interpretation," or—finally—if John F. Kennedy had not been president of the United States. As the president entered the room, his advisers rose to their feet.[173]

Since the United Nations failed to gain Castro's consent for on-site inspection of the removal of the Soviet missiles, Kennedy continued aerial reconnaissance, and told Khrushchev he was doing so. Ex-Comm continued to meet at least daily, though no longer in a crisis atmosphere, to monitor the return of the missiles to the USSR. On October 30 the NSC called a halt to Operation Mongoose. Special Group (5412 Augmented) was abolished. Soon afterward Lansdale went to Miami to close down the CIA station.[174] "After the tumult of the Cuban missile crisis," wrote the deputy DDI, R. Jack Smith, "we went back to the standard flow of international events, an Iraqi coup here, a Soviet provocation there, a governmental collapse there."[175]

Covert action in Cuba, however, did not end. McCone was determined that "the removal of the missiles should not end by giving Castro a sanctuary and thus sustain his subversive threat to other Latin American nations."[176] The president agreed. During November he called for a long-term plan to "keep pressure on Castro and to bolster other regimes in the Caribbean." His aim now was not a CIA-supported invasion to bring Castro down but a program of covert harassment to prevent him from subverting the rest of the hemisphere. He was anxious, nonetheless, not to give a formal guarantee never to support invasion. In his message to Khrushchev on October 27 he had made American "assurances against an invasion" conditional on removal of the Soviet missiles "under appropriate United Nations observation and supervision." Castro's rejection of on-site inspection enabled Kennedy to avoid fulfilling his side of the bargain. At a press conference on November 20 he toughened the conditions for a guarantee against invasion to make them even more unacceptable to Castro, who, he now demanded, must agree to no "export of revolution" from Cuba.[177] Shortly after Christmas the president and First Lady were driven in an open white car to the Orange Bowl in Miami to welcome the survivors of the Cuban brigade captured after the Bay of Pigs, who had just been ransomed from Cuban jails. Bundy and Rusk had tried to persuade Kennedy not to go. His special assistant, Ken O'Donnell, warned him, "It will look as though you're planning to back them in another invasion of Cuba." In the Orange Bowl the brigade commander presented Kennedy with the banner they had carried ashore at the Bay of Pigs. Kennedy told him and his men, "I can assure you that this flag will be returned to this brigade in a free Havana!" The exiles chanted *"Guerra! Guerra! Guerra!"*[178]

At the end of 1962 Ex-Comm was renamed the Standing Group and reduced in size to five members: McNamara, McCone, Bundy, Sorensen, and Robert Kennedy. Bundy was prepared to contemplate an accommodation with Castro. Robert Kennedy was not. He wrote a memo to the president after an NSC meeting in March 1963:

> John McCone spoke at the meeting today about revolt amongst the [Cuban] military. He described the possibilities in rather optimistic terms. What is the basis for that appraisal? What can and should we do to increase the likelihood of this kind of action? . . . I would not like it said a year from now that we could have had this internal breakup in Cuba but we just did not set the stage for it.

The president showed no immediate interest. His brother complained a week later that he had not replied to his memo.[179] Kennedy's attention seems to have focused anew on Cuba as a result of Castro's departure in April for a triumphal five-week tour of the Soviet Union. Dressed, when it was warm enough, in olive-green battle fatigues, Castro addressed huge, enthusiastic crowds from Leningrad to Siberia, inspected a rocket base and the Northern Fleet, reviewed the May Day parade in Moscow's

Red Square, was made a hero of the Soviet Union, and received the Order of Lenin and a Gold Star. A CIA estimate predicted a Soviet campaign of subversion in Latin America: "There is a good chance that Castro's position in Cuba a year from now will be stronger than it presently is, and that in Latin America the Communists will have recovered some of the ground lost in the Missile Crisis." Bundy put the estimate at the top of the president's weekend reading in Hyannisport and warned him that it made "somber reading." Cuba, he added, "continues to be the first item of business for the Standing Group." Kennedy was probably also told that the former KGB resident in Havana, Aleksandr Shitov (alias Alekseev), appointed Soviet ambassador in the previous year, had become one of Castro's trusted advisers. Castro treated the Soviet embassy as a second home; he and Shitov would sometimes cook meals together in the embassy kitchen.[180]

Late in May, at the end of the Cuban leader's Soviet tour, McCone urged a program of sabotage to "create a situation in Cuba in which it would be possible to subvert military leaders to the point of their acting to overthrow Castro." Robert Kennedy argued that the United States "must do something against Castro, even though we do not believe our actions would bring him down." On June 19 the president approved a new sabotage program "to nourish a spirit of resistance and disaffection which could lead to significant defections and other byproducts of unrest."[181] Robert Kennedy later recalled, "There were ten or twenty tons of sugar cane that was being burned every week through internal uprisings."[182] The attorney general's belief in the potential of "internal uprisings" reflected the illusions that continued to inform covert action in Cuba and the unwillingness to recognize the strength of Castro's domestic support. Much of the sabotage was the work of individual agents using such simple and brutal methods as tying burning rags to the tails of terrified cats who were then let loose in sugarcane plantations to set them ablaze.[183] The president was regularly briefed on the progress of the sabotage operations. Bundy forwarded one "after-action report" with the note, "A quick first glance suggests that it is a businesslike report of adventure which you would find interesting."[184]

According to James Reston, Robert Kennedy still "monkeyed around with amateur plots to assassinate Castro."[185] Probably the most serious of the plots involved a disaffected, heavy-drinking, and possibly unbalanced former comrade-in-arms of Castro, Rolando Cubela Secades (code-named Am/Lash by the CIA), who had assassinated Batista's military intelligence chief in 1956 and seized the presidential palace before Castro's triumphant entry into Havana in 1959. Early in September 1962 Cubela told a CIA man in São Paulo that he was willing to make an "inside" attempt on Castro's life. He asked for murder weapons and a personal meeting with Robert Kennedy. On September 7, the day that the report of the meeting with Cubela reached Langley, Castro warned an Associated Press correspondent during a reception at the Brazilian embassy, "United States leaders should think that if they assist in terrorist plans to eliminate Cuban leaders, they themselves will not be safe." The coincidence in timing between Cubela's offer and Castro's warning, as well as the Brazilian connection common to both, caused some anxiety that Am/Lash might be an agent provocateur, but it was decided to maintain contact with him. On October 29 Cubela met the head of the CIA Cuban task force, Desmond Fitzgerald, who claimed to be Robert Kennedy's "personal representative," and asked to be provided with the means of killing Castro.[186]

"Kennedy," wrote Sorensen, "never took his eye off Cuba."[187] He demanded hard evidence of Castro's attempts to export revolution to Latin America. On November 19 Helms and a CIA Latin American expert named Hershel Peake told Robert Kennedy that the agency had discovered a three-ton Cuban arms cache hidden on a Venezuelan beach. The attorney general sent them to see the president. They took a rifle from the arms cache with them to the Oval Office, where Helms showed Kennedy traces of the Cuban coat of arms that had been removed from it. The president congratulated his visitors and reminded them that he was about to leave on an electioneering trip to Texas. "Be sure to have complete information for me when I get back from my trip," he told Helms. "I think maybe we've got him now."[188]

Kennedy did not return to examine the "complete information" he had asked for. He had mentioned several times, almost in passing, to Sorensen and others that complete protection of a president was impossible, particularly from a sniper on a rooftop or in a tall building. That was the Secret Service's problem, not his, he used to say. "Jim Rowley [the head of the Secret Service] is most efficient," he joked. "He has never lost a President." On November 21 he left by helicopter from the South Lawn of the White House to begin his Texas tour.[189]

The next day, November 22, Desmond Fitzgerald of the CIA met Rolando Cubela Secades secretly in Paris and gave him a ballpoint pen containing a poisoned hypodermic needle with which to assassinate Castro. Cubela asked for "something more sophisticated than that." Fitzgerald promised him "everything he needed (telescopic sight, silencer, all the money he wanted)."[190] Over four thousand miles away, Kennedy was being driven through Dallas in an open Lincoln limousine, acknowledging the cheers of the crowd. It was a beautiful day and, on the president's orders, the protective "bubble top" had been removed. Just before

12:30 P.M., as the car passed the Texas School Book Depository, he was shot by an assassin using probably much the same kind of rifle, fitted with a telescopic sight, as that with which Cubela planned to kill Castro. The motorcade sped past the waiting crowds to Parkland Hospital, where, half an hour later, the president was pronounced dead. At 2:15 P.M. Jacqueline Kennedy, her pink suit, white gloves, and stockings streaked with her husband's blood, accompanied the coffin containing his body aboard Air Force One for the return flight to Washington.

CHAPTER 8

Lyndon B. Johnson
(1963-1969)

Lyndon Johnson's presidency began with a major security and intelligence alert. In the Dallas motorcade on November 22, 1963, the vice-president's Lincoln convertible was the second car behind the presidential limousine. Just before 12:30 P.M. Johnson was startled by what sounded like an explosion. Secret Service agent Rufus Youngblood, who was traveling in the front, shouted "Get down!", vaulted into the back-seat, and pushed Johnson onto the floor. With Youngblood sitting on the vice-president's right shoulder, the car sped at over seventy miles an hour to the Parkland Hospital. "When we get to the hospital," Young-blood ordered, "you and Mrs. Johnson follow me and the other agents." At about 1:20 P.M., sitting, in a state of shock, in a small hospital room with the shades pulled down, Johnson learned that Kennedy was dead and that he was now president of the United States. Youngblood's first priority was to move him to a place of safety. He asked the Johnsons to leave for Washington immediately. "We're going to move out fast," he told them. "Please stick close to us." Three unmarked police cars were waiting at the hospital entrance. Surrounded by Secret Service agents, Johnson got into the rear seat of the lead car, kept his head down below window level, and was driven at high speed through red lights by the Dallas police chief to Love Field Airport. At 2:40 P.M., flanked by Lady Bird Johnson and a bloodstained Jacqueline Kennedy in the crowded stateroom of Air Force One, he took the oath of office. Five minutes later, he was airborne.[1]

Behind him, in Dallas, President Johnson left near chaos. The sus-pected assassin, Lee Harvey Oswald, had been arrested less than twenty minutes after Johnson reached Love Field. For the rest of the day he was interrogated with barely believable ineptitude; questions were fired at him almost simultaneously by the Dallas homicide squad, county sheriffs, Texas Rangers, FBI agents, and the Secret Service. There was no recording and no shorthand transcript of the interrogation. The televised shooting of Oswald two days later by the Dallas strip-club owner Jack Ruby, as he was being moved between jails, was an almost appropriate finale to the tragicomic incompetence with which Oswald had been handled since his arrest.[2] Both at the time and since, the combined confusion and horror of the events in Dallas have encouraged the belief that a vast conspiracy had been at work. Even before Johnson took off from Love Field in Air Force One, he had begun to fear that Kennedy's assassination "might be part of a worldwide plot."[3] There was the same fear at Langley. McCone called into session the Watch Committee, whose task in time of crisis was to search out information from every source. CIA stations around the world were asked to report urgently any signs of a conspiracy. According to Helms, "We all went to battle stations over the possibility that this might be a plot. . . ." The main immediate worry was that the agency could not discover the whereabouts of Khrushchev. It was briefly feared that the Soviet leader might be at battle stations in a secret command bunker.[4]

The Pentagon had additional cause for concern. On becoming vice-president in 1961, Johnson had inexplicably—and irresponsibly—refused to be briefed on the secrets of the "football" containing the coded instructions necessary to order nuclear attack, carried by a "bag-man" who accompanied the president wherever he went. With American forces on worldwide alert after the assassination, the United States thus had for a brief period a commander in chief who could not have responded in time to a Soviet missile attack. On the flight from Dallas, Kennedy's former military aide, General Chester V. Clifton, began to explain the contents of the "football" that for the next five years would be constantly at Johnson's side.[5]

The State Department was worried too. Rusk was on his way to Japan when he heard the news of the assassination, stopped in Hawaii, and, at Johnson's request, returned to Washington. Throughout the long flight home, he wondered whether the Russians or the Cubans were behind Kennedy's killing.[6] In Washington, Undersecretary George Ball asked himself the same question. When news came in during the afternoon that Oswald had been arrested, Ball ordered Oswald's name to be checked in State Department files. It was quickly discovered that in 1959 Oswald had gone to live in the Soviet Union, returning in June 1962 with a Russian wife. Ball called in the veteran diplomats Llewellyn Thompson and Averell Harriman, both of whom had served in Moscow.

"Could this be a Soviet move to be followed by a missile attack?" he asked them. Both dismissed the idea. Though the KGB was quite capable of murdering defectors who had fled abroad, they believed that Soviet leaders were unwilling to authorize the killing of Western statesmen for fear of becoming targets themselves.[7]

On Johnson's first morning as president, Saturday, November 23, the president's intelligence checklist was headed "In Honor of President Kennedy, for whom the President's Intelligence Checklist was first written on 17 June 1961," and consisted simply of a tribute to Kennedy:

> For this day, the Checklist staff can find no words more fitting than a verse quoted by the President to a group of newspapermen the day he learned of the presence of Soviet missiles in Cuba.

> *Bullfight critics ranked in rows*
> *Crowd the enormous plaza full;*
> *But only one is there who knows*
> *And he's the man who fights the bull.*[8]

At 9:15 A.M. McCone and R. Jack Smith, head of CIA current intelligence, called at the White House to give Johnson his first intelligence briefing as president. After the alarms of the previous day Johnson was relieved to be told that the international situation seemed relatively calm with "nothing that required an immediate decision."[9] During McCone's survey of global problems, however, the president's attention began to wander. According to Smith:

> Beside the compact, trim McCone, [Johnson] looked massive, rumpled and worried. He had no interest whatever in being briefed, and after some inconsequential chatting, he turned into Bundy's office. We had no way of knowing it, but we just witnessed a preview of McCone's future relationship with Lyndon Johnson.[10]

McCone continued calling at the White House for about ten days. Then the briefings stopped.[11] Johnson's increasingly obvious lack of personal rapport with McCone was compounded by his conspiracy theories about the CIA. He believed, absurdly, that the agency had conspired against him at the 1960 Democratic convention to ensure that Kennedy won the presidential nomination.[12]

Even more remarkable than Johnson's disdain for McCone was his admiration for J. Edgar Hoover. A week after Kennedy's assassination Hoover recorded in his personal file after a visit to the White House:

> The President . . . stated I was more than head of the FBI—I was
> his brother and personal friend; that he knew I did not want any-
> thing to happen to his family; that he has more confidence in me
> than anyone in town. . . .[13]

On May 8, 1964, standing next to a beaming sixty-nine-year-old Hoover
in the White House Rose Garden, Johnson announced that he was
exempting him from compulsory retirement at seventy "for an indefinite
period of time." "The nation cannot afford to lose you," the president
told the FBI director. ". . . No other American, now or in our past, has
served the cause of justice so faithfully and so well."[14] Four and a half
years later, Johnson told his successor, Richard Nixon:

> If it hadn't been for Edgar Hoover, I couldn't have carried out my
> responsibilities as Commander in Chief. Period. Dick, you will come
> to rely on Edgar. He is a pillar of strength in a city of weak men. You
> will rely on him time and again to maintain security. He's the only
> one you can put your complete trust in.[15]

According to Johnson's press secretary, Bill Moyers, Hoover was one
of the very few men whom the president "personally feared." Johnson's
past electoral shenanigans in Texas and his dealings with wealthy supporters may well have left compromising information in the director's
personal file.[16] By continuing Hoover's appointment for an "indefinite
period of time" rather than for a fixed term, however, Johnson acquired
a hold over the FBI director; henceforth his continuance in office was at
the pleasure of the president.

George Ball found Johnson's relations with Hoover "odd and sinister": "Suspicious, and sometimes vindictive, Johnson was fascinated at
the thought of having at his command a man and an institution that
knew so much about so many and he relished Hoover's assiduous tale
bearing."[17] Many of the tales concerned members of the Kennedy clan,
from whom Johnson had suffered a series of real or imagined slights.
Robert Kennedy later claimed to have evidence that Johnson was given
dossiers by Hoover on "everyone that President Kennedy had appointed,
in the White House particularly." Some of the dossiers concerned the
attorney general himself, and probably included reports on his sexual
liaisons. Robert Kennedy later complained, ". . . McNamara used to tell
me that Hoover used to send over all this material on me and that Lyndon Johnson would read it to him."[18] According to Moyers, "gossip about
other men's weaknesses" provided one of Johnson's favorite relax-
ations.[19] Some of the gossip concerned the sex life of the black civil

rights leader Reverend Martin Luther King Jr. Obsessed with the belief that King was "a 'tom cat' with obsessive degenerate sexual urges" as well as dangerously subject to Communist influences, Hoover bugged a series of his hotel bedrooms.[20] Johnson appears to have found recordings of King engaging in adulterous sexual intercourse so entertaining that he played them to some of his confidants.[21] Hoover also sent Johnson what Ball complained was "pornographic gossip" about foreign political leaders; this, he claimed, "tended to influence the President's attitudes to the point of distorting policy."[22]

The director of the president's military office, William Gulley, called Johnson "Big Ears." His appetite for most forms of domestic news and gossip was as insatiable as that of any president in American history. To the left of his desk in the Oval Office he kept two ticker-tape machines constantly churning out news reports. Nearby was a long, low cabinet containing three large TV sets running simultaneously; the president was often to be found restlessly switching news channels with his remote control. There were another three televisions in the small office next door and three more in Johnson's bedroom.[23] His interest in foreign news, however, was much less impressive. The president's intelligence checklist, with which Kennedy had begun the day, failed to find favor with Johnson. On his instructions, the early morning delivery was abandoned in favor of an intelligence summary, renamed the president's daily brief, delivered each evening at 6 P.M. for the president to read later in bed. Johnson insisted that it be no longer than a single sheet. If he read it, he showed—unlike his predecessor—almost no sign of interest detectable by the analysts. He did, however, complain on at least one occasion when the daily brief ran to a second sheet.[24]

Probably on November 28 the president was given the disturbing news by Mac Bundy that, according to a CIA report, Oswald had tried earlier in the year to contact a KGB officer in Mexico City.[25] The next day Johnson made his first major decision directly affecting the intelligence community by appointing a commission to investigate Kennedy's assassination. He told its reluctant chairman, Chief Justice Earl Warren, that "wild rumors" of Soviet or Cuban involvement had to be dispelled as soon as possible: ". . . If the public became aroused against Castro and Khrushchev there might be war."[26] Rusk too believed that the possible involvement of a foreign government "was potentially a matter of war and peace."[27] The former DCI, Allen Dulles, who was one of the seven members of the commission, began an early meeting by circulating a history of previous attempts on the lives of presidents that argued that the typical assassin was a loner and misfit. ". . . You'll find a pattern running through here that I think we'll find in the present case," Dulles said.[28] He may well have been right, but both he and the CIA withheld embarrassing intelligence that might have suggested a conspiracy going far beyond Oswald. The commission was not told of agency plots to kill Castro that included supplying an agent with a murder weapon on the very day of Kennedy's assassination. Nor did the CIA reveal that a Cuban agent was present in Dallas on November 22 on a "sabotage and espionage mission."

Hoover too held back important information. He discovered, to his horror, that Oswald had not been included on the FBI's security index of twenty thousand potentially disloyal citizens, despite having written a threatening letter to the bureau after his return from Russia and making an appointment to see a KGB officer in Mexico City. After reading a report on "investigative deficiencies in the Oswald case," Hoover concluded that, if it became public, it would destroy the bureau's reputation. Not only did he conceal the bureau's failings from the investigation, he also instructed his agents to dig out "all derogatory information on Warren Commission members and staff contained in FBI files." Ironically, therefore, both the CIA and FBI showed themselves anxious to exonerate the United States' two main intelligence and counterintelligence targets, the Soviet Union and Cuba, from any involvement in the assassination.[29]

The commission's report, presented to the president in September 1964, found "very persuasive" evidence that Oswald was the lone assassin, and none of a conspiracy. Though its main conclusions were probably correct, both the gaps in the evidence and the cover-ups by the CIA and FBI were eventually to discredit the report in the eyes of a majority of the American people. At the time, however, the Warren Commission produced the verdict that the president wanted. It was, he claimed in his memoirs, "dispassionate and just."[30] Johnson did not believe his own claim. What he learned from the FBI about the CIA's attempts to use the Mafia to kill Castro persuaded him that there had been a conspiracy. He informed one of his aides in 1967 that "he was now convinced that there was a plot in connection with the assassination." Johnson later told a television newsman, "I'll tell you something that will rock you. Kennedy was trying to get Castro, but Castro got him first!"[31]

Ironically, the CIA had failed to present the Warren Commission with the most compelling evidence for its thesis that Oswald, despite his time in Russia, had no link with the KGB. On February 5, 1964, McCone informed the White House that Lieutenant Colonel Yuri Nosenko of the KGB Second Chief (Counterintelligence) Directorate, who had been recruited as a CIA agent in the summer of 1962, had defected to the United States. Nosenko had seen Oswald's KGB file soon after Kennedy's assassination. The KGB, he reported, considered Oswald mentally unstable and had no dealings with him. Agency analysts took much the same view of Oswald as the KGB. "It is abundantly clear from all the materials reviewed," wrote one of them, "that Lee Oswald was psychiatrically disturbed from his earliest youth." For some CIA officials, however, the timing of Nosenko's defection with information on Oswald that apparently exonerated the KGB was too much of a coincidence. James Jesus Angleton, the head of the Counterintelligence Staff, persuaded McCone to tell the White House that Nosenko might not, after all, be a genuine defector. Yuri Golitsyn, a KGB major who had defected two years earlier, denounced Nosenko as "obviously a KGB provocation." Golitsyn was the most dangerous kind of defector, a man who combined some accurate intelligence with vast conspiracy theories. He persuaded Angleton that the Soviet Union was engaged in a giant global deception, and that even the Sino-Soviet split (whose reality most agency analysts did not doubt) was a charade to deceive the West. The KGB, Golitsyn insisted, would send a series of bogus defectors in an attempt to discredit him and his sensational "revelations." Nosenko, he declared, was one of them. In April 1964 Nosenko was imprisoned by the agency. For the next three and a half years there were constant attempts to persuade him to admit that he was a KGB plant. Since he was, in fact, a genuine defector, Nosenko refused to do so. Few cases in CIA history were more appallingly mishandled.[32]

Johnson was probably never told of Nosenko's incarceration.[33] The activities of the CIA ranked low on the president's agenda during 1964. His main priorities were to win election as president in his own right and to lay the foundations for the "Great Society" that he hoped would secure his place in history and allow him to emerge from the long shadow cast by his martyred predecessor. During his victorious presidential campaign, Johnson spoke eloquently of the war on poverty, of greater educational opportunities for American children, of medical care for the elderly, of building programs to end the housing shortage, and of the protection of the environment. Meanwhile, he read attentively the regular secret reports from Hoover on his political rivals and hostile newspapers. Johnson was determined that his nomination at the 1964 Democratic National Convention in Atlantic City should not be marred by any display of party disunity. At his request, Hoover assigned a squad of thirty FBI agents under Assistant Director Cartha DeLoach, a close friend of the president, to monitor potential dissidents. On August 29 DeLoach reported "the successful completion of the assignment":

By means of informant coverage, by use of various confidential techniques [wiretaps and bugs], by infiltration of key groups through use of undercover agents, and through utilization of agents using appropriate cover as reporters, we were able to keep the

White House fully apprised of all major developments during the Convention's course. For example, through informant coverage and by controlling the situation, we were able to prevent a potentially explosive stall-in and sit-in demonstration planned by [two civil rights organizations].

In a phone call to Hoover, Johnson's aide, Walter Jenkins, praised the bureau's performance in Atlantic City as "one of the finest the President had ever seen." Bill Moyers congratulated DeLoach personally on behalf of the president. DeLoach replied:

Please be assured that it was a pleasure and a privilege to be able to be of assistance to the President and all the boys with me felt honored in being selected for the assignment. I think everything worked out well, and I'm certainly glad that we were able to come through with vital tidbits from time to time which were of assistance to you and Walter [Jenkins]. You know you have only to call on us when a similar situation arises. . . .[34]

In November Johnson won the largest presidential plurality in American history and helped to bring about the biggest Democratic majority in Congress since before the Second World War. In pushing through his domestic reform program, he was able to draw both on his own senatorial record on civil rights, described by Clark Clifford as "the best of any Southerner since Reconstruction," and on his unequaled skill in managing and cajoling Congress. By the end of 1965 Congress had passed eighty-four of the eighty-seven major bills he had submitted to it. Then came growing disappointment. His very success created enormous expectations that were beyond his power to fulfill. Increasingly, the vision of the Great Society was overshadowed by the grisly reality of the Vietnam War. "I knew from the start," claimed Johnson later, "that if I left the woman I really loved—the Great Society—for that bitch of a war on the other side of the world, then I would lose everything at home."[35]

At first, Vietnam had seemed a manageable problem. The overthrow of the lethargic President Ngo Dinh Diem on November 1, with the knowledge but not the active involvement of the CIA, had left the State Department optimistic about the future. Its briefing for Johnson the day after Kennedy's assassination concluded, "The outlook is hopeful. There is better assurance than under Diem that the war can be won. We are pulling out 1,000 American troops by the end of 1963."[36] McNamara, who quickly emerged as Johnson's main adviser on Vietnam, was equally confident.[37] On November 24 Henry Cabot Lodge Jr., the ambassador to

Saigon, visited the Oval Office and quoted a series of military intelligence reports that "left the President with the impression that we are on the road to victory." The CIA disagreed. McCone told Johnson that the agency's "estimate of the situation was somewhat more serious. We had noted a continuing increase in Viet Cong activity. . . ." SIGINT revealed apparent preparations for further "large-scale guerrilla offensives." [38] The CIA assessment was quickly proved right. On a visit to Vietnam shortly before Christmas, McNamara discovered that he had been misled by overoptimistic military intelligence reports. He reported to the president on his return, "The situation is very disturbing. Current trends, unless reversed in the next 2–3 months, will lead to neutralization at best and more likely to a Communist-controlled state."[39] McCone told Johnson, "There is no substantive difference between Secretary McNamara and myself except"—he added ungrammatically—"perhaps I feel a little less pessimistic than he."[40]

Over the next three years, however, McNamara tended to be less pessimistic than agency analysts. According to the DDI, Ray Cline, "The CIA was the bearer of bad tidings throughout the Vietnam War, and was not very happily received by any of the policymakers who tried to make the Vietnam intervention work."[41] Chief among those policymakers was the president himself. McCone noted an immediate difference between what he called the "President Johnson tone" on Vietnam and the "Kennedy tone": "Johnson definitely feels that we place too much emphasis on social reforms; he has very little tolerance on our spending so much time being 'do-gooders'. . . ."[42] McCone tried vainly to persuade the president that Viet Cong attempts to cultivate a reputation as "do-gooders" contributed to their military success:

A standard Viet Cong technique of gaining a foothold among tribal minorities in the highland areas of South Vietnam—where Communist encouragement of tribal autonomy gives them a political appeal—has been to select promising tribesmen, take them to North Vietnam for training in welfare activities as well as for political indoctrination, and return them to tribal villages where their new skills tend to assure them positions of prestige and leadership. The Viet Cong also promote cultural activities—heavily flavored with propaganda—through press, radio and film media, as well as live drama and festivals. A student informant reported attending dramatic performances in a Viet Cong–held area, where plays, song and dances provided entertainment and a dose of propaganda—often enthusiastically received. . . . A Viet Cong document discussing the successful construction of a "combat hamlet" indicates

that primary stress is laid on determining the basic wants and needs
of the inhabitants—frequently their concern for their own land. . . .
The peasants presumably come to regard the Viet Cong as their
protectors and to cooperate voluntarily with the Viet Cong military
effort.[43]

The president, however, showed little interest in the idea of a Southeast
Asian version of the Great Society. His aim in Vietnam was simply to win
the war with as little disruption as possible to his domestic agenda. He
seems to have approved of the maxim crudely enunciated by General
James F. "Holly" Hollingsworth: "Grab the enemy by the balls, and the
hearts and minds will follow."

Johnson was less interested in CIA intelligence on Vietnam than in
its covert operations. On November 26, 1963, he ordered plans to be
drawn up for increased covert action against North Vietnam.[44] On January 13, 1964, the president approved OPLAN 34A-64, jointly prepared
by Defense and CIA. Bundy told him:

Sabotage and propaganda operations in North Vietnam in the last
year and a half have been most disappointing. The operators now
believe that substantial improvements can be achieved, and the policy officers are all in favor of trying. Specific views are as follows:
McNamara is highly enthusiastic. McCone thinks you should understand that no great results are likely from this kind of effort.[45]

McCone's forecast proved, once again, more reliable than McNamara's.
The teams of South Vietnamese and Chinese Nationalist agents who
were parachuted into the North or secretly landed on the coast achieved
little. William Colby, chief of the Far East Division of the CIA Plans
Directorate (and a future DCI), protested to McNamara that most of
their operations were a useless waste of lives. McNamara replied that
more, not fewer, covert operations were needed, and increased their
number. Years later, however, he admitted that the results had been
"very feeble."[46]

From February 1964 onward, Johnson's main decision-making group
for the Vietnam War became not the NSC but the so-called Tuesday
Lunch, where he met, usually but not always at Tuesday lunchtime, with
his key advisers: chief among them McNamara, Rusk, and Bundy (and,
from April 1966, Bundy's successor, Walt W. Rostow). McCone was never
invited. Bundy suggested to the president in June that McNamara's
thinking on Vietnam had gone "a l'ttle stale. Also, in a curious way, he
has rather mechanized the problem so that he misses the real political

flavor."[47] Though one of the most politically astute of all American presidents, Johnson failed to grasp the limitations of McNamara's severely statistical analysis of the war, based on calculations of military might that took too little account of human motivation. McNamara's incomprehension of Vietnam was disguised by the brilliance of his exposition and his mastery of figures. "As a briefer," observed his assistant, Lieutenant Colonel Alexander M. Haig Jr., "he was in a class by himself. . . ." In the early stages of the Vietnam War:

> . . . Men who had been listening to testimony all their lives listened to McNamara's briefings with the rapt faces of religious converts. Standing behind McNamara as I placed the charts on the easel, I saw that Lyndon Johnson was one of them.[48]

Johnson was ensnared by McNamara's statistical wizardry into the fatal error of believing that the increasing level of military pain inflicted by the United States on the Vietnamese Communists would gradually persuade them to give up the fight. Neither the president nor his secretary of defense grasped, until it was too late, that Hanoi was willing to endure greater pain than the United States could bring itself to inflict. It is difficult to avoid the conclusion that both saw the Vietnamese as statistics rather than as human beings. The CIA understood Vietnam better. It did not say that the war could not be won, but its analysts argued that it would be a longer and harder slog than Johnson and McNamara supposed.

During the first major Vietnamese crisis of the Johnson presidency, the CIA was barely consulted. In the early hours (Washington time) of Sunday, August 2, 1964, the USS *Maddox*, while on a SIGINT-gathering mission in the Gulf of Tonkin, was attacked by North Vietnamese torpedo boats. Before breakfast that morning, the duty officer in the White House situation room sent the president an after-action report:

> The Captain of the *Maddox* returned the fire with 5-inch guns and requested air support from the carrier *Ticonderoga* in connection with reconnaissance flights in that area. *Ticonderoga* jets arrived shortly and made strafing attacks on the PT boats resulting in one enemy boat dead in the water, two others damaged and turned tail for home. The *Maddox* reports no personnel or material damages.

After attending church Johnson summoned a meeting of key advisers at 11:30 A.M. Remarkably, although intelligence was involved, he did not invite the DCI. Several NSA personnel, however, were on hand to help interpret the SIGINT evidence. The meeting concluded that the attack had been ordered by an overeager North Vietnamese boat commander or shore station, and decided not to order retaliation.[49]

Two days later, on August 4, McNamara telephoned Johnson shortly after 9 A.M. to tell him that SIGINT "strongly indicated that the North Vietnamese were preparing another attack on our ships in the Tonkin Gulf." Soon afterward the *Maddox* reported that it had made radar contact with two unidentified surface vessels and three unidentified aircraft; it believed it was under torpedo attack and was taking evasive action. Shortly before lunch McNamara and Bundy briefed the NSC, which was holding a previously scheduled meeting. Johnson ordered the NSC to reconvene at 6:15 P.M. to discuss the situation in the Tonkin Gulf. Early in the afternoon, however, the *Maddox* radioed that its previous reports of torpedo attacks and radar contacts with enemy ships and aircraft now appeared "doubtful." It was possible that a combination of "over-eager" sonarmen and "freak weather effects" on radar might have been to blame; there had been "no visual sightings." McNamara, however, assured the president that SIGINT evidence "nails down the incident." One intercepted message from a North Vietnamese boat reported firing at two "enemy airplanes" and damaging one. According to another intercept, a North Vietnamese captain said his unit had "sacrificed two comrades"; NSA interpreted this as a reference either to two enemy boats or to two men in the attack group. A third intercepted message to North Vietnamese torpedo boat headquarters reported, "Enemy vessel perhaps wounded." As on August 2, Johnson did not seek the opinion of McCone and the CIA on the interpretation of these somewhat confusing messages. By the time the NSC reconvened at 6:15 P.M., he had already decided on retaliation.[50] To the CIA, wrote R. Jack Smith later, the intelligence that had convinced the president and his advisers "proved nothing":

> My own guess is that confusion prevailed both on the destroyers in the Tonkin Gulf and in the Oval Office. A strong predisposition to believe the worst, combined with an inadequate understanding of the intelligence the White House was dealing with, did the rest.[51]

McCone's first opportunity to express a view directly to the president came during the thirty-five-minute meeting of the NSC at 6:15 P.M. He had probably not yet had a chance to consider carefully the alleged evidence of a North Vietnamese attack. But he was openly skeptical of the rationale for the retaliatory air strike that Johnson had already decided. The president asked him, "Do they want a war by attacking our ships in the middle of the Gulf of Tonkin?" McCone replied, "No. The North Vietnamese are reacting defensively to our attacks on their off-shore islands. They are responding out of pride and on the basis of defense considerations."[52]

The air strike on North Vietnam was bungled as well as ill-conceived. Johnson had intended to make a televised announcement that the attack was in progress in time for the 7 P.M. news programs. But his advisers had forgotten that the carrier aircraft in the Gulf of Tonkin were equipped only for air-to-air or air-to-ship combat. Some hours were needed to load them with the ordnance for a bombing raid and to brief the pilots on their targets. By 11 P.M. Johnson's patience was exhausted. "Bob," he roared down the phone to McNamara, "I'm *exposed* here! I've got to make my speech *right now!*" When he went before the television cameras just over half an hour later, some of the attack planes had still not taken off. The advance warning given by the president to the North Vietnamese air defenses may help to explain why two aircraft were shot down. Johnson used the charge that North Vietnam had committed "open aggression on the high seas" to win a blank check from Congress to expand the war as he saw fit. The Gulf of Tonkin Resolution, which sailed through both the House and Senate with only two dissenting votes, gave him authority to "use all necessary measures" to "repel any armed attack" on U.S. forces, "prevent further aggression," and assist any member of the Southeast Asia Treaty Organization "in defense of its freedom." The suspicion later spread, after Senate hearings in 1968, that Johnson had fabricated the attack in the Gulf of Tonkin to push the resolution through Congress. It is far more likely that intelligence from the gulf on August 4 was misinterpreted and that the president was badly advised. There was, however, a cover-up when the error was discovered. According to McNamara's assistant, Alexander Haig:

An internal investigation of the incident by the Pentagon soon after it took place established that the noises identified by the *Maddox*'s sonarman as enemy torpedoes were, in fact, the sounds of the destroyer's own wake, and that while some North Vietnamese craft may have sortied from their bases on August 4, they never attacked or threatened to attack the destroyers.[53]

There was a curiously similar episode in the Tonkin Gulf on September 18. While on SIGINT-gathering missions, the destroyers *Morton* and *Edwards* reported radar contact with surface vessels on which they opened fire. As on August 4, there were no visual sightings and the radar evidence was swiftly discredited, but an intercepted North Vietnamese message seemed, at first sight, to indicate the presence of hostile ships. Bundy noted after a meeting in the Oval Office that the president "pressed his own skeptical views and made it clear that he was not interested in rapid escalation on so frail evidence." The doubts expressed by Johnson about the incident on September 18 suggest he had had second thoughts about the reality of the attack six weeks earlier. On September 20 Johnson discussed the most recent incident again with a larger group of advisers, who included McCone's deputy, General Carter. When pressed by Johnson, Carter would say only that it was "possible" the destroyers had made contact with enemy vessels. The discussion ended with an angry outburst by Johnson that reflected his frustration at the confused naval and intelligence reports from the Gulf of Tonkin:

> Secretary Rusk . . . pressed on the President the importance of not seeming to doubt our naval officers on the spot. These officers were convinced that they had been facing the enemy, and an expression of doubt from Washington would be damaging. The President replied somewhat sharply that he was not planning to make a radio broadcast on the matter but that he did think it important to find out exactly what happened.

Bundy noted after the heated discussion in the cabinet room, "The President found only the intercept persuasive (and it is significant that even this evidence was countered by a later analytical report)."[54]

On January 27, 1965, Bundy and McNamara sent Johnson a brief and dramatic memorandum entitled "Basic Policy in Vietnam":

> . . . Both of us are now pretty well convinced that our current policy can lead only to disastrous defeat. . . . *We see two alternatives.* The first is to use our military power in the Far East and to force a change of Communist policy. The second is to deploy all our resources along a track of negotiation, aimed at what little can be preserved with no addition to our present military risks.

Though Bundy and McNamara said that both options should be seriously considered, they made clear that they were in favor of the first.[55] On February 13, after two Viet Cong attacks on U.S. bases, Johnson authorized the beginning of an air war against North Vietnam, code-named Operation Rolling Thunder. The staple diet of the Tuesday Lunch became the JCS target list for the bombing campaign.[56] Rolling Thunder, however, was directed less against the real enemy than against a figment of the Pentagon's imagination. The Tuesday Lunchers failed to grasp that the warmaking capacity of North Vietnam was not a by-product of its industrial infrastructure. Hanoi's war effort survived more bombs than those dropped by all the combatants of World War II.[57] The major policy errors of the Vietnam War were due far less to lack of intelligence than to a failure to understand the nature of Vietnam.

Art Lundahl and the NPIC analysts believed that the imagery shown to LBJ presented a misleadingly optimistic picture of the success of Rolling Thunder. McNamara insisted that, in war conditions, the responsibility for briefing the president on photographic intelligence belonged to the Defense Intelligence Agency (DIA) rather than NPIC. "Lundahl," recalls his assistant, Dino Brugioni, "was cut out by Defense. He was never allowed to brief Johnson on the situation in Vietnam." According to Brugioni, the DIA showed the president briefing boards of huge bomb craters along the Ho Chi Minh Trail through the jungles of Laos and Cambodia that gave the impression that the major supply route from North to South Vietnam was being cut. NPIC briefing boards, based on low-level photographs that showed bicycles and pack animals laden with supplies weaving around the bomb craters, were not brought to Johnson's attention.[58]

On April 1, 1965, the NSC agreed "to change the mission of our ground forces in South Vietnam from one of advice and static defense to one of active combat operations against the Viet Cong guerrillas." McCone played little part in the policy decisions that led to the escalation of the war. He told an aide early in 1965, referring to the CIA's Annual Survey of Soviet Intentions and Capabilities, "I've been trying to get Johnson to sit down and read these papers. When I can't even get the President to read the summaries, it's time to go."[59] Having lost the president's ear as well as his favor, McCone resigned in April 1965. Almost his final act as DCI was to send Johnson a copy of a memorandum he had sent Bundy on April 2 that, he tactfully suggested, "may not have come to your attention." Existing policy in the Vietnam War, he argued, was not working. The only options were to hit the enemy "harder, more frequently, and inflict greater damage," or, he implied, to withdraw. He gave a remarkably accurate forecast of the failures of the next three years:

> I have reported that the [air] strikes to date have not caused a change in the North Vietnamese policy of directing Viet Cong insurgency, infiltrating cadres and supplying material. If anything, the strikes to date have hardened their attitude. . . . It is my personal opinion that this program is not sufficiently severe or damaging to the North Vietnamese to cause them to compromise their present

policy. On the other hand, we must look with care to our position under a program of slowly ascending tempo of air strikes. With the passage of each day and each week, we can expect increasing pressure to stop the bombing. This will come from various elements of the American public, from the press, the United Nations and world opinion. Therefore time will run against us in this operation and I think the North Vietnamese are counting on this. Therefore I think what we are doing is starting on a track which, in all probability, will have limited effectiveness against guerrillas, although admittedly [they] will restrain some VC advances. However, we can expect requirements for an ever-increasing commitment of U.S. personnel without materially improving the chances of victory. . . . Since the contemplated actions against the North are modest in scale, they will not impose unacceptable damage on it, nor will they threaten the DRV's [North Vietnam's] vital interests. Hence, they will not present them with a situation with which they cannot live, though such actions will cause the DRV pain and inconvenience.[60]

McCone was more clearsighted than the president and his main advisers chiefly because he did not commit their fatal error of underestimating the enemy. Johnson could not believe that a small backward Asian power could stand up to the might of the United States. The war, he thought, would be like a filibuster in Congress: "enormous resistance at first, then a steady whittling away, then Ho [Chi Minh] hurrying to get it over with." [61]

McCone was also more prescient than the president about public disillusion with the war. Well before Johnson, he grasped the potential threat to the war effort posed by the growth of domestic opposition. Johnson took seriously McCone's warning that the North Vietnamese and Chinese hoped to intensify the campus antiwar movement. Encouraged by Hoover, however, Johnson greatly exaggerated Communist influence in the Vietnam demonstrations. Hoover noted after a meeting in the Oval Office on April 28:

I informed the President that I had just received word this morning before coming to the White House that plans had been made from May 3 to May 9 to demonstrate in 85 cities in this country by the Students for [a] Democratic Society, which is largely infiltrated by communists and which has been woven into the civil rights situation which we know has large communist influence. I told the President we were preparing a memorandum on the Students for [a] Democratic Society which I would try to get to him by tomorrow. . . .

Hoover effectively dictated to his subordinates what the conclusions of the memorandum were to be:

> While I realize we may not be able to technically state that [Students for a Democratic Society] is an actual communist organization, certainly we do know there are communists in it. . . . What I want to get to the President is the background with emphasis upon the communist influence therein so that he will know exactly what the picture is.[62]

Hoover's alarmist assessment of Communist conspiracy was further exaggerated by the president. Johnson's conspiracy theories extended even to the Senate. He claimed, absurdly, that Senators Fulbright and Wayne Morse, two of the leading opponents of his Vietnam policy, were "definitely under the control of the Soviet embassy."[63] In February 1966 the president instructed the FBI to monitor the televised hearings of the Senate Foreign Relations Committee, chaired by Fulbright. The bureau made detailed comparisons between points raised during the hearings and Communist policy. DeLoach, the FBI liaison with the White House, also interviewed the Senate minority leader, Everett Dirksen, who declared himself convinced that Fulbright and Morse were "very much obligated to Communist interests."[64]

Johnson's choice of his devoted Texan supporter, retired Vice Admiral William F. "Red" Raborn, to succeed McCone as DCI in April 1965 reflected his growing impatience with the discordant notes struck by the CIA's Vietnam estimates. Richard Helms, who became Raborn's deputy, later recalled the president complaining at a private dinner in the White House family quarters:

> Let me tell you about these intelligence guys. When I was growing up in Texas, we had a cow named Bessie. I'd go out early and milk her. I'd get her in the stanchion, seat myself and squeeze out a pail of fresh milk. One day I'd worked hard and gotten a full pail of milk, but I wasn't paying attention, and old Bessie swung her shit-smeared tail through that bucket of milk. Now, you know, that's what these intelligence guys do. You work hard and get a good program or policy going, and they swing a shit-smeared tail through it.[65]

There was no danger that Raborn, like McCone, would be tempted to play the role of Bessie. His loyalty to Johnson was such that after the president had spoken of his confidence in him at the White House swearing-in ceremony on April 28, "tears were coursing down his crimson cheeks and forming tiny drops at the point of his chin."[66] Even if most of the stories told about Raborn on the Washington cocktail circuit are discounted, he still emerges as clearly the least qualified of all DCIs. Though he had managed the Polaris nuclear submarine program efficiently, he knew little about, and had little interest in, foreign affairs. The story spread at Langley that he complained that a classified code word had been left in a report, only to be told that Kuwait was not a code word but a state.[67] According to a Washington wit, "Dulles ran a happy ship, McCone ran a tight ship, and Raborn runs a sinking ship." Johnson, however, was more interested in curbing the CIA's independence than in improving the quality of its intelligence. He saw in Raborn a reliably compliant DCI whose administrative efficiency would ensure that the agency did not rock the presidential boat.

Raborn's arrival at Langley coincided with a sudden crisis in the Dominican Republic. On Saturday, April 24, the president and First Lady visited the annual Azalea Festival at Norfolk, Virginia. Johnson crowned their daughter Luci queen of the festival and, in a speech of the kind that made the Eastern Establishment cringe, declared that she had been *his* queen for a long time. That evening, at Camp David in the Catoctin Mountains of Maryland, he was shown a cable that had just arrived from the embassy in Santo Domingo, capital of the Dominican Republic:

> Santo Domingo is rife with rumors of a coup, promoted by announcement over two radio stations that a number of army officers, including Army Chief of Staff Rivera Cuesta, had been arrested. Word of the overthrow of the Government spread like wildfire and brought crowds into the street, much horn-blowing, and a concentration of some 1,000 persons at the palace who were dispersed by a water truck.

The many rumors of coups that circulated in Latin America did not usually disturb the president's weekends. On this occasion, however, Johnson immediately suspected the hand of Castro. According to intelligence reports, Cuba had backed an attempted invasion several years earlier and was currently training Dominican guerrillas and saboteurs. On Sunday Johnson cut short his weekend and returned to the White House. Over the next few days the situation in Santo Domingo continued to worsen. On the afternoon of Wednesday, April 28, a "critic" (high-priority cable) from the U.S. ambassador warned: "American lives are in danger." That evening, soon after Raborn had been sworn in as DCI, the president announced that marines were being sent in "to give protection to hundreds of Americans" and other nationals.[68] Johnson, noted Rusk, was determined "to stress the Communist threat," though the State Department believed that Communist influence in the rebellion was slight.[69] "Hard pressed in Vietnam," believed George Ball, "President Johnson was giving excessive weight to the small number of alleged Communists dubiously reported to be in the Dominican Republic."[70]

The president did not consult the CIA before sending in the marines. What he demanded from Raborn was evidence to justify a decision he had already made. His close adviser, Jack Valenti, noted in a presidential memorandum, "Show *indisputable evidence* that Castro-types are in charge. This cannot be *just* a statement. Raborn must have *pictures*, *names*, a full dossier."[71] Ray Cline heard Johnson informing Raborn of the marine landings over an amplified telephone in the DCI's office. According to Cline, "Johnson told Raborn; he did not consult him or ask for advice." "Aye, aye, sir!" replied the DCI.[72] Raborn was not the only man required to provide hard evidence to support presidential hyperbole. When Johnson's claims of "headless bodies lying in the streets of Santo Domingo" were challenged by critics of American intervention, he called the ambassador personally and told him, "For God's sake, see if you can find some headless bodies." The embassy obliged with some suitably grisly photographs.[73]

"*One fact is sure*," Valenti warned the president. "If the Castro-types take over the Dominican Republic, it will be the worst domestic political disaster any Administration could suffer."[74] Johnson seems to have taken the warning to heart. He astonished both the State Department and the CIA by his determination to take personal charge of almost every detail of the handling of the Dominican crisis. According to Ball, he became, in effect, "the Dominican desk officer." Hoover pleased the president by supplying him with the names of fifty-three "known Communists" in the Dominican Republic, subsequently adding another twenty-four. A list of fifty-eight "identified and prominent Communist and Castroite leaders" in the rebel forces was published by the administration on May 2. Johnson went on television to declare, "What began as a popular revolution, committed to democracy and social justice, very shortly moved and was taken over and really seized and placed in the hands of a band of Communist conspirators." Though most of the president's advisers probably remained skeptical, only the assistant secretary of state for inter-American affairs, Jack Hood Vaughn, seems to have challenged him directly. At a late night meeting in the White House,

Johnson gave him an angry dressing-down. Vaughn got up and left the room.[75] At Johnson's request, Hoover sent a team of FBI agents to the Dominican Republic with instructions to gather further intelligence on Communist subversion. Their leader sought out the CIA station chief, David Phillips, a veteran of the Guatemalan coup of 1954, and told him, "None of us knows anything of the local political and security situation and our experience is in criminal, not political, investigation. J. Edgar has told us to start churning out reports. What do we do?" Hoover, meanwhile, informed the president that his agents were "producing excellent results." Johnson told him to use the intelligence they provided to "prepare in writing the strongest case [you] can to prove [Communist domination] if and when we have to."[76]

On September 3 a provisional government was installed with the moderate politician Héctor García-Godoy as acting president. Hoover alarmed both Johnson and Raborn by alleging that García-Godoy was appointing secret Communists as ministers. David Phillips and Desmond Fitzgerald, who had succeeded Helms as DDP, had some difficulty in persuading Raborn that this was not the case. Phillips startled Raborn by telling him that one of his agents in Santo Domingo was a member of the rebel underground and had two hundred rifles buried in his cellar. The DCI jumped to his feet. "Have him arrested!" he ordered. Phillips noticed a muscle in Fitzgerald's neck begin to twitch. "Is he a Commie?" Raborn continued. The normally voluble Fitzgerald was reduced to silence. Patiently, Phillips explained to the new DCI the principle of penetration agents, and why it was useful to have one within a Dominican Communist group. "He joined it at our request," he told Raborn, "and now works from within against Communist interests."[77] There were times during the Dominican crisis when the DCI understood less about intelligence than the president.

One Sunday morning, while ill in bed, Johnson summoned Raborn to his White House bedroom. Raborn took Cline, the DDI, with him. "How the hell can I get my troops out of this damned mess?" the president demanded. "Maybe Dr. Cline has a suggestion," Raborn replied. Cline said it would only be possible to withdraw all the marines after the election of a reliably non-Communist president. He reviewed the possible candidates, giving his warmest endorsement to an exiled former president, Joaquín Balaguer, then living in New York. Johnson sat bolt-upright in bed. "That's it!" he declared. "That's our policy. Get this guy in office down there!"[78] During the 1966 Dominican presidential election campaign, Johnson demanded regular reports. The CIA station, unlike the embassy, predicted a Balaguer victory with 57 percent of the vote. In the event, Balaguer was elected with only one percent less. Desmond

Fitzgerald won the White House pool on the election, and Raborn cabled his congratulations to David Phillips. The president was reported to be pleased.[79]

"Cline thought Raborn was a horse's ass," recalls Richard Helms, "and he didn't hesitate to say so." Early in 1966 Raborn told Helms, "I want you to get rid of Ray Cline." Almost simultaneously Cline asked Helms to give him a foreign posting; soon afterward he left to become head of station in Frankfurt. Johnson, meanwhile, had had second thoughts about Raborn's appointment. In April 1965 he had told Helms that he expected him to be the next DCI. In June 1966, without informing Helms in advance, Johnson announced at a press conference that he was to succeed Raborn.[80] Despite his uncertain grasp of both intelligence and international relations, Raborn left behind him one major organizational reform. To meet Johnson's frequent demands for up-to-the-minute intelligence during the Dominican crisis, he established an agency Operations Center, manned twenty-four hours a day, in which for the first time staff from the rival directorates of Plans and Intelligence worked closely together. The president's aides phoned the center a dozen times on its first day. What was happening? Was there really fighting in downtown Santo Domingo? Throughout the crisis, wrote one of the center staff, "Johnson always wanted to know *now*."[81]

Johnson's determination to defeat what he regarded as the Communist challenge in the Dominican Republic had much to do with his concern for the credibility of American policy in Southeast Asia. "What can we do in Vietnam," he said privately, "if we can't clean up the Dominican Republic?"[82] In July 1965 he agreed to a major commitment of U.S. ground forces in the Vietnam War. For the next two and a half years the MACV (U.S. Military Assistance Command, Vietnam) continued to insist that the war was being won, while at the same time making regular requests for more troops and an expansion of the bombing campaign. Throughout that period, overoptimistic MACV intelligence on enemy numbers, supported by the DIA in Washington,[83] was used to sustain the illusion that the United States was winning a war of attrition. MACV's errors derived not from deliberate deception but from wishful thinking. American forces and firepower, it was believed, *must* be defeating Asian peasant soldiers and guerrillas. Order-of-battle (OB) intelligence must therefore reflect that supposed reality.

The bulk and complexity of the MACV computer printouts of enemy OB statistics meant that very few outside the compliant DIA were equipped to dispute their conclusions. According to Colonel Gains B. Hawkins, chief of the MACV OB section from February 1966 to September 1967:

When I arrived [in Saigon], the . . . monthly Order of Battle Summary was about a quarter of an inch thick, and when I left there, a little better than eighteen months later, it was about an inch—a little better maybe than an inch thick, because our requirements had grown during that time along with our capability to process and produce order of battle intelligence.[84]

Johnson's leadership style added to the difficulty of challenging MACV statistics on enemy forces. Unlike Kennedy, he was inclined to treat dissent among his advisers as personal disloyalty. And his standards of loyalty were unusually demanding. "I don't want loyalty . . . ," the journalist David Halberstam reports LBJ as saying about one supporter who failed to meet his exacting standards, "I want him to kiss my ass in Macy's window at high noon and tell me it smells like roses."[85] Though McNamara, for three years Johnson's leading adviser on the Vietnam War, eschewed such exotic comparisons, he reinforced the president's intolerance of dissent. "I don't believe the government of a complicated state can operate effectively," he declared, "if those in charge of the departments of the government express disagreement with the decisions of the established head of that government." George Ball later recalled that McNamara regarded his own dissenting views on Vietnam as "next to treason," and treated his memos like "poisonous snakes." When McNamara too developed doubts about the war, he found it difficult at first to admit them even to himself.[86]

Since the complexities of battle order were the responsibility of military intelligence, it was some time before the CIA began to form an independent view of them. The first to do so was Sam Adams, a youthful analyst distantly related to President John Adams, who had become skeptical of MACV statistics after serving in the CIA Saigon station. On Friday, August 19, 1966, Adams read a captured Viet Cong document reporting that the guerrilla-militia in Binh Dinh province numbered just over fifty thousand. He checked the MACV order of battle and discovered that the figure for Binh Dinh was only forty-five hundred. Another captured document, for Phu Yen province, showed eleven thousand guerrilla-militia. The MACV figure was fourteen hundred. Adams "almost shouted" from his desk, "There goes the whole damn order of battle!" He spent the weekend working in the office, checking more figures. On Monday, August 22, he wrote a memo suggesting that the MACV order-of-battle estimate might be two hundred thousand men too low. Convinced that he had made "the biggest intelligence find of the war—by far," Adams sent it to the director's office on the seventh floor and waited impatiently for the response. He imagined receiving a telephone call to tell him, "The President's got to be told about this, and you'd better be able to defend these numbers!" In fact, it seems to have taken five months for Johnson to be made aware that MACV statistics were contested. For some time Adams found it difficult to get his figures taken seriously even within the agency. His memo of August 22 was returned without comment four days later. The circulation list attached showed that it had been read, or at least glanced at, by Helms and the seventh-floor hierarchy, but they had clearly not been convinced by it. Adams furiously fired off a further memo, containing additional evidence. This time there was no response at all. After a week Adams went to the seventh floor and found his memo in a folder marked "Indefinite Hold." He then wrote a third memo and took it to the seventh floor himself, hoping to find some senior official who would take it seriously. The Asia–Middle East area chief, Waldo Duberstein, exclaimed on seeing him, "It's that Goddam memo again! Adams, stop being such a primadonna!" The official in the next-door office told him that battle-order intelligence was the business of the MACV commander, General William C. Westmoreland, and no concern of the CIA.[87] The initial skepticism with which Adams's case was received reflected both his apparent failure to make adequate allowance for the exaggerated claims contained in captured Viet Cong documents and the impression he conveyed to his superiors of a man who believed he had found the Holy Grail. On September 8 he finally gained permission for a version of his original memo, entitled "The Strength of the Viet Cong Irregulars," to be given restricted circulation as a "draft working paper." It went only to "working-level" analysts and staffers, not to policymakers, and carried the note:

> This working paper is a preliminary study of the evidence available in Washington on the numerical strength of Viet Cong irregulars. We invite your cooperation in further investigation of this subject. Efforts are now underway to arrange for a fuller review of the evidence by MACV.[88]

By now Adams was so angry and exhausted that, by his own admission, he needed two weeks off work to "simmer down."[89]

Adams had launched what became the most fraught part of the Vietnam paper war in Washington: a conflict that was still being bitterly contested on television and in a libel action brought by Westmoreland against CBS a decade after the real war was over. There was comparatively little controversy over the numbers of uniformed soldiers in the Viet Cong army. The dispute centered instead on the guerrilla-militia. The traditional battle-order concepts of the MACV and the DIA found it difficult to take full account of Viet Cong irregulars. For most CIA analysts, clerks and shopkeepers who helped to blow up bridges or plant booby-traps in their spare time qualified as guerrillas. MACV, however, defined a guerrilla as a member of an irregular military unit subordinate to a village or district committee. Its figures for irregular forces were therefore unrealistically low.[90] In Adams's view, they produced a serious distortion in the MACV enemy order of battle. He also believed that the MACV had seriously underestimated both enemy support troops and armed political cadres. In December Adams found his first major supporter within the agency. George Carver, Helms's recently appointed special assistant for Vietnamese affairs, told him he was "on the right track" with his revised OB statistics.[91] On January 11, 1967, Carver sent a memo, drafted by Adams, on "Revising the Viet Cong Order of Battle" to R. Jack Smith, Cline's successor as DDI:

> We believe the MACV Order of Battle of Communist Ground Forces in South Vietnam, which on 3 January carried the number of confirmed Viet Cong, including North Vietnamese, at 277,150, is far too low and should be raised, perhaps doubled. A raising of the OB figure to a more realistic level would allow the intelligence community to make a better informed appraisal of what we are up against. . . .[92]

Smith had mixed feelings about the memorandum. Though he thought that MACV estimates were too low, he also believed that it made little sense to add together the numbers of uniformed soldiers and guerrillas to arrive at an overall total figure of enemy forces. Part-time irregulars did not, in his judgment, have the same military value as regular troops. Nor could their numbers be calculated in the same way:

> We recognized that in reality *there was no right number*. No one, not even the North Vietnamese themselves, knew exactly how many Viet Cong and related irregular units there were in South Vietnam. We were all feeling our way toward an approximation.

Smith had little sympathy with those who "wanted us to rush into battle and carry the fight for Eternal Truth up to the front steps of the White House."[93] Helms agreed with Smith. "Sam Adams," he uncharitably concluded, "was the most acute pain in the ass I've ever met."[94] Carver believed that Adams was undermining his own case by the uncompromising zeal of his attack on the MACV figures: "The idea to Sam that people could review some very spotty evidence and honestly come to a different conclusion than the one he came to was an idea that he rejected totally out of hand."[95]

During January news of the battle-order controversy reached the Oval Office. Mac Bundy's successor, Walt Rostow, sought to reassure the president that all was well:

> . . . A debate continues over the absolute size of the enemy order of battle in Viet Nam. . . . [But,] whatever the size, you should know that the official [MACV] statistics now show for the first time a net decline in both VC main force and North Vietnam army units for the fourth quarter of 1966. This is the first reversal of the upward trend since 1960.

General Earle Wheeler, chairman of the JCS, summoned a conference of OB analysts from the MACV, CIA, and DIA that met at Honolulu in February, in the hope of reconciling the differences between them.[96] Some progress seemed to be made. "You know," said Colonel Hawkins, head of the MACV OB section, "there's a lot more of these little bastards out there than we thought there were!"[97]

The MACV, however, remained under relentless pressure from Washington to show results. Wheeler was alarmed by statistics in March that showed a sharp increase in enemy attacks. He wrote to Westmoreland:

> I can only interpret the new figures to mean that, despite the force buildup, despite our many successful spoiling attacks and base area searches, and despite the heavy interdiction campaign in North Vietnam and Laos, VC/NVA combat capability and offensive activity throughout 1966 and now in 1967 has been increasing steadily. . . . I cannot go to the President and tell him that, contrary to my other reports and those of the other chiefs as to the progress of the war in which we have laid great stress upon the thesis you have seized the initiative from the enemy, the situation is such that we are not sure who has the initiative in South Vietnam. Moreover, the effect of surfacing this major and significant discrepancy would be dynamite, particularly coming on the heels of other recent statistical problems.

During May the conflict between the MACV and the CIA over enemy strength reemerged. The MACV order of battle for May 15 gave a figure of 292,000.[98] "Now, Sam," Carver told Adams, "don't you worry. It's time to bite the bullet."[99] On May 23 the CIA issued a Vietnamese estimate concluding that Viet Cong irregular forces were considerably larger than suggested by the MACV. It was seen by Rostow, McNamara, and Rusk, but not shown to the president. A draft Special National Intelligence Estimate (SNIE) completed by the CIA in mid-June agreed with MACV figures for regular forces but put guerrilla-militia numbers at 185,000–245,000, as compared with the MACV figure of 100,000–120,000; the CIA estimate for support forces and armed political cadres was 155,000–180,000, in contrast with the MACV's 63,000.[100]

During his first three and a half years in office, Johnson had paid less heed than any of his three predecessors either to the DCI or to CIA estimates. In the summer of 1967, however, he raised his opinion of both. He did so as a result of two major agency successes. The first was Operation Black Shield, which for the next twenty-five years remained one of the best-kept secrets of the Vietnam War. By May 1967 the growth of SAM sites in North Vietnam had raised fears that, as in Cuba five years earlier, the Soviet Union might be planning to install surface-to-surface missile bases. Helms proposed a series of reconnaissance missions by a top-secret successor to the U-2, code-named Oxcart, which had become operational six months earlier. In a test flight on December 21, 1966, Oxcart had flown 10,198 statute miles in six hours, a feat beyond the reach of any other aircraft in the world. Helms assured the president that it was far less vulnerable to SAM attack than the U-2, and that its camera was "far superior." A three-year, $2 million development program had devised a highly sophisticated camera that used a quartz glass window, fused into the Oxcart fuselage by a revolutionary process using high-frequency sound waves to prevent optical distortion even at high temperature. On May 16 Helms was invited to the Tuesday Lunch to put the proposal for Operation Black Shield in person. Johnson gave his verbal approval, confirmed in writing later that day by Rostow. The first Black Shield mission was flown from the Kadena Air Force Base in Okinawa on May 31 and photographed 70 of the 190 known SAM sites in North Vietnam in a flight lasting just over three and a half hours; the cruise legs were flown at Mach 3.1. No radar signals were detected, indicating that the mission had gone completely unnoticed by any of the sites. By mid-July Helms was able to report to the White House that it was now almost certain that no surface-to-surface missiles were deployed in North Vietnam. Later in the year the Oxcart's electronic countermeasures equipment enabled it to survive several SAM missile attacks.[101]

The second major CIA success that impressed the president in the summer of 1967 came in the Middle East. Since the beginning of the year an agency task force, headed by the Asia–Middle East area chief, Waldo

Duberstein, had been monitoring growing Arab-Israeli tension. By May it was convinced both that war was imminent and that the Israelis would win in ten to fourteen days. The Israeli government, meanwhile, was telling Washington that without major new U.S. arms shipments it would face defeat by the Arabs. Both Johnson and Rusk were half-convinced by the Israelis' argument. Helms was summoned to the White House to defend the agency estimate. Before the meeting Rusk asked him if he was sure the estimate was right. Helms said he was. "Well," replied Rusk, "in the words of [former New York mayor] Fiorello La Guardia, if this is a mistake, it's a beaut!" Johnson seemed persuaded by Helms's assessment, but asked for the agency estimate to be reworked—or, as he put it, "scrubbed down"—by Helms and General Wheeler. The result was a SNIE on May 26 that predicted an Israeli victory in seven to ten days.[102] On the same day the Israeli foreign minister, who had flown to Washington, told Johnson that, according to Israeli intelligence, Egypt was preparing an all-out attack. "All of our intelligence people are unanimous," the president replied, "that if the UAR [Egypt] attacks, you will whip hell out of them."[103]

Levi Eshkol, the Israeli prime minister, assured Johnson on May 30 that he would wait two weeks to see if international diplomacy could resolve the crisis with Egypt. Helms's discussions in Washington at the end of May with the head of Mossad, General Meri Amit, persuaded him that, on the contrary, Israel intended to launch a preemptive strike. When Amit, accompanied by the Israeli ambassador, suddenly left Washington for Tel Aviv on June 2, Helms warned Johnson that an Israeli attack was imminent.[104] At 4:35 A.M. on June 5 Rostow woke the president with the news that Israel and its Arab neighbors were at war. By 7 o'clock it was becoming clear that Israeli air strikes had destroyed much of the Egyptian, Syrian, and Jordanian air forces on the ground. Just before 8 A.M., still in his White House bedroom, Johnson was telephoned by McNamara with a message unlike any received by any previous president. "Mr. President," he told him, "the hot line is up." Installed after the Cuban missile crisis, the hot line provided a direct teletype link between Moscow and Washington. It had never been used before except to convey test messages and New Year greetings. This time the Kremlin used the hot line to express its outrage at the Israeli offensive. "It took some hard persuading," wrote Rusk later, presumably with tongue in cheek, "to persuade them that we were as surprised by the Israeli attack as they were."[105]

The Arab-Israeli War ended in a sweeping Israeli victory in only six days, rather than the seven to ten predicted by the SNIE of May 26. Throughout the Six-Day War the White House situation room was on twenty-four-hour watch, with senior officers on duty around the clock—the longest major alert of the Johnson presidency.[106] There were two moments of particular tension. The first came early on the morning of June 8 when news reached Washington that a U.S. SIGINT ship, the *Liberty*, had been attacked in international waters off the Sinai coast. Ten of its crew were killed and over a hundred wounded. At 6:40 A.M. Johnson convened an emergency meeting of his advisers in the situation room. At first he assumed that the Russians must be responsible and began dictating a hot-line message to the Kremlin, warning that U.S. aircraft were investigating a serious incident in the area. Before the message had been sent, however, a "flash" arrived from Tel Aviv, reporting an Israeli admission that "maybe" they had attacked an American ship in error. The tone of the hot-line message to Moscow was hurriedly changed. ". . . The ship had been attacked in error by Israeli gunboats and planes," wrote the president later. ". . . This heartbreaking episode grieved the Israelis deeply, as it did us."[107] Johnson is unlikely to have believed his own explanation. The Israelis had almost certainly decided to destroy the *Liberty* rather than allow it to monitor a crucial phase of their operations, though doubt remains about the level at which the attack was authorized. A CIA report of July 27 quoted an Israeli informant as saying that Israeli headquarters had been worried "as to how many people might have access to the information the *Liberty* was intercepting."[108]

The tensest moment in the situation room during the Six-Day War came on the morning of June 10. At 9:05 A.M. Johnson received a message from the Kremlin accusing Israel of breaking a cease-fire with Syria and warning that a "grave catastrophe" was in the making. Unless the Israelis halted operations unconditionally, the Soviet Union would take the "necessary actions, including military." For the first time in his presidency, Johnson believed that there was an imminent danger of superpower confrontation. He decided to move the Sixth Fleet, then in the Mediterranean, toward Syria in the hope of deterring Soviet intervention. Helms told him that ELINT monitoring of the fleet's movement by Russian submarines would ensure that its change of course was immediately reported to the Soviet leaders. He recalled later how the tension of the discussion produced "the lowest voices I ever heard in a meeting of that kind." Johnson ordered the Sixth Fleet to move to take up a position fifty miles off the Syrian coast. Simultaneously he sent a conciliatory message over the hot line, assuring the Kremlin that "we had been pressing Israel to make the ceasefire completely effective and had received assurances that this would be done." By midday, after a series of exchanges with Moscow, the tension in the situation room had subsided. But the memory of it left Johnson with the conviction that the morning of the June 10 had been one of those "times when the wisdom and rightness of a President's judgment are critically important."[109]

After the Six-Day War, Helms was for the first time regularly invited to the Tuesday Lunch. Once he became a member of Johnson's inner circle of advisers:

> . . . It did take a little time to sink in, if I may put it that way—that a President of the United States does not make his decisions in an orderly way or the way that political scientists say they should be done or, in fact, the way ninety-nine per cent of the American people understand that they are done.

Johnson's decision-making was, Helms discovered, "a highly personal affair." He soon learned that if he wanted to get a point across to the president effectively at the Tuesday Lunch he had to do so in the first sixty seconds of what he had to say. Some within the agency complained that Helms did not argue the CIA case strongly enough. Helms, however, believed that he should avoid expressing opinions on policy to preserve the agency's reputation for objective assessment. By gaining the president's trust, he ensured that Johnson would read the main reports Helms submitted to him.[110] That was also the view of the DDI, R. Jack Smith: "To be certain that your reports reach the president's eyes and ears without the intervention of a phalanx of aides and assistants is the ultimate reward. It is seldom achieved. . . ."[111] Johnson agreed at last to the inclusion of the president's daily brief in his early morning papers.[112] Helms's memos to the president were signed simply "Dick"; he insists that "Johnson never bawled me out with a single bad-news report I brought to him."[113]

The long hot summer of 1967 saw the worst race riots in American history. Late July, wrote Johnson in his memoirs, remained "forever etched on my memory." During four days of rioting in Detroit, forty-three people were killed. At a meeting in the Oval Office on the evening of July 24 Hoover forecast imminent catastrophe. "They have lost all control in Detroit," he told the president. "Harlem may break loose within thirty minutes. They plan to tear it to pieces!" (Harlem was not in fact destroyed.) On July 29 Johnson appointed the National Commission on Civil Disorders (the Kerner commission) to inquire into their origins. "Until people realized that all the riots and demonstrations were not the product of conspiracy," he wrote later, "there was little hope of persuading them to focus on fundamental causes—on poverty, discrimination, inadequate schooling, substandard housing, slums and unemployment."[114] But Johnson initially suspected that a large conspiracy did lie behind the race riots as well as the growing antiwar movement, even if he was not greatly impressed by Hoover's continued warnings of Communist influences on Martin Luther King. "There must be a way to predict violence," Johnson believed. "We've got to know more about this." Attorney General Ramsey Clark instructed Hoover to "use the maximum resources" to discover whether there was "a scheme or conspiracy by any group" behind the riots. At Clark's request, the FBI launched a "ghetto informant program" that recruited 4,067 informants over the next two years to provide intelligence on the "racial situation" and "racial activities." Helms started Operation Chaos to examine the extent of foreign influences on domestic dissent. "President Johnson was after this all the time," he later testified; he and his staff returned to it "almost daily." Chaos, Helms recalled, simply happened to be the next code word on the CIA list. "But when it later became public, it made it sound all the worse."[115]

Johnson, meanwhile, struggled to remain optimistic about the outcome of the Vietnam War. At a meeting with the press on August 24 he insisted that MACV reports showed that "the guerrilla infra-structure is on the verge of collapse. All I can say . . . is that if there is a stalemate, as the press reports, then every single one of our men we have out there is wrong."[116] Five days later, however, Helms sent the president an intelligence report suggesting that Rolling Thunder, despite the enormous damage it had inflicted, was indeed approaching stalemate:

> The intensified air war against North Vietnam has shown increased effectiveness in several ways: (1) the cost of bomb damage in the past four months almost equals the total damage inflicted in 1966; (2) most of modern industry is now at a standstill, thus neutralizing a decade of economic growth. . . . At the same time, however, Hanoi continues to meet the needs of the Communists in South Vietnam and essential military and economic traffic continues to move.[117]

Ellsworth Bunker, who had succeeded Henry Cabot Lodge as ambassador in Saigon earlier in the year, disputed the agency view. He complained to the White House that, if CIA battle-order figures became public, "the credibility gap would be enormous." They were, he claimed, "quite inconsistent with all the hard evidence we have about growing enemy losses, declining VC recruitments and the like."[118]

George Carver's deputy, George W. Allen, believed that Helms "was not comfortable . . . disagreeing with the military on a matter in which presumably the military should have expertise."[119] Early in September the DCI dispatched a CIA team, headed by Carver, to Saigon to try to resolve the differences with the MACV and agree on battle-order figures for a Special National Intelligence Estimate (SNIE). Carver cabled Helms on September 12 that he had reached "the inescapable conclusion that General Westmoreland . . . has given instruction tantamount to a direct order that VC strength total will not exceed 300,000 ceiling. Rationale seems to be that any higher figure would not be sufficiently optimistic and would generate unacceptable level of criticism from the press." Helms told Carver to reach a compromise based on the omission from the battle-order statistics of the part-time guerrillas, which the DDI believed were not comparable with the regular forces; the guerrillas were to be discussed separately in the SNIE. Westmoreland agreed to the compromise. Carver cabled Helms, "Circle now squared."[120]

Though it made sense not to lump together full-time regulars and part-time guerrillas in a single statistic, it is difficult not to conclude that the September compromise leaned too far in the direction of the MACV. SNIE 14.3-67, eventually issued in November, accepted that "in many [previous] instances our numerical estimates of Communist forces, other than for regular forces, were too low," but reached a relatively optimistic conclusion.[121] "It comes to this," Walt Rostow told the president:

—manpower is the major problem confronting the Communists;
—there has been a substantial reduction in guerrillas since an
   estimated peak in early 1966;
—there has been a slight reduction in main force units in the
   past year, but this has been possible only by using more
   North Vietnamese replacements in Viet Cong units;
—there is a "fairly good chance" that the Communist military
   strength and political infrastructure will continue to decline;
—Communist strategy is to sustain a protracted war of attrition
   and to persuade the United States that it must pull out or
   settle on Hanoi's terms. Their judgment is that the "Communists still retain adequate capabilities to support this strategy for at least another year."[122]

George Allen privately denounced SNIE 14.3-67 as "the mistake of the century." He told Sam Adams that, in accepting this compromise with the MACV, the CIA "had sacrificed its integrity on the altar of public expediency." Adams was angrier still. He eventually concluded that there had been a conspiracy within MACV to deceive the president about enemy strength in Vietnam in order to persuade him to continue the war—a conclusion later embodied in a CBS documentary. Whatever the failings of the SNIE, however, there had been no conspiracy. Johnson was well aware of the battle-order controversy in the intelligence community and was briefed on it by Helms. According to Rostow, he also studied some of the intelligence at the heart of the dispute: "President Johnson received directly and read voraciously the captured documents . . . as well as reports of CIA, State Department and DIA officers in the provinces; prisoner-of-war interrogations; intercepts; and all manner of basic information. . . . "[123]

The November SNIE did little to keep up morale in the White House. Johnson, who longed to be loved by the American people, was assailed everywhere he went by protesters chanting, "Hey, hey, LBJ, how many kids did you kill today?" On October 21 fifty thousand antiwar protesters, led by Norman Mailer, marched on the Pentagon in an unsuccessful attempt to close it down. McNamara watched from his office window. "Girls were rubbing their naked breasts in the soldiers' faces," he told an interviewer later. "They're spitting on them; they're taunting them. God, it was a mess!"[124] The march on the Pentagon, coinciding with international antiwar demonstrations on the same day, strengthened Johnson's suspicions of a Communist plot. Helms ordered an urgent report on "International Connections of the U.S. Peace Movement" to present to the president.[125] The main conclusions of the report, completed on November 15, based on NSA and FBI as well as CIA files, were relatively reassuring:

> The coordinators of the peace movement—personalities such as [David] Dellinger, [Tom] Hayden, [Rev. James] Bevel and [Nick] Egleson—are tireless, peripatetic, full time crusaders. . . . *Many have close Communist associations but they do not appear to be under Communist direction.* . . . Apart from contacts with the Hanoi officialdom, U.S. peace activists by and large do not deal with foreign governments. Their relations are with foreign, private institutions such as the Bertrand Russell Peace Foundation and other international peace federations. *Moscow exploits and may indeed influence the U.S. delegates to these bodies through its front organizations, but the indications—at least at this stage—of covert or overt connections between these U.S. activists and foreign governments are limited.*

But Helms added that further investigation was required, for example on the funding of the antiwar movement.[126]

The first of Johnson's inner circle of advisers to lose faith in his Vietnamese policy was McNamara. For months the secretary of defense had struggled to reconcile loyalty to the president with deepening despair about the war. At the Tuesday Lunch on October 31 McNamara revealed the full extent of his pessimism for the first time. The next day he delivered personally to the president a memorandum that, he warned him, contained views that "may be incompatible with your own." He had come to the private conclusion that "continuation of our present course of action in Southeast Asia would be dangerous, costly in lives, and unsatisfactory to the American people."[127] Later in November, without telling McNamara in advance, Johnson nominated him as president of the World Bank. "I never knew whether I resigned or I was fired," McNamara told Helms.[128] He stayed on as secretary of defense until his successor, Clark Clifford, was sworn in on March 1.

The year ended with conflicting intelligence assessments. The CIA was adamant that the air war was not achieving its primary objective. On December 13 Johnson received an agency analysis that concluded:

Despite the achievements of the bombing program, . . . no significant deterioration in North Vietnam's military capabilities or its determination to persist in the war can be detected. The flow of men and supplies to the South has been maintained; and the cost of damage has been more than compensated by deliveries of foreign aid.

The Pacific Command year-end review, by contrast, was determinedly optimistic:

The enemy did not win a single battle in Vietnam in 1967. . . . The combination of military operations in South Vietnam, North Vietnam and Laos during 1967 produced a definite shift in the military situation favorable to the U.S. As a result the enemy is no longer capable of a military victory in the South.

Rolling Thunder, claimed CINCPAC, had the capacity to bring about the collapse of the North during 1968.[129] At the beginning of 1968 Clark Clifford, chairman of PFI AB and (from January 18) defense secretary-elect, concluded that "the mood dominating Washington" was "a sense that events were moving in the right direction, and that the Communists were on the defensive."[130]

On January 11 Rostow gave the president a CIA report of an emerging threat to the marine base at Khe Sanh, a mountain plateau position in the northwest corner of South Vietnam. The battle began in the early hours of January 21 with rocket and mortar fire from the encircling

North Vietnamese. For the first time in the war American troops were besieged by larger enemy forces. Two days later Johnson told the Democratic leadership that "intelligence reports show a great similarity between what is happening at Khe Sanh and what happened at Dien Bien Phu," the lengthy siege in 1954 that had culminated in a French defeat and the end of the French empire in Indochina. Johnson became obsessed with the analogy.[131] On Helms's instructions, NPIC constructed a large relief model of the Khe Sanh area, based on photographs taken by SR-71s flying at eighty thousand feet. Placed in the White House situation room, the model became known as "the president's sandbox." Johnson was fascinated by it. Several times a day he would visit the situation room to study the latest positions of enemy troops around Khe Sanh plotted on the sandbox. "Those sons of bitches can't get through there," he told his advisers.[132]

At the Tuesday Lunch on January 23 there was general agreement that the siege of Khe Sanh was about to become the biggest battle of the war. But there was news also of another in the series of incidents involving SIGINT-collection vessels that punctuated the Johnson presidency. The USS *Pueblo* and its crew had been seized in international waters off North Korea—the first U.S. naval vessel captured since the Napoleonic Wars. Two days earlier a North Korean assassination squad had come within two hundred yards of the presidential palace in Seoul. The president and his advisers feared that the two incidents might signal preparations for another North Korean invasion of the South, encouraged by the belief that the United States was tied down in Vietnam and unable to respond. As sometimes happened, Johnson began to develop extravagant conspiracy theories. At first he was convinced that he was facing an international Communist plot, involving the Soviet Union as well as North Vietnam and North Korea, aimed at stretching American resources to the breaking point. The next blow, he warned his advisers, would fall in Berlin. In fact, the brutal regime of the North Korean dictator Kim Il Sung had acted on its own initiative in seizing the *Pueblo* and imprisoning its crew. To the fury of NSA, which had warned about the need to protect it from North Korean attack, state-of-the-art SIGINT equipment had fallen into enemy hands. It was agreed, after an inquiry, that such risks must never be taken again. The unarmed SIGINT-collection fleet was decommissioned and its tasks reassigned to destroyers, other ships capable of defending themselves, and aircraft.[133]

The Tuesday Lunch on January 30 began with a discussion of Khe Sanh. In the middle of the meeting Rostow was called out of the room. He returned a few minutes later with a dramatic announcement: "We have just received a flash message from the National Military Command

Center. We are being heavily mortared in Saigon. The Presidential Palace, our military installations, the American Embassy, and other parts of the city have been hit." "The answer to these mortar attacks," said McNamara, "is success at Khe Sanh. We are inflicting very heavy casualties on the enemy. . . ."[134] Neither Johnson nor his advisers had grasped that the attack on Khe Sanh was part of a North Vietnamese deception strategy designed to divert their attention from preparations for a much larger offensive that was to begin the next day on the Tet (New Year) holiday.[135] In any case, as Rusk later admitted, "We didn't think the enemy would launch an offensive in the middle of the Tet holidays, any more than we would have expected Americans to launch a major offensive on Christmas Day."[136]

In the early hours of January 31 over eighty thousand North Vietnamese and guerrilla forces attacked more than a hundred cities in the South in an offensive that continued until February 24. Johnson later claimed in his memoirs that he had seen the Tet offensive coming since the previous autumn, a statement that reflects the self-delusion that clouded his later attempts to come to terms with the failure of his Vietnam policy. At the very last minute before the offensive, Westmoreland began to cancel leave and put his troops on the alert. But the scale and scope of the offensive that followed took both him and the whole Johnson administration by surprise. For the next two weeks Johnson and Westmoreland continued to believe that Khe Sanh remained the chief objective of the North Vietnamese offensive and that the Tet offensive was a diversion—thus neatly reversing the real strategy of the enemy commander in chief, General Vo Nguyen Giap. By orthodox American military criteria, the Tet offensive was a failure. The North Vietnamese and Viet Cong failed to hold any of the major southern cities, except Hue, for more than a few days. The offensive cost them about fifty-eight thousand men—the majority irregulars rather than regular troops. But, in a broader sense, Giap won—though at a terrible cost—a major victory. He destroyed the credibility of the Johnson administration's claim that it was winning a war of attrition, and thus fatally undermined its ability to continue it.[137]

"The first thing to understand about General Giap's Tet offensive," concludes a textbook used in West Point after the Vietnam War, "is that it was an allied intelligence failure to rank with Pearl Harbor. . . ." This was also the view of Clark Clifford after he had studied the intelligence reports that preceded the offensive.[138] Roberta Wohlstetter's celebrated analysis of the problems of distinguishing the key intelligence "signals" from the mass of distracting background "noise" fits Tet better than Pearl Harbor. In December 1941 the crucial signals were missing; in January 1968 they were present but mostly overlooked or misinterpreted. There was, however, one notable exception to the intelligence failure that preceded Tet. In late November 1967 Joseph Hovey, an analyst at the CIA Saigon station, correctly predicted, largely on the basis of captured documents, an attempt early in the New Year by the Viet Cong and North Vietnamese "to launch the long-promised 'general uprising.' To accomplish this, the VC/NVN have set themselves the task of occupying and holding some urban centers in South Vietnam and isolating many others. . . ." Hovey accepted that his interpretation meant that the enemy had "committed themselves to unobtainable ends in a very specific and short period of time," but correctly emphasized their overoptimistic assessment of their own position. He was also right to point to the possible advantages for the Communists even of an offensive that could not achieve its full objectives. These included:

> A serious effort to inflict unacceptable military and political losses on the Allies regardless of VC casualties during a U.S. election year, in the hopes that the U.S. will be forced to yield to resulting national and international political pressure and withdraw from South Vietnam.

The Directorate of Intelligence at Langley praised Hovey's memorandum as a "useful and provocative analysis," but disagreed with its main conclusions. There was, it said, important intelligence that was unavailable to Hovey.[139] This was probably SIGINT, for which less than 5 percent of the CIA Saigon station were cleared.[140] SIGINT, however, gave a distorted impression of enemy movements. It provided good intelligence on the regular forces preparing the assault on Khe Sanh, but not much on the guerrillas surrounding and infiltrating southern cities, who generated little radio traffic. Reports in captured documents and prisoner interrogation reports of a Viet Cong offensive against the cities did not seem to square with the usually more reliable, but on this occasion misleading, SIGINT evidence.[141]

The main reason, however, that Hovey's analysis was rejected by both the agency and the White House was that it did not fit their preconceptions about enemy strategy. Since they were convinced that a general offensive against southern cities could not succeed, they did not believe that the North Vietnamese would attempt it. The attack on Khe Sanh, by contrast, seemed to make better sense. Johnson was haunted by the fear that it would become what he was apt to call his "Dinbinphoo." Once the siege of Khe Sanh began, both he and Westmoreland interpreted last-minute intelligence on preparations for the Tet offensive as diversionary operations to distract attention from Giap's main target.[142] Underlying the Tet intelligence failure was, once again, a failure to understand North Vietnam. Neither Johnson nor his advisers grasped the terrifying level of casualties that Hanoi was willing to accept. Ho Chi Minh had warned the French in 1946 that the Vietnamese were prepared to suffer ten casualties for every one they inflicted on the imperialists. Twenty years later he was willing to make similar sacrifices against the Americans.[143]

At the end of February 1968 the chairman of the JCS, General Wheeler, returned from a three-day visit to Vietnam in a somber mood. "Pacification is at a halt," he told the president over breakfast at the White House. "The Viet Cong can roam at will in the countryside." Westmoreland, he announced, needed 205,000 additional troops in three phases. That demand began the first fundamental debate over the course of the war among the president and his advisers since the decision to start the air war and commit large numbers of American ground forces in 1965.[144] As part of the debate, the CIA reopened the controversy over enemy order of battle. The MACV figures, which had suggested that the enemy no longer had the capacity to mount a major offensive, seemed discredited even in the eyes of some of the intelligence analysts who had produced them. On March 2 Commander James Meacham of the MACV OB unit wrote bitterly to his wife:

> Tomorrow will be a sort of day of truth. We shall see if I can make the computer sort out the losses since the Tet Offensive began in such a manner as to prove that we are winning the war. If I can't, we shall of course jack the figures around until we *do* show progress. Every month we make progress here.

Meacham added the next day:

> . . . The computer screwed up the whole business and we had to start over. Anyhow about 5:30 we finally got things settled. We *are* winning the war, and now I can prove it, having received sufficient and adequate guidance from my leaders.[145]

The CIA argued that Tet demonstrated that guerrillas played a more important role in the war than the MACV had previously recognized. While it accepted that part-time irregulars did not have the same military significance as regular soldiers, the Directorate of Intelligence contended that traditional order-of-battle calculations failed to reflect the reality of the Vietnam conflict. The most realistic way of judging enemy strength, it argued, was to estimate the total "Communist organized manpower base," including both regular forces and all forms of irregulars. On the eve of the Tet offensive, it believed, this "organized manpower base" had numbered 515,000 to 600,000 men. Though changing the terminology, the CIA had thus come close to adopting Adams's calculations of the previous year. It was also pessimistic about the future. Heavy though enemy losses had been, the agency thought it "entirely possible . . . that within six months their troop strength would be substantially greater than it was prior to Tet":

> There is little question that the Tet offensive has opened a new recruitment base to the Viet Cong in the South Vietnamese countryside. . . . The new pool, consisting of the population of hamlets where the VC formerly have had little or no influence, can be expected to boost 1968 recruitment greatly.[146]

After taking over as defense secretary on March 1 Clark Clifford spent his first few days in office chairing a task force appointed by the president to consider the request for a further 205,000 American troops. The CIA estimate of enemy strength was probably in his mind when he asked military witnesses whether the additional troops would be sufficient. "Nothing," Clifford later recalled, "had prepared me for the weakness of the military's case"; they seemed to have no idea whether 205,000 would be sufficient and no "plan for victory in the historic American sense." On March 4 Clifford reported to the president, "I see more and more fighting on the U.S. side, and no end in sight."[147]

Johnson struggled to remain optimistic. Some of his advisers—Rusk and Rostow, in particular—still urged him to "hang in there."[148] Over the next fortnight, however, the damage done to his chances of reelection by the Tet offensive and the demand for massive reinforcements in Vietnam (leaked to the press on March 10) became obvious. On March 12 he only narrowly won the New Hampshire primary. Four days later Robert Kennedy announced that he was challenging Johnson for the Democratic presidential nomination. On March 17, in one of the toughest speeches of his presidency, Johnson called for "a total national effort to win the war." "My God," thought Clifford, "after only eighteen days in office, am I in such fundamental disagreement with the man who appointed me?" At the Tuesday Lunch on March 19 Clifford proposed that the president convene a senior group of advisers known in Washington as the "Wise Men," sometimes referred to by Johnson as "the bastards from out of town." The shift in their views as a result of the Tet offensive would, hoped Clifford, convince the president of the need for deescalation.[149]

On the evening of March 25 the Wise Men were secretly briefed by Major General William E. DePuy, Philip C. Habib of the State Department, and George Carver of the CIA. Carver argued that in the long term the Tet offensive might prove to have weakened, rather than strengthened, the North Vietnamese offensive. Its tactical success, however, showed that the enemy "had to have more strength than we'd credited them with." The Wise Men, Carver recalls, "showed not much disposition to take the longer view." They fastened instead on what he said about enemy strength.[150] When the Wise Men met the president the next day Dean Acheson, the doyen of the group, whom Johnson had previously regarded as a hawk, told him bluntly, ". . . We must begin to take steps to disengage." To Johnson's surprise, most of the Wise Men agreed with Acheson. "The Establishment bastards have betrayed us," the president muttered as they filed out of the cabinet room. When they were gone, he turned angrily to Clifford and Rusk. "Who poisoned the well with these guys?" he demanded. "I want to hear those briefings myself."[151]

On March 27 DePuy and Carver were summoned to the White House to brief Johnson and a small group of his advisers in the cabinet room.[152] Their briefings had probably not been decisive in shifting a majority of the Wise Men in favor of disengagement, but Carver in particular made a deep impression on the president. Carver recalls that he spoke for about an hour and a quarter, frequently interrupted by Johnson, who repeatedly demanded, "Have you finished?":

I figured "in for a penny, in for a pound," and I kept saying, "Well, no, Mr. President, as a matter of fact I haven't." The more I talked, the less he liked what I said. I kept thinking he was going to pitch me into the Rose Garden without necessarily going through the formality of opening the glass doors before he did so.

As Carver argued that "some of our more roseate estimates of progress and some of the statistical indices thereof were clearly not relating to the real world," he saw the president "getting darker and darker of visage" and "various courtiers turning white because you didn't talk to him like that." "You can't tell the people in Keokuk, Iowa, you want to get out," Carver insisted, "and also tell the North Vietnamese you're going to stick it out for two decades, and make them believe you." As the briefing finished, Johnson rose to his feet, his manner reminding Carver of "an erupting volcano," and stormed out of the room. Carver's immediate reaction was to tell himself, "There's a nice, promising career shot to hell." Helms and Vice-President Hubert H. Humphrey, however, came up to congratulate him on standing his ground:

All of a sudden I sensed a sort of looming presence behind me, and it was LBJ who had stalked back into the room. He slapped me on the shoulder, practically driving me down into the basement, pumped my hand with his paw, almost wrenching my arm out of its socket, and thanked me profusely for my alleged services to the Republic and the Presidency. He said anytime I wanted to talk to him, "Just pick up the phone and call." Then he walked out of the room.[153]

Carver's was probably the longest briefing the president ever received from a CIA official. If it was not the final straw that broke the back of Johnson's Vietnam policy, it was at least one of the final straws. Four days later, on March 31, Johnson went on television to announce a partial suspension of the bombing campaign against North Vietnam: "So, tonight, in the hope that this action will lead to early talks, I am taking the first step to de-escalate the conflict. We are reducing—substantially reducing—the present level of hostilities. And we are doing so unilaterally and at once." Then came an even bigger bombshell:

With America's sons in the fields far away, with America's future under challenge right here at home, with our hopes and the world's hopes for peace in the balance every day, I do not believe that I should devote an hour or a day of my time to any personal partisan causes or to any duties other than the awesome duties of this office—the Presidency of your country. Accordingly, I shall not seek, and I will not accept, the nomination of my party for another term as your President.[154]

"The President's speech of March 31," Humphrey wrote to Carver, "indicated that your briefings had a profound effect on the course of U.S. policy to Vietnam."[155] On April 3 Hanoi announced that it was willing to begin talks.

The initiative in the Washington war of words and paper over the size of enemy forces now passed to Helms. Immediately after Carver's briefing at the White House on March 27 Johnson gave Helms "the task of resolving differences on strength figures." MACV and CINCPAC were ordered to send representatives to Langley to confer with CIA and DIA analysts. Mutual recriminations quickly followed. On April 22 General Wheeler sent formal protests to both Helms and Clifford. Helms replied by accusing Wheeler of "a basic misunderstanding of what we have been trying to accomplish. . . . To my mind MACV's characterization of the basic problems involved in arriving at agreed strength figures—as cited in your memorandum to the Secretary of Defense—is not an accurate representation."[156] The whip hand was now clearly with the DCI. With the change in Johnson's Vietnam policy, MACV's ability to press its own calculations on the CIA had drastically declined. A memo to Helms from the DDI on May 1 spelled out the differences between MACV, DIA, and CINCPAC on the one hand, and the agency on the other. There remained, as before, little argument over the size of North Vietnamese regular forces. But, in the aftermath of the Tet offensive, CIA analysts were no longer prepared to exclude irregulars from overall totals:

> The military [intelligence] services would prefer to include only those elements listed under combat forces—225-260,000—as representing enemy strengths. We agree that this number represents the prime combat threat but prefer to use the total insurgency base of 450-600,000 as the best estimate of enemy strengths. We feel most strongly that the total figure is the one that most accurately describes the enemy forces that are the main target and concern of those charged with the military and political resolution of the Vietnam problem.[157]

Helms accepted, however, that publication of the CIA estimates would widen still further the Johnson administration's "credibility gap." He wrote to Wheeler:

> I share your concern as to the effect a "public announcement" of the figures we are developing would have. . . . I would be happy to join with you in placing the tightest possible restrictions on the dissemination of these figures. . . .[158]

After Johnson's dramatic speech of March 31 his advisers split into two groups. Rusk, Rostow, and the military continued to believe that the war could be won. The other group, led by Clifford, pinned all their hopes on a negotiated peace. At the Tuesday Lunches Clifford justified his position by quoting from pessimistic CIA assessments. When Rusk urged an expansion of the bombing on May 21, Clifford replied: ". . . I don't think we can win the war by military means. . . . The CIA says [the enemy] are not running out of manpower. They can continue at their present rate indefinitely. The Soviets and the Chinese will continue to help them." Anxious for a consensus among his advisers, Johnson found it difficult to deal with the conflict between them. Clifford believed that he was "torn between a search for an honorable exit and his desire not to be the first President to lose a foreign war."[159]

Johnson's understanding of the domestic opposition to his Vietnamese policy continued to be distorted by his belief that an international Communist conspiracy lay behind the antiwar movement. According to Helms, ". . . The only manner in which the CIA could support its conclusion that there was no significant foreign influence on the domestic dissent, in the face of incredulity from the White House, was to continually expand the coverage of [Operation] CHAOS." In August 1968 a number of CIA stations abroad were informed that Chaos was a "high-priority program" and instructed to investigate foreign "contacts" with what was described as the "Radical Left": "radical students, antiwar activists, draft resisters and deserters, black nationalists, anarchists, and assorted 'New Leftists.' "[160]

Throughout the summer of 1968 the Vietnam War seemed locked in military and diplomatic stalemate. While the killing continued, the talks about talks failed to progress to serious peace negotiations. "The break in the stalemate," Johnson recalled, "came during the second week in October." At a secret meeting with American negotiators at a CIA safe house in Paris, the North Vietnamese asked whether, in return for their agreement to include the South Vietnamese government in the peace talks, the United States would call a complete halt to the bombing. After two more weeks of haggling, the bargain was agreed. On October 31, five days before the presidential election, Johnson announced on television that the bombing of North Vietnam would stop on the following day and peace talks would open in Paris on November 6, the day after the American presidential election. President Nguyen Van Thieu of South Vietnam, however, at first declined to send a delegate. Johnson hints darkly in his memoirs that Thieu's attitude "had at least as much to do with American domestic politics as with Saigon politics." Had the peace talks opened on November 2 with the South Vietnamese present, as originally agreed between Washington and Hanoi, the Democratic presidential candidate, Vice-President Hubert Humphrey, would undoubtedly have benefited at the polls. The favored candidate of Thieu and his colleagues, however, was Humphrey's Republican opponent, Richard Nixon. "I had reason to believe," wrote Johnson in his memoirs, "that they had been urged to delay going to the Paris meetings and promised that they would get a better deal from a Nixon administration."[161]

Though Johnson could not mention it in his memoirs, he had made what Clifford later called the "potentially explosive . . . discovery through intelligence channels, of a plot—there is no other word for it—to help Nixon win the election by a flagrant interference in the negotiations." The main intermediaries between Nixon's entourage and Thieu were Bui Diem, the South Vietnamese ambassador in Washington, and

Anna Chennault, the Chinese-born head of Concerned Asians for Nixon and the widow of General Claire Chennault, commander of the celebrated Flying Tigers in China and Burma during the Second World War. There is little doubt that during the final stages of the campaign Anna Chennault passed on a "very important" message from the Nixon camp that was intended to dissuade Thieu from agreeing to attend the Paris peace talks until after the election. According to Clifford, "President Johnson, although furious at Mrs. Chennault, decided not to use the information or make it public in any way." He was deterred in part by a desire not to compromise the highly sensitive intelligence he received from at least three different sources. NSA regularly decrypted diplomatic traffic between the South Vietnamese government and its Washington embassy; the FBI mounted surveillance operations against both Bui Diem and Mrs. Chennault; the CIA provided reports from Thieu's office in Saigon. When Johnson made a conference call to the presidential candidates shortly before his televised address on October 31, he made a remark intended to warn Nixon that he knew what was going on:

> Some old China hands are going round and implying to some of the Embassies and some others that they might get a better deal out of somebody that was not involved in this. Now that's made it difficult and it's held things up a bit, and I know that none of you candidates are aware of it or responsible for it. . . .

Two days before Election Day Johnson told the Republican senator Everett Dirksen that he was fully informed about Anna Chennault's activities. Dirksen warned Nixon that Johnson might be about to go public with the information. Nixon immediately telephoned the president and sought to placate him by insisting that he had nothing to do with Mrs. Chennault's schemes.[162]

On Tuesday, November 5, Richard Nixon was elected president by a plurality of less than half a million votes. Clifford's first reaction was, "We could have won!" If word of the Nixon camp's dealings with Saigon had become public during the final stages of the campaign, Humphrey might well have been elected. Clifford believed, probably correctly, that Johnson made no use of the damning intelligence about the Nixon campaign available to him because, in the last resort, he did not want Humphrey to win badly enough. What mattered most to Lyndon Johnson as his presidency drew to a close was not who was to succeed him but his own place in history.[163]

CHAPTER 9

Richard M. Nixon
(1969-1974)

Richard Nixon entered the White House in January 1969 with a better grasp of international affairs than any previous president of the United States. As congressman and vice-president, he had traveled to over eighty countries and held discussions with many world leaders. As president, Nixon demonstrated a flair for foreign policy still evident twenty years after his resignation. But he also possessed a conspiratorial mindset and a tendency, like many conspirators, to form conspiracy theories about his political opponents: both highly undesirable qualities in an intelligence consumer.

At Nixon's first meeting after his election victory with his future national security adviser, Henry Kissinger, he denounced the CIA as a group of "Ivy League liberals" who "had always opposed him politically." Asked to comment on this mildly paranoid view of the agency, Kissinger was prudently, if uncharacteristically, noncommittal, claiming to know "too little about the CIA to have an opinion."[1] Besides his generalized suspicions of Langley "liberals," Nixon clung to the absurd conspiracy theory that the agency had conspired to make him lose the 1960 presidential election to Kennedy. He was convinced that the CIA had secretly given information intended to undermine the Republican program to Senator Stuart Symington, whom Kennedy had made head of a special committee on the defense establishment during the election campaign. According to Richard Helms, "He believed Allen Dulles had fed Stuart Symington with information on the missile gap—why I never understood, but I want to tell you it lingered."[2] Nixon, writes the DDI, Jack Smith, "never forgot or forgave" the CIA for his defeat by Kennedy.[3] Ironically, in one of his first public addresses as president, he was forced to pay an insincere tribute to Allen Dulles, the man he held chiefly responsible for the agency "conspiracy" against him in 1960. After Dulles's death on January 29, 1969, Nixon solemnly eulogized his "unstinting devotion to duty." "Because of him," he declared, "the world is a safer place today."[4]

Nixon was also suspicious, though to a less remarkable degree, of what he sneeringly called "the little boys in the State Department." The position of national security adviser, he told Kissinger, would be of crucial importance because he planned to run foreign policy from the White House. The new secretary of state, William Rogers, Nixon believed, would "brook no nonsense" from "the little boys," and had the additional advantage of unfamiliarity with international relations, thus ensuring that "policy direction would remain in the White House." As Kissinger dryly observes, "Few Secretaries of State can have been selected because of their President's confidence in their ignorance of foreign policy."[5] Together Nixon and Kissinger transformed the role of the national security adviser.

The Nixon-Kissinger combination was arguably the most talented ever to run American foreign and security policy. Withdrawal from Vietnam, opening the door to Communist China, and the first arms control agreement of the Cold War with the Soviet Union owed much to both of them, and to Nixon in particular. Though Helms increasingly distrusted the president personally, he had no doubt that "Nixon was the architect and Kissinger the construction manager" of American foreign policy.[6] Stephen Ambrose's monumental biography of Nixon concludes, even with a hindsight influenced by the disgrace of Watergate, "When Nixon resigned, we lost more than we gained."[7] The intelligence community, however, gained more than it lost. Kissinger, like Nixon, was a born conspirator. ". . . Intrigue," noted William Safire, one of Nixon's speechwriters, "was second nature to him, an exercise he went through without thinking."[8] Such men do not handle intelligence communities wisely. They lack a sense of proportion in their grasp of the relationship between the secret and nonsecret worlds. Nixon and Kissinger, writes Ambrose, "shared a love of eavesdropping on others (the taps and the tapes), of secrecy, of surprises, of conspiracy, of backbiting, of powerplays. . . . They spent enormous amounts of time together, three or four meetings nearly every day, interspersed with innumerable phone calls. They spent more time together than was good for them."[9] It was Kissinger rather than the DCI who became the president's main intelligence adviser. "Kissinger," says William Colby, who became DCI in 1973, "loved as much intelligence as he could get, but didn't necessarily believe it. 'Bill,' he would tell me, 'give me things that make me think!' "[10]

A senior CIA analyst recalls that ". . . Nixon seemed more interested in the CIA for covert action than for intelligence analysis. Why not? Covert action was an extension of administration policy, while analysis often showed policy to be unwise."[11] As vice-president in 1960 Nixon had been one of the most enthusiastic advocates of using the CIA to overthrow Castro. A decade later, according to Kissinger, Cuba still remained "a neuralgic problem for Nixon." His closest friend, Bebe Rebozo, had a visceral hatred of Castro and close links with the Cuban expatriates in Miami who continued to plot his overthrow.[12] One of Nixon's first acts as president was to order the agency to step up its covert operations against Castro just as they were being wound down.[13] As Kissinger acknowledges, they were a "time-wasting" exercise: "Harassment of Castro had been tried and failed. . . ."[14] Covert action continued to do some damage to the Cuban economy, but far less than either the official embargo on trade with Cuba or Castro's own economic mismanagement.

Both Nixon and Kissinger were naturally drawn to secret back channels as a way of conducting business. Nixon's back channel to Moscow was vastly superior to those established earlier by Harry Hopkins and Robert Kennedy, not least because it ran through the Soviet ambassador, Anatoli Dobrynin, rather than through a Soviet intelligence officer like Akhmerov and Bolshakov. Less than a month after taking office, Nixon told Dobrynin that "matters of special sensitivity" should be handled privately between Kissinger and himself, bypassing Rogers and the State Department. Usually meeting in the White House map room, writes Kissinger, "Dobrynin and I began to conduct negotiations on almost all major issues, he on behalf of the Politburo, I as confidant of Nixon." This was only one, though probably the most important, of a series of back channels to foreign statesmen and U.S. representatives abroad that were intended to circumvent the intelligence community as well as the State Department. Kissinger acknowledges that these "extraordinary procedures" were "demoralizing for the bureaucracy" and "unlikely to be recommended in textbooks on public administration."[15] Colby recalls that agency analysts frequently complained, "How can we do our job if we don't know what's going on?"[16]

The habit of changing the DCI at the beginning of a new administration had not yet taken root when Nixon became president. Kissinger, who was impressed by Helms's professionalism, persuaded Nixon to keep him on. The president, however, felt ill at ease with Helms, whom he suspected of links with "the liberal Georgetown social set." To "keep track" of Helms, Nixon appointed one of his former military aides, Lieutenant General Robert E. Cushman, as deputy DCI. According to John Ehrlichman, the president's assistant and White House special counsel,

Cushman was intended to be (though he did not become) "Nixon's man over there at the Agency." In a further attempt to undermine Helms's position, Nixon at first proposed to exclude him from NSC meetings.[17] On being persuaded that it would be impracticable to keep the DCI away, Nixon set out to put him firmly in his place. Helms began one of the first NSC meetings of the new administration by listing the states that had recognized the breakaway of Biafra during the Nigerian Civil War. Nixon stopped him. "Look, Dick," he said, "you've left out a couple of countries—Zambia and the Ivory Coast." Helms went on to discuss the ethnic rivalries associated with the Biafra problem. Nixon interrupted him again to display his own impressive grasp of the complexities of Nigerian tribal rivalries.[18] Allied to Nixon's remarkable command of world affairs was what some of those present at NSC meetings considered spitefulness toward the DCI.[19] Helms says the president's comments were "not personal."[20] It seems more likely that they sometimes were, but that Helms simply ignored the personal element in Nixon's jibes. Kissinger grew to admire the DCI's "unflappability" as well as his professionalism: "He never volunteered policy advice beyond the questions that were asked him, though never hesitating to warn the White House of dangers even when his views ran counter to the preconceptions of the President or his security adviser."[21]

The CIA quickly discovered that Nixon was paying little or no attention to the president's daily brief. John Mitchell, the attorney general, told Jack Smith, the DDI, "The President is a lawyer. He likes to have the facts first and then the opinion." Henceforth all daily brief items during the Nixon presidency were divided into two sections: fact and comment. "My impression," writes Smith, "is that it accomplished nothing and that Nixon continued to ignore our publication while relying on a daily compilation from Kissinger's staff."[22] The compilation consisted of a three-page intelligence summary prepared every evening by Kissinger's assistant, Colonel Alexander M. Haig Jr. Each morning Haig arrived at his office in the Executive Office Building at 6 A.M., sifted through overnight intelligence reports, added anything of importance to the previous night's summary, and took the revised version to Kissinger. As Haig acknowledges, Kissinger was highly critical of the linguistic contortions of what was later dubbed "Haigspeak," then known by the generic term "Pentagonese": ". . . He would slash it, rewrite it, and redictate it in my presence, crying out as he went along against what he deemed grammatical errors and solecisms." Kissinger took the final product to Nixon himself, waiting while the president read it to see if he had any questions or wanted further information.[23]

The CIA Directorate of Intelligence (DI) believed that Nixon paid little attention to its estimates—giving them less weight, according to Smith, than the opinions of a junior analyst on Kissinger's staff.[24] Kissinger and his staff consumed vast quantities of CIA reports and assessments. What grated most on the DI was their ability to second-guess or modify agency estimates and prevent the CIA's own view from reaching Nixon's desk. Under Truman, Eisenhower, and Kennedy, the DCI had regular, direct access to the president. Even Johnson, despite his disdain for McCone, made Helms a member of the inner circle at the Tuesday Lunch. Nixon, however, kept Helms at arm's length. It was Kissinger, not the president, who maintained regular contact with the DCI.

Nixon frequently gave the DI the impression that he believed its job was to provide detailed intelligence to support conclusions he had already reached. On January 23, 1969, he ordered the NSC to undertake a global study of student revolt. The next day, after television reports of student demonstrations from Paris to Tokyo, he instructed: "I want to have a CIA analysis in depth of communist factors in youth disturbance."[25] Like Johnson, he was convinced that "communist factors" were of great importance, and skeptical of any intelligence estimate that reached a different conclusion. Faced with the incredulity of the president, the only way that the CIA could justify its contention that domestic dissent was not part of an international Communist plot was by continually expanding the scope of Operation Chaos, begun in 1967.[26] "Only by being able to demonstrate that it had investigated *all* anti-war persons and *all* contacts between them and any foreign person could CIA 'prove the negative' that none were under foreign domination." The agency thus became drawn into the dangerous and illegal ground of domestic intelligence collection. On February 18 Helms wrote to Kissinger:

> Herewith is a survey of student dissidence worldwide as requested by the President. In an effort to round out our discussion of this subject, we have included a section on American students. This is an area not within the charter of this Agency, so I need not emphasize how extremely sensitive this makes the paper. Should anyone learn of its existence, it would prove most embarrassing for all concerned.[27]

The agency's failure to discover a vast Communist conspiracy behind campus revolt merely reinforced Nixon's conviction that it was run by feeble-minded "Ivy League liberals." It did not occur to the president that his own convictions rather than CIA intelligence collection might be at fault. On June 5 John Ehrlichman, Nixon's assistant and White House counsel, informed him that "the intelligence community conclusion is that our Government does not have specific information or 'ironclad proof' that Red China or Cuba is funding campus disorders." Nixon was predictably dissatisfied, and instructed, " Keep after this." He ordered that Tom Charles Huston, then working on "special projects" in the White House ("or someone of his toughness and brains"), be given "the job of developing hard evidence on this."[28] The clear implication was that lack of "toughness and brains" had so far prevented the intelligence community unearthing the evidence that the president knew was there. "There was," recalls Helms, "nothing we could do to convince him."[29] During the summer, however, the DCI personally "reviewed the Agency's efforts to monitor those international activities of radicals and black militants which may adversely affect the national security." The main result of Chaos and related operations was to collect huge amounts of useless intelligence, all of which had to be analyzed in a vain attempt to persuade a disbelieving president that it did not contain evidence of a vast international conspiracy. Helms complained in September that "the backlog of undigested raw information" had become "a formidable obstacle."[30]

The SS-9 controversy in the spring of 1969 provided another example of the president's anger with the CIA when its intelligence contradicted his own inner convictions. On March 21 his secretary of defense, Melvin Laird, made the dramatic announcement that the Soviet Union had embarked on an arms buildup that would enable it to wipe out U.S. defenses in a single strike. The basis of this alarmist declaration was the controversial claim that the mammoth Soviet SS-9 missile was a MIRV (multiple independently targeted reentry vehicle) whose multiple warheads would give the Soviet Union a "first-strike capability." The Nixon administration used this alleged capability as the basis of its arguments for the construction of an enormously expensive antiballistic missile (ABM) system. The last NIE (National Intelligence Estimate) of October 1968, however, had concluded that the SS-9 was not a MIRV but a less dangerous MRV (multiple reentry vehicle) without individually targeted warheads. CIA analysts stuck to that view, which leaked to the press. Nixon suspected the agency of plotting to undermine the administration's case for the ABM.[31] The NIE was, in his view, further evidence of the feeblemindedness of the "Ivy League liberals" at Langley. "Those goddam estimates of yours [on the Soviet Union] out of the Agency have been wrong for years," he told Helms, "and they still are."[32]

In public, attempts were made to deny the difference of views between the CIA and the administration. Laird's deputy, John Foster, testified improbably in May that he and Laird had "no disagreements with the Central Intelligence Agency." In private, the CIA was pressured to suppress or change its assessment of the SS-9. According to John W.

Huizenga, deputy director (later director) of the Office of National Estimates (ONE), "There's no doubt that the White House was determined that there should be an intelligence finding that the Soviets were engaged in MIRV testing."[33] In the summer a brief CIA update to the NIE of October 1968 restated its view that the Soviet Union was not aiming a first-strike capability. Laird immediately demanded that this statement be withdrawn. Helms reluctantly agreed on the grounds that the agency's view was clearly stated in the still-current NIE, and that it was therefore unnecessary to "flaunt" the disagreement with Defense. According to Jack Smith, "The reaction among CIA analysts and estimators was intense. As they saw it, one of CIA's fundamental strengths had been violated: the right to state forthrightly any conclusion their intelligence led to regardless of existing U.S. policy."[34] Some also blamed Helms for giving way. According to one senior analyst, "Helms had pulled his punches on the SS-9 issue at considerable cost to his reputation in the Intelligence Directorate."[35] The effect of the president's ill-concealed hostility to the CIA was to degrade, at least slightly, the quality of intelligence analysis. According to Huizenga, "When intelligence producers have a general feeling that they are working in a hostile climate, what really happens is not so much that they tailor the product to please, although that's not been unknown, but more likely, they avoid the treatment of difficult issues."[36] "It became a constant mantra from Nixon," recalls Helms, "that CIA was underestimating the Soviet military threat."[37]

Nixon's early months in office showed not merely a deep distrust of CIA but also a serious lack of understanding of NSA.[38] On April 14, 1969, a North Korean MIG fighter shot down a U.S. Navy aircraft on a routine ELINT collection mission in international airspace ninety miles off the Korean coast. NSA quickly concluded from intercepted North Korean communications that the shoot-down was a command-and-control error involving a single plane. According to an NSA analyst, "There was evidence it was a screw-up. The North Koreans are ruthless but careful. It would be very much out of their pattern." There was no evidence that, as had happened before the seizure of the *Pueblo*, the North Korean government had approved the attack in advance.[39] The CIA suggested that, since April 14 was Kim Il Sung's birthday, the shoot-down with the loss of thirty-one American lives might have been intended by the MIG pilot as a macabre birthday present.[40] The White House, however, had already decided that the shoot-down was a calculated act of deliberate provocation by the North Korean regime. Nixon originally intended to retaliate but, according to Kissinger, "procrastinated too much."[41] At a news conference on April 18 he made the worst public intelligence gaffe of his career. The North Koreans, he insisted, were well aware that the EC-121 was in international airspace:

> There was no uncertainty whatever as to where this plane was, because we know what their radar showed. We, incidentally, know what the Russian radar showed. And all three radars [Russian, North Korean, American] showed exactly the same thing.[42]

Hitherto, the encryption methods used in Soviet, Chinese, and North Korean radar systems had been, by American standards, relatively unsophisticated, and NSA had been able to reveal what the other side was seeing. Had Nixon understood the principles of SIGINT, which evidently he did not, he would have grasped the disastrous consequences of his statement at the press conference. According to an NSA analyst:

> I died when I heard it. This was my business. I just fell out of my chair—I literally did. . . . The Soviet Union and other countries changed every frequency, every net structure—all at once. It took months to work it out.[43]

Helms too was horrified by Nixon's gaffe.[44] Within the White House situation room, Alexis Johnson of the State Department attempted a grim joke. "We're going," he said, "to take the President's clearances away."[45]

Nixon made other, less damaging public use of SIGINT during the SS-9 controversy. Telemetry interception had become an established part of intelligence monitoring of Soviet missile development. Analysis of Soviet telemetry, however, still involved major technical problems. The Thompson-Ramo-Wooldridge (TRW) Corporation, which did telemetry analysis under contract, reported that during Soviet missile tests the triplet warheads of the SS-9 were landing in a triangular pattern or—to use the jargon of the analysts—forming a "footprint" that resembled the deployment pattern of U.S. Minuteman missiles, their presumed target. This was seized on by the White House and Defense to justify their argument that the SS-9 was a MIRV, or at least its functional equivalent, with the capacity to direct its multiple warheads to individual targets. Nixon made a thinly veiled reference to telemetry analysis during a press conference on June 19, at which he sought to justify his ABM program:

> . . . In recommending Safeguard [the ABM program], I did so based on intelligence information at that time. Since that time, new intelligence information with regard to the Soviet success in testing multiple reentry vehicles . . . has convinced me that Safeguard is even

more important. However we may argue that intelligence, as to whether it has an independent guidance system as ours will have, there isn't any question but that it is a multiple weapon and its footprints indicate that it just happens to fall in somewhat the precise area in which our Minuteman silos are located.

In fact, the TRW report was mistaken. (In any case, because of deliberate variations in Minuteman deployment, the same triangular footprint would not have been effective against all the silos.) More and better telemetry analysis later helped to demonstrate that the SS-9 was not, in fact, a MIRV.[46]

Nixon's eleven hundred pages of memoirs include few references to NSA and mention SIGINT only obliquely. Remarkably, the twenty-eight hundred pages devoted by Kissinger to his five and a half years as a member of the Nixon administration make no mention of NSA at all. Despite the silence of their memoirs, however, both Nixon and Kissinger were fascinated by diplomatic decrypts supplied by NSA that contained references to themselves. According to Ray Cline, who became director of State Department intelligence in 1969:

> In the old days that sort of [intercepted] diplomatic traffic was handled by a few officials in each agency, but Henry laid down the law—everything that mentioned him by name had to be cleared through his office. If his name appeared, it was strictly NODIS [not for distribution within the government].

Other evidence suggests that the NODIS category went far beyond decrypts mentioning Kissinger by name. Though Laird, as defense secretary, was responsible for NSA, Kissinger sought to prevent much important diplomatic traffic reaching him. Laird's military assistant, Colonel Robert E. Pursley, said later that he "always had the feeling we weren't getting all the [NSA] stuff the White House was."[47] Pursley, however, seems to have been unaware that, on appointing Vice-Admiral Noel Gayler director of NSA, Laird had come to a secret agreement with him. According to Helms:

> Laird told me more than once he put Gayler in NSA because Gayler assured him he'd keep him fully informed on everything NSA sent the White House. That's how Gayler got four stars and [promotion to] CINCPAC in 1972.

This secret arrangement seems never to have been discovered by Nixon and Kissinger. Nixon did, however, say of Laird on one occasion, "There goes the most devious man in Washington." Helms commented, "It takes one to recognize one."[48]

Though high-grade Soviet cipher systems appear to have remained invulnerable to American cryptanalytic attack, NSA successfully intercepted a number of Soviet communications. One of the most closely guarded secrets of the Nixon White House, not even hinted at in Nixon's or Kissinger's memoirs, was a series of NSA intercepts from the Soviet embassy on Sixteenth Street in Washington. Both Nixon and Kissinger are said to have attached great importance to these intercepts, probably because they provided some sort of check on the working of the back channel and the prospects for détente.[49] The president also took a personal interest in Operation Gamma Guppy, begun shortly before his election victory by an ASA unit working under NSA direction at the U.S. embassy in Moscow, which successfully intercepted the microwave radio and telephone communications between the large black Zil limousines of Politburo members as they drove around Moscow. According to one of the limited number of senior CIA analysts cleared for access to the intercepts:

The White House was not the only fascinated reader of GAMMA GUPPY material. We analysts pored over these routine conversations (largely between *drivers* of Politburo members rather than the members themselves) looking for meaningful insights. There weren't many to be found. Over time, we learned who hunted and fished with whom, and pieced together the existence of close friendships, but the information was so highly sensitive it couldn't be alluded to in routinely disseminated analysis on leadership issues![50]

Gamma Guppy ended in September 1971 after columnist Jack Anderson had revealed in the *Washington Post* that the United States was eavesdropping on Soviet leaders.[51] One senior intelligence officer ruefully recalls, "I had lunch with Jack Anderson. I should have shot him!"[52] Only a small fraction of NSA's vast output of decrypted diplomatic traffic from Latin American and Third World countries seems to have aroused the president's interest. His obsession with Castro, however, was such that he almost certainly read with attention some of the substantial amount of Cuban decrypts.[53]

Nixon's main preoccupation during his first term of office was Vietnam. Though both he and Kissinger had lost hope of a military victory after the Tet offensive,[54] it took three years for the new administration to negotiate an end to the war. When Nixon opened the president's pri-

vate safe on his first morning in the White House, he found that Johnson had left only one document behind: the Vietnam intelligence summary for the previous day. On the last page were the latest casualty figures, showing that in the final week of Johnson's presidency 185
Americans had been killed and 1,237 wounded. Nixon put the intelligence report back in the safe. He did not remove it until the war was
over.[55] The new administration began with a major policy review.
National Security Study Memorandum 1 (NSSM-1), issued on Inauguration Day, put fifty-six questions to government departments and agencies concerned with Vietnam. The answers revealed a sharp divide
between the assessment of the CIA and that of the military and the
Saigon embassy. One of the most basic questions concerned the so-
called domino theory. Would the fall of South Vietnam lead to Communist revolutions among its neighbors? The intelligence departments of
the three armed services thought it would; the CIA was skeptical. Were
B-52 bombing strikes effective? While the military thought they were,
the agency believed they might even be counterproductive; there was,
it claimed, "substantial evidence" that the bombing helped Hanoi "mobi-
lize people behind the Communist war effort." Perhaps the most important question for the immediate future involved enemy supply routes
through Cambodia. The military and the Saigon embassy considered
them very important; CIA "strongly" disagreed.[56]

On February 9 General Creighton Abrams, Westmoreland's successor as U.S. commander in Vietnam, cabled Washington that he had "hard
intelligence" from imagery, confirmed by a deserter, on the location of
the elusive jungle headquarters in the so-called Fish Hook area of Cambodia, about seventy-five miles northwest of Saigon, from which the
North Vietnamese and Viet Cong were believed to be coordinating their
war effort. On March 16, after more than a month's argument within the
administration, Nixon approved B-52 strikes against the enemy's Cambodian "sanctuaries." The bombing campaign, code-named Menu, began
the next day and continued at intervals until May 1970. The various target areas were designated by what Kissinger considered "tasteless"
mealtime code words: Breakfast, Dessert, Snack, Lunch, Supper, Dinner.
Though 3,875 sorties were flown and 108,823 tons of bombs dropped,
the bombing campaign failed to achieve its objectives. By the spring of
1970 Nixon had concluded that only a land invasion by U.S. and South
Vietnamese forces could remove the sanctuaries. Remarkably, Operation
Menu was at first successfully kept secret. North Vietnam did not wish
to advertise the presence of its forces in Cambodia and therefore failed
to mention the bombing attacks on them. Cambodian leader Prince
Sihanouk, anxious not to be drawn into the conflict, also preferred not to

publicize the bombing. One of the reasons for secrecy on the American side, Nixon later acknowledged, "was the problem of domestic antiwar protest." Keeping the Cambodian bombing secret involved an unprecedented form of double bookkeeping. A set of false reports on the bombing raids was sent to the Pentagon through the usual air force channels, while a parallel set of highly classified reports contained the real targets.[57]

In the end, Nixon seems to have become more concerned with keeping the secret of Operation Menu than with the bombing itself. "In the first five months of my presidency," wrote Nixon in his memoirs, "at least twenty-one major stories based on leaks in the NSC files appeared in New York and Washington newspapers."[58] Nixon failed to mention, however, that Kissinger was an experienced leaker himself. Since the national security adviser leaked to journalists on topics of his choosing, it is unsurprising that some NSC staff followed his example.[59] The president's growing obsession with leaks set him on the primrose path that led eventually to Watergate. On April 25 Nixon summoned Hoover and Mitchell to a meeting in the Oval Office to discuss methods of identifying the leakers. Throughout Nixon's years out of office, he and Hoover had kept in touch. According to Ehrlichman, Hoover became "more than a source of information—he was an advisor to whom Nixon listened." Shortly before his inauguration, Nixon told him, "Edgar, you are one of the few people who is to have access to me at all times. I've talked to Mitchell about it and he understands." Nixon did not intend his invitation to be taken literally. He gave Ehrlichman instructions to establish himself as Hoover's confidant and intermediary with the White House.[60] At the meeting on April 25 Hoover told the president that three members of the NSC staff—Morton Halperin, Helmut Sonnenfeldt, and Daniel Davidson—had been identified as "arrogant Harvard-type Kennedy men" and possible leakers. Easily persuaded that doves and Democrats on Kissinger's staff were at the root of his troubles, Nixon approved in principle the tapping of their telephones. Kissinger was summoned to the meeting and given the three men's FBI files. Kissinger, in turn, handed them to Haig and asked him to read them. Haig found evidence of nothing worse than acquaintance with "people with whom I myself would not have wished to be on intimate terms."[61]

Nixon's outrage at the leaks flared up again on May 9 with the publication of a *New York Times* article that began: "American B-52 bombers in recent weeks have raided several Viet Cong and North Vietnamese supply dumps and base camps in Cambodia for the first time, according to Nixon administration sources." Kissinger read the article over breakfast by the swimming pool at the Key Biscayne Hotel in Florida, stood up shaking with rage, and insisted that the president, staying nearby with his friend Bebe Rebozo, be informed at once. Beyond Nixon's immediate entourage, the article aroused remarkably little interest. There were no hostile demonstrations, no protests by congressmen, no sign of interest by other newspapers. Nixon, however, persuaded himself that "The *Times* leak threatened everything." He instructed Kissinger to telephone Hoover at once. "Dr. Kissinger," noted Hoover, "said . . . to put whatever resources I need to do this. I said I would take care of this right away." That same afternoon Hoover reported that the principal suspect was Morton Halperin. Kissinger pledged to "destroy whoever did this if we can find him, no matter where he is." At 6:20 P.M. the FBI placed a tap on Halperin's phone. The next day Haig called Hoover to request "on the highest authority" that the FBI begin "telephone surveillance" of Sonnenfeldt and Davidson, the other two suspected leakers in the NSC. Hoover noted that Haig considered it "a matter of most grave and serious consequence to our national security. He stressed that it is so sensitive it demands handling on a need-to-know basis with no record maintained." As Haig later acknowledged, "The wiretaps began to cross-pollinate and multiply." Over the next twenty-one months the White House ordered a total of seventeen wiretaps on the grounds of national security—seven on NSC staff, three on White House aides, three on State and Defense Department officials, and four on newsmen. Haig read all FBI summaries of the intercepted telephone calls and passed extracts on to Kissinger. As Nixon later complained, the wiretaps "never helped us. Just gobs and gobs of material: gossip and bullshitting—the tapping was a very, very unproductive thing." Though the leaks continued, not a single leaker was discovered. The tapping became common knowledge among NSC staff. Kissinger's personal assistant, Lawrence Eagleburger, warned some of his colleagues, "Don't say anything you don't want [White House chief of staff H. R. "Bob"] Haldeman or Henry to read over breakfast." Another member of Kissinger's staff, Anthony Lake, later President Clinton's national security adviser, recalls that ". . . Every now and then, when we were speaking on the phone we'd wish J. Edgar Hoover a merry Christmas."[62]

Contrary to popular belief, the Nixon administration ordered fewer wiretaps per year for foreign intelligence and national security purposes than any of its predecessors since presidential authorizations had begun under Franklin Roosevelt.[63] The statistics, however, do not tell the full story. Unlike their predecessors, Nixon and Kissinger introduced the wiretap into the heart of the national security organization, with corrosive effects on the morale and confidence of White House staff.[64] Their first victim, Morton Halperin, eventually gained an apology from Kissinger after a nineteen-year lawsuit.[65] Kissinger, claimed another White House victim of the wiretaps, William Safire, was "capable of getting a special thrill out of working most closely with those he spied on most."[66] The conspiratorial mindset of the president and his national security adviser made them increasingly obsessional about the hunt for leakers. Though Kissinger did not know it, he was himself an indirect target of Nixon's hunt. According to Ehrlichman, Nixon was "getting very concerned about Henry, and he knew he was leaking to [columnist Joseph] Kraft." In May 1969, bypassing the FBI and the "national security" wiretaps, Nixon ordered Ehrlichman to arrange for Kraft's telephone to be bugged. Through John Caulfield, a former New York policeman on his staff, Ehrlichman obtained the services of John Ragan, an ex-FBI agent who had become director of security for the Republican National Committee. But the bug planted by Ragan on a telephone in Kraft's Georgetown home disclosed no leaks. According to Haldeman, Caulfield and Ragan "heard nothing but the maid for weeks—and she didn't speak English." On learning that Kraft and his wife were staying at the Hotel George V in Paris, Nixon told Ehrlichman to arrange for the French authorities to bug their bedroom. FBI deputy director William Sullivan flew over to France to oversee the arrangements. The FBI, however, proved curiously obtuse in interpreting the tapes that resulted. After Kraft called the leading French statesman, Jean Monnet, father of the European Community, he was reported as having contacted a Mr. John Monay. Kraft also contacted Kay Graham; on this occasion the FBI recorded the name correctly but, failing to recognize the name of the owner of the *Washington Post*, reported that her identity was "not known." Despite the farce that surrounded it, the surveillance of Joseph Kraft set one important and ominous precedent. Nixon had for the first time authorized the use of White House personnel in an illegal bugging operation.[67]

Nixon also used unconventional methods to acquire intelligence on his freewheeling brother Don. "In another age," writes John Ehrlichman, "F. Donald Nixon might have been a patent-medicine salesman or a carnival barker; when I first met him he was the modern equivalent, a 'consultant.'" Don boasted to friends, after his brother entered the White House, that he would be a millionaire within four years. Anxious about Don's business dealings, the president considered putting him under FBI surveillance, but disliked the idea of allowing Hoover to meddle in his family affairs. Instead, he instructed Ehrlichman to see the deputy DCI, Robert Cushman, and "have the CIA put a 'full cover' on Don." Cushman refused on the grounds that it was illegal for the agency to engage in domestic surveillance. Nixon, who had appointed Cushman to ensure that the CIA did his bidding, was doubtless outraged. He turned to the

Secret Service, which agreed to put Don under surveillance and tap his telephones. "Some of the telephone logs," recalls Ehrlichman, "confirmed our worst concerns. In spite of Don's denials, it was clear that he was up to his ears in the kinds of 'really big deals' . . . that might eventually embarrass his brother."[68]

Most of Nixon's domestic intelligence, however, continued to come from the FBI. In November 1969 Hoover instituted the "FBI Intelligence Letter for the President" to systematize the flow of information to Nixon. Copies also went to the vice-president and attorney general. Codenamed Inlet, the intelligence was divided into six categories. Five concerned "'security related' cases or 'inside' information concerning demonstrations, disorders or other civil disruptions which is of more than local significance." The sixth was devoted to scandal or gossip, euphemistically described as "Items which may be of special interest to the President or Attorney General."[69] Among the sexual scandal with which Hoover sought to titillate the president were transcripts of Martin Luther King's extramarital affairs in hotel bedrooms. Haldeman glanced at the first page of the transcripts and pushed it back in the FBI envelope. Their contents were, he claimed, "almost as disgusting" as Hoover's attempted use of them. Though King had been assassinated in April 1968, Hoover continued a vendetta against him, determined to demonstrate that King was not "such a saint as they're trying to make him out to be today."[70] Nixon sometimes solicited from the FBI compromising personal information on hostile individuals or groups. On one occasion Haldeman called Hoover and "stated the President wanted him to ask, and he would imagine I would have it pretty much at hand so there would be no specific investigation, for a run down on the homosexuals known and suspected in the Washington press corps." Hoover did indeed have the information "pretty much at hand."[71]

The importance attached by Nixon to domestic intelligence gathering was enhanced by a brief but frightening period of terrorist violence by the Black Panthers, Weathermen, and other quasi-revolutionary movements. During the academic year 1969–70 there were 174 campus bombings and bombing attempts. Though the bombing campaign was short-lived, it seemed possible at the time that it was the prelude to an even more serious terrorist offensive. Nixon's decision to order an invasion of Cambodia by U.S. and South Vietnamese forces in April 1970 to destroy enemy bases reenergized the antiwar movement. Amid a new wave of campus protest, there was tragedy at Kent State University in Ohio where, on May 4, 1970, National Guards shot and killed four student demonstrators. On Friday, May 8, close to one hundred thousand demonstrators began converging on the White House for a mass demonstration the following day. After an evening news conference, Nixon spent most of the night in the Lincoln Sitting Room unable to sleep. Between 10:35 P.M. and 1:55 A.M. he made over forty phone calls to advisers and supporters around the country. After dozing for about an hour, he began another round of calls, then just before dawn went to see some of the student demonstrators gathered at the Lincoln Memorial, engaging in rambling conversations on topics that ranged from foreign travel to football. To Kissinger it seemed that "The very fabric of government was falling apart. The Executive Branch was shell-shocked."[72]

Though the administration weathered the crisis, Nixon retreated for a period into a siege mentality, brooding over, among other things, the failures of his intelligence community. He had been outraged not to receive advance warning from the CIA of the overthrow in March of Cambodian leader Prince Sihanouk. "What the hell do those clowns do out there in Langley?" he demanded. He repeated that ill-tempered question in his memoirs published nine years later.[73] Nixon omitted to mention, however, that the agency had so far been denied permission to open a station in the Cambodian capital, Phnom Penh. On April 1 he ordered a station to be opened immediately. On April 15 he discovered that, chiefly because of obstruction from State, his instructions had yet to be carried out. In a towering rage, he summoned Helms, Cushman, Kissinger, and Haig to the Oval Office (but, as a sign of his displeasure, no representative of State), and issued a twenty-four-hour deadline for the station to be opened. More procrastination followed. It took another presidential explosion a week later to achieve results. "Once again," noted Kissinger, "we beheld one of the wonders of the modern state, the relative inability of leaders to dominate their bureaucracy or to cut short its powers of endless exegesis."[74]

Nixon's main intelligence concern, however, was the FBI's lack of energy in dealing with what he believed was the great Communist conspiracy orchestrating domestic dissent. Though Hoover was seventy-five and facing growing criticism even from within his own ranks, Nixon could not bring himself to order his retirement and allowed him to die in office in 1972. In the spring of 1970, just as the antiwar movement was reviving, Hoover's relations with the rest of the intelligence community descended to an all-time low. When the CIA refused to supply him with the name of an FBI agent who had assisted the agency without first seeking his permission, he retaliated by cutting all liaison between the FBI and the CIA. A few weeks later Hoover ended liaison with the rest of the intelligence community as well, maintaining direct contact only with the White House and the Department of Justice.[75] What probably most outraged the president, however, was that to protect the bureau from its congressional critics, Hoover had decided to discontinue the illegal methods of investigation that he had employed under previous presidents, among them mail opening and black bag jobs against American citizens, both regarded by Nixon as essential tools in uncovering the Communist conspiracy. FBI recruitment of campus informants was also restricted, against Nixon's wishes, to men aged over twenty-one.[76]

On June 5, 1970, Nixon's accumulated frustrations with the intelligence community burst forth at a meeting in the Oval Office with Hoover; Helms; Gayler; Lieutenant General Donald V. Bennett of the DIA; Haldeman; Ehrlichman; Tom Huston, a young lawyer and former DIA analyst on the White House staff; and Robert Finch, secretary of health, education and welfare.[77] Nixon had been favorably impressed for some time by Huston's hard-line views on internal subversion.[78] He opened the meeting by reading from a paper prepared by Huston:

> We are now confronted with a new and grave crisis in our country—one which we know too little about. Certainly hundreds, perhaps thousands, of Americans—mostly under thirty—are determined to destroy our society. . . . They are reaching out for the support—ideological and otherwise—of foreign powers and they are developing their own brand of indigenous revolutionary activism which is as dangerous as anything which they could import from Cuba, China, or the Soviet Union.

The administration could deal with the threat, Nixon declared, only if it had more and better intelligence. He then berated his intelligence chiefs for being disorganized and ineffective. According to General Bennett, "The President chewed our butts."[79] Nixon's complaint at the lack of coordination within the intelligence community had considerable justification. He failed to acknowledge, however, that he himself was partly responsible for it. Nixon had denied Helms the authority he required as DCI to become an effective head of the whole intelligence community, and he could not bring himself to replace Hoover with an FBI director prepared for real collaboration with other intelligence agencies. Nor, of course, could he grasp the fact that the scale of the subversive antiwar conspiracy and of its links with international Communism had been greatly magnified by his own conspiratorial imagination.

Nixon instructed his intelligence chiefs to form an interagency committee on intelligence (ad hoc) under Hoover's chairmanship to "recommend steps which would strengthen the capabilities of the government to collect intelligence on radicals." He added that Huston would provide them "with detailed information on the scope of the review which I have in mind." Huston moved quickly to establish his authority. "Operational details will be the responsibility of the chairman," he informed the interagency committee. However, "the scope and direction of the review" was to be decided by Huston himself. At the committee's first meeting in Hoover's office on June 8 Huston announced that the president "wanted the pros and cons of various collection methods spelled out clearly in the form of an options paper," to ensure that he was not "merely the recipient of a *fait accompli*"; he would then decide personally which options were to be selected. At subsequent meetings, Hoover, Helms, Gayler, Bennett, and senior members of their agencies discussed in detail the application of HUMINT, SIGINT, and IMINT collection methods to the surveillance of radical subversion in the United States and its international connections. Privately, Hoover dismissed Huston as a "hippie intellectual" (both words of abuse in Hoover's vocabulary). At the final committee meeting Hoover set out to humiliate Huston by pretending to forget his name. "Any comments, Mr. Hoffmann?" he asked at one stage in the discussion. "Any comments, Mr. Hutchinson?" he inquired soon afterward. According to one of those present, Hoover carried on "getting the name wrong in six or seven different ways." Hoover also insisted that he would no longer take personal responsibility for some of the surveillance methods he had authorized in the past:

> For years and years and years I have approved opening mail and other similar operations, but no. It is becoming more and more dangerous and we are apt to get caught. I am not opposed to doing this. I'm not opposed to continuing the burglaries and the opening of mail and other similar activities, providing somebody higher than myself approves of it. . . . [If] the Attorney General or some high ranking person in the White House [does so]—then I will carry out their decision. But I'm not going to accept the responsibility myself anymore, even though I've done it for many years.

Huston suggested that Nixon engage in a face-to-face "stroking session" with Hoover if he wanted the FBI restrictions lifted. Though the director was "bullheaded as hell" and "getting old and worried about his legend," Huston predicted optimistically that he would "not hesitate to accede to any decision that the President makes."[80]

The intelligence chiefs reported to the president on June 25. According to Nixon's memoirs:

> The report opened with a brief analysis of the problems confronting us, ranging from the Black Panthers and the Weathermen to Com-

munist infiltrators. It differentiated radical terrorist groups from those that merely indulged in incendiary rhetoric. It gave a summary of the available intelligence techniques, the current restrictions on them, and the advantages and disadvantages of lifting those restrictions.[81]

Huston set out to secure Nixon's approval for "the strongest options" in the interagency report, with the aim of removing as many as possible of "the existing restrictions on intelligence collection." At least two of the proposals in what became known as the "Huston plan" were unlawful. "Covert [mail] coverage is illegal, and there are serious risks involved," Huston advised the president. "However, the advantages to be derived from its use outweigh the risks." He took a similar view on the question of "surreptitious entry":

> Use of this technique is clearly illegal: it amounts to burglary. It is also highly risky and could result in great embarrassment if exposed. However, it is also the most fruitful tool and can produce the type of intelligence which cannot be obtained in any other fashion.

Nixon approved the Huston plan on July 14.[82] In his memoirs he makes no reference to its illegality, but says simply that he felt it "necessary and justified by the violence we faced. . . . The express domestic targets—the Black Panthers and the Weathermen—had announced their intentions to kidnap and assassinate and were already building up an arsenal of weapons to carry out their threat."[83] A Senate inquiry six years later gave this assessment of Nixon's decision:

> Henceforth, *with presidential authority*, the intelligence community could at will intercept and transcribe the communications of Americans using international communications facilities; eavesdrop from near or afar on anyone deemed to be a "threat to national security"; read the mail of American citizens; break into the homes of anyone tagged as a security threat; and monitor in various ways the activities of suspicious student groups.

Huston wanted the president to announce his decision to adopt these draconian measures personally to his intelligence chiefs, particularly in the case of Hoover, "because it seemed to me it would be easier maybe [for Nixon] to get him to accept it." Not for the first time, however, Nixon shied away from a difficult confrontation and left Huston to inform Hoover, Helms, Gayler, and Bennett in writing on July 23. Bennett and his assistant, James Stilwell, agreed that Nixon "didn't have the guts" to sign the Huston plan himself. Leaving it to Huston showed "what a hot potato it was."[84]

According to an eyewitness, Hoover "went through the ceiling" when he received instructions to implement the Huston plan, signed by the despised "hippie intellectual" himself. He marched straight into the office of Attorney General Mitchell and confronted him with the document. Though responsible for the FBI, Mitchell had never heard of the interagency committee, let alone of the Huston plan. He told Hoover he would take his objections to the president as soon as Nixon returned from the so-called Western White House in San Clemente. Hoover returned to his office and wrote a memorandum stating that, despite his "clear-cut and specific opposition to the lifting of the various investigative restraints," the FBI would implement the plan—but only on the specific instructions of the president or the attorney general. Hoover's opposition plainly did not derive from ethical objections to the intelligence collection methods embodied in the plan. Rather, he was fearful of the growing risks of exposure and of the possibility that collaboration with other intelligence agencies would undermine the prerogatives of the FBI. At a meeting with Nixon on July 27 Mitchell emphasized "the risk of disclosure of the possible illegal actions." On July 28, four days before the Huston plan was due to come into effect, the president withdrew his approval for it. Huston walked into the White House situation room and complained that Hoover had "pulled the rug out" from under him.[85] Nixon's explanation for his about-face in his memoirs is an extraordinary one:

> I knew that if Hoover had decided not to cooperate, it would matter little what I had decided or approved. Even if I issued a direct order to him, while he would undoubtedly carry it out, he would see to it that I had cause to reverse myself. There was even the remote possibility that he would resign in protest.[86]

The president of the United States thus declared himself powerless to impose his wishes on the seventy-five-year-old director of the FBI, yet unwilling to contemplate his removal from office. The real reason, perhaps, for Nixon's refusal to proceed with the Huston plan was that he was unwilling to accept responsibility for it himself and had hoped to transfer responsibility to his intelligence chiefs.[87] The failure to implement the plan marked a watershed in the Nixon presidency. It would lead in 1971 to Nixon's decision to set up a secret White House intelligence unit, the "Plumbers," who would use some of the techniques resisted by his intelligence chiefs.

During the summer of 1970 the wave of terrorist incidents had passed its peak. Nor were there any major campus protests when students returned to university after summer vacation. The covert operations that preoccupied the president at the beginning of the new academic year were not in the United States but in Chile. Both Nixon's predecessors had displayed at least a passing interest in subverting Chilean democracy to protect it from the Red Peril. In 1962 the Special Group (5412) had gained Kennedy's approval for the start of a covert operation to influence the outcome of the Chilean presidential election two years later. During 1964 Johnson had approved proposals by the 303 Committee (successor to the Special Group) for the expenditure by the CIA of $2.6 million to ensure the defeat of the pro-Castro Marxist Socialist Salvador Allende and the victory of the Christian Democrat Eduardo Frei.[88] How far agency money actually influenced the outcome of the election is debatable, but Helms believed that the operation had been "very successful."[89] Nixon, like his predecessors, regarded the selective use of bribery to influence foreign elections as a routine fact of international relations. He was well aware that Moscow secretly subsidized all pro-Soviet Communist parties and many other movements around the world that it hoped to influence. "As long as the Communists supply external funds to support political parties, factions, or individuals in other countries," Nixon wrote later, "I believe that the United States can and should do the same and do it secretly so that it can be effective."[90]

At a meeting of the 303 Committee on April 15, 1969, Helms argued that if the 1964 success was to be repeated in the presidential elections due in September 1970, at which Frei would be unable to stand again, it was time to begin active preparations. Kissinger was not persuaded that Allende stood a real chance of success. Helms made several further attempts over the next few weeks to win his approval for an immediate start to a new covert operation. "Kissinger wouldn't buy it," he recalls. "He wasn't interested."[91] Kissinger himself acknowledges in his memoirs, "Until well into 1970 I did not focus on the dangers. . . ."[92] While the agency wished to give direct support to Allende's main opponent, the elderly conservative Jorge Alessandri, the State Department wanted to limit covert action to anti-Allende propaganda. In March and June 1970 the 40 Committee (as the 303 Committee had renamed itself) approved a propaganda campaign "to alert Chileans to dangers of Allende and a Marxist government," but "excluded support to either of the candidates opposing Allende."[93] On September 4 Allende came out on top of the presidential poll with 36.3 percent of the vote to Alessandri's 34.9.

According to Kissinger, "Nixon was beside himself." Having berated the Democrats for over a decade for allowing Cuba to go Communist, he now faced the prospect of Chile following suit.[94] Helms blamed Nixon and Kissinger for failing to heed his calls for covert action: "It was their own damn fault for letting things go until it was too late."[95] Nixon, writes Kissinger, now insisted on "doing something, *anything*, that would reverse the previous neglect."[96]

Since no presidential candidate had won an overall majority, Chile's constitution required that a joint session of its congress choose between the two with the most votes, Allende and Alessandri, on October 24, fifty days after the election. Though the Chilean congress was expected to vote for Allende, since he had topped the poll, there remained a final opportunity for covert action to prevent his coming to power. The first possibility for covert action (denoted as Track I) was to find some method of persuading Congress not to vote Allende into office. The CIA suggested what it called "the Rube Goldberg gambit," under which Alessandri would be elected on October 24, resign immediately, and "leave Frei constitutionally free to run in a second election for the presidency."[97] The second possibility (Track II) was to engineer a military coup. Nixon ordered both tracks to be followed simultaneously. On September 15 he summoned Helms, Kissinger, and Mitchell to the Oval Office. As Nixon barked instructions, Helms took notes:

> One in 10 chance perhaps, but save Chile!
> worth spending
> not concerned risks involved
> no involvement of Embassy
> $10,000,000 available, more if necessary
> full time job—best men we have
> game plan
> make the economy scream.
> 48 hours for plan of action[98]

Kissinger's memoirs downplay the significance of this remarkable note. The president's outburst, he argues, should not be interpreted "literally."[99] Helms insists that, on the contrary, "Nixon meant every word he said." He says of Kissinger's account, "Kissinger is trying to protect his own ass. Every man does that, but Henry's been particularly good at it."[100]

The desperate measures ordered by Nixon to keep Allende from becoming president demonstrated, once again, his willingness to step outside established procedures for implementing covert action. He gave instructions that Track II, unlike Track I, was to be kept secret from State, Defense, and the embassy in Santiago. Even the 40 Committee was not told. Probably only four CIA officials in Chile and five at Langley knew of it. David Atlee Phillips, the head of the secret Chilean task force charged with implementing Track II, believed from the outset that the odds against it were "very long indeed." He also had more scruples than the president. "Should the CIA," he wondered, "even responding to a President's ukase, encourage a military coup in one of the few countries in Latin America with a solid, functioning democratic tradition?"[101] Nixon told an audience at Kansas State University on September 16, "There are those who protest that if the verdict of democracy goes against them, democracy itself is at fault, the system is at fault—who say that if they don't get their own way, the answer is to burn a bus or bomb a building."[102] As far as Chile was concerned, the president was himself just such a protester against "the verdict of democracy," though his preferred weapons were violation of the constitution or a military coup rather than small-scale arson or campus bombing.

Track I in Chile involved covertly orchestrating a major propaganda campaign against the Red Peril represented by Allende, as well as putting pressure on Frei to go ahead with the Rube Goldberg gambit. The CIA reported to the White House that by September 28 it had "in place in, or en route to, Chile" fifteen "journalist agents" of ten different nationalities, and a further eight journalists from five countries, who though not agents themselves, were "under the direction of high-level [CIA] agents" in the media. In addition:

> Special intelligence and "inside" briefings were given to U.S. journalists in deference to the international influence of the U.S. media. Particularly noteworthy in this connection was the *Time* cover story which owed a great deal to written materials and briefings provided by CIA. The *Time* correspondent in Chile who was providing much of the background material for the story apparently accepted Allende's protestations of moderation and constitutionality at face value. CIA briefings in Washington [*one line censored*] changed the basic thrust of the story in the final stages according to another *Time* correspondent.

The agency also reported that it had brought direct pressure to bear on Frei from outside as well as inside Chile to agree to the Rube Goldberg gambit: "In Europe and Latin America, prominent and influential members of the Christian Democratic movement as well as of the Catholic Church were prompted to visit Frei or send personal messages to him urging that he save Chile." The names of those "prompted" by the CIA remain classified, but they included "several top-level emissaries" from the West German Christian Democrats and "one of the international figures in Catholicism most respected by Frei." A leading Italian Christian Democrat approached by the agency, however, "said it was a hopeless situation and he saw no point in risking his reputation in a lost cause." Frei's respect for the constitution did indeed make him "a lost cause" as far as Track I was concerned. The CIA reported that it had failed to come up with "any evidence that Frei was responding, politically speaking, to [its attempts at] artificial respiration."[103]

Frei's refusal to violate the constitution left Track II, a military coup, as the only option.[104] The DDP, Thomas Karamessines, later testified that Kissinger "left no doubt in my mind that he was under the heaviest of pressure to get this accomplished, and he in turn was placing us under the heaviest of pressures to get it accomplished."[105] The strongest advocate of Track II was probably the president himself, who was regularly briefed by Karamessines. But, as Karamessines explained, there were formidable obstacles:

> Anti-Allende currents did exist in the military and the Carabineros, but were immobilized by:
>
> —the tradition of military respect for the constitution;
> —the public and private stance of General [Rene] Schneider, Commander in Chief of the Army, who advocated strict adherence to the Constitution;
> —fear of the reaction of non-commissioned officers who tended to harbor pro-Allende sympathies; and
> —a strong propensity to accept Allende blandishments to the effect that the military had little to fear from him.[106]

The CIA reported that all it could do in these circumstances was to "collect intelligence on coup-minded officers"; "create a coup climate by propaganda, disinformation, and terrorist activities intended to provoke the left to give a pretext for a coup"; and "inform those coup-minded officers that the U.S. Government would give them full support in a coup short of direct U.S. intervention." To assist it in its search for "coup-minded officers," the U.S. military attaché in Santiago was placed under the "operational direction" of the CIA station chief, who found his contacts in the Chilean army "invaluable."[107] The most enthusiastic of the candidates for coup leader was a retired Chilean army general, Robert Viaux, who had led a minor insurrection a year before. Viaux, however, struck the agency as rash and ill-prepared. On October 13 the Santiago station cabled Langley: "Viaux plans to kidnap Generals Schneider and Prats [his deputy] within the next 48 hours to precipitate a coup." On

October 15 Karamessines met Kissinger and Haig at the White House to decide what action to take:

> It was decided by those present that the Agency must get a message to Viaux warning him against any precipitate action. In essence the message should state: "We have reviewed your plans and based on your information and ours, we come to the conclusion that your plans for a coup at this time cannot succeed. Failing, they may reduce your capabilities in the future. Preserve your assets. We will stay in touch. The time will come when you with all your friends can do something. You will continue to have our support."

Viaux, however, was not to be dissuaded. On October 22 he went ahead with his attempt to kidnap Schneider, who drew his gun in self-defense and was mortally wounded in the ensuing struggle. Viaux was arrested, and the coup attempt collapsed before it had properly begun. Helms had already warned the White House that there was nothing further that the CIA could do to organize a coup before, as now seemed inevitable, Allende became president.[108] Nixon's memoirs say simply that, having been "informed that our efforts were probably not going to be successful . . . I instructed the CIA to abandon the operation."[109] Kissinger's memoirs claim that Track II was "terminated by me" on October 15.[110] CIA files give a different impression. A note after the meeting on October 15 records instructions from Kissinger "that the agency should continue keeping pressure on every Allende weak spot in sight—now . . . and into the future until such time as new marching orders are given." According to Karamessines, "Track II was really never ended." After Allende became president, it continued as a more general attempt to destabilize his regime. The CIA became the White House scapegoat for failing to stop Allende. One member of the agency's Chilean Task Force observed, "We're there as the whipping boy. Kissinger and Nixon left us holding the bag, but that's what we're in business for."[111]

While Nixon was preoccupied with the apparent threat of a second Castro in Chile, a new crisis developed over Cuba. Late in August U-2 photography had revealed the construction of a wharf and barracks at the Cuban port of Cienfuegos. On September 9 a Soviet flotilla arrived at Cienfuegos, bringing with it vessels of the type used for servicing nuclear submarines. Kissinger ordered daily U-2 missions, when weather conditions allowed, beginning on September 14. NPIC analysis of U-2 photographs taken on September 16 revealed, according to Kissinger, "all the earmarks of a permanent Soviet naval base." He reported to Nixon on September 18, "Today's photography readout confirms that . . .

the Soviets have moved precipitously to establish an installation in Cienfuegos Bay which is probably designed to serve as a submarine staging
post in the Caribbean." Nixon reacted with instant outrage and a handwritten note to Kissinger:

> I want a report on a crash basis on: (1) What CIA can do on a crash
> basis to support *any* kind of action which will irritate Castro; (2)
> What actions we can take which we have not yet taken to boycott
> nations dealing with Castro; (3) Most important, what actions we
> can take, covert or overt, to put missiles in Turkey—or a sub base
> in the Black Sea—anything which will give us some trading stock.

These, as Kissinger observes in his memoirs, were all "time-wasting
options." What is striking, however, is that Nixon's first suggestion for
dealing with the crisis had been to propose the use of covert action. In
the event, the crisis was swiftly settled by diplomacy. In an exchange of
notes early in October, the Soviet Union protested, not very convincingly, that it had never intended to establish a submarine base at Cienfuegos and, more persuasively, that it would not do so in future.[112]

Abroad, despite his moves toward détente, Nixon believed, like the
intelligence community, that the Communist challenge must be
resisted by covert as well as overt means. At home, his addiction to
conspiracy and clandestine operations exceeded that of his intelligence chiefs. He believed that he was faced with a great conspiracy by
the Eastern liberal establishment, which was orchestrating a hostile
press against him. The failure of the wiretaps to identify the traitors
within the White House who were leaking to the enemy media gnawed
at his entrails. As he brooded over the liberal offensive against him, his
mind turned increasingly to plans for covert action. By 1970 his chief
co-conspirator was Charles Colson, an ambitious and aggressive thirty-
nine-year-old lawyer who had joined the White House staff the previous year. "Increasingly," wrote Nixon later, "I turned to Chuck Colson
to act as my political point-man. . . . His instinct for the political jugular
and his ability to get things done made him a lightning rod for my own
frustrations at the timidity of most Republicans in responding to
attacks from the Democrats and from the media."[113] The president
installed him in a room next to his own working office and included
him in his early morning senior staff meetings with Kissinger, Ehrlichman and his chief of staff, Bob Haldeman.[114] Nixon would call in Colson
regularly to discuss, sometimes for hours on end, ways of dealing with
his enemies. The two men fed each other's conspiracy theories. In Colson's view, "Those who say that I fed the President's darker instincts

are only 50 percent correct, because 50 percent of the time he was feeding my darker instincts."[115]

Even at moments of victory, Nixon's mind would sometimes turn to the liberal conspiracy against him. Colson recalls an evening aboard the presidential yacht *Sequoia* on May 19, 1970, to celebrate a breakthrough in the negotiation of the first SALT (Strategic Arms Limitation Talks) treaty with the Soviet Union. The secret talks with China that were to lead to Nixon's visit to Beijing in February 1972 were then at a critical stage. Over dinner Nixon turned on Kissinger: "If those liberals on your staff, Henry, don't stop leaking everything to the *New York Times*, I won't be going anywhere. The leaks, the leaks; that's what we've got to stop at any cost. Do you hear me, Henry?" The president rounded off what had been intended as a relaxed evening of celebration with a gruesome description of the fate that lay in store for the enemies who were plotting against him: "One day we will get them—we'll get them on the ground where we want them. And we'll stick our heels in, step on them hard and twist—right, Chuck, right?" "You're right, sir, we'll get them," replied Colson.[116]

The bizarre evening aboard the *Sequoia* may well have been the beginning of the White House Enemies Project. Soon afterward Colson began asking his colleagues for names to put on a list of enemies selected for unspecified covert retribution. According to one of his assistants, an entire office was devoted to files on the project. Before long Colson handed over the running of the project to the White House counsel, John W. Dean III.[117] On August 16 Dean produced a memorandum entitled "Dealing with Our Political Enemies":

> This memorandum addresses the matter of how we can maximize the fact of our incumbency in dealing with persons known to be active in their opposition to our Administration. Stated a bit more bluntly— how we can use the available federal machinery to screw our political enemies. . . . In brief, the system would work as follows:
>
> - Key members of the [White House] staff should be requested to inform us as to who they feel we should be giving a hard time.
> - The project coordinator should then determine what sorts of dealings these individuals have with the federal government and how we can best screw them (e.g. grant availability, federal contracts, litigation, prosecution, etc.).
> - The project coordinator should have access to and the full support of the top officials of the agency or department in proceeding to deal with the individual.

There had been individual attempts to use similar methods to "screw" political opponents before. Most of them had been unsuccessful, Dean believed, "because of lack of support at the top."[118] That mistake, he insisted, must not be repeated. In the summer of 1971, for the first time in American history, a comprehensive covert action program was prepared, on the instructions of the president, to neutralize his "political enemies."

Colson sent Dean a "priority list" of twenty targets, among them:

> *Picker, Arnold M.*, United Artists Corporation: Top Muskie [Senator Edmund Muskie, who was running for the Democratic presidential nomination] fundraiser. Success here could be both debilitating and very embarrassing to the Muskie machine. . . .
>
> *Halperin, Morton*, [ex-NSC] leading executive at Common Cause: A scandal would be most welcome here.
>
> *Davidoff, Sidney*, [New York Mayor John] Lindsay's top personal aide: A first-class S.O.B. wheeler-dealer and suspected bagman. Positive results would really shake the Lindsay camp and Lindsay's plans to capture youth vote.
>
> *Conyers, John*, Congressman, Detroit: Coming on fast. Emerging as a leading black anti-Nixon spokesman. Has known weakness for white females.
>
> *Schorr, Daniel*, Columbia Broadcasting System: A real media enemy.
>
> *S. Harrison Dogole*, President of Globe Security Systems: Fourth largest private detective agency in U.S. Heavy Humphrey contributor. Could program his agency against us.
>
> *Paul Newman*: Radic-Lib causes. Heavy McCarthy [Eugene McCarthy, who had sought the Democratic presidential nomination] involvement '68. Used effectively in nationwide T.V. commercials. '72 involvement certain.[119]

Both the names on the priority list and Colson's comments on them must surely have reflected his daily discussions with the president.

Nixon's main immediate targets in the summer of 1971 were the leakers. To deal with them, he authorized a more far-ranging program of covert action. On June 13, the wedding day of Nixon's daughter Tricia, the *New York Times* published the first extract from what became known as the "Pentagon Papers," a long and rambling official history of American involvement in Vietnam up to 1968, containing many highly classified documents. The papers, given to the *Times* by Daniel Ellsberg, a former Pentagon aide who had briefly worked for Kissinger, dealt with the policy of previous presidents and made no mention of the Nixon administration. Nixon did not at first seem greatly excited. Kissinger, however, instantly exploded with probably the most spectacular of all his White House rages. Haldeman remembers it as "Kissinger's premier performance." Colson recalls him pounding a Chippendale table as he denounced the "forces at work bent on destroying this government": "There is wholesale subversion of this government underway." Both agree that it was Kissinger who roused the president into a fury. ". . . It could destroy our ability to conduct foreign policy," Kissinger insisted. "If the other powers feel that we can't control internal leaks, they will never agree to secret negotiations." Kissinger concluded with an almost hysterical personal attack on Ellsberg who, he bizarrely claimed, was a sexual pervert who enjoyed taking random potshots from helicopters at Vietnamese peasants. According to Haldeman, "The thought that an alleged weird-o was blatantly challenging the President infuriated [Nixon] far more than it might, let's say, if Ellsberg had been one of those gray-faced civil servants who, according to Nixon, 'still believed Franklin D. Roosevelt was President.' "[120]

When attempts to pursue Ellsberg in the courts failed, Nixon turned to covert action. His face flushed, hammering his desk with his fist, he told Colson and Haldeman at a late night meeting, "I don't care how it's done. I don't want any excuses. Use any means." The president's obsession with the Pentagon Papers became more dangerous to the national interest than the leaks themselves. When Nixon brooded over his enemies, his mind invariably turned to conspiracy theories. Thus it was with the Pentagon Papers. Nixon and Colson persuaded each other that Ellsberg was only the visible tip of a much larger subversive iceberg. "We've got a countergovernment here and we've got to fight it," Nixon insisted. ". . . I want to know who is behind this and I want the most complete investigation that can be conducted."[121] Nixon had lost faith in the ability—or willingness—of Hoover and the FBI to take on the "countergovernment." Rumors were rife in Washington that the president was considering ways to remove its seventy-six-year-old director. On July 12 Assistant Attorney General Robert Mardian warned Nixon that Hoover might try to use the seventeen wiretaps placed on White House staff and others in 1969 as "blackmail leverage" to maintain his position. Nixon claims in his memoirs that he was convinced "Hoover would never deliberately expose national security wiretaps." But he admits to being afraid that someone in the bureau might do just that: ". . . The FBI was in a period of great upheaval, and even though the taps had been discontinued, I could not permit the reports of them to fall into the hands of someone who, like Ellsberg, would see the chance to publicize them and become a media hero." Nixon ordered Haldeman to destroy all the logs from the wiretaps to leave no incriminating evidence in the White House. He allowed the irascible and visibly aging FBI director to stay in office until his death in May 1972, noting in his diary, "It would have killed him had he been forced out of office or had he resigned even voluntarily."[122]

Having lost faith in the FBI, Nixon decided to set up a covert action unit among his own staff to neutralize Ellsberg and the imaginary "countergovernment" that lay behind him. He told Ehrlichman:

> If we can't get anyone in this damn government to do something about the problem that may be the most serious one we have, then, by God, we'll do it ourselves. I want you to set up a little group right here in the White House. Have them get off their tails and find out what's going on and figure out how to stop it.

On July 17 Ehrlichman assigned Egil "Bud" Krogh of his own staff and David Young of Kissinger's staff to a new Special Investigations Unit, soon known as the "Plumbers" because its responsibilities included fixing leaks, in the basement of the Executive Office Building.[123] On Colson's recommendation, they were quickly joined by E. Howard Hunt, formerly of the CIA, and G. Gordon Liddy, formerly of the FBI. Nixon later acknowledged that he had personally instructed Krogh that "as a matter of priority the unit should find out all it could about Mr. Ellsberg and his associates and his motives," and had emphasized "the vital importance to the national security of his assignment."[124] On August 11 Krogh and Young gained Ehrlichman's approval for a covert operation "to examine all the medical files still held by Ellsberg's psychoanalyst." The probability is that the operation had been personally authorized by Nixon but that, following the well-established traditions of plausible deniability designed to protect the president from admitting responsibility for covert operations that become public knowledge, he instructed Krogh to seek authorization from Ehrlichman. According to John Dean, Krogh told him that approval for the break-in "came right out of the Oval Office." Ehrlichman confirms that the order came from the president. In a public statement two years later, Nixon himself denied that he had given the order, but added:

> . . . Because of the emphasis I put on the crucial importance of protecting the national security, I can understand how highly motivated individuals could have felt justified in engaging in specific activities that I would have disapproved of had they been brought to my attention.

Nixon stuck to that position in his memoirs. While writing the memoirs, however, he told Haldeman, "I was so damn mad at Ellsberg in those days. And Henry was jumping up and down. I've been thinking—and maybe I did order that break-in."[125]

During the Labor Day weekend a team of three Cuban-American burglars under the direction of Hunt and Liddy broke into the Beverly Hills office of Ellsberg's psychiatrist. The operation proceeded like an episode in *Beverly Hills Cop*. Liddy was fitted with a "gait altering device" and a long dark brown wig, but abandoned both, the former because "the damn thing was killing me," the latter because he believed it attracted homosexuals. ("'Jesus!' I said under my breath, 'I'm being cruised by a seven-foot Navaho. It's got to be this fucking wig.'") During the break-in, the cut-price walkie-talkies with which Hunt and Liddy, who waited in cars outside the office building, had planned to stay in contact with the burglars inside the office, failed to function. The burglars found no trace of Ellsberg's file but wrecked the psychiatrist's office in the hope of making the break-in look like the work of junkies looking for drugs. Liddy phoned Krogh to report on the operation and found him "so relieved nothing had gone wrong, he wasn't concerned that we hadn't found anything." The break-in team then went off for a champagne celebration. On the flight back from California, Liddy and Hunt tried to impress two stewardesses by boasting that they had just carried out a big national security assignment. When the Watergate scandal broke, the stewardesses recognized their pictures in the papers and called the FBI.

On his return to Washington, Liddy found Krogh upset by Polaroid photographs of the damage done to the psychiatrist's office. Liddy failed to understand Krogh's squeamishness. Krogh also seemed concerned by the Browning knife attached to Liddy's belt. "Would you really have used it—I mean, kill somebody?" he asked. Liddy said he would kill if it was necessary to protect his men. A few days later the CIA called Ehrlichman to complain about Hunt's demands for wigs, voice-masking machines, and other equipment. He was probably further disturbed by a plan proposed by Hunt and Liddy to place a psychedelic drug in Ellsberg's soup before he gave a speech at a fundraising dinner in Washington. Ehrlichman told Krogh to halt operations against Ellsberg. Krogh himself was clearly out of his depth. A friend said unkindly that he was "the kind of guy who, if you put him in charge of a big wedding back in Seattle, wouldn't have known how to call the police and get a couple of cops to help with the traffic." By the end of the year the White House Special Investigations Unit had been disbanded.[126]

The short and farcical history of the Plumbers set two important precedents. For the first time in American history, a president had set up a covert action agency to operate from the White House under the control of his own staff. Its ineptitude gave a foretaste of further farce to come. Nixon and his senior staff had failed to grasp the dangers of inexperienced management and enthusiastic improvisation in the conduct of covert action. The many professional black bag jobs carried out by the FBI within the United States, like the numerous equally professional break-ins organized by the CIA abroad, had almost all passed undetected. By contrast, attempts by Nixon's staff to organize covert action led to one bungle after another. It was, in the end, the White House's direct involvement in covert action, combined with the incompetence of its management and its difficulty in maintaining plausible deniability, that was to destroy the Nixon presidency.

The principal source for Nixon's personal involvement in covert action will one day be the four thousand hours of tape recordings (mostly still embargoed) of his conversations and telephone calls covering the period from early 1971 to the summer of 1973. Similar White House recordings, on a much smaller scale, go back to the era of Franklin Roosevelt, who is said to have had a microphone installed in a lamp in the Oval Office. LBJ had much more elaborate recording systems that were removed on Nixon's orders as soon as he took office. Early in 1971 Nixon changed his mind, probably—as he later claimed—so that he could consult the tapes when writing his memoirs in retirement. In February the Secret Service began installing voice-activated recording devices at various locations in the White House and Camp David.[127] Their existence remained a closely guarded secret for the next two and a half years. Though extracts from the tapes played a crucial part in forcing Nixon's resignation in 1974, legal action by the former president prevented all but forty hours of the tapes from being released before his death twenty years later. Ehrlichman acknowledges that their eventual disclosure "will be uncomfortable and embarrassing for me, as well as others who worked in the Nixon White House." That, no doubt, explains why Nixon went to such lengths to keep the tapes secret. The investigative journalist Seymour Hersh concluded, after interviews with unnamed archivists who have worked on the recordings, that "Nixon on tape is a man who saw himself as a lone warrior surrounded by enemies." His closest friend, Bebe Rebozo, used to tell the president in their tape-recorded discussions, "You're doing a great job," but "Your enemies are out to get you."[128]

Covert action against his "enemies" was part of Nixon's strategy to win reelection in 1972. Though he was not, of course, the first president to use "dirty tricks" against his opponents, none of his predecessors had made them such a central part of his campaign. In the autumn of 1971

Nixon's thirty-year-old appointments secretary, Dwight L. Chapin, hired his friend Donald Segretti, a California lawyer, to organize a dirty tricks campaign against contenders for the Democratic nomination. Soon Segretti had twenty-eight people in seventeen states distributing forged documents on the candidates' letterheads, making phone calls to cancel their appearances, and causing various kinds of confusion. Chapin told him to concentrate on Edmund S. Muskie, whom Nixon regarded as the most impressive of the Democrat contenders. Segretti was nothing if not ingenious. He hired a woman to stand naked outside the Muskie headquarters and shout, "I love Ed Muskie!"[129] Nixon also insisted that CRP (the Committee for the Re-election of the President, irreverently known as CREEP) should set up an intelligence branch. "When are they going to *do* something over there?" he repeatedly demanded of Haldeman, drumming his fingers impatiently on his desk.[130]

When the Plumbers disbanded, Liddy and Hunt went off to work for CRP. On January 27, 1972, in the office of CRP's chairman, former Attorney General Mitchell, Liddy proposed perhaps the most bizarre program in the history of Republican campaigns. Displaying a series of multicolored charts on an easel, Liddy outlined a million-dollar operation codenamed Gemstone to monitor and destabilize the Democrats and other enemies. Among the dirty tricks he proposed was a plan to sabotage the air-conditioning at the Democratic convention. "Can't you see all those delegates sitting there dripping wet in 120-degree heat on national television?" he asked his audience. Specially trained prostitutes ("high-class girls, only the best") would then lure delegates to bedrooms or a pleasure boat fitted with hidden cameras and recording equipment. Trouble at the Republican convention could be avoided by kidnapping radical leaders such as Jerry Rubin and Abbie Hoffmann, drugging them, and holding them in safe houses: "They'd never know who had them or where they were." "Well, Gordon," said Mitchell, "that's all very interesting, but not quite what I had in mind." Jeb Magruder, Mitchell's deputy, told Liddy to tone the program down and come up with something cheaper. A number of CRP staff had already been disturbed by Liddy's sometimes bizarre behavior. He enjoyed explaining to horrified secretaries how to kill a man with a sharpened pencil (sharpen it and thrust it into his neck above the Adam's apple), and wore an ostentatious bandage on his hand (he explained that he had burned it with a candle to prove his ability to withstand pain).[131] Mitchell later concluded that after Liddy's presentation, "I not only should have thrown him out of the office, I should have thrown him out of the window."

CRP kept Liddy on chiefly because of pressure from the White House to develop a program of covert action. On February 4 Liddy presented a half-million-dollar program that omitted the wilder excesses of his previous plan and put the emphasis on wiretapping and electronic surveillance of the Democrats. The office of the head of the Democratic National Committee, Larry O'Brien, at the Watergate building in downtown Washington, was added to the list of targets. Mitchell, however, seems to have remained worried by the problem of "deniability," and deferred a decision on Liddy's proposals. During March Liddy continued to work on his plans. He claims, probably correctly, that on about April 1 he received a message from Magruder to tell him, "You've got a 'go' on your project." Giving Liddy the go-ahead required a massive suspension of common sense as well as of political decency. The decision to entrust as risky and sensitive an operation as the Watergate burglary to a man who held his hand over burning candles and gave instruction in assassination by sharpened pencil appears prima facie evidence that some of Nixon's advisers had taken leave of their senses as well as of their ethics. Liddy's political masters had so little idea of the tradecraft of covert operations, however, that they tended to assume that they necessarily involved bizarre characters like Liddy. On one occasion, when Magruder put his hand on Liddy's shoulder, Liddy shouted, "*Get your hand off me! Get your hand off me or I'll kill you!*" Magruder concluded, "Once you accept the premise of no-holds-barred intelligence-gathering, G. Gordon Liddy is what you end up with."[132]

As long as 98 percent of Nixon's tapes and most of his papers remain inaccessible, any assessment of how much he knew about the details of the "no-holds-barred intelligence-gathering" and covert action program against his political enemies must necessarily be tentative. There is little doubt, however, that Nixon took a direct personal interest in at least some covert operations against the Democrats. The tapes are plausibly alleged to contain, for example, an animated conversation between Nixon and Colson after the attempted assassination on May 15, 1972, of George Wallace, governor of Alabama and contender for the Democratic presidential nomination. Nixon and Colson are said to agree in one of the recordings that Howard Hunt should fly to Milwaukee, enter the apartment of the would-be assassin, Arthur Bremer, and plant McGovern campaign literature to make it appear that the attempted assassination had been inspired by it. Hunt, however, was unable to make the trip because the FBI had sealed Bremer's apartment. He offered to try to break in, but his offer was declined. According to Colson, his frequent discussions with the president on the subject of covert action reflected "the black side to our natures. We were constantly saying, 'Can we do this or that?' Like catching [Senator] Teddy Kennedy in bed. It was both of us. We were spontaneous combustion."[133]

Nixon was a great statesman on the world stage as well as a shabby practitioner of electoral politics in the domestic arena. While the criminal farce of Watergate was in the making, Nixon's inspirational statesmanship was establishing new working relationships with both Communist China and the Soviet Union. His triumphal visit to Beijing in February 1972 was followed by an equally remarkable Moscow summit in May, which began less than a week after the abortive plot to burgle Bremer's apartment. The great achievement of the summit was the conclusion of the SALT I agreements: the ABM treaty that, as Nixon claimed, "stopped what inevitably would have become a defensive arms race, with untold billions of dollars being spent on each side" on antiballistic missile systems; and a five-year interim agreement freezing levels of strategic missiles to those in existence or under construction.[134] Both would have been impossible without the remarkable technical achievements of the intelligence communities of both sides. Since the Soviet leadership refused to contemplate adequate systems of on-site inspection, SALT I fell back on verification by what were euphemistically termed National Technical Means (NTMs): spy satellites, ELINT, and other covert forms of monitoring. Just as advances in intelligence collection and analysis had helped to stabilize the Cold War in the mid-1950s, so in the early 1970s they made possible the first steps in controlling the nuclear arms race. On July 1, 1972, representatives of the CIA, NSA, DIA, NRO, and the service intelligence departments formed the Steering Group on Monitoring Strategic Arms Limitations under the chairmanship of the DCI, Richard Helms.[135]

While Nixon was signing SALT I in Moscow, the burglary of the Watergate offices of the Democratic National Committee was under way in Washington. Once Liddy received the go-ahead from Mitchell, he recruited Howard Hunt, his fellow bungler during the raid on the office of Ellsberg's psychiatrist, to assist in the Watergate break-in. Hunt reenlisted the Cuban burglars whom they had used for the earlier raid. James McCord, an ex-CIA agent hired by CRP as a security consultant, was put in charge of the surveillance equipment. Even by the dismal standards of the Beverly Hills operation, the bungles during the Watergate burglary almost defy belief. The first attempted break-in on May 26 had to be aborted, forcing Hunt to spend the night hiding in a liquor closet at the Watergate Hotel. The next morning Hunt advised Liddy never to order Scotch at the Watergate: "Last night in that damn closet I had to take a leak. . . . I was desperate. Finally I found a nearly empty bottle of Johnnie Walker Red. It's now quite full." In the future, Hunt decided to remain outside with Liddy as one of the lookouts. On the night of May 27 the burglars tried again. This time one of the Cubans turned up with the wrong housebreaking equipment. Liddy furiously ordered him to return to Miami for the correct tools: "I didn't care how tired he was; he could sleep on the plane." On May 28 everything seemed to go well. The burglars photographed material on Larry O'Brien's desk; McCord reported that he had fitted bugs to the phones of O'Brien and a staffer on the Democratic National Committee. Mitchell and Magruder were unimpressed both by the documents and by transcripts of bugged telephone conversations. "This stuff isn't worth the paper it's printed on," Mitchell told Liddy. According to Magruder, Liddy then reported a further "problem": "One of the bugs isn't working. And they put one of them on O'Brien's secretary's phone instead of O'Brien's phone. But I'll get everything straightened out right away."[136]

On the night of June 16 there was another break-in to "get everything straightened out." This time the burglars' luck ran out. One of them left tape used to hold open the lock to a garage-level entrance door to the Watergate building visible on the outside of the door. At about 2:30 A.M. on the morning of June 17 the tape was spotted by a security guard, who called the police. The five intruders were caught red-handed in possession of a bag of burglary tools, a walkie-talkie, forty rolls of unexposed film, two 35-millimeter cameras, pen-size tear-gas guns, bugging devices, a wig, $5,300 in new $100 bills, documents linking them to CRP, and address books containing the name and telephone number of Howard Hunt with the note "W. House." "Oh, God," moaned Magruder when he heard the news. "Why didn't I fire that idiot Liddy when I had the chance? How could we have been so stupid?"[137] Nixon claims, probably correctly, that he first heard of the Watergate break-in in Key Biscayne on the morning of Sunday, June 18, when he glanced at a copy of the Miami *Herald*. The main story was about troop withdrawals from Vietnam, but there was also a short news item headed MIAMIANS HELD IN D.C. TRY TO BUG DEMO HEADQUARTERS.[138]

The Nixon tapes are said to contain no indication that the president knew in advance of the Watergate break-ins. Seymour Hersh argues persuasively, "A dirty tricks operation as significant as that undertaken by Hunt and Liddy would have been repeatedly discussed in Oval Office conversations with Bob Haldeman if word of it had reached the President."[139] Whether or not Nixon was informed in advance of the Watergate break-ins, however, there is no doubt about his ultimate responsibility for them. He told a press conference on June 22, "This kind of activity . . . has no place whatever in our electoral process or in our governmental system." Though Nixon repeated that claim in his memoirs,[140] he did not believe it. Under his administration, he had made covert action against his "enemies" part of his governmental system. While he may not have given his personal approval for the operations against the Democratic National Committee offices, there is no doubt that he authorized the attempted cover-up afterward. Nixon probably thought of the elaborate but unsuccessful deception in which he engaged not as a criminal conspiracy but as part of the traditional process of plausible deniability used to distance presidents from all responsibility for covert operations. What made the cover-up after Watergate so difficult to maintain was that there was so much other incompetent covert action to conceal at the same time.

It was the CIA's refusal to become involved in the cover-up that eventually made it unsustainable. On June 23 Nixon approved a plan put to him by Haldeman for the agency to persuade the FBI to call off its investigation on the pretext that it had been a CIA operation concerned with national security. The CIA background of Hunt and one of the Cuban burglars, Eugenio Martinez, would, the president believed, distract FBI attention from White House responsibility for the break-in. Hunt's involvement in Cuban operations going back to the Bay of Pigs was to be used to blackmail Helms into cooperating with the cover-up. Investigating Hunt, said Nixon, "would uncover a lot of things" that the agency might prefer not to see the light of day: "You open that scab, there's a hell of a lot of things. . . ." Nixon instructed Haldeman to tell Helms and his recently appointed deputy, General Vernon A. Walters, "It would make the CIA look bad, it would make Hunt look bad, and it is likely to make Hunt blow the whole Bay of Pigs thing which we think would be very unfortunate—both for CIA and for the country, at this time, and for American foreign policy." Soon afterward Haldeman met Helms and Walters at the White House. Walters later testified that he was ordered to inform L. Patrick Gray, acting director of the FBI, that bureau investigations could endanger CIA operations in Mexico.[141] While driving back from the White House, Helms told Walters simply to ask Gray to inform the agency of anything he discovered that related to Mexican operations. After seeing Gray and holding further discussions at Langley, Walters telephoned John Dean, who was coordinating handling of the Watergate affair in the White House, to tell him that it was extremely unlikely that FBI investigations would prejudice any agency activities in Mexico. Dean plainly failed to inform the FBI, for on July 5 Gray informed Walters that he could no longer hold off the Watergate investigation without a written request from the CIA. Walters replied that the agency was happy for the investigation to proceed.[142]

By involving the White House first in covert action against his "enemies," then in a complex cover-up, Nixon effectively criminalized his administration. Of his four closest advisers, only Kissinger did not become involved. Haldeman, Ehrlichman, and Colson later served prison terms. So did Mitchell, Dean, Magruder, and many smaller fry, including most of those involved with the Plumbers and the Watergate burglars. Even Watergate did not immediately cure the president of his addiction to covert action as part of his reelection campaign. In a tape-recorded conversation of September 15 Nixon threatened to fire the treasury secretary, George P. Shultz, unless he agreed to use the Internal Revenue Service for political purposes. "If he doesn't do it," threatened the president, "he is out as Secretary of Treasury, and that is the way it is going to be played."[143] The White House's passion for dirty tricks showed a lack of a sense of proportion as well as of scruple. No part of the covert action was remotely worth the risks involved in it. "Everything Nixon's wild men got up to, including the break-in to our own National Committee's headquarters," recalls Senator McGovern, "was low-level, superficial, and utterly peripheral to the mainstream of campaigning. I don't think all those dirty tricks put together changed more than 10,000 votes in either the battle for the nomination or the election itself."[144] Much the most important political consequence of the dirty tricks was the eventual destruction of the Nixon presidency. The early stages of the coverup, however, worked well enough to prevent Watergate from becoming a serious issue in the 1972 campaign. Nixon won by a landslide in November, with over 60 percent of the popular vote to McGovern's 37.5. percent.

"I decided after the election," writes Nixon in his memoirs, "that both Chuck Colson and Dwight Chapin should leave the White House." Colson had become "a lightning rod for criticism" of the dark side of the administration; Chapin's association with Segretti had made him too a political embarrassment. With their departure Nixon hoped to give the White House a cleaner image.[145] But Nixon passes over in silence in his memoirs one equally significant sacking, carried out for different reasons. On November 20, 1972, he summoned Helms to Camp David, ostensibly to discuss the CIA budget. "What happened at Camp David," wrote the future DCI, William Colby, "had nothing to do with the budget. It had to do with Helms's careful distancing of the agency from Watergate, his refusal to allow it to be used in the cover-up. And for that Nixon fired him as DCI, sent him packing to Iran as ambassador. . . ."[146] Asked for his opinion of Nixon twenty years later, Helms said simply, "The man is a shit."[147]

Nixon's second term began with what seemed one of his greatest foreign policy successes. Ten years of war in Vietnam and four years of negotiations ended in Paris on January 27, 1973, with the signing of "The Agreement on Ending the War and Restoring Peace in Vietnam." Both sides agreed on an immediate cease-fire. North Vietnam accepted, at least for the present, the continued existence of the Saigon government. During the final stages of the negotiations, Kissinger sent frequent telegrams to Nixon from Paris, marked "President's eyes only." When they arrived in the White House, Haig would telephone George Carver, assistant to the DCI for Vietnamese affairs. Unknown to Kissinger, Carver and Haig then drafted Nixon's replies. "If Henry had found out," Carver believed, "he'd've killed me." Among the intelligence available to the president and his advisers were decrypted North Vietnamese cables that gave a valuable insight into their negotiating position.[148] Nixon hailed the agreement signed in Paris as "peace with honor."[149] In Carver's view, "The North Vietnamese settled basically on our terms, except that the settlement turned out to be a [Munich] 1938 scrap of paper, which they then promptly ignored."[150] Disillusioned CIA analyst Frank Snepp and some of his colleagues saw the agreement as providing only a "decent interval" between American withdrawal and the fall of South Vietnam. It was not long before Nixon and Kissinger came to the same conclusion. "After the summer of 1973," writes Kissinger, "I knew that Cambodia was doomed and that only a miracle could save South Vietnam."[151]

Helms's successor as DCI, after a brief transition period, was James R. Schlesinger, the dynamic, abrasive forty-four-year-old chairman of the Atomic Energy Commission. Schlesinger arrived at Langley in February 1973 with strong ideas on the future of the CIA. While deputy director of the Office of Management and Budget (OMB) in 1971, he had conducted, on Nixon's orders, a "Review of the Intelligence Community," which argued the case for the streamlining and "centralized management of the community."[152] Nixon seems to have chosen Schlesinger as Helms's successor for three reasons. He wanted to shake up the CIA, to establish the DCI as the effective head of the whole intelligence community, and then to bring the community—the agency in particular—firmly under direct presidential control. Nixon did not believe that CIA should have the same independent standing as State or Defense. His aim was to reduce it to the covert arm of the White House. There is no reason to believe that Schlesinger shared Nixon's third and ultimate objective. But, though he stayed only five months as DCI, he left an indelible mark on the CIA. According to Colby, "he arrived at Langley running, his shirt tails flying, determined . . . to set off a wave of change." He fired or retired fifteen hundred agency employees, one thousand of them from the Directorate of Operations (previously known as Plans). Schlesinger also ordered Colby, whom he made his DDO, to assemble a report on past illegal CIA activities, which became known as the "Family Jewels."[153]

On April 30, as the Watergate cover-up started to unravel, Nixon accepted the resignations of Haldeman and Ehrlichman, and fired Dean. ". . . From that day on," Nixon writes, "the presidency lost all joy for me."[154] Kissinger claims that he found it "difficult to get Nixon to focus on foreign policy, to a degree that should have disquieted me."[155] Still less did Nixon focus on the future of the intelligence community. As he became obsessed by Watergate and the problem of his own survival, his plan to reduce the CIA to the secret arm of the White House withered away. In May 1973 Nixon announced that Schlesinger was to become secretary of defense and that Colby would succeed him as DCI.[156] At the time of his nomination, Colby was preoccupied by the Family Jewels. In agreement with Schlesinger, but apparently without consulting Nixon, he revealed their contents in confidence to the chairmen of the congressional armed services committees and their intelligence subcommittees, assuring them that "we were determined that the CIA would remain within its proper limits in the future."[157] Even this limited revelation of the Family Jewels, however, can scarcely have served to increase congressional confidence in the president.

Colby briefed Nixon about once a month during the remainder of his presidency. "I found him very preoccupied," he recalls. "His mind was somewhere else." Nixon telephoned Colby only once. Out of the blue, he called to ask, "What's going on in China?" Colby summarized the latest intelligence. Nixon thanked him and put the phone down. Colby is still uncertain what prompted the call.[158]

Nixon's difficulty in containing the political damage caused by covert action at home seems to have diminished his enthusiasm for covert action abroad. Three years earlier he had reacted with fury to the prospect of Allende becoming president of Chile and had personally ordered the planning of a military coup. In 1973, preoccupied with his own declining political fortunes, he took little interest in Allende's. "I did most of my business with Kissinger," Colby recalls.[159] Though the CIA spent $8 million secretly financing Allende's opponents during the three years after his election, Allende's own economic mismanagement did more than American covert action to destabilize his regime. By the end of 1972, with the Chilean economy in desperate straits, both the Kremlin and the KGB were secretly pessimistic about his chances of survival.[160] In October 1972, however, the CIA reported to the White House that the odds were sixty to forty against a military coup. Kissinger appears to have endorsed the view of one of his staffers that "60-40 means you are certain something won't happen, but you don't want to be too wrong if it does." Not until May 1973 did the CIA report active preparations for a coup. Kissinger seems to have been skeptical. On June 29, however, there was the first military attempt to overthrow a Chilean government for over forty years. It was quickly suppressed by loyal forces. On September 11 a much larger-scale coup, led by the commanders in chief of the armed forces, succeeded. It has been alleged that "American military attachés were in the field with Chilean army units participating in the coup."[161] The CIA, though not directly involved in the overthrow of Allende, seems to have had advance knowledge of it.[162] Allende himself died during the storming of the presidential palace, whether by assassination or suicide remains unclear. On the day following the coup, the leader of the military junta, General Augusto Pinochet, held a secret meeting with the head of the U.S. Military Assistance Advisory Group in Chile. It was a sign of Nixon's sharply diminished interest in the fate of the Allende regime that Kissinger did not report the meeting to him for another week.[163] On September 22 Kissinger succeeded Rogers as secretary of state, a post he combined for the next two years with that of national security adviser.

The foreign intelligence that made the greatest impact on Nixon during the final year of his presidency concerned the Middle East. On October 6, 1973, the Jewish holy day of Yom Kippur, a simultaneous attack by Syria and Egypt caught Israel off-guard. The Syrians advanced into the Golan Heights; the Egyptians destroyed the much-vaunted Bar-Lev defense line and began crossing the Sinai desert. Thus began the sixteen-day Yom Kippur War. Its outbreak, complained Nixon, "took us completely by surprise." Only the previous day the CIA had reported that war was unlikely, dismissing massive Egyptian troop movements as no more than annual maneuvers. That intelligence failure merely confirmed the president's low opinion of the agency. What "stunned" him was that Israeli intelligence, which he regarded as "among the best in the world," had made the same mistake.[164] The most basic Israeli error was to underrate their opponents. After their sweeping victory in the Six-Day War of 1967, they had ceased to regard Arab forces as serious opposition.[165] Israeli overconfidence affected American assessments too. "Anyone who visited the Bar-Lev line," recalls Richard Helms, "left persuaded that no sensible military would want to attack it, especially the Egyptians. The Israelis were convinced that Egypt couldn't get through that line, and Washington believed them."[166] In the summer of 1973 both CIA and DIA flatly asserted that Egypt was not capable of a major assault across the Suez Canal. On September 30 the agency reported to the White House: "The whole thrust of [Egyptian] President [Anwar] Sadat's activities since last spring has been in the direction of bringing moral, political, and economic force to bear on Israel in tacit acknowledgment of Arab unreadiness to make war." A CIA handbook concluded that the Arab fighting man "lacks the necessary physical and cultural qualities for effective military service."[167]

There was, however, no shortage of intelligence from the Middle East. But the sheer volume of SIGINT came close to swamping the system as analysts were faced with the classic problem of distinguishing the crucial signals pointing to the Egyptian-Syrian attack from the mass of distracting, and sometimes misleading, background noise. According to the later, leaked report of the House select committee on intelligence chaired by Representative Otis Pike:

> In late September, the National Security Agency began picking up clear signs that Egypt and Syria were preparing for a major offensive. . . . NSA's warnings escaped the serious attention of most intelligence analysts responsible for the Middle East. The fault may well lie in the system itself. NSA intercepts of Egyptian-Syrian war preparations were so voluminous—an average of hundreds of reports each week—that few analysts had time to digest more than a small portion of them. Even fewer analysts were qualified by technical training to read raw NSA traffic. Costly intercepts had scant impact on estimates. . . . The Defense Intelligence Agency, having no military contingency plan for the area, proved unable to deal with a deluge of reports from the war zone, and quickly found itself in chaos.

A CIA postmortem on the outbreak of the Yom Kippur War came to similar conclusions. It singled out "two particular problems associated with SIGINT":

> 1. Certain highly classified and specially handled categories of COMINT reached their consumers only several days after intercept, a circumstance which perhaps had unfortunate effects;
> 2. SIGINT reporting is very voluminous; in a typical non-crisis week, hundreds of SIGINT reports on the Middle East cross the desk of the area specialist in the production office. Moreover, partly because of the requirements levied on it by a wide variety of consumers, NSA issues most SIGINT reports (not merely ELINT) in very technical language. SIGINT can thus challenge the ingenuity of even the most experienced all-source analyst searching for meaning and patterns in a mountain of material. . . .

The White House, however, bears part of the responsibility for the confusion. The Pike committee heard testimony from various sections of the intelligence community that "Kissinger's secrecy may also have thwarted effective intelligence analysis." He withheld from analysts notes on his conversations with a series of Middle Eastern and Soviet statesmen "despite the obvious usefulness of this information."[168] According to Lawrence Eagleburger, then on Kissinger's staff, "Henry, reading some fairly raw intelligence, came to the conclusion that Sadat was going to start a war before the intelligence community itself did, but too late all the same."[169] The root cause of the intelligence failure, however, was that, at all levels in Washington from the president to junior analysts, the Egyptians and Syrians were not thought capable of the offensive that they launched on October 6. Had the possibility of such an attack been taken seriously, the SIGINT signals would surely have been noticed earlier.

During the war itself, satellite imagery was judged "of no practical value." A subsequent postmortem concluded that two reconnaissance missions on October 13 and 25 "straddled the most critical phase of the war and were, therefore, of little use."[170] According to another CIA report, however, SR-71 spy planes "provided the intelligence community with up-to-date knowledge of the disposition of Arab and Israeli forces."[171] SIGINT provided the best intelligence. Though nearly all the details remain classified, it is known that decrypted signals on October 16–17 enabled Lieutenant Colonel Ariel Sharon of Israel to trap and destroy Egypt's 25th Armored Brigade on the shore of the Great Bitter Lake, thus opening the way to the crossing of the Suez Canal. Other intercepts revealed that Syria's 47th Armored Brigade was headed toward the Sea of Galilee; its commander was heard boasting that in an hour's time he would "bathe in it."[172] Kissinger devoured "every shred" of intelligence received during the war. Nixon did not. He was preoccupied by the scandal surrounding his vice-president, Spiro Agnew, who was forced to plead no contest to a charge of tax evasion, as well as by the even greater uproar over Watergate. On October 10 Agnew resigned. On October 20, while Kissinger was in Moscow discussing a cease-fire to end the war, came the "Saturday night massacre." Nixon fired Watergate Special Prosecutor Archibald Cox; Attorney General Elliot Richardson and his deputy resigned in protest. Though the president struggled to show that he was still in command of foreign policy, the initiative had passed to Kissinger.[173]

On the morning of October 24, almost eleven years to the day after the beginning of the Cuban missile crisis, Nixon received what he considered "alarming new intelligence reports" on the crisis in the Middle East. Seven Soviet airborne divisions had been put on alert; eighty-five Soviet ships, including landing craft and vessels carrying troop helicopters, had been deployed in the Mediterranean.[174] Soon after 9:30 P.M. EST, Dobrynin announced the arrival of an urgent letter from the Soviet leader, Leonid Brezhnev, for the president. Haig, who had replaced Haldeman as Nixon's chief of staff, took the letter to him. In it Brezhnev claimed that Israel was breaking the cease-fire and proposed that the Soviet Union and the United States jointly send forces to the battle zone to take up positions on, respectively, the Egyptian and Israeli sides of the cease-fire line. "I will say it straight," Brezhnev added, "that if you find it impossible to act jointly with us in this matter, we should be faced with the necessity urgently to consider the question of taking appropriate steps unilaterally." Nixon treated the letter as an ultimatum. "We've got a problem, Al," he said. "This is the most serious thing since the Cuban Missile Crisis. Words won't do the job. We've got to act." On Nixon's instructions, Kissinger, Haig, Colby, Schlesinger, the chairman of the JCS, and other members of the interagency Special Action Group met at 11 P.M. to consider how to respond. According to Haig, "We all knew what [Nixon] wanted: a worldwide military alert of United States military forces tied to a strong reply to Brezhnev." Remarkably, however, the president did not attend the meeting that had to deal with what he considered potentially the most serious crisis since the Cuban missiles.[175] Exhausted by the strain of Watergate, Nixon went to bed. At 11:41 P.M., while the president slept, his advisers put American forces around the world on DEFCON III (the highest state of readiness in peacetime conditions, short of an announcement that war is imminent). Nixon awoke the next morning to discover that his forces were on nuclear alert. Later that day Brezhnev backed down and accepted an American suggestion that nonmilitary observers rather than troops be sent to monitor the cease-fire.[176]

Nixon's biographer, Stephen Ambrose, concludes that if Nixon had faced the facts, he would have resigned in October 1973. Instead he hung on for another ten months, fighting an exhausting and unwinnable rearguard action to save his presidency.[177] During that period there was a series of real or alleged intelligence failures. On April 25, 1974, Washington was taken by surprise when a group of left-wing army officers ousted the Caetano regime in Portugal. Agency officials later told the Pike committee that "the CIA Station in Lisbon was so small, and so dependent upon the official Portuguese security service for information that very little was picked up." The six officers in the defense attaché office at the U.S. embassy were far better placed to learn of moves afoot but were said by the Pike committee to have shown little initiative:

> The Committee was . . . told that a serious problem in DIA is a tendency to reward senior officers nearing the end of their careers, by assigning them to attaché posts. Not only were these officers often untrained and unmotivated for intelligence duties, but the Director

of Attaché Affairs testified that he was powerless to assign substantive duties to the attachés in any case.

The intelligence community also failed to provide advance warning of the first nuclear test in the Third World—by India on May 18. There had been a flurry of reports two years earlier that India was capable of testing a nuclear device or that it was about to do so. But between August 1972 and May 1974 there were only two further reports, neither of which was followed up.[178] "We knew that they were fooling around with the nuclear stuff," Colby recalls, "but that they would go ahead and blow one seemed a little farfetched."[179] The last DIA assessment before the test concluded that India might already possess a nuclear device but that "A nuclear weapons program will not likely be pursued in the near term." A CIA report of April 17, 1974, which indicated that India might have already carried out an unsuccessful nuclear test in the Rajasthan desert, attracted little attention at Langley and was not disseminated to other agencies. The threat of nuclear proliferation in the Third World had yet to capture the sustained attention of either the administration or the intelligence community. Immediately after the Indian test, Colby informed Kissinger that the CIA would henceforth devote "a more aggressive effort" to this problem. NPIC analysts were able to identify the Indian test site from previously unexamined satellite photography.[180] Preoccupied by moves for his impeachment, Nixon paid little attention to the intelligence failures in Portugal and India.[181] There is no mention of them either in his own memoirs or in the even lengthier biography by Stephen Ambrose.

Nixon's last major foreign policy initiatives were his tour of the Middle East and his visit to the Soviet Union in June and July 1974. The voluminous NSA decrypts that played a major part in his intelligence briefings before he left for the Middle East are unlikely to be declassified before the twenty-first century. Throughout his travels, Nixon kept up a remarkable front of outward calm but, by the time he began his second Moscow summit, he was in acute pain from phlebitis as well as preoccupied by the now desperate problems of his own political survival.[182] The extraordinary stress under which he was living may help to account for his intermittent failure to pay due attention to the fact (of which he had been warned) that his rooms in the Kremlin palace and elsewhere in his Soviet travels were bugged. Former KGB colonel Oleg Gordievsky recalls that the KGB teams responsible for the surveillance of the president were decorated for their success after the Moscow summit.[183] The Nixon White House tapes stopped in the summer of 1973. Ironically, therefore, the very last of the Nixon tapes, recorded in the summer of 1974, is now located not in Washington but in Moscow, in the archives of the KGB.

The last international crisis of the Nixon presidency came only twelve days after his return from Moscow. On July 15 the government of Archbishop Makarios in Cyprus was overthrown in a coup led by the Greek contingent in the National Guard, acting with the blessing of the ruling military junta in Athens. Once again, Washington was taken by surprise. There had, however, been many warning signs in intelligence reports over the previous few months. On June 3 General Dimitrios Ioannides, leader of the Athens junta, boasted to a CIA official, "Greece is capable of removing Makarios and his key supporters from power in twenty-four hours with little if any blood being shed." If Makarios continued to "provoke" Athens, Ioannides said he would have to consider whether to remove him "once and for all." On July 3 Makarios outraged the junta by demanding the immediate withdrawal of the Greek contingent in the National Guard. A CIA cable from Athens on the same day, however, based on what was later acknowledged as "an untested source," reported that Ioannides had changed his mind and that there would be no coup after all. That report remained the basis of agency assessments until the day of the coup. A CIA postmortem concluded that the Athens station had probably been the victim of a deception. Though there had been no shortage of Greek and Cypriot SIGINT, analysts had been overwhelmed once again by its sheer amount. According to the postmortem:

> As in past crises, most of the Customers interviewed complained of the volume of . . . [SIGINT] reporting, as well as its frequent redundancy. Many also complained of too little analysis of the facts, too few assessments of the significance of reported developments.

Not until after the coup was there any attempt to intercept Greek National Guard communications.[184] Events moved quickly after the overthrow of Makarios. On July 19 a Turkish invasion of Cyprus began. On July 22 the Athens junta was overthrown. After a period of unsuccessful negotiations, a further Turkish invasion on August 14 led to the occupation of one-third of the island and its effective partition. During Nixon's first term he would have followed reports on the Cyprus crisis with close attention, probably complaining of intelligence failures by "the clowns out at Langley." In July 1974, however, Kissinger found it difficult even to ensure that the president was adequately briefed. From July 12 to July 28, while Nixon was in San Clemente, so many documents on Watergate were relayed to him from Washington that Kissinger had to insist that space be found for material on Cyprus too.[185] Nixon did not respond to the intelligence reports.[186]

At the heart of both the Watergate affair and the downfall of the president lay the misuse of intelligence operations and the attempted misuse of the intelligence community. The Articles of Impeachment voted by the House Judiciary Committee declared that the Watergate break-in had been "for the purpose of securing political intelligence":

> Subsequent thereto, Richard M. Nixon, using the powers of his high office, engaged personally and through his subordinates and agents, in a course of conduct or plan designed to delay, impede, and obstruct the investigation of such unlawful entry; to cover up, conceal and protect those responsible; and to conceal the existence and scope of other unlawful covert activities.

The means employed by Nixon, declared the Articles of Impeachment, had included "endeavoring to misuse the Central Intelligence Agency."[187] In May 1973 Nixon had insisted in a public statement, "At no time did I attempt, or did I authorize others to attempt, to implicate the CIA in the Watergate matter."[188] In a taped conversation with Haldeman on June 23, 1972, however, he had attempted to do just that. On July 24, 1974, the Supreme Court ordered the president to hand over that and other subpoenaed tapes to the Watergate special prosecutor Leon Jaworski, who had succeeded Archibald Cox. From that moment Nixon's last faint hope of survival disappeared. His counsel, Fred Buzhardt, told him that the taped conversation with Haldeman was "the smoking gun" for which the prosecution had been searching. By seeking to use the CIA to halt the FBI investigation, the president had clearly obstructed the course of justice. The tape was made public on Monday, August 5, and enraged even some of Nixon's closest supporters. Senator Barry Goldwater read the transcript as he walked from the Senate to his office building, becoming steadily more angry as he did so. "I was mad," he said. "I was mad as hell. I was goddamned mad when I got to the office." Some of Nixon's advisers feared Nixon might do something desperate. At the end of July James Schlesinger, the defense secretary, had instructed all military commanders to accept no orders from the White House without his countersignature. Haig asked the president's physicians not to give him sleeping pills or tranquilizers. Their fears, however, proved to be unfounded. In a televised address on August 8 Nixon announced his resignation. He left the White House the next day with dignity and tears.[189] It was a unique moment in the history of intelligence operations as well as of the presidency. The most powerful government ever to fall as a result of American covert action was the administration of Richard Nixon.

CHAPTER 10

Gerald R. Ford
(1974-1977)

During a career in the House of Representatives lasting almost a quarter of a century, Gerald Ford had concentrated on the nuts and bolts of administration rather than the great issues of national and international policy. At the time of Nixon's resignation, he had been vice-president for only eight months in succession to the disgraced Spiro Agnew. "The reality was," he later admitted, "I wasn't ready to be President. . . . By the time I realized that I really wanted the job, and could do the job, it was too late."[1] On September 8, after less than a month in the White House, Ford announced that he was granting Nixon an unconditional pardon. At that very moment the Watergate prosecutor was exploring ten areas of possible criminal conduct by the former president. If Ford had waited for an indictment, he could have made the pardon conditional on Nixon's admission of his guilt. In the event, the unconditional pardon enabled Nixon to acknowledge nothing more than errors of judgment "in not acting more decisively and more forthrightly in dealing with Watergate."[2] In place of the old doctrine of plausible deniability that had protected previous presidents from having to accept responsibility for covert action, Nixon now substituted implausible denial. Nixon's pardon probably cost Ford the 1976 presidential election.

Ford's reputation for integrity survived the public outcry that followed the pardon of his predecessor. His intellect was far more frequently maligned than his probity. One of Lyndon Johnson's most frequently quoted comments was his dismissive quip, "Jerry Ford is so dumb he can't fart and chew gum at the same time" (an aphorism usually bowdlerized in public to "can't walk and chew gum at the same time").

Though less intelligent than Johnson, however, Ford understood more about intelligence. From 1957 to 1965 he had been a diligent member of the intelligence subcommittee of the House Appropriations Committee, paying careful attention to briefings by the CIA. Louis Tordella, the long-serving deputy director of NSA, found him equally attentive during SIGINT briefings.[3] Ford had also followed the phenomenal progress in IMINT; he was proud to have been one of the few people informed about the secret U-2 overflights of the Soviet Union. His supportive attitude to the CIA showed itself in his public defense of Allen Dulles after the Bay of Pigs fiasco. Ford was content that his intelligence briefers should decide how much he ought to know. "When I served in the House," he later claimed, "the system we had for monitoring the CIA worked well."[4] He did not welcome proposals for greater congressional oversight, but eventually accepted them as a political necessity.

"As soon as Ford became vice-president," Colby recalls, "I briefed him on absolutely everything. So there was no transition problem when he became president."[5] Unlike Johnson and Nixon, Ford paid careful attention to the president's daily brief, though he relied heavily on the interpretation of it by Kissinger and his staff. The brief was delivered to him each morning shortly after his alarm rang at 5:15 A.M., together with the *New York Times*, the *Washington Post*, and a news digest. He spent over an hour reading them in bed, before doing his early morning exercises and having breakfast. The president's first caller after he arrived in the Oval Office at about 7:30 A.M. was usually Brent Scowcroft, Kissinger's deputy at the NSC, sometimes accompanied by David Peterson of the CIA, who answered questions arising from the daily brief.[6] Colby saw Ford, rarely alone, about twice a month.[7] In retrospect, Colby felt he had been wrong not to establish more direct contact with the president:

> But my own reluctance to push into the Oval Office unless I was invited or had something I thought demanded my personal presence, combined with a lively awareness of the probable reaction if I had tried to elbow past Henry Kissinger, kept me from pressing for personal access. . . .[8]

Colby was well aware that Kissinger's influence with the president was incomparably greater than his own. Ford found it "hard . . . to overstate the admiration and affection I had for Henry." According to Kissinger's son, David, "President Ford made it clear that he considered my father intellectually superior to him, but he was comfortable with that." In

October 1975, to Kissinger's annoyance, Ford appointed his deputy, Brent Scowcroft, to succeed him as national security adviser. Kissinger, however, remained secretary of state. Ford writes in his memoirs, "I think we worked together as well as any President and Secretary of State have worked throughout our history."[9]

Ford's first major decision on an intelligence issue came on only his second morning in the White House. While vice-president he had been personally briefed by Colby on Project Jennifer, an unprecedented attempt to raise a sunken Soviet submarine from the seabed of the Pacific at a depth of sixteen thousand feet. "Like everyone who knew about the project," Colby recalls, "he was fascinated by it."[10] Ford concluded that, if the operation could recover the submarine's nuclear weapons systems and codes, it would be well worth its estimated $300 million cost. A purpose-built vessel, the *Glomar Explorer*, equipped with giant claws that could be lowered to the seabed, was constructed for the operation by a mining company owned by the billionaire recluse Howard Hughes, ostensibly to prospect for manganese nodules in the depths of the Pacific. On the morning of August 11 Kissinger, Colby, Scowcroft, and Schlesinger came to the Oval Office to tell Ford that the *Glomar Explorer* was ready to go ahead with the operation, but was being shadowed by a Soviet trawler that might try to stop it. Ford decided that, "having progressed as far as we had, we should gamble and proceed."[11]

It is usually forgotten now just how great the gamble appeared at the time. Colby's mind went back to the Soviet protest after the U-2 shoot-down in 1960. "We could have had a screaming crisis on our hands," he believes. "But though the Soviets sent a ship to sit on top of the thing, they didn't say a word."[12] On August 12 the *Glomar Explorer* succeeded in raising the submarine from the seabed. Five thousand feet from the surface, it broke in two, and the stern section sank back to the ocean floor. The salvaged section, however, yielded two nuclear torpedoes and valuable intelligence on the submarine's technology and weapons systems, including the journal of the nuclear weapons officer.[13] With Ford's approval, the bodies of the thirty Soviet seamen recovered from the submarine were secretly buried at sea near Hawaii with full naval honors, draped in Soviet flags sent from Washington. Fifteen years later, after the end of the Cold War, the then DCI, Robert Gates, took a film of the ceremony to Moscow.[14]

Ford's main priority on succeeding Nixon was to rehabilitate the presidency and the Republican party. Before long, however, he was faced with the additional problem of restoring public confidence in the CIA. On September 8, the day of Nixon's pardon, confidential evidence on covert action in Chile given by Colby to the intelligence subcommit-

tee of the House Armed Services Committee earlier in the year leaked to
the press. The *New York Times* denounced the White House and the
State Department for having "repeatedly and deliberately misled the
public and the Congress about the extent of U.S. involvement in the
internal affairs of Chile." Ford was asked at a press conference on
September 16, "Is the policy of your administration to attempt to destabilize the governments of other democracies?" He replied with the first
ever presidential defense of peacetime covert action:

> Our government, like other governments, does take certain actions
> in the intelligence field to help implement foreign policy and pro-
> tect national security. I am informed reliably that Communist
> nations spend far more than we do for the same kind of purposes.

Ford's comments about Chile, however, were disingenuous. He implied
that American covert action had been uniquely devoted to resisting
attempts by the Allende government to destroy democratic opposition to
his regime:

> And the [U.S.] effort that was made in this case was to help and
> assist the preservation of opposition newspapers and electronic
> media and to preserve opposition political parties. I think this is in
> the best interest of the people of Chile, and certainly in our best
> interest.

Ford then tried to damp down further controversy by officially revealing
for the first time both the existence of the 40 Committee and Congress's
knowledge of its decisions:

> That Committee reviews every covert operation undertaken by our
> Government, and that information is relayed to the responsible
> Congressional committees where it is reviewed by House and Sen-
> ate committees.
>   It seems to me that the 40 Committee should continue in exis-
> tence, and I am going to meet with the responsible Congressional
> committees to see whether or not they want any changes in the
> review process so that the Congress, as well as the President, are
> fully informed and are fully included in the operations for any such
> action.[15]

Ford did not mention that congressional committees had usually been
content hitherto to receive only such intelligence briefings as the CIA

and the White House chose to give them. The controversy concerning the previous administration's covert action in Chile, however, was overshadowed by far more vociferous protests against Ford's pardon of Nixon. Within a few weeks Colby believed that the agency had weathered the brief storm over its Chilean operations.[16]

By December Colby's main preoccupation was the removal of James J. Angleton, the long-serving head of the CIA Counterintelligence Staff. Though admired by many of his staff for his professional skill and encyclopedic knowledge, Angleton had become increasingly obsessed by vast and implausible conspiracy theories. Both the Sino-Soviet split and the Prague Spring of 1968, he believed, were mere playacting—part of a vast Soviet strategic deception designed to mislead the West. Because Angleton's theories were largely ignored by the analysts who prepared the intelligence estimates that reached the White House, they had negligible impact on successive presidents. Kissinger said later, "We never crossed paths while [Angleton] was in office, and none of his memos crossed my desk." Neither he nor Ford had any idea that Angleton suspected Kissinger of being a Soviet mole. Angleton's conviction that all Soviet defectors and intelligence sources for the past decade were KGB plants had come close to paralyzing agency operations against the Soviet Union. The last straw as far as Colby was concerned was to be told by the head of French foreign intelligence, Alexandre de Marenches, that Angleton had warned him that the head of the CIA station in Paris was a Soviet mole. "It was another indication," Colby believed, "that Jim was totally out of control." On December 17 Colby summoned Angleton to his office, told him that he was to be replaced as head of the Counterintelligence Staff, offered him the choice of a consultancy or retirement, and gave him a few days to think it over. Angleton later told journalists that Kissinger had ordered his expulsion from the CIA and was out to destroy the agency.[17]

The problem of removing Angleton was soon to be overshadowed by the biggest public controversy in the history of the American intelligence community. On December 18 Colby received a telephone call that, as he later recalled, had the effect of "ruining not only the Christmas season for me but nearly all of the next year as well." The caller was the journalist Seymour Hersh, who said that he was working on the biggest story of his career. At a meeting on December 20 Hersh told Colby that he had been informed of vast, illegal CIA operations against the antiwar movement. Among the operations he had discovered was Chaos, which had been run by Angleton. Colby insisted that there had been only "a few incidents of the Agency straying from the straight and narrow." For Hersh, however, the DCI's admission of these "incidents" provided confirmation of his story. The first casualty of Hersh's story was Angleton.

Soon after seeing Hersh, Colby summoned him to his office and told him, "This story is going to be tough to handle. We've talked about you leaving before. You will now leave, period."[18]

The lead story in the *New York Times* on December 22 was a report by Hersh that began:

> The Central Intelligence Agency, directly violating its charter, conducted a massive illegal domestic intelligence operation during the Nixon Administration against the antiwar movement and other dissident groups in the United States, according to well-placed Government sources.

When Colby telephoned Ford to discuss the article, the president was on board Air Force One en route to Vail, Colorado, to spend his Christmas vacation. Speaking over an open circuit that he feared might be monitored by the KGB, Colby assured Ford that "Hersh had mixed a few disconnected aspects of CIA's past but that any such actions had been fully terminated"; he promised to prepare a full written report. Colby assumed that the president was already acquainted with the Family Jewels list of agency misdeeds prepared on the instructions of the previous DCI, James Schlesinger. Shortly after speaking to Ford on Air Force One, however, he discovered from Schlesinger that neither Ford nor Kissinger had ever seen it. Colby attributes the embarrassing failure to brief the White House on the skeletons in the agency's closet to an error "which I cannot explain to this day other than by saying it fell between Schlesinger's directorate and mine, during our transition, and that it was deep in the past by the time Ford became President."[19]

On Christmas Eve Colby delivered his report on Hersh's article personally to Kissinger at the State Department for transmission to Ford in Colorado. It concluded:

> . . . Mr. President, you have my full assurance that the Agency is not conducting activities comparable to those alleged in *The New York Times* articles. Even in the past, I believe the Agency essentially conformed to its mission of foreign intelligence. There were occasions over the years in which improper actions were taken . . . , but I believe these were few, were quite exceptional to the thrust of the Agency's activities, and have been fully terminated.

Colby correctly implied that the CIA's involvement in domestic surveillance, in defiance of the National Security Act of 1947, which prohibited it from engaging in "internal security functions," was an outgrowth of the Johnson and Nixon administrations' exaggerated fear that "domestic dissidence" was being orchestrated from abroad:

> Because of CIA's effort during these years, some CIA employees, not directly involved in the program, misinterpreted it as being more focused on American dissidents than on their possible connections with foreign governments. In addition, however, there were individual cases in which actions were taken which overstepped proper bounds. For example, the Agency recruited or inserted individuals into American dissident circles to establish their credentials for operations abroad against those foreign elements which might be supporting, encouraging, or directing dissidence in the United States.

In all, the agency had set up "counterintelligence files" on 9,944 U.S. citizens, including 14 past or present members of Congress.[20]

Colby also took Kissinger a copy of the full Family Jewels report. Kissinger studied the section dealing with assassination attempts against foreign leaders. "Well, Bill," he told Colby, "when Hersh's story first came out I thought you should have flatly denied it as totally wrong, but now I see why you couldn't." Kissinger took Colby's report on the Hersh article to Colorado, discussed it at length with Ford over the Christmas holiday, and briefed him on other items in the Family Jewels. Others of Ford's advisers were also summoned to take part in the discussions, but no invitation arrived for the DCI. Colby spent a lonely Christmas week in Washington while his family went skiing in Pennsylvania. The White House, he concluded, "planned to 'distance' itself from the CIA and its troubles (as the CIA had distanced itself from the White House during Watergate)."[21]

While Ford and his advisers were working out a strategy for damage control in Colorado, Congress was showing signs of a new assertiveness in the intelligence field. The Hughes-Ryan amendment to the Foreign Assistance Act, passed on December 30, required the president, when authorizing a covert action, to certify by a written "finding" that it was "important to the national security of the United States," and to report, "in timely fashion, a description and scope of such operation to the appropriate committees of Congress." In practice, the amendment did little to limit Ford's freedom of action. It did not require him to give Congress prior notification or to obtain its approval.[22] But it was a portent of more serious congressional challenges to the president's intelligence prerogatives in the New Year.

In fact, 1975 was to become known as the "Year of Intelligence." ". . . The CIA," Colby later claimed, "came under the closest and harshest public scrutiny that any such service has ever experienced not only in this country but anywhere in the world."[23] Though sympathetic to the agency, Ford faced a difficult dilemma. The best way to defend the CIA would have been to emphasize that, in the words of a later congressional report, "far from being out of control," it had been "utterly responsive to the instructions of the President and the Assistant to the President for National Security Affairs."[24] Such a defense, however, would have conflicted with Ford's primary aim of rehabilitating the presidency. To restore confidence in the White House, the president and his advisers felt it necessary to distance themselves from the charges leveled against the agency. After the trauma of Watergate, Colby "saw a certain logic in the Ford administration's determination not to take on almost thirty years of CIA's sins."[25]

On January 3, 1975, Ford returned to Washington from Colorado. That evening in the Oval Office, Colby briefed him on the Family Jewels, paying particular attention to the assassination plots.[26] Ford's strategy, worked out during his Christmas holiday, was to preempt a major congressional investigation of the agency by setting up an inquiry of his own. On January 4 he announced the establishment of a blue-ribbon Commission on CIA Activities Within the United States. After paying tribute to the agency's "notable record of many successes" that could not be publicly revealed, he added:

> It is essential in this Republic that we meet our security requirements and at the same time avoid impairing our democratic institutions and fundamental freedoms. Intelligence activities must be conducted consistently with both objectives.
>
> To that end, in addition to asking the panel to determine whether the CIA has exceeded its statutory authority, I have asked the panel to determine whether existing safeguards are adequate to preclude Agency activities that might go beyond its authority and to make appropriate recommendations.

The chairmanship of the commission was entrusted to Ford's vice-president, Nelson Rockefeller. Among its other members was future president Ronald Reagan.[27]

The commission's remit was strictly limited to the CIA's domestic misbehavior and excluded the assassination attempts and other foreign Family Jewels, which had yet to be discovered by the media. Though Ford was anxious to avoid any appearance of a cover-up, he acknowledges in his memoirs that he sought to prevent "unnecessary disclosures [that] could cripple the agency's effectiveness, lower its morale and make foreign governments extremely wary about sharing vital information with us."[28] He doubtless also wished to avoid any suggestion that past presidents had approved assassination plots against foreign leaders. Colby, however, annoyed the White House by being franker than Ford had intended. After the DCI's second or third appearance before the commission, Rockefeller took him aside and asked:

> Bill, do you really have to present all this material to us? We realize that there are secrets that you fellows need to keep and so nobody here is going to take it amiss if you feel that there are some questions you can't answer quite as fully as you seem to feel you have to.[29]

Colby failed to take the hint.

On January 27 the Senate established a Select Committee to Study Governmental Operations with Respect to Intelligence Activities, with Frank Church as chairman. On February 19 the House of Representatives set up its own Select Committee on Intelligence, chaired by Lucien Nedzi. The White House grew increasingly irritated by Colby's relative openness in dealing with the committees. "Every time Bill Colby gets near Capitol Hill," groaned Kissinger, "the damn fool feels an irresistible urge to confess to some horrible crime."[30] It was Ford himself, however, who inadvertently revealed the most sensational crimes of all. At a White House lunch for the publisher and editors of the *New York Times* on January 16 the president revealed that the intelligence files contained material that it was against the national interest to reveal because it would "blacken the reputation of every President since Truman." "Like what?" asked one of the editors. "Like assassinations!" replied Ford, adding hastily, "That's off the record!"[31] It was, by any standards, an astonishingly ill-judged remark. Colby was told what Ford had said the next day. "I was stunned," he recalls. "I just couldn't figure out how it had happened. My conclusion is that it was just Ford being the straightforward guy he is. He's not a Machiavellian, . . . and he was being pressed."[32]

Though all the CIA's assassination plots had either failed or been abandoned, the president's unguarded comment gave the erroneous impression that some had succeeded. After a "spirited argument," the *New York Times* editors agreed to comply with Ford's insistence that his remark was "off the record." Unsurprisingly, however, the story leaked to Daniel Schorr of CBS News, who wrongly assumed that it referred to CIA assassinations within the United States. For several weeks CBS followed a number of false trails, among them a New York automobile accident in Central Park several years earlier that had killed two Soviet diplomats. On February 27 Schorr had a background interview with Colby. After half an hour's discussion of Watergate and other matters, Schorr mentioned as casually as he was able that he had heard Ford was concerned about the agency's role in assassinations. "Has the CIA ever killed anyone in this country?" he asked. "Not in this country," replied Colby. Schorr suddenly realized he had been on the wrong track, and that Ford had been referring to assassinations abroad. Colby refused to supply names. Schorr suggested Dag Hammarskjöld, the UN Secretary General killed in an air crash in Africa in 1961. "No, of course not!" said Colby. But when Schorr mentioned the name of the Congolese leader Patrice Lumumba, also killed in 1961, Colby refused to comment. As the Church committee later revealed, there had indeed been a plot to poison Lumumba.

Schorr returned to his office, his head "spinning with the names of dead foreign leaders." A series of bizarre conspiracy theories swept the CBS newsroom. The political editor, Martin Plissner, asked Schorr, "How do we know it wasn't someone generally believed to have died from natural causes? Stalin? De Gaulle?" Schorr began his news broadcast the next day: "President Ford has reportedly warned associates that if current investigations go too far they could uncover several assassinations of foreign officials involving the CIA. . . ." The White House refused to comment.[33] Leaks to the press and media speculation, however, made it impossible for Ford to remain silent. On March 9, for example, *Time* reported that "credible sources" within the agency had confirmed that "the CIA enlisted the hired-gun help of U.S. Mafia figures in several unsuccessful attempts to kill Cuban Premier Castro."[34] The Rockefeller commission's original brief had been carefully framed to exclude the assassination plots. Two weeks after Schorr's broadcast, however, Ford asked the vice-president to include the plots in his investigations. He told a press conference on March 17:

> I will not condone—in fact I condemn—any CIA involvement in any assassination planning or action. . . . I am personally looking at, analyzing all of the more recent charges of any assassination attempts by the CIA or actual assassinations from its inception to the present.[35]

Ford made matters worse by appearing to acknowledge that there had been "actual assassinations," and he caused further damage to the agency's declining morale by seeming to shift the entire responsibility for the plots from the White House to Langley. The CIA now had to face widespread public anger not merely over its involvement in domestic espionage but also over its homicidal foreign operations.

The public outcry over the assassination plots persuaded the president to come, slightly incoherently, to the defense of the CIA in a series of speeches during April. He declared on April 7:

> . . . We certainly will not adopt such a naive vision of this world in which we live that we dismantle our essential intelligence gathering agencies. I can assure you, I can reassure you that other superpowers are increasing, not decreasing, their military and intelligence capacities.

Three days later Ford told a joint session of Congress that the CIA had been "of maximum importance" both to him and to previous presidents: "I think it would be catastrophic for the Congress or anyone else to destroy the usefulness by dismantling, in effect, our intelligence systems upon which we rest so heavily." At a press conference on April 21 he made a rare public defense of covert action: "A good intelligence covert activity you don't go around talking about. . . . There have been some most successful ones, and I don't think it is wise for us today to talk about the good ones or even the bad ones in the past."[36] Ford could not bring himself to ease the public pressure on the CIA by revealing that "the bad ones" had had the blessing of the White House.

While Ford was defending the CIA, Cambodia and South Vietnam were falling to the Communists. During the previous winter the agency had predicted a new North Vietnamese offensive early in 1975, but had expected it to be only the beginning of a two-year campaign that was intended to reach its climax during the 1976 presidential election.[37] The unexpectedly rapid success of the offensive led Kissinger to order George Carver, then Colby's deputy for national intelligence, to accompany the army chief of staff, General Frederick Weyand, on a tour of inspection to Vietnam in mid-March. Carver found the tour a "heartrending" experience. A South Vietnamese friend commanding a division in the Mekong Delta told him that, because of the cutbacks in American aid, his men were desperately short of ammunition. "Why do you make us fight so lonely?" he asked in broken English. The normally voluble Carver found himself unable to reply. On their return from Saigon, Carver and Weyand landed at Palm Springs to brief Ford and Kissinger. Carver's conclusions were deeply pessimistic:

> I argued that heavy utilization of American military force *might* check the North Vietnamese long enough to give the South Viet-

namese the time to organize themselves: "We can't guarantee it's going to work. What we can guarantee is that if we don't inject American military force the whole thing's going to be collapsed within a few weeks."[38]

The predicted collapse duly came. The final siege of Saigon started on April 25. At 7:30 P.M. on April 28 Ford convened an emergency meeting of the National Security Council, which agreed to evacuate remaining Americans and as many of their South Vietnamese allies as possible by helicopter from the roof of the American embassy in Saigon.[39] "The most dangerous thing right now," Carver told Colby bitterly, "is to be an ally of the United States."[40] On April 30 the South Vietnamese government surrendered. The CIA estimates of only a few months earlier seemed to have been comprehensively discredited. It later became known, however, that the victorious North Vietnamese commander, General Van Tien Dung, had also expected his final campaign to last two years. The speed of the South Vietnamese collapse took Hanoi as well as Washington by surprise.[41]

After the sudden and humiliating American withdrawal from Cambodia and Vietnam, writes Ford in his memoirs, "our allies around the world began to question our resolve." He was shown a front-page editorial in the *Frankfurter Allgemeine Zeitung* headed AMERICA—A HELPLESS GIANT. Ford was determined to provide "proof of our resolve" as soon as possible. What he considered a suitable opportunity to do so came out of the blue on the morning of May 12. At 7:40 A.M. Scowcroft entered the Oval Office with the news that the U.S. merchant ship SS *Mayaguez* had been seized by the Cambodians in international waters. Ford could easily have delegated the handling of the emergency to Kissinger and the crisis management team, the Washington Special Action Group. Instead, he decided to take personal charge himself to reassert his own authority. An NSC meeting, summoned by the president in the cabinet room at noon, began with a briefing by Colby. The *Mayaguez*, he reported, had been fired on and intercepted by Cambodian gunboats sixty miles off the Cambodian coast, about six and a half miles from Poulo Wai Island. Its crew of thirty-nine had been taken captive.[42] Intelligence was scanty. CIA had no sources inside Cambodia, said Colby, and "the SIGINT wasn't giving us much." Aerial reconnaissance by U.S. planes based in the Philippines offered the best means of obtaining further intelligence on the *Mayaguez* and its crew.[43] To demonstrate his own authority, Ford instructed that all news about the *Mayaguez* was to be issued by the White House and that the State Department was to refer all media inquiries to it. In order not to overshadow the president,

Kissinger was to go ahead with speaking engagements in Missouri rather than remain in Washington to deal with the crisis.⁴⁴

Throughout the day there were contradictory reports on the fate of the *Mayaguez*, due chiefly to the difficulties of nighttime reconnaissance. Cambodian time was eleven hours ahead of Eastern Daylight Time, and it was not until dawn on May 14 (the evening of May 13 in Washington) that U.S. naval planes established the ship's location. At 10:30 P.M. Scowcroft informed the president that the *Mayaguez* was anchored off Poulo Wai. Shortly afterward the ship was ordered to weigh anchor by its Cambodian captors. At 1:30 A.M. and again an hour later, Scowcroft telephoned the president to report its latest movements. Ford had little sleep that night. At 5:52 A.M. he began a telephone conversation with Schlesinger lasting over an hour. Determined not to allow the *Mayaguez* to go the way of the *Pueblo* seven years earlier, Ford insisted that it must not be allowed to reach the Cambodian mainland, where its crew could not be rescued. At a midmorning meeting of the NSC, Colby reported that at least some of the crew of the *Mayaguez* were believed to have been transferred to the island of Koh Tang. Ford ordered U.S. fighter jets based in Thailand to interdict all naval traffic in the region headed for the coast. At 10:40 P.M. the president convened the NSC again. Colby's briefing suggested that Cambodia was in an aggressive mood; Khmer Rouge forces had seized a Thai freighter at a Cambodian port and fired on a Swedish merchant vessel. But, the DCI reported, a Chinese official in Paris had said that his country would not intervene if the United States decided to take military action against the Khmer Rouge. During the meeting a message arrived that an air force pilot believed he had seen Caucasians huddled on the deck of a Cambodian ship leaving Koh Tang. Ford instructed the chief of naval operations, "You get a message to that pilot to shoot across the bow but do not sink that boat."

Shortly before 4 P.M. the next day, May 14, the NSC met to discuss the crisis for the fourth time. The latest intelligence, Colby reported, indicated that some of the crew might still be on board the *Mayaguez*, that some were on Koh Tang, and that others had left for the mainland. (In reality, all were on the island of Rong Sam Lem, in the Bay of Kompong Som.) After an hour's discussion, Ford gave instructions for the destroyer escort *Holt* to seize the *Mayaguez*, for the aircraft carrier *Coral Sea* to launch air strikes against military installations near Kompong Som, and for marines to land on Koh Tang and rescue crew members there. The operation quickly ran into trouble. Intelligence reports had put the number of Cambodian forces on Koh Tang at fewer than two dozen. In fact, there were 150 to 200 Khmer Rouge well dug in. Three of the eight marine helicopters were shot down, and no Americans were discovered either on Koh Tang or aboard the *Mayaguez*. Ford had a working dinner scheduled that evening with the Dutch prime minister, Johannes den Uyl, but by his own admission was totally preoccupied throughout the meal. Den Uyl was visibly irritated and "annoyed the hell" out of the president. Scowcroft interrupted dinner with a report from the CIA's Foreign Broadcast Information Service that a Cambodian minister had denied any "intention to detain the *Mayaguez* permanently," but had made no mention of the crew. Unknown to the CIA or the White House, however, the Cambodians had already released their prisoners. After the disgruntled den Uyl had departed, Ford assembled his advisers in the Oval Office. In the middle of the meeting, news arrived that a reconnaissance aircraft had spotted a fishing vessel heading for Koh Tang carrying Caucasians waving white flags. Confirmation soon followed that the Caucasians were the crew of the *Mayaguez*. "We got them all out. Thank God!" said Ford, and added overenthusiastically, "It went perfectly. It just went great!" Whoops of joy went around the Oval Office. Shortly before 12:30 A.M. Ford broadcast live from the White House to announce that "the vessel has been recovered intact and the entire crew has been rescued." In the cold light of dawn, the triumph seemed less spectacular. Forty-one Americans had died and another fifty had been wounded in the rescue operation. Ford complained of "high-level bumbling at the Defense Department."[45] The stream of contradictory reports about the location of the *Mayaguez* and its crew had also left him unhappy with the quality of intelligence supplied by the service intelligence departments during the crisis.[46]

Ford remained anxious, however, to subdue public controversy about the intelligence community. He opened a news conference on June 9 by announcing optimistically, "I believe that the credibility of the CIA can be and will be restored by the report of the Rockefeller Commission and the recommendations of the several Congressional Committees." Though Ford released the Rockefeller commission report on CIA activities within the United States the next day, he withheld material on its investigation of assassination plots on the grounds of its extreme sensitivity. "It remains my deep personal conviction," Ford declared, "that the CIA and other units of the intelligence community are vital to the survival of this country."[47] The Rockefeller report concluded that "the great majority of the CIA's domestic activities comply with its statutory authority," and that some of its illegal activities had been "initiated or ordered by Presidents either directly or indirectly." As Ford had hoped, the report remained studiously vague over the extent of White House responsibility.[48] The president warned against "Monday morning quarterbacking" about presidential involvement in assassination plots. On NBC's "Meet the Press," however, Rockefeller acknowledged that there was "White House knowledge and/or approval of all major [covert] undertakings."[49]

Among the most disturbing of the Rockefeller revelations was the disclosure that:

> As part of a [CIA] program to test the influence of drugs on humans, research included the administration of LSD to persons who were unaware that they were being tested. This was clearly illegal. One person died in 1953, apparently as a result.

The unnamed individual, subsequently identified in the press, was Frank R. Olson, a researcher in biological warfare, who, a month after being given LSD in a glass of Cointreau, had jumped to his death from a tenth-floor hotel bedroom in New York. Ford decided to respond personally to the public outcry that the case provoked. On July 21 he invited Olson's widow and three children to the Oval Office and apologized in person for "the wrong that's been done to you." In 1976 Congress passed a bill to pay Mrs. Olson $750,000 in compensation.[50]

Senator Frank Church declared, with his usual flair for media sound bites, "The Rockefeller report is just the tip of the iceberg." By exposing the rest of the iceberg at hearings of the Senate select committee, Church hoped to establish himself as a leading contender for the Democratic nomination in the next presidential election. He had no wish, however, to compromise his political ambitions by undermining the reputations of past Democratic presidents. Daniel Schorr noted in his diary, "Church, now obviously nurturing presidential dreams, would find life more comfortable if he could exonerate the Kennedys and pin all the assassination plots on Helms and his cloak-and-dagger band." It was politically much safer to blame the CIA than the White House. "The Agency," declared Church on July 18, "may have been behaving like a rogue elephant on the rampage."[51]

While Church pursued his investigation of past CIA operations, the agency was embarking on a major new covert action in Angola. Earlier in the year the 40 Committee had approved $300,000 support to forces opposing the pro-Marxist MPLA (Popular Movement for the Liberation of Angola). In June the threat that the MPLA would sweep all before it led the NSC to set up an interagency task force on Angola chaired by Nathaniel Davis, assistant secretary for African affairs at the State Department. Davis argued strongly against covert intervention. Kissinger and the 40 Committee, however, were convinced that covert action was the only way to "prevent an easy victory by communist forces in Angola," and won the approval of the president. On July 18, while Church was publicly describing the CIA as a "rogue elephant," Ford secretly approved an Angolan operation code-named IA Feature with an initial budget of $6 million. "Go ahead and do it," the president told Colby. Nathaniel Davis resigned in protest from his post as assistant secretary. In his "finding" to the congressional committees, Ford made no specific reference to Angola; he described the purpose of the operation in vague and anodyne terms as the provision of material, support, and advice to moderate nationalist movements in order to promote self-determination in newly emerging African states. On July 27 he approved an additional $8 million for IA Feature. During August the total budget was increased to $25 million.[52]

IA Feature contained from the outset an element of wishful thinking. Davis had warned Kissinger on July 16:

> We have evidence the Soviets are introducing more, heavier and more sophisticated weapons [into Angola]. . . . If it were not true before, it seems clear that it is now unrealistic to think in terms of a program that could be both effective and covert.

There were doubts about IA Feature even within the CIA. One agency assessment warned, "Soviets enjoy greater freedom of action in the covert supply of arms, equipment and ammunition . . . [and] can escalate the level of their aid more readily than we."[53] The arrival of Cuban troops in Angola during the summer of 1975 to support the MPLA and establish Fidel Castro as a great revolutionary leader on the world stage should have made it plain that no conceivable program of covert action could defeat the MPLA. John Stockwell, the increasingly disillusioned commander of the CIA's Angolan task force, who later resigned from the agency, warned that IA Feature was too small to achieve victory but too large to be kept secret.[54] Colby's aim, however, was not to defeat the MPLA but to deny it total control of Angola by supporting two rival groups: UNITA, led by Jonas Savimbi, and the FNLA, led by Holden Roberto. According to Colby:

> Ford was convinced we should help the other two outfits. What we were trying to do was lay the basis for some sort of confederation, call it what you will, leaving the MPLA in Luanda [the capital] and Savimbi and Roberto with their own separate areas and some autonomy. There was a strong tribal base to each of the three groups.[55]

The main impetus for IA Feature, however, came from the White House. As the fighting in Angola intensified, the stakes increased. Kissinger persuaded Ford that, after the humiliations of Vietnam and Cambodia, it was essential to draw the line at Communist expansion in Africa.[56]

As well as covertly pouring arms into Angola during the autumn of 1975, Ford was also engaged in low-intensity conflict with the congressional select committees on intelligence. He declared on August 19:

> Sweeping attacks, overgeneralization against our intelligence activities jeopardize vital functions necessary to our national security. Today's sensations must not be the prelude to tomorrow's Pearl Harbor. . . . Any reckless Congressional action to cripple our intelligence services in legitimate operations would be catastrophic.[57]

Some, perhaps most, senior CIA officials believed that over the next few weeks Ford missed a major opportunity to take the initiative away from Congress by announcing that he was implementing the main recommendations of the Rockefeller commission. "By mid-summer 1975," according to a White House aide, "it was apparent that the intelligence community was quite willing to accept implementation" of the recommendations. The president's counsel, Philip Buchen, took the lead in drafting an executive order, based on the Rockefeller report, imposing restrictions on foreign intelligence operations and giving the President's Foreign Intelligence Advisory Board (PFIAB) responsibility for policing the intelligence community. The executive order, however, was never issued. Langley blamed "lack of direction" and "poor staff work" in the White House: "Those who counseled that Congress would never act and that therefore issuance of restrictions was in the long term an unnecessary limitation of foreign intelligence won the day."[58]

The first "reckless Congressional action" on intelligence to arouse the ire of the president came on September 11, when the House select committee, now chaired by Otis Pike, released a Middle East intelligence summary dated October 6, 1973. One passage in the summary included four words referring to SIGINT whose omission had been formally requested by both CIA and NSA:

> EGYPT—The [deleted] large-scale mobilization exercise may be an effort to soothe internal problems as much as to improve military capabilities. Mobilization of some personnel, increased readiness of isolated units, and greater communication security are all assessed as part of the exercise routine. . . .

The phrase "and greater communication security" revealed NSA's ability to monitor Egypt's tactical communications so closely that it was able to tell when Egyptian tanks were observing radio silence. Ford shared NSA's outrage at the revelation. His SIGINT briefings over the past two decades had accustomed him to the idea that the whole subject was undiscussable in public. On September 12 Assistant Attorney General Rex Lee announced that the president was asking the House select committee to return all secret papers issued to it, and would refuse to provide further documents until assured that it would not release any part of them without his permission. Chairman Pike angrily declared, "The Executive Branch is telling this Committee of the House that it may not continue to operate!"[59]

Senator Church was determined not to be upstaged by the Pike committee. He told one of his staffers on September 4, "We must focus on abuses. That's what this committee is for: to investigate wrongdoing. We need to begin hearings with something dramatic." There was no shortage of drama when the Church committee began public hearings on September 15. Over the next three days Colby, Helms, and CIA scientists gave evidence revealing that over the past eighteen years the agency had spent $3 million developing poisons and biological weapons. Church and the committee members posed for the cameras, holding a silent electrically powered gun designed to fire lethal poisoned darts (absurdly designated, in CIA official jargon, a "Nondiscernible Microbioinoculator"). As notes suggesting possible questions to be addressed to witnesses were passed to the committee, Daniel Schorr and other TV correspondents signaled their potential news value to the publicity-conscious senators either by making circular motions with their index fingers ("roll 'em") or by drawing fingers across the throat ("cut"). By the time the committee hearings appeared on television news, Colby knew that his days as DCI were numbered. For Ford and his advisers, already angered by Colby's relative openness in dealing with the select committees, the sight of senators queuing to be photographed with the Nondiscernible Microbioinoculator was the last straw. Colby wrote later in his memoirs, ". . . The impact of the toxin spectacular, and especially the fact that I delivered the dart gun when Congress demanded it, blew the roof off."[60]

On September 26 Ford, flanked by Kissinger and Colby, met Church and Pike in the Oval Office to try to settle differences over disclosure of classified information. It was agreed that disputes between the CIA and the select committees would be referred to Ford, who would then give formal notification if he believed disclosure was against the national interest. The compromise did not last long. The president's first major clash with the Senate select committee came, as in the case of the

House committee, over SIGINT. On October 7 Ford phoned Church to try to convince him personally of the danger to SIGINT operations that would result from public hearings on NSA. He then dispatched Attorney General Edward H. Levi to put the same case in greater detail to a closed meeting of the committee, but to no avail. The committee voted 5–4 in favor of open hearings. Hitherto, NSA's existence had been almost unknown to the public. But on October 29 its director, Lieutenant General Lew Allen Jr., who appeared to Daniel Schorr "like a meek professor in uniform," was obliged to testify that from 1966 to 1973, during Operation Minaret, NSA had intercepted the communications of 1,680 U.S. citizens and groups placed on a "watch list" by other sections of the intelligence community and the former Bureau of Narcotics and Dangerous Drugs. Allen stressed that none of the communications had been purely domestic; all had involved at least one foreign "terminal." Though he gave no details of NSA's awesome technology, his answers gave the American people their first glimpse of its phenomenal ability to pluck messages from the ether.[61]

The president's next clash with the Church committee came over its report on assassination plots. He had written to the committee on October 9, urging it not to publish the report on the grounds that it would provide the Soviet Union with an unprecedented propaganda weapon against the United States. On October 31 Ford sent strongly worded three-and-a-half-page letters to each member of the committee, emphasizing that publication would do serious damage to national security. Church responded with an angry press statement: "I am astonished that President Ford wants to suppress the committee's report on assassinations and keep it concealed from the American people. They have a right to know what their government has done."[62]

In the early hours of Sunday, November 2, Colby arrived back at Washington National Airport after a visit to Florida. He found a message asking him to see the president in the Oval Office at 8 A.M. Ford came quickly to the point. "We are going to do some restructuring of the national-security structure," he announced. Colby realized at once that his thirty-year career in intelligence was at an end and that he was about to be fired as DCI. Ford offered him a new post as ambassador to NATO, which he later turned down. Schlesinger was sacked along with Colby in what became known as the "Halloween massacre," and Kissinger lost his post as national security adviser to Scowcroft, though he stayed on as secretary of state. Ford told Colby that the next DCI was to be the ambassador to China, George Bush, the former chairman of the Republican National Committee. The Halloween massacre, however, was bungled as well as rushed. The president and his advisers had failed to realize that Bush could scarcely return from Beijing in the midst of arranging a presidential visit to China scheduled for December. While clearing his desk at Langley on November 5, Colby thus found himself unexpectedly summoned back to the Oval Office and asked to stay on as DCI for a few more months. He agreed on condition his authority remained undiminished. "Certainly, Bill," said Ford with evident relief. "You have my full authority, of course. Do you want me to put that in writing?" Colby declined the president's offer. His last three months as DCI before handing over to Bush at the end of January were to be among the busiest of his intelligence career.[63]

Until November the president's counsel, Philip Buchen, had been in charge of coordinating White House policy on relations with the congressional select committees. The continuing clashes with the committees, however, persuaded Ford that better organization and more detailed planning was required. In mid-November he set up an Intelligence Coordinating Group (ICG), chaired by presidential counselor Jack Marsh, and including representatives of the intelligence agencies, the NSC, and the Office of Management and Budget (OMB). The ICG met daily for a month to work out proposals for an executive order on intelligence reform to lay before the president. While it did so, the conflict with Congress continued. Kissinger refused to supply the Pike committee with the State Department documents on covert action it requested. The White House claimed executive privilege. Kissinger, argued Buchen, was right to withhold the documents because they revealed "to an unacceptable degree the consultation process involving advice to previous Presidents Kennedy, Johnson, and Nixon." On November 14 the Pike committee responded by issuing three contempt-of-Congress citations against Kissinger. The dispute was later settled when Kissinger grudgingly handed over most of the documents.[64] When the Church committee rejected Ford's request not to publish its report, *Alleged Assassination Plots Involving Foreign Leaders*, he asked it to delete the names of twelve individuals whose lives would, he claimed, be put at risk. On November 20 a closed session of the Senate endorsed the committee's decision to publish the full report.[65]

While battling with the select committees, Ford and Kissinger were simultaneously preoccupied by the failure of covert action in Angola to prevent the MPLA winning the civil war. On November 14 the 40 Committee instructed the CIA to come up with a program capable of overthrowing the MPLA. In the meantime, it recommended spending the last $7 million in the agency's contingency reserve fund, thus bringing the total budget for Operation IA Feature to almost $32 million. On November 21 Kissinger testified to a closed session of the Church committee about covert action in Angola. If Russian and Cuban intervention succeeded, he claimed, other African dominoes would start to fall. The 40 Committee, however, was dithering. Presented by the CIA on November 24 with programs costing up to an additional $100 million, it hesitated to recommend massive new expenditure but could not bring itself to abandon the secret war against the MPLA and its well-equipped Cuban allies.[66] On December 13 covert action in Angola finally ceased to be covert. A front-page story in the *New York Times* by Seymour Hersh revealed both the scale of IA Feature and the fact that five months earlier Nathaniel Davis had resigned in protest against it. On December 19 the Senate voted 54–22 to cut off funds for Angolan covert operations. Ford reacted angrily, denouncing the vote as "a deep tragedy for all countries whose security depends upon the United States. . . . This abdication of responsibility by a majority of the Senate will have the gravest consequences for the long-term position of the United States and for international order in general."[67] For the first time in American history, a president had been forced by Congress to stop a covert operation abroad to which he was personally committed. "Instead of getting mad at the Senate," Ford complained, "people tended to blame me. Angola was going down the drain, they said, and, as President, Ford was responsible."[68] Among the "people" Ford had in mind was his secretary of state. In a remarkable off-the-record briefing, Kissinger condemned the president for allowing Congress to ride roughshod over his foreign policy.[69]

Within a few days Ford had unexpectedly regained the initiative. On December 23 the CIA station chief in Athens, Richard S. Welch, was killed by masked gunmen as he returned home with his wife from a Christmas party. Colby's immediate reaction was to blame an underground newspaper, *Counter-Spy*, which sought to expose CIA operations and had published the names of a number of agency personnel serving abroad. Some CIA supporters, like Charles Bartlett in the Washington *Star*, were quick to claim—unfairly—that Welch's killing was "a direct consequence of the stagey hearings of the Church Committee." Colby too alleged that "the sensational and hysterical way the CIA investigations had been handled and trumpeted around the world" had contributed to the murder. Both the Church and Pike committees quickly found themselves forced on the defensive. On December 30 Welch's body was flown back to Andrews Air Force Base. The plane carrying his coffin circled for fifteen minutes so that it could land promptly at 7 A.M., thus enabling the reception ceremony to appear live on TV morning news. "Welch, in death," reported Daniel Schorr on CBS, "may have started the rollback of investigations that President Ford, Secretary Kissinger and the whole CIA seemed unable to accomplish." Ford directed that Welch be buried with full military honors at Arlington National Cemetery, and attended the funeral service on January 6. The coffin was carried to the Cemetery Chapel on the horse-drawn caisson that had borne the body of President Kennedy. At the graveside Colby personally presented the folded flag to Welch's widow.[70]

In his State of the Union address on January 19, 1976, the president launched an indirect but blistering attack on the alleged irresponsibility of the select committees:

> The crippling of our foreign intelligence services increases the danger of American involvement in direct armed conflict. Our adversaries are encouraged to attempt new adventures, while our own ability to monitor events and to influence events short of military action is undermined. Without effective intelligence capability, the United States stands blindfolded and hobbled. In the near future, I will take actions to reform and strengthen our intelligence community. I ask for your positive cooperation. It is time to go beyond sensationalism and ensure an effective, responsible and responsive intelligence capability.[71]

Ford's attempts to regain the initiative in the intelligence debate were assisted by the virtual self-destruction of the Pike committee. On January 23 the committee, having rejected by a vote of 9–4 the 150 deletions requested by the CIA, sent its final report to the printers. Three days later extracts appeared in the *New York Times*. On January 29 the House voted 246–124 not to release the report until it had been "certified by the President as not containing information which would adversely affect the intelligence activities of the CIA." A dejected Pike told reporters that the vote had made the work of his committee "an exercise in futility." Ford's authority had been further enhanced on January 28 when, despite the opposition of Church, the Senate confirmed Bush as DCI by a majority of 64–27. Church had attacked Bush's nomination on the grounds that his Republican background made him too political an appointment. He blanched visibly when a reporter asked whether, in that case, "the investigation of the CIA and other intelligence agencies [should] be headed by a man whose aides say he is 80 percent certain to enter politics and run for the presidency?"[72] When Ford arrived at the CIA auditorium in Langley for Bush's swearing-in on January 30, agency morale seemed to be on the mend. "Mr. President and Mr. Bush," declared Colby, "I have the great honor to present to you an organization of dedicated professionals. Despite the turmoil and tumult of the past year, they continue to produce the best intelligence in the world."[73]

Ford's relations with Bush were far closer than they had been with Colby. The president and his new DCI had private meetings in the Oval Office at least once a week.[74]

Conscious that he had lost the initiative to Ford, Church complained to reporters that "the issue has become how to keep secrets rather than how to preserve freedom." The leaking of the Pike report played into the president's hands. On February 16 the *Village Voice*, a radical New York weekly, began publishing the full text under the headline THE REPORT ON THE CIA THAT PRESIDENT FORD DOESN'T WANT YOU TO READ. The discrediting of the Pike committee gave Ford the perfect opportunity to present his own proposals for intelligence reform. On the evening of February 17 he denounced on national television the "irresponsible and dangerous exposure of our nation's secrets," and went on to announce what he claimed was "the first major reorganization of the intelligence community since 1947." The three main innovations contained in Executive Order 11905, issued by Ford the next day, however, scarcely amounted to a major reorganization. A new NSC Committee on Foreign Intelligence, chaired by the DCI, was intended to give greater central coordination to the "management of intelligence." The 40 Committee was replaced by a five-man Operations Advisory Group with similar responsibilities, composed of senior representatives of the White House, the CIA, State, Defense, and the military. EO 11905 also created a part-time three-member Intelligence Oversight Board (IOB), chaired by former ambassador Robert Murphy, which was instructed to report possible illegalities to the attorney general and improprieties to the president. With an average age of just under seventy, the membership of the IOB led one columnist to comment, "Rip Van Winkle guards the CIA."[75] An article on the reforms in the summer 1976 issue of the classified CIA in-house journal *Intelligence Studies* commented:

> [An] intriguing aspect of the emphasis on accountability is that it should have become the focus of Executive Branch intelligence reform after the revelations that many of the abuses of the intelligence agencies were caused not by too little, but rather by too much, accountability to the President. Often the agencies had wandered from their statutory roles precisely in an effort to be responsive to Presidents who sought (or ordered) their help either in covert operations overseas or in dissident surveillance on the home front. . . . It was perhaps symptomatic of the Ford Administration's image of itself—and indeed largely its reality—that no doubt would ever enter its mind that Presidents could be trusted, were honest, and always proceeded by legal means.[76]

The Pike report similarly concluded, "All the evidence in hand suggests that the CIA, far from being out of control, has been utterly responsive to the instructions of the President and the Assistant to the President for National Security Affairs."[77]

Though Ford had regained the initiative in the intelligence debate, he was well aware that it was no longer possible to prevent increased congressional oversight, and he endorsed the idea of a joint congressional intelligence committee. The Senate and the House, however, proceeded along separate paths at different speeds. During the summer of 1976 the House Committee on Standards of Official Conduct conducted eleven days of hearings, summoning all thirteen members and thirty-two staffers of the Pike committee to testify under oath in an unsuccessful attempt to discover who had leaked its report. Congressman Ron Dellums declared when giving evidence, "The investigator has now become the investigatee." It was to be another year before the House proceeded to set up a permanent intelligence oversight committee.[78] The fate of the Pike committee left the Church committee less inclined than at the time of its report entitled *Alleged Assassination Plots* to challenge the president's judgment on the potential threats to national security from the publication of intelligence material in its final report. "The object of the exercise," complained one staffer, "was to prove that we were not Pike." On April 22 Ford wrote to Church:

> It is my understanding that the Select Committee expects to publish in its final report the budget figure for the Intelligence Community. It is my belief that the net effect of such a disclosure could adversely affect our foreign intelligence efforts and therefore would not be in the public interest.

By a vote of 6–5, the committee reversed its earlier decision to reveal the total size of the intelligence budget.[79]

The six-volume final report of the Church committee, published on April 26, acknowledged the dilemma posed by all public discussion of secret intelligence in democracies:

> The fundamental issue faced by the Committee in its investigation was how the requirements of American democracy can be properly balanced in intelligence matters against the need for secrecy. Secrecy is essential for the success of many important intelligence activities. At the same time, secrecy contributed to many of the abuses, excesses and inefficiencies uncovered by the Committee.

Secrecy also makes it difficult to establish a public consensus for the future conduct of certain intelligence operations.

There was no sweeping condemnation of the intelligence community. The final report concluded, "United States foreign and military intelligence agencies have made important contributions to the nation's security, and generally have performed their missions with dedication and distinction." It also accepted that Congress bore part of the responsibility for past intelligence abuses:

The Committee finds that Congress has failed to provide the necessary statutory guidelines to ensure that intelligence agencies carry out their missions in accord with constitutional processes. Mechanisms for, and the practice of, congressional oversight have not been adequate.[80]

No phrase in the final report, however, lingered as long in the memories of most Americans who read newspaper summaries of it as Church's description of the CIA nine months earlier as "a rogue elephant." Now campaigning (unsuccessfully) for the Democratic presidential nomination, Church was unwilling to withdraw that charge publicly. In private he admitted that the study of the assassination plots had convinced him that the real rogue elephant had been in the White House: "The CIA operated as an arm of the presidency. This led presidents to conclude that they were 'super-godfathers' with enforcers. It made them feel above the law and unaccountable."[81] Ford's off-the-record admission earlier in the year that the intelligence files contained material that would "blacken the reputation of every President since Truman"[82] seems to have led him to a similar conclusion.

Perhaps the harshest criticisms in the Church committee's final report concerned FBI rather than CIA operations. The most detailed case study in the report, 115 pages long, concerned "the program to destroy Dr. King as the leader of the civil rights movement."[83] Most of the excesses of the CIA examined by the committee had taken place abroad, where—in the words of one staffer—"laws and ethical standards were frequently different from our own and the boundaries of rectitude obscure." The misdeeds of the FBI, however, had mostly been directed against Americans.[84] The committee welcomed recent guidelines for the bureau issued by Attorney General Edward Levi as "a major step forward in creating safeguards and establishing standards," but criticized them as incomplete.[85] Its report may have had some influence on the further guidelines for the FBI issued by Levi on May 28 dealing with domestic security, counterintelligence, and foreign intelligence activities.

"Ironically," noted the *Washington Post*, "the [Church committee] findings come at a time when the impetus for reform appears to be only a shadow of what it was last year." On May 19, however, the Senate voted by a large majority to implement perhaps the most important recommendation and set up a standing Select Committee on Intelligence. The result was to subject the presidency for the first time to serious, sustained congressional scrutiny of its management of the intelligence community.[86]

If 1975 had been the Year of Intelligence, 1976 was, for most Americans, Bicentennial and presidential election year. These two events prompted Ford to set records for presidential loquaciousness, uttering over a million rarely inspirational words on official occasions.[87] The Bicentennial worried the KGB, which feared that it would improve the worldwide image of the United States after the Watergate and intelligence scandals of the past two years. Among the intelligence shown to Ford was evidence of KGB plans "to expose the reactionary internal and external policies of American ruling circles in connection with the U.S. bicentenary" by arranging for the publication in Europe and the Third World of articles and pamphlets prepared in Moscow denouncing American crimes at home and abroad during the two hundred years since independence. Some of the intelligence came from a KGB officer in Copenhagen, Oleg Gordievsky, who had been working for British intelligence since 1974. Operating from Copenhagen under the cover of a fictitious "European Bicentennial Committee," the KGB distributed pamphlets attacking the Bicentennial around the world.[88]

At the beginning of Bicentennial year, however, Ford was far more concerned by attacks from his main rival for the Republican presidential nomination, Ronald Reagan, than by those of the KGB. "Under Kissinger and Ford," declared Reagan, "this nation has become Number Two in a world where it is dangerous—if not fatal—to be second best. . . . There is little doubt in my mind that the Soviet Union will not stop taking advantage of détente until it sees that the American people have elected a new President and appointed a new Secretary of State." Kissinger urged the president to reply in kind and say that Reagan's reckless rhetoric was endangering the United States' position in the world. Ford refused. "If I criticized Reagan personally," he believed, "I would infuriate conservatives whose support I would need in November." But, in an attempt to counter Reagan's attacks, Ford stopped using the word "détente" in his speeches and began to campaign instead on a policy of "peace through strength."[89]

The desire to fend off charges that the administration was underestimating the Red Menace also influenced Ford's unprecedented decision to approve "competitive analysis" of intelligence on Soviet strategic strength and intentions. In June 1976 a "B Team," composed of conservative critics of CIA's alleged "arms control bias," was asked to make an independent assessment of the intelligence being examined by an "A Team" of agency analysts.[90] Chaired by Richard Pipes, professor of Russian history at Harvard, the B Team also included the recently retired director of the DIA, Lieutenant General Daniel D. Graham, who resented the lack of attention paid by the White House to DIA estimates. Due chiefly to errors by the CIA, Graham complained, National Intelligence Estimates had disastrously underestimated Soviet military might, while some DIA analysts, ignored by the agency, had been "right on the mark":

> CIA analysts have . . . created and fed the myth that military intelligence agencies consistently produced bloated, self-serving intelligence, and that only by feeding these deliberate Pentagon distortions through the cool medium of CIA could the nation get honest military intelligence.

Unsurprisingly, the B Team differed sharply from the A Team, arguing that, contrary to long-held CIA assumptions, the Soviet Union was bent on building a first-strike, "war-winning" capability. "Despite wounded cries," claimed Graham, "the authors of the NIEs, unable to contradict the B-Team, changed their own views."[91] A later study of the A Team/B Team experiment by the Senate Select Committee on Intelligence disputed that conclusion.[92] Competition from the B Team may have made agency analysts more conscious of the dangers of underestimating Soviet strength, but it did not persuade them that the Soviet Union intended to use its military might to secure global dominance.

At the Republican convention in August, Ford narrowly defeated Reagan for the party nomination. In the presidential election on November 2 he lost to Jimmy Carter by only 2 percent of the popular vote. The first question Ford asked himself as he pondered the reasons for his narrow defeat was, "What if I hadn't pardoned Nixon? How many people had voted against me because of that?"[93] The most contentious intelligence issue in what remained of Ford's presidency was the A Team/B Team dispute. Only three days after the election, the two teams confronted each other across a table at Langley. On November 11 Paul Nitze, a leading member of the B Team, took part in founding the Committee on the Present Danger to alert the nation to the grave peril posed by the Soviet "drive for dominance." "Our country," it warned, "is in a period of danger and the danger is increasing." The classified B Team report, submitted on December 2, contained the same controversial message. Within a few weeks the main conclusions of the report had leaked to the press.[94] The Ford administration responded gingerly to the controversy that followed. Though refusing to comment on the report itself, George Bush said on December 26 that there was worrying intelligence on Soviet strategic objectives. In his last State of the Union address to Congress on January 12 Ford gave strong support to the negotiation of a further SALT treaty with the Soviet Union. But he added a warning clearly related to the controversy aroused by the B Team report:

> The United States can never tolerate a shift in [the] strategic balance against us, or even a situation where the American people or our allies believe the balance is shifting against us. The United States would risk the most serious political consequences if the world came to believe that our adversaries have a decisive margin of superiority.[95]

The B Team report found no favor with the incoming Carter administration. Cyrus Vance, the new secretary of state, dismissed the claim that the Soviet Union was achieving military superiority, and declared that "general parity" prevailed.[96] The B Team's conclusions, however, made a deep impression on Ronald Reagan, who became a founder-member of the board of directors of the Committee on the Present Danger.[97] Four years later Reagan entered the White House convinced that "The Soviets were more dedicated than ever to achieving Lenin's goal of a Communist world."[98]

CHAPTER 11

Jimmy Carter
(1977-1981)

When James Earl "Jimmy" Carter, governor of Georgia, told his mother that he was going to run for president, she replied, "President of what?"[1] Probably the only political observer to predict, two years before his inauguration, that Carter would be the next president of the United States was a Soviet analyst who argued that Wall Street capitalists needed to install a puppet from the agrarian South in the White House to control the restless American peasantry.[2] His foolish but accurate forecast is a reminder that the best predictions are not always produced by the best analysts.

Carter seemed the ultimate outsider: the first Southerner to be elected since Zachary Taylor in 1848 and the first president without previous experience of Washington since Woodrow Wilson. He began to study international relations only in 1972 to prepare for the presidential race he had privately decided to enter four years later. In 1976, however, Carter turned his inexperience of foreign policy into an electoral asset, condemning the national disgraces of "Watergate, Vietnam and the CIA," promising to return the nation to the paths of reighteousness, and vowing never to "do anything as President that would be a contravention of the moral and ethical standards that I would exemplify in my own life as an individual." Covert action, it appeared, would be against the spirit of a Carter presidency:

> Our Government should justify the character and moral principles
> of the American people, and our foreign policy should not short-cir-
> cuit that for temporary advantage. I think in every instance we've

done that it's been counterproductive. When the CIA undertakes covert activities that might be justified if they were peaceful, we always suffer when they're revealed. . . .³

The DCI, George Bush, privately complained that Carter's attacks on the CIA were "frequent and vituperative."⁴

The first CIA briefing prepared for Carter after he secured the Democratic nomination in August 1976 assumed little or no previous knowledge of the workings of the U.S. intelligence community. In view of his success in transforming the fortunes of his ailing family peanut producing and processing firm, the agency decided to appeal to Carter's business instincts:

> Essentially the intelligence process can be likened to an industrial one. Raw material—fragments of information of various types and degrees of detail and validity—is collected and fed into a factory—an analytic or *production* organization. The factory distills its raw input into a variety of products, *finished intelligence,* designed for the use of a variety of *consumers.* Intelligence *managers* seek to determine the needs of their consumers, to translate these into *requirements* for collection, to direct collection in response to these requirements, and to shape the finished intelligence product so as best to meet consumer needs.⁵

No such briefing was required for Walter Mondale, Carter's vice-president. Mondale had been probably the most active and best-informed senator on the Church committee. His priorities, however, were the regulation of CIA activities and the protection of civil liberties rather than the improvement of intelligence collection.⁶ Several times during the campaign and the transition period, Bush traveled to Carter's home in Plains, Georgia, to brief him personally. The DCI found the president-elect "all concentration, soaking up data" but with "his guard up." "I felt," writes Bush, "that beneath his surface cool, he harbored a deep antipathy to the CIA."⁷

Carter's inauguration as thirty-ninth president of the United States on January 20, 1977, coincided with one of the greatest technical breakthroughs in intelligence history. Early that morning, only a few hours before Carter took the oath of office at the Capitol, the CIA received the first pictures from the revolutionary KH-11 satellite, launched a month before. Pictures from all previous spy satellites had been taken on film jettisoned in capsules that had to be snared in mid-air over the Pacific before they were delivered to Washington. The KH-11, then code-named

Kennan, began the era of what became known as "real-time imagery." Motion pictures were transmitted, without the need for film, in digital code that was converted by computer into high-resolution screen images. Each image could be enhanced or manipulated to highlight features of particular interest. It took little more than an hour to get imagery from the orbiting satellite to the White House. Henceforth, under good conditions, the president could see the test firing of Soviet ICBMs and wars being waged on other continents almost as they happened. The acting DCI, E. Henry "Hank" Knoche, formerly Bush's deputy, was so excited by the first pictures from the KH-11 that his initial instinct was to take them to Carter on Inauguration Day. He quickly thought better of it. The new president's priority that day was to demonstrate what he intended to be the openness of his administration. He broke with precedent after taking the oath of office by walking, hand in hand with the First Lady, from the Capitol to the White House.

Knoche saw the president and his national security adviser, Zbigniew Brzezinski, at 3:20 P.M. the next day, January 21, in the White House map room. The acting DCI spread some of the first pictures from the KH-11 satellite on a large ornate table in the middle of the room. Carter studied them closely, shook his head in amazement, laughed, and congratulated Knoche. "Of course," he said, turning to Brzezinski, "this will also be of value to our arms control work." Verification remained at the heart of the Strategic Arms Limitation Talks that Carter was anxious to pursue with the Soviet Union. The SALT I treaty was due to expire in October 1977. In September Carter was to reach agreement with the Soviet foreign minister, Andrei Gromyko, on the framework for SALT II. When Knoche finished his briefing on KH-11 on January 21, the president asked him to provide some of its imagery for his first meeting of the National Security Council on the following day.[8] Initially the new pictures were so highly classified that they were withheld even from most of those allowed access to other satellite imagery.[9]

Carter's choice of DCI set an unhappy precedent. Since the foundation of the CIA, all newly elected presidents except Eisenhower had kept the incumbent DCI in office. (Ike had made Truman's last DCI, Bedell Smith, undersecretary of state.) George Bush tried to persuade Carter to keep him on, at least for a few months, to preserve the principle that the office of DCI was above partisan politics. Carter, however, failed to grasp the importance of the principle, and was anxious to make a visible break with the past.[10] For the first time, the DCI was dismissed simply because there was a change of administration. It has been assumed ever since that a newly elected president will automatically sack a DCI appointed by a president of the other political party.

Carter's selection of Bush's successor reflected his inexperience both of intelligence and of Washington. His first choice was President Kennedy's former aide, Theodore Sorensen. Neither Carter nor his transition team had thought to check Sorensen's background. When he had registered for the draft in 1946, Sorensen had asked for noncombatant status as a conscientious objector. It was inevitably, though unfairly, claimed that as DCI he might oppose the use of force in defense of national security. Sorensen was also accused of taking classified material from the White House to use in his biography of John Kennedy. At his confirmation hearing before the Senate Select Committee on Intelligence on January 17 he made a dignified defense against the charges leveled against him, then withdrew his nomination.[11]

According to one of his advisers, Carter concluded after Sorensen's withdrawal that "he had better get a military man for the job and hit the pacifism in the neck." The first military man he approached was the army chief of staff, General Bernard W. Rogers, who had gotten to know Carter while Rogers was commander at Fort McPherson in Atlanta. Rogers turned down the job of DCI but suggested the name of Admiral Stansfield Turner, commander of NATO's southern flank.[12] Turner had been in Carter's class at Annapolis Naval Academy, though the two men had scarcely known each other. The president modestly told a high school audience:

> Stan Turner was so far above me in academics and in leadership that I just admired him from a distance. He was a star football player. He was the top officer in the Naval Academy Brigade of Midshipmen, and he was right at the top in our class. He was a Rhodes Scholar afterwards and had a brilliant career in the Navy.

As president of the Naval War College in Newport, Rhode Island, claimed Carter, Turner had "completely transformed a relatively dormant organization into one that is vibrant and aggressive."[13] On February 2, 1977, Turner received at his Naples headquarters an unexpected summons to the White House. The next day, having crossed the Atlantic by Concorde, he accepted Carter's offer of the post of DCI.[14] Addressing a packed house in the CIA auditorium, Knoche warned the audience that Turner came from a different "culture."[15] The "vibrant and aggressive" style that impressed the president was to make the new DCI unpopular with much of the agency.

On February 10 Turner had a working lunch with Carter beside the fireplace in the Oval Office. He was disconcerted to notice that he was served one more course than the abstemious president. It was agreed that he should brief Carter twice a week, on Tuesday and Friday mornings from 10:30 to 11 A.M. Turner took ten to twelve hours to prepare for each thirty-minute session in the Oval Office. In addition to dealing with major items of current intelligence, Turner also used the briefings to give the president "tutorials" on IMINT, SIGINT, and HUMINT. Much of the content of the tutorials was new to the DCI as well. "I would study the characteristics and capabilities of one or two of the means of collecting intelligence each week," Turner later recalled, "and then pass on what I thought would be useful to him." He discovered that Carter, like himself, had "a technical bent." Both men were deeply impressed by the advanced technology of imagery and signals intelligence collection, but regarded what Turner called "the traditional human spy" as largely outmoded.[16]

Turner considered the extent of IMINT and SIGINT sharing with the British both "excessive" and a potential security risk.[17] When he proposed varying the UKUSA agreement on collaboration between NSA and GCHQ, the British prime minister, James Callaghan, appealed personally to Carter to ensure that the terms remained unchanged. Carter did, however, support Turner's refusal to give the British the latest satellite imagery. While DCI, Bush had promised to share the photography of the revolutionary new KH-11 system with Britain. Turner told the British some of what the KH-11 discovered but refused to provide the imagery itself. It was important, Turner argued, not to "take any more risks than necessary with this absolutely fantastic system that the Soviets don't know about." He recalls:

> Once a month some British intelligence officer appeared in my office and talked for half an hour, and would then say, "I'm sorry to raise this, old chap, you know, but I'm under instruction, you know. This is a difficult question, but when *are* we going to get those photographs?"

The imagery began to be supplied to the British early in 1978, after it was discovered that a former CIA employee, William Kampiles, had given the KGB a copy of the KH-11 manual.[18]

Turner's continuing unease about British security derived from the history of the penetration agents recruited by Soviet intelligence forty years earlier. The KGB considered five of these moles—all graduates of Cambridge University and sometimes described as the Magnificent Five—as the ablest group of foreign agents in its history. Two of the five—the British diplomats Guy Burgess and Donald Maclean—had fled to Moscow in 1951. The so-called Third Man, Kim Philby, defected in 1963. The identity of the other two members of the Magnificent Five gave rise to intense media speculation and, inevitably, to numerous conspiracy theories. British intelligence informed the CIA that the art historian and wartime MI5 officer Sir Anthony Blunt had secretly confessed to being the fourth, and that the fifth was John Cairncross, who, after a varied intelligence and civil service career, had left Britain in 1951. (Blunt was exposed in 1979; Cairncross was not publicly identified as the Fifth Man until 1990.)[19] Turner was not satisfied that the problems of Soviet penetration had been fully resolved by British counterintelligence. When Prime Minister Callaghan asked him, "Do you trust us again?" Turner's reply was polite but, by his own admission, "not too positive." "I did have reservations," he acknowledges.[20] Those reservations were also made known to Carter.

Initially Carter found the mountain of classified and unclassified documents that arrived on his desk each day almost impossible to cope with. Thanks to weekly speed-reading classes in the cabinet room, however, the pace of the president's reading doubled in the space of a fortnight, and eventually quadrupled. Among the first documents that he saw each day was the president's daily brief, which was brought to him in the Oval Office by Brzezinski at about 8 A.M. Carter instructed that copies should also be sent to the vice-president and to Cyrus Vance and Harold Brown, the secretaries of state and defense.[21] "From the very first day of the Presidency," writes Brzezinski, "I insisted that the morning intelligence briefing be given to the president by me and by no one else." To counter Turner's insistence that he, not the national security adviser, was the president's principal intelligence officer, Brzezinski ordered that the president's morning intelligence briefing should be retitled the "national security briefing." He resisted pressure from the CIA that an agency analyst should accompany him to the Oval Office at 8 A.M. to respond to questions about the daily brief. Brzezinski added to the brief other intelligence items such as NSA decrypts selected by his staff and occasional newspaper articles. The total written brief, always conscientiously digested by Carter, came to around twenty pages. On a sheet of White House stationery, Brzezinski would jot down about five to eight points that he wished to make to the president during his oral briefing. As Brzezinski acknowledges in his memoirs, he was anxious to allow Turner only "relatively limited access to the President." Once the initial tutorials on intelligence methods were over, the DCI's meetings with the president were reduced to one a week, later to one every two weeks—always with Brzezinski present. "In brief," claims Brzezinski, "the CIA was effectively supervised by the NSC. . . ." Each week he discussed "the most sensitive internal CIA matters" privately with Turner, then reported what he judged "appropriate" to Carter.[22]

The practical problems of protecting intelligence sources and methods somewhat diminished Carter's enthusiasm for greater openness about the intelligence community. When confronted at a press conference on February 23 with an embarrassing question about past CIA payments to King Hussein of Jordan, he replied, "Well, I've adopted a policy, which I am not going to leave, of not commenting directly on any specific CIA activity."[23] At a meeting with publishers, editors, and broadcasters on March 4 Carter complained that one of the main surprises during his first six weeks as president had been "the almost total absence of any sort of confidentiality around Washington":

> I've been quite disconcerted at some of the CIA revelations, for instance, and I believe it's damaged us considerably in our capability of obtaining adequate intelligence information from other countries.[24]

Carter's surprise was further evidence of his inexperience. "They're very smart," said one old D.C. hand of Carter and his aides, "but it's almost impossible to exaggerate their ignorance of what's been going on in government the last twenty years."[25]

At the outset of his administration, Carter showed less interest in promoting covert action than any president since Truman. But he lacked the rooted objection to it implied by his campaign rhetoric. "Carter never turned down a covert action that I took to him," Turner recalls. "I never turned down a covert action either, though I modified one or two." For the first two years of the Carter administration, however, the Directorate of Operations was in a cautious mood. According to Turner:

> The professionals were so shook by the Church committee that they weren't bringing much forward. They were protecting their hides and weren't proposing risky things in intelligence collection, let alone covert action. It wasn't till [the Soviet invasion of] Afghanistan that they began to get in the Cold War mold.[26]

In 1977 the proportion of the CIA budget allocated to covert action fell to less than 5 percent—the lowest since 1948.[27]

Carter's first major policy initiative as president was in the field of energy—an issue barely mentioned during his election campaign. The dizzy rise in oil prices that began with the angry response of Arab oil producers to the Yom Kippur War raised the price of crude oil almost fifteen-fold in less than a decade, while American imports continued to grow. "Throughout my entire term," Carter wrote later, "Congress and I struggled with energy legislation." The struggle started in earnest with his televised address to the nation on April 18, which began in an almost apocalyptic mood:

> Tonight I want to have an unpleasant talk with you about a problem that is unprecedented in our history. With the exception of preventing war, this is the greatest challenge that our country will face during our lifetime. The energy crisis has not yet overwhelmed us, but it will if we do not act quickly.

Two days later Carter paid his first visit to the House chamber to address a joint session of Congress, calling for a "comprehensive national energy plan" that would be the "moral equivalent of war" (a phrase irreverently abbreviated to the acronym MEOW).[28] "I don't expect much applause," the president declared at the beginning of his speech. "This was one time Congress lived up to my expectations," he later recalled.[29] Among the allies whom Carter summoned to his aid in his battle with Congress was the CIA. On April 18 the White House Press Office released a newly declassified eighteen-page agency report, "The International Energy Situation: Outlook to 1985."[30] The report accurately identified the increasing problems of the Soviet oil industry in keeping pace with growing domestic demand but wrongly suggested that by 1985 the Soviet Union would need to import 3.4 to 4.5 million barrels a day—a conclusion fiercely disputed by experts who gave evidence to the Senate Select Committee on Intelligence. Some accused the CIA of having "cooked the facts to fit the President's recipe." The Senate committee, while criticizing the conclusions of the agency's report, found "no evidence that the integrity and independence of the analytical process . . . was compromised in any way." Carter's use of the CIA assessment to justify his energy policy had, however, "understandably given rise to questions about his use of intelligence."[31]

On May 13 Carter and his senior advisers met the Senate committee, chaired by Daniel Inouye, and agreed to cooperate in producing a legislative charter for the intelligence community. Five days later the committee produced its first annual report. The intelligence agencies, it concluded, were "now functioning under the control of the President and the DCI" and "fully and properly accountable to Congress." The committee's next annual report expressed satisfaction at its "professional and productive relationship on intelligence matters with President Carter."[32] In July 1977, over a year after the Senate, the House created its own Permanent Select Committee on Intelligence. Whereas the Senate committee was determinedly bipartisan, with the Democrats having only one more member than the Republicans, the House committee began with nine Democrats to four Republicans. Intelligence professionals some-times complained, probably with good reason, about "micromanage-ment" by the congressional committees. Carter, however, shared Turner's conviction that "If we want good intelligence in the long run, our only option is to make oversight work."[33] Both rightly judged that, in the post-Watergate era, Congress would never again allow the president a virtually free hand in using the intelligence community.

There was less friction between Carter and the congressional com-mittees than between his two main foreign policy advisers. As Brzezinski later acknowledged, there was a "prolonged and intense" debate over policy toward the Soviet Union between him and Vance. The result, according to Vance, was an unstable balance between the "visceral anti-Sovietism" of the Polish-born Brzezinski and his own "attempt to regu-late dangerous competition" between the superpowers. Brzezinski, for his part, complained of Vance's tendency "to shy away from the unavoid-able ingredient of force in dealing with contemporary international reali-ties." The two men also differed over the role of intelligence. Brzezinski wanted to "revitalize" CIA foreign operations and complained that Vance's approach was too "gentlemanly." In particular, Vance was reluc-tant to approve covert operations against foreign embassies designed to assist NSA in breaking diplomatic ciphers. Brzezinski accused him of going back to the days in 1929 when Stimson had closed the Black Chamber on the grounds that gentlemen should not read each others' mail.[34] At least initially, Carter seems to have shared the squeamishness of the secretary of state.

Both Turner and Carter saw the CIA's thirtieth anniversary in September 1977 as an opportunity to improve its public image by an unprecedented display of openness. On Monday, September 19, ABC television's "Good Morning America" devoted its entire two-hour pro-gram to an unprecedented "inside look at the CIA." Interviews with Turner and "some men and women of the CIA" were followed by a "first-time ever look" at the work of the photographic analysts of NPIC.[35] The DCI and probably the president, whom he briefed the next day,[36] were delighted with the result. Turner wrote to congratulate the producers on "a terrific show":

> A great many people, both within the Agency and from other spots
> all over the country, have voiced the opinion that it was a very
> objective program which gave the viewer a balanced view of the
> CIA. We greatly appreciate having the opportunity to work with you
> and have great admiration for the manner in which you put all the
> pieces together to form such an interesting mosaic.

... All the people here at CIA who worked with your *Good Morning America* staff were greatly impressed with the professionalism and cooperation evident at every juncture. Please pass along my personal thanks and congratulations to all concerned for a job extremely well done.[37]

Behind the scenes, however, morale at Langley was declining. For many of his officials, the glass of lemon and hot water that Turner took for breakfast seemed to symbolize his astringent management style. He had not hidden his view on becoming DCI that "the place was a shambles in administration and needed somebody to take charge of it." By the time he took over, the Operations Directorate had already declined from a peak of about 8,000 employees to 4,730.[38] There was probably scope for further cutbacks, but Turner's method of achieving them was brusque. In August he announced within the agency that another 820 posts in Operations were to go over the next two years; there would have to be 147 immediate early retirements. In what became known as another Halloween massacre, abrupt dismissal notices were sent out on October 31. "I regret to this day," writes Turner, "not having seen to it that these letters were written and delivered properly."[39] Carter supported the cutback in the Operations Directorate. If he was aware of the damage done to agency morale, he gave no public sign of it. A few months later he made the remarkable claim that when Turner took over from Bush, "the CIA had very low morale," and that the new DCI had actually improved it: ". . . I am completely satisfied and totally pleased with the performance of Admiral Turner."[40]

Immediately after taking office, the Carter administration had begun to revise EO 11905, Ford's directive of February 1976 on the intelligence community. A number of piecemeal reforms during 1977 were brought together in EO 12036 of January 24, 1978 on "United States Foreign Intelligence Activities." The signing ceremony in the White House cabinet room, with speeches by Carter, Mondale, and seven members of the congressional committees, produced a remarkable display of unity between executive and legislature. Senator Walter D. Huddleston wondered aloud whether any executive order had ever had "as much congressional input as this particular one." Carter responded, amid laughter, "I doubt if ever before in history an Executive Order has had so much input from the president. I have had to send it back three or four times to be redrafted so I could understand it." EO 12036 laid down the duties and membership of two cabinet-level NSC committees set up by Carter in the previous year. The Policy Review Committee (PRC), chaired by the DCI, and including the vice-president, the national security adviser, the secretaries of state and defense, and the chairman of the Joint Chiefs, was given responsibility for defining priorities for intelligence collection, analysis, and budget allocations. The Special Coordination Committee (SCC), the successor to Ford's Operations Advisory Group and its predecessors, was to review proposals for covert action and other particularly "sensitive" intelligence operations, and to make recommendations to the president. Chaired by the national security adviser, the SCC had much the same membership as the PRC—with the significant addition of the attorney general, who became in effect its main legal adviser. EO 12036 also included a long list of restrictions on intelligence activities, described by Carter as a means of ensuring "full compliance with the laws of the United States." Carter himself took a degree of personal responsibility. The executive order specified that no intelligence operations should be undertaken against U.S. citizens without a warrant "unless the President has authorized the type of activity involved."

Other measures were intended to strengthen the role of the DCI as head of the intelligence community. The National Foreign Intelligence Board, including representatives of all sections of the community, chaired by the DCI, was established to assist him in "the production, review and coordination of national foreign intelligence." The National Foreign Intelligence Center, also chaired in peacetime by the DCI, was responsible for coordinating tasking among the various agencies. The DCI and agency heads were also instructed to keep the congressional committees "fully and currently" informed of their operations. EO 12036 went beyond Hughes-Ryan in ordering prior notification of "any significant anticipated [covert] activities." In keeping with the remarkable display of harmony that Carter had succeeded in orchestrating between the executive and legislative branches, he announced that the order was to be no more than an interim measure, effective only "until appropriate charter legislation can be introduced and enacted by Congress." "I intend," he declared, "to work closely with congressional leaders to enact such legislation."[41]

On February 9 Senator Huddleston introduced S.2525, the 263-page National Intelligence Reorganization and Reform Act of 1978. Besides seeking to regulate intelligence activities in enormous detail, it proposed to create a new post of director of national intelligence who would be "the principal foreign intelligence officer of the United States," accountable to Congress as well as to the president. The president was to be authorized, if he so wished, to appoint an assistant director of national intelligence to head the CIA. Hearings on S.2525 began in April and continued intermittently for two months.[42] Partly because of its sheer bulk and complexity, it failed to become law and served merely as a basis for yet further discussion. On October 25 Carter signed the Foreign Intelligence Surveillance Act, which, as he explained at the signing ceremony, required for the first time "a prior judicial warrant for *all* electronic surveillance for foreign intelligence or counterintelligence purposes in the United States in which communications of U.S. persons might be intercepted." The signing was an occasion for platitudinous mutual congratulation by the president and the congressional committees. The act, said Carter, was proof that "our country benefits when the legislative and executive branches of Government work together toward a common goal."[43] The Senate select committee commended the president for abandoning the claim of previous administrations that the executive possessed "inherent" power to conduct surveillance without a judicial warrant.[44]

Events abroad during 1978 shifted the president's priorities from the regulation to the performance of the foreign intelligence agencies. Early in the year satellite imagery and SIGINT revealed a massive airlift of Soviet arms to the quasi-Marxist regime in Ethiopia headed by Lieutenant Colonel Mengistu Haile Mariam. By February, according to intelligence reports supplied to the president, about four hundred Soviet tanks and fifty MIG fighters had been sent to Ethiopia for use in its war against Somalia. In addition, over ten thousand Cuban troops had been airlifted from Angola to join one thousand Soviet military advisers and four hundred East Germans who were training internal security forces.[45] In a major foreign policy address on March 17 Carter warned of the "ominous inclination on the part of the Soviet Union to use its military power—to intervene in local conflicts with advisers, with equipment, and with full logistical support and encouragement for mercenaries from other Communist countries, as we can observe today in Africa."[46] In May the CIA reported that Cuban mercenaries in Angola were stirring up tribal warfare in the copper- and cobalt-producing area of Zaire. Vance considered the intelligence ambiguous and unconvincing, but, probably influenced by Brzezinski, Carter took it seriously.[47] On June 7 the president told the graduating class at Annapolis, where he had studied over thirty years before, that the Russians were waging "an aggressive struggle for political advantage" that threatened a dangerous escalation of international tension: "The Soviet Union can choose either confrontation or cooperation. The United States is adequately prepared to meet either choice."[48] Carter remained anxious for progress toward another SALT agreement. But he was increasingly concerned by the intelligence presented to him on Soviet and Cuban involvement with the self-styled Marxist-Leninist regimes of Angola, Ethiopia, and Mozambique.

On August 16 Carter paid his first visit to Langley since the swearing in of Turner eighteen months before. His praise for the agency went well beyond the necessary courtesies. Speaking outside the main entrance of the headquarters building, he congratulated his audience on the "superb job" they were doing:

> I've told many groups that one of the most pleasant surprises that I have had as President of our country has been the quality of the work done by the Central Intelligence Agency, and I want to thank you for that.[49]

Just over a week before his visit to the CIA, President Anwar Sadat of Egypt and Prime Minister Menachem Begin of Israel had accepted Carter's invitation to Middle Eastern peace talks at Camp David, beginning on September 5. Not since Woodrow Wilson crossed the Atlantic to attend the Paris Peace Conference after the First World War had an American president thrown himself so deeply into diplomatic negotiations. Carter impressed all his advisers by his detailed grasp of the vast and complex briefs on the negotiating issues.[50] During his final preparations for the Camp David talks, at a retreat on the shores of Jackson Lake in Wyoming, Carter concentrated on reading lengthy psychological studies and viewing videos on Sadat and Begin prepared by the CIA, based on both open and classified sources. The agency provided detailed analysis of the two leaders' medical histories, political ambitions, religious beliefs, relations with colleagues and family, negotiating techniques, behavior under stress, constraints under which they were operating, views about each other, and attitudes toward the United States and Carter personally. His close study of the CIA assessments, said Carter later, paid "rich dividends" at Camp David.[51]

One of the president's secret fears during the thirteen days of negotiations was the threat to Sadat's life if he made the concessions to Israel that would permit agreement with Begin. The CIA had a number of contacts within the PLO, including one of Yasser Arafat's leading aides, Ali Hassan Salameh, whom the agency believed had plotted the massacre of Israeli athletes at the Munich Olympics.[52] Intelligence reports warned Carter that some of Sadat's entourage were "deeply committed to the goals of the Palestine Liberation Organization and other radical groups." While going for an early morning bicycle ride in the Camp David grounds on September 12, Carter saw Sadat engaged in a heated argument with some of his advisers on the front porch of the lodge in which he was staying. During the talks later that day, Sadat appeared preoccupied. Carter believed that he was under pressure to break off negotiations. The next day, according to Carter, in Sadat's absence one of his key advisers "directly misrepresented" his views. Carter tried to see Sadat but was told by his aides that, uncharacteristically, he had gone to bed early and could not be disturbed. The president spent a sleepless night, turning over in his mind intelligence reports of PLO influences in Sadat's entourage and worrying about the possibility of an assassination attempt. At 4:15 A.M. he telephoned Brzezinski and asked him to come and see him. The national security adviser left his cabin in his pajamas and found the president, looking "terribly worried," sitting in his living room with the First Lady and the head of the Secret Service detail. "Zbig," said Carter, "I am very much concerned for Sadat's life." "I was obviously quite startled by that," Brzezinski confided to his diary. The president and his advisers agreed that all that could be done was to strengthen security around Sadat's lodge and keep careful track of comings and goings. "Later, my concerns seemed groundless," Carter admitted, "but . . . I was greatly relieved to see President Sadat in good shape next day."[53]

The subsequent few days were among the most dramatic of Carter's presidency. On the morning of September 15 Vance burst into the president's room and announced, his face white with tension, "Sadat is leaving. He and his aides are already packed. He asked me to order him a helicopter!" With difficulty Carter persuaded Sadat to stay. On September 17 Sadat and Begin, with Carter as witness, signed "A Framework for Peace in the Middle East" and "A Framework for the Conclusion of a Peace Treaty Between Egypt and Israel." The next day, in the presence of Sadat and Begin, Carter gave an address to a joint session of Congress that concluded, ". . . I would like to say to these two friends of mine, the words of Jesus, 'Blessed are the peacemakers, for they shall be the children of God.'"[54] During the Camp David negotiations Carter, unlike Brzezinski and Vance, had been rashly optimistic that the Arab states would acquiesce in an agreement.[55] He quickly realized his error. The Middle Eastern diplomatic traffic decrypted by NSA vividly displayed the disarray and anger in the Arab world.

If the Middle East produced the greatest triumph of the Carter presidency, it also inflicted a humiliation that may well have cost him a second term in the White House. While relations between Egypt and Israel were improving, the shah's hold on the Iranian throne was weakening. As Brzezinski later admitted, "until the [Iranian] crisis became very grave, the attention of the top decision makers, myself included, was riveted on other issues. . . . Our decision-making circuits were heavily overloaded."[56] Carter had visited Teheran at the beginning of 1978, declaring in a New Year toast, "Iran is an island of stability in one of the more troubled areas of the world." Ill-judged though it proved to be, the toast merely reflected the prevailing view in Washington.[57] Though unrest grew steadily during 1978, there was no sense even in midsummer that the shah himself was threatened. A CIA assessment in August, later quoted by Carter in his memoirs, concluded that Iran was "not in a revolutionary or even a prerevolutionary situation." Turner reinforced that message during his briefings of the president. The shah, he told Carter, was in full control of a powerful army, police force, and intelligence service (SAVAK), which were more than equal to any challenge from opposition groups.[58]

That confidence declined rapidly during the autumn. Early in September the shah was forced to install a military government. Embassy telegrams reported that the social fabric was visibly crumbling, with almost continuous riots and demonstrations in every major city.[59] Brzezinski noted in his journal after a meeting of the SCC on November 2: ". . . I was really appalled by how inept and vague Stan Turner's comments on the crisis in Iran were. This reinforces my strong view that we need much better political intelligence."[60] Gary Sick, the NSC desk officer for Iran, complained to Brzezinski four days later, "The most fundamental problem at the moment is the astonishing lack of hard information we are getting about developments in Iran. . . . This has been an intelligence disaster of the first order."[61]

Hitherto, Carter's view of intelligence collection had been dominated by the high-tech wonders of IMINT and SIGINT. The Iranian crisis brought home to him for the first time the importance of political intelligence from human sources. On November 9 the U.S. ambassador in Teheran, William Sullivan, sent a cable to Washington, entitled "Thinking the Unthinkable," which concluded that the shah might be forced to abdicate. Carter reacted to Sullivan's telegram with a sense of personal shock. Only a few days earlier he had congratulated Turner on doing "a fine job." Now he felt badly let down by the CIA. Probably at Brzezinski's suggestion, he sent a sealed envelope to Langley with instructions that it be opened personally by Turner. Inside was a short, reproachful handwritten note. Though addressed to Vance and Brzezinski as well as to Turner, it was clearly directed chiefly at the DCI:

> To Cy, Zbig, Stan: I am not satisfied with the quality of our political intelligence. Assess our assets and as soon as possible give me a report concerning our abilities in the most important areas of the world. Make a joint recommendation on what we should do to improve your ability to give me political information and advice. J.C.[62]

Turner read the note, put it back in the envelope, resealed it, and placed it in his "hold" basket. His attitude at the time, he recalls, was, "I'll take the rap and I'll take responsibility for doing something about it, but I don't have to tell people we've been chewed out by the president. That won't help with morale out here." When the contents of the note leaked to the press a few days later, Turner was convinced that he had been "set up as the scapegoat." He discovered that three journalists had been invited to the White House and shown copies of the note addressed, not to "Cy, Zbig, Stan," but simply to "Stan."[63]

As the Iranian crisis worsened and the shah's position became steadily more untenable, Carter became increasingly convinced that there had been a major intelligence failure. The roots of the intelligence failure, however, lay as much within the White House as within the intelligence community. For the past decade and more, American policy had been governed by what Gary Sick called "the unspoken but unanimous view . . . that the shah was Iran and Iran was the shah."[64] In order not to offend the shah, the CIA had been discouraged from establishing links with opposition figures. The first priority for intelligence gathering in Iran had been the monitoring of Soviet missile testing and development by the SIGINT stations that the shah had allowed NSA to establish at Kabkan and Behshahr. Most domestic intelligence gathered by the CIA in Iran came from SAVAK, the shah's own brutal intelligence service. According to one of Carter's advisers:

> Our understanding was that the deal with the Shah was, "You rely on me for what goes on here, and I'll let you have all the telemetry and monitoring equipment up north that you want." Most people decided that it was not a bad deal—it was more important to monitor Soviet missiles and so forth than have agents keeping tabs on the political situation inside Iran.[65]

In the Oval Office, as elsewhere, the CIA tended to become a scapegoat for the failure to foresee the fall of the shah and the rise of the seventy-eight-year-old Ayatollah Khomeini, who had lived in exile for the past fourteen years. The main failure, however, was far less a shortage of secret intelligence than a broader incomprehension of Iranian society and the appeal of Islamic fundamentalism. It did not require a covert operation to obtain copies of Khomeini's tape-recorded sermons that drew such an emotional response in Iranian mosques. But the appeal of his call for the establishment of a religious philosopher-king, the *velayat-e faqih*, was almost beyond the understanding of the secularized West—even of a devoutly Christian president of the United States. As Gary Sick noted in retrospect, ". . . The notion of a popular revolution leading to the establishment of a theocratic state seemed so unlikely as to be absurd." Even had the CIA been able to keep track of the shah's domestic opposition, it would have been unlikely to concentrate on the mullahs. "Whoever took religion seriously?" demanded one State Department official after Khomeini's rise to power.[66]

On December 29 the shah appointed the moderate opposition politician Shahpour Bakhtiar as head of a new civilian government. The shah himself, Brzezinski told Carter, was doomed. The question now was whether the Bakhtiar government could survive in the face of much more radical opposition. Much, Brzezinski believed, would depend on the attitude of the Iranian armed forces. On January 3, 1979, Carter agreed to send Lieutenant General Robert Huyser to Teheran to urge the military to back "a strong and stable government which keeps close ties with the United States." Brzezinski hoped that Huyser's mission would encourage the leaders of the Iranian armed forces to "take firm action when the moment of truth arrives." He tried to persuade the president to approve covert encouragement for an Iranian military coup to prevent Khomeini's supporters from coming to power. Carter, however, found the proposal "morally troublesome."[67] Halfway through his presidency, Carter still had greater scruples about the use of covert action than any of his predecessors—Truman included—since the founding of the CIA.

Brzezinski's proposal was also vigorously opposed by Vance and the State Department. Faced with internecine warfare within his own administration as well as "morally troublesome" proposals from his national security adviser, Carter became unusually short-tempered. Vance and Sullivan sought to persuade the president to make direct contact with Khomeini in Paris and try to establish a working relationship with him. Carter initially refused in order not to undermine further the rapidly dwindling authority of the Bakhtiar government, but agreed to an indirect approach via the French president, Giscard d'Estaing. On January 16 the shah left Iran—not, as had been expected, for the United States, but for Egypt, vainly hoping that the military would succeed in restoring order and thus enable him to return. Though not willing to promote a military coup, Carter would have been happy if one had taken place. "The threat of a military coup," he told his advisers, "is the best way to prevent Khomeini from sliding into power."[68]

On February 1 Khomeini returned in triumph to Teheran, greeted by over a million of his supporters, and demanded Bakhtiar's resignation. On February 5 Huyser gave a pessimistic report to Carter and his advisers in the White House cabinet room. Though Sullivan believed that Khomeini would eventually install a democratic regime, Huyser predicted that his rise to power would play into the hands of the Communists. At the end of Huyser's briefing, Brzezinski asked him whether "the military would and could execute a coup if given a signal from Washington." Huyser replied in the affirmative. Intelligence reports on the state of the Iranian armed forces, however, were increasingly mixed. On February 9 units in air bases outside Teheran rebelled against their officers and declared their allegiance to Khomeini. Two days later Bakhtiar resigned, surrendering power to Khomeini's nominee, Mehdi Bazargan. At an emergency meeting of the SCC Brzezinski put the case for a military coup, though he accepted that it would now be a "very risky action." Huyser argued that a coup could not succeed "without a massive U.S. commitment." Carter turned the proposal down as "historically and morally wrong." In retrospect, Brzezinski believed that Khomeini's victory had been made possible by three failures of will: "The Shah did not act; the military did not move; Washington never ordered a coup."[69] Given Khomeini's enormous popular support, however, the most likely result of the American-sponsored military coup that Brzezinski vainly urged on Carter would have been an Iranian bloodbath.

Though the CIA had prepared a psychological profile on the shah, it had none on Khomeini. "We weren't tracking Khomeini the way we should have done," Turner believes. "None of us understood the internal dynamics of the Khomeini regime." Even with better intelligence, however, predicting Khomeini's policies after his return from exile would have been enormously difficult. "He was," says Turner, "an irrational, irascible bastard. None of us knew how to predict what his reactions would be."[70]

One almost immediate consequence of the fall of the shah and Bakhtiar was the loss of the NSA listening posts in Iran that had monitored Soviet missile testing and development. On January 31 American personnel abandoned the Behshahr station, though it continued for some time to relay SIGINT automatically via satellite to the United States. (An Iranian supervisor explained, "It might hurt the machinery if we switch off the electricity.")[71] On March 1 the Kabkan listening post was also abandoned. The loss of the two Iranian SIGINT stations added to Carter's difficulties in gaining congressional support for the conclusion of SALT II, which he described as "among our top priorities." In his State of the Union message at the beginning of the year, he had insisted that SALT II would be fully verifiable: "We have very sophisticated, proven means, including our satellites, to determine for ourselves whether or not the Soviet Union is meeting its treaty obligations. I will sign no agreement which cannot be verified."[72] Immediately after the loss of the Kabkan listening post, however, an unidentified official told the *New York Times*:

Kabkan is not replaceable. No tricks are going to overcome that in the short run, and the short run could be three or four years. It is going to affect our capability on verification. I don't think people realize how important that base was, not just for SALT, but generally for keeping up with the Soviet missile program.

Worse still from Carter's point of view was the reaction of the former astronaut, Senator John Glenn, who had made a special study of SALT verification. "I'm not satisfied as of now," Glenn declared, "that we can get by any other means what we got out of Iran."[73]

Helped by his engineering background, Carter had studied in detail the highly classified IMINT and SIGINT methods used to monitor Soviet compliance with the SALT agreements. He was well-enough briefed to discuss personally with Gromyko the technical problems for verification caused by Soviet encryption of some of its missile telemetry. By April 1979 the Soviet Union had agreed not to encode most of its missile-test data.[74] After detailed consultations with his intelligence advisers, Carter publicly insisted that, despite the loss of the Behshahr and Kabkan listening posts:

> We are very secure in our belief that we do have adequate technical means to confirm the SALT agreement, not based on mutual trust, but based on our own ability, with or without the Iran monitoring stations. They were important. We'd like to have them back, or an adequate replacement for them, but they're just one element in an all-inclusive, complex, adequate means by which we can assure compliance with SALT.[75]

Carter was almost beside himself with fury at what he saw as Senator Glenn's attempt to undermine the SALT negotiations by casting doubt on the adequacy of intelligence monitoring. He was about to phone him on the evening of April 6 when his wife persuaded him, with some difficulty, to wait until he had calmed down. The president's temper had only partly subsided when he called Glenn the following morning. Speaking in what he perhaps euphemistically describes as "the most forceful possible language," Carter accused him of "trying to kill the arms limitation process while still claiming to be a strong supporter of SALT."[76]

At a summit meeting in Vienna on June 18 Carter and Brezhnev signed SALT II. The president regarded it as a historic moment. The treaty placed, for the first time, equal ceilings on the strategic nuclear arsenals of both sides. Flying back to Washington immediately after the signing ceremony, Carter addressed a joint session of Congress and a television audience later the same day. He laid heavy emphasis on the ability of the intelligence community to ensure that the treaty was honored:

Compliance will be ensured by our own Nation's means of verification, including extremely sophisticated satellites, powerful electronic systems, and a vast intelligence network. Were the Soviet Union to take [the] enormous risk of trying to violate this treaty in any way that might affect the strategic balance, there is no doubt that we would discover it in time to respond fully and effectively. It's the SALT II agreement itself which forbids concealment measures—many of them for the first time—forbids interference with our monitoring, and forbids the encryption or the encoding of crucial missile-test information.[77]

Turner was put under heavy presidential pressure to support Carter's arguments. Before he gave evidence to the Senate, his testimony was rehearsed at a meeting of the SCC. The DCI considered it "insulting to an agency head to have his testimony subjected to this kind of advance scrutiny. . . . The real reason was clearly to get me under control and to push me to testify that the treaty was adequately verifiable."[78] By late summer both the president and his advisers believed that the campaign for the ratification of SALT II was making steady progress.[79]

Ratification, however, was derailed by an intelligence fiasco for which the White House, State Department, the intelligence community, and Senator Frank Church all bore varying degrees of responsibility. Early in July, in response to pressure from Brzezinski for more intelligence on Soviet activities in Cuba, NSA produced a Cuban intercept that referred to the presence of a Soviet *brigada*. Jumping to the conclusion that the unit had a combat function, NSA coined the term "combat brigade" to describe it—thus giving the false impression that it might be intended to move out of Cuba and help to spread revolution in Central America.[80] On July 24 Brzezinski told Carter that the presence of the brigade "could have serious repercussions for SALT." The CIA, however, was still doubtful as to the significance of the NSA report, uncertain whether the brigade was "a combat force, a training structure for Cuban forces, or a facility for Soviet development and testing of tropical combat tactics." The president thus found himself faced, in the middle of the SALT hearings, with increasing rumors in Congress about the discovery of Soviet troops in Cuba but no hard information about what the troops were up to. Brzezinski sent an angry note (or, in his own words, "a crisply worded memorandum") to Turner demanding better intelligence.[81]

Early in August an exercise by the Soviet brigade offered an opportunity to discover more about its role. All the resources of the intelligence community—imagery, SIGINT, and agent reports—were focused on the brigade in what Turner claimed was an example of "superb" teamwork.

Proof was quickly obtained that the Soviet troops were engaged in field exercises on their own, not in training Cubans. An agency assessment a few days after the exercise concluded that NSA had been right to describe the Soviet unit as a "combat brigade." CIA analysts, however, had wrongly jumped to alarmist conclusions. As Turner later acknowledged:

> Our playing up this combat unit as something new was misleading. It was new to us, but such exercises might have been going on unnoticed. After all, we detected the one in August only because we had begun paying special attention to the brigade. . . .

The consequence of the intelligence report on the brigade exercise was to create, in Turner's words, "as much panic as can be generated in Washington in mid-August, when most officials are away on holiday."[82] On August 14 Brzezinski warned the president that the situation was now "extremely serious."[83] At the end of the month a number of congressional leaders were briefed, including Frank Church, chairman of the Senate Foreign Relations Committee. His presidential ambitions now well behind him, Church was fighting to save his Senate seat in Idaho. Having been widely criticized for going to Cuba to meet Castro, Church saw the Soviet brigade as an opportunity to gain welcome publicity and counter claims that he was soft on Communism. On August 31 the press carried Church's call for SALT to be scrapped unless the whole brigade was promptly withdrawn. "The President must make it clear," he insisted, "[that] we draw the line on Russian penetration of this hemisphere." A week later, privately indignant at Church's "absolutely irresponsible" behavior, Carter went on television to try to "reassure the nation." In the event, his confused statement only made the crisis worse:

> We have concluded, as the consequences [sic] of intensified intelligence efforts, that a Soviet combat unit is currently stationed in Cuba. We have some evidence to indicate that such a unit has been in Cuba for some time, perhaps for quite a few years. . . . It is not an assault force. It does not have airlift or sea-going capabilities and does not have weapons capable of attacking the United States. The purpose of this combat unit is not yet clear. However, . . . we consider the presence of a Soviet combat brigade in Cuba to be a very serious matter and that this status quo is not acceptable.

That ill-judged final phrase proved, as Carter later acknowledged, to be "troublesome." It was widely interpreted as a demand for the removal of the Soviet brigade.[84]

The Washington panic, of which Turner complained, resulted from an extraordinary lapse of collective memory on the part of both the administration and the intelligence community. The White House and the State Department had somehow forgotten that in 1963 Kennedy had agreed to a Soviet military unit remaining in Cuba. CIA and NSA had overlooked Cuban decrypts buried in their files going back to the late 1960s that used the term *brigada* to refer to the Soviet unit.[85] These failures, however, also reflected Carter's own ahistorical mindset. One of his speechwriters, James Fallows, was repeatedly struck by "his view of problems as technical, not historical, [and] his lack of curiosity about how the story turned out before." Harvard professors Richard Neustadt and Ernest May conclude that in the summer of 1979:

> U.S. intelligence agencies did not have the historical data at hand, because they were not accustomed to answering historical questions. Carter did not ask them. So his aides did not ask them either.[86]

As the past history of the Soviet brigade began to reemerge in mid-September, Brzezinski found the president "deeply perplexed."[87] To help resolve his confusion, he summoned the elder statesman, Clark Clifford, and asked him to convene a high-level advisory group modeled on the Wise Men of 1968. Clifford's group, officially known as the Citizens Advisory Committee on Cuba, spent a day at Langley, grilling agency analysts on the background to the crisis. At Clifford's request, McGeorge Bundy, a member of his group, drew up a report on the intelligence failure, completed on September 26, which concluded:

> The present crisis over a Soviet infantry brigade in Cuba is the product of internal accident and error in the United States. It should be ended mainly by American good sense. . . . We would not have made the brigade a *cause célèbre* if we had known its full history; we should not make it so because we did not.

On September 29 Carter met Clifford's committee, listened to their conclusions, then left for Camp David to work on a speech designed to bring the crisis to an end. Clifford recommended that the president "simply tell the truth." Carter, however, could not bring himself to admit the almost farcical incompetence with which his administration had conjured a crisis out of thin air.[88] Instead, in a confused televised address to the nation, he sought to defuse the crisis and made clear that there would be no demand for the brigade's withdrawal. But his description of the threat posed by it was woefully inept:

Just recently, American intelligence obtained persuasive evidence that some of these Soviet forces [in Cuba] had been organized as a combat unit. . . . This is not a large force, nor an assault force. It presents no direct threat to us. . . . Nevertheless, the Soviet brigade in Cuba is a serious matter. It contributes to tension in the Caribbean and Central American region. . . . The Soviet Union does not admit that the unit in question is a combat unit. . . . They have said that the Soviet personnel in Cuba are not and will not be a threat to the United States or any other nation. . . . Although we have persuasive evidence that the unit has been a combat brigade, the Soviet statements about the future noncombat status of the unit are significant.

Clifford found Carter's explanation "almost unintelligible." The president sought to regain public confidence by announcing intensified intelligence surveillance of the brigade:

We are enhancing our intelligence capability in order to monitor Soviet and Cuban military activities—both in Cuba and throughout the world. We will increase our efforts to guard against damage to our crucial intelligence sources and our methods of collection, without impairing civil and constitutional rights.[89]

But for the fiasco of the Soviet brigade, Clifford believed that SALT II would have been speedily ratified by the Senate.[90] The delay proved fatal, for the Soviet invasion of Afghanistan at the end of the year destroyed all prospect of pushing the treaty through, though its terms were substantially honored by both sides without ratification. From early December onward, Carter received intelligence reports of the buildup of Soviet forces on the Afghan border.[91] At nightfall on Christmas Day Soviet military transport planes began a massive airlift to Kabul International Airport. On December 27 an assault group of specially trained KGB commandos stormed the presidential palace, killed President Hafizullah Amin, and installed as his successor the exiled Afghan Communist and veteran KGB agent, Babrak Karmal.[92] Carter publicly refuted Brezhnev's claim that the Soviet forces had entered Kabul at the invitation of the Afghan government: ". . . The person that he claimed invited him in, President Amin, was murdered or assassinated after the Soviets pulled their coup." "My opinion of the Russians," said Carter, "has changed more drastically in the last week than even the previous two and one half years before that."[93]

The war in Afghanistan gave rise to what Turner calls "the first big covert action of the Carter administration." During the first few days after the Soviet invasion Turner worried that supplying arms to the Afghan Mujahideen resistance fighters would simply encourage them to commit suicide in a hopeless struggle against a much more powerful opponent. By the New Year, however, he had been convinced that the Mujahideen were determined to fight on whether or not they received outside help. It was, Turner remembers, "not a big struggle" to gain Carter's approval for covert support to the Mujahideen:

> The primary thing we discussed was how we were going to pull it off, and that meant getting Pakistani cooperation. I explained to him how we were going to send Soviet-made weapons [through Pakistan] because we didn't want knowledge of our own involvement to get out.[94]

The president was determined to make the Russians pay a heavy price for the Afghan war. "Soviet involvement," Carter directed, was to be made "as costly as possible."[95] "The funny thing here," Turner recalls, "is this was Carter and Turner pushing the CIA":

> We couldn't get them interested in this. I was mad. I wanted to show we could react. They [the Soviet-made arms supplies] were still in Texas or someplace, and I couldn't get these people to move them off, so I set a deadline myself. They didn't really appreciate that Turner and Carter would back this thing. They figured we'd get them [the Mujahideen] started and then leave them hanging down there. Personally, I had to beat people over the head to get the program moving.[96]

The president also became personally involved. In January 1980 Sadat agreed to a secret personal request from Carter to assist the CIA in channeling Soviet-made arms to the Mujahideen.[97]

It was Iran, however, rather than the war in Afghanistan, that dominated Carter's last year in the White House and may well have lost him the 1980 election. The shah's best-kept secret, even after he went into exile, was probably the state of his own health. Until the autumn of 1979 the CIA was unaware that the shah had cancer. Even more remarkably, French intelligence did not know—despite the fact that the shah's two doctors were French. According to Gary Sick, "despite the rumor mill in Teheran, after the news of the shah's illness came out . . . the revolutionaries said they had heard every rumor in the world except that one."[98] On October 1 Carter learned for the first time that the shah, then in Mexico, might be seriously ill and might wish to seek treatment in the United States. At Camp David on October 20 the president received a "super sensitive" memorandum, reporting that the shah had malignant lymphoma, which was not responding satisfactorily to chemotherapy. Carter decided, on compassionate grounds, to allow the shah to enter a New York hospital. Bazargan's government reacted to the news with apparent "moderation," and Carter saw "no reason for alarm about the safety of Americans" in Iran.[99] One of the errors of American policy since the fall of the shah, however, had been to place exaggerated confidence in what it was hoped was the growing pragmatism of the Bazargan regime.

Sunday, November 4, 1979, said Carter later, was a date he would never forget. Early that morning he was awakened by Brzezinski with the news that the Teheran embassy had been overrun by several thousand militant "students," and that over fifty U.S. personnel had been taken hostage. Carter was worried but "reasonably confident" that the embassy staff would soon be freed. An invasion of the embassy the previous February had been quickly ended after intervention by Bazargan's government. When the SCC met on the morning of November 5 none of its members yet had any inkling that the hostage crisis was to last for the reminder of the Carter presidency. The next day, however, hopes of an early end to the crisis were dashed when Khomeini publicly endorsed the seizure of the hostages and refused to negotiate with any American emissaries. Bazargan's government collapsed, and Khomeini transferred power to the Revolutionary Council of clerics and religious militants. Thus began what Carter considered "the most difficult period of my life."[100] The hostage crisis had more intensive television coverage than any event since the Second World War, even including Vietnam. Carter, however, saw pictures denied to almost all other Americans. The phenomenal technology of the KH-11 satellite made it possible for him to look down on the Teheran embassy compound from above, though not to peer inside the rooms in which the hostages were being held.[101] The fact that, unlike any previous president, he had access to real-time imagery gave the crisis an extraordinary immediacy. As Carter lay awake at night or paced the White House Rose Garden early in the morning, worrying over the fate of the hostages, the latest pictures of Teheran from the KH-11 must have been imprinted on his mind.

"For the next six months," Turner recalls, "75 percent of my time was taken up by the hostage crisis."[102] Brzezinski ordered contingency planning for a secret rescue mission to begin on November 6. Within two days an outline plan had been worked out for an airborne helicopter assault on the embassy compound to rescue the hostages and take them to an airfield near Teheran from which they could be flown out of the country. It was clear from the outset that the logistics would be enormously complex. Preparations for the rescue mission were overseen by a small group chaired by Brzezinski, consisting of Brown; Turner; General David C. Jones, chairman of the Joint Chiefs; and a number of their aides, which met in Brzezinski's room several times a week. For almost five months Carter refused to give the go-ahead, hoping instead to end the hostage crisis by negotiation.[103]

The president quickly gave his consent, however, to a covert operation to rescue six U.S. diplomats who, unknown to the Iranians, had taken refuge in the homes of Canadian diplomats in Teheran. Some American reporters had calculated that there were more embassy personnel in Teheran than had been taken hostage and began working on stories about those who had evaded capture. Carter and Vance personally telephoned editors and newspaper publishers to make sure that there was no mention of the "missing" Americans. Turner told Carter that there were two possible methods of exfiltrating the Americans from the Canadian embassy. Either they could be given false identities and fly out of Teheran airport on scheduled flights, or they could each be helped to cross some deserted part of the Iranian border. "Maybe, Mr. President," said Turner, "we should give each one his choice." "I disagree, Stan," replied Carter. "There is no telling about the mental and emotional state of those people. Some speak Farsi, some don't. Some can stand up under pressure better than others." Turner agreed that the best exit route was through the airport.[104]

Carter followed preparations for the escape of the American diplomats hiding in the Canadian embassy with mounting excitement. It was, he said later, "a real cloak-and-dagger story." He was given detailed briefings on the "many adventures" of the CIA agents dispatched to Teheran with false passports to supply the diplomats with disguises and forged documents, and give them the training required to pose successfully as non-American travelers and businessmen when they arrived to catch their flights out of the country. One of the agents had a close escape. Carter was told that, when he landed at Teheran airport with a German passport, an alert Iranian customs official asked him why the passport, instead of giving the whole of his middle name, uncharacteristically contained only the initial "H." The agent replied quick-wittedly that his parents had given him the middle name "Hitler," and that ever since the war he had been allowed to use only the initial in his passport. The customs officer waved him through. The escape plan was put into operation on January 28. At 4 A.M. that morning, a Canadian embassy van took the six diplomats and their CIA escorts to Teheran airport to catch an early morning Air France flight to Switzerland. A few hours later Carter was brought the good news that all were safely out of Iran.[105]

The president continued to hope, however, that secret negotiations with the Iranians through intermediaries would secure the release of the hostages in the American embassy and make a further covert operation unnecessary. On several occasions during January and February Brzezinski and Turner sought Carter's approval for a secret CIA flight into Iran to reconnoiter possible landing sites for a rescue mission. The president refused for fear of jeopardizing the negotiations. On March 7 he refused again. Had Carter approved the reconnaissance flight early in the year, Turner believes that the prospects for a successful rescue mission would have been greatly improved: "If we'd done that flight in January, we'd have had much more time to plan. That could have turned the whole thing around."[106]

By late March, faced with the declining prospects for a negotiated settlement, Carter's opposition to a rescue mission was weakening. After a detailed briefing on plans for the mission on March 22, he approved a reconnaissance flight. On April 2 Carter was told that the flight had been a complete success. Without being detected by the Iranians, the pilot had landed in the desert at night, inspected a possible staging post by the light of a full moon, and reported that it was ideal for the mission—in an isolated position with a smooth, flat surface. At that stage, writes Carter in his memoirs, "I still believed the rescue mission would not have to be launched." He changed his mind after breaking off diplomatic relations with Iran on April 7, telling a meeting of the NSC on April 11, "It is time for us to bring our hostages home." The decision to approve Operation Eagle Claw was deliberately made at a time when Vance was out of Washington, since the secretary of state was known to believe the mission stood virtually no chance of success. At a secret meeting of the NSC on April 15 a grim-faced Carter invited Vance to offer his objections to the mission, then announced, "I will stick with the decisions I made." Two days later Vance told the president that he would resign as soon as the operation was over, whether or not it succeeded.[107]

On April 16 Carter met the mission commanders in the White House situation room and spent two and a half hours going through the details of Eagle Claw. In the first stage of the operation, eight helicopters were to fly to the remote desert site in Iran (code-named Desert One) reconnoitered earlier. There they would be met by six C-130s bringing fuel for the helicopters and a crack unit of Green Berets known as the Delta Force, commanded by Colonel Charles "Chargin' Charlie" Beckwith. Delta Force was to travel by helicopter to a mountain hideout southeast of Teheran (Desert Two), transfer to trucks, descend on the embassy under cover of darkness, and liberate the hostages. In Teheran, a CIA agent masquerading as an Irish businessman had arranged the purchase of the vehicles needed for the operation and concealed them in a rented warehouse. After the rescue, the hostages and the Green Berets were to be airlifted by helicopter out of the embassy compound, then flown out of the country by two C-141s from an abandoned airstrip near Teheran. Carter ended the review of the operation in a confident mood. "Because I was so clear in my resolve," he writes in his memoirs, "I looked forward to the mission." He told the mission commanders that he wished to be kept fully informed of preparations for Eagle Claw, scheduled to begin April 24, but would not interfere once it was under way.[108]

Henceforth Brzezinski's planning group met daily, consulting frequently with Carter. The final intelligence reports before the mission reinforced the president's optimism. CIA agents in Teheran, disguised as foreign businessmen and media employees, reported that the guards at the U.S. embassy had become lax, and convinced Carter that "security around the compound was no longer a serious obstacle to a surprise entry by force." Almost real-time satellite imagery enabled him to see the movements of the guards and identify individual cars and trucks as they entered and left the compound. Carter believed the night-vision equipment of Beckwith's Delta Force would enable it to distinguish the Iranian guards from their captives when they stormed the compound. On April 23 the president received a final intelligence briefing. ". . . Everything," he concluded, "was favorable for the rescue mission." That evening there was a last-minute piece of intelligence good fortune. By a remarkable coincidence, a Pakistani cook who had been working in the American embassy took the same flight out of Teheran as a deep-cover CIA agent. The cook said that he had taken the hostages their breakfast that very morning and revealed their precise locations within the embassy.[109]

Carter remembers the day of April 24 as "one of the worst of my life." Eagle Claw began, however, amid a mood of optimism. At 10:30 A.M. EST (night in Iran), General Jones reported that the weather for the operation was good and all eight helicopters were on their way. Carter's instinct was to spend the whole day trying to follow the progress of the mission minute by minute, but he forced himself to stick to a series of prearranged morning meetings, trying to behave as if he were merely following his usual routine. The first sign of trouble came during lunch with his advisers when Brown was called out of the room and returned with the news that two helicopters had failed to arrive at Desert One. At that stage, it was still possible that they had merely been delayed. At 3:15 A.M., however, he reported that both helicopters were out of the operation. One had returned to the carrier *Nimitz* after navigational problems in an unexpected dust storm; the other had been abandoned when its instruments indicated possible mechanical failure. There was also an unanticipated problem at Desert One. Soon after the landing of the three C-130s, an Iranian bus appeared on a nearby road with forty people on board who were temporarily taken captive; another vehicle escaped across the desert. Though Carter was shaken by the news, Brzezinski assured him that the operation could go ahead with a minimum of six helicopters. Brzezinski was still confident of success.

After a phone call from Brown at 4:45 P.M. Brzezinski's confidence evaporated. "I think we have an abort situation," Brown told him. "One helicopter at Desert One has a hydraulic problem. We thus have less than the minimum six to go." Brzezinski went to the Oval Office and told the president. Carter muttered, "Damn, damn!", called Brown, and asked what Beckwith recommended. On being told that Beckwith favored aborting the mission, Carter replied, "Let's go with his recommendation." He put down the phone, leaned forward onto his desk, and put his head in his hands. There was worse news still to come. At 5:58 P.M. General Jones telephoned to say that one of the helicopters at Desert One had crashed into a C-130, setting both ablaze. It was later learned that eight Americans and an Iranian interpreter, whose identity was kept secret, had been killed. Carter's mind turned to the Bay of Pigs. He asked to see a copy of the speech Kennedy had made afterward. Soon after 8 P.M. Carter met his senior advisers in the cabinet room. The president's expression was haggard but his manner was controlled and businesslike. Turner pressed strongly that there be no public announcement of the mission until he had made certain that the CIA team in Iran was safe. Carter agreed that a statement from the White House would be delayed until 1 A.M.[110]

On April 27 Carter flew to meet the Delta Force rescue team. His reunion with Colonel Beckwith was probably the most emotional moment in the history of presidential involvement in covert action. Beckwith struck Carter as one of the toughest men he had ever met. But, as the president disembarked from his helicopter, tears were streaming down Beckwith's cheeks. "Mr. President," he said, "I'm sorry we let you down." Carter put his arms around him, and the two men wept together. Carter found the memorial service two weeks later for the eight servicemen killed in Iran one of the most painful moments of his presidency. "It was so difficult to see those pretty young wives all dressed up, and the children in their best clothes, and to realize their fathers would never see them again," he told Hamilton Jordan, his chief of staff. "I thought I was going to be able to make it through the ceremony all right, but when I looked up and saw the single jet formation, it was just too much."[111]

In his televised address after the failure of the mission, Carter took personal responsibility: "It was my decision to attempt the rescue operation. It was my decision to cancel it. . . ." "Intensive planning and intensive training and repeated rehearsal" had, he said, given the operation an "excellent chance of success."[112] An inquiry by Admiral James L. Holloway for the JCS, however, discovered that there had been no rehearsal integrating all elements of the operation. Worse still, some of the key participants met each other for the first time at Desert One. There were thus inevitable weaknesses of command, control, and communications. These were all the more serious because, as Holloway concluded, ". . . People and equipment were called upon to perform at the upper limits of human capacity and equipment capability. There was little margin to compensate for mistakes or plain bad luck." At Desert One the rescue mission experienced for the first time "the pressures of a full-scale combination of airplanes, helicopters, troops, and vehicles, maneuvering in the crowded parking area under the confusing conditions of noise, dust, and darkness."[113]

It is difficult to avoid the conclusion that Carter as well as his advisers made too little allowance for the limitations of high technology. One (unnamed) member of the White House staff was reported as wondering after the rescue attempt whether "we've psyched ourselves into putting too much faith in machines." "Little did I dream," admitted Brzezinski, "that our failure would involve technology, an area where America normally excels." During the six-hundred-nautical-mile flight to Desert One over unknown desert and mountain ranges, the eight helicopter pilots were ordered to maintain strict radio silence. When they ran into a dust storm, they were thus forced to fly solely by instruments. The commander of the helicopter who turned back because of problems with his instruments in the dust storm would have continued if he had been informed by radio that he was only half an hour from Desert One. Holloway concluded that the helicopters could have been provided with secure communication systems that would have made them less completely dependent on their instruments. The use of a C-130 pathfinder plane would also have "decreased the probability of a mission abort due to weather."[114] Carter, however, failed to learn the lesson of excessive reliance on high technology. He continued to believe that the planning of the mission had not been at fault, and that it had failed only as the result of a strange series of "almost completely unpredictable" mishaps.[115]

The long drawn-out Iranian crisis strengthened the shift of emphasis in both the White House and Congress from the regulation of the intelligence community to the enhancement of its performance. Carter had declared in his State of the Union message on January 21, 1980, "Our national interests are critically dependent on a strong and effective intelligence capability. We will not shortchange the intelligence capabilities needed to assure our national security." He told a news conference soon afterward, ". . . There's been an excessive restraint on what the CIA and other intelligence groups could do."[116] On May 8 the Senate Select Committee on Intelligence approved a 750-word bill, the Intelligence Oversight Act of 1980. This was all that now remained of the absurdly bulky 263-page bill introduced two years earlier. By proposing to restrict intelligence oversight to the Senate and House intelligence committees, it sought to reduce the number of congressional committees with the right to be informed about covert action. Although laying down the principle of prior notification to the committees, it allowed the president in case of emergency to take covert action first and inform the committees afterward. There were no new statutory constraints on intelligence operations. The bill became law in October.[117]

The hostage crisis and the Soviet invasion of Afghanistan together converted Carter to covert action as a major instrument of his foreign policy. "In considering how much to turn again to covert action," Turner noted, "the administration was buffeted between Vance's skepticism and Brzezinski's enthusiasm."[118] Well before Vance's resignation, it was clear that Brzezinski's enthusiasm had prevailed. Carter told a student audience in 1982 that covert action had been the best way to resist Soviet aggression in Afghanistan, short of "going to war, which wasn't possible."[119] The revival of covert action against the Soviet Union was not confined to Afghanistan. Carter also sought ways of responding to what he saw as Soviet-sponsored aggression by the quasi-Marxist regimes in Angola, Ethiopia, Mozambique, and South Yemen. "Thus it was," writes Turner, "that the Carter administration, despite its dedication to human rights and its considerable reservations about the morality of covert actions, turned easily and quickly to covert devices. . . ." During 1980 Carter approved what Turner discreetly describes as "a wide variety of covert operations."[120] The future DCI, Robert Gates, who served on Carter's NSC staff, concludes that in his dealings with the Soviet Union, "Jimmy Carter laid the foundations for Ronald Reagan."[121]

The covert action that had by far the most important consequences for Carter himself, however, was Eagle Claw. Had the mission to rescue the hostages succeeded, he might well have been reelected for a second term. In the event, after defeating a challenge by Senator Edward Kennedy for the Democratic nomination, he lost to Reagan on November 4 by over eight million votes. If Nixon was the first president to lose office as the result of an unsuccessful covert operation, Carter was probably the second (though the two operations were, of course, of very different kinds). Looking back on his last year in office, Carter told Hamilton Jordan, "1980 was pure hell—the Kennedy challenge, Afghanistan, having to put the SALT Treaty on the shelf, the recession, Ronald Reagan, and the hostages . . . always the hostages!"[122]

Two days before Carter's election defeat, formal negotiations with the Iranians through Algerian intermediaries opened in Algiers. The talks, of labyrinthine complexity, dominated the ten weeks of his lame-duck presidency. Though the basis of a settlement was agreed on January 18, tension continued until Inauguration Day two days later. Carter spent a final sleepless night in the Oval Office, hoping for news that the hostages would be released during the last hours of his presidency. At 7:55 A.M. on Inauguration Day he received a message on his secure red telephone that NSA monitoring of the radio traffic of Teheran Airport control tower had disclosed that Flight 133 was at the end of a runway. Carter already knew that the flight consisted of a commercial 727 airliner carrying the American hostages, a second 727 intended either as a backup or as a possible decoy, and a small corporate jet transporting the Algerian medical team that had examined the hostages before their departure for the airport. The president put down the phone and announced to cheers from those present in the Oval Office, "Flight 133 is ready for takeoff!" A further intelligence message at 8:28 A.M. reported that the flight was still at the end of the runway and that a possible Iranian fighter escort had been identified. No president during his final hours in office has ever hung so eagerly on the latest intelligence reports. During the next hour there were reports of escort planes circling the airport and of a jeep checking the runway, but Flight 133 remained immobile. In frustration, Carter gave orders for the numbers of the 727s to be checked to make sure that there had been no mistake about their identity. At 9:45 A.M. Warren Christopher, the chief American negotiator in Algiers, phoned to say that takeoff had been delayed but that it would definitely take place before Reagan took the oath of office. He was to be mistaken. At 10:45 A.M. Rosalynn Carter told her husband that it was time for him to change into his morning clothes to greet the Reagans when they arrived at 11 A.M. As Carter combed his hair in front of the bathroom mirror and looked at his lined face, he wondered if he had aged more than he had realized over the past four years or whether he was simply exhausted. His ride with Reagan to the Capitol and the inauguration ceremony passed in a blur. All he could think about, Carter told Jordan, "was whether the hostages had taken off—and whether the message would come." A few minutes after he ceased to be president, Flight 133 became airborne.[123]

CHAPTER 12

Ronald Reagan
(1981-1989)

Forty years before he entered the White House, Ronald Reagan spent several undemanding years as commander of the Junior Secret Service Club. Founded by Warner Brothers to publicize a series of films featuring the future president as Brass Bancroft, Secret Agent J-24, the club gave each of its members a secret code and a membership card signed by Reagan. Cinema managers were encouraged to "fingerprint new members under the supervision of local police officials," play up the "spying angle" of the films, and sponsor school essay contests with the title, "What steps do you think our government must take to combat sabotage and spying?"

By the time Reagan began his Hollywood career in 1937, the secret struggle against subversion (mostly by fascists) was already established as a major theme of Warner Brothers movies. Ten of his first thirty films, some made in cooperation with military authorities, dealt with threats to national security. The Brass Bancroft films were advertised as "thinly disguised dramatizations of actual adventures." Reagan, it was claimed, was "ideal for the part [of Bancroft], for he is, both in appearance and personality, the representative of all that is admirable in young American manhood. While he is tall and handsome, there is nothing of the pretty boy about him, for virility is his outstanding characteristic." Warner Brothers claimed in 1940 that Secret Service roles were those that "Reagan feels he can do best and which he thoroughly enjoys playing." Studio publicity went too far, however, in claiming that he was "tall, *blond*, and handsome." The Secret Service films, said Reagan later, made him "the Errol Flynn of the B's": "I was as brave as Errol," he recalls, "but in a low-budget fashion."¹ His last picture before he was drafted in 1942 was *Desperate Journey*, in which he and Flynn played the parts of Royal Air Force pilots shot down behind German lines.²

A few months after being drafted, Reagan joined Army Air Force Intelligence, becoming adjutant and personnel officer of a Los Angeles unit making training films, documentaries for public screening, and classified films about the progress of the war for the General Staff. The unit's greatest achievement, he believed, was to devise a new method of briefing pilots and bombardiers before bombing missions in the Pacific war. Using intelligence reports and prewar photographs, it constructed on a studio floor a large scale-model of Tokyo, complete with thousands of buildings and the nearby coastline, which was regularly updated to show the latest bomb damage revealed by aerial photography. Films taken by a camera mounted on a movable overhead derrick simulated what air crews could expect to see as they approached and flew over Tokyo.³ When he gained access as president to the latest state-of-the-art satellite imagery, Reagan must surely have thought back to his wartime experience.

At the end of the war Reagan, then a Democrat, considered Communists simply as "liberals who were off track." Within a few years, however, he had become convinced that "Moscow was trying to take over the picture business." Using well-tried techniques of Communist subversion orchestrated by Soviet intelligence, "Joseph Stalin had set out to make Hollywood an instrument of propaganda for his program of Soviet expansionism aimed at communizing the world." Both as president of the Screen Actors Guild and as an FBI informant, Reagan took an active combat role against the Red Menace. He quotes with pride in his memoirs a description of him by a fellow actor as a one-man anti-Communist battalion. "In the end," he writes, "we stopped the Communists cold in Hollywood. . . ." But there was, he acknowledges, a "dark side" to the victory. Despite his attempts to save some of them, "Many fine people were wrongly accused of being Communists simply because they were liberals." When he ran for the governorship of California in 1966, Reagan was outraged when a rival candidate during the Republican primary campaign accused him of havi ɩg been a member of Communist fronts during his time in Hollywood.⁴

Reagan's first serious involvement with peacetime foreign intelligence came almost a decade later, immediately after the end of his eight-year term as governor of California. In January 1975 President Ford made him a member of the Rockefeller commission on CIA activities within the United States.⁵ Reagan took a tolerant view of the abuses uncovered by the commission. After its report was published, he said in defense of the CIA, "In any bureaucracy of about sixteen thousand people there are going to be individuals who make mistakes and do things they shouldn't."⁶ The agency, he believed, needed more dynamism rather than more regulation. During the presidential campaign in 1980 he promised to "unleash" the CIA. The Republican platform promised an administration that would "seek to improve U.S. intelligence capabilities for technical and clandestine collection, cogent analysis, coordinated counterintelligence, and covert action." A transition team report of November 1980 concluded, "Decisive action at the CIA is the keystone to achieving a reversal of the unwise policies of the past decade."⁷

The man chosen by Reagan to "unleash" the agency was his sixty-eight-year-old campaign manager, William J. Casey. An OSS veteran who had made a fortune from the stock market and a Park Avenue law practice in New York, Casey was both the wealthiest and the oldest man ever to be appointed DCI. Though he had held several posts in the Nixon and Ford administrations, his only direct involvement in postwar intelligence had been as a member of PFIAB from 1976 to 1977. Casey, however, was the first DCI to be given cabinet rank. He shared both Reagan's passionate conviction that the Soviet Union was the root of all evil in the international system and his faith in the CIA as a means of turning back Soviet expansionism.⁸ One of the few mildly embarrassing moments during Casey's generally undemanding Senate confirmation hearings came when he was asked about Reagan's call to "unleash" the CIA. He claimed that he had never used the phrase himself, and promised "to comply with the spirit as well as the letter of the Intelligence Oversight Act."⁹ Casey, however, had a natural tendency to bend intelligence rules as far as they would go. Along with his freewheeling style went a disregard of bureaucratic procedure that his staff found both endearing and perplexing. According to Casey's executive assistant, Robert M. Gates (later his deputy and a future DCI):

> Actually for the first several years, it was something of an adventure to work for him, because he would pick up the phone and punch a button without much concern for who was at the other end of the line and start shouting instructions. . . . He would also fail to change the buttons when he'd call again. So he'd call and then about thirty seconds later he'd call again, and you'd say, "Yes?" and he'd say, "Who's this?" and you'd say, "Well, this is Bob, and you just talked to me." And he'd say, "Oh, I didn't want you," and then he'd hang up. . . .
>
> I don't think he would have recognized the CIA organization chart, the first several years he was there, if a lot depended on it. . . .¹⁰

Like most postwar presidents, Reagan began each day with the president's daily brief. Knowing his dislike of lengthy documents, agency analysts usually limited themselves to four 150-word main stories, set out in two columns (headlines on the left, text on the right), with a few shorter pieces and the occasional anecdote.[11] Among the first imagery shown to the president was an album of satellite photographs of his California ranch. Reagan was able to identify his and the First Lady's horses, El Alamein and No Strings, grazing in a field.[12] Video briefings, which had begun on a small scale under Carter, were rapidly expanded under Reagan.[13] Before most of his major foreign visits he watched videos that combined intelligence assessments with film of people he would be meeting and places he would be visiting.[14]

Unlike Stansfield Turner, who reviewed the daily brief before it went to the White House, Casey saw it at about the same time as the president.[15] Reagan's copy was delivered by his national security adviser, Richard V. Allen, who sometimes added items to it.[16] Allen, however, was a far less influential figure than Kissinger and Brzezinski, and was replaced after only a year. (In all, Reagan had six national security advisers in eight years.) The DCI became once again, in practice as well as in theory, the president's chief intelligence adviser. Casey had an office in the Old Executive Office Building next to the White House as well as at Langley. Though he shared the president's determination to roll back international Communism, however, their personal relations—contrary to popular belief—were never close.[17] Casey was rarely invited to the White House socially. According to Gates, "Mrs. Reagan didn't like him at all from the beginning, partly—perhaps mostly—because of his manners. He was a slob, and watching Bill Casey eat was not for the queasy." Casey would phone Reagan from time to time on issues such as the budget and political appointments. He also periodically wrote the president letters. But, says Gates, "I sort of had the feeling there was nobody listening at the other end."[18] Casey saw the vice-president and former DCI, George Bush, as a potential rival. Soon after the appointment of Admiral Bobby Ray Inman as deputy DCI, Casey told him, "George Bush isn't welcome here."[19]

At Reagan's first presidential press conference on January 29 he made a savage attack on Soviet policy:

> I know of no leader of the Soviet Union since the revolution, and including the present leadership, that has not more than once repeated in the various Communist congresses they hold their determination that their goal must be the promotion of world revolution and a one-world Socialist or Communist state, whichever word you want to use. . . . They, at the same time, have openly and publicly declared that the only morality they recognize is what will

further their cause, meaning they reserve unto themselves the right to commit any crime, to lie, to cheat, in order to attain that, and that is moral, not immoral. . . .[20]

Both Casey and Reagan believed that the main immediate threat to American security lay in Soviet designs on Central America. A few days before his first press conference Reagan had received what he believed was "firm and incontrovertible" intelligence that the Sandinista Liberation Front, which had taken power in Nicaragua six months earlier, was passing hundreds of tons of Soviet arms from Cuba to rebel forces in El Salvador:

Although El Salvador was the immediate target, the evidence showed that the Soviets and Fidel Castro were targeting all of Central America for a Communist takeover. El Salvador and Nicaragua were only a down payment. Honduras, Guatemala and Costa Rica were next, and then would come Mexico.[21]

Casey and Reagan, however, had mistaken the grandiose ambitions of Fidel Castro and some KGB officers for the policy of the Soviet government. At a meeting of senior KGB foreign intelligence officers at Moscow Center in 1979, General Nikolai Leonov, who twenty years earlier had been the first to grasp Castro's potential as a revolutionary leader, claimed that the next decade would provide important new opportunities for exploiting the weakness of the "main adversary" (the United States) in Latin America. He called for support for the Sandinistas and other non-Communist liberation movements that, he claimed, could be turned into allies of the Soviet Union. Despite Cuban backing and Leonov's advocacy, Moscow did not immediately rush to the Sandinistas' aid. Though welcoming Sandinista support for the Soviet military presence in Afghanistan, and attracted by their anthem that denounced the *yanqis* as "enemies of mankind," the Kremlin hoped for some time that the small but orthodox Nicaraguan Communist party would replace the unorthodox Sandinistas as the dominant force in the new regime. Not till late in 1981 did Castro and the KGB persuade the Kremlin that the Sandinistas were genuine revolutionaries who would follow the Cuban path to Soviet loyalism.[22] Casey and Reagan, however, were convinced that, from the outset, the Sandinistas had been part of a sixty-year-old Soviet master plan to take over the Western Hemisphere. Reagan was greatly impressed by an alleged saying of Lenin:

First, we will take Eastern Europe, then we will organize the hordes of Asia . . . then we will move on to Latin America; once we have

Latin America, we won't have to take the United States, the last bastion of capitalism, because it will fall into our outstretched hands like overripe fruit.

Though the saying was of doubtful authenticity, Reagan liked it so much that he later included it in his memoirs—twice.[23] Early in March Casey presented to the NSPG (National Security Planning Group, successor to Carter's SCC) an ambitious plan for covert action to counter the Soviet advance in the Third World, which included a $19 million operation against the Sandinistas. "If we can't stop Soviet expansionism in a place like Nicaragua," demanded Casey, "where the hell can we?" Reagan approved the Nicaraguan plan on March 9, but, to make it more palatable to the congressional intelligence committees, described it in his finding as covert action to defend El Salvador against a Communist takeover.[24]

During Reagan's early months as president there was no shortage of secret intelligence that seemed to justify his public denunciation of Soviet policy. In 1980 the KGB had installed the brutal Mohammed Najibullah as head of a new Soviet-trained Afghan security service, Khedamat-e Etala'at-e Dawlati (better known as KHAD). During the war against the Mujahideen, the KGB revived on Afghan soil some of the horrors of its Stalinist past. Amnesty International later published horrifying evidence of "widespread and systematic torture of men, women and children" at KHAD interrogation centers, some of it supervised by Soviet advisers.[25] From the moment Reagan became president, he also received a series of intelligence reports on possible Soviet preparations for an invasion of Poland to crush the Solidarity movement, much as Russian troops had ended the Prague Spring in 1968.[26] During the spring of 1981 intelligence reports from Colonel Ryczard Kuklinski, a CIA agent on the Polish General Staff, indicated that the invasion might be imminent. Reagan sent a secret letter to Brezhnev, warning him to expect "the harshest possible economic sanctions" if the invasion went ahead. Brezhnev replied, predictably, that what went on in Poland was the responsibility of the Polish government.[27]

Reagan's secretary of state, Alexander Haig, was determined to signal the dawn of a new era in Soviet-American relations:

In the morning of an Administration, the air is fresh and still relatively quiet, and friends and adversaries are alert and watchful. It is the best time to send signals. Our signal to the Soviets had to be a plain warning that their time of unrestricted adventuring in the Third World was over. . . .[28]

Reagan and his main advisers failed, however, to understand the Kremlin's reaction to its signals. Moscow had interpreted his anti-Soviet speeches in 1980 largely as campaign rhetoric. Not till he entered the White House did it fully grasp that his denunciations of the Soviet Union sprang from deep conviction. The effect of Reagan's speeches was to inflame the paranoid tendency never far below the surface of Soviet policy. Their impact was heightened by the 10 percent increase in the U.S. defense budget—a figure double Reagan's campaign promise. Carter had suspended development of the MX missile and the B-1 bomber. Reagan resumed work on both. In May 1981 Brezhnev denounced Reagan's policies in a secret address to a major KGB conference in Moscow. The most dramatic speech, however, was given by the KGB chairman, Yuri Andropov. The new American administration, he declared, was actively preparing for nuclear war. It was even possible that Reagan was planning a nuclear first strike against the Soviet Union. The Politburo had therefore decided that the overriding priority of Soviet foreign intelligence operations must henceforth be to collect intelligence on the nuclear threat from the United States and its NATO allies. Andropov announced that, to discover Reagan's (in reality, nonexistent) preparations for a nuclear first strike, the KGB and GRU (Soviet military intelligence) would, for the first time, collaborate in a worldwide operation codenamed RYAN: a newly devised acronym for Raketno-Yadernoye Napadenie (Nuclear Missile Attack).[29] No intelligence on the secret KGB meeting that launched RYAN seems to have reached Washington until much later. It barely occurred to Reagan at the beginning of his presidency that the Soviet Union might be genuinely afraid of his intentions. "During my first years in Washington," he later acknowledged, "I think many of us in the administration took it for granted that the Russians, like ourselves, considered it unthinkable that the United States would launch a first strike against them."[30] Both Reagan and Casey dismissed most signs of Soviet alarm as propaganda.

Reagan's presidency came within a whisker of being the shortest in American history. On March 30, 1981, a bullet fired by a deranged would-be assassin, John W. Hinckley Jr., narrowly missed the president's heart. Though Reagan made a full recovery, intelligence on other assassination plots during the remainder of the year understandably made a deep impression on him. Only six weeks later Pope John Paul II survived an attempt on his life in St. Peter's Square. Casey, unlike most of his analysts, was convinced that the KGB had been involved in the shooting, and probably led Reagan to the same conclusion.[31] The assassination plotter who caused Reagan most concern, however, was the Libyan dictator Colonel Muammar Qaddafi, whom Reagan reasonably regarded as an unpredictable fanatic. In his memoirs Reagan gives personal credit to Casey for expanding intelligence collection in the Middle East (partly, though he does not mention it, by expanding collaboration with the Israelis), and for providing detailed information on Soviet arms supplies to Libya and Qaddafi's support for terrorist groups around the world. The Libyan embassy in Washington was ordered to close in May after the FBI had implicated a Libyan terrorist in a Chicago murder.[32] Following a clash on August 19 between two F-14 jets from the USS *Nimitz* and Libyan planes sixty miles off the coast of Libya, Qaddafi decided to target Reagan personally. On August 22 Qaddafi visited the Marxist leader of Ethiopia, Lieutenant Colonel Mengistu Haile Mariam, in Addis Ababa. According to a senior Ethiopian official working for the CIA, Mengistu was convinced after the meeting that the Libyan death threat was in deadly earnest. Shortly afterward NSA decrypts provided further evidence of Qaddafi's homicidal intentions. At the insistence of the Secret Service, Reagan wore a bullet-proof vest whenever he appeared in public.[33]

On October 6 President Sadat of Egypt was assassinated by Islamic fundamentalists. A few hours later Reagan watched television film of a jubilant Qaddafi, "almost doing a jig" as he led Libyan celebrations in the streets of Tripoli. Intelligence reports convinced him that Qaddafi had been told in advance of plans for Sadat's murder. "As I prayed for Sadat," writes Reagan, "I tried to repress the hatred I felt for Qaddafi, but I couldn't do it."[34] Three days later Reagan received an intelligence report that Qaddafi had enlisted the support of four Syrian-based terrorist groups in attacking American targets in Europe. Soon afterward a Libyan hit squad was reported to be planning attacks on the U.S. embassies in Paris and Rome. On November 12 a gunman in Paris (believed to be working for the Libyans) fired six shots at the U.S. chargé d'affaires, but narrowly failed to hit him.[35] Reagan was warned that a Libyan terrorist group had entered the United States, armed with a hand-held heat-seeking missile capable of shooting down the presidential helicopter, Marine One. Henceforth, the route taken by his helicopter was decided only minutes in advance.[36] Bush, Haig, Casey, and Caspar Weinberger, the defense secretary, were reported to have been selected as alternative targets if Reagan proved too difficult to reach.[37]

Qaddafi's links with Moscow only served to reinforce Reagan's acute suspicion of Soviet policy. Since 1979, under the terms of a secret Soviet-Libyan accord, the KGB had provided training for Libyan intelligence officers at the Andropov Institute in Moscow and supplied Qaddafi with reports on U.S. activities in the Eastern Mediterranean through a KGB liaison officer in Tripoli. In return Libya assisted KGB operations targeted against Western diplomats in Tripoli and provided intelligence on Egypt, Israel, and North Africa.[38] Though the KGB was not suspected of involvement in the Libyan assassination plots, Reagan received intelligence reports that Soviet intelligence had embarked on "active measures" operations designed to discredit him. During 1981, for example, the KGB sought to fuel Spanish opposition to seeking membership in NATO by planting media stories that Reagan was putting pressure on the king of Spain. In November Spanish journalists were sent copies of a forged letter from the president, urging the king "to act . . . with dispatch to remove the forces obstructing Spain's entry into NATO."[39]

Probably the most remarkable intelligence on the scale of Soviet espionage to reach Reagan during his first year in office came from the French. In the early summer of 1981 Vice President Bush received a secret visit from Marcel Chalet, the head of Direction de la Surveillance du Territoire (DST, the French security service), who briefed him on the intelligence provided by a French mole, Vladimir Vetrov (code-named Farewell), working in the scientific and technological (S&T) division of the KGB First Chief Directorate.[40] During a private meeting with Reagan and Haig at the Ottawa economic summit meeting of the heads of the seven leading industrialized nations in July, President François Mitterrand gave further details.[41] Vetrov had access not merely to much operational detail but also to the annual statistics for Soviet S&T operations. During 1980 a total of 3,617 "acquisition tasks" had been under way, of which 1,085 had been successfully completed in the course of the year, producing over four thousand "samples" and more than twenty-five thousand technical documents. The main S&T target, as in the case of political and military intelligence collection, had been the United States.[42] According to Mitterrand, Reagan and Haig told him that the Vetrov revelations were "the biggest affair of its kind since the Second World War."[43]

At the end of the year Reagan stepped up covert action against what he called "the Communist threat in Central America." On December 1 he approved a $19 million plan prepared under Casey's personal direction to use Argentinian officers to arm and train an anti-Sandinista guerrilla force in Honduras. Casey misleadingly presented the operation to the congressional intelligence committees as an attempt to interdict Nicaraguan arms shipments into El Salvador.[44] On December 4 Reagan issued two executive orders intended "to revitalize America's intelligence system":

These orders are designed to provide America's intelligence community with clearer, more positive guidance and to remove the aura of suspicion and mistrust that can hobble our nation's intelligence efforts. . . . The men and women of our intelligence community . . . cannot be fully thanked in public, but I want them to know that their job is vital and that the American people, and their President, are profoundly grateful for what they do.

Executive Order 12333 gave the CIA the exclusive right to conduct covert action (euphemistically termed "special activities") "unless the President determines that another agency is more likely to achieve a particular objective."[45] It was generally assumed at the time that the "other agency" would be a unit of the armed forces, but the phrasing of the order provided a loophole allowing the White House itself, through the NSC staff, to engage directly in covert action—with disastrous consequences in the Iran-Contra affair a few years later.

Events in Poland were soon to produce a new crisis in Soviet-American relations. Plans for the establishment of martial law in Poland had been in progress for several months. The CIA had probably learned from Colonel Kuklinski, its agent on the Polish General Staff, of visits to Warsaw by General Vladimir Kryuchkov, head of the KGB First Chief (Foreign Intelligence) Directorate, and Marshal Viktor Kulikov, commander in chief of Warsaw Pact forces, to discuss the crackdown with the Polish leader, General Wojciech Jaruzelski.[46] Early in November, fearful that he had fallen under suspicion, Kuklinski had to be exfiltrated from Poland by the agency.[47] Partly as a result, the timing of the declaration of martial law on December 13 took Washington by surprise. For some days previously, heavy cloud cover over Poland had prevented satellite photography of the troop and militia movements that would have revealed that martial law was imminent.[48] Intelligence reports to Reagan persuaded him that "the entire exercise had been ordered from and orchestrated by Moscow. . . . The Soviets were acting more like international brigands than ever."[49] On December 29 he ordered trade sanctions "directed at the Governments of Poland and of the Soviet Union . . . to convey to those regimes how strongly we feel about their joint attempts to extinguish liberty in Poland."[50] By the end of 1981 Casey was established as Reagan's main policy adviser on Poland as well as Central America.

Reagan's policy toward Nicaragua was far less popular than his tough line on Poland. ". . . One of my greatest frustrations," he writes in his memoirs, ". . . was my inability to communicate to the American people and to Congress the seriousness of the threat we faced in Central America."[51] His sense of frustration led him to approve the public use of classified imagery on a scale unparalleled since the Cuban missile crisis, in a despairing attempt to prove the administration's case. On March 9, 1982,

Inman and John T. Hughes of DIA displayed overhead photographs of the military buildup in Nicaragua at a press briefing. Inman told the assembled journalists, "I'm angry because I've watched, over the past couple of weeks, public servants trying to grapple with the difficulty of conveying information while protecting critical intelligence sources and methods and finding that they're standardly greeted with, 'How can we believe you unless you show us all the detailed evidence?'" In order not to reveal the high resolution of the latest satellite imagery, the photographs shown at the briefing had been taken by an SR-71A spy plane, using satellite photographs as a guide.[52]

The public relations benefit of the press briefing, however, was nullified by the revelation in the *Washington Post* the next day that Reagan had secretly authorized $19 million to train a paramilitary force of five hundred Latin Americans to target Nicaraguan power plants and bridges, and "disrupt the Nicaraguan arms supply line to El Salvador." During April the House Select Committee on Intelligence, chaired by Representative Edward Boland, adopted a classified addition to the Intelligence Authorization Bill for the 1983 financial year, specifically prohibiting the use of U.S. funds to overthrow the Sandinista government and restricting CIA covert operations to the interdiction of Nicaraguan arms supplies. The prohibition eventually became public eight months later when it was publicly enacted by Congress as the Boland amendment.[53]

During the spring of 1982, however, the focus of Washington's attention in Latin America shifted temporarily from Nicaragua to the conflict between Britain and Argentina in the South Atlantic that followed the Argentinian invasion of the Falklands on April 2. Against the wishes of some members of his administration, Reagan privately assured the British prime minister, Margaret Thatcher, of his full support.[54] As so often before, the most special part of the special relationship between Britain and the United States was the secret intelligence alliance. The SIGINT attack on Argentinian communications, which yielded the best intelligence of the Falklands War, was conducted virtually as a combined operation by GCHQ (the British SIGINT agency) and NSA. There were inevitable problems in selecting which of the large number of intercepted Argentinian signals should be given priority by the cryptanalysts and in rapidly communicating the intelligence obtained to British commanders.[55] After British forces had retaken the Falklands on June 14, however, the director of GCHQ, Sir Brian Tovey, was formally congratulated on its performance by the British government. "Never," Tovey told NSA and his own senior staff, "has such praise been accorded."[56] CIA is also plausibly alleged to have provided SIS with intelligence from its

Buenos Aires station. There was, however, one tense moment during the conflict when Reagan was alarmed to receive intelligence reports that the British were preparing to escalate the conflict by attacking military bases on the Argentinian mainland. The president immediately telephoned Mrs. Thatcher, but failed to persuade her to abandon plans for the attack. ". . . For several days," writes Reagan in his memoirs, "we waited for a nightmare attack by British planes on the mainland—one that never came."[57] George Shultz, who succeeded Haig as secretary of state at the end of June, concluded that the retaking of the Falklands left the Anglo-American alliance "closer than at any time since World War II." Like Reagan, Shultz welcomed the British victory as "the first marker laid down by a democratic power in the post-Vietnam era to state unambiguously that a free world nation was willing to fight for a principle"—and a sign to the Soviet Union of the growing strength of Western resolve.[58]

Reagan was also encouraged by briefings on the growing problems of the Soviet economy. "They are in very bad shape," he noted with satisfaction in his diary on March 26, "and if we can cut off their credit they'll have to yell 'Uncle' or starve."[59] In May Reagan signed a secret National Security Decision Directive (NSDD 32), providing for covert action as well as economic and diplomatic pressure designed to "neutralize efforts of the USSR" to maintain its hold on Eastern Europe. The covert action was to be concentrated on Poland, which both Reagan and Casey were convinced was the weak link in the Soviet bloc.[60] Casey knew from a number of intelligence sources that the KGB privately agreed.[61] Polish experts in Moscow Centre traced the origins of the Polish crisis to the election of the Polish cardinal Karol Wojtyla as Pope John Paul II in 1978. The following year John Paul II had made a triumphal nine-day tour though Poland. At the end of his visit, as he bade farewell to his home city of Krakow, where, he said, "every stone and brick is dear to me," men and women wept uncontrollably in the streets. The contrast between the political bankruptcy of the Polish Communist regime and the moral authority of the Church and the Polish pope was plain for all to see.[62] It was partly because Casey and Reagan knew Moscow Center's assessment of the potential threat posed by the pope to the stability of the Soviet bloc that they so strongly suspected the KGB of involvement in the attempt on his life in 1981.

On June 7, 1982, Reagan met the pope for the first time in the Vatican Library, where they discussed ways of giving clandestine support to the outlawed Solidarity movement and hastening the collapse of the Soviet empire, which both believed to be doomed. "We both felt that a great mistake had been made at Yalta and something should be done,"

MISSILE READY BLDGS

ERECTOR ON LAUNCH PAD

PROB HYDROGEN PEROXIDE TANKS

OXIDIZER VEHICLES

MISSILE READY BLDGS

FUELING VEHICLES

TENTS

ERECTOR ON LAUNCH PAD

MISSILE ON TRAILER

Above: One of the U-2 photographs that revealed the construction of Soviet missile bases in Cuba.

Right: U-2 photo of Russian soldier at a Cuban base using three-hole latrine. Kennedy had complained at the description of MRBM launch positions with launchers as "occupied." NPIC analysts amused the president by producing this photo as another example of an "occupied" position. *(Both courtesy of the Central Intelligence Agency)*

In honor of President Kennedy
for whom the President's Intelligence Checklist
was first written on 17 June 1961

For this day, the Checklist Staff can
find no words more fitting than a
verse quoted by the President to a
group of newspapermen the day he
learned of the presence of Soviet
missiles in Cuba.

Bullfight critics ranked in rows
Crowd the enormous plaza full;
But only one is there who knows
And he's the man who fights the bull.

THE PRESIDENT'S
INTELLIGENCE CHECKLIST

ISSUED BY THE
CENTRAL INTELLIGENCE AGENCY

22 NOVEMBER 1963
TOP SECRET

For The President Only · Top Secret

Left: The President's Intelligence Checklist (later renamed theDaily Brief) pays tribute to Kennedy after his assassination. *(Courtesy of the Walter Pforzheimer Collection on Intelligence Service, Washington, D.C.)*

Below: Lyndon B. Johnson shows his top-secret Daily Brief to his grandchild. *(Courtesy of CIA Exhibit Center)*

LBJ at the swearing in as DCI of (*above*) his ill-qualified Texan supporter
Adm. William "Red" Raborn in 1965 and (*below*) Richard Helms in 1966.
(Both courtesy of the Central Intelligence Agency)

Soviet Communist Party General Secretary Leonid Brezhnev toasts President Nixon in Moscow. Because of the stress of Watergate, Nixon failed to pay adequate attention during his second visit to Russia, in June 1974, to the fact that his rooms were bugged. The KGB team responsible for the bugging was decorated for its success shortly after Nixon's departure. *(Courtesy of UPI/Bettman)*

Above: President Ford at George Bush's swearing-in as DCI in 1976; behind is Bush's predecessor, William Colby.

Right: President Carter congratulates DCI Admiral Stansfield Turner on his swearing-in in 1977. *(Both courtesy of the Central Intelligence Agency)*

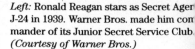

UNCLE SAM'S FIRST LINE OF DEFENSE ...AGAINST CRIME!

Watch America's fearless secret agents plunge into their most dangerous assignment ... risking their lives to protect you and yours!

"Code of the SECRET SERVICE"

with
RONALD REAGAN
ROSELLA TOWNE
EDDIE FOY, Jr.
Directed by NOEL SMITH
Presented by WARNER BROS.
A First National Picture

Original Screen Play by Lee Katz and Dean Franklin • Based Upon Material Compiled by W. H. Moran, Ex-Chief of U. S. Secret Service

Left: Ronald Reagan stars as Secret Agent J-24 in 1939. Warner Bros. made him commander of its Junior Secret Service Club. *(Courtesy of Warner Bros.)*

Below left: President Reagan and his first DCI, William Casey, look forward to "rolling back" Communism. *(Courtesy of UPI/Bettman)*

Below: An example of the KGB disinformation campaign against Reagan: a forged letter designed to suggest that he was putting pressure on the King of Spain to join NATO.

NATIONAL SECURITY AGENCY WELCOMES PRESIDENT RONALD REAGAN

Above: In September 1986 Reagan became the first president to enter NSA headquarters at Fort Meade; NSA had tried without success to persuade previous presidents to visit. Reagan made unprecedented public use of SIGINT.

Right: Bush at NSA in May 1991. He was the first president to use the word SIGINT in public; it was, he claimed, a "prime factor" in his foreign policy. *(Both courtesy of the National Security Agency)*

Above: The first encounter between a former KGB chief
and a former DCI: General Secretary Yuri Andropov meets Vice President Bush
after Brezhnev's funeral in November 1982. *(Courtesy of UPI/Bettman)*

Below: During his farewell visit as president to CIA headquarters in January 1993,
Bush presents DCI Robert Gates with the National Security Medal.
(Courtesy of the Central Intelligence Agency)

said Reagan later. "Solidarity was the very weapon for bringing this about."[63] As Reagan left the Vatican Library, a group of Armenian priests sang "America the Beautiful." Tears streamed down the president's cheeks.[64] The president's former national security adviser, Richard Allen, later claimed that Reagan and the pope had concluded "one of the great secret alliances of all time."[65] Gates insists that there was no "alliance." The Vatican and the CIA were, he says, "more or less knowledgeable" about each other's activities in Eastern Europe, but "the threads never crossed." Over the next few years Casey visited the pope several times. The usual emissary sent by Reagan and Casey to discuss Polish affairs with John Paul II, however, was the former deputy DCI, Vernon Walters, whose visits were usually unannounced.[66] According to William Clark, who had succeeded Allen as national security adviser, "The President and Casey and I discussed the situation on the ground in Poland constantly: covert operations; who was doing what, where, why and how; and the chances of success." The president's daily brief included a regular supplement on events and covert action in Poland. Casey and Clark also had regular meetings with the apostolic delegate in Washington, Archbishop Pio Laghi, often over breakfast or cappuccino, to discuss the Polish situation. On several occasions Laghi was smuggled into the White House through the southwest gate to meet Reagan. His main role, however, was to arrange Walters's secret visits to the Vatican. The problems of secretly helping Solidarity to stay alive were, Laghi recalls, very complex: "But I told Vernon, 'Listen to the Holy Father. We have 2,000 years experience of this.'"[67] In September 1982 the KGB embarked on Operation Sirena 2, intended to expose American interference in Polish affairs with the help of a forged NSC directive. The operation, which was discovered by the CIA, achieved little.[68] The fact that popular support for the Polish Church was clearly so much greater than for the Communist regime effectively undercut Soviet attempts to blame the opposition movement on the Americans.

Brezhnev's last speech, delivered in the Kremlin on October 27, only a fortnight before his death, was a deeply pessimistic denunciation of the threat to peace posed by the Reagan administration. Casey sent the president a prescient assessment of the contenders for the Soviet succession. "As for me," he wrote, "I bet Andropov on the nose and Gorbachev across the board."[69] Yuri Andropov, the former KGB chief who succeeded Brezhnev, reminded Shultz of Professor Moriarty, the evil genius of the Sherlock Holmes stories, "all brain in a disregarded body . . . a formidable adversary."[70] Under Andropov, as under Brezhnev, Reagan, like most of his advisers, remained more impressed by intelligence on hostile Soviet operations—some of it directed personally against him and members of his administration—than by evidence of Soviet alarm at his aim of beginning the "rollback" of the Communist system. Probably early in November the president was informed that the KGB residency in Washington was implementing Operation Golf, designed by Moscow Center to discredit Jeane Kirkpatrick, the U.S. ambassador to the United Nations, by the use of forged documents linking her with the South African regime. A hostile article on Kirkpatrick, entitled "A Girl's Best Friend," written by the unsuspecting Washington correspondent of the British *New Statesman*, reproduced a bogus letter to her concocted by the KGB, containing "best regards and gratitude" from the head of South African military intelligence, and allegedly enclosing a birthday present as "a token of appreciation from my government."[71]

By the end of 1982 Reagan's covert action program against the Sandinistas was in serious trouble. On November 8 *Newsweek* blew the administration's cover. Its lead story, entitled "America's Secret War: Target Nicaragua," revealed a covert operation to overthrow the Nicaraguan government and the involvement of the U.S. ambassador to Honduras in training and organizing Contra rebels. The administration was forced to admit its covert support for Contra operations, but claimed that their purpose was to put pressure on, rather than to overthrow, the Sandinistas. Congress was, predictably, unconvinced. On December 8, by a majority of 411–0, the House passed the Boland amendment, prohibiting both Defense and CIA from providing military equipment, training, or advice for the purpose of overthrowing the Nicaraguan regime. The experience of Operation Zapata and the Bay of Pigs should have made clear that paramilitary operations on the scale planned against the Sandinistas could not reasonably be expected to remain secret. "A *covert* operation," writes Shultz, "was being converted to *overt* by talk on Capitol Hill and in the daily press and television news coverage." By the summer of 1983 the CIA favored making public American support for Contra guerrilla operations and transferring management of it to the Defense Department. Defense, however, successfully resisted taking responsibility for such a controversial program, and the Latin American governments involved in assisting the Contras opposed any public admission of their role in helping to destabilize a neighboring regime. Reagan's covert action in Central America had thus become riddled with contradictions. What had become an overt program of support to the Contras was still being implemented as a covert operation—with the result, as Shultz complained, that "the administration could not openly defend it."[72] Reagan himself added to the contradictions by publicly proclaiming one policy while secretly following another. The stated aim of support for the Contras was to prevent the Sandinistas from undermining their neighbors "through the export of subversion and violence." ". . . Let us be clear as to the American attitude toward the Government of Nicaragua," the president told a joint session of Congress on April 27. "We do not seek its overthrow."[73] Reagan's real aim, however, was precisely that—the overthrow of the government of Nicaragua.

The year 1983 marked the most dangerous moment in U.S.-Soviet relations since the Cuban missile crisis. Top-secret KGB directives sent to its American and other major residencies around the world on February 17 decreed that Operation RYAN, intended to uncover plans by Reagan and NATO for a nuclear first strike, now had "an especial degree of urgency": "It is thus fully evident that the problem of uncovering the threat of RYAN must be dealt with without delay." The importance of the directives was emphasized by the fact that they were addressed to each KGB resident by name, and marked strictly personal. Though residents were ordered to keep the directive securely in their "special" (most secret) files, Oleg Gordievsky, the British agent in the London residency, succeeded in copying the entire text.[74] The substance of the directive, though not the text itself, was relayed to the CIA by SIS under the usual liaison arrangements. Following usual procedures, to protect Gordievsky, the identity of the source was not disclosed to the agency by the British, though the clues gradually multiplied.[75]

Intelligence on Soviet fears of an American first strike continued to make less impression on Reagan and his advisers than what they saw as the Soviet grand design for the Communist conquest of Central America. ". . . I wanted to get Andropov's attention," writes Reagan in his memoirs; ". . . I wanted to remind the Soviets we knew what they were up to." He did so in a remarkable speech on March 8, denouncing the Soviet Union as "an evil empire" whose end was almost at hand: "I believe that Communism is another sad, bizarre chapter in history whose last pages even now are being written."[76] Two weeks later Reagan announced the Strategic Defense Initiative (SDI), popularly known as "Star Wars," a plan to construct a defensive shield in space that would use laser technology to destroy Soviet missiles in flight. To underscore the Soviet threat in Latin America during his televised address, the president displayed a remarkable range of imagery intelligence. He began with the first photograph to be declassified of the large Soviet SIGINT station covering twenty-eight square miles at Lourdes in Cuba, with fifteen hundred Soviet personnel and acres of antennae fields targeted on the United States. Reagan went on to show aerial photographs of the Soviet arms shipments contributing to the "massive military buildup" in Cuba and Nicaragua. To illustrate "the Soviet-Cuban militarization of Grenada," he displayed a photograph of the construction of an airfield with a massive runway, despite the fact that Grenada itself had no air force. There was, said Reagan, other important intelligence that he could not reveal "without compromising our most sensitive intelligence sources and methods."[77] The intelligence that the president did not reveal included instructions to KGB residencies to embark on a large-scale (though unsuccessful) operation designed to hinder Reagan's reelection in 1984. American residencies were told to acquire contacts in the staffs of all likely presidential candidates and in both party headquarters, with the aim both of acquiring information with which to discredit Reagan during the campaign and of opening up new channels for its dissemination. Residents outside the United States were ordered to report on the possibility of sending agents to take part in this operation. KGB officers around the world were told to use their media contacts to popularize the slogan "Reagan means war!"[78]

Moscow interpreted the Star Wars speech both as further evidence of Reagan's belief that the United States could win a nuclear conflict and as part of the psychological preparation of the American people for war. On June 16, 1983, Andropov told the Central Committee that they were witnessing an "unprecedented sharpening of the struggle" between East and West: "The threat of nuclear war overhanging mankind causes one to reappraise the principal goals of the activities of the entire Communist movement." Five days later Moscow Center sent an alarmist telegram to American and other NATO residencies, stressing the high priority of Operation RYAN and claiming that the Reagan administration was continuing preparations for nuclear war. On August 12 it dispatched a further major directive "relating to intelligence and counterintelligence indications of enemy preparations for a nuclear attack":

> . . . Attention should be concentrated particularly on signs of any secret measures which, in conjunction with other factors, may point to a decision being taken by the military and political leadership of the member-countries of the [NATO] bloc to begin immediate preparations for a nuclear missile strike against the USSR.

The checklist of suspicious activities provided by the Moscow Center was largely a mirror image of Soviet contingency plans for war with the West. They included an expansion of "disinformation operations"; infiltration of sabotage teams armed with nuclear, bacteriological, and chemical weapons; and an increase in "repressive measures."[79]

The most serious moment of East-West tension since Reagan's election followed the shooting down in the early hours of September 1 of a South Korean airliner, KAL 007, which had blundered badly off course over Soviet airspace. An NSA listening post in Japan heard a Soviet fighter pilot say that he had fired a missile, then announce at 3:26 A.M. Tokyo time, "The target is destroyed." At about 9 A.M. EDT, a transcript of the pilot's reports to ground control reached the president, then on vacation in California, and his senior advisers in Washington. Reagan agreed that, while he was flying back to the White House, Shultz should announce the shoot-down at a press conference. The State Department immediately became embroiled in a heated argument with CIA and NSA over the public use of SIGINT material. With Reagan's support, Shultz insisted that "the stakes were so high that they must agree I could use it, both with the Soviets and in public."[80] Visibly angry and waving an intelligence report in his hand, Shultz told a press conference at 10:45 A.M. that there was no possible doubt that the Soviet fighter pilot had identified KAL 007 as a civilian 747 and shot it down in cold blood. For the first time in State Department history a secretary of state was directly, and unmistakably, quoting SIGINT reports. The airliner, he announced, had been tracked by Soviet radar for two hours, and the pilot had reported the shoot-down to ground control. "The United States reacts with revulsion to this attack," Shultz concluded. ". . . We can see no excuse whatsoever for this appalling act."

In the immediate aftermath of the shoot-down, the Reagan administration experienced what Henry E. Catto Jr., assistant secretary of defense, later called the "joy of total self-righteousness." The Evil Empire had shown itself to be just that. Its initial fumbling attempts to evade responsibility only added to Reagan's sense of moral outrage.[81] Within twenty-four hours of Shultz's press conference, however, the intelligence picture began to seem less clear. Both CIA and NSA analysts reported that they now thought it possible that the Soviet air force had mistaken the 747 for an American spy plane. Having publicly insisted that such an error was impossible, Shultz reacted with both anger and disbelief. ". . . A case of mistaken identity," he insisted, "was not remotely plausible." The intelligence community, he told his staff, "have no compunctions about fooling you."[82] The director of NSA, General Lincoln Faurer, seems not to have shared the doubts of some of his own analysts. There was "absolutely no way," he claimed, that the Soviet pilot could have failed to realize what he was shooting at.[83] On the morning of Sunday, September 4, Reagan called congressional leaders to the Oval Office and played them SIGINT recordings of the pilot reporting that he was arming his plane's air-to-air missile system, locking its radar onto the target, firing the missile, and announcing the target's destruction. In order "to show the American people the utter callousness of this act," Reagan decided to broadcast excerpts from the recordings the next day.

The president had planned to spend most of Monday, September 5, Labor Day, beside the White House pool. But, dissatisfied with the insufficiently ferocious text of his televised address prepared by his speechwriters, he repaired to his study, still in damp swimming trunks, laid a towel over the chair at his desk, and rewrote most of the speech himself.[84] At 8 P.M. that evening, speaking from the Oval Office, Reagan declared that the shoot-down was "an act of barbarism born of a society which wantonly disregards individual rights and the value of human life and seeks constantly to expand and dominate other nations." After playing extracts from the Soviet pilot's intercepted communications before and after firing a missile, he insisted, "There is no way a pilot could mistake this for anything other than a civilian airliner."[85]

Reagan had become the first president to quote SIGINT in a public address. The next day Jeane Kirkpatrick incorporated lengthier recordings of the Soviet pilot in a remarkable audiovisual presentation of the shoot-down before the United Nations General Assembly. She supplied a curiously prudish English transcript that deleted Russian expletives, absurdly rendering the pilot's exclamation before he fired the missile, "*Yolki palki!*" (roughly "Holy shit!"), as "Fiddlesticks!" Despite the squeamishness of its translation, however, the Reagan administration—not for the first time—damaged a powerful case against the Soviet Union by overstating it. A closed hearing of the Senate Foreign Relations Committee was told that NSA analysts believed the Soviet pilot did not know that his target was a civilian airliner. Public controversy over the shoot-down gradually shifted from Soviet responsibility for the deaths of 269 passengers and crew to the credibility of the American indictment. The language of official spokesmen became increasingly tortured as they struggled to defend the original charge of deliberate, cold-blooded murder. Robert M. McFarlane, who succeeded Clark as national security adviser in October, was reduced to arguing incoherently, "We believe that those levels of command and decision . . . who were involved [in the shoot-down] were levels that at least we expect and believe must reflect a maturity and judgment that would foreclose this kind of thing."[86]

Shortly before the shoot-down Andropov, now seriously ill, had disappeared from public view, never to reemerge. From his sickbed on September 28 he issued a denunciation of Reagan's "extreme adventurism. . . . If anyone had any illusions about the possibility of an evolution for the better in the policy of the present American administration, recent events have dispelled them once and for all." The violence of his attack on Reagan's America as "a country where extreme militarist psychosis is being imposed" was unprecedented since the depths of the

Cold War.[87] Tension continued to mount during October. On October 6 Lech Walesa, the leader of Solidarity, seen by Moscow as a central part of Reagan's plan to destabilize the Soviet bloc, was awarded the Nobel Peace Prize. On October 19 Maurice Bishop was murdered, and his regime in the former British colony of Grenada overthrown, by another group of self-styled Marxist-Leninists. Reagan and Thatcher disagreed sharply in their interpretation of the coup. British intelligence assessments concluded that, though Castro was heavily involved in Grenada, the Soviet Union had only a "peripheral interest" in it. The new regime, Mrs. Thatcher believed, though it contained more obvious thugs, was not fundamentally different from its predecessor.[88] Reagan, like Casey, regarded the coup as a serious escalation of the Communist threat to the Caribbean. Grenada, he believed, was "a Soviet-Cuban colony, being readied as a major military bastion to export terror and undermine democracy."[89]

Reagan was also genuinely concerned by the threat to eight hundred American medical students in Grenada. On October 22 he approved, in principle, an operation to rescue the students and overthrow the regime. At about 6 P.M. on October 24 he gave the go-ahead for intervention on the following day.[90] Despite the loss of nineteen American lives and injuries to a hundred more, Reagan was elated by the success of the operation. It had, he believed, "not only stopped the Communists in their tracks in that part of the world but perhaps helped all Americans stand a little taller."[91] The operation further fueled Soviet paranoia. Vice-President Vasili Kuznetsov accused the Reagan administration of "making delirious plans for world domination" that were "pushing mankind to the brink of disaster." The Soviet press depicted Reagan himself as a "madman."[92] The Sandinistas feared that Nicaragua might be the next target for an American invasion. So did the KGB.[93]

Paranoia in the Kremlin reached its peak during the NATO command post exercise Able Archer 83, held from November 2 to 11 to practice nuclear release procedures. Soviet contingency plans for a surprise attack on the West envisaged the use of training exercises as cover for a real offensive. Moscow was haunted by the fear that Western plans might be the mirror image of its own.[94] At the start of the exercise, NSA and its SIGINT allies discovered a sudden and dramatic increase in the volume and urgency of Warsaw Pact communications.[95] The most important intelligence during the exercise, however, almost certainly came via SIS from Gordievsky at the KGB London residency. Gordievsky provided the text of a directive from the Moscow Center on November 5 that revealed, for the first time, what Moscow believed was the likely timetable for a Western first strike:

Surprise is the key element in the main adversary's [the United States'] plans and preparations for war in today's conditions. As a result it can be assumed that the period of time from the moment when the preliminary decision for RYAN [a nuclear first strike] is taken, up to the order to deliver the strike will be of very short duration, possibly 7–10 days.

The London residency was ordered to "keep a constant watch" on key individuals and locations "in order to discover any possible contacts and consultations between the U.S. government and the British leadership before RYAN."[96] During Able Archer 83, imaginary NATO forces were moved through all the alert phases from normal readiness to general alert. Though there was no real alert involving any NATO forces, alarmist KGB reporting in the tense atmosphere generated both by the exercise and by the crises and rhetoric of the last few months persuaded Moscow that there was. Surveillance teams around some American bases in Europe reported changed patterns of officer movement and the observation of an hour's radio silence between 10 and 11 P.M. Moscow time. On November 8 or 9 emergency "flash" telegrams were sent to both KGB and GRU residencies in the West reporting a (nonexistent) alert at American bases. Moscow Center suggested that possible reasons for the alert might be heightened security following the death of over 240 U.S. marines in a Beirut bombing two weeks earlier, and forthcoming U.S. Army maneuvers. But it clearly implied that an alternative explanation was the beginning of the countdown toward a nuclear first strike. Residencies were ordered to report as a matter of urgency on reasons for the supposed alert and on other RYAN indicators.[97]

With the end of Able Archer, the alarm at Moscow Center eased somewhat. The intelligence over the past ten days on the paranoia in the Kremlin left a profound impression on Reagan. Though his memoirs contain no reference to the NATO exercise, he identifies November 1983 as the moment at which he finally grasped "something surprising about the Russians": "Many people at the top of the Soviet hierarchy were genuinely afraid of America and Americans. Maybe this shouldn't have surprised me but it did." A few days after the end of Able Archer, Reagan wrote in his diary, "I feel the Soviets are . . . so paranoid about being attacked that without in any way being soft on them, we ought to tell them no one here has any intention of doing anything like that." Following discussion with Shultz, he approved the creation of a small group within the National Security Planning Group (NSPG) "with the goal of opening new channels to the Kremlin" and calming Soviet fears of an American first strike."[98] Reagan did not learn the identity of the British agent, Oleg Gordievsky, who had provided probably the most important intelligence on Operation RYAN and the fears aroused by Able Archer until after Gordievsky's defection in July 1985. Late in 1986 Reagan received Gordievsky in the Oval Office and thanked him for what he had done. Putting his arm around Gordievsky's shoulder, the president promised to try to persuade Gorbachev to allow his family to leave Moscow and join him in Britain.[99]

After the shock of Soviet reaction to Able Archer in November 1983 Reagan abandoned the rhetoric of the Evil Empire virtually overnight. He began 1984 with his most conciliatory speech on East-West relations since he had entered Republican politics. The president expressed astonishment that his views on the Soviet system should have "come as a surprise to Soviet leaders who've never shied from expressing their view of our system." "But," he insisted, "that doesn't mean we can't work with each other":

> We must and will engage with the Soviets in a dialogue as serious and constructive as possible. . . . We have a long way to go, but we're determined to try and try again. We may have to start in small ways but start we must.[100]

Reagan's and Shultz's comments on the death of Andropov and his succession by Konstantin Chernenko in February 1984 struck Strobe Talbott, diplomatic correspondent of *Time* and future diplomat, as "extraordinarily conciliatory" by the previous standards of the Reagan administration.[101] But the new tone of the president's rhetoric produced no instant thaw in East-West relations. CIA assessments warned Reagan to expect no response from the Russians until after the 1984 presidential election. Chernenko and the Soviet leadership, they concluded, had decided not to agree to a summit meeting for fear that it might help Reagan's chances of reelection.[102] The KGB directives supplied by Gordievsky showed that Operation RYAN was taking time to wind down. When the London residency grew lax in early summer about sending in its regular fortnightly RYAN reports, it received a reprimand from the Moscow Center and was told to adhere strictly to its original instructions. On July 10 residencies were informed of new "combat readiness" procedures that would operate in an emergency. Gordievsky reported, however, that KGB officers returning from leave in Moscow during the summer of 1984 had the sense that the priority of Operation RYAN was steadily declining. It continued to decline for the remainder of the year. But though the Kremlin's fear of surprise nuclear attack had receded, its suspicions of the Reagan administration remained acute.[103]

During 1984 Shultz increasingly replaced Casey as the main influence on Reagan's policy to the Soviet Union. According to Gates:

> Casey's war against the Soviets and Weinberger's military buildup had an important part in Reagan's first term. But when Reagan felt that the situation on the ground vis-à-vis the Soviets had been reversed and the United States began to be seen to have the upper hand in a number of situations, Casey and Weinberger both became increasingly irrelevant. From the beginning of his second term . . . the president was prepared to go down the negotiating path with the Soviets that Shultz was pointing to.[104]

The shift in Reagan's policy to the Soviet Union did not, however, diminish his enthusiasm for the secret war against the Red Menace in Central America. In January 1984, with the president's approval, the CIA began to place magnetic mines in three Nicaraguan harbors. The mining was attributed to the Contras, who, at the agency's instigation, were happy to claim credit for it. Casey's briefing to the congressional intelligence committees was deliberately perfunctory. In a two-and-a-half-hour session with the Senate select committee on March 8, he included one sentence on the mining in a list of Contra actions not specifically identified as CIA operations. The committee failed to realize that the CIA itself had mined the harbors until its involvement was revealed by the *Wall Street Journal* on April 6. By then the mines had struck ships from six different states, among them a Soviet oil tanker. The Senate committee chairman, Senator Barry Goldwater, usually one of the agency's strongest supporters, wrote to Casey on April 9:

> All this past weekend, I've been trying to figure out how I can tell you my feelings about the discovery of the President having approved mining some of the harbors of Central America.
>
> It gets down to one, little, simple phrase: I am pissed off!

The Republican-controlled Senate condemned the mining by a majority of 84–12. On April 26 Casey made a formal apology to the Senate committee. The words almost stuck in his throat. ". . . The Nicaraguan operation was on the ropes," he said later. "I only apologized to save the Contras." The Nicaraguan operation remained on the ropes. On May 24 the House voted another Boland amendment, more drastic than its predecessor. Signed into law by Reagan five months later, Boland II (as it became known) prohibited military or paramilitary support for the Contras by the CIA, Defense, "or any other agency or entity involved in intelligence activities" during the period from October 1984 to December 1985.[105]

Foreseeing the congressional ban on funding, the national security adviser, Robert McFarlane, had been trying since March, with the support of Reagan and Casey, to find support for the Contras from abroad. McFarlane later testified that in the spring and summer of 1984 Reagan "let us know very clearly that we were to do all that we could to make sure that the movement, the freedom fighters, survived and . . . to keep them together body and soul."[106] From Reagan's determination that covert means be found to keep the Contras together "body and soul," despite the Boland amendments, there eventually developed the whole Iran-Contra imbroglio. An attempt by McFarlane to seek support for the Contras from Israel failed. The South Africans expressed interest, but their involvement was rejected by the White House because of the political risks of accepting support from the apartheid regime. In May, however, the Saudi Arabian ambassador, Prince Bandar bin Sultan, agreed to provide a million dollars a month to support the Contras until the end of the year. According to McFarlane, Reagan sent him a note expressing "satisfaction and pleasure" at the Saudi offer. On June 25 the president chaired an NSPG meeting to discuss seeking foreign funding for the Contras. Shultz reported the view of James Baker, then chief of staff, that this would be an "impeachable offense." Neither Reagan nor McFarlane revealed that Saudi support had already been obtained. (The congressional intelligence committees were not informed until 1987.) The meeting failed to reach a firm conclusion. With CIA operations in Nicaragua prohibited by Boland II, the responsibility for supporting the Contras passed to the NSC. "The President had made it clear that he wanted a job done," McFarlane later testified. "The net result was that the job fell to National Security Council staff."[107]

The "job," however, was impossible. The disorganized Contras had no prospect of defeating the Sandinistas. Their inept guerrilla campaign served chiefly to discredit themselves and their American supporters. The DDI, Robert Gates, wrote to Casey on December 14, 1984:

> The course we have been on (even before the funding cut-off)— as the last two years will testify—will result in further strengthening of the regime and a Communist Nicaragua which, allied with its Soviet and Cuban friends, will serve as the engine for the destabilization of Central America. Even a well funded Contra movement cannot prevent this; indeed, relying on and supporting the Contras as our only action may actually hasten the ultimate unfortunate outcome.

The only way to bring down the Sandinistas, Gates argued, was overt military assistance to their opponents, coupled with "air strikes to destroy a considerable portion of Nicaragua's military buildup." Covert action could not do the job.[108] Neither Casey nor Reagan was willing to face up to this uncomfortable truth.

The element of fantasy in the Contra operation was personified in the role of the NSC staff officer responsible for it, marine Lieutenant Colonel Oliver L. North. When North was assigned to the White House in 1981 he was, by his own admission, "unprepared and inexperienced": "I was over my head at the NSC, and I knew it." Most military officers in the White House, he discovered, had "advanced degrees in foreign studies or political science." North did not. Though he had a reputation as a "can-do" officer with a dynamic leadership style, he had a limited grasp of international relations. He also confessed to knowing "nothing about covert operations" and "little about Central America" when he arrived at the NSC, but later claimed to have learned "a great deal" from Casey about the former and to have "read like crazy" about the latter. If North had few qualifications for the Contra assignment, however, he also faced limited competition. As he acknowledges in his memoirs, ". . . NSC staff members were not exactly standing in line to work on Latin America."[109] Clair George, CIA deputy director of operations, was struck by the naïveté of North's plans for Contra operations against the Sandinistas. Many of them were, he claimed, "crazy" or "harebrained." But, as McFarlane's deputy (and successor), Vice Admiral John M. Poindexter, later testified, "[O]nce the CIA was restricted," North became the "switching point that made the whole system work . . . the kingpin to the Central American opposition. . . ." North was nothing if not determinedly optimistic. "With adequate support," he claimed, "the [Contra] resistance could be in Managua by the end of 1985."[110] Reagan, too, convinced himself that the Contras could win. On March 1, 1985, he described them as "the moral equal of the Founding Fathers."[111] "Amidst all the turmoil and infighting," writes North, ". . . only one thing was clear and steadfast: Ronald Reagan's support for the Nicaraguan resistance."[112]

Reagan's other great foreign preoccupation during 1985 was the hostage crisis in Lebanon. By the beginning of the year Hizballah, the pro-Iranian "Party of God," had kidnapped five Americans, including the CIA station chief in Beirut, William Buckley, whom it brutally tortured. Four more Americans were taken prisoner over the next six months. Their fate preyed on the president's mind. The scenes on television of the hostages in captivity and Reagan's emotional meetings with their families moved him deeply. He took to opening his morning national security briefings by repeating the same question, "Any progress on getting the hostages out of Lebanon?"[113] The attempt to rescue the hostages, like that to support the Contras, led Reagan to approve covert operations run not by the professionals of the CIA, but by the amateurs of the NSC—though, thanks chiefly to Casey, both operations had access to varying amounts of agency expertise. The eventual merging of these two operations in the Iran-Contra affair was to produce by far the most serious crisis of the Reagan presidency.

"The United States gives terrorists no rewards and no guarantees," Reagan declared on June 30, 1985. "We make no concessions, we make no deals."[114] A few weeks later he authorized the sale by Israel of American TOW antitank missiles to Iran, a state formally designated by the State Department as a supporter of international terrorism. The decision may have been made while Reagan was recovering from major surgery in Bethesda Naval Hospital. One of his first questions when he recovered consciousness after his operation on July 13 was "Any word on the hostages?"[115] On July 18 he was visited in the hospital by McFarlane, who told him that Iranian "moderates" had told the Israelis they wanted a dialogue with the United States, and had offered to use their influence to persuade Hizballah to release the hostages. Reagan found this "exciting" news. No record was made of his discussion with McFarlane, and it is uncertain whether at this meeting he agreed to the sale by Israel of TOW missiles to Iran for use in the war against Iraq. But, as Reagan acknowledges, he certainly did so in August:

> The truth is, once we had information from Israel that we could trust the people in Iran, I didn't have to think thirty seconds about saying yes to their proposal. . . . But I said there was one thing we wanted: The Moderate Iranians had to use their influence with the Hizballah and try to get our hostages freed.[116]

Reagan was both deceived and humiliated by the allegedly moderate Iranians. Though Iran received a total of over two thousand TOW missiles, as well as spare parts for its HAWK antiaircraft missiles, only three Americans were released—fewer than the number of new hostages taken in Beirut while negotiations were in progress. The fiasco was due partly to the gullibility of NSC staff—and, ultimately, of the president himself. The NSC's main initial contact with Iran, the arms dealer Manucher Ghorbanifar, who arranged the first TOW shipments, had been condemned by the CIA in a "burn notice" of July 1984, warning agency personnel and other intelligence agencies that he was "an intelligence fabricator and a nuisance."[117] The most basic problem, however, was the lack of reliable intelligence from within Iran. Reagan and the NSC never really knew who they were dealing with. Gates believes that Casey went along with the arms sales to Iran not, as has been claimed, because of concern for the fate of William Buckley, the station chief taken hostage by the Hizballah, but essentially because the president was so committed to the whole disastrous enterprise:

> Reagan had been bugging him so insistently on getting the hostages out—"Why can't we find them?" sort of thing—that Casey was willing to support anything that showed some promise of bringing the problem to a conclusion. I think most of what's been written about Casey's preoccupation with Bill Buckley is bilge. Casey regretted Buckley's capture and regretted his death. But Casey was a tough old bird who'd gone through the OSS and saw Buckley as a casualty of war. I never, ever heard him muse on the tragedy of Bill Buckley or convey in any way that what needed to be done on the arms sales to Iran or anything else was motivated by concern about Buckley.[118]

By December 1985 North was working on a plan to divert profits from arms sales to Iran to the Contras. During 1986 arms supplies to the Contras dramatically increased. By the summer, in defiance of Boland II, weapons purchased with Iranian money were being dropped to guerrilla forces in northern Nicaragua; by the autumn, drops were being made in the south as well. Poindexter, who succeeded McFarlane as national security adviser at the end of 1985, made plausible deniability a cardinal principle of the whole operation. He later claimed at the congressional Iran-Contra hearings that he had made "a very deliberate decision" not to consult the president about the diversion of funds to the Contras to "insulate" him from a "politically volatile issue" and "provide some future deniability for the President if it ever leaked out." But Poindexter also testified to his conviction that the diversion was fully in accord with Reagan's wishes: "I was convinced that I understood the president's thinking on this, and that if I had taken it to him that he would have approved it." North claimed that he always "assumed that the President was aware of [the diversion]." ". . . I find it hard to believe that he didn't know," he later wrote in his memoirs.[119] North's tendency to fantasy, however, weakens the credibility of his evidence.

Though Reagan was poorly supplied with intelligence on the Iranian-Hizballah terrorist connection, he received plentiful intelligence from both CIA and NSA during 1985 on a dramatic upsurge in Libyan-sponsored terrorism. In the autumn Reagan ordered a review of the options for military action against Libya. The Pentagon came forward with a plan for a seaborne attack that to Gates "looked a very great deal like D-Day. Most objective observers would conclude that there wasn't a lot in common between Hitler's Fortress Europe and Qaddafi's Libya. But, [according to the Defense Department,] the force requirements were roughly similar."[120] The only practicable option thus appeared to be an air strike. On December 27 twenty people, five of them Americans, were killed in simultaneous terrorist attacks at Rome and Vienna airports. Though the attacks were carried out by Palestinians of the Abu Nidal Organization, it was clear that they had been supported by Qaddafi, who hailed them as "heroic." Three of the terrorists in Vienna were found to be using Tunisian passports supplied by Libya. A meeting of the Crisis Pre-Planning Group at the White House on January 5, 1986, began discussing possible targets for a retaliatory air attack on Libya. Soon afterward the CIA set up a new Counter-Terrorism Center, in which, for the first time, analysts and operations officers worked side by side, together with representatives of NSA and other sections of the intelligence community. According to Charles Cogan, a senior member of the Operations Directorate, "The improvement in the quality of finished intelligence was quickly noticeable, as was the agency's overall ability to respond to and disrupt terrorist planning."[121]

Reagan made the final decision to go ahead with an air strike against Libya after the bombing of La Belle Discothèque in West Berlin in the early hours of April 5. An American sergeant and a Turkish woman were killed and 230 were wounded, including over 50 American servicemen. Intercepted Libyan cables decrypted by NSA and its British ally, GCHQ, provided proof of Libyan responsibility. On March 25 the Libyan "People's Bureaux" (embassies) in East Berlin, Rome, Madrid, and other European capitals had been ordered to prepare terrorist attacks on U.S. military installations and civilian targets frequented by Americans. On the night of April 4 the People's Bureau in East Berlin had cabled Tripoli, predicting an imminent "joyous event." At almost the moment when the discothèque bomb exploded, another decrypted cable from the People's Bureau in East Berlin reported that the operation had been successfully carried out "without leaving clues."[122] Reagan took a personal part in selecting the targets for the American air strike, poring over large-scale satellite photographs of Tripoli, spread out on the floor of the Oval Office.[123] The JCS opposed including in the targets the Azizia Barracks Compound, which included Qaddafi's residence and operational headquarters as well as elements of the elite Jamahiriya Guards, because of the danger of civilian casualties. Reagan personally overrode their objections.[124] On April 14, just before the air strike, Reagan briefed congressional leaders on the decrypts that proved Libyan responsibility for the discothèque bombing. Following media reports that the operation was about to begin, writes Reagan in his memoirs, ". . . I really lost my patience with the press." "Seldom in military history," thought Shultz, "had a punch been so clearly telegraphed."[125] At 9 P.M., in a televised address from the Oval Office, Reagan announced that the air strikes had taken place two hours earlier. He irritated both GCHQ and his own cryptanalysts by his thinly veiled references to SIGINT:

> The evidence is now conclusive that the terrorist bombing of La Belle Discothèque was planned and executed under the direct orders of the Libyan regime. On March 25th, more than a week before the attack, orders were sent from Tripoli to the Libyan People's Bureau in East Berlin to conduct a terrorist attack against Americans to cause maximum and indiscriminate casualties. Libya's agents then planted the bomb. On April 4th the People's Bureau alerted Tripoli that the attack would be carried out the following morning. The next day they reported back to Tripoli on the great success of their mission.
>
> Our evidence is direct; it is precise; it is irrefutable.[126]

The air strike achieved only some of its objectives. According to intelligence reports, however, Qaddafi was traumatized by the attack, which killed one of his infant children and was said to have blown out a door to him in his underground command bunker. Reagan was told that Qaddafi had taken his revenge by paying "a fortune" for one of the American hostages in Beirut, then ordering his execution along with that of two Britons. The president believed the air strike had been a success. ". . . We didn't," he claims, "hear much more from Qaddafi's terrorists." One intelligence assessment later concluded that Qaddafi "hunkered down" for about eighteen months before recovering sufficient nerve to resume terrorist operations.[127] It was probably partly to express his gratitude for NSA's success in decrypting Libyan communications that in September Reagan became the first president to visit its Fort Meade headquarters. He told its staff:

> The simple truth is: Without you, I could not do my job; nor could Secretary Shultz conduct diplomacy; nor could Secretary Weinberger, nor Admiral [William J.] Crowe [Chairman of the JCS], muster the forces that defend us. . . . You carry on the struggle for freedom, and you, too, are heroes.[128]

No world leader had ever paid such a public tribute to the work of peacetime cryptanalysts.

There was a striking contradiction between the bombing of the Libyan terrorist center and Reagan's support for an arms-for-hostages deal with Middle Eastern terrorists. Reagan resolved the contradiction by refusing to admit that it existed. On the flimsy pretext that weapons were being offered not to the Hizballah but to the Iranians, he insisted that the arms and the hostages were not linked. Absurd though the argument was, Reagan managed to convince himself of it. "I had seen him like this before on other issues," writes Shultz. "He would go over the script of an event, past or present, in his mind, and once that script was mastered, that was the truth—no fact, no argument, no plea for reconsideration, could change his mind."[129] The president, in other words, possessed an alarming capacity for self-delusion on issues that really mattered to him. He so desperately wanted the release of the hostages that at the beginning of 1986 he continued to pin his hopes on the allegedly "good connections" in Iran of the egregious Ghorbanifar, preferring the ill-informed confidence of the NSC staff to the well-founded skepticism of his secretaries of state and defense. "[Shultz and Weinberger] argued forcefully that I was wrong," Reagan acknowledges, "but I just put my foot down." Throughout February he lived in almost daily expectation of news that the hostages had been released.[130]

The climax of the arms-for-hostages negotiations came in a series of farcical secret meetings with Iranian representatives. The first was a four-day visit to Teheran in May by an American delegation headed by the former national security adviser, Robert McFarlane, and including Oliver North, to negotiate the release of the hostages. North told Poindexter that he was confident of the mission's success, adding piously, "Thank God—he answers prayers." McFarlane absurdly compared the importance of his mission to Kissinger's historic secret meeting with Chou En-Lai, which had paved the way for Nixon's state visit and the reconciliation of China and the United States. Ghorbanifar had led McFarlane to believe that the hostages would be released on his arrival in Teheran, and that the Speaker of the Majlis, Ali Akbar Hashemi Rafsanjani, would be at the airport to greet him. In fact, the delegation initially found no one at the airport who knew they were coming. Revolutionary Guards, famished by the fast of Ramadan, ate a chocolate layer cake purchased by North from an Israeli bakery. They also confiscated the delegation's false Irish passports, two presentation pistols (intended, like the cake, as a gift), and a consignment of missile spare parts that McFarlane had intended to hand over only after the hostages were released. The Americans met only middle-ranking Iranian officials and failed to secure the return of any of the hostages. McFarlane twice telephoned the president from Teheran to report the lack of progress of the mission. North blamed the "duplicitous sneak," Ghorbanifar, for deceiving both the Americans and the Iranians about what the other side was prepared to offer. At the root of the whole farcical encounter, however, was the gullibility of the White House and its NSC staff. Given Ghorbanifar's record and his repeated failure of CIA lie-detector tests, it almost passes belief that any trust was still placed in him. Reagan, however, had had high hopes for McFarlane's mission. His return without the hostages, wrote Reagan in his diary, "was a heart breaking disappointment for us all."[131]

After the release of one of the hostages, Father Lawrence Jenco, on July 26, Reagan's hopes revived. Poindexter's optimism, like Reagan's, owed more to self-delusion than to hard intelligence. He told the president that the release was a direct result of McFarlane's mission, that the Iranian "moderates" had shown "they could deliver," and that they "expected to arrange the release of all the hostages shortly." Both Casey and the NSC staff recommended another shipment of spare missile parts as a demonstration of goodwill. Then Poindexter announced the opening up of a promising "second channel" to the Iranian leadership through Ali Hashemi Bahramani, usually dubbed "the Relative," allegedly the nephew of Speaker Rafsanjani. So far from being a "moderate," however, Bahramani was a member of the Revolutionary Guard, the military arm of the radicals seeking to replace the regular Iranian army. He visited Washington secretly on September 19 for two days of talks with North and others. North gave him a tour of "every corner of the White House," including the Oval Office. A small group of American negotiators, including North, met the Relative again at Frankfurt from October 6 to 8. The Relative was accompanied by another Revolutionary Guard, nicknamed "the Engine" by the Americans. North took with him a Bible, inscribed at his request by Reagan in his spidery hand with a verse from Galatians: "And the Scripture, foreseeing that God would justify the Gentiles by faith, preached the Gospel beforehand to Abraham, saying 'All the nations shall be blessed in you.'" This passage, North believed, would demonstrate to the Iranians the strength of the president's religious faith and underline how much Muslims and Christians had in common. The Frankfurt encounter recaptured the farcical absurdity of the Teheran meeting. North shamelessly invented a series of meetings with, and statements by, the president:

> . . . I flew up to Camp David to talk to the President, and I showed him the list [of arms requested by the Iranians], and he said, "Why are you thinking so small?" . . . And he banged on the table, "I want to end the war!"

In a further, comic attempt to impress the Relative and the Engine, North announced as he presented them with the Bible inscribed by Reagan:

> We inside our Government had an enormous debate, a very angry debate inside our government over whether or not my President should authorize me to say, "We accept the Islamic Revolution of Iran as a fact. . . ." He went off one whole weekend and prayed about what the answer should be and he came back almost a year ago with that passage I gave you that he wrote in front of the Bible I gave you. And he said to me, "This is the promise that God gave to Abraham. Who am I to say that we should not do this?"

Never before had a secret White House emissary so shamelessly invented statements by the president. As North later admitted, he made a habit of lying to the Iranians.[132]

A further meeting with the Relative and the Engine took place in Mainz at the end of October. By then, however, the whole Iran-Contra imbroglio had begun to unravel. On October 5 a C-123K cargo plane carrying ammunitions and other supplies for the Contras was shot down over Nicaragua. One crew member survived and was captured by the Sandinistas. At almost the same moment Casey was informed that three businessmen who claimed to have lost $10 million on the arms sales to Iran were threatening to sue, alleging that the money had been used by the U.S. government for operations in Central America. Casey warned North, who began shredding documents. On November 3 the Lebanese weekly *Al-Shiraa* published an account of McFarlane's secret mission to Teheran and unleashed a torrent of news reports and media speculation in the United States.[133] Rafsanjani exposed Reagan to international ridicule by publicly displaying the Bible inscribed by him and giving an embroidered account of McFarlane's mission to Teheran as the president's representative. The immediate reaction of the White House to the revelations was to attempt a cover-up—though there was confusion about how much to conceal. Reagan's initial instinct was to stonewall.[134] He declared, in response to a reporter's question on November 6, that the *Al-Shiraa* story had "no foundation at all."[135] By the time the president convened a meeting of his senior advisers on November 10, however, he was convinced that "[we] must say something because I'm being held out to dry." The discussion was dominated by Reagan, and the simplistic formula that emerged from it was also his. The president had persuaded himself that the secret approaches to the alleged Iranian moderates were not in any sense an offer either of arms for hostages or of a ransom to terrorists. A press release after the meeting implausibly declared, ". . . Our policy of not making concessions to terrorists remains intact." At Shultz's insistence, however, a proposed reference to the advisers' "unanimous support for the President's decisions" was changed to "unanimous support for the President."[136]

The disorientation that resulted from the NSC staff's bizarre and muddled secret dealings with Iran was reflected in the confusion in the president's mind. His televised address from the Oval Office on the evening of November 13 persuaded Shultz that "Ronald Reagan still truly did not believe that what had happened had, in fact, happened." There had been no illegality, the president told a largely skeptical nation, and no trading of arms for hostages.[137] Shultz sympathized with Senator Pat Moynihan's description of the secret negotiations with Iran as "the worst handling of an intelligence problem in our history." He agreed, too, with an article in the *Wall Street Journal* that concluded that Reagan had "cuckolded his own secretaries of state and defense."[138] As Reagan tried to defuse the crisis and restore his own credibility, he only became more confused. His performance at a press conference on November 19 was probably the most inept of his political career. He began by announcing: ". . . To eliminate the widespread but mistaken perception that we have been exchanging arms for hostages, I have directed that no further arms sales of any kind be sent to Iran." Thereafter, he was repeatedly caught by reporters' questions. Having twice insisted that "We did not condone and do not condone the shipment of arms [to Iran] from other countries," he was reminded that his chief of staff, Donald Regan, had already revealed the administration's approval for the Israeli shipment of TOW missiles in September 1985. The president was reduced to replying lamely, "Well, no, I've never heard Mr. Regan say that, and I'll ask him about that."[139] Regan believed that the president was "stumbling all over the place and looking very inept and weak and willful during that press conference" because he was confused about how much he should admit to knowing.[140] Scarcely had the press conference concluded than Reagan was persuaded by his advisers to issue a correction. "There was," he acknowledged, "a third country [Israel] involved in our secret project with Iran." But he repeated his inaccurate claim at the press conference that he had "authorized or condoned" the shipment of only "token amounts of defensive arms and parts"—all of which could have been carried in "a single cargo aircraft."[141]

Though convinced of the rightness of his cause and apparently unable to grasp that he had approved arms-for-hostages negotiations, Reagan nonetheless believed in the need, as Shultz put it, to "rearrange the record." For the past two weeks, on Poindexter's instructions, North had been preparing, with some assistance from the CIA and the Pentagon, a doctored narrative of the negotiations with Iran. The most important excision from the narrative—"the secret within a secret," as North described it—was any hint of the Iran-Contra diversion of funds. North found falsifying history an unusually demanding enterprise. Confused record-keeping within the NSC meant that, particularly in the early stages of the negotiations, it proved difficult to establish what had really happened. It was even harder, however, to gauge how much fabrication would successfully withstand congressional inquiry. At least a dozen times, North and his helpers wrote and rewrote their narrative. Like some of his other covert operations, North's shredding and doctoring of documents degenerated into the theater of the absurd, with his secretary, Fawn Hall, smuggling compromising papers out of his office concealed in her boots and clothing. Hundreds of incriminating documents, however, remained to assist future investigators. Though Reagan remained in ignorance of the criminal farce taking place in North's office, the independent counsel for Iran-Contra matters, Lawrence E. Walsh, later concluded that he "permitted the creation of a false account of the Iran arms sales to be disseminated to members of Congress and the American people."[142]

After Reagan's disastrous press conference on November 19 it was clear that the attempt to contain the crisis was not succeeding. Two days later he agreed to Attorney General Edwin Meese's proposal that he prepare "a coherent overview of all the facts" by November 24. Walsh's controversial final report later claimed that Meese's investigation was "more of a damage-control exercise than an effort to find the facts":

> Meese was conducting the November 21-24 investigation as "counselor" and "friend" to the President, not as the nation's chief law enforcement officer. Independent Counsel concluded that he was not so much searching for the truth . . . as he was building a case of deniability for his client-in-fact, President Reagan.[143]

By far the most alarming discovery in the course of Meese's investigation was evidence in North's papers of the diversion of money from Iranian arms sales to the Contras. At about 4:30 P.M. on November 24 Meese informed Reagan in the Oval Office. According to Donald Regan, the only other person present, "The color drained from [the president's] face leaving his skin pasty white."[144] Regan's first priority was to distance the president from the new scandal that was about to break. A memo that he wrote that day became the basis of White House strategy:

> Tough as it seems[,] blame must be put at NSC's door—rogue operation, going on without President's knowledge or sanction. When

suspicions arose he took charge, ordered investigation, had meeting of top advisers to get at facts, and find out who knew what. Try to make the best of a sensational story. Anticipate charges of "out of control" "President doesn't know what's going on". . . .[145]

The conduct of covert operations and the role of the NSC staff in the Reagan administration had put in doubt his survival as president. The ultimate responsibility for both, however, lay with Reagan himself. Walsh concluded at the end of his investigation:

The tone in Iran/contra was set by President Reagan. He directed that the contras be supported, despite a ban on contra aid imposed on him by Congress. And he was willing to trade arms to Iran for the release of Americans held hostage in the Middle East, even if doing so was contrary to the nation's stated policy and possibly in violation of the law.[146]

During the Iran-Contra crisis, the word "impeachment" was probably never uttered either by the president himself or by his advisers in their conversations with him.[147] It was, however, in all their minds. Faced with the knowledge on November 24 that the Iran-Contra affair was about to become headline news, Reagan's nerve seems to have cracked. He handed over management of the crisis to Meese and Regan.[148] The White House press conference on November 25 was probably the most humiliating moment of his presidency. Unable to cope with questions, Reagan made only a brief statement. He announced that an inquiry by the attorney general had revealed that he had not been "fully informed" by NSC staff on "one of the activities undertaken in connection with [the Iranian] initiative." Though he could not bring himself to say what the activity was, Reagan acknowledged that it raised "serious questions of propriety." He announced that North had been "relieved of his duties," and that Poindexter, who, he inaccurately claimed, was "not directly involved," had resigned:

While I cannot reverse what has happened, I'm initiating steps . . . to assure that the implementation of all future foreign and national security policy initiatives will proceed only in accordance with my authorization. . . . And now, I'm going to ask Attorney General Meese to brief you.

Pandemonium followed. As a barrage of questions descended on him, Reagan first insisted that he would not answer, then gave a few fragmentary replies, quickly thought better of it, handed over to Meese, and departed.[149] The public shambles of the press conference aptly mirrored the secret confusion of the covert action that had put Reagan's presidency at risk.

Meese had two roles to fulfill at the press conference. Though he was officially present as attorney general, the independent counsel later charged that he acted chiefly as the president's defense lawyer, seeking to protect his client from possible impeachment. Meese acknowledged that Reagan had been "informed generally" of the Israeli sale of American arms to Iran in the late summer or early fall of 1985, but said that he had learned the "details" of the November 1985 shipment of antiaircraft missiles only in February 1986. Walsh's final report on Iran-Contra makes much—perhaps too much—of Meese's statement. An admission that the president had been aware at the time of the November 1985 shipment would, he claims, have exposed Reagan to charges of illegal conduct, given his failure either to sign a covert-action finding or to observe the requirements of the Arms Export Control Act.[150] Meese's most important function at the press conference was to make the first public admission that the proceeds of arms sales to Iran had been diverted to the Contras. Relying on an inaccurate account supplied by North, Meese placed most of the responsibility for the diversion on the Israelis. "So far as we know at this stage," he declared, "no American person actually handled any of the funds which went to the forces in Central America." On the American side, Meese pinned most of the blame on North—"the only person in the United States government that knew precisely about this"—and exonerated all higher ranks: "I don't think anyone can be responsible if someone on the lower echelons of government does something that we don't feel—or that—objectively viewed is not correct." The reporters—whom Regan watched "shouting and leaping and gesticulating"—had other ideas. They were, he believed, "thinking a single thought: another Presidency was about to destroy itself."[151] That evening Bush dictated for his diary a series of staccato phrases that summed up the despondency in the White House: "The administration is in disarray—foreign policy in disarray—cover-up—Who knew what when?"[152]

The November revelations and the firing of North and Poindexter brought the Iran-Contra "diversion" to an end. But they did not immediately lead to the breaking off of secret contacts with the Iranians. Shultz agreed to a further meeting with the second channel at Frankfurt on December 13, on condition that the meeting was for intelligence purposes only, that there were no policy discussions, and that it was made clear to the Iranians that the arms-for-hostages negotiations were at an end. Casey, however, gained Reagan's approval for policy discussions to continue with the second channel. At an angry meeting in the Oval Office on December 15 Shultz claimed that, at Casey's insistence, "the CIA was *still* trying to trade arms for hostages," and was putting pressure on Kuwait to release jailed Iranian-backed terrorists. While the meeting was taking place, the DCI was being rushed to hospital with what proved to be terminal brain cancer. With Casey's departure, the last influential voice in favor of continuing the arms-for-hostages negotiations disappeared.[153]

Though Reagan sought to evade as much personal responsibility as possible for the Iran-Contra diversion of funds, he was also anxious to avoid all appearance of a cover-up on the Watergate model. On November 26 he appointed a special review board, chaired by Senator John Tower, to conduct "a comprehensive study of the future role and procedures of the National Security Council staff." On December 2 the president ordered the appointment of an independent counsel to investigate arms supplies to Iran, aid to the Contras, and the connection between the two. Two days later the House and the Senate agreed to establish a joint panel to investigate the Iran-Contra scandal. Despite its confused beginnings in November, the White House damage-control exercise to distance the president as far as possible from responsibility for the scandal was largely successful. At difficult moments of the inquiries, Reagan fell back on what the historian Theodore Draper calls an "innocence-by-ignorance" defense. Despite his passionate commitment to the Contra cause, he told the Tower commission that he "did not know the NSC staff was engaged in helping the Contras." But the president's protestations of ignorance were sometimes weakened by confusion. He first told the Tower commission that he had approved the initial Israeli missile shipments, then changed his mind and said that he had not, and finally claimed that he could not remember whether he had or not. Both the Tower and congressional inquiries largely supported the White House view of the scandal as the work of subordinates who had escaped executive control.[154] The congressional committees had no stomach for an impeachment crisis on the Watergate model. Except for the "diversion" issue, they chose not to investigate any potentially illegal acts involving the president. They were also much criticized by the independent counsel for giving North and Poindexter guarantees that nothing said by either in their hearings could be used in future legal proceedings, thus making more difficult investigation of the role of the president and his cabinet:

> Immunity is ordinarily given by a prosecutor to a witness who will incriminate someone more important than himself. Congress gave

immunity to North and Poindexter, who incriminated only themselves and who largely exculpated those responsible for the initiation, supervision and support of their activities.[155]

The hearings of North and Poindexter, seen on television around the
world, made the Iran-Contra affair—once "the secret within the
secret"—the best publicized foreign covert action in American history.
The congressional inquiry pinned most of the blame on North, Poindexter, McFarlane, and Casey. It concluded, however, that "ultimate responsibility" lay with Reagan: "If the President did not know what his
National Security Advisers were doing, he should have."[156] Walsh's later
verdict on the president and his cabinet was much harsher:

> The underlying facts of Iran/contra are that, regardless of criminal-
> ity, President Reagan, the secretary of state, the secretary of
> defense, and the director of central intelligence and their necessary
> assistants committed themselves, however reluctantly, to two pro-
> grams contrary to congressional policy and contrary to national pol-
> icy. They skirted the law, some of them broke the law, and almost all
> of them tried to cover up the President's willful activities.[157]

Another distinguishing characteristic of Iran-Contra was its sheer incompetence. For that too, the ultimate responsibility rested with the president, who had allowed his national security staff to engage in operations
for which they lacked the expertise. "The problem was," said one scorn-
ful senior member of the CIA Directorate of Operations, "there was no
adult supervision."[158]

While the Iran-Contra operation was ending in ignominy, the Reagan
administration was simultaneously conducting in Afghanistan what
became one of the most successful covert operations since the Second
World War. There were two critical differences between Iran-Contra and
Afghanistan. First, the secret help to the Afghan Mujahideen, unlike the
arms supplied to Iran and the Contras, was in line with the publicly
stated policy of the administration. Secondly, the Afghan operation,
though far from flawless, was run by experienced CIA professionals
rather than by the bungling amateurs of the NSC. Reagan's decision in
April 1986, despite the opposition of the Pentagon, to supply the
Mujahideen with hand-held Stinger heat-seeking missiles, never previously used in combat, was one of the turning points in the Afghan War.[159]
Stingers were first used on September 25 by three Mujahideen concealed near Jelalabad airfield not far from the Khyber Pass. As a group
of Soviet Hind helicopter gunships approached the airfield, each

Mujahideen selected a target and waited until a pinging noise from the launcher indicated that the missile was locked onto its target. To shouts of *"Allah o Akhbar!"* ("God is Great!"), five missiles were fired and three Hinds were shot down. A video of the attack was rushed to Washington and shown to Reagan in the Oval Office. Its quality was disappointing. The Mujahideen cameraman had become so excited during the attack that he had been unable to stand still. Much of the video thus consisted of blurred images of sky, scrub, and ground. The cameraman steadied himself after the shoot-down, and the president was able to see black smoke billowing from the wrecks of three helicopter gunships.[160]

With the arrival of the Stingers, the Soviet air force lost most of its ability to use helicopters and low-level aircraft against Mujahideen positions. The tide of the war began to turn. The author witnessed one air attack in northeastern Afghanistan in August 1987 that vividly illustrated the Soviet loss of air supremacy. The aircraft dropped flares intended to confuse the heat-seeking Stingers, then departed rapidly after one hasty bombing run. On this occasion, the Mujahideen had no missiles. Had they been equipped with Stingers, however, the flares would, almost certainly, have been ineffective against them.[161] By early 1987 there were already signs that the Soviet Union was planning a withdrawal from Afghanistan. After a visit to Moscow at the end of 1986 the Afghan leader, Mohammad Najibullah, reported to the Communist Central Committee in Kabul that Soviet troops were to be withdrawn in one and a half to two years' time. A few weeks later a member of the Central Committee defected to France and revealed what had been said. Most CIA analysts, however, were deeply skeptical of this and similar intelligence.[162]

Though intelligence had played a major part in persuading Reagan to abandon his Evil Empire rhetoric at the end of 1983, it had a much smaller influence on the remarkable Soviet-American rapprochement that gathered pace during his second term. The rise to power of Mikhail Gorbachev in March 1985, followed by his summit meetings with Reagan at Geneva in November 1985 and Reykjavik in October 1986, changed the atmosphere of East-West relations. But though progress was made at Reykjavik in negotiations on nuclear arms reductions, no U.S.-Soviet agreements were signed during Gorbachev's first two years in power. Throughout that period, Reagan received increasingly pessimistic reports on the Soviet economy. Some of these reports came from the CIA. According to Gates:

> We credited Gorbachev with making a serious effort to implement reform during his first two and a half years. But . . . we consistently

and accurately predicted that his attempts to reform the centrally planned economic system would not work. . . . By 1987, the Agency was describing in considerable detail the failure of Gorbachev's reforms and the growing crisis in the Soviet Union. The Agency's pessimism with respect to Gorbachev's approach crystallized in a December, 1987 paper that stated, "The reform package as now constituted is a set of half-measures that leaves in place the pillars of socialist central planning. . . ." That same study also accurately predicted much of the damage done to the economy by basic flaws in Gorbachev's inadequate reforms.[163]

Reagan claims in his memoirs that evidence of the "Soviet economic tailspin" helped to persuade him that Gorbachev would have to come around to "an arms reduction agreement we could both live with."[164]

Though the president's daily brief correctly predicted the failure of Gorbachev's economic reforms, it underestimated his growing willingness to transform East-West relations. According to Shultz's jaundiced reading of the briefs:

When Gorbachev appeared at the helm, the CIA said he was "just talk," just another Soviet attempt to deceive us. As that line became increasingly untenable, the CIA changed its tune: Gorbachev was serious about change, but the Soviet Union had a powerfully entrenched and largely successful system that was incapable of being changed. . . . When it became evident that the Soviet Union was, in fact, changing, the CIA line was that the changes wouldn't really make a difference.[165]

But there was no consensus within the CIA on how to interpret the beginning of the Gorbachev era. In the mid-1980s there was a bitter clash between Gates and Mel Goodman, division chief in SOVA (the Office of Soviet Analysis of the CIA), a passionate exponent of the view that real change was under way. Goodman, who resigned from the agency in 1986, later accused Gates in congressional hearings of politicizing intelligence by seeking to suppress dissent to his hard-line views—a charge supported by some analysts and refuted by others.[166] In 1986 Gates made public his own uncompromising assessment of Gorbachev's Soviet Union in a speech entitled "War by Another Name":

It is imperative that at long last Americans recognize the strategic significance of the Soviet offensive, that it is in reality a war, a war waged between nations and against Western influence and presence, against economic development, and against the growth of democratic values. It is war without declaration, without mobilization, without massive armies.[167]

Gates told Shultz that the Kremlin was seeking only "a period of dampened tensions with the West" while they sought to rejuvenate the Soviet system and gather strength for another era of conflict.[168]

Though Reagan thought Gorbachev "sincere in wanting to end the threat of nuclear war," his intelligence briefings helped to keep alive his deep suspicions of Soviet policy. SIGINT and IMINT revealed what he believed were "dozens of violations of the SALT and ABM treaties." (Some were later admitted by the Soviet Union.) In September 1986 the arrest by the KGB of Nicholas Daniloff, an American journalist in Moscow, to use him as a bargaining chip to secure the release of a Soviet spy arrested in the United States, made Reagan, as he noted in his diary, "mad as hell." "Once we have [Daniloff] back," he wrote, "I propose we kick half a hundred of their UN KGB agents out of the country." In the end Reagan reduced the number of expulsions of Soviet intelligence officers attached to their UN delegation to twenty-five.[169] The president's intelligence briefings also showed that there was no let-up in the KGB's campaign of anti-American "active measures." Probably the most successful Soviet "active measure" during the early years of the Gorbachev era, promoted around the world by a mixture of covert action and overt propaganda, was the claim that the AIDS virus had been manufactured by the Pentagon during genetic engineering experiments at Fort Detrick in Maryland. In the first six months of 1987 alone, the story received major news coverage in over forty Third World countries. The KGB also continued to produce forgeries of U.S. official documents designed to discredit American policy. Some were so-called silent forgeries, shown confidentially to Third World leaders to alert them to (nonexistent) American conspiracies against them. Other forgeries were used to promote anti-American media campaigns, among them, as late as 1988, bogus instructions signed by Reagan for the destabilization of Panama.[170] Reagan's penchant for picturesque anecdote must surely have ensured that some of the "active measures" mentioned in the daily brief lodged in his memory. His apparently inexhaustible fund of stories reminded Donald Regan of "the morgue of one of his favorite magazines, *Readers Digest*,"[171] but there was also a classified section to the president's memory store stocked with items from his intelligence briefings.

After Casey's resignation as DCI in January 1987 (followed by his death on May 5), Reagan nominated Gates as his successor. Gates, however, had to withdraw amid controversy concerning his alleged knowledge of Iran-Contra. He stayed on as an influential deputy DCI. After three other candidates had turned down, or been unable to accept, the job of DCI, it went eventually to the director of the FBI, Judge William Webster, like Stansfield Turner a teetotal Christian Scientist.[172] Because of his better table manners, Webster was allowed by Nancy Reagan to attend more social occasions at the White House than his predecessor.[173] But, unlike Casey, Webster was not given cabinet rank. Nor did his influence on foreign policy ever rival his predecessor's. Webster was an able administrator, but as even his supporter, Admiral Inman, conceded, "Foreign policy wasn't his strong suit, and everyone understood that. And it took him a long time to pick it up."[174] Reagan's memoirs contain a one-line reference to Webster's appointment but no other mention of him.[175] According to a senior CIA official:

> Reagan and Webster were never close personally. Some of the people in the White House just didn't like Bill, and he was too much of a gentleman to force his way in. He was a straight arrow, not all that colorful, not all that forceful.[176]

Casey's disappearance confirmed Shultz's role as the chief architect of Reagan's policy to the Soviet Union. There was some initial friction between Shultz and Frank Carlucci, a former deputy DCI who became national security adviser in January 1987. As Shultz acknowledges, he "offended" Carlucci by his hostility to the CIA. Shultz got on much better with Lieutenant General Colin Powell, who became national security adviser in October, when Carlucci succeeded Weinberger at Defense. Powell joked that no national security adviser and secretary of state had worked so well together since Kissinger had held both jobs at the same time.[177]

During the early months of 1987, in the wake of the Iran-Contra scandal, Reagan was prematurely dismissed by many political commentators as a lame-duck president. When Margaret Thatcher visited Washington in July, she found Reagan still "hurt and bemused by what was happening." She was appalled to discover that the First Lady was depressing the president with daily briefings on the latest media attacks. "Cheer up! Cheer up!", the prime minister instructed an interviewer on CBS's "Face the Nation." "America is a strong country with a great president, a great people and a great future!" Reagan interrupted a cabinet meeting to phone Mrs. Thatcher and thank her for what she had said. He then held up the receiver so that she could hear loud and long applause from the cabinet members.[178] Reagan owed more to Gorbachev, however, than to Thatcher. His political recovery was intimately linked to the dramatic improvement in Soviet-American relations that reached a climax with Gorbachev's state visit to Washington in December 1987. Among the many hopeful signs that preceded the visit was some decline in Soviet active measures. Gorbachev was bitterly critical of a State Department publication entitled *Soviet Influence Activities: A Report on Active Measures and Propaganda, 1986–87*, based on CIA and other intelligence reports, which gave pride of place to Soviet attempts to blame the Pentagon for the AIDS virus. Despite Gorbachev's denunciation of the report, however, Soviet press coverage of the AIDS story was abruptly halted in the autumn of 1987.[179] Reagan's briefings by Shultz before the Washington summit were more optimistic than those of the CIA. The Soviet Union, Shultz concluded, wanted to leave Afghanistan and was causing fewer problems in "other regional hot spots." Gates believed that, on the contrary, "Gorbachev . . . has poured in more weapons to regional conflicts."[180]

Reagan's preparations for the Washington summit included astrological as well as intelligence briefings. Both Shultz and the Soviet delegation were puzzled as to why the White House insisted, some weeks in advance of the summit, that the INF treaty eliminating intermediate and shorter-range missiles should be signed by the president and Gorbachev at precisely 1:45 P.M. on Tuesday, December 8. Only later did they discover that the time had been picked by Nancy Reagan's California astrologer.[181] "My friend," as the First Lady mysteriously referred to her, regularly provided lists of "good," "bad," and "iffy" days for presidential activities (all indicated on the White House chief of staff's calendar in, respectively, green, red, and yellow ink). She played a part not only in scheduling all four of Reagan's summit meetings with Gorbachev on astrologically auspicious days, but also in providing horoscopes of the Soviet leader that purported to reveal secrets of his character and probable behavior.[182] The president, it appears, took this nonsense seriously. His sources of information on the Soviet Union thus ranged from hightech intelligence to ancient superstition.

Unnoticed by the media, but reported to the president, Gorbachev took the unprecedented step of taking with him to Washington, traveling incognito, General Vladimir Kryuchkov, head of the KGB First Chief Directorate for the past thirteen years. Never before had a Soviet leader been accompanied on a visit to the West by his foreign intelligence chief. Kryuchkov was understandably regarded with considerable distrust by Western intelligence agencies. Earlier in the decade he had helped to plan the military crackdown in Poland and had been responsible for directing Operation RYAN during the period of acute U.S.-Soviet tension in Reagan's first term. More recently his directorate had organized a series of "active measures" designed to discredit both the United States and Reagan personally.[183]

Agency analysts were unaware of one major reason for Gorbachev's confidence in Kryuchkov. In the spring of 1985 the KGB First Chief Directorate had succeeded in recruiting a middle-ranking CIA official, Aldrich Ames, whose career included a spell as head of the Soviet section of agency counterintelligence. Ames's recruitment was perhaps the KGB's most important coup against the United States in the final years of the Cold War. Almost his first act as a KGB mole was to betray the most important Western agent of the last decade inside the KGB, Oleg Gordievsky. Despite being under KGB surveillance, Gordievsky made a remarkable escape from the Soviet Union with the assistance of British intelligence in July 1985, but was forced to leave his family behind. When he visited Washington for the first time in February 1986, Ames was among those who debriefed him.[184] Gordievsky took to Ames immediately:

> His face radiated gentleness and kindness. . . . In fact, I was so impressed by him that I thought I had encountered the embodiment of American values: here was the openness, honesty and decency of which I had heard so much.[185]

During Gorbachev's visit to Washington in December 1987 Gates, the deputy DCI, had dinner with Kryuchkov at the Maison Blanche restaurant near the White House and pressed him to allow Gordievsky's family to join him in Britain. Kryuchkov refused, but said that he would guarantee Gordievsky "a good job with a lot of security" if he returned to Moscow. Gorbachev's decision to bring Kryuchkov to the Washington summit reinforced the skepticism of those agency analysts who doubted the possibility of fundamental change in Soviet foreign policy. Early in 1988 Gates and Fritz Ermath, the CIA national intelligence officer for the Soviet Union, both laid wagers with Undersecretary of State Michael Armacost that the Soviet Union would not withdraw from Afghanistan. Gates and Ermath lost their bets. "It was the best $25 I ever lost," Gates recalls. "It was one of those bets that I considered a win-win. I was either right or I was wrong. In either case I won."[186] On February 8, 1988, Gorbachev announced that Soviet forces would start withdrawing from Afghanistan by mid-May and would complete their departure within ten months. The CIA, having previously forecast that Soviet troops would remain, now predicted—also wrongly—that the Najibullah regime would collapse soon after, if not before, the Soviet withdrawal.[187]

Scarred by forty years of Cold War, CIA assessments failed to keep pace with the sea-change in Soviet-American relations during the last two years of Reagan's presidency. By the time Reagan arrived in Moscow for his fourth summit on May 29, 1988, Soviet troops had begun to leave Afghanistan. As Reagan strolled across Red Square with Gorbachev a few days later, a reporter asked him whether he still thought the Soviet Union was an "evil empire." "No," replied the president. "I was talking about another time, another era." What had influenced Reagan most were probably his own meetings with Gorbachev. Despite the ideological gulf between them, "There was a chemistry," Reagan believed, "that kept our conversations on a man-to-man basis. . . ." The very crudeness of his stereotype of previous Soviet leaders strengthened his conviction that Gorbachev marked a break the past. Every one of Gorbachev's predecessors, Reagan was convinced, "had vowed to pursue the Marxist commitment to a one-world Communist state." Gorbachev was "the first not to push Soviet expansionism."[188] It was Gorbachev himself who did most to change Reagan's perception of the Soviet Union. The CIA struggled to keep up. "Looking back on the Gorbachev period," says Gates, "I think I underestimated the degree to which Gorbachev was prepared to depart from the past. I think I got absolutely on the mark his refusal to embrace genuine change at home, but underestimated his tolerance for dramatic change in foreign affairs."[189]

Reagan also brought back from Moscow a renewed sense of the power of the KGB. During a walk in Arbat Street he had been surrounded by a friendly crowd that was suddenly broken up by the KGB. "I've never seen such brutal mishandling," Reagan wrote in his diary.[190] In October General Kryuchkov, who had accompanied Gorbachev incognito to the Washington summit, became the first foreign intelligence chief ever to be appointed chairman of the KGB.[191] (Also for the first time, both the KGB and the CIA were headed by teetotalers.) Kryuchkov's appointment (which Gorbachev would later bitterly regret) served as another reminder to Reagan of the priority that Gorbachev continued to attach to Soviet foreign intelligence. In his farewell televised address from the Oval Office in January 1989 Reagan paid tribute to Gorbachev and emphasized the need "to work together to lessen and eliminate tension and mistrust." The moment he chose to recall from the Moscow summit, however, was not his walk through Red Square but the incident in the Arbat. Though the words were the speechwriter's, the sentiments were Reagan's:

> We were just about swept away by the warmth [on Arbat Street]. You could almost feel the possibilities in all that joy. But within seconds a KGB detail pushed their way toward us and began pushing

and shoving the people in the crowd. It was an interesting moment. It reminded me that while the man on the street in the Soviet Union yearns for peace, the government is Communist. And those who run it are Communists, and that means we and they view such issues as freedom and human rights very differently.[192]

The intelligence that made the greatest impression on Reagan during his final months in office, however, concerned not the fate of the Soviet Union but the spread of chemical weapons. He made the centerpiece of his final address to the United Nations on September 26 an emotional appeal for "all civilized nations to ban, once and for all, and on a verifiable and global basis, the use of chemical and gas warfare":

. . . Even as diplomatic and technological progress holds out the hope of at last diminishing the awful cloud of nuclear terror we've lived under in the postwar era, another ominous terror is loose once again in the world, a terror we thought the world had put behind, a terror that looms at us now from the long-buried past, from ghostly, scarring trenches and the haunting, wan faces of millions dead in one of the most inhumane conflicts of all time: poison gas, chemical warfare. Mr. Secretary-General, distinguished delegates, the terror of it! The horror of it![193]

Though the words, once again, were a speechwriter's, there is no doubt that Reagan had been deeply affected by intelligence and news reports of the use of chemical weapons in the recently concluded Iran-Iraq War and, within the past few weeks, by Saddam Hussein against Kurdish rebels in northern Iraq. He felt so strongly on this issue that, as after the shoot-down of KAL 007 in 1983 and the Libyan bombing in 1986, he decided to make public use of SIGINT. To prove that, despite their denials, Iraqi armed forces *had* used poison gas against the Kurds, Reagan ordered the disclosure of NSA decrypts of Iraqi military communications.[194] Though Shultz supported the president's decision, he was well aware that, at least in the short term, the result would be to compromise NSA's Iraqi operations.[195]

Reagan was also deeply concerned by imagery and other intelligence that revealed the construction by Qaddafi of a chemical weapons plant at Rabta in Libya.[196] The world, he believed, "had good reason to worry about the next move by this unpredictable clown."[197] Reagan was worried by intelligence disclosing West German involvement in the construction of the Rabta plant. According to one senior CIA official, West German chancellor Helmut Kohl "didn't want to know."[198] During a visit to Washington in mid-November by Kohl and his foreign minister, Hans-Dietrich Genscher, Reagan asked them to attend a briefing by Webster and Shultz on Qaddafi's chemical weapons program. Shultz found the occasion profoundly irritating. Webster's intelligence briefing was, he considered, not nearly tough enough. Shultz repeatedly interrupted him to, so he claimed, "make key points as sharp as possible." The secretary of state was even more annoyed with Kohl, who, he believed, was going through the motions of listening to the briefing only because Reagan had asked him to attend. An American intelligence mission to Bonn discovered that West German intelligence had already informed its government about the role of German firms in the Rabta plant, but that no action had been taken. The final days of the Reagan administration witnessed a bitter dispute between Genscher and Shultz. Genscher accused the United States of leaking intelligence about West German involvement in Libyan chemical weapons production. Shultz denied the charge and told Genscher, "It's up to Germany to look into it and do something about it."[199]

Reagan, meanwhile, engaged in a personal war of nerves with Qaddafi. In his last televised news interview as president, broadcast by ABC on December 22, he told David Brinkley that Qaddafi was building a poison gas plant of "tremendous size," and that the United States knew its precise location. Brinkley recalled that Libya had been bombed in 1986 "as a punishment for terrorism," and asked whether another air strike was being planned. Reagan's reply was intended to frighten Qaddafi. There would, he implied, be no advance warning of any attack. But, though no decision had been made yet, he confirmed that an air strike was a possibility: "We're in communication with our allies and with NATO forces and all, and we're watching very closely that situation."[200]

On January 20, 1989, however, Reagan's presidency came to a peaceful conclusion. When his national security adviser, General Colin Powell, arrived to give him his morning briefing, Reagan tried to hand over the white laminated card containing the secret codes necessary for the president to launch a nuclear attack. Powell gently reminded him that the codes remained his responsibility until Bush took the oath of office at noon. Reagan's last national security briefing was a reassuring one. "Mr. President," said Powell, "the world is quiet today."[201]

CHAPTER 13

George Bush
(1989-1993)

George Bush was the first former intelligence chief to become leader of a major Western state. Thirteen years before he was elected president, the opportunity to serve as DCI had taken him completely by surprise. On November 1, 1975, while serving as ambassador in Beijing, he had received a telegram from President Ford's secretary of state, Henry Kissinger, announcing "some major personnel shifts": "Among those shifts will be the transfer of Bill Colby from CIA. The President asks that you consent to his nomination of you as the new Director of the Central Intelligence Agency." Bush's first thought was of the possible damage to his political ambitions. "As far as future prospects for elective office were concerned," he feared, "the CIA was marked DEAD END." He decided, nonetheless, to accept. As Chairman Mao reminded him, his new job was, after all, a promotion. But Bush made two conditions, both of which were accepted. He was to have direct access to the president, and he was to pick his own deputy and staff.[1]

The first major political influence on Bush had been his own father, Prescott Bush, Republican senator for Connecticut from 1952 to 1963. Asked in 1988 how his own early views on politics had differed from those of his father, Bush replied, "It never occurred to me to differ."[2] Prescott Bush had been a fervent supporter of the CIA. He told an interviewer in 1966, "I was always and still am a great admirer of Allen Dulles." Even the Bay of Pigs, he believed, had been "a well-planned, well-thought-out operation" that failed only because Kennedy had refused to give it air support. Prescott Bush continued to support covert action in Cuba: "If it was to bring about a revolution in Cuba right now,

and throw Castro out, I'd be in favor of that." Among past agency successes, he singled out the U-2 program.[3] Like his father, George Bush
entered politics untroubled by doubts about the CIA.

When Bush was sworn in as DCI in January 1976, many at Langley initially regarded him as an ambitious politician who might misuse the
agency for his own partisan purposes. Bush quickly dispelled most of their
suspicions. "As DCI, and later as president," one senior official recalls,
"George was not a reader of long tomes. He wanted to meet the people
and was always interested in what they had to say."[4] Cord Meyer, who
returned to Langley from a foreign posting in July 1976, found morale at
the agency much improved after the battering of the past two years.
According to Meyer, Bush "leaned over backward to protect the objectivity
and independence of the agency's estimates and to avoid slanting the
results to fit some preconceived notion of what the President wanted to
hear."[5] His experience as DCI was to give him a clearer grasp than perhaps
any previous president of what it was reasonable to expect from an intelligence estimate. Once in the White House, Bush made plain his frustration
with those who confused intelligence with clairvoyance:

> I am sick and tired with those in the political arena or, yes, in the
> media who do nothing but carp and criticize and second-guess the
> intelligence community of the United States. Measuring intentions . . .
> is an extraordinarily difficult task, and no one can expect every esti-
> mate to turn out to be 100 percent correct or 100 percent perfect.[6]

As ambassador to the United Nations in 1971 Bush had been celebrated for his ability to meet several hundred strangers at a cocktail
party and "greet each as if he had just met a new brother-in-law."[7] He
showed the same advanced social and networking skills at Langley. A
number of Bush's personal contacts as DCI were to play an important
part in his presidency. His working relationship with Ford's national
security adviser, Brent Scowcroft, was so successful that Bush later
appointed him as his own national security adviser. Bush's success in
winning the confidence of the Saudi intelligence chief, Prince (later
King) Fahd ibn Abdul Aziz, was to be a major element in Fahd's decision
to allow U.S. troops into Saudi Arabia before the Gulf War.[8] While at
Langley, however, Bush had a bizarre introduction to the special relationship between British and American intelligence. During his last
months in office the British prime minister, Harold Wilson, who resigned
in March 1976, became increasingly obsessed with the idea that a plot
had been organized against him bv MI5, CIA, and the South African
security service BOSS. During a visit to London, Bush was asked to reas-

sure him. For once, his ability to strike a rapport with foreign allies seems to have failed him. Bush emerged from a meeting with Wilson asking, "Is that man mad? He did nothing but complain about being spied on!"[9]

Bush became so attached to the post of DCI that, after Ford's electoral defeat in November, he tried to persuade Carter to keep him on for a full term, promising to give up his political ambitions in exchange. When that offer was turned down, Bush attempted—also unsuccessfully—to convince the president-elect that he should stay on for at least a few months to preserve the principle that the post of DCI was above elective politics.[10] To his successor, Stansfield Turner, Bush seemed to exude "enthusiasm and admiration for the CIA." The post of DCI, which he had occupied for slightly under a year, was, he told Turner, "the best job in Washington."[11] Bush's predecessor as DCI, William Colby, estimates—doubtless with some exaggeration—that if the 1980 primaries and presidential election had been decided at Langley, "Bush would have had 98 percent of the vote."[12]

Bush's political style after his election as president in 1988 depended heavily on the telephone as well as on personal contact. During his first year in the White House, he held 190 phone conversations and 135 meetings with world leaders.[13] CIA analysts also had an unprecedented amount of contact with the president. In addition to being briefed by Scowcroft, his national security adviser, Bush usually met CIA briefing staff, frequently headed by Webster, at 8 A.M. each day.[14] The president regularly phoned analysts with questions and comments about their reports. No other president had provided so much of the feedback that analysts craved and for which they had in the past frequently felt starved.[15] "Another thing we loved him for," a member of the Operations Directorate recalls, "is that in any crisis he always wanted to know what the local station chief thought." But though Bush's contact with Langley was unusually close, his relations with Webster were never intimate.[16] Increasingly, the president's chief intelligence adviser was Webster's former deputy, Bob Gates, whom Bush made his deputy national security adviser. Webster was not a member of Bush's inner circle. Gates was.[17]

At the beginning of the Bush presidency, CIA analysts began for the first time to suggest the possibility that Gorbachev's attempts to reform the unreformable Soviet system, combined with its accelerating economic decline, might cause the collapse of the entire Communist edifice.[18] Though Bush did not speculate in public about the future prospects of Gorbachev and the Soviet Union, his anxiety was evident at his first White House press conference on January 27, 1989. Asked about relations with the USSR, he replied:

Our administration position . . . is: Let's take our time now. . . . Do
we still have problems; are there still uncertainties; are we still
unsure in our predictions on Soviet intentions? I'd have to say, yes,
we should be cautious.[19]

The new administration decided on what Gates called a "conscious
pause" in its Soviet policy to give it time to consider its options. A
month-long "national security review" by the State Department on relations with the Soviet Union concluded portentously on March 14, "We
are in a transition period potentially as important as the immediate postwar period." Bush and his main advisers found the report's recommendations unhelpfully vague and cautious.[20] In April the CIA raised for the
first time the possibility of a conservative coup in Moscow. Growing
political opposition, nationalist unrest, and the "near disastrous state" of
the Soviet economy were, it reported, undermining Gorbachev's position. The next few years threatened to be "some of the most turbulent in
Soviet history":

> . . . The political stability of the Soviet system could be fundamen-
> tally threatened. . . . Should a sharp polarization of the leadership
> prevent it from acting resolutely to deal with a growing crisis, the
> prospects would increase for a conservative coup involving a minor-
> ity of Politburo members supported by elements of the military and
> the KGB.[21]

Bush seems to have been impressed by the assessment (which later
proved to be remarkably accurate), but he objected to the analysts' use
of the word "conservative" to describe Soviet hard-liners. He was, he
complained, a conservative himself. The Directorate of Intelligence
began to use the word "traditionalist" instead. George Kolt, the director
of SOVA (CIA Office of Soviet Analysis), preferred "Leninist'; Fritz
Ermath, now of the National Intelligence Council, suggested simply "bad
guys."[22]

In a speech in Brussels on April 1 Gates predicted "prolonged turbu-
lence" in the Soviet Union. Neither Gorbachev nor his power structure,
he claimed, was irrevocably committed to reform. The secretary of state,
James Baker, privately complained about Gates's outspokenness.[23] A CIA
estimate in May predicted that Gorbachev had only a fifty-fifty chance of
survival over the next three to four years unless he gave up his reform
policies.[24] (In fact, an attempted hard-line coup against him was only two
and a quarter years away.) On May 10, in the Lenin Hills outside
Moscow, Baker had his first talks with his Soviet opposite number,

Eduard Shevardnadze. The next day he had an hour's private discussion with Gorbachev in the Kremlin. When Gorbachev was introduced to members of Baker's entourage, he told Gates: "I understand that the White House has a special cell assigned to the task of discrediting Gorbachev. And I've heard that you are in charge, Mr. Gates." Gorbachev then turned to Baker: "Perhaps if we are able to work out our problems, Mr. Gates will be out of a job!"[25] As deputy DCI under Reagan during the early years of *perestroika*, Gates had failed to grasp the extent of Gorbachev's "new thinking" in foreign policy. As deputy national security adviser under Bush, he played a much more important role in constantly drawing attention to the domestic obstacles in Gorbachev's path.

Bush seems to have been as curious about KGB influences on Gorbachev as Gorbachev was about Gates's role in the Bush White House.[26] CIA speculation about the possibility of "a conservative coup" backed by elements of the KGB assumed the involvement of Vladimir Kryuchkov, who had accompanied Gorbachev to the Washington summit in December 1987.[27] On becoming KGB chairman in October 1988 Kryuchkov had admitted that traditional Soviet interpretations of the capitalist world had been "submerged in clichés and stereotypes," but he had publicly denounced the American intelligence community:

> They have retained in full measure their role as a shock detachment of right-wing forces, one of the sharp instruments of the imperialist "brake mechanism" on the road to improvement of the international position. It is no chance occurrence that in the West the wide-ranging campaign of spy mania and brutal provocation employed against Soviet institutions abroad has not lost its impetus.[28]

At the beginning of 1989 Kryuchkov began an unprecedented charm offensive, becoming the first KGB chairman ever to invite the American ambassador to visit him in his office. Over the next few months Kryuchkov and other senior KGB officers gave interviews and press conferences to Western correspondents and starred in a film, *The KGB Today*, which was offered for sale to foreign television companies. Kryuchkov's increasing influence (doubtless assisted by the KGB's continued success in running the CIA official Aldrich Ames as an agent) was demonstrated by his promotion to the Politburo in September 1989.[29] The appointment of the fifty-three-year-old Leonid Shebarshin as head of the KGB First Chief (Foreign Intelligence) Directorate in January 1989 provided further evidence of the importance that Gorbachev attached to foreign intelligence. One of Shebarshin's main jobs had been to prepare intelligence assessments for the party leadership. The fact that, after some bureaucratic infighting, he leapfrogged several more senior candidates for his new post is a certain indication that his briefing had impressed Gorbachev. Shebarshin later claimed that his main initial brief as foreign intelligence chief was "to ensure the West did not cheat on arms control."[30]

In a speech on May 12, 1989, Bush announced some conclusions of his administration's "review of U.S.-Soviet relations," based, though he did not mention it, on a classified National Security Directive, NSD-23. The forty-year-old policy of containment, said the president, had proved successful. He added cautiously:

> While we hope to move beyond containment, we are only at the beginning of our new path. Many dangers and uncertainties are ahead. We must not forget that the Soviet Union has acquired awesome military capabilities.

A new East-West relationship would require important changes in Soviet policy: among them a willingness to "support self-determination for all the nations of Eastern Europe and Central Europe" and abandon the Brezhnev doctrine. It did not occur to Bush or any of his advisers that the Brezhnev doctrine would be formally denounced in less than six months' time. In the course of the president's speech the White House press corps had been told to expect a major policy initiative. All that Bush offered, however, was a slightly updated version of Eisenhower's Open Skies proposal first put in 1955:

> Such surveillance flights, complementing satellites, would provide regular scrutiny for both sides. Such unprecedented territorial access would show the world the true meaning of the concept of openness.

Most experts dismissed the proposal as out of date. Advances in satellite imagery intelligence meant that aircraft overflights of the Soviet Union no longer served much purpose.[31]

Bush had shown, once again, his problem with the "vision thing." A *New York Times* editorial concluded that an alien spaceship, approaching Planet Earth with a request to "take me to your leader," would without doubt be directed to Gorbachev. Bush privately complained to Scowcroft that he was "sick and tired of getting beat up every day for having no vision and letting Gorbachev run the show."[32] The clearest American vision of the future of the Soviet bloc in the spring of 1989 came not from the Bush administration, and probably not from its intelligence community, but rather from a handful of experienced outside observers. Carter's former national security adviser, Brzezinski, proclaimed the dawn of "the postcommunist era": "This is a massive, monumental transformation. Communism shaped much of this century. And now it is coming to an end." Former CIA and NSC official William Hyland stressed the impact of change in the Soviet Union "spilling over into Eastern Europe." If it reached East Germany, he asked with impressive foresight, "aren't you just a step away from the unification of Germany altogether?"[33] Bush saw some of the changes in Eastern Europe firsthand during a visit to Poland and Hungary in July. "There's big stuff, heavy stuff going on here," he told his aides—and, he added, it could not have happened without Gorbachev. During his return flight across the Atlantic aboard Air Force One on July 18 Bush wrote a secret invitation to Gorbachev to meet him at the end of the year. The small circle of those let into the secret included Vice-President Dan Quayle, Baker, Scowcroft, and Gates—but not Webster or Secretary of Defense Richard Cheney.[34] Bush was later embarrassed to be asked why he had not informed Webster or Cheney. "No, it didn't occur to me they couldn't be trusted," he told a press conference.[35]

CIA assessments in the summer of 1989 paid increasing attention to the remarkable political comeback of Boris Yeltsin, the mercurial former Moscow party chief who had been sacked by Gorbachev two years earlier for demanding too radical reforms. In March Yeltsin was elected as a people's deputy for Moscow by a large majority. "The Agency," Gates recalls, "came across to the White House as having a crush on Boris Yeltsin." When Yeltsin visited the United States on a speaking tour in September, however, Gates urged Bush to meet him. "The difference between Gorbachev and Yeltsin," he argued, "is that Gorbachev still believes the system can be fixed, and Yeltsin has come to understand it has to be replaced." Though Bush was anxious not to damage his relations with Gorbachev, he agreed that Yeltsin should be invited to meet Scowcroft and Gates at the White House, and that he would drop in during the meeting. Yeltsin's behavior during his trip to the United States strengthened Bush's suspicion that CIA assessments of Yeltsin were "too uncritical." In Gates's view:

It's hard to overstate what a disaster that trip was. That was the visit where Yeltsin got drunk at Johns Hopkins [University]. That was the visit when Condy Rice [the NSC Soviet expert] brought him into the ground floor of the White House, and he folded his arms and refused to go forward without a guarantee he would see the president. Condy basically kicked him upstairs, and he stopped

midway on the stairs and refused to go further unless all his aides
be included. She kicked him a little harder, and he came in and sat
on the couch and laid out the most extraordinary ideas on the role
of the West in the economic development of Russia, beginning with
the building of two million apartments and turning over one entire
province of Russia to the West as an experimental farm. If the truth
be told, Scowcroft fell asleep.

As arranged, Bush dropped by for a quarter of an hour during this
bizarre encounter.[36] Yeltsin's first visit to the White House did nothing to
diminish what some in the agency considered the president's "Gorbocen-
tric" tendencies.

By the time the news that Bush and Gorbachev were to meet at
Malta in December became public at the end of October, change in Eastern Europe was proceeding more rapidly than any analyst could have
predicted. Gorbachev had expected that reforms in Eastern Europe
would lead not to the collapse of the Soviet bloc but to reformist Communist regimes. That was also the expectation of the White House. "The
Soviets thought they were creating lots of little Gorbachevs," an
unnamed Bush aide was later quoted as saying. "So did we." When the
tide of history swept away even reformist Communists, Gorbachev did
not resist it. Thanks in large part to his leadership, the Eastern European revolution of 1989 was, save in Romania, remarkably bloodless. In
the White House the turning point in the collapse of the Communist
order was believed to be a telephone call on August 22 from Gorbachev
to the general secretary of the Polish party, Mieczyslaw Rakowski,
encouraging him to participate in a Solidarity-led government. According to "a senior U.S. intelligence official," speaking on the condition of
anonymity, "the Rubicon was crossed with the Gorbachev phone call to
Rakowski. Its real meaning was that Soviet power would not be used to
maintain communist power in Eastern Europe."[37] Two days after the
telephone conversation, Tadeusz Mazowiecki was elected prime minister
of a Solidarity-led government. Bush publicly gave much of the credit to
Gorbachev:

> I think that Mr. Gorbachev's reaction to the changes in Poland were
> [sic] extraordinarily understanding. . . . And I hope that would be
> the tone as the rapid change that's taking place in Eastern Europe
> goes forward—not just in Poland, but in other countries as well.[38]

A CIA assessment in September forecast an acceleration in "the
decay of Communist systems and the growth of regional instability in

Eastern Europe."[39] For the rest of the year, analysts struggled to keep pace with the daily images on television news of the disintegration of Communist rule. On October 25 the Soviet Foreign Ministry press spokesman, Gennadi Gerasimov, formally pronounced the Brezhnev doctrine dead. Recalling that "Hungary and Poland are doing it their way," he announced: "We now have the Sinatra doctrine." Bush, by now, was visibly disconcerted by the speed of change. As the Berlin Wall was coming down on November 9 a reporter asked him why he did not "seem elated." The president lamely replied, "I am not an emotional kind of guy."[40] Intelligence reports on the Soviet Union in fact gave Bush good reason to moderate his euphoria. The collapse of Communism in the Soviet bloc drove an increasingly dangerous wedge between Gorbachev and the hard-liners. The KGB devised a series of "active measures" intended to stave off the downfall of the regimes in East Germany, Czechoslovakia, and Bulgaria, but was not allowed to implement them. The Communist leaders of Eastern Europe, Shebarshin complained, could not be expected to fend for themselves: "They were educated only to be friends of the Soviet Union; they were never prepared to stand on their own feet. They were just thrown to the wolves."[41] Behind the exhilarating spectacle of Eastern Europe throwing off its chains, both Bush and the intelligence analysts discerned the terrifying possibility that its liberation would destabilize the Soviet nuclear superpower.

Before his December meeting with Gorbachev, Bush was extensively briefed both by the official bureaucracy and by outside experts. Scowcroft gave him a list of twenty topics from which to select. "It's back-to-school time, Brent," said the president, and chose them all. The national intelligence officer for the Soviet Union, Robert Blackwell, supervised the preparation of a relatively optimistic National Intelligence Estimate predicting that, though Gorbachev might sometimes react with toughness to ethnic unrest or attempts at secession, his reform program was likely to continue. George Kolt, the director of SOVA, and his leading analysts took a much more somber view, arguing that the failure of Gorbachev's economic reforms and the threatened breakaway of some Soviet republics might produce a hard-line coup against him. Their assessment was sent to Bush along with the NIE. Gates told the president that he tended to agree with the SOVA view. Almost all Bush's advisers, however, agreed that it was important for him to avoid any action at Malta that could be construed by hard-liners as an attempt to exploit Soviet difficulties, thus making Gorbachev more vulnerable to an attempted coup.[42]

Bush's elaborate briefings, however, failed to take account of meteorology. Malta had been chosen as the site for the meeting on the recommendation of the president's younger brother, William (nicknamed "Bucky"), who had seen it only in summer. When the news reached a secretary on the NSC staff who had spent two years at the U.S. embassy in Malta, she commented, "Gee, that's kind of odd, especially doing it on ships. The weather can be really awful at that time of year." And so it was. The Malta meeting passed into history as the "sea-sick summit." Bush and Gorbachev had planned to hold the meeting on Soviet and U.S. warships in Marsaxlockk Bay. Because of stormy seas, the two leaders were forced to meet instead on a Soviet cruise liner, the *Maxim Gorky*, which had tied up to the dock in Malta as a floating hotel for Soviet officials and journalists. When Bush returned by navy launch to the USS *Belknap* in Marsaxlockk Bay after his first meeting with Gorbachev on the morning of December 2, the launch required half a dozen passes (all shown on television) before the president was able to climb aboard. Bush then found himself stranded aboard the *Belknap*, tossed in sixteen-foot seas, for the remainder of the day.[43]

The results of the Malta meeting, when it resumed on December 3, were largely symbolic. It ended with the first joint press conference, given by Bush and Gorbachev, in the history of Soviet-American summits.[44] But the meeting also had an important influence on Bush's Soviet policy. Personal contact probably did more to shape Bush's attitude to Gorbachev than intelligence briefings. The president felt much more comfortable with the measured and controlled manner of Gorbachev than with the more temperamental and less predictable Yeltsin. He left Malta resolved to do what he could both to help Gorbachev remain in power and to maintain his commitment to reform.[45] Gates believes that "ironically CIA probably slowed the acceptance of Yeltsin by Bush" by appearing too enthusiastic.[46]

Intelligence reports at the end of 1989 made clear that, in one important respect, Gorbachev had been less than honest. In October a leading Soviet scientist, Vladimir Pasechnik, had secretly defected to Britain with detailed intelligence on a Soviet biological warfare program being secretly carried out in violation of international agreements.[47] The intelligence was passed on to the CIA under liaison agreements and shown to the president. Bush, however, plainly regarded Gorbachev's unwillingness to stop the Soviet biological warfare program (whose existence he was never willing to admit at summit meetings) as far less important than his decision not to use force to try to prevent the rapid disintegration of the Soviet bloc and the Warsaw Pact in the closing months of the year. It is unlikely that any intelligence report on the changes in Eastern Europe had quite the impact on Bush of the television pictures of the downfall of Nicolae and Elena Ceausescu in Romania, culminating in their execution on Christmas Day, or of the jubilant crowds in Prague celebrating the election four days later of the former dissident playwright, Vaclav Havel, as president of the Czechoslovak parliament.

The intelligence reports to which Bush paid closest attention at the end of 1989 were probably those on Panama. Since the beginning of the year the brutal and corrupt Panamanian dictator General Manuel Noriega, formerly a CIA asset, had been a thorn in the administration's side, waging a campaign of intimidation against American citizens. After Noriega had rigged the results of elections in May and organized attacks on leading opposition candidates, Bush had approved an attempt to overthrow him by covert action. On May 13 the president publicly encouraged the Panama Defense Force (PDF) to organize a coup. "I would love to see them get [Noriega] out," Bush told reporters.[48] It proved frustratingly difficult to do so. According to one of those involved, almost all the potential Panamanian plotters fell into one of two groups. Either they wanted to assassinate Noriega—in which case the CIA was disbarred from cooperating with them—or they were too "spineless" to succeed.[49] The intelligence files on senior PDF officers failed to identify any attractive alternative to Noriega. On October 3 there was an unsuccessful coup attempt. Expecting it to fail, the CIA gave no serious support.[50] There were promptly allegations in Washington that an opportunity had been missed. At a press conference on October 13 Bush began by insisting that there was no "intelligence gap that would have made me act in a different way," then gave a garbled reply that implied that there might have been:

Everyone knows that when you have a combat situation—and there was with the PDF and the coup people—it isn't all that clear. But to the degree we can improve our communications, fine. . . . When I hear that there was, you know, a phone number given and nobody answers—we'll find out what's the significance of that.

Though Bush claimed he was "not in the blame business,"[51] leaked recriminations from the White House quickly followed. An article in the *Washington Post* headlined CIA DIRECTOR UNDER FIRE quoted Bush's chief of staff, John Sununu, as claiming he had "learned more about the attempted coup in Panama from watching Cable News Network than from Webster's Central Intelligence Agency." An anonymous source claimed that "[Webster] is not close to Bush. He's not close to Baker. He's not close to Scowcroft. There's no reason for him to be treated with any great weight." "This is Sununu's work," Webster angrily told his aides.[52] According to one of Webster's senior officials, "Sununu and Baker cut down Webster every chance they got. They just didn't want him to be in the inner circle."[53]

The failure of covert action in Panama led Bush to order an overt military attack to topple Noriega's regime and bring him to trial on drug charges in the United States. Operation Just Cause began at 12:45 A.M. on December 20. Shortly before 1 A.M. Bush arrived in the Oval Office, wearing, so reporters were later informed, a dark blue sweater over a shirt and tie. For the next three hours he was brought regular progress and intelligence reports on the operation.[54] Among the first successes reported to the president was the freeing of a CIA contract agent, Kurt Muse, imprisoned by Noriega earlier in the year. In September Bush had received a personal plea for help from Muse, smuggled out of his prison cell in a book. The surveillance team in Panama watching Noriega's movements, however, had lost track of him at about 6 P.M. on the previous evening. It was later discovered that he had gone to a brothel in Tocumen and had made a hasty exit after hearing the gunfire that marked the beginning of Just Cause. At 3:39 A.M. a SIGINT report based on an intercepted phone conversation by a member of Noriega's entourage revealed that he had gone to ground at an undisclosed location.[55] Shortly afterward Bush went to bed, returning to the Oval Office at 6:30 A.M. to prepare for a televised address at 7:20 A.M. "Most organized resistance has been eliminated," he announced, "but the operation is not over yet; General Noriega is in hiding." At a press conference the next day the president was asked, "Why is it that tens of thousands of American fighting men, and with all our intelligence, were still unable to snatch one bad guy from Panama?" Bush's garbled reply reflected his embarrassment that the most technically advanced intelligence community in the world had still failed to find Noriega's hiding place:

> . . . Intelligence is imperfect. . . . It's good. Sometimes it's counting numbers—very sure. The intention of a person to be some place or move—very difficult, but it's still sophisticated. I'm convinced we've got the best, but that's why it's imperfect.[56]

Noriega finally materialized on December 24 when he presented himself at the papal nunciature in Panama City and asked for political asylum. There followed a somewhat farcical Christmas and New Year standoff that included attempts to blast Noriega out of the nunciature by playing heavy-metal music at full volume. On January 3, 1990, Noriega emerged from the nunciature and surrendered to members of Delta Force. Noriega cursed the nuncio, the nuncio blessed Noriega, and the Panamanian ex-dictator was taken to face drug charges in the United States.[57]

Operation Just Cause was the largest U.S. military action since the Vietnam War. It occurred to no one at the beginning of 1990 that by the end of the year the United States would be committed to a far larger operation in the Persian Gulf. Iraq had emerged from the end of its eight-year war with Iran in August 1988 as the dominant power in the region. But despite intelligence reports demonstrating the brutal nature of Saddam Hussein's regime and his involvement in terrorism, Bush mistakenly believed that a mixture of aid and diplomacy would gradually moderate the Iraqi dictator. In October 1989 he had signed the still-secret National Security Directive 26, which ordered a continuing attempt to "improve and expand our relationship with Iraq."[58] The first public warning that Saddam Hussein was preparing for another conflict in the Persian Gulf came in a bellicose speech on April 1, 1990. Saddam boasted of his arsenal of chemical weapons and struck a series of heroic postures intended to establish his reputation as leader of the Arab world. "By God," he boasted, "we will make the fire eat up half of Israel if it tries to do anything against Iraq!" Bush's response was curiously understated. ". . . I found those statements to be bad," he told reporters, "and I would strongly urge Iraq to reject the use of chemical weapons. And," he added superfluously, "I don't think it helps peace in the Middle East."[59] Shortly before Saddam's speech, satellite imagery had revealed that Iraq possessed launchers capable of firing missiles against Tel Aviv and Riyadh. Lke Scowcroft, and Gates, however, Bush believed that, despite Saddam's vainglorious rhetoric, he was in no position to start another major conflict so soon after his war with Iran. Both the White House and the State Department labored under the delusion that the United States could exercise a moderating influence on Iraq, a belief interpreted as weakness by Saddam. In early May the CIA issued its first warning of possible Iraqi designs on Kuwait. The White House was skeptical.[60]

In the spring of 1990 Bush was preoccupied by apparently more pressing concerns than the threat from Saddam Hussein. On March 11 the Lithuanian parliament declared independence from Moscow—an act immediately denounced by Gorbachev as "illegitimate and invalid." The CIA forecast that the Soviet leadership was facing "a general inability to implement its directives in many national republics, a loss of control over society in general, and the precipitous decline of the Communist party of the Soviet Union, secessionist movements in the Baltic Republics and elsewhere, serious interethnic strife and continued economic deterioration." Whatever Gorbachev's response, it concluded, "It is likely that political instability, social upheaval and interethnic conflict will persist and could intensify."[61] "It is an extraordinarily complicated situation," Bush complained on April 24. On the one hand, the United States had "a fundamental stake" in self-determination for Lithuania and the other Baltic states. On the other hand, he was afraid that American support for their independence might play into the hands of Gorbachev's hard-line opponents who wanted to return to the Cold War.[62] As one of Bush's advisers put it, "He's afraid to light a match in a gas-filled room."[63] On May 29, the day before Gorbachev arrived in Washington for a Soviet-American summit meeting, his more radical rival, Yeltsin, was elected parliamentary president of the Russian Republic—despite Gorbachev's active lobbying against him.

In the run-up to the summit, Bush had to deal with an even more dangerous crisis in the Indian subcontinent. India had massed two hundred thousand troops, including five brigades of its main attack force, in the disputed territory of Kashmir, close to the Pakistan border. In a conventional war, Pakistan would risk a repetition of the disastrous two-week defeat of December 1971, which had led to the loss of Bangladesh (then East Pakistan). Intelligence reports to Bush concluded that, by mid-May, Pakistan had assembled at least six, perhaps ten, nuclear weapons, and might already have deployed them on its American-built F-16s. Nuclear planning, analysts suspected, was in the hands not of Prime Minister Benazir Bhutto, but of President Ghulam Ishaq Khan and the army chief of staff, General Mirza Aslam Beg. Both, the CIA believed, were capable of ordering a nuclear strike against New Delhi rather than run the risk of another humiliation at the hands of the Indian army. India, with a larger nuclear arsenal than Pakistan, would certainly respond in kind. "The intelligence community," recalls Gates, "was not predicting an immediate nuclear war. But they *were* predicting a series of clashes that would lead to a conventional war that they believed would then inevitably go nuclear." The deputy DCI, Richard J. Kerr, who coordinated the intelligence assessment in May 1990, was convinced that "We were right on the edge. . . . The intelligence community believed that without some intervention the two parties could miscalculate—and miscalculation could lead to a nuclear exchange."[64]

During talks in Moscow in mid-May to prepare for the Washington summit, Baker and Gates tried unsuccessfully to persuade the Soviet leadership to take part in a joint approach to the Indians and Pakistanis. Bush then ordered Gates to fly from Moscow as his personal representative on an urgent mission first to President Khan and General Beg in Islamabad, then to the Indian prime minister, Vishwanath Pratap Singh, in New Delhi. Gates took with him personal letters from Bush appealing for restraint from both sides. "The card that I played heavily," he recalls, "was that I was not a diplomat but an intelligence officer by training, and that the reason I was there was that the American government, watching the two sides, had become convinced that they were blundering toward a war and that they [might] not even know it." To demonstrate the accuracy of American intelligence, Gates "told the Pakistanis and the Indians in excruciating detail what their own forces were doing—right down to the deployment of individual aircraft and units down to the company level, distances between artillery units, and numbers of tanks in various places." At his first stop in Islamabad, Gates told General Beg, in the presence of President Khan, "General, our military has war-gamed every conceivable scenario of conflict between you and the Indians, and there isn't a single one you win." "I would never want to play poker with Beg," Gates said later. "He never changed his expression."[65] Khan told Gates that he could give the Indians a secret assurance that Pakistani training camps for Kashmiri "freedom fighters" would be closed down. At a meeting with Indian leaders in New Delhi on May 21 Gates gained permission for American military attachés to visit the frontier region in Kashmir and neighboring Rajasthan. They were able to report that Indian forces were ending their exercises and that no invasion was imminent.[66]

Gates described to both sides some of the confidence-building measures devised by the Americans and the Russians to guard against military miscalculation, then added: "If, as is the case between Egypt and Israel, you would like for us to brief both of you on the same satellite imagery so you know what the other side is doing, we are prepared to do that." Both the Pakistanis and the Indians turned down the offer.[67] "This wasn't one of Bob's great trips," claims a senior CIA official. "He irritated both sides."[68] Bush saw things differently and congratulated Gates on the success of his mission. About two weeks after he left New Delhi, intelligence reports revealed that the leading officials in the Indian and Pakistani foreign ministries had begun regular meetings and that the two governments had agreed to other confidence-building measures.[69] The crisis was successfully kept secret from the American media, and had been largely defused by the time the Bush-Gorbachev summit began in Washington at the end of May. But, for a brief period, the intelligence reaching Bush had suggested perhaps the most serious threat of nuclear conflict since the Cuban missile crisis.

The cordial atmosphere of the Soviet-American summit from May 30 to June 2 was in striking contrast to the tension of the previous few weeks. According to an opinion poll taken a fortnight before his arrival in Washington, 73 percent of Americans had a favorable opinion of Gorbachev—a higher approval rating than that enjoyed by most U.S. presidents. Scowcroft found Gorbachev's manner, despite his domestic difficulties, "serene." The warmth in his relations with Bush was noted by all.

Once again, personal contact overcame at least some of the president's doubts about Gorbachev's future.[70] The CIA followed the summit, however, with its bleakest forecast yet of the danger of a hard-line coup:

> President Gorbachev is losing control over the political process. . . .
> The continuing drift toward crisis could produce growing pressure
> from traditionalist elements for an attempt to reimpose authoritar-
> ian controls. They could conspire to take action on their own, mov-
> ing against Gorbachev in the process.[71]

Early in July, during the Twenty-eighth Congress of the Soviet Communist party, Yeltsin attacked Gorbachev for failing to "neutralize" the hardline forces that, he claimed, were "on the offensive." Shortly before the end of the congress, he announced his resignation from the party and strode dramatically down the center aisle out of the hall.

The main focus of the president's attention, however, was soon to shift to the Middle East. By July more IMINT technology—four KH-11 ("keyhole") satellites and a Lacrosse radar satellite—was focused on the Iraq-Kuwait border than had ever previously been devoted to a single target. On July 17 the CIA reported to Bush that over thirty thousand Iraqi soldiers were moving toward the Kuwaiti border. Agency analysts were convinced that Saddam Hussein was planning more than a show of force. That conviction was strengthened by further IMINT showing Iraqi troop movements. Infrared imagery from a KH-11 in the early hours of July 27 revealed Iraqi trucks carrying ammunition, fuel, and water to troops poised on Kuwait's northern border. By the end of the month both CIA and DIA believed that an Iraqi invasion was imminent. Bush was skeptical. The intelligence evidence, he believed, was circumstantial. There was no intercepted message from Saddam or report from an agent in his entourage to provide proof that he intended to invade. President Hosni Mubarak of Egypt, to whom Bush spoke over the phone, assured him that Saddam was bluffing—seeking to put pressure on Kuwait but not planning an invasion. King Hussein of Jordan told Bush the same story. The president put more faith in his own high-level Middle Eastern contacts than in the conclusions of his intelligence analysts.[72]

On the morning of August 1 Gates submitted to the president a draft national security directive, agreed to by his senior advisers, setting out American aims in the event of a new gulf war. It omitted any mention of forcing a change of government in Iraq because, says Gates, "we weren't sure we could bring it about." To Gates it seemed a historic document. Bush glanced at it and signed it without comment.[73] At about 9 P.M. that evening (early the next morning in the Persian Gulf), Scowcroft brought Bush the news that Iraqi forces were pouring across the Kuwaiti border. The president called a meeting of the NSC in the cabinet room for 8 A.M. the next morning. Before the meeting began he made a brief statement condemning the invasion to reporters and answered a few questions. Probably still shocked by the invasion, Bush failed to appear resolute. "We're not discussing intervention," he told reporters. Asked if he had been "taken by surprise," he replied somewhat evasively, "Not totally by surprise because we have good intelligence, and our intelligence has had me concerned for some time here about what action might be taken."[74] After the reporters were shown out of the cabinet room the NSC meeting opened with an intelligence briefing by the DCI. When Webster announced that all contact had been lost with the American embassy in Kuwait, he was interrupted by General Norman Schwarzkopf, the commander in chief of Central Command (the Middle East and Southwest Asia). A military intelligence officer on the roof of the embassy, Schwarzkopf reported, had been providing a running commentary by radio of the battle for Kuwait City. He had spotted Iraqi agents in civilian clothes directing helicopters containing special forces troops to prearranged landing sites. The invasion had been well prepared.[75] At a press conference a few days later Bush denied that there had been an intelligence failure. Asked if "our intelligence let us down," he replied:

> No, I don't feel let down by the intelligence at all. . . . And I think the intelligence community deserves certain credit for picking up what was a substantial buildup and then reporting it to us. . . . I really can't blame our intelligence in any way—fault them in this particular go-around.[76]

On the evening of August 2 Bush met Margaret Thatcher at the Aspen Institute in Colorado, where both had speaking engagements. According to one boastful British adviser, "The Prime Minister performed a successful backbone transplant."[77] The president returned to Washington with a new sense of resolve. On August 3 he chaired a meeting of the NSC that discussed a CIA report on the consequences of the invasion of Kuwait. Saddam, the agency concluded, intended to turn Iraq into an Arab superpower. It would take him only three days to advance his forces from Kuwait to the Saudi capital, Riyadh. Scowcroft argued for a two-track policy. The United States must make clear that it was prepared to use force to stop Iraqi aggression. But it must also embark urgently on a covert operation to overthrow Saddam. Bush ordered the CIA to begin immediate planning for covert action to destabilize the Iraqi regime, strangle its economy, provide support for Saddam's opponents inside and outside Iraq, and identify alternative leaders. He recognized, however, that the efficiency with which the brutal Iraqi police state crushed all opposition might make it impossible for Saddam to be toppled.[78] Webster told Bush of one instance in which Saddam had a group of twenty-six people killed because he believed that there was one unidentified traitor among them.[79] In the Persian Gulf as in Panama, American military intervention was the result of the failure of covert action to overthrow a hostile dictator. Saddam was to prove a far tougher nut than Noriega.

Returning on Marine Corps One from a weekend with his advisers at Camp David on the afternoon of Sunday, August 5, Bush announced to waiting reporters on the South Lawn of the White House, "This will not stand, this aggression against Kuwait." The president's statement took even some of his closest advisers by surprise. General Colin Powell, now chairman of the Joint Chiefs of Staff, was struck by the change in Bush's attitude since his hesitant response to the invasion only three days earlier. It seemed now "almost as if the President had six-shooters in both hands and he was blazing away."[80] Bush's speeches personalized the conflict into a struggle of will between himself and Saddam. In time of crisis, past presidents had spoken of the United States or of the national interest. Bush regularly used the first person singular: "I've had it"; "Consider me provoked"; "I am more determined than ever before in my life"; "I will never—ever—agree to a halfway effort." The conflict in the gulf was to be George Bush's war. Powell was initially reluctant to go beyond sanctions against Iraq. Baker sought a compromise settlement. Bush was set on military victory.[81]

"My worry about the Saudis," Bush had told his advisers at Camp David, "is that they're going to be the ones who bug out at the last minute and accept a puppet regime in Kuwait." NSA decrypts and other intelligence reports revealed that some Saudi leaders were getting cold feet and considering paying millions of dollars of their oil revenue to buy off Saddam.[82] To persuade King Fahd to accept American forces on his soil, Bush sent a delegation headed by Cheney, including Schwarzkopf, Gates, and an NPIC representative carrying the latest satellite photographs. At the royal palace in Jidda on August 6 Cheney presented greetings from the president, briefly summarized the situation in Kuwait, then told the king, "General Schwarzkopf is going to brief you on the intelligence situation as we see it and on the military options that we have available." Schwarzkopf displayed a series of satellite photographs showing Iraqi tanks on the Saudi border, and in two instances actually on Saudi territory. Though Iraqi forces were currently regrouping and reequipping, they had their best units forward and were, he claimed, poised to attack. Schwarzkopf went on to describe the U.S. forces that could be used to defend Saudi Arabia from Iraqi attack. Cheney ended the briefing by assuring Fahd, on behalf of Bush, "If you ask us, we will come. We will seek no permanent bases. And when you ask us to go home, we will leave."[83]

While Cheney and Schwarzkopf were briefing Fahd, Mrs. Thatcher was in the White House discussing the crisis with Bush and examining the same KH-11 imagery showing Iraqi troops on the Saudi border. During the discussion Cheney phoned from Jidda with the news that Fahd had agreed to Operation Desert Shield, a massive airlift of American forces to Saudi Arabia. Thatcher and Bush engaged in perhaps the most detailed discussion of intelligence and military planning by a British prime minister and an American president since the Second World War. "For all the friendship and co-operation I had had from President Reagan," writes Mrs. Thatcher in her memoirs, "I was never taken into the Americans' confidence more than I was during the two hours or so I spent that afternoon at the White House." During her visit to Aspen the prime minister had been flown by helicopter, on Bush's instructions, to visit the Strategic Air Defense Monitoring Center inside Cheyenne Mountain. Mrs. Thatcher was not easily impressed, but, as she was shown how the center monitored both U.S. and Soviet satellites, she "felt awed by the sophistication of America's scientific and technological achievement."[84]

On August 7 Bush visited the CIA Operations Center, attending briefings and staying for a working lunch to underline the importance he attached to agency operations in the Persian Gulf. The president continued his telephone diplomacy even during the visit, calling King Hussein of Jordan from Webster's desk.[85] A CIA briefer is said to have explained to the president how to taunt Saddam by mispronouncing his name. By placing the emphasis incorrectly on the first rather than the second syllable, Bush changed the Arabic meaning of the Iraqi leader's name from "one who confronts" to "little boy who cleans the shoes of old men."[86] Webster usually headed the CIA team that met Bush daily during the gulf crisis to discuss the president's daily brief. He was not, however, one of the "Gang of Eight" (Bush, Baker, Cheney, Gates, Powell, Quayle, Scowcroft, and Sununu) that managed the crisis.[87]

Bush was deeply influenced by intelligence reports on Iraqi atrocities and depredations inside Kuwait and on Saddam's attempts to build an arsenal of weapons of mass destruction. Together with reports on the growing crisis in the Soviet Union, Gates believes that this was the intelligence that made the greatest personal impact on the president:

All this contributed to energizing Bush into not doing what I think his secretaries of state and defense wanted—which was to establish a defensive line [in Saudi Arabia] and stay there. I don't think Margaret Thatcher ever needed to worry about George Bush going "wobbly." George Bush was prepared to be impeached. He was going to throw Saddam Hussein out of Kuwait come hell or high water—and I heard him say that. So it was fortunate that the votes in Congress went the way they did.[88]

By mid-September satellite imagery and other intelligence made clear that Iraq had no intention of invading Saudi Arabia. In place of the Republican Guards and armored units that had moved up to the border after the invasion of Kuwait, tens of thousands of Iraqi infantry arrived to dig trenches and build barricades to defend themselves against attack.[89] Bush successfully concealed the fact that Schwarzkopf's forces were preparing the recapture of Kuwait until after the November midterm election, by which time public opinion was ready to accept the possibility of war. The president's great achievement during the intervening period was to use his personal rapport with other world leaders and mastery of telephone diplomacy to put together a coalition against Iraq of a kind unprecedented since the Second World War.[90] ". . . This is not a matter between Iraq and the United States of America," Bush declared. "It is between Iraq and the entire world community."[91] Most remarkable of all was backing from the Soviet Union of a kind that would have been barely conceivable only a year before. After a meeting at Helsinki on September 8–9 Bush and Gorbachev publicly declared that they would be "united against Iraq's aggression as long as the crisis lasts."[92] The president failed, however, to win over King Hussein. In monitoring the complex reactions of Middle Eastern leaders to the crisis, Bush seems to have relied heavily on NSA's success in decrypting their communications.[93]

At the end of October Bush called for a briefing on what would be required to launch a military offensive to expel Saddam from Kuwait. Gates believes that the Pentagon briefing, given in the presence of Cheney and Powell, was designed to deter Bush from going ahead:

The first thing the briefer says is, "We will require the Seventh Corps to move from Germany." Well, good God! two heavy divisions and all the logistical requirements—this alone is enough to scotch the whole thing. Then they said, "We'll need six carrier battle groups." Then the true poison pill: "And you'll have to activate the National Guard and Army Reserve"—in other words, disrupt every American community.

I'll never forget it. Bush pushed back his chair, smiled, said, "*Done!* Come back if you need more," and walked out of the room. And these guys' jaws were absolutely on their chests, as though they were saying to themselves, "Has this guy any *idea* what he has just approved?"[94]

On November 27 the UN Security Council passed Security Resolution 678, authorizing the use of force to liberate Kuwait. The first phase of Operation Desert Storm, a massive aerial bombardment of Iraq and Iraqi positions in Kuwait, began on January 16, 1991. The ground assault opened on February 23 and ended in a crushing victory after only a hundred hours of fighting. A later inquiry by the House Armed Services Committee concluded that intelligence on the units, locations, and equipment of Iraqi troops, though not their numbers, had been excellent. It was equally complimentary about intelligence identification of military targets within Iraq for attack during the air war, concluding that there were "few, if any errors." Intelligence on Iraq's chemical warfare capability was also good, but there were major gaps in information on Saddam's nuclear program. Estimates by individual analysts of the time it would take Iraq to construct a nuclear device ranged from six months to ten years. On January 23 Bush rashly announced in a speech to the Reserve Officers Association, "Our pinpoint attacks have put Saddam out of the nuclear bomb-building business for a long time to come." That, however, was wishful thinking. It emerged after the war that the intelligence community had been completely unaware of more than half the major nuclear weapons installations in Iraq. Bush had been warned in his briefings that information on Saddam's nuclear capability was seriously incomplete. The rash claim that the capability had been destroyed was the responsibility not of the intelligence analysts but of the president and his speechwriters.[95]

IMINT provided the most striking intelligence collection successes of the Gulf War. The House Armed Services Committee later praised the performance of three new tactical collection platforms—JSTARS, ASARS, and the UAV—as outstanding. The air force–army Joint Surveillance and Target Attack Radar System (JSTARS), though still at the development stage when Desert Shield began, succeeded in providing commanders with near real-time target information in all weather conditions. The air force also deployed U-2 aircraft equipped with the Advanced Synthetic Aperture Radar System (ASARS) to track moving vehicles and provide high-resolution imagery of fixed targets at night as well as by day. The Pioneer unmanned aerial vehicle (UAV) provided excellent tactical IMINT for marine, army, and navy units. On one occasion Iraqi troops tried to surrender to a UAV hovering above them. The very success of imagery collection, however, created problems of its own. The demand for IMINT far exceeded what anyone had anticipated. The problem was exacerbated by a chronic, though traditional, failure of interservice coordination. Only a third of the secondary image dissemination systems (SIDS) used in operations could communicate with one another. The problem of SIDS from different services being unable to talk to one another had been identified when the systems were first introduced in the early 1980s, but a decade of interservice wrangling had produced no solution.[96] IMINT units in the army, navy, air force, and marines had shown the same reluctance to collaborate as service SIGINT agencies forty years before. The chairman of a House inquiry later complained, "When it came to intelligence imagery, it was like we had four separate countries out there rather than four services from one country." The failure to disseminate much of the remarkable imagery available within the theater of operations was one of the major intelligence failures of operations Desert Shield and Desert Storm.[97] Both the Pentagon and the White House had forgotten the intelligence lessons of the Korean War.[98]

Bush did not interfere with most aspects of military and intelligence operations during Desert Storm. The one major exception became known as the "Great Scud Chase." The Scud was a clumsy, out-of-date Soviet missile originally designed to lob a half-ton warhead a distance of 190 miles. By welding two Scuds together, the Iraqis had produced a missile with almost twice the range but capable of delivering a warhead of only 160 pounds within about two miles of the intended target. Though of little military significance, the Scuds fired against Israel and Saudi Arabia made a major political impact. Fearful that Saddam might use the Scuds to provoke the Israelis into entering the war, thus alienating Arab opinion from the allied side, Bush ordered a major diversion of resources into the hunt for Scud launchers. From January 18 one-third of the two thousand combat and support missions flown each day in the strategic air campaign were devoted to the Great Scud Chase. Special operations teams deep inside Iraq were ordered to search for mobile launchers.[99] During the first land battle of the war, at Al-Khafji on the Saudi coast just south of the border with Kuwait, a JSTARS plane monitoring the battle was ordered to fly west to join the search for Scud launchers being used against Israel. Though several fixed Scud launch sites were destroyed, the mobile launchers proved perhaps the most elusive targets of the war.[100] The DIA had reported that it took thirty minutes to drive a Scud launcher away after it had launched its missile. The Egyptians, who had firsthand experience of using Soviet equipment, revealed that it required only six minutes. Schwarzkopf complained, ". . . By the time we detected a launch and were able to relay the coordinates to our pilots, who then flew to the target, the Iraqis had scrammed."[101] Though politically necessary, the Great Scud Chase proved militarily futile. There is no evidence that it destroyed a single mobile launcher. A film shown on television, billed as showing the destruction of Scud launchers, was later discovered to show an attack on fuel trucks.[102]

Potentially the most dangerous intelligence failures were the errors of tactical battle damage assessment (BDA). Military intelligence officers in Schwarzkopf's command greatly exaggerated the amount of Iraqi tanks, armored personnel carriers, and artillery destroyed before the ground offensive began. Both DIA and CIA analysts in Washington believed that the BDA was giving the White House and the Pentagon misleading assessments of the achievements of the air campaign. Though experience in previous wars should have made clear that theater BDA was almost certain to disagree with the estimates of Washington analysts, there had been no serious attempt to arrive at an agreed methodology. Schwarzkopf defended the BDA produced by his command and took deep offense at the skepticism of Washington. "The national intelligence agencies," he complained, "were all distancing themselves from Schwarzkopf. . . ." His army G-2, however, later accepted that much of the skepticism was justified. The number of Iraqi vessels reported sunk eventually amounted to three times the size of the Iraqi navy. The total number of claimed Scud kills was probably wrong by a similar order of magnitude. Had the Iraqi army been as formidable as some commentators suggested, such errors might well have had serious consequences, and Bush's decision to approve the beginning of the land offensive on February 23 might have proved dangerously premature. In the event, however, faulty BDA made no difference to the success of Desert Storm. Though Schwarzkopf had counted on destroying 50 percent of Iraqi frontline tanks and equipment before beginning his advance, a far lower attrition rate proved more than adequate. The fourth largest army in the world was routed in a hundred hours of land fighting with the loss of only 148 American lives. While the level of material destruction inflicted on the Iraqis in the air war had been exaggerated, the damage done to their morale had been underestimated. Not till U.S. reconnaissance teams, crossing the Kuwaiti border in the few days before the land offensive, discovered empty bunkers was it realized that massive numbers of Iraqi troops had fled. The intelligence from the reconnaissance teams gave Bush the first solid evidence that Iraqi resistance might crumble quickly.[103]

When Bush addressed a joint session of Congress on March 6, a week after victory in the gulf, he was at the pinnacle of his political career. Members of the Congress waving small American flags gave him a three-minute standing ovation. Polls recorded almost 90 percent approval ratings. It can scarcely have occurred to Bush or his audience that day that Saddam Hussein would outlast him as president. Covert action designed to destabilize the Iraqi regime continued. Had it succeeded, Bush might have retained just enough of the popularity generated by victory in Desert Storm to be reelected in 1992.

Both publicly and privately, Bush was generous in his tribute to the role of the intelligence community in the Gulf War. ". . . The intelligence," he declared, "was outstanding and the community performed fantastically." "Be assured," he told OSS veterans, "that victory in Desert Storm cost so few lives because, in my view at least, our intelligence community did its work with characteristic brilliance." Bush summoned to the White House all the CIA heads of station for the Middle East and congratulated them in person.[104] Even more unusually, he visited NSA headquarters and praised its staff as "the unsung heroes of Desert Storm." Bush probably had in mind their success in decrypting Middle Eastern diplomatic traffic as well as Iraqi military communications. During his visit to Fort Meade he became the first president to use the word "SIGINT" in public:

My association with NSA goes back many years. And over the years I've come to appreciate more and more the full value of SIGINT. As President and Commander-in-Chief, I can assure you, signals intelligence is a prime factor in the decisionmaking process by which we chart the course of this nation's foreign affairs.[105]

During operations Desert Shield and Desert Storm, the Soviet Union had, for the first time since the beginning of the Cold War, lost its place as the prime "collection target" of the United States intelligence community.[106] In the spring and summer of 1991 it returned to center stage. On April 25 a major CIA assessment, entitled "The Soviet Cauldron," concluded: "Economic crisis, independence aspirations and anti-communist forces are breaking down the Soviet Empire and system of governance." In a situation of growing chaos, a coup attempt by "reactionary leaders" was becoming "increasingly possible." But the agency also predicted, accurately, that the coup might not succeed. The number of troops that could be counted on to enforce repression was limited, and Yeltsin and the democrats might emerge victorious. A further CIA assessment in May concluded that Gorbachev's domination of the political system had ended and "will not be restored." The danger of a coup was increasing:

> The current political situation is highly volatile and could quickly unravel and throw the country into a succession crisis with little warning. The security services are feeling increasingly desperate and there is a possibility that they could act against Gorbachev at any time.

The agency correctly forecast that the danger would be greatest if the hard-line conspirators believed Gorbachev was sacrificing Soviet interests to the Republics.[107]

On May 14 Bush announced that he was nominating Gates to succeed Webster as DCI. In a public tribute to Gates, he cited his "wisdom and precision in laying out the options for Presidential action" during Desert Storm.[108] Gorbachev was plainly unhappy with the nomination, telling the U.S. ambassador, Jack Matlock, that Gates was a "well-known anti-Soviet." Matlock retorted, "Mr. Gates is less anti-Soviet than Chairman Kryuchkov is anti-American." "I've got my opinion about Gates just as you've got yours of Kryuchkov," Gorbachev replied.[109] The CIA's assessment of Kryuchkov turned out to be more accurate than Gorbachev's. Because Kryuchkov owed his promotion as KGB chairman to him, Gorbachev seems to have believed that Kryuchkov would never be involved in a plot to overthrow him.[110] CIA warnings of a possible coup correctly assumed the involvement of the KGB leadership.

In December 1990, probably at about the time when he began preliminary planning for the coup, Kryuchkov had issued a public warning of an American plot, which he described as "akin to economic sabotage," to "deliver impure and sometimes infected grain, as well as products with an above-average level of radioactivity or containing harmful substances" in food exports to the Soviet Union. Agency analysts recognized this as a recycled version of a conspiracy theory contained in a top-secret 1985 directive sent by the KGB First Chief Directorate (then headed by Kryuchkov) to the Washington residency.[111] What they did not realize was that Aldrich Ames, the Soviet mole within the CIA, was passing some of their assessments on to the KGB.

During the eight months that led up to the abortive coup of August 1991 there was ample evidence of the resurgence of traditional KGB conspiracy theories about the United States. In a remarkable speech to the Supreme Soviet on June 17 Kryuchkov read out a hitherto classified report entitled "On CIA Plans To Recruit Agents Among Soviet Citizens," which he had submitted to the Politburo as far back as 1977. The report described an imaginary CIA master plan to use agents recruited in the Soviet Union to sabotage the administration, the economy, and scientific research. This plan, Kryuchkov insisted, remained in force, and some of the sabotage agents had achieved "certain results." Gorbachev, he implied, was turning a blind eye to the danger. Speeches to the Supreme Soviet by other hard-liners who were later to take a leading part in the August coup also accused Gorbachev of failing to recognize the threat from the West. Kryuchkov privately concluded that, having tamely accepted the collapse of the Soviet bloc in 1989, Gorbachev was now presiding over the disintegration of the Soviet Union.[112] Bush's attempts to warn Gorbachev of preparations for a coup made little impression on him. Gorbachev thanked the president for his "friendly gesture" but told him he "need not worry."[113]

On June 12 Yeltsin was elected president of Russia, thus becoming the first democratically elected leader in Russian history. Bush continued, however, to feel a deep sense of personal loyalty to Gorbachev. When Yeltsin visited the White House on June 20 Bush's welcoming speech contained more frequent and more favorable references to the president of the Soviet Union than to the president of Russia. "I want to be very clear about this," he told reporters, "the United States will continue to maintain the closest possible official relationship with the Soviet Government of President Gorbachev."[114] Bush was impressed nonetheless with the change in Yeltsin's demeanor since the disastrous White House visit of September 1989. "Yeltsin came back," Gates recalls, "with a gravity, a seriousness, and a dignity that were absolutely unmistakable."[115] At Gates's request, a ranking senator (whose identity has still to be revealed) took the president of Russia aside and raised with him American intelligence forecasts of an impending coup in Moscow. "There will be a coup before the end of the calendar year," Yeltsin agreed. "Gorbachev deosn't believe it, but I'm preparing for it." With Bush's approval, a team of U.S. intelligence experts left for Moscow to help improve Yeltsin's personal and communications security. [116]

The main achievement of the fourth and final Bush-Gorbachev summit, held in Moscow from July 29 to August 1, was the signing of the START treaty, which for the first time cut strategic nuclear arsenals—by about 30 percent. It remained Gorbachev, not Yeltsin, who controlled the mighty Soviet nuclear arsenal, and it was with him that arms control agreements had to be negotiated. The START treaty provided, in unprecedented detail, for each side to verify the other's compliance with it by both IMINT and SIGINT, described by the now traditional diplomatic euphemism "national technical means." Each party undertook "not to interfere with the national technical means of verification of the other Party" and "not to use concealment measures that impede verification by national technical means." A protocol laid down detailed conditions intended to ensure that each side was able to monitor the other's missile telemetry.[117] The INF and START negotiations had made verification a steadily more important part of the intelligence community's work, in which Bush appears to have taken a personal interest. The Arms Control Intelligence Staff (ACIS) had begun in 1981 with six professionals housed in the CIA Directorate of Intelligence. In 1989 ACIS was attached to the office of the DCI. By the time the START Treaty was signed, its staff had grown to almost a hundred.[118]

Less than three weeks after signing the START Treaty Gorbachev was briefly removed from power by a coup carried out in Moscow while he was on holiday in the Black Sea. The timing of the coup was chiefly determined by the publication on August 15 of the Union Treaty providing for a major shift of power from the central government of the Soviet Union to the republics. The plotters decided to act before the treaty was signed on August 20. On Saturday, August 17, the president's daily brief reported in detail on preparations by hard-liners for a coup. The plotters "would hope to co-opt Gorbachev as part of the effort, but this time he may turn against them and side with the democrats." The next day Gorbachev was placed under house arrest in his Black Sea dacha. U.S. satellite monitoring of Gorbachev's movements, though it did not reveal the house arrest, disclosed that he had failed to fly back to Moscow, as planned, for the signing ceremony of the Union Treaty.[119] Gates discussed the latest intelligence reports with Bush on the deck at Kennebunkport, where the president was vacationing.[120] Shortly after 6 A.M. (Moscow time) on Monday, August 19 (the previous evening in Washington), TASS and Radio Moscow announced that Gorbachev was prevented by "ill health" from performing his duties, and that Vice-President Gennadi Yanayev had become acting president at the head of an eight-man "State Committee for the State of Emergency in the USSR." Yanayev, who drank heavily throughout the crisis, was little more than a figurehead. The chief planner of the coup had been Kryuchkov, and his chief associates the defense and interior ministers, Dmitri Yazov and Boris Pugo. Bush first heard of the coup announcement in a telephone call at 11:45 P.M EDT on Sunday, August 18, from Scowcroft, who had seen the news on CNN.

At Langley, George Kolt, the director of SOVA, set up a task force to monitor the cables and intelligence on the coup that were flooding in. Both he and Fritz Ermath of the National Intelligence Council, who arrived at the agency at about 1 A.M., were struck by the evidence of scanty preparations for the coup. There had been no major troop deployments, no roundup of leading democrats, and no clampdown on communications. Ermath drafted a SPOTCOM (spot commentary) for the president that described the coup as poorly prepared and estimated the odds on the outcome as a 10 percent chance of a return to the Soviet regime of a decade earlier, a 45 percent chance of a prolonged stalemate between reformers and hard-liners, and a 45 percent chance of an "early fizzle." Bush's reaction to the coup at an early morning press conference was cautious, but—reflecting the conclusions of his intelligence brief- ing—he said that Yanayev was not "calling the shots" and that the coup was apparently "backed by the KGB and the military." In the course of the day the evidence of news as well as intelligence reports shortened the odds on an "early fizzle." While Yeltsin rallied his supporters, the Soviet prime minister, Valentin Pavlov, resigned from his post and from the emergency committee on "health grounds." At a shambling press conference of the emergency committee, the heavy-drinking Yanayev, though not the teetotal Kryuchkov, seemed decidedly the worse for wear. Having returned to the White House, Bush chaired a committee of departmental deputy heads at 5 P.M. The deputy DCI, Richard Kerr, summed up the CIA assessment of the coup thus far as "not very profes- sional. They're trying to take control of the major power centers one at a time, and you can't pull off a coup in phases."[121]

The best and most highly classified intelligence available to Bush during the coup derived from NSA's success in monitoring communica- tions from Kryuchkov and Yazov in Moscow to military command posts around the Soviet Union. SIGINT showed little military support for the coup. A majority of theater commanders refused even to take calls from Moscow. Bush, it is claimed, took the unprecedented decision to pass this intelligence on to Yeltsin. A communications expert at the U.S. embassy in Moscow was assigned to help Yeltsin make secure telephone calls to military leaders. NSA opposed Bush's desision to share SIGINT with Yeltsin on the grounds that it would compromise its future ability to monitor Russian military communications.[122] For the president, however, the overriding priority was to do everything possible to defeat the coup. In the event, the coup collapsed more rapidly than had been expected even by those analysts who predicted an "early fizzle." On the night of August 20–21 the elite KGB Alpha Group refused orders to storm Yeltsin's headquarters in the Russian parliament building. "We have all kinds of intelligence coming in," Bush told a reporter, but prudently declined to be specific.[123] On August 21 the coup petered out in farce. Kryuchkov and Yazov flew to see Gorbachev in the Crimea, only to be arrested soon after their arrival. Pugo shot himself. Gorbachev returned to Moscow, not quite comprehending what had happened. Yeltsin was the hero of the hour.

Bush did not require secret intelligence to grasp how profoundly the coup had changed the balance of power between Gorbachev and Yeltsin. On August 23 he and Scowcroft watched a televised session of the Russian parliament in which Gorbachev was ordered about by Yeltsin. "I'm afraid he may have had it," said Bush. Though it took Gorbachev almost till the end of the year to accept the now inevitable disintegration of the Soviet Union and the disappearance of his own job as president, Bush remained loyal to him. He was rightly apprehensive at the rapidly approaching end of the Gorbachev era, which would bring with it, as intelligence reports made clear, the unpredictable dangers attendant on the emergence of four new nuclear powers—Russia, Belorus, Ukraine, and Kazakhstan—on the territory of the former Soviet Union. Gorbachev's last telephone call as president to Bush, at Christmas 1991, was to reassure him that the *chemodanchik* ("little suitcase") containing the codes necessary to authorize the use of Soviet nuclear weapons had been safely transferred to Yeltsin.[124]

In September and October 1991, while the Soviet Union was approaching its end, the Senate Select Committee on Intelligence held its hearings on the nomination of Gates as DCI. The hearings were unusually dramatic. Though Gates had strong supporters, including two retred former deputy DCIs, Inman and John N. McMahon, three former analysts accused him of tailoring assessments to fit the political prejudices of the White House—a charge strongly denied by Gates. Among the arguments that Gates urged in his own favor was the strong support for his nomination from Bush, "with whom I have worked so closely during these revolutionary times": "This uncommon relationship between us and his expectations, having himself been Director, offer a unique opportunity to remake American intelligence. . . ."[125] The president publicly agreed:

> Bob Gates . . . is an independent thinker with a passion for excellence. And he has served by my side through [the] Panama crisis, through Desert Storm, through the drama of August in Moscow, and I have the fullest trust in his integrity and ability.

Bush dismissed the charge that Gates had politicized intelligence as "an outrageous assertion against a very honest man, a thorough-going professional. . . . I know Bob Gates, and I know he would never cook the estimates."[126] The committee approved Gates's nomination by a vote of 11–4. The Senate voted 64–31 in his favor. Not since the days of Eisenhower and Allen Dulles had a president and a DCI worked as closely together as Bush and Gates. "Bush had as president," Gates later claimed, "a unique understanding of what intelligence could do for him and what it could not."[127]

At Gates's swearing-in ceremony on November 12 Bush told the audience at Langley that the intelligence community would have to change "as rapidly and profoundly as the world itself has changed": "The collapse of the Warsaw Pact and Soviet communism allows us to make different use of some of the assets that we once needed to penetrate Soviet and East European security."[128] Three days later the president signed National Security Review 29 (NSR-29), calling for "a top to bottom transformation of the mission, role and priorities of the intelligence community," and directing twenty federal agencies and departments to identify their expected intelligence needs up to the year 2005. The review was to go beyond traditional intelligence categories and include global problems such as the environment, scarce natural resources, and health problems. As well as helping to define future priorities, the exercise was intended to provide ammunition to limit calls for intelligence cutbacks by producing evidence of continuing demand for a wide variety of intelligence from government departments. After reports from fourteen task forces, Gates presented the results of the review and his recommendations for changes in the intelligence community to Bush late in March 1992.[129]

The review identified the republics of the former Soviet Union as the major target for intelligence collection—no longer because of Cold War confrontation with the United States but because of the risks of internal destabilization and the dangers of the dispersal of nuclear weapons among four of the successor states.[130] Intelligence also continued to accumulate on the Russian biological warfare program.[131] The proportion of the intelligence community budget allocated to the former Soviet republics, however, declined from about half in fiscal year 1990 to a third in 1993. The greater part of the intelligence budget devoted to the successor republics was spent on IMINT and SIGINT. By 1993 only 15 percent of the CIA budget was allocated to the former Soviet Union.[132]

The next major priority identified by the review was "intelligence on the proliferation of nuclear, chemical and biological weapons, and the means to deliver them."[133] Bush called this "a life and death mission" for the intelligence community.[134] The crisis on the Indian subcontinent in May 1990 had dramatically underlined the increasing threat of nuclear conflict in the Third World. So had the discovery after Desert Storm that more than half the major nuclear weapons installations in Iraq were previously undetected. The use of chemical weapons in the Iran-Iraq War and Saddam's threat to use them in the next gulf war further emphasized the danger of proliferation. In September 1991 a Non-Proliferation Center had been founded within the Directorate of Intelligence.[135]

Following the review ordered by NSR-29, Bush approved proposals by Gates for four structural changes in the intelligence community. The first was another attempt to address the old problem of strengthening the DCI's ability to coordinate the work of the community as a whole. The small Intelligence Community Staff was abolished and replaced by a DCI Community Management Staff, headed by an executive director for community affairs. The 1993 Intelligence Authorization Bill gave the president (in practice, usually the DCI) authority to move resources for foreign intelligence collection from one agency to another. The second change approved by Bush consisted of measures to improve the coordination of intelligence analysis within the community. The National Intelligence Council (NIC) and National Intelligence Officers (NIOs), who were responsible for the production of National Intelligence Estimates (NIEs), were moved out of the CIA into a building of their own, and given additional staff to strengthen their independence.[136]

A third set of measures was intended to enhance the coordination of intelligence collection—HUMINT and IMINT in particular. The Gulf War had led to a renewed appreciation of the importance of human intelligence in a high-tech era. The technological wizardry deployed against Saddam had revealed the deployment of his armed forces but not his political and military aims. Though a limited number of agents had been recruited in Iraqi diplomatic and trade missions abroad, none seems to have had access to Saddam's thinking or to his inner circle.[137] The increased priority of intelligence on proliferation also enhanced the importance of recruiting agents in the entourage of other Third World leaders anxious to acquire chemical, biological, or nuclear weapons. In March 1992 Bush approved the creation of a National Human Intelligence Tasking Center, managed by the CIA deputy director for operations and including representatives from Defense and State's Bureau of Intelligence and Research. According to Gates:

> For the first time in the history of U.S. intelligence, we will have an integrated interagency mechanism for tasking human intelligence requirements to that part of the Community that has the best chance of acquiring the information at least cost and least risk.[138]

Postmortems on Desert Storm repeatedly identified failures of IMINT coordination.[139] On May 6 Cheney ordered the creation of a new Central Imagery Office in the Defense Department to coordinate distribution to the armed services and ensure that in future operations their secondary image dissemination systems (SIDS) could communicate with one another. A thirteen-member panel headed by the arms negotiator and future DCI R. James Woolsey was instructed to investigate ways to "streamline, consolidate, reduce or enhance" imagery collection by the National Reconnaissance Office (NRO). Its classified report, completed at the end of August, was officially described as "well received" by the intelligence community and the White House. The end of the Cold War faced the NRO with both budget cutbacks and increasing demands for its services by consumers outside the intelligence community. In May Bush ordered "appropriate" IMINT "technology and data" to be made available for unclassified research on global ecology and the environment.[140]

The fourth major change prompted by the Gulf War and the NSR-29 review concerned intelligence community support for military operations. According to the former director of NSA, General William Odom, CIA military intelligence, was "almost never used by the military services."[141] In an attempt to bridge the gap between the CIA and the military, the agency established a new Office of Military Affairs. Gates optimistically described its mission thus:

> . . . This Office will be responsible for coordinating military and CIA planning; strengthening the role of DCI representatives at the major commands and at the Pentagon; developing procedures so that CIA is regularly informed of military needs for intelligence support; developing plans for CIA support in national, theater and joint intelligence centers during crises; and the availability of CIA officers for participation with the military on selected exercises.[142]

It will take another Operation Just Cause or Desert Storm to demonstrate how much of that ambitious program proves practicable.

During the final year of Bush's presidency, the CIA sought, with his enthusiastic support, both to redefine its mission in a post–Cold War world and to change its public image. Having been accused by some former analysts during his confirmation hearings of slanting intelligence analysis to conform to the views of the White House, Gates appointed a task force to consider the whole question of politicization. The task force reported that half those it had questioned in the Directorate of Intelligence "said that forcing a product to conform to a view higher up the chain of command occurs often enough to be of concern." In March 1992 Gates reported its findings in an unusually frank address to analysts in the CIA auditorium:

> In the short time I have been back at the Agency, I have become more aware of the profound impact the issue of politicization has

had on the morale of analysts and managers alike. It is not a concern to be dismissed with token gestures. Politicization is a serious matter, and it has no place in the CIA or in the Intelligence Community. . . . Getting the policymaker to read our product should not jeopardize our objectivity; it does not mean sugarcoating our analysis. On the contrary, it means providing a frank, evenhanded discussion of the issues.

Among the measures announced by Gates to deal with the problem was the appointment of a full-time ombudsman to investigate complaints of politicization and produce an annual report. Though Gates acknowledged that "senior-level rhetoric" tended to generate "skepticism—even cynicism" within the Directorate of Intelligence, he insisted: "This will be no paper exercise."[143]

Gates's decision to publish his address on politicization was part of a much broader "openness initiative" backed by Bush. "We are under no illusions," he told the press, "that CIA, whatever the level of its efforts, will be able to win recognition as an 'open' institution." But to improve its image and broaden its horizons, the agency was to provide the media with more background briefings and on-the-record interviews by senior officials; strengthen its links with universities through the encouragement of intelligence studies courses; support academic conferences on issues of mutual interest; adopt "a bias toward declassification of historical documents" in its files; and publish some of the articles in its hitherto-classified in-house journal, *Studies in Intelligence*.[144] In the course of 1992, according to the calculations of two former agency analysts, "the DCI had given more briefings to, and testimony in, Congress than all his predecessors did during their combined tenure."[145] Among the consequences of the openness initiative was the lifting in September 1992 of the outdated official ban on acknowledging the existence of the NRO. Ever since its foundation soon after the shoot-down of Gary Powers's U-2 in 1960, even retired DCIs had been refused permission to make any public reference to the NRO—to the visible frustration of Stansfield Turner in particular.[146] In October the director of the NRO, Martin C. Faga, a former imagery specialist at the CIA, gave his first media interview.[147]

The ambitious series of reforms announced by Gates in the course of 1992 reflected Bush's vision of the future shape of the intelligence community during what he hoped would be his second term. The reforms failed, however, to address one major problem within the CIA. It occurred to virtually none either of the agency's supporters or of its critics that, despite the collapse of the Soviet Union, the CIA might be penetrated by a major Russian agent. But, as Bush had embarked on his reelection campaign, the hunt was on for a mole within the agency. Had Aldrich Ames been arrested in 1992, rather than two years later, the running of the CIA would doubtless have figured much more prominently as a campaign issue.

In November 1992 Bush lost a presidential election that, a year earlier, he had been widely expected to win. American victories in the Cold War and the Gulf War failed to compensate for the sluggishness of economic recovery and Bush's own uninspired campaigning. One further foreign policy success in Iraq might just have tipped the balance in Bush's favor. Earlier in the year he had sent Gates on an unpublicized mission to discuss with President Mubarak and King Fahd measures to bring about the overthrow of Saddam Hussein. Bush's decision to send his DCI to Cairo and Riyadh was a certain indication that the measures discussed included covert action as well as economic and diplomatic pressure.[148] But the strength and ruthlessness of Saddam's security service successfully resisted all attempts to topple him from power. The fact that Saddam's most determined Iraqi opponents hoped to assassinate him added to the CIA's problems. Since the agency was not permitted, as it had been a generation earlier, to plot the assassination of foreign leaders, it could not collaborate with potential assassins.[149] Saddam's survival contributed to Bush's electoral defeat. In 1992, as in 1980, the failure of a covert operation in the Middle East may have helped to prevent the president from winning a second term. Gates, however, thinks otherwise:

> If we'd been lucky enough that there'd been a coup against Saddam, it [the covert action] would have had to be deniable. The credit would have been taken by the Iraqi generals who accomplished the act. I think it would have had minimal political impact in the United States.[150]

Intelligence After the Cold War

Over the past two centuries only four American presidents—Washington, Eisenhower, Kennedy (briefly), and Bush—have shown a real flair for intelligence. But whether presidents have used intelligence and the intelligence community well or badly, *how* they have used it is an essential—though frequently neglected—part of the history of every administration since the Second World War. Much of the story still remains officially secret. Hardly any of the president's daily briefs are yet available to historians. Not a single decrypt produced by the National Security Agency, the largest and most expensive intelligence agency in the history of Western civilization, has so far been declassified. When NSA files for the Cold War period finally become available some time during the twenty-first century, they are certain to generate thousands of doctoral dissertations and some interesting reassessments of American foreign policy.

Since the Second World War, presidents have had access to global intelligence on a scale that their predecessors would have found unimaginable. Though Franklin Roosevelt failed to grasp the full significance of the intelligence revolution that the war produced, he was the first president to see the need for "the establishment of a central intelligence agency" in peacetime. No postwar president has been nearly as ignorant of intelligence as Truman was when he succeeded FDR. Yet it was his administration, more than any other, that shaped today's intelligence community. In retirement, Truman sometimes seemed amazed, even appalled, at the size and "strange activities" of the secret agencies that he had brought into being. Eisenhower, by contrast, relished the covert power that the intelligence community appeared to give him.

Less than two decades separated the amateur espionage of Vincent Astor and the Room from the age of the U-2. Before the Second World War, Roosevelt had been woefully ignorant of the real strength of the German Luftwaffe. Twenty years later, Eisenhower was well informed on the deployment of the Soviet ICBM nuclear strike force. Ike took a personal part in promoting the dramatic advances in imagery intelligence that helped to change the history of the Cold War. Kennedy was stunned to discover, after his election as president, what IMINT could do. The Cuban missile crisis showed that he was right to be impressed. Without a remarkable combination of imagery and human intelligence, it would have been far harder to bring to a peaceful conclusion the most dangerous crisis of the Cold War.

Since the missile crisis, however, presidents have tended, more often than not, to take for granted their daily diet of all-source global intelligence. Indeed, they have frequently seemed disappointed by it. All remember international crises that took them by surprise, and most are inclined to treat the surprises as intelligence failures.[1] "What the hell do those clowns do out there in Langley?" Nixon demanded after the unexpected overthrow of the Cambodian leader Prince Sihanouk in 1970. Eight years later Carter asked much the same question, more politely phrased, when he was suddenly informed that the shah of Iran was in danger of losing his throne.[2]

The intelligence community has had its fair share of failures. Presidents' recurrent disappointment with the intelligence they receive, however, has derived, at least in part, from their own exaggerated expectations. Good intelligence diminishes surprise, but even the best cannot possibly prevent it altogether. Human behavior is not, and probably never will be, fully predictable. Robert Gates displayed on his desk in the DCI's office the maxim, "As a general rule, the best way to achieve complete strategic surprise is to commit an act that makes no sense or is even self-destructive." There will always be statesmen and generals who achieve surprise by these simple yet effective methods. Some intelligence analysts during the Cold War, argues Gates, showed "a confidence in their judgments they [could] not reasonably justify."[3] Anxious to impress each incoming president with the sophistication of its product, the intelligence community was reluctant to emphasize its own limitations. It was thus partly responsible for raising unrealistic expectations in the White House.

"Of all the presidents I worked for [from 1968 to 1993]," says Gates, "only Bush did not have exaggerated expectations of intelligence."[4] Bush's experience as DCI gave him a clearer grasp than perhaps any previous president of what could reasonably be expected from an intelligence estimate. "Measuring intentions," he rightly emphasized, ". . . is an extraordinarily difficult task."⁵ Bush's own electoral defeat in November 1992, forecast by almost no political pundit after his triumph in the Gulf War eighteen months earlier, aptly illustrated the difficulties of political prediction. Some of the columnists who failed to foresee Bush's demise castigated the CIA for failing to predict political change in the Soviet Union with greater accuracy than they themselves had shown in forecasting the outcome of a presidential election in the United States.

As former presidents and their advisers look back on the Cold War, they tend to forget the truth of Eisenhower's dictum that intelligence on "what the Soviets *did not* have" was often as important as information on what they did. If all presidents had possessed as little intelligence on the Soviet Union as Truman, there would have been many more missile gap controversies and much greater tension between the superpowers. From 1972 onward, secret "national technical means" made it possible first to limit, and then to control, the nuclear arms race. Intelligence played a crucial part in stabilizing the Cold War.

Though presidents often underestimated the value of the intelligence they received during the Cold War, they frequently overestimated the secret power that covert action put at their command. Even Truman, after at first opposing covert action, approved a series of secret operations in the Soviet bloc that were doomed to failure. Eisenhower's exaggerated faith in covert action led him to bequeath the disastrous Cuban operation to his inexperienced successor. Despite the fiasco at the Bay of Pigs, Kennedy, Johnson, and Nixon continued secret attempts to destabilize (if not assassinate) Castro, the only significant result of which was to lower the international reputation of the United States. Nixon's attempt to cover up the farcically incompetent domestic covert operations run by the White House led to his own fall from power. The fate of Nixon's successors has also, though in different ways, been powerfully affected by covert action. By pardoning Nixon, and thus appearing to condone his attempted cover-up of Watergate, Ford probably sacrificed the 1976 presidential election. The failure of the covert operation to rescue the Teheran hostages may have cost Carter a second term. Iran-Contra, which revived both the illegality and the bungling of White House covert action in the Nixon era, reduced Reagan's presidency to its lowest ebb.

Victory in the Cold War produced some disorientation in both Langley and the White House. To a greater extent than most other modern intelligence communities, that of the United States was a product of the

Cold War. In its main intelligence ally, Britain, both the major collection agencies, SIS and GCHQ, and the main assessment system, the JIC, were already in place during the Second World War. The United States's principal postwar intelligence adversaries, the KGB and the GRU, went back, despite changes in their names, almost to the foundation of the Soviet state. By contrast, the main American agencies, CIA, NSA, NRO, and DIA, as well as the National Security Council, though drawing on some earlier precedents, were all founded during the Cold War. The end of the Cold War thus produced greater uncertainty about the future role of foreign intelligence in the United States than in most other Western states.

The enormous budget of the intelligence community—an estimated $28 billion at the beginning of the 1990s—added to the uncertainty. The United States spent approximately twenty times as much on SIGINT as Britain.[6] Despite the growing number of foreign satellites in orbit, it possessed a monopoly of state-of-the-art satellite imagery. With the disintegration of the Soviet Union and the Soviet bloc, Russian foreign intelligence lost much of its hard-currency budget, most of its allies, and about 150 SIGINT stations in countries of the former Warsaw Pact (though not in Cuba).[7] The United States remained the only intelligence superpower. At the end of the Cold War, as after the two world wars, there was pressure for cuts in the intelligence budget. The Clinton administration discussed plans to cut about a quarter of the total by 1998. There were, inevitably, calls for even larger savings. The problem, as Gates observed a few months after being succeeded as DCI by James Woolsey in January 1993, was that the leading budget-cutters had failed "to identify what they don't want to know about the world."[8] Some of those who demanded major budget cuts were simultaneously calling for a wider range of intelligence.

For all the talk of new intelligence horizons, the main priority for the future remains the traditional need to monitor threats to American security. "In sum," Bush told an audience at Langley in November 1991, "intelligence remains our basic national instrument for anticipating danger, military, political and economic. Intelligence is and always will be our first line of defense, enabling us to ward off emerging threats whenever possible before any damage is done."[9] Russia and the other successor states of the former Soviet Union are still necessary intelligence targets. The disintegration of the Soviet system carries with it even greater potential risks than the fall of the Turkish and Austro-Hungarian empires earlier in this century. Among those risks is the emergence of one or more aggressively nationalist—or even neo-fascist leaders—with large nuclear arsenals at their command. When Clinton succeeded Bush, however, such dangers still appeared remote. To many in Congress, and perhaps to the incoming president, the CIA seemed to have lost its traditional enemy and not yet found a role. The Ames affair in 1994 brought dissatisfaction with the agency to a head, and prompted the announcement of a congressional investigation of the CIA.

In the euphoria generated by the end of the Cold War, there was a tendency to forget that the nuclear age had not also ended. Though the prospect of an Armageddon between nuclear superpowers has—at least temporarily—receded, other dangers remain. The threat of nuclear confrontation between Pakistan and India, which so alarmed both the White House and the CIA in May 1990, undoubtedly foreshadows some of the international crises that will preoccupy the presidents of the next century. The head of U.S. naval intelligence, Rear Admiral Edward Scheafer Jr., warned in 1993 that "somewhere, sometime in this decade, someone is going to set off a nuclear weapon."[10] Scheafer's prediction may prove too pessimistic, at least in its timing, but, like all previous inventions in human history, chemical, biological, and nuclear weapons will—sooner or later—inevitably proliferate. DCI Woolsey told the House Select Intelligence Committee in 1993 that by the year 2000 twenty states are likely to possess IRBMs.[11] Without a combination of traditional human spies and advanced technical intelligence, the United States will find it impossible either to monitor or to slow down the proliferation of weapons of mass destruction.

A merciful providence allows us, even with good intelligence, to foresee the future only as Saint Paul glimpsed heaven—"through a glass, darkly." Were it otherwise, we might lack the courage to confront all the trials that await us. Many of the threats to American security in the twenty-first century are still unpredictable at the end of the twentieth. But, as the world becomes increasingly compressed into a global village, these threats will surely become both more numerous and more varied than during the Cold War. Woolsey warned in March 1994:

> The Cold War has ended, but history has not, and neither has conflict. . . . The term ethnic cleansing has become part of the language of international politics—hardly a reassuring thought when less than 10 per cent of the 170 nations around the globe are ethnically homogeneous.[12]

Bush may well have been right to argue during his valedictory address to the CIA in January 1993 that "We need more intelligence, not less."[13] The presidents of the twenty-first century, like their Cold War predecessors, will continue to find an enormously expensive global intelligence system both fallible and indispensable.

ACKNOWLEDGMENTS

I first had the idea of writing an article on presidents and intelligence while I was Visiting Professor in the Department of History at the University of Toronto and Provost's Visitor at Trinity College, Toronto, in the first semester of the 1991–92 academic year. During the second semester, when I was Visiting Michael Beton Kaneb Professor of National Security in the Olin Institute and the Department of History at Harvard University, the article turned into the outline of a book that I began to write after my return to Cambridge University at the beginning of the 1992–93 academic year. I am grateful both to the students who took my courses and to the colleagues in Toronto, Harvard, and Cambridge who encouraged me to develop my research far beyond the scope I originally envisioned.

I owe a debt also to the staff of the university libraries of Cambridge, Toronto, Harvard, Princeton, and Yale; of the presidential libraries (especially those of Harry S. Truman and John F. Kennedy); of the Public Record Office at Kew, England; and of the National Archives in Washington, D.C., who have made it possible for me to write this book. Documents in the Public Record Office and other Crown copyright material are quoted by permission of the Controller of HM Stationery Office. Extracts from the Henry L. Stimson papers are published by permission of Yale University Library.

For information and help with my research and/or permission to quote from their papers and publications, I am grateful to the Barker family, Colonel Charles Brower, Ms. Kathryn Brown, Mr. Dino Brugioni, the late Dr. George Carver, Dr. Ray S. Cline, Dr. Charles Cogan, Professor Elliot Cohen, Ambassador William Colby, Dr. Cleveland Cram, Dr. Robert M. Gates, Mr. Oleg Gordievsky, Professor Michael Handel, Mr. John L. Hart, Mr. John Helgerson, Ambassador Richard Helms, Professor Sir Harry Hinsley, Dr. Rhodri Jeffreys-Jones, Dr. David Kahn, Professor Warren Kimball, Mr. Franklin Lindsay, Dr. Kenneth McDonald, Mr. Yuri Nosenko, Mr. Walter Pforzheimer, Dr. John

Ranelagh, Dr. David Reynolds, Dr. Jeff Richelson, Mr. Anthony Schinella, Mr. R. Jack Smith, Mr. Charles A. Sorrels, Dr. Zara Steiner, Dr. John Thompson, Dr. Louis Tordella, Mr. Thomas Troy, Admiral Stansfield Turner, Mr. Chris Van Houten, Professor Wesley Wark, Professor Brad Westerfield, and Mr. Jim Worthen. I am grateful, too, to those former intelligence officers who gave me interviews but have asked not to be identified.

For the errors and omissions that remain, I am responsible. I shall be grateful to readers kind enough to bring them to my attention at Corpus Christi College, Cambridge CB2 1RH, England.

NOTES

Abbreviations Used in the Notes

CCAC	Churchill College Archive Centre, Cambridge (UK).
Church Committee, *Alleged Assassination Plots*	*Alleged Assassination Plots Involving Foreign Leaders: An Interim Report of the Select Committee to Study Governmental Operations with Respect to Intelligence Activities* [Church Committee]. U.S. Senate, 94 Cong., 1 Sess., Report no. 94-465 (Nov. 20, 1975).
Church Committee, *Final Report*	*Final Report of the Select Committee to Study Governmental Operations with Respect to Intelligence Activities* [Church Committee]. U.S. Senate, 94 Cong., 2 Sess., Report no. 94-755 (April 26, 1976).
CMC (CIA)	*CIA Documents on the Cuban Missile Crisis, 1962,* ed. Mary S. McAuliffe (Washington, D.C.: CIA, 1992).
CMC (NSA)	Lawrence Chang and Peter Kornbluh (eds.), *The Cuban Missile Crisis (1962): A National Security Archive Documents Reader* (New York: New Press, 1992).
DDEL	Dwight D. Eisenhower Library, Abilene, Kansas
DDRS	Declassified Document Reference System
FDRL	Franklin D. Roosevelt Library, Hyde Park, New York
FRUS	*Foreign Relations of the United States* (Washington, D.C.: U.S. Government Printing Office).
HCL	Harvard College Library
HSTL	Harry S. Truman Library, Independence, Missouri
JFKL	John F. Kennedy Library, Boston, Massachusetts
KSG	John F. Kennedy School of Government, Harvard University
LBJL	Lyndon B. Johnson Library, Austin, Texas
MBPH	*The "Magic" Background of Pearl Harbor* (Washington, D.C.: Department of Defense, 1978).
NAW	National Archives, Washington, D.C.
OH	Oral History
PHA	Joint Committee on the Investigation of the Pearl Harbor Attack, *Pearl Harbor Attack: Hearings.* 79

Cong., 1 and 2 Sess. (Washington, D.C.: U.S. Government Printing Office, 1946).

PP　　　　*Public Papers of the Presidents* (Washington, D.C.: U.S. Government Printing Office).

PRO　　　Public Record Office, Kew, England

PWW　　Arthur S. Link (ed.), *The Papers of Woodrow Wilson* (Princeton, N.J.: Princeton University Press, 1966–1992).

SLYU　　Sterling Library, Yale University

Introduction: The President and Intelligence

1. Joseph E. Persico, *Casey: From the OSS to the CIA*, paperback ed. (New York: Penguin Books, 1991), p. 363.

2. *PP Reagan 1986*, vol. 2, p. 1275.

3. Robert M. Gates, "An Opportunity Unfulfilled: The Use and Perceptions of Intelligence at the White House," *Washington Quarterly*, Winter 1989, pp. 38–39.

4. The term "signals intelligence" or SIGINT (the intelligence derived from analyzing intercepted signals) came into general use only in the 1950s. I have followed the practice of the official history of British Intelligence in the Second World War and other authorities in using the term retrospectively.

5. Gates, "An Opportunity Unfulfilled," p. 36.

Chapter 1: From George Washington to the Twentieth Century

1. David Jackson (ed.), *The Diaries of George Washington* (Charlottesville: University Press of Virginia, 1976), vol. 1, pp. 144–45.

2. Washington had, however, been secretly supplied with an accurate plan of Fort Duquesne by Major Robert Stobo. *Memoirs of Major Robert Stobo of the Virginia Regiment* (Pittsburgh: John S. Davidson, 1854), pp. x, 20–23.

3. James T. Flexner, *George Washington: The Forge of Experience (1732–1775)* (London: Leo Cooper, 1973), chs. 5, 6. John E. Ferling, *The First of Men* (Knoxville: University of Tennessee Press, 1988), ch. 2. Thomas A. Lewis, *For King and Country* (New York: HarperCollins, 1992), chs. 9, 10.

4. Washington to Robert Hunter Morris, Jan. 5, 1766: John C. Fitzpatrick (ed.), *The Writings of George Washington* (Washington, D.C.: U.S. Government Printing Office, 1931–44), vol. 1, p. 268.

5. Washington to John Hancock, July 21, 1775: Philander D. Chase (ed.), *The Papers of George Washington. Revolutionary War Series* (Charlottesville: University Press of Virginia, 1985), vol. 1, p. 138.

6. Fitzpatrick (ed.), *Writings of Washington*, vol. 3, p. 407n.

7. Chase (ed.), *Papers of Washington*, vol. 1, p. 38. Cf. pp. 57, 79, 91, 138, 306, 332–33, 399, 410, 421, 437, 458, 459.

8. Ibid., vol. 3, pp. 528–59.

9. Francis Wharton (ed.), *The Revolutionary Diplomatic Correspon-*

dence of the United States (Washington, D.C.: U.S. Government Printing Office, 1889), vol. 2, pp. 63–64.

10. On Washington's strategy, see, inter alia, Thomas Fleming, "George Washington, General," in Robert Cowley (ed.), *Experience of War* (New York: W. W. Norton, 1992), pp. 140–50.

11. Robin W. Winks, *Cloak and Gown* (New York: William Morrow, 1987), pp. 15–19.

12. Robert McConnell Hatch, *Major John André: A Gallant in Spy's Clothing* (Boston: Houghton Mifflin, 1986).

13. Morton Pennypacker, *General Washington's Spies on Long Island and in New York* (Brooklyn, N.Y.: Long Island Historical Society, 1939). *Intelligence in the War of Independence* (Washington, D.C.: CIA, 1976), p. 21. G. J. A. O'Toole, *Honorable Treachery* (New York: Atlantic Monthly Press, 1991), ch. 4.

14. Washington to Col. Elias Dayton, July 26, 1777. The original of this letter is in the Walter L. Pforzheimer Collection on Intelligence Service, Washington D.C.; I am grateful to Mr. Pforzheimer for allowing me to reproduce a section of it. The text also appears in Fitzpatrick (ed.), *Writings of Washington*, vol. 8, pp. 478–89.

15. Pennypacker, *Washington's Spies*, pp. 58–59. O'Toole, *Honorable Treachery*, pp. 46–47.

16. Pamela Kessler, *Undercover Washington* (McLean, Va.: EPM Publications, 1992), p. 123.

17. O'Toole, *Honorable Treachery*, p. 42. Fleming, "George Washington, General."

18. Pennypacker, *Washington's Spies*. O'Toole, *Honorable Treachery*, ch. 4.

19. Edmund R. Thompson, "Intelligence at Yorktown," *Defense 81*, Sept. 1981. John C. Miller, *The Triumph of Freedom, 1775–1783* (Boston: Little, Brown & Co., 1948), p. 606. O'Toole, *Honorable Treachery*, pp. 59–60.

20. Fitzpatrick (ed.), *Writings of Washington*, vol. 23, p. 189; cf. pp. 210, 308n.

21. Fitzpatrick (ed.), *Writings of Washington*, vol. 24, p. 98.

22. Edward F. Sayle, "The Historical Underpinning of the U.S. Intelligence Community," *International Journal of Intelligence and CounterIntelligence*, vol. 1 (1986), no. 1, p. 9.

23. Like the fictional Birch, one of Washington's spies, James Rivington, who had posed as a British propagandist during the war, was afterward hounded by American patriots unaware of his true role. On the publishing history of *The Spy*, see the introduction by J. E. Morpurgo to the Oxford University Press edition, first published in 1968.

24. Donald R. Hickey, *The War of 1812* (Urbana and Chicago: University of Chicago Press, 1989), pp. 37–39. Samuel Eliot Morison, "The Henry-Crillon Affair of 1812," *Proceedings of the Massachusetts Historical Society*, 69 (1947–1950), pp. 207–31.

25. Hickey, *War of 1812*. O'Toole, *Honorable Treachery*, ch. 7.

26. Milo M. Quaife (ed.), *The Diary of James K. Polk* (Chicago: A. C. McClurg & Co., 1910), vol. 1, pp. 328–40.

27. Lyman B. Kirkpatrick Jr., "Intelligence and Counterintelligence," in Alexander De Conde (ed.), *Encyclopedia of American Foreign Policy* (New York: Charles Scribner's Sons, 1978), vol. 2, pp. 418–19. A. Brooke Caruso, *The Mexican Spy Company* (Jefferson, N.C.: McFarland, 1991).

28. Peter Maslowski, "Military Intelligence Sources During the American Civil War: A Case Study," in Walter T. Hitchcock (ed.), *The Intelligence Revolution: A Historical Perspective* (Washington, D.C.: U.S. Air Force Academy, 1991). J. Cutler Andrews, *The North Reports the Civil War* (Pittsburgh: University of Pittsburgh Press, 1955). Idem, *The South Reports the Civil War* (Princeton, N.J.: Princeton University Press). O'Toole, *Honorable Treachery*, pp. 131–33.

29. John Y. Simon (ed.), *The Papers of Ulysses S. Grant* (Carbondale and Edwardsville: Southern Illinois University Press, 1985), vol. 14, pp. 80–81.

30. Stephen B. Oates, *With Malice Toward None: The Life of Abraham Lincoln* (London: George Allen & Unwin, 1978), pp. 210–13.

31. Roy P. Basler (ed.), *The Collected Works of Abraham Lincoln* (New Brunswick, N.J.: Rutgers University Press, 1953–55), vol 6, p. 263.

32. Oates, *With Malice Toward None*, p. 235.

33. Basler (ed.), *Works of Lincoln*, vol. 4, p. 353.

34. Allan Pinkerton, *The Spy of the Rebellion, Being a True Story of the Spy System of the United States Army During the Late Rebellion* (New York: G. W. Dillingham, 1888).

35. Basler (ed.), *Works of Lincoln*, vol. 4, p. 372

36. Sayle, "Historical Underpinning," pp. 18–19. There is a detailed, but somewhat uncritical, account of Lloyd's career in Alan Axelrod, *The War Between the Spies: A History of Espionage During the American Civil War* (New York: Atlantic Monthly Press, 1992), ch. 2.

37. Letter from Pinkerton to McClellan, cited in Axelrod, *War Between the Spies*, pp. 57–70.

38. Mrs. [Rose] Greenhow, *My Imprisonment and the First Year of Abolition Rule at Washington* (London: Richard Bentley, 1867). Ishbel Ross, *Rebel Rose* (New York: Harper & Brothers, 1954).

39. The best study of the Peninsula campaign is Stephen W. Sears, *To the Gates of Richmond* (New York: Ticknor & Fields, 1992).

40. Edwin C. Fishel, "The Mythology of Civil War Intelligence," *Civil War History*, vol. 10 (1964), no. 4, pp. 345–47.

41. General Lafayette Charles Baker, *The History of the United States Secret Service* (Philadelphia: private printing, 1867), pp. 242–43, 252, 593. William R. Corson, *The Armies of Ignorance* (New York: Dial Press, 1977), pp. 528–59.

42. David Homer Bates, *Lincoln in the Telegraph Office* (New York: Century Co., 1907). David Kahn, *The Codebreakers* (New York: Macmillan, 1967), pp. 214–20.

43. Dino A. Brugioni, "Arlington and Fairfax Counties: Land of Many Reconnaissance Firsts," *Northern Virginia Heritage*, Feb. 1985, pp. 3–8. G. J. A. O'Toole, *The Encyclopedia of American Intelligence and Espionage* (New York: Facts on File, 1988), pp. 385–88. John W. Stepp and I. William Hill, *Mirror of War: The Washington Star Reports the Civil War* (Washington, D.C.: Castle Books, 1961), p. 52.

44. Jay Luvaas, "Lee at Gettysburg: A General Without Intelligence," *Intelligence and National Security*, vol. 5 (1990), no. 2, pp. 116–35.

45. Jay Luvaas, "The Role of Intelligence in the Chancellorsville Campaign, April-May, 1863," *Intelligence and National Security*, vol. 5 (1990), no. 2, pp. 99–115.

46. Luvaas, "Lee at Gettysburg."

47. Fishel, "Mythology." O'Toole, *Encyclopedia*, pp. 83–84, 463–64.

48. Paul H. Bergeron (ed.), *The Papers of Andrew Johnson* (Knoxville: University of Tennessee Press), vol. 8 (1991), p. 542; vol. 9 (1989), pp. 126–27.

49. Ibid., vol. 9, pp. 370–72.

50. Baker, *Secret Service*, p. 602.

51. Bergeron (ed.), *Papers of Andrew Johnson*, vol. 8, p. 99n.

52. Milton Lomask, *Andrew Johnson: President on Trial* (New York: Octagon Books, 1973); quotation from House Report no. 7, 40 Cong., 1 Sess., pp. 110–11.

53. William Hanchett, *The Lincoln Murder Conspiracies* (Urbana and Chicago: University of Illinois Press, 1983).

54. Walter S. Bowen and Henry Edward Neal, *The United States Secret Service* (Philadelphia: Chilton, 1960). O'Toole, *Encyclopedia*, pp. 413–14. The round-the-clock protection at the beginning of the twentieth century, however, was not quite what it has since become. When President Theodore Roosevelt spent holidays at his Pine Knot cabin, his Secret Service "protector" lodged in a village several miles away.

55. Sayle, "Historical Underpinning," p. 19.

56. Jeffrey M. Dorwart, *The Office of Naval Intelligence* (Annapolis, Md.: Naval Institute Press, 1979), ch. 2.

57. Bruce W. Bidwell, *History of the Military Intelligence Division, Department of the Army General Staff: 1775–1941* (Frederick, Md.: University Publications of America, 1986), ch. 6.

58. Mark Shulman, "The Rise and Fall of American Naval Intelligence," *Intelligence and National Security*, vol. 8 (1993), no. 2, pp. 215–16.

59. Elting E. Morison (ed.), *The Letters of Theodore Roosevelt* (Cambridge, Mass.: Harvard University Press, 1951–54), vol. 1, p. 742.

60. Dorwart, *Office of Naval Intelligence*, chs. 7, 8. The author of the Kimball Plan, Lieutenant (later Rear Admiral) William W. Kimball, served in ONI from 1894 to 1897.

61. G. J. A. O'Toole, *The Spanish War: An American Epic* (New York: W. W. Norton, 1984).

62. Morison (ed.), *Letters of Theodore Roosevelt*, vol. 6, p. 1498.

63. Theodore Roosevelt, *An Autobiography* (New York: Charles Scribner's Sons, 1920), p. 512.

64. Samuel Eliot Morison, Henry Steele Comager, and William E. Leuchtenberg, *The Growth of the American Republic*, 7th ed. (New York: Oxford University Press, 1980), vol. 2, pp. 312–13. David McCullough, *The Path Between the Seas* (New York: Simon and Schuster, 1977), chs. 12, 13.

65. Morison (ed.), *Letters of Theodore Roosevelt*, vol. 6, p. 1444.

66. McCullough, *Path Between the Seas*, pp. 382–83. Philip C. Jessup, *Elihu Root* (New York: Dodd, Mead & Co., 1938), pp. 404–405.

67. Gates, Memo to DCI, Dec. 14, 1984; text in *New York Times*, Sept. 20, 1991, p. A14.

68. Morison (ed.), *Letters of Theodore Roosevelt*, vol. 6, p. 1444.

69. Shulman, "American Naval Intelligence," pp. 220–24.

70. Ibid. Dorwart, *Office of Naval Intelligence*, ch. 10.

71. They were, however, more interested in the diplomatic traffic of their European rivals. See Christopher Andrew, "France and the German Menace," in Ernest May (ed.), *Knowing One's Enemies: Intelligence Assessment Before the Two World Wars* (Princeton, N.J.: Princeton University Press, 1984), pp. 127–49; and Christopher Andrew and Oleg Gordievsky, *KGB: The Inside Story of Its Foreign Operations from Lenin to Gorbachev*, paperback ed. (New York: HarperPerennial, 1991), pp. 26–32.

Chapter 2: The First World War and After:
From Woodrow Wilson to Herbert Hoover

1. Arthur S. Link, *Woodrow Wilson: Revolution, War and Peace* (Arlington Heights, Ill.: AMH Publishing Corporation, 1979), pp. 6–7.

2. Speech of Sept. 5, 1919, in *PWW*, vol. 63, pp. 46–47.

3. Christopher Andrew, *Her Majesty's Secret Service*, paperback ed. (New York: Penguin Books, 1987), chs. 2, 4, 5.

4. Introduction by Arthur S. Link to Reinhard R. Doerries, *Imperial Challenge: Ambassador Count Bernstorff and German-American Relations, 1908–1917* (Chapel Hill: University of North Carolina Press, 1989), p. xiv.

5. Kathleen Burk, *Britain, America and the Sinews of War, 1914–1918* (London: George Allen & Unwin, 1985). David Dimbleby and David Reynolds, *An Ocean Apart* (London: BBC Books, 1988), ch. 3.

6. *PWW*, vol. 30, pp. 393–94.

7. *PWW*, vol. 31, pp. 467–68.

8. Arthur S. Link, *Wilson: The Struggle for Neutrality, 1914–1915* (Princeton, N.J.: Princeton University Press, 1960), pp. 558–60.

9. Burke's report appears in William G. McAdoo, *Crowded Years* (New York: Houghton Mifflin, 1931), ch. 21.

10. Ibid., pp. 554–56.

11. Rintelen's own account is in Captain Franz von Rintelen, *The Dark*

Invader (London: Lovat Dickson, 1933). On German wartime covert operations in the United States, see Doerries, *Imperial Challenge*, ch. 5, and Jules Witcover, *Sabotage at Black Tom: Imperial Germany's Secret War in America, 1914–1917* (Chapel Hill, N.C.: Algonquin Books, 1989).

12. The original of this letter, missing from the usually comprehensive *PWW*, is in RG 59, NAW. Doerries, *Imperial Challenge*, p. 341.

13. *PWW*, vol. 33, p. 473.

14. Link, *Struggle for Neutrality*, pp. 562–64.

15. Rintelen, *Dark Invader*, pp. 80, 126.

16. *New York Times*, August 16-17, 1915. Link, *Struggle for Neutrality*, pp. 563–64.

17. *PWW*, vol. 34, p. 79.

18. Ibid., p. 309.

19. Rintelen, *Dark Invader*, part III. Patrick Beesly, *Room 40* (London: Hamish Hamilton, 1982), pp. 229–31.

20. Admiral Sir William James, *The Eyes of the Navy* (London: Methuen, 1955), p. xvii.

21. Beesly, *Room 40*, pp. 229–31.

22. *PWW*, vol. 34, pp. 403–404, 426, 429, 435, 503.

23. *PWW*, vol. 35, pp. 264–65. Lansing and Wilson also initially favored the expulsion of the Austro-Hungarian consul in New York, who was in the end reprieved.

24. Ibid., p. 306.

25. Stephen Gwynn (ed.), *The Letters and Friendships of Sir Cecil Spring Rice* (London: Constable, 1929), pp. 301–302.

26. Beesly, *Room 40*, p. 232.

27. Andrew, *Her Majesty's Secret Service*, pp. 246–48. The allegation that the diary extracts were forged has been comprehensively disproved.

28. There is no contemporary record of the foundation of the State Department intelligence unit. However, in a note to Wilson on April 8, 1917, Lansing gave the date of its creation as "8 or 9 months ago." *PWW*. Polk's diary for June 16, 1916 (SLYU), records that he "saw McAdoo re Secret Service," presumably to gain his approval for his unit to receive Secret Service reports.

29. George F. Kennan, *Russia Leaves the War*, paperback ed. (Princeton, N.J.: Princeton University Press, 1989), pp. 28–31.

30. Admiral Sir Guy Gaunt, *The Yield of the Years* (London: Hutchinson, 1940), pp. 135, 167–69.

31. Andrew, *Her Majesty's Secret Service*, pp. 73–84, 131–32. On the purchase of the autoped, see Thwaites to Wiseman, Oct. 1, 1918, Wiseman papers, series I, box 3, folder 84, SLYU.

32. "Memorandum on Scope and Activities of MI1c in New York," April 27, 1918, series I, box 6, folder 174, SLYU.

33. Andrew, *Her Majesty's Secret Service*, pp. 208–209.

34. Norman Thwaites, *Velvet and Vinegar* (London: Grayson & Grayson, 1932).

35. See note 32.

36. W. B. Fowler, *British-American Relations, 1917–1918: The Role of Sir William Wiseman* (Princeton, N.J.: Princeton University Press, 1969), pp. 10, 13, 19.

37. *PWW*, vol. 41, p. 26.

38. John Bruce Lockhart, "Sir William Wiseman, Bart., Agent of Influence," unpublished talk to the British Study Group on Intelligence.

39. Thwaites, *Velvet and Vinegar*, pp. 154–55. Thwaites's account is confirmed by Gaunt, *Yield of the Years*, pp. 192–94.

40. Kahn, *Codebreakers*, pp. 284–85. Andrew, *Her Majesty's Secret Service*, pp. 107–108.

41. Kahn, *Codebreakers*, p. 351. Ray Stannard Baker, *Woodrow Wilson, Life and Letters* (London: Heinemann, 1928–39), vol. 5, pp. 204ff, 307, 317–18; vol. 6, pp. 52–3, 143ff.

42. Herbert O. Yardley, *The American Black Chamber* (London: Faber, 1931), p. 4.

43. Kahn, *Codebreakers*, pp. 284–96. Andrew, *Her Majesty's Secret Service*, pp. 108–13. Beesly, *Room 40*, ch. 13.

44. *FRUS 1917*, supplement 1, pp. 147–48.

45. Arthur S. Link, *Campaigns for Progressivism and Peace, 1916–1917* (Princeton, N.J.: Princeton University Press, 1965), pp. 345–46.

46. Lansing, "Memorandum on the Message of Zimmermann to the German Minister to Mexico," March 4, 1917, Robert Lansing papers, Library of Congress, Washington, D.C. *PWW*, vol. 41, pp. 322–23.

47. Link, *Progressivism and Peace*, pp. 354–57.

48. *FRUS 1917*, supplement 1, pp. 155–58.

49. Andrew, *Her Majesty's Secret Service*, p. 113.

50. *FRUS 1917*, supplement 1, p. 158.

51. See note 46.

52. Andrew, *Her Majesty's Secret Service*, p. 114.

53. *PWW*, vol. 41, pp. 519–27.

54. Andrew, *Her Majesty's Secret Service*, p. 114.

55. Fowler, *British-American Relations, 1917–1918*, pp. 111–12.

56. Wiseman, Report 91(0), "Russian Affairs," May 26, 1917, Wiseman papers, series I, box 10, folder 255, SLYU. On the MI1c station in Petrograd, see Andrew, *Her Majesty's Secret Service*, ch. 6.

57. *PWW*, vol. 42, pp. 527, 529–30.

58. *PWW*, vol. 42, pp. 551–52.

59. *PWW*, vol. 43, p. 20.

60. W. Somerset Maugham, "Looking Back," *Sunday Express*, Sept. 30, Oct. 7, 1962. Andrew, *Her Majesty's Secret Service*, pp. 209–11.

61. Sir Arthur Willert, *The Road to Safety* (London: Derek Verschoyle, 1952), p. 61.

62. *PWW*, vol. 43, p. 24.

63. *PWW*, vol. 43, pp. 172, 183, 195.

64. Northcliffe to Reading, Sept. 2, 1917, Wiseman papers, series I, box 3, folder 59, SLYU.

65. Burk, *Sinews of War*, pp. 162–72. Dr. Burk's generally excellent account fails to identify Wiseman as a British intelligence officer.

66. The impending delivery of the intercepts by Wiseman was announced in cables from Page to Wilson (which discreetly described Wiseman simply as "a trustworthy messenger personally known to you') and from Wiseman to House. *PWW*, vol. 44, pp. 140, 164.

67. Beesly, *Room 40*, pp. 237–41.

68. *PWW*, vol. 44, p. 201.

69. Fowler, *British-American Relations, 1917–1918*, p. 124.

70. "His Excellency" and "Mr Harrington's Washing," in W. Somerset Maugham, *Collected Short Stories* (London: Pan, 1976). Andrew, *Her Majesty's Secret Service*, pp. 211–12.

71. [Wiseman to Cumming], "American Section M.I.1.c.," [?Oct. 1917], Wiseman papers, series I, box 6, folder 172, SLYU.

72. Wiseman to "C," Dec. 18, 1917, Wiseman papers, series I, box 6, folder 173, SLYU.

73. *PWW*, vol. 46, pp. 155ff.

74. Ibid., p. 389.

75. House noted in his diary in June: "Sir William thought the President could never be on as confidential terms with Reading as he was, for instance, with himself, for the reason that he had observed that Reading always approached the matter with the air and caution of a lawyer." *PWW*, vol. 48, p. 381.

76. Memorandum, March 28, 1918, Wiseman papers, series I, box 6, folder 172, SLYU.

77. Wiseman to Cumming, Sept. 6, 1918, Wiseman papers, series I, box 6, folder 171, SLYU.

78. Gaunt, *Yield of the Years*, pp. 172, 270–71.

79. "Memorandum on Scope and Activities of MI1c in New York," April 27, 1918, Wiseman papers, series I, box 6, folder 174, SLYU.

80. Wiseman to Cumming, Sept. 6, 1918, Wiseman papers, series I, box 6, folder 171, SLYU.

81. *PWW*, vol. 42, pp. 16–17.

82. Dorwart, *Office of Naval Intelligence*, p. 117.

83. Robert G. Angevine, "Gentlemen Do Read Each Other's Mail: American Intelligence in the Interwar Era," *Intelligence and National Security*, vol. 7 (1992), no. 2, p. 2.

84. Major Herbert O. Yardley, "A History of the Code and Cipher Section During the First World War, Prepared in 1919," p. 6, RG 457: SRH-030, NAW.

85. *Historical Background of the Signal Security Agency*, vol. 2, p. 21, RG 457: NC3-457-77-1, NAW.

86. The reports, which fill thirty volumes, are reprinted in Richard D. Challener (ed.), *United States Military Intelligence Weekly Summaries* (New York: Garland Publishing, 1978); the examples cited are from vol. 1.

87. Joan M. Jensen, *The Price of Vigilance* (New York: Rand McNally, 1968).

88. McAdoo probably hoped to have responsibility for the proposed agency. When Lansing discussed with him his proposal for an intelligence supremo, McAdoo "advocated strongly the appointment of Chief Flynn of the Secret Service." *PWW*, vol. 42, p. 16.

89. *PWW*, vol. 43, pp. 154–55.

90. *PWW*, vol. 44, pp. 480–81.

91. *PWW*, vol. 45, pp. 28–29.

92. Ibid., pp. 74–75, 101–102.

93. *PWW*, vol. 49, pp. 497–503.

94. *PWW*, vol. 47, p. 307.

95. Ibid., pp. 433, 444.

96. Wiseman to Reading, July 26, 1918, Wiseman papers, series I, box 3, folder 74, SLYU.

97. Arthur C. Murray, *At Close Quarters* (London: John Murray, 1946), pp. 40–41, 50.

98. Murray to Wiseman, Oct. 8, 1918, Wiseman papers, series I, box 2, folder 53, SLYU.

99. Wiseman to Murray, Sept. 14, 1918, ibid. Fowler, *British-American Relations, 1917–1918*.

100. *PWW*, vol. 47, p. 440.

101. George F. Kennan, "The Sisson Documents," *Journal of Modern History*, vol. 28 (1956), no. 2. Idem, *Russia Leaves the War*, pp. 446–48.

102. *PWW*, vol. 51, pp. 246–47, 352.

103. Kennan, *Russia Leaves the War*, ch. 22.

104. Wiseman to Reading, Sept. 5, 1918, Wiseman papers, series I, box 3, folder 74, SLYU. Fowler, *British-American Relations, 1917–1918*, p. 215.

105. *PWW*, vol. 51, pp. 345–48.

106. Ibid., pp. 527–28.

107. Ibid., pp. 594–95.

108. *PWW*, vol. 43, p. 238.

109. Fowler, *British-American Relations, 1917–1918*, p. 228.

110. Challener (ed.), *Weekly Summaries*, vols. 6, 7, 8.

111. Charles Seymour (ed.), *The Intimate Papers of Colonel House* (Boston: Houghton Mifflin, 1926), vol. 4, p. 263.

112. *PWW*, vol. 55, pp. 164–77.

113. Ibid., pp. 238–42.

114. Yardley noted on Dec. 25, 1918, ". . . Churchill wants to keep M.I.8, and [Leland] Harrison of the State Department tells me that Secretary Lansing wants to take it over." *Historical Background of the Signal Security Agency*, vol. 3, pp. 40–42, RG 457: NC3-457-77-1, NAW. Yardley, *Black Chamber*, pp. 160–63.

115. Yardley, *Black Chamber*, pp. 163–64.

116. *Historical Background of the Signal Security Agency*, vol. 3, pp. 42–54, RG 457: NC3-457-77-1, NAW.

117. Robert K. Murray, *Red Scare: A Study in National Hysteria, 1919–1920* (Minneapolis: University of Minnesota Press, 1955). Stanley

Coben, *A. Mitchell Palmer: Politician* (New York: Columbia University Press, 1963). Curt Gentry, *J. Edgar Hoover* (New York: W. W. Norton, 1991), ch. 6.

118. *PWW*, vol. 63, pp. 174–75.

119. *PWW*, vol. 64, p. ix.

120. Ibid.

121. Fowler, *British-American Relations, 1917–1918*, pp. 239–40.

122. Edith Bolling Wilson, *Memoirs of Mrs Woodrow Wilson* (London: Putnam, 1939), p. 342.

123. Thwaites to Wiseman, Nov. 22, 1918, Wiseman papers, series I, box 3, folder 84, SLYU.

124. Churchill to Military Intelligence Officer, Eastern Department, Sept. 13, 1918, RG 165: File 11013-4, NAW.

125. Wiseman to Churchill, April 19, 1919, RG 165: File 11013-7, NAW.

126. "Reduction of Estimates for Secret Services," March 19, 1920, Lloyd George papers, F/9/2/16, House of Lords Record Office. Andrew, *Her Majesty's Secret Service*, chs. 7, 8, 9.

127. Wiseman, Draft Memorandum for Lieut. Grossmith and Mr. Del Campo, Dec. 5, 1918, Wiseman papers, series I, box 6, folder 125, SLYU.

128. "Reduction of Estimates for Secret Services," March 19, 1920, Lloyd George papers, F/9/2/16, House of Lords Record Office. The budget details in this document show that the main SIS postwar targets, after Russia and Germany, were the United States and the Far East.

129. A well-informed obituary in the *New York Times* (June 18, 1962) reported discreetly that "Sir William continued to serve the British Government as a private citizen" and "was frequently consulted by the Foreign Office" (a euphemism for the unavowable SIS).

130. *PWW*, vols. 64, 65.

131. A. Mitchell Palmer, "The Case Against the 'Reds,'" *Forum*, Feb. 1920, pp. 173–76; reprinted in David Brion Davis (ed.), *The Fear of Conspiracy* (Ithaca, N.Y.: Cornell University Press, 1971), pp. 226–27.

132. Murray, *Red Scare*, pp. 190–222, 247–50. Coben, *Palmer*, pp. 196–245.

133. *PWW*, vol. 65, pp. 186–88.

134. Ibid. Josephus Daniels, *The Wilson Era: Years of War and After, 1917–1923* (Chapel Hill: University of North Carolina Press, 1946), pp. 545–46.

135. Gentry, *Hoover*, pp. 97–98.

136. Kennan, *Russia Leaves the War*, pp. 452–54.

137. Angevine, "Gentlemen Do Read Each Other's Mail," pp. 5–7.

138. See the 30 vols. of Challener (ed.), *Weekly Summaries*.

139. Yardley, *Black Chamber*, p. 215.

140. *Documents on British Foreign Policy, 1919–1939*, 1st series, vol. 14, p. 297. The British ambassador did not reveal that Britain was also able to decrypt Japanese diplomatic traffic.

141. Yardley, *Black Chamber*, ch. 16, publishes the text of a number of the Japanese telegrams decrypted during the conference, including a photograph

of the original decrypt of the telegram of November 28. For a useful commentary on Yardley's account, see David Kahn, "The Annotated 'The American Black Chamber,'" in Cipher A. Deavours et al. (eds,), *Cryptology Yesterday, Today and Tomorrow* (Norwood, Mass.: Artech House, 1987), pp. 55–98.

142. Yardley, *Black Chamber*, p. 224.

143. *Historical Background of the Signal Security Agency*, vol. 3, p. 68, RG 457: NC3-457-77-1, NAW.

144. Thomas H. Buckley, *The United States and the Washington Conference, 1921–1922* (Knoxville: University of Tennessee Press, 1970), pp. 176, 139. *New York Times*, Dec. 21, 1921.

145. Kahn, "The Annotated 'The American Black Chamber,'" pp. 83–84.

146. Andrew, *Her Majesty's Secret Service*, pp. 260–61.

147. J. Edgar Hoover to MID, Feb. 21, 1921, RG 165: File 9944-A-178, NAW. Major W.. Hicks (MID), "Memorandum on British Secret Service Activity in This Country," Nov. 2, 1920, RG 165: File 9771-145.

148. Yardley, *Black Chamber*, pp. 232–34.

149. Ibid., pp. 244–48. The original typescript of *The American Black Chamber* reveals that Yardley was summoned to the State Department by Undersecretary of State Joseph P. Grew, who discussed the case with him at some length. (Grew's name, along with those of a number of other living U.S. diplomats, was deleted by the publisher before publication.) The episode is undated, but Grew was undersecretary from March 7, 1924 to May 18, 1927. William F. Friedman's annotated copy of *Black Chamber* (in the George C. Marshall Library, Lexington, Va.), which contains a number of hostile comments and criticisms of various of Yardley's claims, does not challenge his account of this episode. Kahn, "The Annotated 'The American Black Chamber,'" p. 87.

150. *Historical Background of the Signal Security Agency*, vol. 3, pp. 73–118, RG 457: NC3-457-77-1, NAW.

151. W. F. Friedman, "A Brief History of the Signal Intelligence Service," June 29, 1942, pp. 9–10, RG 457: SRH-029, NAW.

152. Stimson Diary, June 1, 1931, SLYU. Stimson kept no diary during his early months as secretary of state, and thus left no contemporary record of the closure of the Black Chamber. This account comes from his diary comments on the publication of Yardley's memoirs.

153. See note 151.

154. Stimson Diary, June 31, 1931, SLYU.

155. *Historical Background of the Signal Security Agency*, vol. 3, p. 144n, RG 457: NC3-457-77-1, NAW.

156. Stimson Diary, Dec. 4, 1930, SLYU.

157. Michael Medved, *The Shadow Presidents: The Secret History of the Chief Executives and Their Top Aides* (New York: Times Books, 1975), p. 185. Gentry, *Hoover*, pp. 125, 152–53.

158. Jeffrey M. Dorwart, *Conflict of Duty* (Annapolis, Md.: Naval Institute Press, 1983), pp. 3–5.

Chapter 3: Franklin D. Roosevelt: The Path to Pearl Harbor

1. Kahn, *Codebreakers*, pp. 114–16.

2. Roosevelt Diary 1901–03, FDR Papers: Family, Business & Personal, box 39, FDRL.

3. On Roosevelt's romance with Alice Sohier, see Ted Morgan, *FDR: A Biography* (London: Grafton Books, 1986), p. 83; Geoffrey C. Ward, *Before the Trumpet: Young Franklin Roosevelt*, paperback ed. (New York: Harper & Row, 1986), pp. 252–55.

4. Diary entries for July 8, 9, 1902, FDR Papers: Family, Business & Personal, box 39, FDRL. It seems unlikely that Roosevelt used the cipher only for brief diary entries. He may also have used it for letters to Alice (all of which she later destroyed) and for other purposes, but the diary entries appear to be the only examples that survive.

5. Ward, *Before the Trumpet*, p. 253. Morgan and Ward differ on their interpretation of the romance. Morgan's suggestion that Alice Sohier's purpose in going to Europe was to have an abortion is convincingly contradicted by family evidence. On the other hand, the family suggestion that all that Alice "confided" in her doctor were fears about her future capacity for childbearing seems an inadequate explanation for Roosevelt's ciphered reference to his sleepless night. (She later had two children after her marriage to an insurance executive.)

6. Diary entry, Oct. 8, 1902, FDR Papers: Family, Business & Personal, box 39, FDRL.

7. Diary entries, July 7, Nov. 22, 1903, ibid.

8. Morgan, *FDR*, pp. 103–105. Geoffrey C. Ward, *A First-Class Temperament: The Emergence of Franklin Roosevelt*, paperback ed. (New York: HarperPerennial, 1990), ch. 1.

9. John Gunther, *Roosevelt in Retrospect* (London: Hamish Hamilton, 1950), pp. 97–99.

10. Ward, *First-Class Temperament*, pp. 433, 476–78.

11. Dorwart, *Office of Naval Intelligence*, pp. 104–111.

12. See above, p. 37.

13. Dorwart, *Office of Naval Intelligence*, p. 117.

14. See, e.g., FDR, Memos to Lt. Comm. McCauley, March 6 and 14, 1917, Papers as Assistant Secretary of the Navy, box 2, "Official Files, Naval Department: I General," FDRL.

15. ONI, Memos for FDR, May 12 and 27, 1917, ibid.

16. PSF Anecdotes, FDRL. Ward, *First-Class Temperament*, p. 350n.

17. Frank Freidel, *Franklin D. Roosevelt: The Triumph* (Boston, Little, Brown & Co., 1956), p. 66.

18. Dorwart, *Office of Naval Intelligence*, pp. 106–107.

19. Beesly, *Room 40*, pp. 245–46.

20. Elliott Roosevelt (ed.), *The Roosevelt Letters* (London: Harrap, 1950), vol. 2, p. 311.

21. Papers as Assistant Secretary of the Navy, FDRL; cited Morgan, *FDR*,

pp. 194–95, Hall's fraudulent story made such an impression on FDR that he repeated it to Hall's Second World War successor, Admiral John Godfrey, over twenty years later; Godfrey, unpublished memoirs, vol. 5, pp. 136–37, CCAC. See below, p. 100.

22. Frank Freidel, *Franklin D. Roosevelt: The Ordeal* (Boston: Little, Brown & Co., 1954), pp. 18, 30–31, 77.

23. Niblack, confidential memorandum, Dec. 20, 1919, Papers as Assistant Secretary of the Navy, box 2, "Official Files, Naval Department: I General," FDRL.

24. The best secondary accounts of Roosevelt's involvement in the Newport scandal (which differ in their assessment of his responsibility for it) are in Morgan, *FDR*, ch. 9, and Ward, *First-Class Temperament*, pp. 437–44, 459–61, 487–555, 568–75. The main documentary sources are the "Newport Case" files in the FDR Papers: Papers as Assistant Secretary of the Navy, and Family, Business and Personal, FDRL.

25. Morgan, *FDR*, p. 369. Subsequent inaugurations took place in January rather than in March.

26. Dorwart, *Conflict of Duty*, pp. 55–56, 65, 68.

27. PSF, John Franklin Carter Files, FDRL.

28. Orville H. Bullitt (ed.), *For the President, Personal and Secret: Correspondence Between Franklin D. Roosevelt and William C. Bullitt* (London: André Deutsch, 1973), ch. 2.

29. Jeffrey M. Dorwart, "The Roosevelt-Astor Espionage Ring," *New York History*, vol. 62 (1981), no. 3, pp. 309–11.

30. Elliott Roosevelt (ed.), *Roosevelt Letters*, vol. 3, p. 100.

31. Astor to FDR, Sept. 26, 1934, PSF 92, Astor File, FDRL.

32. FDR to Astor, Sept. 26, 1934, Astor Papers, FDRL.

33. Astor to FDR, n.d., PSF 92, "Amusing Things" File, FDRL.

34. My account is based on three undated (1938) letters in the FDR papers: two written by Astor before the trip from 130 East 80th Street, New York (one located in PSF 92, Astor File; the other, marked "Thursday night," in PPF 40, Astor File); the third sent from the *Nourmahal*, making a preliminary report on the result of the voyage, in PSF 92, Astor File. FDRL.

35. Andrew, *Her Majesty's Secret Service*, chs. 1, 2.

36. Astor to FDR, n.d. [1938], PSF 92, Astor File, FDRL.

37. Anthony Cave Brown, *The Last Hero: Wild Bill Donovan*, Vintage Books ed. (New York: Random House, 1984), part I. Anthony Cave Brown, *"C": The Secret Life of Sir Stewart Menzies, Spymaster to Winston Churchill* (New York: Macmillan, 1987), pp. 123–24.

38. Brian R. Sullivan, "'A Highly Commendable Action': William J. Donovan's Intelligence Mission for Mussolini and Roosevelt, December 1935—February 1936," *Intelligence and National Security*, vol. 7 (1991), no. 2. Professor Sullivan's pathbreaking article probably exaggerates the degree to which, "given the sycophants that surrounded him," Mussolini sought an objective view from Donovan (p. 347).

39. Stimson Diary, Dec. 18, 1940, SLYU. On FDR's policymaking, see War-

ren F. Kimball, *The Juggler: Franklin Roosevelt as Wartime Statesman* (Princeton, N.J.: Princeton University Press, 1991), ch. 1.

40. Memorandum of White House conference, Nov. 14, 1938, RG 165, box 281, NAW; cited by Mark M. Lowenthal, "Searching for National Intelligence: U.S. Intelligence and Policy Before the Second World War," *Intelligence and National Security*, vol. 6 (1991), no. 4.

41. *FRUS 1938*, vol. 1, pp. 72–73. There is little doubt about Lindbergh's influence on FDR. In February 1938 he had sent an earlier memo from Lindbergh to both the army chief of staff and the chief of naval operations; PSF 87, File "Navy," FDRL.

42. Bullitt (ed.), *For the President*, pp. 295–99 (cf. pp. 276, 305–306); Donald B. Schewe (ed.), *Franklin D. Roosevelt and Foreign Affairs*, 2nd series (New York: Clearwater Publishing Co., 1980), vol. 11, nos. 1306, 1306A.

43. Memorandum of White House conference, Nov. 14, 1938, RG 165, box 281, NAW. Lowenthal, "Searching for National Intelligence," pp. 736–38.

44. Wesley K. Wark, *The Ultimate Enemy: British Intelligence and Nazi Germany 1933–1939* (London: Tauris, 1985), pp. 68–69, 245.

45. Don Whitehead, *The FBI Story* (London: Frederic Muller, 1957), pp. 153–54, 334.

46. Athan Theoharis (ed.), *From the Secret Files of J. Edgar Hoover* (Chicago: Ivan R. Dee, 1991), pp. 180–81.

47. No such document has been discovered either in the Roosevelt Library or in the National Archives. Ibid. Gentry, *Hoover*, p. 206n.

48. Theoharis (ed.), *Secret Files*, pp. 182–83. Gentry, *Hoover*, p. 207.

49. Henry Julian Wadleigh, "Why I Spied for the Communists," part 7, New York *Post*, Home News, July 19, 1949. Andrew and Gordievsky, *KGB*, pp. 226–32.

50. Ladislas Farago, *The Game of the Foxes* (London: Hodder and Stoughton, 1972), ch. 6. Thomas F. Troy, *Donovan and the CIA* (Washington, D.C.: CIA Center for the Study of Intelligence, 1981), p. 11. *New York Times*, Dec. 3, 10, 1938.

51. Schewe (ed.), *Roosevelt and Foreign Affairs*, 2nd series, vol. 11, pp. 315–16.

52. Theoharis (ed.), *Secret Files*, p. 183. Troy, *Donovan and the CIA*, p. 11. *New York Times*, Dec. 10, 1938.

53. Whitehead, *FBI Story* p. 159.

54. Ibid., p. 158.

55. Church Committee, *Final Report*, book 2, pp. 26–27, 34. Troy, *Donovan and the CIA*, pp. 12–13.

56. Samuel I. Rosenman (ed.), *The Public Papers and Addresses of Franklin Roosevelt 1928–1945* (New York: Random House/Macmillan/Harper & Brothers, 1938–50), *1939*, pp. 478–79, 485–86.

57. Troy, *Donovan and the CIA*, p. 13.

58. Ibid., pp. 15–16.

59. Astor to FDR, "Sunday night," n.d. [1939], PSF 92 Astor File, FDRL.

60. Unsigned report (marked "from V Astor, Oct 30 '39"), PSF 92 Astor File, FDRL.

61. Astor to FDR, Nov. 20, Dec. 1, 1939, Feb. 5, 1940; FDR to Treasury Secretary (copy), Feb. 8, 1940. Ibid.

62. Astor to FDR, April 18, 1940, ibid.

63. Ibid. Astor gives the date of his meeting with Paget as "shortly after the 'club''s formation."

64. Thomas F. Troy, "The Coordinator of Intelligence and British Intelligence" [partially declassified CIA study], DDRS, 1990, no. 92, pp. 17, 19, 25. Stephenson visited the United States in April 1940, went back to England for several weeks, then returned to New York as head of station in June.

65. Troy, Donovan and the CIA, ch. 3. Cave Brown, Last Hero, chs. 9, 10. For the first eight months of the war in Europe, Donovan was preoccupied by family problems, first the serious illness of his wife, then the death of their daughter Pat in a road accident in April 1940.

66. Anthony Cave Brown (ed.), The Secret War Report of the OSS, paperback ed. (New York: Berkley, 1976), pp. 42–43.

67. Andrew, Her Majesty's Secret Service, pp. 477–78.

68. David Reynolds, The Creation of the Anglo-American Alliance 1937–41 (London: Europa Publications, 1981), chs. 3, 4.

69. The chapter in the CIA study by Thomas F. Troy, "The Coordinator of Intelligence and British Intelligence," DDRS, 1990, no. 92, which deals with Donovan's visit, remains classified. The first section of the missing chapter is, however, appropriately entitled "An Angry U.S. Ambassador."

70. Godfrey, unpublished memoirs, vol. 5, pp. 129–32, GDFY 1/6, CCAC.

71. H. Montgomery Hyde, The Quiet Canadian (London: Hamish Hamilton, 1962), pp. 34–43. Reynolds, Anglo-American Alliance, ch. 5. Martin Gilbert, Winston S. Churchill (London: Heinemann, 1966–88), vol. 6, p. 738.

72. Godfrey, unpublished memoirs, vol. 5, p. 131, GDFY 1/6, CCAC.

73. Stimson Diary, July 15, 16, 1940, SLYU.

74. COS(40)289, CAB 79/6, PRO. Bradley F. Smith, The Ultra-Magic Deals (Novato, Calif.: Presidio, 1993), pp. 38, 43–44. Sir F. H. Hinsley et al., British Intelligence in the Second World War (London: HMSO, 1979–88), vol. 1, pp. 312–13. On September 5 Roosevelt also signed a presidential order giving British official representatives access to State Department and consular reports.

75. William Stevenson, A Man Called Intrepid, paperback ed. (London: Sphere Books, 1971). (Sir William Stephenson is not to be confused with his biographer, William Stevenson.) David Stafford, "'Intrepid': Myth and Reality," Journal of Contemporary History, vol. 22 (1987). Nigel West, A Thread of Deceit: Espionage Myths of the Second World War, paperback ed. (New York: Dell, 1986), ch. 10. Timothy J. Naftali, "Intrepid's Last Deception: Documenting the Career of Sir William Stephenson," Intelligence and National Security, vol. 8 (1993), no. 3.

76. Troy, "The Coordinator of Intelligence and British Intelligence," DDRS, 1990, no. 92, p. 63.

77. Ibid., pp. 64–74. Cave Brown, Last Hero, pp. 153–55.

78. Stimson, "Notes After Cabinet Meeting, April 4, 1941," cited by Troy,

"The Coordinator of Intelligence and British Intelligence," DDRS, 1990, no. 92, pp. 89–90.

79. On Swinton, see Andrew, *Her Majesty's Secret Service*, pp. 478–80. On the role of "C," see ibid., passim.

80. Miles to Marshall, April 8, 1941, RG 319: File 310.11, NAW. Troy, "The Coordinator of Intelligence and British Intelligence," DDRS, 1990, no. 92, p. 88.

81. Stimson Diary, March 25, 1941, SLYU.

82. Astor to FDR, March 14, [1941], PSF 92, Astor File, FDRL.

83. Troy, "The Coordinator of Intelligence and British Intelligence," DDRS, 1990, no. 92, pp. 105–106.

84. Godfrey, "Intelligence in the United States," July 7, 1941, CAB 122/1021, PRO: published, with an introduction by Bradley J. Smith, in *Intelligence and National Security*, vol. 1 (1986), pp. 445–50.

85. Godfrey, unpublished memoirs, vol. 5, pp. 132–37, GDFY 1/6, CCAC.

86. Godfrey, "Intelligence in the United States," July 7, 1941, CAB 122/1021, PRO.

87. Troy, *Donovan and the CIA*, appendix B.

88. Troy, "The Coordinator of Intelligence and British Intelligence," DDRS, 1990, no. 92, pp. 107–109.

89. Stevenson, *A Man Called Intrepid*, pp. 14, 107–108, 158, 161, 204. Sir William Stephenson, introduction to H. Montgomery Hyde, *Secret Intelligence Agent* (London: Constable, 1982), pp. xv–xvi.

90. See below, p. 130.

91. Hyde, *Quiet Canadian*, pp. 2, 236–37.

92. Stephenson's assistant, the late H. Montgomery Hyde, who took a leading part in the Belmonte forgery, gave me permission to examine the papers on this and other episodes of his career that he had deposited in the Churchill College Archive Centre. Unhappily, Whitehall's historical censors beat me to it; by the time I was able to go through the Hyde papers, they had closed many items to historical research. For the time being, the most revealing account of the Belmonte forgery is in Hyde, *Secret Intelligence Agent*, pp. 150–60.

93. Rosenman (ed.), *Public Papers . . . 1941*, p. 387.

94. Adolf Berle, Memo to Sumner Welles, Sept. 27, 1941, Berle Diary, FDRL.

95. Stephenson continued even after the war to maintain that the map was genuine; Stevenson, *Man Called Intrepid*, p. 317. Among those studies that conclude that it was a BSC forgery is a recent CIA history, *The Intelligence War in 1941: A 50th Anniversary Perspective* (Washington, D.C.: CIA Center for the Study of Intelligence, 1992), p. 19.

96. Rosenman (ed.), *Public Papers . . . 1941*, pp. 439–40. Though the consequences of a German victory would have been appalling for organized religion, as for the rest of civilized life, there was no written master plan for its formal abolition of the kind quoted by FDR.

97. The isolationist senator Burt Wheeler immediately smelled a rat, and told the Senate where it came from:

It originated in the office of Colonel Donovan, in the office of the Coordinator of Information of the United States Government. Perhaps I should say it originated in New York, in the minds of gentlemen closely associated with the British Government . . .

Stephenson responded with a covert operation to discredit Wheeler. His later recollection of the operation was somewhat confused. Stevenson, *Man Called Intrepid*, pp. 318–19.

98. Declassification of the decrypts supplied to Churchill began only in 1993. They are located in the HW1 series at the PRO.

99. Christopher Andrew, "Churchill and Intelligence," *Intelligence and National Security*, vol. 3 (1988), no. 2; reprinted in Michael Handel (ed.), *Leaders and Intelligence* (London: Frank Cass, 1988), pp. 181–93.

100. *Historical Background of the Signal Security Agency*, part 3, p. 308, RG 457: SRH-001, NAW. Christopher Andrew, "Codebreakers and Foreign Offices," in Christopher Andrew and David Dilks (eds.), *The Missing Dimension: Governments and Intelligence Communities in the Twentieth Century* (London: Macmillan, 1984), p. 52.

101. David Kahn, "Pearl Harbor and the Inadequacy of Cryptanalysis," *Cryptologia*, vol. 15 (1991), pp. 280–81.

102. Ibid., pp. 283–85. Andrew, "Codebreakers and Foreign Offices," p. 53.

103. Edwin T. Layton et al., *And I Was There* (New York: William Morrow, 1987), p. 81.

104. See above, pp. 72–73.

105. James Bamford, *The Puzzle Palace* (Boston: Houghton Mifflin, 1982), p. 40.

106. Stimson Diary, Sept. 25, Oct. 23, 1940, SLYU.

107. *Historical Background of the Signal Security Agency*, part 3, p. 308, RG 457: SRH-001, NAW. Andrew, "Codebreakers and Foreign Offices," pp. 52–53.

108. See above, p. 96. Smith, *Ultra-Magic Deals*, pp. 43–44. Hinsley et al., *British Intelligence in the Second World War*, vol. 1, pp. 312–13.

109. Stimson wrote "Hull." It is clear from the context that he intended to write "Knox."

110. Stimson Diary, Oct. 23, 1940, SLYU.

111. Ibid., Oct. 24, 1940. Stimson noted in his diary (SLYU) on Dec. 17, 1940, that "the Navy had gone back on the agreement. . . . I called up Knox at once and told him about it and it made him angry too and he said he'd settle it."

112. For examples of the occasional U.S. decrypts included in Churchill's "golden eggs," see decrypts no. 094864, Aug. 26, 1941, HW1/28; no. 095432, Sept. 13, 1941, HW1/64; no. 095510, Sept. 15, 1941, HW1/66; no. 096090, Oct. 2, 1941, HW1/107; no. 097126, Oct. 30, 1941, HW1/179; no. 098061, Nov. 23, 1941, HW1/251, PRO. On British interception of U.S. diplomatic traffic, see the forthcoming article by Kathryn Brown in *Intelligence and National Security*, scheduled for publication in 1995.

113. Thomas Parrish, *The Ultra Americans* (New York: Stein and Day, 1986), pp. 61–66. Smith, *Ultra-Magic Deals*, pp. 53–58.

114. Stimson Diary, Jan. 2, 1941, SLYU.

115. *PHA*, part 2, p. 288; part 4, p. 1734. David Kahn, "Roosevelt, MAGIC, and ULTRA," *Cryptologia*, vol. 14 (1992), p. 292.

116. *PHA*, part 11, pp. 5278–81.

117. Morgan, *FDR*, pp. 606–607.

118. *PHA*, part 11, p. 5475. Watson had never been given the unrestricted access to Magic enjoyed by the naval aide; *PHA*, part 2, pp. 788–89. On Watson's role in the White House, see Morgan, *FDR*, p. 444.

119. Ruth R. Harris, "The 'Magic' Leak of 1941 and Japanese-American Relations," *Pacific Historical Review*, vol. 50 (1981), no. 1. *PHA*, part 4, pp. 1860–63.

120. *PHA*, part 11, p. 5475.

121. *PHA*, part 14, pp. 1337f, 1343. Roberta Wohlstetter, *Pearl Harbor: Warning and Decision* (Stanford, Calif.: Stanford University Press, 1962), pp. 120–24.

122. Lloyd C. Gardiner and Warren F. Kimball, "The United States: Democratic Diplomacy," in David Reynolds, Warren F. Kimball, and A. O. Chubarian (eds.), *Allies at War* (London: Macmillan, 1994).

123. Hinsley et al., *British Intelligence in the Second World War*, vol. 2, pp. 55, 174–75. Smith, *Ultra-Magic Deals*, p. 87.

124. Kahn, *Codebreakers* p. 29.

125. *FRUS 1941*, vol. 4, pp. 299–300.

126. *PHA*, part 11, pp. 5475–76.

127. Ibid.

128. *MBPH*, vol. 4, no. 16A; vol. 4, appendix, nos. 44, 114, 162.

129. Stimson Diary, Nov. 25, 26, 1941, SLYU. Layton et al., *And I Was There*, p. 202. Layton implausibly suggests that Stimson's account was a cover story, that Russian espionage had obtained (despite Sorge's arrest) "details of the Japanese war plans," and that Churchill might have obtained this information "from a British penetration of Soviet cipher traffic" and passed it on to FDR via Stephenson (ibid., pp. 203–205). Bletchley Park was not in fact able to read Soviet traffic; the main Soviet intelligence from Japan at this point came, as in Washington, from SIGINT (Andrew and Gordievsky, *KGB*, pp. 271–72).

130. *MBPH*, vol. 4, appendix, nos. 192–96.

131. Stimson Diary, Nov. 27, 1941, SLYU.

132. *MBPH*, vol. 4, appendix, no. 210.

133. Morgan, *FDR*, pp. 611–12.

134. Stimson Diary, Nov. 28, 1941, SLYU.

135. Gordon W. Prange, *At Dawn We Slept*, paperback ed. (New York: Penguin Books, 1982), p. 424.

136. *MBPH*, vol. 4, no. 70.

137. *MBPH*, vol. 4, appendix, no. 214.

138. Stimson Diary, Nov. 30, 1941, SLYU.

139. *MBPH*, vol. 4, appendix, nos. 216, 217.

140. Stimson Diary, Nov. 30, 1941, SLYU.

141. Prange, *At Dawn We Slept*, p. 428. A British decrypt of the same telegram reached Churchill on December 2; HW1/288, PRO.

142. *PHA*, part 9, p. 4072.

143. Gwen Terasaki, *Bridge to the Sun* (London: Michael Joseph, 1957), pp. 75–77.

144. Stimson Diary, Dec. 2, 1941, SLYU.

145. Terasaki, *Bridge to the Sun*, pp. 78–79.

146. Wohlstetter, *Pearl Harbor*, pp. 207–208. Layton et al., *And I Was There*, pp. 253, 269–70.

147. Beardall later remembered the date as "about the 4th or 5th"; given the importance of the decrypt, it is unlikely that it was not shown to FDR until two days after it was decrypted. *PHA*, part 11, p. 5284. The same decrypt also reached Churchill on December 4; HW1/297, PRO.

148. Ibid.

149. Morgan, *FDR*, pp. 613–14.

150. Stimson Diary, Dec. 7, 1941, SLYU.

151. *PHA*, part 14, pp. 1413–15.

152. *PHA*, part 9, pp. 4002–03.

153. Details in *PHA*, part 14, pp. 1413–15.

154. *PHA*, part 9, pp. 4003–39.

155. *PHA*, part 14, pp. 1240–45.

156. *PHA*, part 10, pp. 4660–64.

157. Details in *PHA*, part 14, pp. 1415–16.

158. *PHA*, part 11, pp. 5281–84.

159. Prange, *At Dawn We Slept*, p. 553.

160. *PHA*, part 9, p. 4099; part 11, pp. 5283–84.

161. Stimson Diary, Dec. 7, 1941, SLYU.

162. Cordell Hull, *Memoirs of Cordell Hull* (New York: Macmillan, 1948), vol. 2, pp. 1096–97.

163. Robert E. Sherwood, *Roosevelt and Hopkins: An Intimate History* (New York: Harper, 1948), pp. 430–31.

164. Prange, *At Dawn We Slept*, p. 555.

165. Frances Perkins OH, Oral History Project, Columbia University, New York.

166. *PHA*, part 12, pp. 200–202.

167. Prange, *At Dawn We Slept*, p. 558.

168. Berle Diary, Dec. 7, 1941, FRDL.

169. Ronald Lewin, *The Other Ultra* (London: Hutchinson, 1982), p. 67.

170. Wohlstetter, *Pearl Harbor*, p. 387.

171. Kahn, "Pearl Harbor and the Inadequacy of Cryptanalysis." Idem, "The Intelligence Failure at Pearl Harbor," *Foreign Affairs*, Winter 1991–92, pp. 138–52.

172. The findings of the still-classified NSA study are summarized in an article by the NSA historian, Frederick D. Parker, "The Unsolved Messages of Pearl Harbor," *Cryptologia*, vol. 15 (1991), no. 4.

173. John Ferris, "From Broadway House to Bletchley Park: The Diary of Captain Malcolm Kennedy, 1934–1946," *Intelligence and National Security*, vol. 4 (1989), no. 3.

174. John Dower, *War Without Mercy: Race and Power in the Pacific War* (New York: Pantheon Books, 1986), p. 105.

Chapter 4: Roosevelt at War (1941–1945)

1. Stimson Diary, Dec. 31, 1941, Jan. 19, 1942, SLYU.

2. Smith, *Ultra-Magic Deals*, p. 95.

3. The history of the Special Branch is covered by a series of mostly declassified in-house histories in RG 457: SRH-035, SRH-116, SRH-117, SRH-185, SRH-276, NAW.

4. RG 456: SRH-035, NAW.

5. Kahn, "Roosevelt, MAGIC, and ULTRA," pp. 306–308.

6. Lewin, *Other Ultra*, ch. 4.

7. *PHA*, part 3, p. 1158.

8. On Midway, see Kahn, *Codebreakers*, pp. 566–73; Lewin, *Other Ultra*, ch. 4; Layton et al., *And I Was There*, chs. 31, 32; Gordon Prange, *Miracle at Midway* (New York: Penguin Books, 1983).

9. Kahn, "Roosevelt, MAGIC, and ULTRA," p. 312.

10. Andrew and Gordievsky, *KGB*, pp. 271–72.

11. Kahn, "Roosevelt, MAGIC, and ULTRA," p. 312.

12. McCrea, Memorandum for the President, Feb. 18, 1942; Roosevelt, Memoranda for Captain McCrea, May 28, Nov. 30, 1942, PSF 62, Departmental File Navy: McCrea, John L., FDRL.

13. Gilbert, *Churchill*, vol. 6, chs. 10–15. Hinsley et al., *British Intelligence in the Second World War*, vol. 2, part 6.

14. Andrew, "Churchill and Intelligence."

15. FDR to Donovan, Feb. 9, 1942, Confidential File, box 10, FDRL. Bradley F. Smith, *The Shadow Warriors* (London: André Deutsch, 1983), pp. 102–103.

16. See above, p. 100.

17. Smith, *Shadow Warriors*, pp. 90–91.

18. Troy, *Donovan and the CIA*, pp. 118–20.

19. Morgan, *FDR*, pp. 625–29.

20. Berle Diary, Jan. 6, 1942, FDRL.

21. Berle Diary, Sept. 27, 1941, FDRL.

22. Berle Memo, Feb. 13, 1942, Berle Diary, Feb. 13, 1942, FDRL.

23. Berle Diary, Feb. 1, 4, 1942, FDRL.

24. Berle to FDR, Feb. 5, 1942, FDRL.

25. Berle Memo, Feb. 13, 1942, Berle Diary, FDRL; abbreviated version in Beatrice B. Berle and Travis B. Jacobs (eds.), *Navigating the Rapids, 1918–1971: From the Papers of Adolf A. Berle* (New York: Harcourt Brace Jovanovich, 1973), p. 402.

26. Berle Memo, Feb. 26, 1942, Berle Diary, FDRL.

27. Berle Memorandum of Conversation, March 5, 1942, Berle Diary, FDRL.

28. Troy, "The Coordinator of Intelligence and British Intelligence," DDRS, 1990, no. 92, p. 15.

29. Berle Memorandum of Conversation, March 10, 1942, Berle Diary, FDRL.

30. Troy, *Donovan and the CIA*, ch. 6. Berle and Jacobs (eds.), *Navigating the Rapids*, p. 412.

31. Smith, *Shadow Warriors*, ch. 3.

32. Theoharis (ed.), *Secret Files*, ch. 4. Gentry, *Hoover*, pp. 304–306.

33. Stimson Diary, Nov. 9, 1943, SLYU.

34. Dorwart, *Conflict of Duty*, pp. 200–201.

35. Stimson Diary, Nov. 9, 1943, SLYU.

36. Troy, *Donovan and the CIA*, p. 209.

37. Andrew, "Churchill and Intelligence."

38. JIC Memo, M.M.(S)(44)75, Sept. 27, 1944, CAB 122/1417, PRO.

39. J. F. Carter, "Report on Stalin's 'Secret' Board of Strategy, Etc.," Jan. 7, 1942, PSF 98, FDRL.

40. Carter Report, Oct. 8, 1942, PSF 98, FDRL. Smith, *Shadow Warriors*, p. 185.

41. Carter Reports in PSF 98-100; Carter OH, pp. 11–23, FDRL.

42. Carter OH, p. 23, FDRL.

43. Troy, *Donovan and the CIA*, p. 226.

44. There are numerous examples in FDRL.

45. Ray S. Cline, *Secrets, Spies and Scholars* (Washington, D.C.: Acropolis Books, 1976), p. 58. The Americans adopted the British term "Ultra" to denote all high-grade SIGINT. Magic (technically one form of Ultra) remained in use to refer to Japanese diplomatic decrypts, but was occasionally used inaccurately almost as a synonym for Ultra.

46. Robert Murphy, *Diplomat Among Warriors* (New York: Pyramid Books, 1965), pp. 119–20.

47. Cave Brown (ed.), *Secret War Report*, p. 145.

48. Stephen E. Ambrose, *Ike's Spies: Eisenhower and the Espionage Establishment* (Garden City, N.Y.: Doubleday, 1981), p. 44.

49. Morgan, *FDR*, p. 648. Roosevelt and Churchill had agreed on Torch in June 1942 in the teeth of opposition from the president's military advisers, whose sights were set on an early cross-Channel landing in France.

50. See, e.g., Churchill's minute on decrypt no. 104768, May 24, 1942, HW1/592, PRO. To judge from the decrypts so far released in the PRO, the supply of American decrypts to the prime minister ceased after Pearl Harbor. The argument from silence or lack of evidence, however, is never conclusive.

51. Ambrose, *Ike's Spies*, ch. 1.

52. Marshall, Memorandum for the President, July 11, 1942, MR 162, Naval Aide's Files: A-6 Communications, FDRL. The phrasing of the memo suggests that it was a response to an inquiry from FDR. It begins: "I have taken up the question of interchange of information between cipher experts in the British and American Armies with Sir John Dill."

53. Hinsley et al., *British Intelligence in the Second World War*, vol. 2, p. 56.

54. On the breaking of the U-boat Enigma, see David Kahn, *Seizing the Enigma* (Boston: Houghton Mifflin, 1991).

55. Hinsley et al., *British Intelligence in the Second World War*, vol. 3, p. 4n.

56. Kahn, *Seizing the Enigma*, pp. 242–43.

57. Interviews with Sir Harry Hinsley, March-April 1994.

58. Hinsley et al., *British Intelligence in the Second World War*, vol. 2, p. 48.

59. Ibid., chs. 16, 19. Kahn, *Seizing the Enigma*, chs. 20–23.

60. See above, p. 106.

61. "Operations of the Military Intelligence Service War Department London (MIS WD London)," June 11, 1945, pp. 36–37, RG 457: SRH-110, NAW.

62. Interviews with Sir Harry Hinsley, March-April 1994.

63. "Operations of the Military Intelligence Service War Department London (MIS WD London)," June 11, 1945, Tab A, RG 457: SRH-110, NAW.

64. Ibid., p. 38.

65. Lewin, *Other Ultra*, pp. 112–27, 187–91. Layton et al., *And I Was There*, pp. 453–56, 474–76. Ronald H. Spector, *Eagle Against the Sun* (London: Viking, 1985), pp. 451–54.

66. Stimson Diary, Nov. 10, 1943, SLYU.

67. See below, pp. 161–63.

68. For details, see box 370, File 385, RG 218, NAW.

69. Hinsley et al., *British Intelligence in the Second World War*, vol. 2, ch. 16; vol. 3, part 1, appendix 1.

70. Unpublished X-2 History, Entry 176, box 2, File 16, RG 226, NAW.

71. Hinsley et al., *British Intelligence in the Second World War*, vol. 3, part 1, appendix 1.

72. Information from Air and Space Museum, Washington, D.C. See photo insert.

73. Ambrose, *Ike's Spies*, chs. 6, 7. Hinsley et al., *British Intelligence in the Second World War*, vol. 3. Michael Howard, *British Intelligence in the Second World War*, vol. 5.

74. Sherwood, *Roosevelt and Hopkins*, p. 685.

75. Cave Brown, *Last Hero*, pp. 556–58.

76. Charles de Gaulle, *Mémoires de Guerre*, paperback ed. (Paris: Plon, 1956), vol. 2: *L'Unité: 1942–1944*, pp. 291–95.

77. Cave Brown, *Last Hero*, pp. 278–86. Cave Brown (ed.), *Secret War Report*, pp. 318–23.

78. Donovan, Memorandum for the President (enclosing telegram from Allen Dulles of April 12, 1944), April 15, 1944. Unusually, a copy of the memo, marked by Leahy for the president's attention and initialed by Rear Admiral Wilson Brown, is included in the naval aide's file; MR 163, Naval Aide's Files: Intelligence Matters A 8-3, FDRL. From 1942 to 1949 Leahy served under FDR and Truman as "Chief of Staff to the Commander in Chief of the Army and Navy." The post of civilian chief of staff in the White House did not yet exist.

79. Gilbert, *Churchill*, vol. 7, ch. 44.

80. Marshall to Dewey, Sept. 25, 1944, SRH-043, NAW.

81. Marshall, "Memorandum for the President. Subject: 'Magic,'" Feb. 12, 1944, Leahy papers, folder 126, RG 276, NAW.

82. The text of Marshall's letter to Dewey of Sept. 25, 1944, is in George A. Brownell, *The Origin and Development of the Naional Security Agency* (Laguna Hills, Calif.: Aegean Park Press, 1981), Exhibit D. For the rest of the story, see "Statement for Record of Participation of Brigadier General Carter W. Clarke, GSC, in the Transmittal of Letters from General George C. Marshall to Gov. Thomas E. Dewey, the Latter Part of September 1944," RG 457: SRH-043, NAW. See also Lewin, *Other Ultra*, ch. 1.

83. Lewin, *Other Ultra*, p. 13.

84. Troy, *Donovan and the CIA*, appendix M.

85. Andrew and Gordievsky, *KGB*, pp. 284–85. Smith, *Shadow Warriors*, pp. 353–54.

86. G. Edward Buxton (acting director, OSS) to General Deane (U.S. Military Mission in Moscow), Jan. 5, 1945; Fitin to Deane, Feb. 15, 1945; Deane to Fitin, Feb. 15, 1945. Records of U.S. Military Mission in Moscow, box 18, RG 334, NAW.

87. Andrew and Gordievsky, *KGB*, pp. 284–85, 373–74. See below, pp. 178, 195.

88. Troy, *Donovan and the CIA*, pp. 255–59. Cave Brown, *Last Hero*, pp. 627–33.

89. Smith, *Shadow Warriors*, pp. 399–400.

90. Troy, *Donovan and the CIA*, p. 263.

Chapter 5: Harry S. Truman (1945–1953)

1. Harry S. Truman, *Memoirs*, paperback ed. (New York: Signet Books, 1965), vol. 1: *1945, Year of Decision*, p. 31.

2. Speech to the final session of the CIA's Eighth Training Orientation Course, Nov. 21, 1952, Official File 1290-B, HSTL. Until after his election victory in 1948, when Alben Barkley was his running mate, Truman had no vice-president. Thereafter he took the initiative in making sure no future vice-president would be as ignorant as he had been. He promoted a National Security Act Amendment of 1949 (Public Law 81-216) making the vice-president a statutory member of the National Security Council. Interview with Walter Pforzheimer, former CIA legislative counsel, March 15, 1994.

3. Margaret Truman, *Harry S. Truman* (New York: William Morrow, 1973), p. 241.

4. Truman, *Memoirs*, vol. 1, pp. 20–21.

5. Stimson Diary, April 15, 1941, SLYU.

6. Truman, *Memoirs*, vol. 1, pp. 20–21. According to Clark Clifford, Truman "always emphasized that no one had told him anything about the Manhattan Project before he became President." Clark Clifford, *Counsel to the President* (New York: Doubleday, 1992), p. 57.

7. "Memorandum Discussed with the President," April 25, 1945, Stimson Diary, SLYU.

8. Clifford, *Counsel*, p. 58.

9. Stimson Diary, April 12, 13, 18, 20–22, 1945, SLYU.

10. On Vaughan, see OH John R. Steelman, HSTL; Robert H. Ferrell (ed.), *Off the Record: The Private Papers of Harry S. Truman* (New York: Harper & Row, 1980), p. 11; Robert J. Donovan, *Tumultuous Years: The Presidency of Harry S. Truman, 1949–1953* (New York: W. W. Norton, 1982), pp. 115–18; David McCullough, *Truman* (New York: Simon and Schuster, 1992), pp. 365–66, 745–46.

11. Special Log Map Room, April 17, 1945, MR 195, FDRL.

12. Marshall to Truman, April 17, 1945, Marshall papers 81/33, Marshall Library, Lexington, Va. Smith, *Ultra-Magic Deals*, p. 196.

13. Clifford, *Counsel*, p. 3.

14. Special Log Map Room, April 17, 19, 1945, MR 195, FDRL. On the plotting of Japanese fleet movements, see Clifford, *Counsel*, p. 50.

15. See above, pp. 144–45.

16. Smith, *Ultra-Magic Deals*, p. 208.

17. "Japan's Reaction to German Defeat," RG 457: SRH-075, NAW.

18. Travis and Hinsley arrived in Washington on April 26, Loehnis (later director-general of the postwar British SIGINT agency, GCHQ, from 1960 to 1964) a day later. Their times of arrival and departure are recorded on a map in the papers of Sir Harry Hinsley entitled, "Round the World Tour by Sir Edward Travis and Rear-Admiral Rushbrooke and Staffs, 14th March–27th April 1945," prepared by an admiralty cartographer. The earlier part of the world tour—to the Middle East, Indian subcontinent, and Australasia—had been concerned with the transfer of SIGINT resources to the war against Japan with the approach of victory in Europe. Rushbrooke went to Canada instead of the United States. Interviews with Sir Harry Hinsley, March-April 1994.

19. Interviews with Sir Harry Hinsley, March-April 1994. On March 10 the Army-Navy Communications Intelligence Board (ANCIB), reporting directly to Marshall and King, had been founded to oversee cryptanalysis by the armed services and had made some progress in resolving Army-Navy disputes. King refused, however, to envisage an interservice SIGINT agency on the Bletchley Park model. Smith, *Ultra-Magic Deals*, pp. 195–96.

20. Smith, *Ultra-Magic Deals*, pp. 202–203.

21. Walter Millis (ed.), *The Forrestal Diaries* (London: Cassell, 1952), pp. 86–89.

22. "Preliminary Report to Pacific Order of Battle Conference," Aug. 15, 1945, RG 457: SRH-056, NAW.

23. Truman, *Memoirs*, vol. 1, pp. 464–65.

24. "Japan's Surrender Maneuvers," RG 457: SRH-090, NAW.

25. OH George M. Elsey, p. 344, HSTL.

26. An intercept of August 12 from an unidentified source (believed to be "a Tokyo Postal Official whose dispatches in the past regarding inner circle doings have often been confirmed by other sources") did, however, report that the Supreme War Council had met from 3 P. M. on August 9 to 4 A.M. on August 10, and that the armed forces had "held out" on a number of points. An intercepted message from the navy minister on August 15 gave further

information about the council meeting. "Japan's Surrender Maneuvers," RG 457: SRH-090, NAW.

27. Ibid.

28. Ibid. Literally, "banzai" means "hurrah."

29. Truman, *Memoirs*, vol. 1, p. 480.

30. "Japan's Surrender Maneuvers," RG 457: SRH-090, NAW.

31. Truman, *Memoirs*, vol. 1, pp. 480–82.

32. "Japan's Surrender Maneuvers," RG 457: SRH-090, NAW.

33. Colonel Richard Park Jr., "Memorandum for the President," Rose Conway File, n.d., box 15, File OSS/Donovan, HSTL. Park had begun working on the report at the end of 1944, while working as Pa Watson's assistant. At least some of his allegations of waste and "orgies" were exaggerated or ill-founded. On OSS activities at the Congressional Country Club, see *The OSS Assessment of Men: Selection of Personnel for the Office of Strategic Services* (New York: Rinehart & Co., 1948).

34. Donovan to Truman, April 30, 1945, Research File 5, HSTL.

35. Ferrell (ed.), *Off the Record*, p. 24.

36. Cave Brown, *Last Hero*, pp. 775–82. Troy, *Donovan and the CIA*, pp. 270–82.

37. G. Edward Buxton, "Memorandum for the President," June 22, 1945, White House Central Files: OSS, HSTL.

38. Troy, *Donovan and the CIA*, p. 267.

39. Theoharis (ed.), *Secret Files*, pp. 202–209.

40. Gentry, *Hoover*, p. 321.

41. Drew Pearson, *Diaries 1949–1959*, ed. Tula Abell (New York: Holt, Rinehart, 1974), p. 284.

42. OH George M. Elsey, pp. 460–61, HSTL.

43. Donovan, "Memorandum for the President," Aug. 25, 1945, White House Central Files: OSS, HSTL. Donovan's memo somewhat exaggerates the long access of foreign intelligence services "to the highest echelons of their Governments." Bradley F. Smith, to whose research on wartime intelligence all scholars in the field are indebted, makes an uncharacteristic error in asserting (*Shadow Warriors*, p. 405) that, when Donovan wrote to the budget director, he did not also "appeal directly to the White House."

44. Donovan, "Memorandum for the President," Sept. 4, 1945, White House Central Files: OSS, HSTL.

45. RG 226, Entry 99, box 7, folders 28, 29, NAW.

46. Donovan to Truman, Sept. 4, 1945, White House Central Files: OSS, HSTL.

47. Corson, *The Armies of Ignorance*, pp. 245–48.

48. Cline, *Secrets, Spies and Scholars*, pp. 86–87,

49. Smith, *Ultra-Magic Deals*, pp. 202–203.

50. "Memorandum for the President, Subject: Collaboration with the British in the Communications Intelligence Field, Continuation and Extension of," Sept. 12, 1945, Naval Aide Files, box 10, file 1, HSTL.

51. Truman, Memorandum for the Secretaries of State, War, and the Navy, Sept. 12, 1945, ibid. Smith, *Ultra-Magic Deals*, p. 212.

52. Admiralty to Cominch, Sept. 16, 1945, Naval Aide Files, box 10, file 1, HSTL.

53. Andrew and Gordievsky, *KGB*, chs. 8, 10.

54. Interviews with Sir Harry Hinsley, March-April 1994.

55. Minutes of Canadian JIC (attended by Travis, Jones, and Hinsley), Oct. 22, 1945, minute 763: "Peacetime Sig Int [*sic*] Policy"; RG 24: vol. 2469, Public Archives of Canada, Ottawa. I am grateful to Professor Wesley Wark for this reference.

56. Interviews with Sir Harry Hinsley, March-April 1994. On Poulden and the postwar reorganization of Australian SIGINT, see Andrew, "The Growth of the Australian Intelligence Community and the Anglo-American Connection," *Intelligence and National Security*, vol. 4 (1989), no. 2, pp. 223–24.

57. Interviews with Sir Harry Hinsley, March-April 1994.

58. Andrew, "The Growth of the Australian Intelligence Community and the Anglo-American Connection," pp. 223–24. The date of the UKUSA agreement is often wrongly given as 1947. Dr. Louis Tordella, deputy director of NSA from 1958 to 1974, who was present at the signing, confirms that the date was 1948. The other American participants in the 1948 UKUSA negotiations were Colonels Kirby and Hayes of the army, Captain Rocder (U.S. Navy), John Morrison (U.S. Air force), Benson K. Buffham (later deputy director of NSA) and Robert Packard of State. Interviews with Dr. Tordella, November 1987 and April 1992. For details of subsequent UKUSA collaboration, see Jeffrey T. Richelson and Desmond Ball, *The Ties That Bind*, 2nd ed. (Boston: Unwin Hyman, 1990).

59. Truman to Byrnes, Sept. 20, 1945; Troy, *Donovan and the CIA*, appendix T.

60. Troy, *Donovan and the CIA*, p. 303.

61. Truman, *Memoirs*, vol. 1. pp. 117, 253; vol. 2: *Years of Trial and Hope, 1946–1952*, p. 74.

62. Dean Acheson, *Present at the Creation* (New York: W. W. Norton, 1969), pp. 159–60.

63. OH George M. Elsey, pp. 4, 120–21. Interview with Admiral Sidney W. Souers, Dec. 15, 1954, p. 9, Post-Presidential Memoirs, HSTL. Truman wrote at the top of the Souers interview, "You can depend on this guy. He was one of my greatest assets."

64. Interview with Admiral Sidney W. Souers, Dec. 15, 1954, Post-Presidential Memoirs, HSTL. Souers, "Memorandum for Commander Clifford," Clark M. Clifford papers, HSTL.

65. Daniel Yergin, *Shattered Peace: The Origins of the Cold War and the National Security State* (Boston: Houghton Mifflin, 1977), pp. 216–17. R. James Woolsey, Address to Conference on "The Origins and Development of the CIA in the Administration of Harry S. Truman," March 17, 1994.

66. Interview with Admiral Sidney W. Souers, Dec. 15, 1954, pp. 9–10, Post-Presidential Memoirs, HSTL.

67. Russell Jack Smith, *The Unknown CIA* (New York: Berkley, 1992), pp. 27–30, 37–39.

68. CIA, *The CIA Under Harry Truman*, ed. Michael Warner (Washington, D.C.: CIA, 1994), p. 337.

69. Philip S. Meilinger, *Hoyt S. Vandenberg* (Bloomington and Indianapolis: Indiana University Press, 1989).

70. *New York Times*, July 16, 1946. Clifford's assistant, George M. Elsey, noted on the copy of Krock's article in his papers, "Clifford and Vandenberg were the source of this column." George M. Elsey papers, HSTL.

71. Undated memo by Elsey attached to Krock article, ibid.

72. Smith, *Unknown CIA*, p. 42.

73. CIA, *The CIA Under Harry Truman*, p. 337.

74. Andrew and Gordievsky, *KGB*, pp. 369–70.

75. Ibid., pp. 229–30, 278, 281–82, 286, 335–37. Robert J. Donovan, *Conflict and Crisis: The Presidency of Harry S. Truman, 1945–1948* (New York: W. W. Norton, 1977), pp. 173–75. Gentry, *Hoover*, pp. 351–52.

76. Theoharis (ed.), *Secret Files*, pp. 134–35. For Truman's opinion of Tom Clarke, see Merle Miller, *Plain Speaking*, paperback ed. (New York: Berkley Medallion, 1974), p. 418.

77. Church Committee, *Final Report*, book 2, pp. 42–44. Donovan, *Conflict and Crisis*, ch. 31. McCullough, *Truman*, pp. 551–53.

78. Elsey, Memorandum for the File, July 17, 1946, Elsey papers, HSTL.

79. Clifford, *Counsel*, p. 168.

80. Ibid., pp. 146–47, 167–69.

81. Arthur Darling, *The Central Intelligence Agency: An Instrument of Government, to 1950* (University Park: Pennsylvania State University Press, 1990), pp. 14–17.

82. Elsey, Memorandum of Conversations on Jan. 8–9, 1947, Elsey papers, HSTL.

83. Clifford, *Counsel*, p. 169.

84. Truman, *Memoirs*, vol. 2, p. 69.

85. Ibid., p. 77. Interview with Admiral Sidney W. Souers, Dec. 15, 1954, p. 14, Post-Presidential Memoirs, HSTL.

86. Smith, *Unknown CIA*, p. 51.

87. Truman says in his *Memoirs* (vol. 2, p. 76) that the DCI was "usually my first caller of the day," but does not identify Hillenkoetter by name.

88. Truman to Hillenkoetter, Oct. 10, 1950, filed with undated memo on Hillenkoetter; Official File, HSTL.

89. *Washington Post*, Dec. 22, 1963.

90. Clifford, *Counsel*, pp. 169–70.

91. Allen Dulles to Souers, Feb. 10, 1964, Souers papers, box 1, Correspondence—general, HSTL.

92. Allen Dulles, "Memorandum for Mr. Lawrence Houston, General Counsel CIA," April 21, 1964, Miscellaneous Historical Documents Collection, HSTL.

93. "The Position of the United States with Regard to Italy," NSC 1/1, Nov. 14, 1947; Robert J. Lovett, Memorandum for the President, Nov. 20, 1947; Truman, Memorandum for the Executive Secretary, NSC, Nov. 17, 1947; White House Central Files (Confidential), bo.: 27, HSTL.

94. Church Committee, *Final Report*, book 4, pp. 28–29. Allen Dulles

later reminded Truman that he had taken a personal interest in NSC 4/A. Allen Dulles, "Memorandum for Mr.Lawrence Houston, General Counsel CIA," April 21, 1964, Miscellaneous Historical Documents Collection, HSTL.

95. Paper by Dr. Mary McAuliffe of the CIA Center for the Study of Intelligence to CIA/Truman Library Conference on "The Origins and Development of the CIA in the Administration of Harry S. Truman," March 17, 1994.

96. O'Toole, *Honorable Treachery*, pp. 436–37. Townsend Hoopes and Douglas Brinkley, *Driven Patriot: The Life and Times of James Forrestal* (New York: Knopf, 1992), pp. 314–16. Clinton P. Anderson, *Outsider in the Senate* (New York: World Publishing, 1970), pp. 70–71.

97. Paper by Dr. Mary McAuliffe of the CIA Center for the Study of Intelligence to CIA/Truman Library Conference on "The Origins and Development of the CIA in the Administration of Harry S. Truman," March 17, 1994.

98. Church Committee, *Final Report*, book 4, p. 29.

99. NSC 10/2, 18 June 1948: text in William M. Leary (ed.), *The Central Intelligence Agency: History and Documents* (University: University of Alabama Press, 1984), pp. 131–33.

100. NSC, Aug. 20, 1948; cited by Hoopes and Brinkley, *Driven Patriot*, p. 312.

101. Church Committee, *Final Report*, book 4, p. 30.

102. Dulles-Jackson-Correa report, Jan. 1, 1949; partial text in Leary (ed.), *Central Intelligence Agency*, pp. 134–42.

103. Robert M. Blum, "Surprised by Tito: Anatomy of an Intelligence Failure," DDRS, 1987, no. 2738.

104. Franklin Lindsay, *Beacons in the Night* (Stanford, Calif.: Stanford University Press, 1993), pp. 336–37. Interview with Franklin Lindsay, June 1992. "United States Policy Toward the Conflict Between the USSR and Yugoslavia," NSC 18/4, Nov. 17, 1949, PSF box 207, HSTL.

105. "United States Policy Toward the Soviet Satellite States in Eastern Europe," NSC 58/2, Dec. 13, 1949, PSF box 207, HSTL.

106. Donovan, *Conflict and Crisis*, pp. 413–14.

107. Allen Weinstein, *Perjury: The Hiss-Chambers Case* (New York: Knopf, 1978), pp. 174–88, 300–301.

108. Hillenkoetter, Memorandum for the President, July 6, 1948, PSF 249, HSTL.

109. *FRUS 1949*, vol. 1, p. 491.

110. "History of Long Range Detection Program," July 21, 1948, PSF 199, HSTL. Truman, *Memoirs*, vol. 2, pp. 350–51. Richard G. Hewlett and Francis Duncan, *Atomic Shield 1947–1952* (University Park: Pennsylvania University Press, 1969), pp. 362–67. Richard G. Neustadt, "Truman in Action: A Retrospect," in Marc Landy (ed.), *Modern Presidents and the Presidency* (Lexington, Mass.: Lexington Books, 1985), pp. 4–5.

111. *FRUS 1949*, vol. 1, p. 536.

112. Robert J. Lamphere and Tom Schachtman, *The FBI-KGB War*, paperback ed. (New York: Berkley, 1987), pp. 80–88, 137–39. Andrew and Gordievsky, *KGB*, pp. 312–15, 373.

113. Lamphere and Schachtman, *FBI-KGB War*, pp. 140–42. Acheson, *Present at the Creation*, pp. 321, 354–61.

114. Donovan, *Tumultuous Years*, pp. 162–63. McCullough, *Truman*, pp. 764–67. Richard M. Fried, *Nightmare in Red* (Oxford, England: Oxford University Press, 1990), ch. 5.

115. Miller, *Plain Speaking*, pp. 446–47.

116. Richard M. Nixon, *RN: The Memoirs of Richard Nixon*, paperback ed. (New York: Touchstone, 1990), p. 70.

117. Fried, *Nightmare in Red*, p. 121.

118. Among them were the Rosenbergs and the British spy Donald Maclean. Andrew and Gordievsky, *KGB*, pp. 379–81, 395–96.

119. David C. Martin, *Wilderness of Mirrors*, paperback ed. (New York: Ballantine Books, 1981), p. 46. Peter Wright, *Spycatcher* (New York: Viking, 1987), pp. 184–85. Andrew and Gordievsky, *KGB*, pp. 374–75.

120. For the text of NSC 68, see *FRUS 1950*, vol. 1, pp. 234–92. It is reprinted, with a useful series of commentaries, in Ernest R. May (ed.), *American Cold War Strategy: Interpreting NSC 68* (Boston: Bedford Books, 1993). Other commentaries include John L. Gaddis, *Strategies of Containment* (Oxford, England: Oxford University Press, 1982), ch. 4; Melvyn P. Leffler, *A Preponderance of Power* (Stanford, Calif.: Stanford University Press, 1992), pp. 355–60.

121. Andrew and Gordievsky, *KGB*, pp. 387–90.

122. *FRUS 1950*, vol. 1, pp. 234–35.

123. Truman formally approved NSC 68 on September 30, 1950. Ibid., p. 400.

124. Truman, *Memoirs*, vol. 2, pp. 377–79. Acheson, *Present at the Creation*, pp. 402–406. Miller, *Plain Speaking*, ch. 23. Truman's language, as reported in Miller's oral history, is somewhat less presidential than in his memoirs.

125. Acheson, *Present at the Creation*, p. 405.

126. Sergei N. Goncharov, John W. Lewis, and Xue Litai, *Uncertain Partners: Stalin, Mao and the Korean War* (Stanford, Calif.: Stanford University Press, 1993), pp. 213–15. Kathryn Weathersby (ed.), "From the Russian Archives: New Findings on the Korean War," *Cold War International History Project Bulletin* (Washington, D.C.: Woodrow Wilson Center), Fall 1993. pp. 14–17.

127. Dean Rusk, *As I Saw It*, paperback ed. (New York: Penguin Books, 1991), p. 161.

128. Brownell Committee Report, June 13, 1952, p. 41. References are to the published version: George A. Brownell, *The Origin and Development of the National Security Agency* (Laguna Hills, Calif.: Aegean Park Press, 1981).

129. Ibid., pp. 3, 17, 26.

130. See above, p. 169

131. Brownell Committee Report, pp. 17–18. Meilinger, Vandenberg, p. 124.

132. Brownell Committee Report, p. 3.

133. Ibid. Interview with Dr. Louis Tordella (later deputy director of the NSA from 1958 to 1974), April 1992.

134. Ludwell Lee Montague, "General Walter Bedell Smith as Director of Central Intelligence," vol. 5, p. 53; DCI Historical Series, DCI-1, DDRS, 1991, no. 60.

135. Interview with Dr. Louis Tordella, April 1992.

136. Brownell Committee Report, pp. 40–43.

137. Montague, "Bedell Smith," vol. 1, p. 14.

138. Ibid., vol. 2, pp. 5–7.

139. Ibid., vol. 2, p. 26.

140. Ibid., vol. 2, pp. 27–38. Church Committee, *Final Report*, book 4, pp. 30–31.

141. Information on ONE staff. From Mr R. Jack Smith. Margaret Truman, *Harry S. Truman*, p. 484. Rusk, *As I Saw It*, pp. 168–69

142. Rusk, *As I Saw It*, pp. 167–68.

143. Interview with Dr. Louis Tordella, April 1992.

144. "U.S. Minutes Truman-Attlee Conversations," Dec. 4, 1950, *FRUS* 1950, vol. 3, pp. 1711–14.

145. CIA, "Review of the World Situation," Nov. 15, 1950, PSF 250, HSTL.

146. *FRUS* 1950, vol. 3, p. 1714.

147. Brownell Committee Report, pp. 37–39, 54–55.

148. Montague, "Bedell Smith," vol. 5, p. 55.

149. Edward J. Drea, *MacArthur's ULTRA* (Lawrence, Kans.: University of Kansas Press, 1992), pp. 228–31.

150. *FRUS* 1950, vol. 7, pp. 1308–10.

151. "Probable Soviet Moves to Exploit the Present Situation," NIE-15, Dec. 11, 1950, Research File B, HSTL.

152. *PP Truman 1950*, pp. 746–47.

153. Montague, "Bedell Smith," vol. 5, pp. 2–7.

154. Ibid., pp. 35–42.

155. Ibid., vol. 2, p. 83; vol. 4, pp. 54–72.

156. Church Committee, *Final Report*, book 4, pp. 30–32. O'Toole, *Encyclopedia*, p. 267.

157. Smith emphasized to senior staff that "he would not go along with any committee that would interpose itself between the President and him." Montague, "Bedell Smith," vol. 5, p. 1.

158. John L. Hart, "CIA's Russians: Triumph and Tragedy," (unpublished study kindly made available to the author by Mr. Hart), pp. 16–23. Interview with Mr. Hart, April 1992.

159. Interview with John L. Hart, April 1992.

160. Interview with Dr. Louis Tordella, April 1992.

161. Robert F. Futrell, "U.S. Air Force Intelligence in the Korean War," in Hitchcock (ed.), *The Intelligence Revolution: A Historical Perspective* (Washington, D.C.: U.S. Air Force Academy, 1991).

162. O'Toole, *Encyclopedia*, p. 266.

163. Andrew and Gordievsky, *KGB*, pp. 379–81, 395–401. Though suspicion began to fall on Philby immediately after Burgess's defection, conclusive evidence was lacking until the eve of his defection to Moscow in 1963.

164. Interview with Dr. Louis Tordella, April 1992.

165. Smith, "Proposed Survey of Comunications Intelligence Activities," Dec. 10, 1951; approved by Truman, Dec. 13, 1951; PSF 250, File Central Intelligence, HSTL.

166. James S. Lay, Jr., "Proposed Survey of Communications Intelligence Activities," Dec. 13, 1951, ibid.

167. Montague, "Bedell Smith," vol. 5, pp. 54–55.

168. Ibid., p. 55.

169. Brownell Committee Report, part 5.

170. "Communications Intelligence Activities," RG 457: SRH-271, NAW.

171. Bamford, *Puzzle Palace*.

Chapter 6: Dwight D. Eisenhower (1953–1961)

1. James R. Killian, *Sputnik, Scientists and Eisenhower: A Memoir of the First Assistant to the President for Science and Technology* (Cambridge, Mass.: MIT Press, 1967), p. 68.

2. Ambrose, *Ike's Spies*, ch. 1.

3. F. W. Winterbotham, *The Ultra Secret*, paperback ed. (London: Futura, 1975), p. 116.

4. Eisenhower to Menzies, July 12, 1945, Eisenhower papers 1916–52, box 77, File "Melo-Men (misc.)," DDEL.

5. Sir Kenneth Strong, *Intelligence at the Top* (London: Cassell, 1968), pp. 112–17, 176. Ambrose, *Ike's Spies*, pp. 125–29, 319–20.

6. Interview with Eisenhower by imagery expert George W. Goddard of Itek Corporation, January 1967; copy kindly supplied by the former Itek chairman, Franklin Lindsay. In 1939 Eisenhower had become the first future president to gain a pilot's license. On the PIU see Andrew, *Her Majesty's Secret Service*, pp. 469–70.

7. Montague, "Bedell Smith," vol. 2, pp. 85–86; vol. 5, pp. 107–12, DDRS, 1991, no. 60. Interview with Walter Pforzheimer, March 15, 1994.

8. Montague, "Bedell Smith," vol. 5, pp. 112–14, DDRS, 1991, no. 60. Smith might well have opposed the Bay of Pigs. But in 1953–1954 he supported the covert action in both Iran and Guatemala.

9. Fred I. Greenstein, *The Hidden-Hand Presidency* (New York: Basic Books, 1982).

10. Stephen E. Ambrose, *Eisenhower* (New York: Simon and Schuster, 1984), vol. 2, pp. 110–11. Michael R. Beschloss, *Mayday: Eisenhower, Khrushchev and the U-2 Affair* (London: Faber, 1986), pp. 130–32.

11. Leonard Mosley, *Dulles: A Biography of Eleanor, Allen, and John Foster Dulles and Their Family Network* (New York: Dial Press, 1978), pp. 323–25.

12. Acheson, *Present at the Creation*, ch. 52.

13. Mark J. Gasiorowski, "The 1953 Coup d'Etat in Iran," *International Journal of Middle East Studies*, no. 19 (Aug. 1987), pp. 264, 267.

14. C. M. Woodhouse, *Something Ventured* (London: Granada, 1982), p. 117.

15. Anthony Eden, *Full Circle: The Memoirs of Sir Anthony Eden* (London: Cassell, 1960–65), p. 235.

16. Kermit Roosevelt, *Countercoup* (New York: McGraw-Hill, 1979), ch. 1

17. Ibid., pp. 155–57. Woodhouse, *Something Ventured*, pp. 126–27.

18. Gasiorowski, "The 1953 Coup d'Etat," pp. 275, 285.

19. Roosevelt, *Countercoup*, chs. 9–11. Woodhouse, *Something Ventured*, pp. 126–29.

20. *Saturday Evening Post*, Nov. 6, 1954.

21. Roosevelt, *Countercoup*, chs. 12, 13. Woodhouse, *Something Ventured*, pp. 129–31.

22. Ambrose, *Eisenhower*, vol. 2, p. 129. Ambrose, *Ike's Spies*, p. 213.

23. Eisenhower Diary, Sept. 23, 1953, DDEL.

24. Clinc, *Secrets, Spies and Scholars*, p. 132.

25. Berle, "The Guatemalan Problem in Central America," March 31, 1953, Berle Diary, FDRL.

26. Richard Immerman, *The CIA in Guatemala: The Foreign Policy of Intervention* (Austin: University of Texas Press, 1982), pp. 134–35, 142–43.

27. *FRUS 1952–1954*, vol. 4, p. 1173.

28. Immerman, *The CIA in Guatemala*, p. 161.

29. *FRUS 1952–1954*, vol. 4, pp. 1174–76.

30. David Atlee Phillips, *The Night Watch* (New York: Atheneum, 1977), pp. 43–44.

31. Eisenhower's appointment book indicates that the meeting was off the record; *FRUS 1952–1954*, vol. 4, p. 1177. The only available account of it is in Dwight D. Eisenhower, *The White House Years: Mandate for Change, 1953–56* (London: Heinemann, 1963), pp. 424–25.

32. *FRUS 1952–1954*, vol. 4, pp. 1188–93.

33. Immerman, *The CIA in Guatemala*, pp. 176–77.

34. Phillips, *Night Watch*, pp. 49–51.

35. Immerman, *The CIA in Guatemala*, p. 180.

36. *PP Eisenhower 1955*, pp. 191–92.

37. Thomas Powers, *The Man Who Kept the Secrets* (London: Weidenfeld and Nicolson, 1979), p. 88.

38. Report of the Special Study Group [Doolittle Committee] on the Covert Activities of the Central Intelligence Agency, Sept. 30, 1954: extract in Leary (ed.), *Central Intelligence Agency*, pp. 143–45.

39. Church Committee, *Final Report*, book 4, pp. 52–53, 62. John Prados, *Presidents' Secret Wars* (New York: William Morrow, 1986), pp. 109–12.

40. Ambrose, *Ike's Spies*, p. 187.

41. Church Committee, *Final Report*, book 4, p. 51.

42. *FRUS 1952–1954*, vol. 2, part 1, p. 268. Cf. Andrew and Gordievsky, *KGB*, pp. 383–90.

43. Richard Harris Smith, "The First Moscow Station: An Espionage Footnote to the Cold War," *International Journal of Intelligence and Counter-Intelligence*, vol. 3 (1989), no. 3.

44. Charles E. Bohlen, *Witness to History, 1919–1969* (London: Weidenfeld and Nicolson, 1973), p. 456.

45. John L. Hart, "Popov: A Man Who Was Faithful," *Intelligence and National Security*, vol. 10 (1995), no. 1; and further information from Mr. Hart.

46. *FRUS 1952–1954*, vol. 2, part 1, p. 778.

47. Martin, *Wilderness of Mirrors*, pp. 72–90. John Ranelagh, *The Agency* (London: Weidenfeld and Nicolson, 1986), pp. 138–42, 288–96. Andrew and Gordievsky, *KGB*, pp. 437–38. Cline, *Secrets, Spies and Scholars*, pp. 161–62.

48. Brownell Committee Report, pp. 63,71.

49. JCEC (Joint Communications–Electronics Committee) 1371/1, July 10, 1956: cited by Richelson and Ball, *The Ties That Bind*, p. 144.

50. Victor Marchetti and John D. Marks, *The CIA and the Cult of Intelligence*, revised ed. (New York: Dell, 1989), pp. 170–71; and unattributable interviews.

51. FBI Memo, April 26, 1954; Theoharis (ed.), *Secret Files*, pp. 127–28. This memo describes "black bag" techniques in general without specific reference to embassies. One paragraph remains classified.

52. Wright, *Spycatcher*, pp. 84–85.

53. Selwyn Lloyd to E. M. Jones, Sept. 20, 1956, PRO, AIR 20/10621.

54. Interview with Dr. Louis Tordella, April 1992.

55. Bamford, *Puzzle Palace*, pp. 153–54.

56. Andrew and Gordievsky, *KGB*, p. 405.

57. Wright, *Spycatcher*, pp. 110–12.

58. The other sources were Bentley, Chambers, and Guzenko. Ambrose, *Eisenhower*, vol. 2, p. 139. Andrew and Gordievsky, *KGB*, pp. 281–82, 370.

59. Unattributable interview.

60. Memorandum of conversation, n.d., Ann Whitman Diary, box 9, folder "October 1957," DDEL. *Aviation Week*, Oct. 21, 1957. John Prados, *The Soviet Estimate*, revised ed. (Princeton, N.J.: Princeton University Press, 1986), pp. 35–37.

61. Interviews in *U.S. News and World Report*, March 15, 1993.

62. On "ferret" losses, see ibid., pp. 32–33. A limited number of missions by British Canberras during Ike's first term were able to penetrate further into Soviet airspace.

63. Dino A. Brugioni, *Eyeball to Eyeball: The Inside Story of the Cuban Missile Crisis* (New York: Random House, 1991), p. 7.

64. Dwight D. Eisenhower, *The White House Years, 1956–61: Waging Peace* (London: Heinemann, 1966), p. 544.

65. Brugioni, *Eyeball to Eyeball*, p. 9.

66. Killian, *Sputnik, Scientists and Eisenhower*, pp. 67–71.

67. Brugioni, *Eyeball to Eyeball*, pp. 15–18.

68. Ambrose, *Ike's Spies*, p. 268.

69. Killian, *Sputnik, Scientists and Eisenhower*, p. 84.

70. Eisenhower, *Waging Peace*, pp. 544–55.

71. Ibid. Cline, *Secrets, Spies and Scholars*, pp. 156–57.

72. Church Committee, *Final Report*, book 4, p. 59.

73. Ibid.

74. Eisenhower, *Mandate for Change*, pp. 520–21.

75. Eisenhower, *Waging Peace*, pp. 545–46.

76. Ambrose, *Ike's Spies*, pp. 279–80.

77. Brugioni, *Eyeball to Eyeball*, pp. 30–31.

78. Beschloss, *Mayday*, p. 158. President Bush somewhat cryptically told reporters in July 1990, "There's a plain mystery by a guy named Beschloss called 'Mayday' that I started to read and put aside because Barbara gave me [an]other one." *PP Bush 1990*, vol. 2, p. 1021.

79. Brugioni, *Eyeball to Eyeball*, p. 31.

80. Eisenhower, *Waging Peace*, p. 547n.

81. Prados, *The Soviet Estimate*, ch. 4.

82. W. Scott Lucas, *Divided We Stand: Britain, the United States and the Suez Crisis* (London: Hodder and Stoughton, 1991), pp. 109–13.

83. Evelyn Shuckburgh, *Descent to Suez: Diaries, 1951–56* (London: Weidenfeld and Nicolson, 1986), pp. 346.

84. Wilbur C. Eveland, *Ropes of Sand* (New York: W. W. Norton, 1980), pp. 168–71, 180–82.

85. Ibid., chs. 18, 19.

86. *FRUS 1955–57*, vol. 16, pp. 9–11.

87. Eden to Macmillan, Sept. 23, 1956, FO 800/740, PRO.

88. Alistair Horne, *Macmillan 1891–1956* (London: Macmillan, 1988), pp. 420–22.

89. Lucas, *Divided We Stand*, p. 217.

90. Ibid., p. 326.

91. Eisenhower, *Waging Peace*, p. 53.

92. Horne, *Macmillan 1891–1956*, pp. 428–34. Lucas, *Divided We Stand*, ch. 20.

93. Allen Dulles OH, p. 73. John Foster Dulles Oral History Collection, Mudd Library, Princeton University.

94. Eisenhower refers obliquely but unmistakably to the interception of diplomatic traffic between France and Israel (*Waging Peace*, pp. 73, 82); he considered NSA, however, too secret to mention at any point in his memoirs.

95. Brugioni, *Eyeball to Eyeball*, p. 33.

96. Eisenhower, *Waging Peace*, p. 677.

97. Allen Dulles OH, p. 73.

98. Lucas, *Divided We Stand*, p. 254. Among those spreading the disinformation were Eden and Lloyd.

99. Eisenhower, *Waging Peace*, p. 676.

100. John Foster Dulles papers, telephone call series, box 5, Oct. 18, 1956, DDEL.

101. Eisenhower, *Waging Peace*, p. 58.

102. NIE 11-3-55; quoted in Raymond L. Garthoff, *Assessing the Adversary* (Washington, D.C.: Brookings Institution, 1991), p. 19.

103. Cord Meyer, *Facing Reality* (New York: Harper & Row, 1980), pp. 126–27.

104.   Eisenhower, *Waging Peace*, pp. 64–65. *FRUS 1955–57*, vol. 16, pp. 774n, 775.

105.   Eisenhower, *Waging Peace*, p. 65.

106.   *FRUS 1955–57*, vol. 25, pp. 280–86.

107.   *FRUS 1955–57*, vol. 16, p. 784.

108.   *FRUS 1955–57*, vol. 25, p. 299. Eisenhower, *Waging Peace*, pp. 67–68.

109.   Eisenhower, *Waging Peace*, p. 68.

110.   Ibid., pp. 68–70. *FRUS 1955–57*, vol. 25, pp. 309–13, 317; vol. 16, p. 795.

111.   Eisenhower, *Waging Peace*, p. 70. *FRUS 1955–57*, vol. 16, pp. 798–801.

112.   Lucas, *Divided We Stand*, p. 255.

113.   Piers Brendon, *Ike: The Life and Times of Dwight D. Eisenhower* (London: Secker and Warburg, 1987), p. 327.

114.   *FRUS 1955–57*, vol. 25, p. 321.

115.   Eisenhower, *Waging Peace*, pp. 71–72. *FRUS 1955–57*, vol. 16, pp. 815–16.

116.   *FRUS 1955–57*, vol. 16, pp. 833–39.

117.   Eveland, *Ropes of Sand*, p. 227.

118.   *FRUS 1955–57*, vol. 16, pp. 848–52. On British fears that the Americans had "cracked the Paris-Tel Aviv correspondence," see William Clark, *From Three Worlds* (London: Sidgwick & Jackson, 1980), p. 202.

119.   Horne, *Macmillan 1891–1956*, p. 438.

120.   Lucas, *Divided We Stand*, p. 263.

121.   *FRUS 1955–57*, vol. 25, p. 342.

122.   *FRUS 1955–57*, vol. 16, p. 884.

123.   Eisenhower, *Waging Peace*, p. 79.

124.   *FRUS 1955–57*, vol. 25, p. 351.

125.   Richard Bissell OH, p. 23; John Foster Dulles Oral History Collection, Mudd Library, Princeton University.

126.   Brugioni, *Eyeball to Eyeball*, p. 34.

127.   *FRUS 1955–57*, vol. 25, p. 358.

128.   *FRUS 1955–57*, vol. 16, pp. 902–16.

129.   Ibid., pp. 944–45.

130.   Ibid., pp. 968–72.

131.   Brendon, *Ike*, p. 329.

132.   *FRUS 1955–57*, vol. 16, p. 918.

133.   Chester Cooper, *The Lion's Last Roar: Suez 1956* (New York: Harper & Row, 1978), p. 181.

134.   Eisenhower, *Waging Peace*, pp. 87–89.

135.   *FRUS 1955–57*, vol. 16, pp. 989, 1000–01. Emmet Hughes, *The Ordeal of Power: A Political Memoir of the Eisenhower Administration* (London: Macmillan, 1963), p. 223.

136.   *FRUS 1955–57*, vol. 16, p. 1004.

137.   Eisenhower, *Waging Peace*, p. 91.

138.   Ibid.

139.   Horne, *Macmillan 1891–1956*, p. 440.

140. Eisenhower, *Waging Peace*, pp. 91–92.

141. *FRUS 1955–57*, vol. 16, pp. 1025–27.

142. Eisenhower, *Waging Peace*, p. 93.

143. *FRUS 1955–57*, vol. 16, pp. 1052–53, 1077, 1080, 1101, 1114, 1121.

144. Ibid., p. 1136.

145. Ibid., pp. 1249–71. Preparation of the report was overseen by W. Park Armstrong, special assistant for intelligence to Foster Dulles, and "reviewed by the Central Intelligence Agency."

146. *FRUS 1955–57*, vol. 24, p. 142.

147. See Allen Dulles's (still partly classified) briefing to the NSC on the Soviet missile program on Jan. 24, 1957. *FRUS 1955–57*, vol. 19, pp. 409–10.

148. *FRUS 1955–57*, vol. 24, p. 162.

149. Ambrose, *Ike's Spies*, p. 273.

150. Beschloss, *Mayday*, p. 155. John Ranelagh, *CIA: A History* (London: BBC Books, 1992), p. 149.

151. Prados, *The Soviet Estimate*, p. 65.

152. *FRUS 1955–57*, vol. 19, pp. 571, 594.

153. *FRUS 1955–57*, vol. 24, p. 162.

154. Eisenhower, *Waging Peace*, pp. 211, 216. Killian, *Sputnik, Scientists and Eisenhower*, pp. 1–10.

155. Prados, *The Soviet Estimate*, p. 65.

156. Eisenhower, *Waging Peace*, pp. 223–25.

157. Ambrose, *Eisenhower*, vol. 2, pp. 434–5. Killian, *Sputnik, Scientists and Eisenhower*, pp. 96–101.

158. *FRUS 1955–57*, vol. 19, p. 712.

159. Killian, *Sputnik, Scientists and Eisenhower*, pp. xv, 20–37, 144–45.

160. Eisenhower, *Waging Peace*, p. 547n.

161. Brugioni, *Eyeball to Eyeball*, pp. 36–37.

162. Ambrose, *Eisenhower*, p. 563.

163. Memorandum of conference, Feb. 5, 1960; memorandum for record, Feb. 8, 1960, WHO 88 Alpha, DDEL. Ambrose, *Eisenhower*, vol. 2, p. 568.

164. Brugioni, *Eyeball to Eyeball*, pp. 43–44.

165. "A New Look at the U-2 Case," *U.S. News and World Report*, March 15, 1993.

166. Brugioni, *Eyeball to Eyeball*, p. 44.

167. Eisenhower, *Waging Peace*, pp. 543, 547–48.

168. Beschloss, *Mayday*, p. 41.

169. Ibid., pp. 42–45. Eisenhower, *Waging Peace*, p. 548.

170. Beschloss, *Mayday*, pp. 53–54.

171. Ibid., pp. 58–61.

172. Ibid., pp. 64–65. Eisenhower, *Waging Peace*, pp. 549–50.

173. Ambrose, *Ike's Spies*, p. 279.

174. Brugioni, *Eyeball to Eyeball*, p. 44.

175. Beschloss, *Mayday*, p. 27.

176. Ibid., pp. 243–50.

177. Ibid., pp. 250–55.

178. Brugioni, *Eyeball to Eyeball*, pp. 46–47.

179.   Beschloss, *Mayday*, pp. 257–58.

180.   *PP Eisenhower 1960–61*, pp. 403–4.

181.   Beschloss, *Mayday*, p. 266.

182.   Eisenhower, *Waging Peace*, pp. 533–37.

183.   *PP Eisenhower 1960–61*, p. 163.

184.   Brugioni, *Eyeball to Eyeball*, p. 53.

185.   Beschloss, *Mayday*, pp. 341–42.

186.   Eric Schmitt, "Spy-Satellite Unit Faces a New Life in Daylight," *New York Times*, Nov. 3, 1992.

187.   Prados, *Presidents' Secret Wars*, pp. 132–45. Powers, *Man Who Kept the Secrets*, pp. 89–92. Ambrose, *Ike's Spies*, pp. 249–51. Ranelagh, *CIA*, pp. 103–105. Cline, *Secrets, Spies and Scholars*, pp. 181–83. Mosley, *Dulles*, pp. 436–38.

188.   *FRUS 1958–60*, vol. 6, p. 1002.

189.   Ambrose, *Ike's Spies*, pp. 304, 308–309.

190.   *FRUS 1958–60*, vol. 6, p. 789.

191.   Ambrose, *Ike's Spies*, p. 309.

192.   *FRUS 1958–60*, vol. 6, pp. 850–51, 861–63. Much of the four-point plan remains classified.

193.   Church Committee, *Alleged Assassination Plots*, pp. 72–81, 92–97, 109. Ambrose, *Ike's Spies*, pp. 303–306.

194.   Church Committee, *Alleged Assassination Plots*, pp. 13–18. Ambrose, *Ike's Spies*, pp. 293–301.

195.   *FRUS 1958–60*, vol. 14, pp. 443, 490, 496–97, 528. The report alleging that Lumumba was "a drug fiend" came from the secretary-general of the UN, Dag Hammarskjöld.

196.   Church Committee, *Alleged Assassination Plots*, pp. 19–33. Ambrose, *Ike's Spies*, pp. 301–303.

197.   *FRUS 1958–60*, vol. 6, p. 1050.

198.   Macmillan to Eisenhower, July 22, 1960, Whitman File (International), DDEL.

199.   *FRUS 1958–60*, vol. 6, pp. 1032–33.

200.   Ibid., pp. 1057–60. Ambrose (*Ike's Spies*, p. 311) puts the Cuban covert action budget at $13 million.

201.   Gregory F. Treverton, *Covert Action* (New York: Basic Books, 1987), p. 87.

202.   *FRUS 1958–60*, vol. 6, p. 1128.

203.   Ibid., p. 1175.

204.   Eisenhower, *Waging Peace*, p. 614.

205.   *PP Eisenhower 1960–61*, p. 925.

206.   Brugioni, *Eyeball to Eyeball*, pp. 55, 568–69.

Chapter 7: John F. Kennedy (1961–1963)

1.   Theodore Sorensen, *Kennedy* (New York: Harper & Row, 1965), p. 309.

2.   The most important available sources for the history of the Bay of

Pigs operation are the sanitized records and report (dated June 13, 1961) of the inquiry of the Cuban Study Group appointed by Kennedy and chaired by General Maxwell D. Taylor, in NSF: boxes 61A and 61B, JFKL. The inquiry concluded that, by the time of Kennedy's election, "the impossibility of running [the invasion] as a covert operation under CIA should have been recognized" (Memorandum no. 3., "Conclusions of the Cuban Study Group," box 61A). The sanitized version declassified in 1977 was published as *Operation ZAPATA: The "Ultrasensitive" Report and Testimony of the Board of Inquiry on the Bay of Pigs* (Frederick, Md.: University Publications of America, 1981), cited hereafter as *Zapata*. Since this publication, some further sections of the Taylor report have been declassified. See, e.g., the record of the first meeting of the Cuban Study Group in DDRS, 1991, no. 653. The most detailed secondary account is Peter Wyden, *Bay of Pigs* (London: Jonathan Cape, 1979).

3. Case Study C14-80-280, KSG.

4. Nigel Hamilton, *JFK: Restless Youth* (London: Century Co., 1992), pp. 407–409, 450, 493.

5. Michael McClintock, *Instruments of Statecraft: U.S. Guerrilla Warfare, Counter-Insurgency, and Counter-Terrorism, 1940–1990* (New York: Pantheon Books, 1992), pp. 161–65. Arthur M. Schlesinger Jr, *A Thousand Days* (London: André Deutsch, 1965), pp. 282–83, 309–10.

6. *Life*, March 17, 1961. Rhodri Jeffreys-Jones, *The CIA and American Democracy* (New Haven: Yale University Press, 1989), p. 128.

7. Brugioni, *Eyeball to Eyeball*, pp. 56–57.

8. 1990 interview with McNamara, quoted in Jerrold L. Schecter and Peter S. Deriabin *ie Spy Who Saved the World* (New York: Charles Scribner's Sons, 1992) pp. 280–81.

9. Brugioni, *Eyeball to Eyeball*, pp. 56–58.

10. Robert Amory OH, pp. 19–20, JFKL.

11. The recollection is that of Richard Neustadt, while intervewing Walt Rostow: Rostow OH, p. 39, JFKL.

12. Schlesinger, *Thousand Days*, p. 218.

13. Arthur M. Schlesinger Jr., Memorandum for the President, June 30, 1961, NSF: box 271, File "CIA," JFKL.

14. Robert Amory OH, pp. 16–17, JFKL.

15. Hamilton, *JFK: Reckless Youth*, p. 450.

16. Interview with Dr. Louis Tordella, deputy-director of NSA from 1958 to 1974, in April 1992.

17. The precise figures remain classified.

18. *Zapata*, pp. 8–9. Wyden, *Bay of Pigs*, pp. 68–69.

19. Sorensen, *Kennedy*, p. 295.

20. Schlesinger, *Thousand Days*, pp. 218, 263.

21. Schlesinger, *Thousand Days*, p. 211.

22. Richard G. Neustadt and Ernest May, *Thinking in Time: The Uses of History for Decision-Makers* (New York: Free Press, 1986), p. 1.

23. *Zapata*, p. 9. Michael R. Beschloss, *Kennedy v. Khrushchev: The Crisis Years, 1960–63* (London: Faber, 1991), p. 104.

24. NSAM 2, 3 Feb. 1961; McNamara to Bundy, "Development of Counter-Guerilla Forces," Feb. 23, 1961, NSF: box 328, JFKL.

25. Memorandum for Mr. Bundy, Feb. 6, 1961, NSF: box 328, JFKL.

26. Beschloss, *Kennedy v. Khrushchev*, p. 105.

27. Sorensen, *Kennedy*, p. 296.

28. Schlesinger, *Thousand Days*, p. 224.

29. Amory OH, p. 24, JFKL.

30. Schlesinger, *Thousand Days*, p. 232.

31. Ibid., pp. 217–20. *Zapata*, pp. 12–15. NSAM 31, NSF: box 329, JFKL.

32. Beschloss, *Kennedy v. Khrushchev*, pp. 89, 107–109.

33. Rusk, *As I Saw It*, pp. 209–10.

34. Cline, *Secrets, Spies and Scholars*, p. 187.

35. Beschloss, *Kennedy v. Khrushchev*, pp. 89, 138–39. Smathers OH, tape 2, pp. 6b, 7b, JFKL. Richard Reeves, *President Kennedy: Profile of Power* (New York: Simon and Schuster, 1993), pp. 265–66, 336–37, 713–14. Thomas C. Reeves, *A Question of Character: A Life of John F. Kennedy* (Rocklin, Calif.: Prima Publishing, 1992), pp. 259–62, though taking an ungenerous view of Kennedy, counters effectively some of the objections of members of the administration who, ignorant themselves of the assassination plots, cannot accept that the president could have known. Kennedy was good at keeping secrets from his advisers. Most were stunned to discover in 1982 that the president had taped 325 conversations. Arthur Schlesinger had previously called the idea that such tapes existed "absolutely inconceivable." It is known that Smathers had a number of discussions with Kennedy about the Cuban operation. A large part of the Smathers oral history in the Kennedy Library is closed to researchers, as are most of the tapes.

36. *Zapata*, pp. 127–30.

37. Amory OH, pp. 121–22.

38. *Zapata*, pp. 18–21. Rusk, *As I Saw It*, pp. 210–12. Schlesinger, *Thousand Days*, ch. 11. Wyden, *Bay of Pigs*, chs. 5, 6.

39. Phillips, *Night Watch*, p. 109.

40. Clifford, *Counsel*, p. 349.

41. *Zapata*, pp. 21–35. Wyden, *Bay of Pigs*, ch. 6. Phillips, *Night Watch*, pp. 108–11.

42. *PP Kennedy 1961*, p. 313.

43. Schlesinger, *Thousand Days*, p. 234.

44. Wyden, *Bay of Pigs*, p. 311.

45. Following six months' preparatory work by the CIA and the General Services Administration, the situation room opened for business in January 1962, exactly twenty years after the inauguration of the map room. Schlesinger, *Thousand Days*, pp. 268–70. John Prados, *Keepers of the Keys: A History of the National Security Council from Truman to Bush* (New York: William Morrow, 1991), pp. 104–106.

46. Smith, *Unknown CIA*, pp. 173–74. The first checklist was dated June 17, 1961; see photo insert.

47. Beschloss, *Kennedy v. Khrushchev*, p. 3. The great majority of the

checklists prepared for Kennedy, as for other presidents, remain classified. There are, however, some sanitized checklists in NSF: Chester V. Clifton series, Intelligence Checklists, JFKL.

48. Beschloss, *Kennedy v. Khrushchev*, ch. 9.

49. Schecter and Deriabin, *Spy*, chs. 5–10. The authors are the first to gain access to Penkovsky's debriefs and associated CIA reports, which are extensively quoted in their book. Previous accounts of the Berlin crisis fail to take account of Penkovsky's intelligence. Studies of Kennedy generally underestimate the impact of Penkovsky's intelligence on him. There is, for example, no mention of Penkovsky at all in the two thousand pages of Schlesinger's *Thousand Days* and *Robert Kennedy and His Times* (New York: Ballantine Books, 1979), or in the most recent biography of JFK by Richard Reeves.

50. Schecter and Deriabin, *Spy*, pp. 225–26.

51. Beschloss, *Kennedy v Khrushchev*, pp. 272–73. Schlesinger, *Thousand Days*, pp. 356–57.

52. Schecter and Deriabin, *Spy*, p. 226.

53. Beschloss, *Kennedy v. Khrushchev*, p. 291.

54. Schecter and Deriabin, *Spy*, pp. 92–93, 225–72.

55. Rusk, *As I Saw It*, p. 226.

56. Cline, *Secrets, Spies and Scholars*, pp. 191–95. Smith, *Unknown CIA*, pp. 176–78.

57. *Zapata*, pp. 1, 44–45. Church Committee, *Final Report*, book 4, p. 51. NSF: NSAM 57, 28 June 1961, JFKL.

58. U. Alexis Johnson OH, pp. 37–39, JFKL.

59. Memorandum for DDP, "Policy Coordination Status of Covert Action Projects," Jan. 16, 1963: DDRS, 1984, no. 81.

60. Roswell Gilpatric OH, p. 38, JFKL.

61. NSF: NSAM 124, Jan. 2, 1962, JFKL. McClintock, *Instruments of Statecraft*, pp. 166–67.

62. Clifford, *Counsel*, pp. 349–56. Schlesinger, *Robert Kennedy*, pp. 493–94. On the foundation of the DIA, see Patrick Mescall, "The Birth of the Defense Intelligence Agency," in Rhodri Jeffreys-Jones and Andrew Lownie (eds.), *North American Spies* (Edinburgh: Edinburgh University Press, 1991), pp. 158–201.

63. Clifford, *Counsel*, pp. 351–52. Prados, *The Soviet Estimate*, pp. 178–80. Brugioni, *Eyeball to Eyeball*, p. 57.

64. NIE 11-8/1-61.

65. Roger Hilsman, *To Move a Nation* (New York: Doubleday, 1967), pp. 163–64.

66. Beschloss, *Kennedy v. Khrushchev*, pp. 329–31.

67. Clifford, *Counsel*, p. 352.

68. Phillips, *Night Watch*, p. 112.

69. Schlesinger, *Robert Kennedy*, pp. 508–509. Idem, *Thousand Days*, pp. 227–28.

70. Church Committee, *Alleged Assassination Plots*, p. 142n.

71. Schecter and Deriabin, *Spy*, p. 249.

72. Ranelagh, *The Agency*, pp. 385–90. Beschloss, *Kennedy v. Khrushchev*, pp. 375–77. Schlesinger, *Robert Kennedy*, pp. 518–22. On the question of Kennedy's knowledge of assassination plots, Beschloss is more persuasive than Schlesinger.

73. U. Alexis Johnson OH, p. 38, JFKL.

74. Cline, *Secrets, Spies and Scholars*, pp. 188–89.

75. Beschloss, *Kennedy v. Khrushchev*, p. 147.

76. Schlesinger, *Thousand Days*, chs. 6, 12, 13.

77. Theoharis (ed.), *Secret Files*, pp. 15–51. Gentry, *Hoover*, pp. 467–74. On JFK's affair with Inga Arvad, see Hamilton, *JFK: Reckless Youth*, pp. 417–92.

78. Clifford, *Counsel*, pp. 331–32.

79. Theoharis (ed.), *Secret Files*, pp. 35–47. Judith Campbell Exner, *My Story* (New York: Grove, 1977). Reeves, *Question of Character*, pp. 240–44, 318–27. Beschloss, *Kennedy v. Khrushchev*, pp. 141–43.

80. Andrew and Gordievsky, *KGB*, pp. 470–71

81. Georgi Bolshakov, "The Hot Line," *New Times* [Moscow], 1989, nos. 4–6.

82. Schlesinger, *Thousand Days*, pp. 537–39. On this point, Schlesinger seems to share Robert Kennedy's naïveté.

83. Edwin O. Guthman and Jeffrey Shulman (eds.), *Robert Kennedy in His Own Words: The Unpublished Recollections of the Kennedy Years* (New York: Bantam Books, 1988), pp. 258–61.

84. Bolshakov, "Hot Line," *New Times*, 1989, no. 4.

85. Andrew and Gordievsky, *KGB*, pp. 470–73.

86. Beschloss, *Kennedy v. Khrushchev*, pp. 155–57.

87. Andrew and Gordievsky, *KGB*, pp. 287–90, 332–34, 349–50. On Hopkins and Akhmerov see also *The Intelligence War in 1941*, pp. 20–22. Some KGB veterans apparently still mistakenly believe that Hopkins was a conscious NKVD agent. See Brian Crozier, *Free Agent* (London: HarperCollins, 1993), pp. 1–2.

88. Beschloss, *Kennedy v. Khrushchev*, pp. 255, 280.

89. Bolshakov, "Hot Line," *New Times*, 1989, nos. 4–6.

90. *CMC (NSA)*, pp. 5–6, 36, 40–51.

91. NIE 85-2-62, *CMC (CIA)*, pp. 9–12.

92. Robert F. Kennedy, *Thirteen Days* (London: Macmillan, 1969), p. 32. Beschloss, *Kennedy v. Khrushchev*, p. 419n. As well as seeking to diminish McCone's role, Robert Kennedy tended to exaggerate his own (undoubtedly significant) role in the missile crisis at the expense of his brother's. When challenged on this point in 1968 by Kenneth O'Donnell, he replied, "Well, he's not running for President this year, and I am."

93. *CMC (CIA)*, pp. 9–24, 31–32.

94. Ibid., pp. 25–26.

95. *CMC (NSA)*, pp. 5–6.

96. *CMC (CIA)*, pp. 27–29.

97. Brugioni, *Eyeball to Eyeball*, pp. 84–86.

98. Between May 31 and October 5, 138 "raw reports" of missile sightings were referred to NPIC for comment. According to a later memo to the DCI, "Of this total, only three cited missile activity which could not be linked directly to the SA-2 and cruise missile deployments. NPIC's evidence negated those three." *CMC (CIA)*, p. 100.

99. Ibid., pp. 13, 35, 39, 127, 366.

100. Beschloss, *Kennedy v. Khrushchev*, p. 420.

101. *CMC (CIA)*, p. 40. Brugioni, *Eyeball to Eyeball*, pp. 120–27. Brugioni gives the date of the briefing on Banes as September 7. According to CIA records, it took place "late" on September 6. The USIB was briefed on September 7.

102. *CMC (CIA)*, pp. 71–73.

103. Ibid., pp. 14, 40, 51, 56, 62, 127–35.

104. Ibid., p. 41.

105. Ibid., pp. 83–84, 87–93.

106. Ibid., pp. 99, 101, 103–4. Samuel Halpern, "Revisiting the Cuban Missile Crisis," *Society for Historians of American Foreign Relations Newsletter,* vol. 25 (1994), no. 7, p. 2.

107. *CMC (CIA)*, p. 115.

108. Schecter and Deriabin, *Spy*, pp. 318–37.

109. *CMC (CIA)*, pp. 111–13.

110. Ibid., pp. 115–17.

111. Ibid., pp. 123–25.

112. Ibid., pp. 149–51.

113. Schlesinger, *Thousand Days*, p. 685. Brugioni, *Eyeball to Eyeball*, p. 208.

114. *CMC (CIA)*, p. 150.

115. Schlesinger, *Thousand Days*, p. 685.

116. *CMC (CIA)*, p. 151.

117. A sanitized transcript of the meeting, which omits all reference to SIGINT, is now available in the Kennedy Library. At the request of the Kennedy family, Caroline's conversation with her father also remains closed. The available transcript reveals, however, that each of them spoke three times before she left the room. There are significant differences between the transcript and those secondary accounts of the meeting that rely in whole or in part on the memories of participants. Part of the transcript is published in *CMC (NSA)*, pp. 85–96.

118. Ibid. On Lundahl's use of the briefing boards, see Brugioni, *Eyeball to Eyeball*, ch. 17. Brugioni also demonstrates the unreliability of Robert Kennedy's account of the meeting in *Thirteen Days*.

119. Brugioni, *Eyeball to Eyeball*, p. 232.

120. Rusk, *As I Saw It*, p. 232.

121. Robert Kennedy, *Thirteen Days*, pp. 35–37. Schlesinger, *Robert Kennedy*, p. 546. Ex-Comm was not, as is sometimes claimed, an abbreviation invented only later. McCone used it at the time; see *CMC (CIA)*, p. 333.

122. *CMC (CIA)*, pp. 153–54. Halpern, "Revisiting the Cuban Missile Crisis," p. 5.

123. Brugioni, *Eyeball to Eyeball*, pp. 251–53, 284. *CMC (CIA)*, p. 157.

124. Even the four-line summary on the "substantial contribution" of SIG-INT operations in the later PFIAB report on the missile crisis remains classified; *CMC (CIA)*, p. 363. Brugioni, then an NPIC analyst, confirms that they were on a "massive" scale; *Eyeball to Eyeball*, pp. 251, 281. For a rare uncensored indication of CIA's insistence on being informed "immediately if NSA came up with further information" on Cuba, see *CMC (CIA)*, p. 40.

125. Robert Kennedy, *Thirteen Days*, p. 85. Like all Ex-Comm members, Kennedy was unable to refer directly to SIGINT operations in his memoirs; he therefore refers to the ELINT ship as "a United States military ship with extremely sensitive equipment (similar to the *Liberty* that was struck by Israel during the Israeli-Arab war)."

126. Brugioni, *Eyeball to Eyeball*, pp. 281–82. Cf. the later PFIAB comments on the value of "intelligence previously obtained concerning strategic missile and air defense installations within the Soviet Union in determining the nature and extent of similar capabilities in Cuba"; *CMC (CIA)*, p. 363.

127. *CMC (CIA)*, pp. 203–208, 227–34, 261–62, 281–82, 293–94. On Ironbark, see above, p. 270.

128. *CMC (CIA)*, pp. 187–91.

129. Ibid., pp. 193–94.

130. Ibid., pp. 203–208.

131. Beschloss, *Kennedy v. Khrushchev*, pp. 460, 469.

132. *CMC (CIA)*, pp. 221–26. Brugioni, *Eyeball to Eyeball*, pp. 311–15.

133. Chester L. Cooper OH, pp. 23–32, JFKL.

134. Sherman Kent papers, series III, box 4, folder 37: "Trip to Paris 1962"; Sherman Kent, "Reminiscences of a Varied Life," pp. 305–10, SLYU .

135. Brugioni, *Eyeball to Eyeball*, pp. 330–32.

136. Smith, *Unknown CIA*, pp. 183–84.

137. Brugioni, *Eyeball to Eyeball*, pp. 333–34.

138. Ibid., p. 351.

139. *CMC (CIA)*, pp. 271–73.

140. Brugioni, *Eyeball to Eyeball*, pp. 353–62.

141. *CMC (CIA)*, pp. 275–79.

142. Schlesinger, *Thousand Days*, p. 694.

143. *CMC (NSA)*, pp. 150–54.

144. Beschloss, *Kennedy v. Khrushchev*, p. 500.

145. Rusk, *As I Saw It*, p. 235.

146. *CMC (CIA)*, p. 353.

147. Ibid., pp. 289–90.

148. Though the briefing itself remains classified, a later summary of McCone's Ex-Comm briefings reveals its subject. Ibid., pp. 292, 353.

149. Ibid., p. 291.

150. Brugioni, *Eyeball to Eyeball*, pp. 382–83, 389–91.

151. Chester L. Cooper OH, pp. 26–30. Cooper's recollection was that permission had been given by Bundy's assistant, Michael J. Forrestal.

152. Brugioni, *Eyeball to Eyeball*, p. 398.

153. Robert Kennedy, *Thirteen Days*, pp. 69–71. Ex-Comm "Record of Action," Meeting no. 3, 10 A.M., Oct. 24, 1962, NSF: box 315, JFKL. As the censored sections in the Ex-Comm record indicate, not all the secrets of this critical meeting have yet been revealed; they include instructions given by Kennedy to McCone, probably concerning SIGINT operations.

154. Ms. note written that evening, Oct. 24, 1962, by Robert Kennedy; Schlesinger, *Robert Kennedy*, p. 554.

155. See the sources cited in note 153. On the role of NSA, omitted in the sanitized version of the Ex-Comm records, see Brugioni, *Eyeball to Eyeball*, p. 399.

156. Rusk, *As I Saw It*, p. 237. Rusk wrongly dates the meeting as October 25.

157. Bolshakov "Hot Line," *New Times*, 1989, no. 6. Andrew and Gordievsky, *KGB*, pp. 472–73. Beschloss, *Kennedy v. Khrushchev*, pp. 500–502.

158. CIA, "The Crisis USSR/Cuba. Information as of 0600, 25 October 1962"; Ex Comm "Record of Action," Meeting no. 4, 10 A.M., Oct. 25, 1962, NSF: box 315, JFKL.

159. Brugioni, *Eyeball to Eyeball*, pp. 425–29. Beschloss, *Kennedy v. Khrushchev*, pp. 505–506.

160. Ex-Comm, "Summary Record," Meeting no. 6, 10 A.M., Oct. 26, 1962, NSF: box 316, JFKL.

161. *CMC (CIA)*, pp. 317–21.

162. Andrew and Gordievsky, *KGB*, p. 473. *CMC (NSA)*, p. 184. Beschloss, *Kennedy v. Khrushchev*, pp. 514–16, 521–22.

163. *CMC (NSA)*, pp. 185–88. Rusk, *As I Saw It*, pp. 238–39.

164. Robert Kennedy, *Thirteen Days*, p. 91.

165. Bundy said during the discussion, "It's very odd, Mr. President, if he's [Khrushchev's] changed his terms from a long letter to you and an urgent appeal from the counselor [Feklisov] only last night . . . I would answer back saying I would prefer to deal with your interesting proposals of last night." Ex-Comm transcript, Oct. 27, 1962, JFKL; abbreviated version in *CMC (NSA)*, pp. 200–20 (Bundy's proposal is on p. 201). Cf. Robert Kennedy, *Thirteen Days*, p. 99, and Schlesinger, *Robert Kennedy*, p. 561.

166. Brugioni, *Eyeball to Eyeball*, pp. 457–58.

167. *CMC (NSA)*, p. 209.

168. Brugioni, *Eyeball to Eyeball*, pp. 461–63.

169. Ex-Comm Minutes, 10 A.M. Oct. 23, 1962, NSF: box 315, JFKL.

170. *CMC (NSA)*, pp. 210–17.

171. Robert Kennedy, *Thirteen Days*, pp. 100–107. Schlesinger, *Robert Kennedy*, pp. 561–63. Beschloss, *Kennedy v. Khrushchev*, pp. 536–37.

172. *CMC (NSA)*, p. 226. McGeorge Bundy, *Danger and Survival* (New York: Random House, 1988), p. 406.

173. Sorensen, *Kennedy*, pp. 716–17.

174. Prados, *Presidents' Secret Wars*, p. 214. Church Committee, *Final Report*, book 4, p. 71.

175. Smith, *Unknown CIA*, p. 188.

176. *CMC (CIA)*, pp. 347, 354; the second document cited corrects a minor typing error in the first.

177. Beschloss, *Kennedy v. Khrushchev*, pp. 564–66, 595.

178. Schlesinger, *Robert Kennedy*, pp. 579–80.

179. Ibid., pp. 580–81.

180. Andrew and Gordievsky, *KGB*, p. 509. CIA Cuban estimate, April 22, 1963, NSF, JFKL (cited by Beschloss, *Kennedy v. Khrushchev*, p. 595). Bundy, "Week-end Reading—April 27, 1963," NSF: box 318, JFKL.

181. Church Committee, *Alleged Assassination Plots*, pp. 171–73, 337.

182. Robert Kennedy OH, JFKL (cited by Beschloss, *Kennedy v. Khrushchev*, p. 639).

183. These and other methods were described by some of those who had used them in the 1992 BBC TV series "CIA" (writer and executive producer John Ranelagh).

184. Beschloss, *Kennedy v. Khrushchev*, p. 639.

185. James Reston, *Deadline: A Memoir* (New York: Random House, 1991).

186. Church Committee, *Alleged Assassination Plots*, pp. 86–88, 174–75. Church Committee, *Final Report*, book 5, pp. 14, 17, 74–75. Schlesinger, *Robert Kennedy*, pp. 589–90.

187. Sorensen, *Kennedy*, p. 722.

188. Beschloss, *Kennedy v Khrushchev*, pp. 666–67.

189. Sorensen, *Kennedy*, p. 749.

190. Church Committee, *Alleged Assassination Plots*, pp. 88–89. Church Committee, *Final Report*, book 5, pp. 17–19.

Chapter 8: Lyndon B. Johnson (1963–1969)

1. Lyndon B. Johnson, *The Vantage Point* (London: Weidenfeld and Nicolson, 1972), ch. 1.

2. William Manchester, *Death of a President* (London: Michael Joseph, 1967), pp. 491, 523–27, 593–99.

3. Schlesinger, *Robert Kennedy*, p. 656. On the conspiracy theories generated by the assassination, see Gerald Posner, *Case Closed: Lee Harvey Oswald and the Assassination of John F. Kennedy* (New York: Random House, 1993).

4. Beschloss, *Kennedy v. Khrushchev*, p. 672.

5. Manchester, *Death of a President*, p. 401. Beschloss, *Kennedy v. Khrushchev*, p. 673.

6. Rusk, *As I Saw It*, p. 321.

7. George W. Ball, *The Past Has Another Pattern* (New York: W. W. Norton, 1982), pp. 311–12.

8. Perhaps to mark the date of the assassination, the checklist is dated November 22, 1963; Walter Pforzheimer Collection on Intelligence Service, Washington D.C. See photo insert.

9. Johnson, *Vantage Point*, p. 22.

10. Smith, *Unknown CIA*, p. 190.

11. Richard Helms OH, p. 8, LBJL.

12. In an interview given for the LBJ Library Oral History Collection in 1970, while Johnson was still alive, McCone referred discreetly to this conspiracy theory. Johnson, he said, entered the White House with "some concern over how to handle the men in the organization [CIA] whose competence he recognized, but also whose allegiance to President Kennedy— [McCone failed to finish the sentence]. And, of course, you know the background of issues that arose that dated way back to the [1960 Democratic] Convention here in Los Angeles and even before." McCone OH, p. 17, LBJL.

13. Theoharis (ed.), *Secret Files*, p. 222.

14. *PP Lyndon Johnson 1963–64*, pp. 654–55.

15. Nixon, *Memoirs*, pp. 358, 596.

16. Gentry, *Hoover*, p. 559.

17. Ball, *Past Has Another Pattern*, p. 321.

18. Schlesinger, *Robert Kennedy*, pp. 678–79. Deborah Shapley, *Promise and Power: The Life and Times of Robert McNamara* (Boston: Little, Brown & Co., 1993), pp. 279–80.

19. Gentry, *Hoover*, p. 558.

20. Michael Friendly and David Galen, *Martin Luther King, Jr.: The FBI File* (New York: Carroll & Graf, 1993), ch. 2. Theoharis (ed.), *Secret Files*, pp. 100–103. Gentry, *Hoover*, pp. 568–76. Church Committee, *Final Report*, book 3, pp. 120–63.

21. Hugh Sidey, "L.B.J., Hoover and Domestic Spying," *Time*, Feb. 10, 1975.

22. Ball, *Past Has Another Pattern*, pp. 321–22.

23. Larry Berman, *Lyndon Johnson's War*, paperback ed. (New York: W. W. Norton, 1991), p. 111. Nixon, *Memoirs*, p. 368.

24. Hugh Sidey, *A Very Personal Presidency* (New York: Atheneum, 1968), p. 250. Cline, *Secrets, Spies and Scholars*, p. 201. Almost all the daily briefs for Johnson's presidency remain classified. Later in his presidency, Johnson agreed to read an early morning brief; see below, p. 335.

25. McCone told Bundy on November 28, "I had intended to discuss this with President Johnson but ran out of time." He recommended that "the President should be advised on the generalities of the Oswald–Mexico City development." McCone to Bundy, Nov. 28, 1963, DDRS, 1988, no. 8, LBJL.

26. Manchester, *Death of a President*, p. 717.

27. Rusk, *As I Saw It*, p. 356.

28. Transcript of meeting of Warren Commission, Dec. 16, 1963, JFKL. Kai Bird, *The Chairman: John J. McCloy and the Making of the American Establishment* (New York: Simon and Schuster, 1992), p. 549.

29. Edward J. Epstein, *Legend: The Secret World of Lee Harvey Oswald* (New York: Reader's Digest Press, 1978), pp. 17, 232, 254, 264. Henry Hurt, *Reasonable Doubt: An Investigation into the Assassination of John F. Kennedy* (New York: Henry Holt, 1985), pp. 420–22. Bird, *Chairman*, pp. 553–62, 566–67. Gerald Posner, *Case Closed*, pp. 407–9.

30. Johnson, *Vantage Point*, p. 27.

31. Bird, *Chairman*, p. 566. Powers, *Man Who Kept the Secrets*, p. 157. Helms denies claims that Johnson instructed him to initiate a new investigation into the assassination in 1967; interview with the author, April 1992. Posner, *Case Closed*, demolishes most of the conspiracy theories generated by Kennedy's assassination.

32. Interview with Yuri Nosenko, Nov. 15, 1987. Tom Mangold, *Cold Warrior: James Jesus Angleton, the CIA's Master Spy Hunter* (New York: Simon and Schuster, 1991), ch. 12. David Wise, *Molehunt: The Secret Search for Traitors That Shattered the CIA* (New York: Random House, 1992), ch. 11. The CIA assessment of Oswald cited was prepared by Arthur Dooley, dated March 20, 1964 (declassified August 1993). Angleton's conspiracy theories were formed at second hand. Nosenko said during my interview with him, "Never once Angleton has seen me; never once Angleton has spoken to me." On the damage done by Golitsyn's and Angleton's conspiracy theories, see below, pp. 401.

33. Letter to the author from Cleveland Cram, December 1993. Dr. Cram investigated the Nosenko case during the 1970s while preparing a lengthy CIA study of Angleton's period as counterintelligence chief.

34. Theoharis (ed.), *Secret Files*, pp. 220–40. Athan G. Theoharis and John Stuart Cox, *Boss: J. Edgar Hoover and the Great American Inquisition*, paperback ed. (New York: Bantam Books, 1990), pp. 395–97.

35. Clifford, *Counsel*, ch. 23. Robert Shogan, *The Riddle of Power* (New York: Plume, 1992), ch. 5.

36. *FRUS 1961–63*, vol. 4, pp. 629–30. Ambassador Lodge told Johnson that "we were not involved in the coup" that overthrew Diem and "were in no way responsible for the death of Diem," but that American "pressures . . . encouraged the coup." Ibid., p. 635.

37. Shapley, *Promise and Power*, pp. 261–62, 293.

38. *FRUS 1961–63*, vol. 4, pp. 635–36.

39. Ibid., pp. 721–35. Shapley, *Promise and Power*, pp. 292–94.

40. *FRUS 1961–63*, vol. 4, p. 735.

41. Cline, *Secrets, Spies and Scholars*, p. 199.

42. *FRUS 1961–63*, vol. 4, p. 637.

43. Ibid., pp. 641–45.

44. NSAM 273, ibid., pp. 637–40.

45. *FRUS 1964–68*, vol. 1, pp. 4–5.

46. Shapley, *Promise and Power*, p. 294.

47. *FRUS 1964–68*, vol. 1, p. 473.

48. Alexander M. Haig Jr., *Inner Circles* (New York: Warner Books, 1992), pp. 145–46.

49. Ibid., pp. 589–93. Johnson, *Vantage Point*, pp. 112–13. Johnson excluded all mention of NSA from his memoirs; he refers to the NSA personnel as "experts in technical intelligence."

50. *FRUS 1964–68*, vol. 1, pp. 604–11. Johnson, *Vantage Point*, pp. 114–15. Johnson's account makes clear that the intelligence that was believed

to "nail down the incident" came from intercepted North Vietnamese communications.

51. Smith, *Unknown CIA*, pp. 197–98.

52. *FRUS 1964–1968*, vol. 1, p. 611.

53. Haig, *Inner Circles*, ch. 9.

54. *FRUS 1964–68*, vol. 1, pp. 778–81.

55. Memorandum for the President, Jan. 27, 1965, NSF Country File, Vietnam, LBJL.

56. Prados, *Keepers of the Keys*, pp. 218–19.

57. Mark Clodfelter, *The Limits of Airpower: The American Bombing of North Vietnam* (New York: Free Press, 1989), pp. 25–38.

58. Telephone interview with Dino A. Brugioni, March 15, 1994.

59. Powers, *Man Who Kept the Secrets*, p. 167.

60. McCone, Memorandum, April 2, 1965, DDRS, 1989, no. 3206.

61. George C. Herring, *America's Longest War* (New York: John Wiley & Sons, 1979), pp. 143–44.

62. Church Committee, *Final Report*, book 3, pp. 483–85.

63. Gentry, *Hoover*, p. 605n.

64. Theoharis (ed.), *Secret Files*, pp. 237–38.

65. Gates, "An Opportunity Unfulfilled," p. 42.

66. Smith, *Unknown CIA*, pp. 183–84.

67. Recollection of Walter Pforzheimer. Whether or not the report was entirely accurate, it is significant that it was thought credible.

68. Johnson, *Vantage Point*, pp. 180–96.

69. Rusk, *As I Saw It*, p. 373.

70. Ball, *Past Has Another Pattern*, p. 330.

71. Valenti, Memorandum for the President, April 30, 1965, WHCF, Gen FG 11-2, folder "Central Intelligence Agency," LBJL; Jeffreys-Jones, *CIA*, p. 149.

72. Cline, *Secrets, Spies and Scholars*, p. 212.

73. Rusk, *As I Saw It*, p. 374.

74. See note 71.

75. Ball, *Past Has Another Pattern*, pp. 326–31. Charles Roberts, *LBJ's Inner Circle* (New York: Delacorte, 1965), pp. 204–10.

76. Phillips, *Night Watch*, ch. 6. Theoharis and Cox, *Boss*, p. 446.

77. Phillips, *Night Watch*, pp. 160–61.

78. Cline, *Secrets, Spies and Scholars*, p. 213.

79. Phillips, *Night Watch*, pp. 176–81.

80. Interview with Richard Helms, April 1992.

81. Cline, *Secrets, Spies and Scholars*, pp. 212–13. Phillips, *Night Watch*, pp. 146–47.

82. John B. Martin, *Overtaken by Events* (Garden City, N.Y.: Doubleday, 1966), p. 661.

83. In testimony during the *Westmoreland v. CBS* libel case in 1985, Colonel Williams, the DIA officer in charge of order-of-battle intelligence, said, ". . . DIA was basically parroting what came out of the field and supporting

MACV." (Williams Dep. Tr. 122) A CIA analyst gave evidence that "We at CIA were convinced that the DIA and CINCPAC spokesmen were simply rubber stamping the MACV position. . . ." (Blascak affidavit; I owe these references to Anthony Schinella.) Microfilm W2709, HCL.

84. T. L. Cubbage II, "Westmoreland vs. CBS: Was Intelligence Corrupted by Policy Demands?," *Intelligence and National Security*, vol. 3 (1988), no. 3, p. 123.

85. David Halberstam, *The Best and the Brightest* (New York: Fawcett Crest, 1972), p. 434.

86. George C. Herring, *"Cold Blood": LBJ's Conduct of Limited War in Vietnam* (Washington, D.C.: U.S. Government Printing Office, 1990), p. 8.

87. Sam Adams, "Vietnam Cover-Up: Playing War with Numbers," *Harper's*, May 1975, pp. 41–44.

88. "The Strength of the Viet Cong Irregulars," Sept. 8, 1966, CIA Documents on Vietnam, microfilm A413.6, reel 6, pp. 474–83, HCL.

89. Adams, "Vietnam Cover-Up," p. 44.

90. Smith, *Unknown CIA*, p. 223.

91. Adams, "Vietnam Cover-Up," p. 62.

92. Carver, Memorandum for DDI, Jan. 11, 1967 ("Drafted: Sam Adams 11/1/67"), CIA Documents on Vietnam, microfilm A413.6, reel 4, pp. 54–55, HCL.

93. Smith, *Unknown CIA*, pp. 223–25.

94. Interview with Ambassador Richard Helms, April 1992.

95. Interview with Dr. George Carver, March 16, 1994.

96. Berman, *Lyndon Johnson's War,* pp. 29–30.

97. Adams, "Vietnam Cover-Up," pp. 62–64.

98. Berman, *Lyndon Johnson's War*, pp. 30–39.

99. Adams, "Vietnam Cover-Up," p. 64.

100. Berman, *Lyndon Johnson's War*, pp. 38–39, 49–51.

101. CIA, "The OXCART Story"; this previously classified study, prepared for the agency's in-house journal, *Studies in Intelligence*, in 1982, was made available to the author in May 1992. A decision to terminate the Oxcart program was confirmed by Johnson at the Tuesday Lunch on May 21, 1968. It was succeeded by the SR-71, which continued the Black Shield missions.

102. Smith, *Unknown CIA*, pp. 219–21. Richard Helms, "Remarks at Donovan Award Dinner," May 24, 1983, cited by Ranelagh, *The Agency*, p. 474.

103. Johnson, *Vantage Point*, p. 293.

104. Smith, *Unknown CIA*, p. 221. Ian Black and Benny Morris, *Israel's Secret Wars* (London: Hamish Hamilton, 1991), pp. 220–22. Following the convention of not naming Mossad leaders publicly, Smith does not identify General Amit by name, referring only to the visit to Washington of an Israeli "key military leader."

105. Johnson, *Vantage Point*, pp. 287, 297–98. Rusk, *As I Saw It*, p. 386.

106. Prados, *Keepers of the Keys*, p. 178.

107. Clifford, *Counsel*, pp. 445–47. Johnson, *Vantage Point*, pp. 300–301.

108. Bamford, *Puzzle Palace*, pp. 218–29.

109. Johnson, *Vantage Point*, pp. 301–304. Prados, *Keepers of the Keys*, pp. 182–83.

110. Interview with Richard Helms, April 1992. Helms OH, p. 25, LBJL.

111. Smith, *Unknown CIA*, p. 222.

112. Information kindly supplied by John Helgerson. Since both the CIA history of the president's daily briefs and almost all Johnson's daily briefs remain classified, the precise date at which LBJ moved from an evening to a morning brief cannot at present be determined. Cf. above, p. 311. Unusually, the daily brief for April 1, 1968 has been partly declassified; DDRS, 1990, no. 2531, LBJL.

113. Interview with Richard Helms, April 1992.

114. Johnson, *Vantage Point*, pp. 168–73.

115. Church Committee, *Final Report*, book 2, pp. 75–76; book 3, pp. 491–99, 688–89. Interview with Richard Helms, April 1992.

116. Berman, *Lyndon Johnson's War*, pp. 74–75.

117. Helms, Memorandum for the President, Aug. 29, 1967, DDRS, 1988, no. 2031, LBJL.

118. Berman, *Lyndon Johnson's War*, p. 75.

119. George Allen, Deposition Tr. 909, *Westmoreland v. CBS*, microfilm W2709, HCL.

120. Berman, *Lyndon Johnson's War*, pp. 81–82. Cubbage, "Westmoreland vs. CBS," pp. 130—3-2. James J. Wirtz, *The Tet Offensive* (Ithaca, N.Y.: Cornell University Press, 1991), p. 160.

121. SNIE 14.3-67, Nov. 13, 1967, CIA Documents on Vietnam, microfilm A413.6, reel 7, pp. 281–309, HCL. The "conclusions" to the SNIE gave no overall total for enemy forces, but estimated regular force strength at 118,000 and guerrillas at 70,000–90,000. The detailed discussion of enemy forces concluded (p. 16):

> In sum, the Communist military and political organization is complex, and its aggregate numerical size cannot be estimated with confidence. . . . The VC/NVA Military Force (Main and Local Forces, administrative and service elements and guerrillas) can be meaningfully presented in numerical totals and . . . we estimate that this Military Force is now at least 223,000– 248,000. It must be recognized, however, that this Military Force constitutes but one component of the total Communist organization. Any comprehensive judgment of Communist capabilities in South Vietnam must embrace the effectiveness of all the elements which comprise that organization, the total size of which is of course considerably greater than the figure given for the Military Force.

122. Rostow, Memorandum for the President, Nov. 15, 1967, DDRS, 1986, no. 1167, LBJL.

123. Cubbage, "Westmoreland vs. CBS," pp. 142–43, 157, 167.

124. Shapley, *Promise and Power*, p. 435.

125. Church Committee, *Final Report*, book 3, pp. 691–92.

126. Helms, Memorandum for the President, Nov. 15, 1967, DDRS, 1984, no. 755, LBJL.

127. Clifford, *Counsel*, pp. 456–58. Shapley, *Promise and Power*, pp. 436–37.

128. Interview with Richard Helms, April 1992.

129. Larry Cable, *Unholy Grail: The U.S. and the Wars in Vietnam, 1965–8* (New York: Routledge, 1991), pp. 212–15.

130. Clifford, *Counsel*, p. 469.

131. Cable, *Unholy Grail*, p. 215. Berman, *Lyndon Johnson's War*, pp. 139–42.

132. Dino A. Brugioni, "The President, Khe Sanh, and the 26th Marines," *Leatherneck*, Sept. 1986, pp. 22–25. Telephone interview with Mr. Brugioni, March 15, 1994. The Khe Sanh model is now in the LBJL.

133. Clifford, *Counsel*, pp. 465–67. Rusk, *As I Saw It*, ch. 24. Bamford, *Puzzle Palace*, pp. 233–35. The crew of the *Pueblo*, but not the ship, were returned eleven months later.

134. Clifford, *Counsel*, pp. 472–73.

135. Wirtz, *Tet Offensive*, pp. 80–84. On North Vietnamese strategy in the Tet offensive, see also Ronnie E. Ford, "Tet Revisited: The Strategy of the Communist Vietnamese," *Intelligence and National Security*, vol. 9 (1994), no. 1, pp. 242–86.

136. Rusk, *As I Saw It*, p. 476.

137. Clifford, *Counsel*, pp. 467–68, 473–79.

138. Ibid., p. 469.

139. Wirtz, *Tet Offensive*, pp. 172–76.

140. Interview with John L. Hart (Saigon station chief 1966–68), April 1992.

141. Wirtz, *Tet Offensive*, p. 274.

142. Ibid., pp. 133–35, 205–206. Berman, *Lyndon Johnson's War*, pp. 140–41. Clifford, *Counsel*, pp. 476–77.

143. Stephen G. Rabe, "Vietnam: The War America Tried to Lose?," in T. G. Fraser and Keith Jeffery (eds.), *Men, Women and War* (Dublin: Lilliput Press, 1993), pp. 227–36.

144. Clifford, *Counsel*, pp. 479–86.

145. *Westmoreland v. CBS*: JX 214D, 214E, microfilm W2709, HCL. (I am grateful to Anthony Schinella for these references).

146. CIA Memorandum, "The Communists' Ability to Recoup Their Tet Military Losses," March 1, 1968, DDRS, 1990, no. 2559; the copy in the LBJL carries the notation "Sec Def has seen."

147. Clifford, *Counsel*, pp. 492–96.

148. Herring, *America's Longest War*, p. 204.

149. Herring, *America's Longest War*, p. 206. Powers, *Man Who Kept the Secrets*, pp. 191–92. Clifford, *Counsel*, pp. 507–508.

150. Interview with Dr. Carver, March 16, 1994.

151. Clifford, *Counsel*, pp. 507–18.

152. LBJ Diary, March 27, 1968, LBJL.

153. Interview with Dr. Carver, March 16, 1994.

154. *PP Lyndon Johnson 1968–69*, pp. 469–76.

155. Humphrey to Carver, April 19, 1968; letter in the possession of Dr. Carver.

156. Helms to Wheeler, April 24, 1968, DDRS, 1991, no. 192, LBJL.

157. Memo for DCI, "Results of [Intelligence] Community Negotiations on Enemy Troop Strength," May 1, 1968, CIA Documents on Vietnam, HCL, microfilm A413.6, reel 6, pp. 208–10. Controversy over OB figures still continues. James Wirtz concludes, "Even though MACV analysts may have underestimated total enemy strength by as much as 20 percent, they were closer to the mark than CIA analysts"; *Tet Offensive*, p. 251.

158. Helms to Wheeler, April 24, 1968, DDRS, 1991, no. 192, LBJL.

159. Clifford, *Counsel*, pp. 527–28, 539–41.

160. Church Committee, *Final Report*, book 2, pp. 100–101.

161. Johnson, *Vantage Point*, pp. 515–29.

162. Clifford, *Counsel*, pp. 573–95. Gentry, *Hoover*, p. 608. Anna Chennault, *The Education of Anna* (New York: Times Books, 1980), pp. 174–76, 190.

163. Clifford, *Counsel*, pp. 584, 595–96.

Chapter 9: Richard M. Nixon: (1969–1974)

1. Henry Kissinger, *White House Years* (Boston: Little, Brown & Co., 1979), p. 11.

2. Interview with Ambassador Richard Helms, April 1992.

3. Smith, *Unknown CIA*, pp. 148–49.

4. *PP Nixon 1969*, p. 36.

5. Kissinger, *White House Years*, p. 26.

6. Interview with Richard Helms, April 1992.

7. Stephen E. Ambrose, *Nixon* (New York: Simon and Schuster, 1987–91), vol. 3, p. 597.

8. William Safire, *Before the Fall* (New York: Doubleday, 1975), p. 437.

9. Ambrose, *Nixon*, vol. 2, pp. 490–91.

10. Colby regarded that as "a brilliant comment by a[n intelligence] customer." Interview with Ambassador William Colby, March 14, 1994.

11. Letter to author, dated April 23, 1992, from senior CIA analyst.

12. Kissinger, *White House Years*, pp. 633, 641–42.

13. Ambrose, *Nixon*, vol. 2, pp. 379–80.

14. Kissinger, *White House Years*, p. 642.

15. Kissinger, *White House Years*, pp. 138ff. Len Colodny and Robert Gettlin, *Silent Coup*, paperback ed. (New York: St. Martin's Press, 1992), pp. 8–9.

16. Interview with William Colby, March 14, 1994. Colby was irritated by the back channels but "finally decided I wasn't going to worry about them. I told the analysts, 'You do your job the best way you can.'"

17. Kissinger, *White House Years*, pp. 36–37. John Ehrlichman, *Witness*

to Power: The Nixon Years (New York: Simon and Schuster, 1982), p. 175.

18. Seymour M. Hersh, *Kissinger: The Price of Power* (New York: Summit, 1983), pp. 104–105.

19. Powers, *Man Who Kept the Secrets*, p. 202.

20. Interview with Richard Helms, April 1992.

21. Kissinger, *White House Years*, pp. 37.

22. Smith, *Unknown CIA*, p. 240.

23. Haig, *Inner Circles*, pp. 195–96.

24. Smith, *Unknown CIA*, p. 248.

25. Ambrose, *Nixon*, vol. 2, p. 262.

26. Interview with Richard Helms, April 1992. See above, pp. 322–23, 336, 338, 348.

27. Church Committee, *Final Report*, book 2, p. 100–102; book 3, p. 697.

28. Ambrose, *Nixon*, vol. 2, p. 264.

29. Interview with Richard Helms, April 1992.

30. Helms, Memo to DDI, DDP et al., Sept. 6, 1969, DDRS, 1987, no. 111.

31. "The SS-9 Controversy: Intelligence as Political Football," Case Study C16-89-884.0, KSG. Prados, *The Soviet Estimate*, ch. 13.

32. Interview with Richard Helms, April 1992.

33. Hersh, *Kissinger*, p. 159.

34. Smith, *Unknown CIA*, p. 243. Interview with Richard Helms, April 1992.

35. Unattributable interview with senior CIA analyst.

36. Church Committee, *Final Report*, book 1, p. 82.

37. Interview with Richard Helms, April 1992.

38. Interview with Richard Helms, April 1992.

39. Hersh, *Kissinger*, pp. 69–70.

40. Haig, *Inner Circles*, p. 205.

41. Kissinger, *White House Years*, p. 320.

42. *PP Nixon 1969*, p. 305.

43. Hersh, *Kissinger*, pp. 73–74.

44. Interview with Richard Helms, April 1992.

45. Hersh, *Kissinger*, p. 74.

46. "The SS-9 Controversy: Intelligence as Political Football," Case Study C16-89-884.0, KSG. Prados, *The Soviet Estimate*, ch. 13.

47. Hersh, *Kissinger*, p. 207.

48. Interview with Richard Helms, April 1992.

49. Hersh, *Kissinger*, p. 257n.

50. Unattributable letter to author from senior CIA analyst, April 23, 1992.

51. Jack Anderson, "CIA Eavesdrops on Kremlin Chiefs," *Washington Post*, Sept. 16, 1971. Jeffrey Richelson, *American Espionage and the Soviet Target* (New York: Quill, 1987), p. 98.

52. Unattributable interview.

53. Hersh, *Kissinger*, p. 257n.

54. Walter Isaacson, *Kissinger: A Biography* (New York: Simon and Schuster, 1992), pp. 159–60.

55. Nixon, *Memoirs*, p. 368.

56. Isaacson, *Kissinger*, pp. 164–65. NSSM-1 and the responses to it were read into the Congressional Record of May 10, 1972, by Congressman Ron Dellums.

57. Kissinger, *White House Years*, pp. 239–50. Nixon, *Memoirs*, pp. 380–302. Isaacson, *Kissinger*, pp. 172–77.

58. Nixon, *Memoirs*, p. 387.

59. Hersh, *Kissinger*, pp. 94, 116.

60. Ehrlichman, *Witness to Power*, pp. 156–59.

61. Haig, *Inner Circles*, pp. 212–13. Isaacson, *Kissinger*, pp. 214–18.

62. H. R. Haldeman, *The Ends of Power* (London: Sidgwick & Jackson, 1978), pp. 100–102. Nixon, *Memoirs*, pp. 388–90. Theoharis (ed.), *Secret Files*, pp. 243–45. Haig, *Inner Circles*, ch. 15. Isaacson, *Kissinger*, ch. 11.

63. The annual statistics for the period 1940 to 1974 inclusive are to be found in Church Committee, *Final Report*, book 3, p. 301.

64. Nixon was well aware "that a leak about the wiretaps would be a blow to the morale of the White House staff." Nixon, *Memoirs*, p. 389.

65. "Kissinger Apologizes for a 1969 Wiretap," *International Herald Tribune*, Nov. 14–15, 1992.

66. Safire, *Before the Fall*, p. 169.

67. Haldeman, *Ends of Power*, pp. 103–104. Isaacson, *Kissinger*, pp. 228–29. David Wise, *The American Police State* (New York: Random House, 1976), pp. 3–30.

68. Ehrlichman, *Witness to Power*, ch. 11.

69. Theoharis (ed.), *Secret Files*, p. 243. Theoharis and Cox, *Boss*, p. 459.

70. Haldeman, *Ends of Power*, p. 102.

71. Theoharis (ed.), *Secret Files*, p. 249.

72. Nixon, *Memoirs*, pp. 445–67. Kissinger, *White House Years*, pp. 509–17. Ambrose, *Nixon*, vol. 2, pp. 347–61. Isaacson, *Kissinger*, pp. 268–84.

73. Nixon, *Memoirs*, pp. 446–47.

74. Kissinger, *White House Years*, pp. 464–66.

75. Church Committee, *Final Report*, book 3, pp. 933–34. Nixon, *Memoirs*, p. 473.

76. Ambrose, *Nixon*, vol. 2, p. 361.

77. Nixon, *Memoirs*, p. 473. Interview with Richard Helms, April 1992.

78. See above, p. 355.

79. Church Committee, *Final Report*, book 3, pp. 936–37.

80. Ibid., pp. 938–55.

81. Nixon, *Memoirs*, pp. 473–74.

82. Church Committee, *Final Report*, book 3, pp. 951–55.

83. Nixon, *Memoirs*, p. 474.

84. Church Committee, *Final Report*, book 3, pp. 955–56.

85. Ibid., pp. 956–59.

86. Nixon, *Memoirs*, pp. 474–75.

87. Richard Helms did not demur when I put that possibility to him in April 1992.

88. CIA, "Background for Chilean Hearings," March 1972, DDRS, 1989, no. 614. CIA, "Chronology [of Chilean Covert Action]," July 20, 1972, ibid., no. 620. Treverton, *Covert Action*, pp. 20–21.

89. Interview with Richard Helms, April 1992.

90. Nixon, *Memoirs*, pp. 489–90.

91. Interview with Richard Helms, April 1992.

92. Kissinger, *White House Years*, p. 665.

93. CIA, "Chronology [of Chilean Covert Action]," July 20, 1972, DDRS, 1987, no. 620. Treverton, *Covert Action*, pp. 101–103.

94. Kissinger, *White House Years*, p. 671.

95. Interview with Richard Helms, April 1992.

96. Kissinger, *White House Years*, p. 671.

97. Church Committee, *Alleged Assassination Plots*, p. 230.

98. Helms memo on meeting with the president, Sept. 15, 1970: exhibit 2 in Covert Action: *Hearings before the Select Committee to Study Governmental Operations with Respect to Intelligence Activities of the United States Senate*, 94 Cong., 1 Sess., pursuant to S. res. 21, vol. 7, Dec. 4 and 5, 1975, p. 96.

99. Kissinger, *White House Years*, pp. 673–74.

100. Interview with Richard Helms, April 1992.

101. Phillips, *Night Watch*, pp. 220–23. Ranelagh, *The Agency*, pp. 514–20. Treverton, *Covert Action*, pp. 22–23, 104–107.

102. *PP Nixon 1970*, p. 758.

103. CIA, "Report on CIA Chilean Task Force Activities, 15 September to 3 November 1970," Nov. 18, 1970, DDRS, 1988, no. 1226.

104. Those running Track I, who were unaware of Track II, would also have been prepared to work for a military coup, had Frei been willing to support it.

105. Church Committee, *Alleged Assassination Plots*, p. 235.

106. CIA, "Report on CIA Chilean Task Force Activities, 15 September to 3 November 1970," Nov. 18, 1970, DDRS, 1988, no. 1226. Kissinger confirms that Nixon was briefed personally by Karamessines, "always pessimistically"; *White House Years*, p. 674.

107. Ibid. Ranelagh, *The Agency*, p. 517.

108. Church Committee, *Alleged Assassination Plots*, pp. 240–476. Phillips, *Night Watch*, p. 223. Ranelagh, *The Agency*, pp. 517–19.

109. Nixon, *Memoirs*, p. 490.

110. Kissinger, *White House Years*, p. 674.

111. Church Committee, *Alleged Assassination Plots*, pp. 242, 254. Ranelagh, *The Agency*, pp. 519–20.

112. Kissinger, *White House Years*, ch. 16.

113. Nixon, *Memoirs*, p. 496.

114. Charles W. Colson, *Born Again* (London: Hodder and Stoughton, 1976), pp. 56–57.

115. Jonathan Aitken, *Nixon: A Life* (London: Weidenfeld and Nicolson, 1992), p. 414.

116. Colson, *Born Again*, pp. 43–45.

117. John Robert Greene, *The Limits of Power: The Nixon and Ford*

Administrations (Bloomington and Indianapolis: Indiana University Press, 1992), pp. 135–36.

118. *Watergate: Chronology of a Crisis* (Washington, D.C.: Congressional Quarterly, 1975), p. 153.

119. Ibid. The other names on the list were Alexander E. Barkan, Ed Guthman, Maxwell Dane, Charles Dyson, Howard Stein, Leonard Woodcock, S. Sterling Munro Jr., Samuel M. Lambert, Stewart Rawlings Mott, Ronald Dellums, and Mary McGrory.

120. Haldeman, *Ends of Power*, pp. 110–13. Colson, *Born Again*, pp. 57–60. Ehrlichman, *Witness to Power*, pp. 300–302.

121. Colson, *Born Again*, p. 60. Haldeman, *Ends of Power*, pp. 115–16.

122. Nixon, *Memoirs*, pp. 596–99. Ambrose, *Nixon*, vol. 2, pp. 448–49.

123. Haldeman, *Ends of Power*, p. 112.

124. Nixon statement, May 22, 1973, *Watergate: Chronology*, p. 92.

125. Ibid. Ambrose, *Nixon*, vol. 2, pp. 465–66. John W. Dean, *Blind Ambition* (New York: Simon and Schuster, 1976), p. 199. Haldeman, *Ends of Power*, pp. 114–15.

126. G. Gordon Liddy, *Will* (London: Severn House, 1981), pp. 157–71. Jeb Stuart Magruder, *An American Life* (New York: Atheneum, 1974), p. 173. Greene, *Limits of Power*, pp. 140–42.

127. Nixon, *Memoirs*, pp. 500–502.

128. Seymour M. Hersh, "Nixon's Last Cover-Up: The Tapes He Wants the Archives To Suppress," *New Yorker*, Dec. 14, 1992, pp. 76–95.

129. *Watergate: Chronology*, pp. 8–9. Ambrose, *Nixon*, vol. 2, pp. 477, 502. Greene, *Limits of Power*, pp. 142–43.

130. Haldeman, *Ends of Power*, pp. 10–11.

131. Dean's and Magruder's accounts are in substantial agreement. Dean, *Blind Ambition*, ch. 3. Magruder, *An American Life*, ch. 9. Cf. Liddy, *Will*, chs. 18, 19.

132. Ibid. Ambrose, *Nixon*, vol. 2, p. 562. Greene, *Limits of Power*, pp. 144–45.

133. Hersh, "Nixon's Last Cover-Up," p. 76. Colson, now a born-again Christian, has confirmed the existence of the plot to enter Bremer's apartment.

134. Nixon, *Memoirs*, pp. 559–80, 609–21.

135. Prados, *The Soviet Estimate*, ch. 14. *CIA: The Pike Report* (Nottingham, England: Spokesman Books, 1977), pp. 65–68.

136. Liddy, *Will*, chs. 19, 20. Magruder, *An American Life*, ch. 10. The most recent study of Watergate is Fred Emery, *Watergate: The Corruption of American Politics and the Fall of Richard Nixon* (New York: Times Books, 1994).

137. Magruder, *An American Life*, p. 214.

138. Nixon, *Memoirs*, pp. 625–26.

139. Hersh, "Nixon's Last Cover-Up," p. 79. The Haldeman diaries, published as this volume was going to press, provide further evidence that Nixon did not know of the break-ins beforehand. H. R. Haldeman (with introduction

and afterword by Stephen E. Ambrose), *The Haldeman Diaries: Inside the Nixon White House* (New York: Putnam, 1994). Theodore Draper, "Nixon Redivivus," *New York Review of Books*, July 14, 1994.

140. Nixon, *Memoirs*, p. 639.

141. *Watergate: Chronology*, appendix, pp. 89A–91A.

142. William Colby, *Honorable Men: My Life in the CIA* (New York: Simon and Schuster, 1978), pp. 323–24.

143. *Watergate: Chronology*, p. 764. Shultz resigned for different reasons in March 1974.

144. Aitken, *Nixon*, p. 447.

145. Nixon, *Memoirs*, pp. 773–75.

146. Colby, *Honorable Men*, p. 328.

147. Interview with Richard Helms, April 1992.

148. Interview with Dr. Carver, March 16, 1994. Dr. Carver, who died on June 26, 1994, did not wish his part in drafting Nixon's telegrams to Kissinger to be revealed until after his death.

149. Nixon, *Memoirs*, pp. 750–57.

150. Interview with Dr. Carver, March 16, 1994.

151. Henry Kissinger, *Years of Upheaval* (Boston: Little, Brown & Co., 1982), ch. 2, p. 369. Frank Snepp, *Decent Interval* (New York: Random House, 1977).

152. Schlesinger, "A Review of the Intelligence Community" [sanitized version], March 10, 1971, National Security Archive, MF W3893, no. 00867, HCL.

153. Colby, *Honorable Men*, pp. 330–42. Ranelagh, *The Agency*, pp. 548–49, 551.

154. Nixon, *Memoirs*, p. 849.

155. Kissinger, *Years of Upheaval*, pp. 77–78.

156. Schlesinger left Langley on July 2. Colby did not formally take over until September 4, after his confirmation by the Senate. General Walters was nominally acting DCI during the interim.

157. Colby, *Honorable Men*, pp. 345–46.

158. Interview with William Colby, March 14, 1994.

159. Interview with William Colby, March 14, 1994.

160. Andrew and Gordievsky, *KGB*, pp. 512–13.

161. Kissinger, *Years of Upheaval*, ch. 9. The CIA had correctly predicted that a successful coup would require the cooperation of all the armed services. Interview with William Colby, March 14, 1994.

162. Prados, *Presidents' Secret Wars*, p. 320.

163. Kissinger, *Years of Upheaval*, p. 407. Kissinger informed the president of the secret meeting with Pinochet on September 19. He says in his memoirs that he can offer no explanation for this unusual delay, except his preoccupation with his Senate confirmation hearings as newly appointed secretary of state (a post that he added to that of national security adviser). It is inconceivable that such a delay could have occurred in 1970.

164. Nixon, *Memoirs*, p. 920.

165. Black and Morris, *Israel's Secret Wars*, ch. 9.

166. Interview with Richard Helms, April 1992.

167. *Pike Report*, p. 142.

168. Ibid., pp. 143–48.

169. Ranelagh, *The Agency*, pp. 582–83.

170. *Pike Report*, p. 145.

171. Briefing notes for DCI Turner, September 1977, "U-2 and SR-71," DDRS, 1985, no. 2445.

172. Black and Morris, *Israel's Secret Wars*, pp. 314–16.

173. Kissinger and Haig, now Nixon's chief of staff, differ somewhat over the extent of Kissinger's initiative. Kissinger, *Years of Upheaval*, ch. 11. Haig, *Inner Circles*, ch. 31.

174. Nixon, *Memoirs*, p. 937.

175. Haig, *Inner Circles*, pp. 414–17.

176. Kissinger, *Years of Upheaval*, pp. 586–99. Ambrose, *Nixon*, vol. 3, pp. 255–57. Isaacson, *Kissinger*, pp. 531–33.

177. Ambrose, *Nixon*, vol. 3, pp. 241–42.

178. *Pike Report*, pp. 149–55.

179. Interview with William Colby, March 14, 1994.

180. *Pike Report*, pp. 155–57.

181. Colby has no recollection of any reference by Nixon to either. Interview with William Colby, March 14, 1994.

182. Kissinger, *Years of Upheaval*, pp. 1163–64.

183. Interviews with Oleg Gordievsky. Nixon was clearly aware of the danger of bugging (*Memoirs*, p. 1027) but preoccupied and insufficiently cautious. On a number of occasions during the summit his attention seemed to wander; Ambrose, *Nixon*, vol. 3, p. 373.

184. *Pike Report*, pp. 158–67.

185. Kissinger, *Years of Upheaval*, pp. 1189–93.

186. Interview with William Colby, March 14, 1994. Colby recalls: "We were making a vigorous effort to stop the Congress infuriating the Turks enough to close our listening stations. The Turks did turn a couple of them off for a short time. Congress, of course, was heavily influenced by the Greek lobby."

187. The text of the Articles of Impeachment appears in Theodore H. White, *Breach of Faith: The Fall of Richard Nixon* (London: Jonathan Cape, 1975), appendix A.

188. *Watergate: Chronology*, p. 91.

189. Ambrose, *Nixon*, vol. 3, chs. 17, 18. Nixon, *Memoirs*, pp. 1049–90. Haig, *Inner Circles*, chs. 35, 36. White, *Breach of Faith*, ch. 1. Michael Schudson, *Watergate in American Memory* (New York: Basic Books, 1992), ch. 1.

Chapter 10: Gerald R. Ford (1974–1977)

1. Haig, *Inner Circles*, p. 519.

2. Shogan, *Riddle of Power*, ch. 7.

3. Interview with Dr. Louis Tordella, April 1992.

4. Jeffreys-Jones, *CIA*, p. 195. Ranelagh, *The Agency*, pp. 585, 616.

5. Interview with William Colby, March 14, 1994.

6. Gerald R. Ford, *A Time to Heal* (London: W. H. Allen, 1979), p. 149.

7. Interview with William Colby, March 14, 1994.

8. Colby, *Honorable Men*, p. 373.

9. Ford, *Time to Heal*, p. 129. Isaacson, *Kissinger*, p. 603.

10. Interview with William Colby, March 14, 1994.

11. Ford, *Time to Heal*, pp. 135–36. Colby, *Honorable Men*, pp. 413–14.

12. Interview with William Colby, March 14, 1994.

13. Ranelagh, *The Agency*, pp. 602–603.

14. Interview with William Colby, March 14, 1994. *Komsomolskaya Pravda*, July 24, 1992 (translation in FBIS-SOV-92-145).

15. *PP Ford 1975*, pp. 150–51.

16. Colby, *Honorable Men*, p. 392.

17. Angleton also handled intelligence liaison with Israel; Colby told him he must give that up too. Ibid., pp. 244, 364–65, 387. Mangold, *Cold Warrior*, chs. 20, 21. Wise, *Molehunt*, chs. 15, 16.

18. Colby, *Honorable Men*, pp. 388–91. Mangold, *Cold Warrior*, pp. 316–17.

19. Colby, *Honorable Men*, pp. 391–98.

20. Colby to Ford, Dec. 24, 1974, DDRS, 1987, no. 38.

21. Colby, *Honorable Men*, pp. 394–98.

22. Church Committee, *Final Report*, book 4, p. 89. Treverton, *Covert Action*, pp. 237–38.

23. Ibid., p. 391.

24. *Pike Report*, p. 189.

25. Colby, *Honorable Men*, p. 398.

26. Ibid. Ford, *Time to Heal*, pp. 229–30.

27. *PP Ford 1975*, pp. 19–20.

28. Ford, *Time to Heal*, p. 230. .

29. Colby, *Honorable Men*, p. 400.

30. Isaacson, *Kissinger*, p. 669.

31. Daniel Schorr, *Clearing the Air* (Boston: Houghton Mifflin, 1977), pp. 143–45.

32. Interview with William Colby, March 14, 1994.

33. Schorr, *Clearing the Air*, pp. 143–47.

34. On media revelations and allegations about CIA assassinations, see Judith F. Buncher (ed.), *The CIA and the Security Debate* (New York: Facts on File, 1976), pp. 22–24.

35. *PP Ford 1975*, pp. 367–68.

36. *PP Ford 1975*, pp. 447, 471, 551.

37. William Colby, *Lost Victory* (Chicago: Contemporary Books, 1989), p. 359.

38. Interview with Dr. Carver, March 16, 1994. "I drafted most of Freddie's report for him," Carver recalled.

39. Ford, *Time to Heal*, p. 256.

40. Interview with Dr. Carver, March 16, 1994.

41. Colby, *Lost Victory*, p. 359.

42. Ford, *Time to Heal*, pp. 275–76. Richard G. Head, Frisco W. Short, and Robert C. McFarlane, *Crisis Resolution: Presidential Decision Making in the Mayaguez and Korean Confrontations* (Boulder, Co.: Westview Press, 1978). "The Mayaguez Incident," KSG Case Study C14-82-443.0.

43. Interview with William Colby, March 14, 1994.

44. Isaacson, *Kissinger*, p. 649.

45. Ford, *Time to Heal*, pp. 276–93. "The Mayaguez Incident," pp. 9–22. *PP Ford 1975*, vol. 1, p. 668.

46. A Defense University study, based on interviews with Ford several years later, found him still doubtful about the "reliability of intelligence monitoring" during the *Mayaguez* crisis. Head, Short, and McFarlane, *Crisis Resolution*, p. 113.

47. *PP Ford 1975*, vol. 1, pp. 789–94.

48. Commission on CIA Activities Within the United States, *Report to the President* (Washington, D.C.: U.S. Government Printing Office, 1975).

49. Schorr, *Clearing the Air*, p. 155.

50. Buncher (ed.), *CIA and the Security Debate*, pp. 29–32. It was reported in 1994 that the Olson case was being reopened as a homicide investigation.

51. Schorr, *Clearing the Air*, pp. 151, 157.

52. Nathaniel Davis, "The Angola Decision of 1975: A Personal Memoir," *Foreign Affairs*, Fall 1978, pp. 109–24. John Stockwell, *In Search of Enemies: A CIA Story* (New York: W. W. Norton, 1978). Interview with William Colby, March 14, 1994.

53. Davis, "The Angola Decision of 1975," pp. 114–16.

54. Stockwell, *In Search of Enemies*, p. 68.

55. Interview with William Colby, March 14, 1994.

56. Isaacson, *Kissinger*, ch. 30. Treverton, *Covert Action*, pp. 153–54.

57. *PP Ford 1975*, vol. 2, p. 492.

58. Timothy S. Hardy, "Intelligence Reform in the Mid-1970s," pp. 5–6, DDRS, 1989, no. 1247. Hardy's article originally appeared in the classified CIA in-house journal, *Studies in Intelligence*, in the summer of 1976.

59. Schorr, *Clearing the Air*, p. 188.

60. Loch K. Johnson, *A Season of Inquiry: The Senate Intelligence Investigation* (Lexington: University Press of Kentucky, 1985), pp. 72–77. Colby, *Honorable Men*, pp. 440–44.

61. Schorr, *Clearing the Air*, pp. 183–84. Johnson, *Season of Inquiry*, pp. 91–108. Bamford, *Puzzle Palace*, pp. 297–302.

62. Johnson, *Season of Inquiry*, pp. 98, 108–109.

63. Colby, *Honorable Men*, pp. 7–11, 445–47.

64. Johnson, *Season of Inquiry*, pp. 194, 123.

65. Frank J. Smist Jr., *Congress Oversees the United States Intelligence Community, 1947–1989* (Knoxville: University of Tennessee Press, 1990), pp. 51–52.

66. Stockwell, *In Search of Enemies*, p. 21. *Pike Report*, p. 199. Johnson, *Season of Inquiry*, pp. 138–39.

67. *PP Ford 1975*, vol. 2, p. 1981.

68. Ford, *Time to Heal*, p. 346.

69. Isaacson, *Kissinger*, p. 683.

70. It later emerged that Welch had failed to follow agency advice to change address because his house had been "previously identified as belonging to the former station chief." Schorr, *Clearing the Air*, p. 191. Johnson, *Season of Inquiry*, pp. 161–62. Colby, *Honorable Men*, pp. 450–51. Smist, *Congress Oversees the United States Intelligence Community*, pp. 64, 82ff, 187.

71. *PP Ford 1976–77*, vol. 1, no. 16.

72. Schorr, *Clearing the Air*, pp. 192–93. Johnson, *Season of Inquiry*, pp. 111–12, 116, 180–82. Smist, *Congress Oversees the United States Intelligence Community*, pp. 136, 162, 169–70.

73. Colby, *Honorable Men*, p. 452.

74. "The Organization of American Intelligence" [CIA briefing paper for Carter], Aug. 12, 1976, p. 11, DDRS, 1986, no. 2477.

75. Johnson, *Season of Inquiry*, chs. 16, 17. *PP Ford 1976–77*, vol. 1, nos. 110, 118, 124.

76. Hardy, "Intelligence Reform," p. 11, DDRS, 1989, no. 1247.

77. *Pike Report*, p. 189.

78. Smist, *Congress Oversees the United States Intelligence Community*, pp. 136–37.

79. Johnson, *Season of Inquiry*, pp. 215–20.

80. Church Committee, *Final Report*, book 1, pp. 423–25.

81. Smist, *Congress Oversees the United States Intelligence Community*, p. 70.

82. See above, p. 405.

83. Church Committee, *Final Report*, book 3, pp. 70–184.

84. Johnson, *Season of Inquiry*, p. 225.

85. Church Committee, *Final Report*, book 2, pp. 135–36.

86. Johnson, *Season of Inquiry*, ch. 20. Smist, *Congress Oversees the United States Intelligence Community*, ch. 3.

87. Robert T. Hartmann, *Palace Politics: An Inside Account of the Ford Years* (New York: McGraw-Hill, 1980), p. 404. Mary E. Stuckey, *The President as Interpreter-in-Chief* (Chatham, N.J.: Chatham House Publishers, 1991), p. 99.

88. Christopher Andrew and Oleg Gordievsky (eds.), *Instructions from the Centre: Top Secret Files on KGB Foreign Operations, 1975–1985* (London: Hodder and Stoughton, 1991), pp. 91–97. Though the intelligence provided by Gordievsky was passed by SIS to CIA on a need-to-know basis, following usual liaison procedures, his identity was not disclosed.

89. Ford, *Time to Heal*, pp. 373–74. Raymond L. Garthoff, *Détente and Confrontation: American-Soviet Relations from Nixon to Reagan* (Washington, D.C.: Brookings Institution, 1985), pp. 544–49.

90. The PFIAB chairman, George W. Anderson Jr., had written to Ford suggesting "competitive analysis" of CIA estimates of Soviet intentions and capabilities in August 1975, but probably had in mind a more balanced B Team. *The National Intelligence Estimates A-B Team Episode Concerning*

Soviet Strategic Capability and Objectives. Report of the Subcommittee on Collection, Production and Quality of the Senate Select Committee on Intelligence, 95 Cong., 2 Sess. (Washington, D.C.: U.S. Government Printing Office, 1978). Prados, *The Soviet Estimate*, pp. 248–57.

91. *National Intelligence Act of 1980.* Hearings before the Senate Select Committee on Intelligence, 96 Cong., 2 Sess. (Washington, D.C.: U.S. Government Printing Office, 1980), pp. 369–72.

92. *National Intelligence Estimates A-B Team Episode.* The reports of both teams remain classified.

93. Ford, *Time to Heal*, p. 437.

94. Prados, *The Soviet Estimate*, pp. 252–53. Strobe Talbott, *The Master of the Game: Paul Nitze and the Nuclear Race*, paperback ed. (New York: Vintage Books, 1989), pp. 146–47. Paul H. Nitze, *From Hiroshima to Glasnost: At the Centre of Decision* (London: Weidenfeld and Nicolson, 1990), pp. 351–54. Daniel Callaghan, *Dangerous Capabilities* (New York: HarperCollins, 1990), p. 378.

95. Garthoff, *Détente and Confrontation*, pp. 551–52.

96. Prados, *The Soviet Estimate*, pp. 253–54.

97. Talbott, *Master of the Game*, p. 151.

98. Ronald Reagan, *An American Life*, paperback ed. (New York: Pocket Books, 1992), p. 266.

Chapter 11: Jimmy Carter (1977–1981)

1. Walter Lafeber, *The American Age: United States Foreign Policy at Home and Abroad Since 1750* (New York: W. W. Norton, 1989), pp. 645–46.

2. Evidence by Professor Ernest R. May to Senate Select Committee on Intelligence, March 31, 1980, *Hearings on S.2284*, p. 376.

3. G. Barry Golson (ed.), *The Playboy Interview* (New York: Wideview Books, 1981), pp. 478–79. Gaddis Smith, *Morality, Reason and Power: American Diplomacy in the Carter Years* (New York: Hill and Wang, 1986), ch. 1.

4. George Bush, *Looking Forward* (New York: Doubleday, 1987), p. 178.

5. "The Organization of American Intelligence," Aug. 12, 1976, DDRS, 1986, no. 2477. The briefing began, "This paper is designed to give Governor Carter an outline of our intelligence system and how it works."

6. Zbigniew Brzezinski, *Power and Principle: Memoirs of the National Security Adviser* (London: Weidenfeld and Nicolson, 1983), pp. 34–35.

7. Bush, *Looking Forward*, p. 179.

8. William E. Burrows, *Deep Black* (New York: Berkley, 1988), ch. 10.

9. Richelson, *American Espionage and the Soviet Target*, p. 236.

10. Ranelagh, *The Agency*, p. 633.

11. Clifford, *Counsel*, pp. 622–23.

12. Ranelagh, *The Agency*, p. 634.

13. *PP Carter 1978*, vol. 1, p. 372.

14. Stansfield Turner, *Secrecy and Democracy: The CIA in Transition* (London: Sidgwick & Jackson, 1985), ch. 1.

15. Charles G. Cogan, "The In-Culture of the DO," *Intelligence and National Security*, vol. 8 (1993), p. 80. Turner sacked Knoche after four months and replaced him as DDCI with an outsider, Frank C. Carlucci, then ambassador to Portugal.

16. Turner, *Secrecy and Democracy*, pp. xviii, 128–31.

17. Unattributable interview with senior official of the CIA Operations Directorate.

18. Interview with Admiral Turner, March 18, 1994.

19. On the Magnificent Five and the unmasking of Cairncross as the fifth man, see Andrew and Gordievsky, *KGB*. After the publication of *KGB*, Cairncross at first denied being the fifth man but admitted it a year later.

20. See the introduction by Turner to the 1986 British edition of *Secrecy and Democracy*, p. xv. Turner's introduction (p. xiv) cites approvingly two books by the British journalist Chapman Pincher, that erroneously accused the former director-general of MI5, Sir Roger Hollis, of having been a Soviet mole. The front of Turner's dust jacket prominently features an endorsement by Pincher. While Turner does not comment on the allegations against Hollis, which were publicly denied by Mrs. Thatcher's government, he would scarcely have associated Pincher so visibly with the publication of his British edition had he accepted the official British view on Hollis's innocence. Ironically, the KGB suspected that the erroneous charges made against Hollis by Pincher and the former MI5 officer, Peter Wright, were "a British plot"; Andrew and Gordievsky, *KGB*, p. 8.

21. Jimmy Carter, *Keeping Faith* (London: Collins, 1982), pp. 51–57.

22. Brzezinski, *Power and Principle*, pp. 64–65, 72–73. Brzezinski does not mention that Turner initially saw the president twice a week. At Carter's request, the margin of the daily brief was widened to leave more room for the president's comments. A CIA analyst remembers these as "small in quantity but high in quality." Unattributable interview.

23. *PP Carter 1977*, vol. 1, pp. 218, 220–21.

24. Ibid., p. 282.

25. Neustadt and May, *Thinking in Time*, p. 68.

26. Interview with Admiral Turner, March 18, 1994. A senior operations official confirmed Turner's account in an unattributable interview.

27. Loch K. Johnson, *America's Secret Power: The CIA in a Democratic Society* (Oxford, England: Oxford University Press, 1989), p. 103.

28. *PP Carter 1977*, vol. 1, pp. 656–72.

29. Carter, *Keeping Faith*, pp. 97–98.

30. *PP Carter 1977*, vol. 1, p. 649.

31. Senate Select Committee on Intelligence, *The Soviet Oil Situation: An Evaluation of CIA Analyses of Soviet Oil Production*, 95 Cong., 2 Sess. (Washington, D.C.: U.S. Government Printing Office, 1978). Senate Select Committee on Intelligence, *Report to the Senate Covering the Period May 16, 1977–December 31, 1978*, 96 Cong., 1 Sess. (Washington, D.C.: U.S. Government Printing Office, 1979), pp. 35–36.

32. Senate Select Committee on Intelligence, *Annual Report to the Senate*, 95 Cong., 1 Sess. (Washington, D.C.: U.S. Government Printing Office, 1977). Senate Select Committee on Intelligence, *Report to the Senate Covering the Period May 16, 1977–December 31, 1978*.

33. Turner, *Secrecy and Democracy*.

34. Brzezinski, *Power and Principle*, pp. 35, 42–44, 146. Cyrus Vance, *Hard Choices: Critical Years in America's Foreign Policy* (New York: Simon and Schuster, 1983), pp. 84, 394. On the closure of the Black Chamber, see above, pp. 72–73.

35. DDRS, 1985, no. 2445.

36. Turner's meeting with Carter on September 20, 1977, is recorded in *PP Carter 1977*, vol. 2, p. 1649. Turner does not remember Carter's comments on the TV program, but recalls the president's support for his openness initiative. Interview with Admiral Turner, March 18, 1994.

37. Turner to Forrest L. Fraser, Sept. 23, 1977, DDRS, 1985, no. 2454.

38. Jeffreys-Jones, *CIA*, pp. 218–19. Ranelagh, *CIA*, pp. 209–11.

39. Turner, *Secrecy and Democracy*, pp. 197–99.

40. *PP Carter 1978*, vol. 1, p. 372.

41. *PP Carter 1978*, vol. 1, pp. 189–216.

42. Senate Select Committee on Intelligence, *Report to the Senate Covering the Period May 16, 1977–December 31, 1978*, pp. 23–31.

43. *PP Carter 1978*, vol. 2, pp. 851–53.

44. Senate Select Committee on Intelligence, *Report to the Senate Covering the Period May 16, 1977–December 31, 1978*, p. 12.

45. Brzezinski, *Power and Principle*, pp. 184–85. Andrew and Gordievsky, *KGB*, pp. 557–58.

46. *PP Carter 1978*, vol. 1, pp. 529–35.

47. Turner, *Secrecy and Democracy*, p. 86. Vance, *Hard Choices*, p. 90. Brzezinski, *Power and Principle*, p. 209.

48. *PP Carter 1978*, vol. 1, pp. 1054–57.

49. *PP Carter 1978*, vol. 2, p. 1435.

50. Smith, *Morality, Reason and Power*, p. 165. Brzezinski, *Power and Principle*, p. 238.

51. Unattributable interviews with two CIA analysts. Carter, *Keeping Faith*, pp. 319–21.

52. Information from Charles G. Cogan, former senior CIA operations officer.

53. Carter, *Keeping Faith*, pp. 383, 389. Brzezinski, *Power and Principle*, p. 267.

54. Carter, *Keeping Faith*, pp. 389–405. *PP Carter 1978*, vol. 2, pp. 1519–37.

55. Brzezinski, *Power and Principle*, p. 274.

56. Ibid., p. 358.

57. Gary Sick, *All Fall Down: America's Fateful Encounter with Iran* (London: Tauris, 1985), p. 30.

58. Carter, *Keeping Faith*, p. 438. Turner, *Secrecy and Democracy*, p. 115.

59. Zachary Karabell, " 'Inside the U.S. Espionage Den': The U.S. Embassy and the Fall of the Shah," *Intelligence and National Security*, vol. 8 (1993), no. 1.

60. Brzezinski, *Power and Principle*, p. 367.

61. Sick, *All Fall Down*, p. 90.

62. Turner, *Secrecy and Democracy*, pp. 113–14. Brzezinski, *Power and Principle*, p. 367. Vance, *Hard Choices*, p. 329.

63. Interview with Admiral Turner, March 18, 1994.

64. Sick, *All Fall Down*, p. 31.

65. Ranelagh, *The Agency*, p. 649. On SAVAK see Abbas W. Samii, "The Role of SAVAK in the 1978–79 Iranian Revolution," Ph.D. thesis (Cambridge University, 1994).

66. Sick, *All Fall Down*, pp. 164–65. Karabell, "Inside the U.S. Espionage Den," pp. 54–55. Even SAVAK concentrated on secular rather than religious opposition to the shah; Samii, "The Role of SAVAK."

67. Brzezinski, *Power and Principle*, pp. 376–82.

68. Vance, *Hard Choices*, pp. 336–38. Carter, *Keeping Faith*, p. 446. Brzezinski, *Power and Principle*, pp. 386–87.

69. Brzezinski, *Power and Principle*, pp. 385–98. Vance, *Hard Choices*, pp. 341–43. Carter, *Keeping Faith*, pp. 448–50.

70. Interview with Admiral Turner, March 18, 1994.

71. Dial Torgeson, "U.S. Spy Devices Still Running at Iran Post," *International Herald Tribune*, March 7, 1979. Richelson, *American Espionage and the Soviet Target*, p. 91.

72. *PP Carter 1979*, vol. 1, pp. 107, 158.

73. Vance, *Hard Choices*, p. 342. Richelson, *American Espionage and the Soviet Target*, pp. 91–92. Hedrick Smith, "U.S. Aides Say Loss of Post in Iran Impairs Missile-Monitoring Ability," *New York Times*, March 2, 1979.

74. Carter, *Keeping Faith*, pp. 231, 238.

75. *PP Carter 1979*, vol. 1, pp. 749, 934.

76. Carter, *Keeping Faith*, pp. 238–39.

77. *PP Carter 1979*, vol. 1, p. 1090.

78. Turner, *Secrecy and Democracy*, pp. 240–41.

79. Brzezinski, *Power and Principle*, p. 344.

80. Turner, *Secrecy and Democracy*, pp. 230–31.

81. Brzezinski, *Power and Principle*, pp. 346–47. Vance, *Hard Choices*, pp. 359–60.

82. Turner, *Secrecy and Democracy*, pp. 232–34.

83. Brzezinski, *Power and Principle*, p. 347. Clifford, *Counsel*, p. 636.

84. Carter, *Keeping Faith*, pp. 263–64. *PP Carter 1979*, vol. 2, p. 1602.

85. Turner, *Secrecy and Democracy*, p. 234.

86. Neustadt and May, *Thinking in Time*, pp. xiv, 96.

87. Brzezinski, *Power and Principle*, p. 350.

88. Clifford, *Counsel*, pp. 637–39.

89. Ibid., p. 638. *PP Carter 1979*, vol. 2, pp. 1802–06.

90. Clifford, *Counsel*, pp. 636.

91. Vance, *Hard Choices*, p. 387.

92. Andrew and Gordievsky, *KGB*, pp. 573–78.

93. Smith, *Morality, Reason and Power*, pp. 222–24.

94. Interview with Admiral Turner, March 18, 1994.

95. Vance, *Hard Choices*, p. 389.

96. Interview with Admiral Turner, March 18, 1994. In an unattributable interview, a senior official in the Operations Directorate supported the general thrust of Turner's argument:

> There is a syndrome of the operators, not just in the DO, perhaps whining a little bit, if you want to put it in a pejorative way, at being left in the lurch when the politicians decide to go off some other place, so I don't quarrel with the general premise that there was a feeling, "Do these guys really mean it? Are they in for the long haul?"

97. Garthoff, *Détente and Confrontation*, pp. 962–63. In February 1980 Brzezinski visited Saudi Arabia and Pakistan to negotiate further covert arms supplies.

98. "The Fall of the Shah of Iran," p. 6, KSG Case Study C16-88-794.0. Sick, *All Fall Down*, pp. 181–87.

99. Carter, *Keeping Faith*, pp. 454–56.

100. Ibid., pp. 457–59. Brzezinski, *Power and Principle*, pp. 477–79.

101. Though unable, for security reasons, to mention the KH-11, Brzezinski reveals in his memoirs that the there was "inadequate intelligence regarding the disposition of the hostages." Brzezinski, *Power and Principle*, p. 488.

102. Interview with Admiral Turner, March 18, 1994.

103. Brzezinski, *Power and Principle*, pp. 487–89.

104. Hamilton Jordan, *Crisis: The Last Year of the Carter Presidency* (London: Michael Joseph, 1982), pp. 142–43.

105. Carter, *Keeping Faith*, pp. 483–84. Stansfield Turner, *Terrorism and Democracy* (Boston: Houghton Mifflin, 1991), pp. 90–94.

106. Interview with Admiral Turner, March 18, 1994.

107. Carter, *Keeping Faith*, pp. 504–507. Brzezinski, *Power and Principle*, pp. 489–94. Turner, *Terrorism and Democracy*, pp. 98, 102–9. Vance, *Hard Choices*, pp. 410–11. After the failure of the rescue mission Vance was succeeded as secretary of state by Senator Edmund Muskie.

108. Carter, *Keeping Faith*, pp. 507–10. Turner, *Terrorism and Democracy*, pp. 110–14. Brzezinski, *Power and Principle*, p. 495. Paul B. Ryan, *The Iranian Rescue Mission: Why It Failed* (Annapolis, Md.: Naval Institute Press, 1985), ch. 2.

109. Carter, *Keeping Faith*, pp. 509, 513. Turner, *Terrorism and Democracy*, pp. 115–18. Brzezinski, *Power and Principle*, pp. 495–96.

110. Carter, *Keeping Faith*, pp. 514–18. Brzezinski, *Power and Principle*, pp. 496–99. Turner, *Terrorism and Democracy*, pp. 118–25. Jordan, *Crisis*, pp. 270–75. Ryan, *Iranian Rescue Mission*, chs. 4, 5.

111. Carter, *Keeping Faith*, pp. 519–22. Jordan, *Crisis*, pp. 281–82, 290–91.

112. *PP Carter 1980*–1981, vol. 1, pp. 772–73.

113. [Admiral James L. Holloway], Rescue Mission Report, Aug. 1980, pp. 58–59, DDRS, 1987, no. 1839.

114. Ibid., pp. 29, 59. Ryan, *Iranian Rescue Mission*, pp. 75–76, 133, 166.

115. Carter, *Keeping Faith*, p. 518. Jordan, *Crisis*, pp. 277–78.

116. *PP Carter 1980–81*, vol. 1, pp. 167, 241.

117. John M. Oseth, *Regulating U.S. Intelligence Operations* (Lexington: University Press of Kentucky, 1985), p. 147. See above, p. 435.

118. Turner, *Secrecy and Democracy*, pp. 87–88.

119. *Washington Post*, Oct. 7, 1982. Prados, *Presidents' Secret Wars*, p. 355.

120. Turner, *Secrecy and Democracy*, pp. 86–89.

121. Interview with Dr. Gates, March 14, 1994.

122. Jordan, *Crisis*, p. 7. Conspiracy theorists later predictably alleged that the Reagan election team had plotted with the Iranians before the presidential election to delay the release of the hostages to ensure that Carter was defeated. Equally predictably, later investigations by committees of both the House and the Senate found no evidence to support this implausible theory.

123. Carter, *Keeping Faith*, pp. 3–14. Jordan, *Crisis*, pp. 395–406. Brzezinski, *Power and Principle*, pp. 507–508. Sick, *All Fall Down*, pp. 336–41. None of these accounts was allowed to make specific reference to the role of NSA.

Chapter 12: Ronald Reagan (1981–1989)

1. Stephen Vaughn, "Spies, National Security, and the 'Inertia Projector': The Secret Service Films of Ronald Reagan," *American Quarterly*, vol. 39 (1987), no. 3.

2. Reagan, *An American Life*, pp. 96–97.

3. Ibid., pp. 97–99.

4. Ibid., pp. 111–15, 149. Theoharis (ed.), *Secret Files*, pp. 115–17.

5. See above, p. 404.

6. Bob Woodward, *Veil: The Secret Wars of the CIA 1981–1987* (New York: Simon and Schuster, 1987), p. 32.

7. Jeffreys-Jones, *CIA*, pp. 227–78. Ranelagh, *The Agency*, pp. 600–601.

8. Persico, *Casey*. The PFIAB was abolished by Carter but revived by Reagan.

9. *Nomination of William J. Casey*: Hearing before the Select Committee on Intelligence of the United States Senate, 97 Cong., 1 Sess. (Washington, D.C.: U.S. Government Printing Office, 1981), p. 25.

10. *Nomination of Robert M. Gates*: Hearing before the Select Committee on Intelligence of the United States Senate, 102 Cong., 1 Sess. (Washington, D.C.: U.S. Government Printing Office, 1992), hearing of Sept. 17, 1991.

11. Unattributable interview with senior CIA analyst. Despite suggestions to the contrary, Reagan did actually read the PDB. According to his later chief of staff, Donald Regan, "he loved to read the daily intelligence summary." Don-

ald T. Regan, *For the Record: From Wall Street to Washington*, paperback ed. (London: Arrow Books, 1988), p. 12.

12. Reagan, *An American Life*, p. 490.

13. Unattributable interview with senior CIA analyst. Video briefings were, of course, not confined to the president.

14. Reagan, *An American Life*, p. 368.

15. Persico, *Casey*, p. 221.

16. Prados, *Keepers of the Keys*, pp. 455–57.

17. According to Gates, "I probably spent more time with Casey than anyone else in the agency, and I just never had the sense that he had what I would call a close personal relationship [with Reagan]. I think that his relationship with the president was in a considerable way a distant one." Interview with Dr. Gates, March 14, 1994.

18. Interview with Dr. Gates, March 14, 1994.

19. Persico, *Casey*, pp. 222, 226–27.

20. *PP Reagan 1981*, p. 37.

21. Reagan, *An American Life*, pp. 238–39.

22. Andrew and Gordievsky, *KGB*, pp. 560–62.

23. Reagan, *An American Life*, pp. 239, 474.

24. Persico, *Casey*, pp. 264–65.

25. Andrew and Gordievsky, *KGB*, pp. 577–78.

26. Caspar Weinberger, *Fighting for Peace: Seven Critical Years in the Pentagon* (New York: Warner Books, 1990), pp. 24–30. Margaret Thatcher, *The Downing Street Years* (London: HarperCollins, 1993), p. 252.

27. Reagan, *An American Life*, p. 302. On Kuklinski, whom Reagan does not identify by name, see Valery Masterov, "Spy Kuklinski: Traitor or Patriot?" *Moscow News*, 1992, no. 43; Woodward, *Veil*, pp. 33, 177–786.

28. Alexander M. Haig Jr., *Caveat* (London: Weidenfeld and Nicolson, 1984), p. 96.

29. Andrew and Gordievsky, *KGB*, pp. 582–83.

30. Reagan, *An American Life*, p. 588.

31. According to Gates, ". . . Casey was convinced of Soviet involvement in the assassination attempt. . . . I was agnostic." *Nomination of Robert M. Gates*, testimony by Gates on Oct. 4, 1991.

32. Reagan, *An American Life*, pp. 280–81. On Soviet relations with Qaddafi, see Andrew and Gordievsky, *KGB*, pp. 550–51.

33. Woodward, *Veil*, p. 167. Reagan, *An American Life*, pp. 290–91.

34. Reagan, *An American Life*, pp. 291–92.

35. Woodward, *Veil*, p. 182.

36. Reagan, *An American Life*, p. 291.

37. Ibid. Woodward, *Veil*, p. 182. Persico, *Casey*, p. 298.

38. Andrew and Gordievsky, *KGB*, pp. 550–51.

39. Andrew and Gordievsky (eds.), *Instructions from the Centre*, pp. 148–52. See photo insert.

40. Information from Dr. Charles Cogan, then a senior member of the CIA Operations Directorate. Bush had first met Chalet during his term as DCI.

41. Pierre Favier and Michel Martin-Roland, *La décennie Mitterrand*, vol. 1 (Paris: Seuil, 1990), pp. 94–96. Vetrov had been given the Anglophone code name 'Farewell' by the French in the hope that if the KGB heard any reference to it, they would assume that it referred to an American or British operation. His identity was first publicly revealed by Oleg Gordievsky in 1990. Christopher Andrew and Oleg Gordievsky, *Le KGB dans le monde* (Paris: Fayard, 1990), pp. 619–23.

42. Andrew and Gordievsky, *KGB*, pp. 621–63. Philip Hanson, *Soviet Industrial Espionage: Some New Information* (London: Royal Institute of International Affairs, 1987).

43. Favier and Martin-Roland, *La décennie Mitterrand*, vol. 1, p. 95.

44. Reagan, *An American Life*, p. 300. Woodward, *Veil*, pp. 173–74. Theodore Draper, *A Very Thin Line: The Iran-Contra Affair*, paperback ed. (New York: Touchstone, 1992), pp. 16–17.

45. *PP Reagan 1981*, pp. 1126–40.

46. Andrew and Gordievsky, *KGB*, p. 581.

47. Masterov, "Spy Kuklinski." Woodward, *Veil*, p. 178.

48. Haig, *Caveat*, p. 247.

49. Reagan, *An American Life*, pp. 303, 306.

50. *PP Reagan 1981*, p. 1202.

51. Reagan, *An American Life*, p. 471.

52. Burrows, *Deep Black*, pp. 275–81. *New York Times*, March 10, 1982.

53. *Washington Post*, March 10, 1982. Peter Kornbluh, *Nicaragua: The Price of Intervention* (Washington, D.C.: Institute for Policy Studies, 1987), p. 55.

54. Reagan, *An American Life*, pp. 358–59.

55. Lawrence Freedman, "Intelligence Operations in the Falklands," *Intelligence and National Security*, vol. 1 (1986), no. 1. Lawrence Freedman and Virginia Gambia-Stonehouse, *Signals of War: The Falklands Conflict of 1982* (London: Faber, 1990), pp. 131–32.

56. The congratulations to Tovey, and his comment on them, were later revealed in a House of Commons speech by Denis Healey.

57. Reagan, *An American Life*, pp. 359–60.

58. George P. Shultz, *Turmoil and Triumph: My Years as Secretary of State* (New York: Charles Scribner's Sons, 1993), p. 152.

59. Reagan, *An American Life*, pp. 316, 320.

60. Carl Bernstein, "The Holy Alliance," *Time*, Feb. 24, 1992, p. 32.

61. Among those sources was the British agent Oleg Gordievsky, who, after four years working in Moscow Center, was posted in June 1982 to the KGB residency in London, where he was able to renew contact with British intelligence.

62. Andrew and Gordievsky, *KGB*, p. 639.

63. Bernstein, "The Holy Alliance," pp. 28–29.

64. Reagan, *An American Life*, p. 387.

65. Bernstein, "The Holy Alliance," p. 28.

66. Interview with Dr. Gates, March 14, 1994. According to Gates, Wal-

ters's meetings with the pope "were more in the form of briefing than dialogue." His briefings also included Central America and Afghanistan.

67. Bernstein, "The Holy Alliance," pp. 31–34.

68. Andrew and Gordievsky (eds.), *Instructions from the Centre*, p. 152. Gordievsky revealed Operation Sirena 2 to SIS who, under normal liaison arrangements, informed the CIA. The agency may also have discovered it from other sources.

69. William Safire, "The Trial of Casey," *New York Times*, Sept. 19, 1991.

70. Shultz, *Turmoil and Triumph*, p. 126.

71. Andrew and Gordievsky (eds.), *Instructions from the Centre*, pp. 152–54.

72. Shultz, *Turmoil and Triumph*, pp. 288–89.

73. *PP Reagan 1983*, vol. 1, pp. 603–604.

74. Andrew and Gordievsky (eds.), *Instructions from the Centre*, pp. 114–28.

75. Information from Oleg Gordievsky. On the failure by SIS to reveal Gordievsky's identity, a senior member of the CIA Operations Directorate said in an unattributable interview, "I don't fault them for that. We wouldn't have told them."

76. Reagan, *An American Life*, pp. 568–70. *PP Reagan 1983*, vol. 1, p. 364.

77. *PP Reagan 1983*, vol. 1, pp. 437–43.

78. Some of the best intelligence on KGB "active measures" against Reagan came from Gordievsky; Andrew and Gordievsky, *KGB*, pp. 589–90.

79. Andrew and Gordievsky (eds.), *Instructions from the Centre*, pp. 129–33.

80. Shultz, *Turmoil and Triumph*, pp. 361–62.

81. Seymour M. Hersh, *The Target Is Destroyed* (London: Faber, 1986), chs. 9–13.

82. Shultz, *Turmoil and Triumph*, pp. 363–64.

83. Hersh, *The Target Is Destroyed*, pp. 151–52.

84. Reagan, *An American Life*, pp. 583–84.

85. *PP Reagan 1983*, vol. 2, pp. 1227–30.

86. Hersh, *The Target Is Destroyed*, ch. 13.

87. The text of Andropov's statement is reprinted in Strobe Talbott, *The Russians and Reagan* (New York: Vintage Books, 1984), pp. 119–27.

88. Thatcher, *Downing Street Years*, pp. 328–32.

89. *PP Reagan 1983*, vol. 2, p. 1521.

90. Shultz, *Turmoil and Triumph*, pp. 328–41.

91. Reagan, *An American Life*, pp. 455–58.

92. Don Oberdorfer, *The Turn: How the Cold War Came to an End* (London: Jonathan Cape, 1992), pp. 64–65.

93. Andrew and Gordievsky, *KGB*, p. 599.

94. Ibid.

95. Oberdorfer, *The Turn*, p. 65.

96. Andrew and Gordievsky (eds.), *Instructions from the Centre*, pp. 134–36.

97. Andrew and Gordievsky, *KGB*, p. 600.

98. Reagan, *An American Life*, pp. 588–59. Reagan identifies the date of the diary entry as "less than a week before the Soviets walked out of the INF talks" on November 23; he also implies that it was several days before November 20.

99. Information from Oleg Gordievsky. Reagan's appeal to Gorbachev, like that of Mrs. Thatcher, was unsuccessful. Gordievsky's wife and children were not allowed to leave Russia until after the failed coup of August 1991.

100. *PP Reagan 1984*, vol. 1, pp. 40–44.

101. Talbott, *The Russians and Reagan*, pp. 83–84.

102. Reagan, *An American Life*, p. 602.

103. Andrew and Gordievsky (eds.), *Instructions from the Centre*, pp. 137–40. Andrew and Gordievsky, *KGB*, pp. 601–605.

104. Interview with Dr. Gates, March 14, 1994.

105. Draper, *A Very Thin Line*, pp. 19–24. Persico, *Casey*, pp. 372–80.

106. Lawrence E. Walsh, *Final Report of the Independent Counsel for Iran/Contra Matters* (Washington, D.C.: U.S. Court of Appeal for the District of Columbia Circuit, 1994), vol. 1, p. 81.

107. Joel Brinkley and Stephen Engelberg (eds.), *Report of the Congressional Committees Investigating the Iran-Contra Affair with the Minority View* (New York: Times Books, 1988), pp. 48–52.

108. The text of Gates's memo was published in the *New York Times*, Sept. 20, 1991, p. A14.

109. Oliver L. North, *Under Fire: An American Story* (London: Fontana, 1992), pp. 152, 180, 223–28.

110. Brinkley and Engelberg (eds.), *Report of the Congressional Committees*, pp. 47, 52, 55, 59.

111. *PP Reagan 1985*, vol. 1, p. 229. According to some press reports, Reagan used the phrase "moral equivalent."

112. North, *Under Fire*, p. 229.

113. Reagan, *An American Life*, p. 492. Cf. Regan, *For the Record*, pp. 10–11.

114. *PP Reagan 1985*, vol. 2, p. 886.

115. Regan, *For the Record*, pp. 10–11.

116. Reagan, *An American Life*, pp. 504–507. Brinkley and Engelberg (eds.), *Report of the Congressional Committees*, pp. 148–51. Draper, *A Very Thin Line*, ch. 8.

117. Brinkley and Engelberg (eds.), *Report of the Congressional Committees*, p. 145.

118. Interview with Dr. Gates, March 14, 1994.

119. Brinkley and Engelberg (eds.), *Report of the Congressional Committees*, pp. 125, 235–36. North, *Under Fire*, pp. 10–14. The fullest collection of documents on Iran-Contra is the microfiche collection, *The Iran-Contra Affair: The Making of a Scandal, 1983–1988*, published in 1989 by the National Security Archive, Washington, D.C., in association with Chadwyck-Healey. Another National Security Archive publication, Peter Kornbluh and

Malcolm Byrne (eds.), *The Iran-Contra Scandal: The Declassified History* (New York: New Press, 1993), though shorter, contains some recently declassified documents not included in the microfiche collection.

120. Interview with Dr. Gates, March 14, 1994.

121. Charles G. Cogan, "The Response of the Strong to the Weak: The American Raid on Libya, 1986," *Intelligence and National Security*, vol. 6 (1991), pp. 611–15. Interview with Dr. Cogan, May 1992.

122. Cogan, "The Response of the Strong to the Weak," p. 611. Shultz, *Turmoil and Triumph*, p. 683. David C. Martin and John Walcott, *Best Laid Plans: The Inside Story of America's War Against Terrorism* (New York: Harper & Row, 1988), pp. 284–86.

123. Interview with Reagan's military aide, Colonel Charles Brower, Sept. 18, 1993.

124. Cogan, "The Response of the Strong to the Weak," pp. 614–15. Reagan, *An American Life*, pp. 518–20.

125. Reagan, *An American Life*, pp. 518–19. Shultz, *Turmoil and Triumph*, p. 686.

126. *PP Reagan 1986*, vol. 1, pp. 468–69.

127. Cogan, "The Response of the Strong to the Weak," pp. 615–18. Reagan, *An American Life*, p. 520. Shultz, *Turmoil and Triumph*, p. 687.

128. *PP Reagan 1986*, vol. 2, pp. 1274–76.

129. Shultz, *Turmoil and Triumph*, p. 819.

130. Reagan, *An American Life*, pp. 516–17.

131. Brinkley and Engelberg (eds.), *Report of the Congressional Committees*, pp. 203–13. Draper, *A Very Thin Line*, ch. 15. North, *Under Fire*, ch. 3. Reagan, *An American Life*, pp. 520–21.

132. Reagan, *An American Life*, pp. 522–26. Brinkley and Engelberg (eds.), *Report of the Congressional Committees*, ch. 14. Draper, *A Very Thin Line*, chs. 19, 20. North, *Under Fire*, ch. 13.

133. Brinkley and Engelberg (eds.), *Report of the Congressional Committees*, pp. 227–32, 239–54. Draper, *A Very Thin Line*, ch. 21.

134. Walsh, *Final Report*, vol. 1, pp. 457–58.

135. *PP Reagan 1986*, vol. 2, pp. 1521–22

136. Draper, *A Very Thin Line*, pp. 464–70. Kornbluh and Byrne (eds.), *The Iran-Contra Scandal*, pp. 315–17. Shultz, *Turmoil and Triumph*, pp. 812–16.

137. *PP Reagan 1986*, vol. 2, pp. 1546–48.

138. Shultz, *Turmoil and Triumph*, pp. 818–28.

139. *PP Reagan 1986*, vol. 2, pp. 1567–75.

140. Walsh, *Final Report*, vol. 1, p. 508.

141. *PP Reagan 1986*, vol. 2, p. 1575.

142. Walsh, *Final Report*, vol. 1, pp. 112–20, 444–46. Draper, *A Very Thin Line*, pp. 486–90, 550–51. North, *Under Fire*, pp. 312–28.

143. Walsh, *Final Report*, vol. 1, pp. xviii, 525–45.

144. Regan, *For the Record*, pp. 38–39. Reagan, *An American Life*, p. 530.

145. Walsh, *Final Report*, vol. 1, p. 516.

146.   Ibid., pp. 565–66.

147.   According to Regan, impeachment was "a no-no word" in the White House. Ibid., p. 507.

148.   Draper, *A Very Thin Line*, p. 530.

149.   *PP Reagan 1986*, vol. 2, pp. 1587–88.

150.   Walsh, *Final Report*, vol. 1, ch. 31. In his response to Walsh, Meese claimed that his statement at the press conference indicated that Reagan had been aware of the November 1985 shipment at the time, though he learned the "details" only later; ibid., vol. 3, p. 411. Meese's interpretation seems unconvincing. So does Walsh's argument that his statement was an important part of a high-level cover-up "conspiracy" of top officials, orchestrated by Meese. Cf. Theodore Draper, "Walsh's Last Stand," *New York Review of Books*, March 3, 1994.

151.   Draper, *A Very Thin Line*, pp. 542–50. North, *Under Fire*, pp. 5–7.

152.   "Extracts from Vice-President Bush Diary Transcripts, November 4, 1986–January 2, 1987" (released by the Bush White House, Jan. 15, 1993); copy in National Security Archive, Washington, D.C.

153.   Shultz, *Turmoil and Triumph*, pp. 848–57. Draper, *A Very Thin Line*, pp. 552–57.

154.   Draper, *A Very Thin Line*, pp. 596–98. Kornbluh and Byrne (eds.), *The Iran-Contra Scandal*, part III. *The Tower Commission Report* (New York: Times Books, 1987).

155.   Walsh, *Final Report*, vol. 1, p. 561.

156.   Brinkley and Engelberg (eds.), *Report of the Congressional Committees*, pp. 32–33.

157.   Walsh, *Final Report*, vol. 1, p. 561.

158.   Unattributable interview with senior member of CIA Operations Directorate.

159.   Shultz, *Turmoil and Triumph*, pp. 692, 1087. Mohammad Yousaf and Mark Adkin, *Bear Trap: Afghanistan's Untold Story* (London: Leo Cooper, 1992), p. 182. Brigadier Yousaf, head of the Afghan Bureau of Pakistani Inter-Services Intelligence from 1983 to 1987, cooperated with the CIA in supplying the Mujahideen with Stingers.

160.   Yousaf and Adkin, *Bear Trap*, pp. 174–76.

161.   Christopher Andrew, "Moscow Terror Tactics in the Afghan War," *Daily Telegraph*, Aug. 10, 1987.

162.   Oberdorfer, *The Turn*, pp. 240, 274. Cf. Shultz, *Turmoil and Triumph*, pp. 872–73.

163.   Robert M. Gates, "CIA and the Collapse of the Soviet Union: Hit or Miss?": address to the Foreign Policy Association, New York, May 20, 1992, pp. 3–4 (transcript supplied to the author by CIA Public Liaison Staff). Though pessimistic, CIA reports on the Soviet economy during most of Reagan's presidency were not pessimistic enough. According to Gates, ". . . Our statistical analysis, while the best available East or West, in absolute terms, described a stronger, larger economy than our own analysis portrayed and than existed in reality. . . . Our quantitative data failed adequately to capture the growing

qualitative disparity between the Soviet economy and the West. We were aware of this and repeatedly emphasized the point to our readers. . . . I would contend also that our quantitative analysis always considerably underestimated the real burden economically of the Soviet military." Ibid., p. 7.

164. Reagan, *An American Life*, p. 660.

165. Shultz, *Turmoil and Triumph*, pp. 864–65, 1002–03.

166. *Nomination of Robert M. Gates*, hearings of Oct. 2–3, 1991. Gates's confirmation as DCI in 1991 indicates that the main charges that he had politicized intelligence assessment were rejected by a majority of the Senate select committee.

167. Ibid, hearing of Oct. 3, 1991. Gates's speech was quoted by Senator Bill Bradley.

168. Shultz, *Turmoil and Triumph*, p. 1003.

169. Reagan, *An American Life*, pp. 661, 665–68, 719.

170. Andrew and Gordievsky, *KGB*, pp. 630–31.

171. Regan, *For the Record*, p. 249.

172. After Gates's withdrawal, Reagan initially favored the appointment of former Senator Howard Baker, but instead made him his chief of staff in succession to Donald Regan. Reagan's next choice was a Washington lawyer, Edward Bennett Williams, who was discovered to be dying of cancer (Reagan, *An American Life*, p. 536). Senator Tower was then approached, at first accepted the post of DCI, then changed his mind (Mark Perry, *Eclipse: The Last Days of the CIA* [New York: William Morrow, 1992], pp. 59–60). Gates's first private meeting with Vice-President Bush came shortly after the withdrawal of his own nomination. "I urged him to use his influence to avoid having a political hack appointed as Casey's replacement," Gates recalls. "I recommended three people: Howard Baker, Bill Webster, and Edward Bennett Williams. Bush said he didn't have much influence." Interview with Dr. Gates, March 14, 1994.

173. Interview with Dr. Gates, March 14, 1994.

174. Perry, *Eclipse*, p. 324. This view was supported by a senior CIA official, also a Webster supporter, in an unattributable interview.

175. Reagan, *An American Life*, p. 536.

176. Unattributable interview.

177. Shultz, *Turmoil and Triumph*, pp. 864, 877, 924, 991, 1138.

178. Thatcher, *Downing Street Years*, pp. 770–71.

179. Shultz, *Turmoil and Triumph*, pp. 997–98. Andrew and Gordievsky, *KGB*, pp. 630–31. Oberdorfer, *The Turn*, pp. 249–51.

180. Shultz, *Turmoil and Triumph*, p. 1003.

181. Ibid., p. 1005. Oberdorfer, *The Turn*, p. 259.

182. Regan, *For the Record*, pp. 3–5, 70–74, 300–301, 344, 359, 367–70.

183. Andrew and Gordievsky, *KGB*, pp. 581, 625. Andrew and Gordievsky (eds.), *Instructions from the Centre*, chs. 4, 5.

184. Information from Oleg Gordievsky. Ames was arrested on March 22, 1994. On Gordievsky's escape, see Andrew and Gordievsky, *KGB*, pp. 8–16.

185. Oleg Gordievsky, "Aldrich Ames, My Would-Be Killer," *The Spectator*, March 5, 1994.

186. Interview with Dr. Gates, March 14, 1994.

187. Oberdorfer, *The Turn*, p. 274. Shultz, *Turmoil and Triumph*, pp. 1003, 1087–94.

188. Reagan, *An American Life*, p. 707.

189. Interview with Dr. Gates, March 14, 1994.

190. Reagan, *An American Life*, p. 709. On his way back from Moscow, Margaret Thatcher found Reagan still "upset" by the behavior of the KGB; *Downing Street Years*, p. 776.

191. Andrew and Gordievsky, *KGB*, p. 625.

192. *PP Reagan 1988–89*, vol. 2, p. 1721. Cf. the diary entry recorded in Reagan, *An American Life*, p. 709.

193. *PP Reagan 1988–89*, vol. 2, pp. 1223–24.

194. According to one of the intelligence officials involved, "There was great strain in trying to use some of this information. A great effort was made to try to sterilize it and disguise it. But, of course, the policymakers were saying, 'Look, I can't use it in this bland form. People will say, Where's the beef?'" Unattributable interview.

195. Shultz, *Turmoil and Triumph*, p. 242.

196. According to an unattributable CIA source, "a lot of good intelligence" on Rabta also came from the British.

197. Reagan, *An American Life*, p. 704.

198. Unattributable interview.

199. Shultz, *Turmoil and Triumph*, pp. 244–45

200. *PP Reagan 1988–89*, vol. 2, p. 1648.

201. Oberdorfer, *The Turn*, p. 325. Reagan, *An American Life*, pp. 722–23.

Chapter 13: George Bush (1989–1993)

1. Bush, *Looking Forward*, pp. 153–56, 166. Bush gave the same account of his nomination in a number of speeches.

2. Garry Wills, "Father Knows Best," *New York Review of Books*, Nov. 5, 1992, p. 36.

3. OH Prescott Bush, pp. 405–11; Columbia University Oral History Project, Butler Library, Columbia University, New York.

4. Unattributable interview.

5. Meyer, *Facing Reality*, pp. 225–26.

6. *PP Bush 1991*, vol. 2, p. 1319.

7. Kerry Mullins and Aaron Wildavsky, "The Procedural Presidency of George Bush," *Political Science Quarterly*, vol. 107 (1992), no. 1, p. 43.

8. Dick Cheney, interviewed on "The Choice," BBC2, Nov. 1, 1992.

9. Philip Ziegler, *Wilson* (London: Weidenfeld and Nicolson, 1993), p. 478. Ben Pimlott, *Wilson* (London: HarperCollins, 1992), p. 721. There was one serious plotter against Wilson in MI5, Peter Wright, who claimed in his memoirs that thirty other officers in MI5 "had given their approval to a plot."

Wright later admitted in a television interview that this claim was "exaggerated." When asked, "How many people were still serious in joining you in trying to get rid of Wilson?," he replied, "One, I should say."

10. Ranelagh, *Agency*, p. 633.

11. Turner, *Secrecy and Democracy*, pp. 24–25.

12. Interview with William Colby, March 14, 1994.

13. Mullins and Wildavsky, "The Procedural Presidency of George Bush," p. 43.

14. *PP Bush 1991*, vol. 1, p. 1267. See also the partial list of appointments published in appendix A of the volumes of *PP Bush*.

15. Unattributable interview with senior member of the Directorate of Intelligence.

16. Unattributable interview with DO officer. "I think George Bush liked Bill Webster but he [Webster] was never in there," says the same source.

17. At the end of his presidency, Bush referred to Gates as "my right-hand person and trusted adviser when at the White House." He told the audience at Langley when presenting Gates with the National Security Medal in January 1993 that he wanted them to know "how much I trust him, admire him and respect him." *PP Bush 1992–93*, vol. 2, pp. 2239–40.

18. Gates, "CIA and the Collapse of the Soviet Union," p. 7.

19. *PP Bush 1989*, vol. 1, p. 23.

20. Michael R. Beschloss and Strobe Talbott, *At the Highest Levels: The Inside Story of the End of the Cold War* (Boston: Little, Brown & Co., 1993), pp. 24–25, 28–29, 43–45.

21. Gates, "CIA and the Collapse of the Soviet Union," p. 4.

22. Beschloss and Talbott, *At the Highest Levels*, p. 309n.

23. Ibid., pp. 47–48.

24. Gates, "CIA and the Collapse of the Soviet Union," p. 5.

25. Beschloss and Talbott, *At the Highest Levels*, pp. 61–66.

26. One example of Bush's curiosity about the KGB was his invitation to Oleg Gordievsky early in his presidency to visit the White House for a briefing session. Bush also questioned him about his estimate of Gorbachev's future prospects. Information from Oleg Gordievsky.

27. See above, p. 498.

28. Andrew and Gordievsky (eds.), *Instructions from the Centre*, pp. 294–301.

29. Andrew and Gordievsky, *KGB*, p. 627.

30. Christopher Andrew, "KGB Foreign Intelligence from Brezhnev to the Coup," *Intelligence and National Security*, vol. 8 (1993), no. 3, pp. 62–63.

31. *PP Bush 1989*, vol. 1, pp. 540–43. The speech drew on some of the conclusions and phraseology of a secret National Security Directive, NSD-23; Beschloss and Talbott, *At the Highest Levels*, pp. 69–71.

32. Beschloss and Talbott, *At the Highest Levels*, pp. 73–74.

33. Oberdorfer, *The Turn*, p. 346.

34. Beschloss and Talbott, *At the Highest Levels*, pp. 84–94, 126.

35. *PP Bush 1989*, vol. 2, p. 1471.

36. Interview with Dr. Gates, March 14, 1994.

37. Oberdorfer, *The Turn*, pp. 353–62.

38. *PP Bush 1989*, vol. 2, p. 1116.

39. Gates, "CIA and the Collapse of the Soviet Union," p. 5.

40. *PP Bush 1989*, vol. 2, pp. 1489–90.

41. Andrew, "KGB Foreign Intelligence from Brezhnev to the Coup," p. 63.

42. Beschloss and Talbott, *At the Highest Levels*, pp. 139–44.

43. Ibid., pp. 128–30, 153–68. Oberdorfer, *The Turn*, pp. 377–84.

44. *PP Bush 1989*, vol. 2, pp. 1625–35.

45. Beschloss and Talbott, *At the Highest Levels*, pp. 103–104, 165–68.

46. Interview with Dr. Gates, March 14, 1994.

47. James Adams, *The New Spies* (London: Hutchinson, 1994), ch. 19 (citing interviews with Pasechnik and others).

48. *PP Bush 1989*, vol. 1, p. 547.

49. Unattributable interview.

50. Bob Woodward, *The Commanders*, paperback ed. (New York: Simon and Schuster, 1992), chs. 11, 12. Perry, *Eclipse*, ch. 11.

51. *PP Bush 1989*, vol. 2, pp. 1335–41.

52. Ann Devrot and David B. Ottaway, "CIA Director Under Fire," Washington *Post*, Oct. 16, 1989. Perry, *Eclipse*, pp. 285–93.

53. Unattributable interview.

54. *PP Bush 1989*, vol. 2, pp. 1724–25.

55. Woodward, *The Commanders*, pp. 136–37, 184–86, 193–94.

56. *PP Bush 1989*, vol. 2, pp. 1722–25, 1731.

57. Woodward, *The Commanders*, pp. 191–93.

58. Leslie H. Gelb, "Bush's Iraqi Blunder," *New York Times*, May 4, 1992.

59. *PP Bush 1990*, vol. 1, p. 450.

60. Woodward, *The Commanders*, ch. 16. Perry, *Eclipse*, pp. 349–53.

61. Gates, "CIA and the Collapse of the Soviet Union," p. 5.

62. *PP Bush 1990*, vol. 1, pp. 556–57.

63. Beschloss and Talbott, *At the Highest Levels*, p. 205.

64. Seymour M. Hersh, "On the Nuclear Edge," *New Yorker*, March 29, 1993. Interview with Dr. Gates, March 14, 1994.

65. Interview with Dr. Gates, March 14, 1994.

66. Hersh, "On the Nuclear Edge."

67. Interview with Dr. Gates, March 14, 1994.

68. Unattributable interview.

69. Interview with Dr. Gates, March 14, 1994.

70. Beschloss and Talbott, *At the Highest Levels*, ch. 11. Oberdorfer, *The Turn*, pp. 410–33.

71. Gates, "CIA and the Collapse of the Soviet Union," p. 5.

72. Perry, *Eclipse*, pp. 353–55. Woodward, *The Commanders*, pp. 216–23. H. Norman Schwarzkopf, *It Doesn't Take a Hero* (New York: Bantam Press, 1992), pp. 291–95.

73. Interview with Dr. Gates, March 14, 1994.

74. *PP Bush 1990*, vol. 2, pp. 1083–85.

75. Schwarzkopf, *It Doesn't Take a Hero*, pp. 295–98.

76. *PP Bush 1990*, vol. 2, p. 1113.

77. Jean Edward Smith, *George Bush's War* (New York: Henry Holt, 1992), pp. 67–68. Cf. *PP Bush 1991*, vol. 1, p. 226.

78. Woodward, *The Commanders*, pp. 236–37.

79. Adams, *The New Spies*, p. 48 (citing interview with William Webster).

80. Woodward, *The Commanders*, pp. 260–61. *PP Bush 1990*, vol. 2, p. 1102.

81. Smith, *George Bush's War*, pp. 4, 6.

82. Woodward, *The Commanders*, pp. 251–53.

83. Schwarzkopf, *It Doesn't Take a Hero*, pp. 302–305.

84. Thatcher, *Downing Street Years*, pp. 819–21.

85. Unattributable interview. The visit is recorded in *PP Bush 1990*, vol. 2, p. 1831.

86. Smith, *George Bush's War*, p. 232n.

87. See photo insert.

88. Interview with Dr. Gates, March 14, 1994.

89. Schwarzkopf, *It Doesn't Take a Hero*, p. 346.

90. Smith, *George Bush's War*, pp. 161–63.

91. *PP Bush 1990*, vol. 2, p. 1158.

92. *PP Bush 1990*, vol. 2, pp. 1203–04.

93. See below, p. 526.

94. Interview with Dr. Gates, March 14, 1994.

95. House of Representatives Committee on Armed Services, Subcommittee on Oversight and Investigations, *Intelligence Successes and Failures in Operations Desert Shield/Storm*, 103 Cong. 1 Sess., August 1993, pp. 3–4, 35–36. *PP Bush 1991*, vol. 1, p. 61.

96. House of Representatives Committee on Armed Services, *Intelligence Successes and Failures*, pp. 12–13, 19–25.

97. Ibid., p. 3. House Armed Services Committee, News Release, Aug. 16, 1993.

98. See above, pp. 185–87, 196–97.

99. Schwarzkopf, *It Doesn't Take a Hero*, pp. 417–18.

100. House of Representatives Committee on Armed Services, *Intelligence Successes and Failures*, pp. 3, 17.

101. Schwarzkopf, *It Doesn't Take a Hero*, p. 419.

102. House of Representatives Committee on Armed Services, *Intelligence Successes and Failures*, p. 17. Before the publication of the committee report, Schwarzkopf had claimed that ten mobile launchers had been destroyed; *It Doesn't Take a Hero*, p. 417.

103. House of Representatives Committee on Armed Services, *Intelligence Successes and Failures*, pp. 27–33, 39–41, 43–44.

104. *PP Bush 1991*, vol. 1, p. 486; vol. 2, p. 1319.

105. Ibid., vol. 1, pp. 448–49.

106. House of Representatives Committee on Armed Services, *Intelligence Successes and Failures*, p. 7.

107. Gates, "CIA and the Collapse of the Soviet Union," p. 6.

108. *PP Bush 1991*, vol. 1, pp. 503–504.

109. Beschloss and Talbott, *At the Highest Levels*, p. 381.

110. Andrew, "KGB Foreign Intelligence from Brezhnev to the Coup," p. 65.

111. A copy of the 1985 directive had been obtained by Oleg Gordievsky; Andrew and Gordievsky (eds.), *Instructions from the Centre*, pp. 155–59, 302.

112. Ibid., pp. 302–307. Andrew, "KGB Foreign Intelligence from Brezhnev to the Coup," pp. 64–65.

113. Beschloss and Talbott, *At the Highest Levels*, pp. 398–99.

114. *PP Bush 1991*, vol. 1, pp. 702–704. Beschloss and Talbott, *At the Highest Levels*, pp. 399–401.

115. Interview with Dr. Gates, March 14, 1994.

116. Seymour M. Hersh, "The Wild East," *Atlantic Monthly*, June 1994, p. 85.

117. START Treaty, July 31, 1991: articles IX, X; protocol on telemetric information (text published by U.S. Arms Control and Disarmament Agency).

118. *Does the Arms Control and Disarmament Agency Have a Future?* (Washington, D.C.: Henry L. Stimson Center, 1992), pp. 2–3.

119. Gates, "CIA and the Collapse of the Soviet Union," p. 6. Beschloss and Talbott, *At the Highest Levels*, p. 421.

120. Interview with Dr. Gates, May 1, 1992.

121. Beschloss and Talbott, *At the Highest Levels*, ch. 21. *PP Bush 1991*, vol. 2, p. 1058.

122. Hersh, "The Wild East," pp. 85–86. Details of SIGINT operations during the coup attempt still remain highly classified.

123. *PP Bush*, vol. 2, p. 1072.

124. Beschloss and Talbott, *At the Highest Levels*, pp. 433–38, 461. On nuclear proliferation, see below, p. 532.

125. *Nomination of Robert M. Gates;* quotation from testimony by Gates on Oct. 3, 1991.

126. *PP Bush 1991*, vol. 2, pp. 1266, 1318.

127. Interview with Dr. Gates, March 14, 1994.

128. *PP Bush 1991*, vol. 2, p. 1437.

129. Gates, "Statement on Change in CIA and the Intelligence Community," April 1, 1992, p. 4; text supplied by CIA Public Liaison Staff.

130. Ibid.

131. Confronted with American intelligence on the Russian biological warfare program in March 1992, Yeltsin admitted its existence for the first time. In April he signed a decree closing down the program. Two years later it was still continuing. Vadim Chelikov, "A Weapon Against their Own People," *Moscow News*, 1992, no. 23. Adams, *New Spies*, p. 278. "Russia Fails To End Germ Warfare Research," *The Times* (London), April 9, 1994.

132. Gates, "CIA and the Collapse of the Soviet Union," p. 1.

133. Gates, "Change in CIA and the Intelligence Community," p. 4.

134. *PP Bush 1991,* vol. 2, pp. 1319, 1438.

135. *A Consumer's Guide to Intelligence* (Washington, D.C.: CIA, 1994), p. 14.

136. Gates, "Change in CIA and the Intelligence Community," pp. 10–13. The structure of the intelligence community, as modified by these reforms, is set out in the CIA pamphlet, *A Consumer's Guide to Intelligence.*

137. Unattributable interview.

138. Gates, "Change in CIA and the Intelligence Community," p. 13.

139. Ibid., p. 14.

140. Eric Schmitt, "Spy-Satellite Unit Faces a New Life in Daylight," *New York Times,* Nov. 3, 1992. Allan E. Goodman and Bruce D. Berkowitz, "Intelligence Without the Cold War," *Intelligence and National Security,* vol. 9 (1994), no. 1, pp. 302–303.

141. Douglas Waller, "The CIA's New Spies," *Newsweek,* April 12, 1993, p. 36. Goodman and Berkowitz, "Intelligence Without the Cold War," p. 307.

142. Gates, "Change in CIA and the Intelligence Community," p. 16.

143. Robert M. Gates, "Guarding Against Politicization," *Studies in Intelligence,* vol. 36 (1992), no. 5, pp. 5–13. *Studies in Intelligence* is the usually classified CIA in-house journal; this issue has been declassified.

144. Robert M. Gates, "CIA and Openness," Feb. 21, 1992; text supplied by CIA Public Liaison Staff. Gates, "Change in CIA and the Intelligence Community," pp. 8–9.

145. Goodman and Berkowitz, "Intelligence Without the Cold War," p. 303.

146. Interview with Admiral Turner, March 18, 1994.

147. Schmitt, "Spy-Satellite Unit Faces a New Life In Daylight."

148. Patrick E. Tyler, "Gates, in MidEast, Is Said To Discuss Ouster of Hussein," *New York Times,* Feb. 7, 1992.

149. Unattributable interview.

150. Interview with Dr. Gates, March 14, 1994.

Conclusion: Intelligence After the Cold War

1. Gates, "An Opportunity Unfulfilled," pp. 35, 38.

2. See above, p. 365.

3. Gates, "An Opportunity Unfulfilled," p. 38.

4. Interview with Dr. Gates, March 14, 1994.

5. See above, p. 504.

6. Unattributable interview.

7. Christopher Andrew, "The Nature of Military Intelligence," in Keith Neilson and B. J. C. McKercher (eds.), *Go Spy the Land: Military Intelligence in History* (Westport, Conn.: Praeger, 1992), pp. 4–5. Desmond Ball and Robert Windren, "Soviet Signals Intelligence (Sigint): Organization and Management," *Intelligence and National Security,* vol. 4 (1989), no. 4.

8. Waller, "The CIA's New Spies," p. 36.

9. *PP Bush 1991,* vol. 2, p. 1438.

10. Ted Galen Carpenter, "Closing the Nuclear Umbrella," *Foreign Affairs*, March-April 1994, p. 13.

11. Seth Cropsey, "The Only Credible Deterrent," ibid., p. 17.

12. R. James Woolsey, Address to Conference entitled "The Origins and Development of the CIA in the Administration of Harry S. Truman," March 17, 1994.

13. *PP Bush 1992-93*, vol. 2, pp. 2239-40.

A. Unpublished Sources

The greater part of the vast archive of the American intelligence community remains classified. There are, however, large numbers of intelligence and intelligence-related documents in the National Archives, presidential libraries, and a number of other libraries and archives. Detailed references to the main files consulted are given in endnotes. Declassified official documents may be consulted in microfiche form in the Declassified Document Reference System.

B. Published Works

Works listed are limited to those cited in the notes.

1. PUBLISHED DOCUMENTS

Christopher Andrew and Oleg Gordievsky (eds.), *Instructions from the Centre: Top Secret Files on KGB Foreign Operations, 1975–1985* (London: Hodder and Stoughton, 1991): published in the United States as *Comrade Kryuchkov's Instructions: Top Secret Files on KGB Foreign Operations, 1975–1985* (Stanford, Calif.: Stanford University Press, 1993).

Roy P. Basler (ed.), *The Collected Works of Abraham Lincoln* (New Brunswick, N.J.: Rutgers University Press, 1953–55).

Paul H. Bergeron (ed.), *The Papers of Andrew Johnson*, vols. 8–10 (Knoxville: University of Tennessee Press, 1989–92).

Beatrice B. Berle and Travis B. Jacobs (eds.), *Navigating the Rapids, 1918–1971: From the Papers of Adolph A. Berle* (New York: Harcourt Brace Jovanovich, 1973).

Joel Brinkley and Stephen Engelberg (eds.), *Report of the Congressional Committees Investigating the Iran-Contra Affair with the Minority View* (New York: Times Books, 1988).

George A. Brownell, *The Origin and Development of the National Security Agency* (Laguna Hills, Calif.: Aegean Park Press, 1981).

Orville H. Bullitt (ed.), *For the President, Personal and Secret: Correspondence Between Franklin D. Roosevelt and William C. Bullitt* (London: André Deutsch, 1973).

Judith F. Buncher (ed.), *The CIA and the Security Debate* (New York: Facts on File, 1976).

Anthony Cave Brown (ed.), *The Secret War Report of the OSS*, paperback ed. (New York: Berkley, 1976).

Richard D. Challener (ed.), *United States Military Intelligence Weekly Summaries* (New York: Garland Publishing, 1978).

Lawrence Chang and Peter Kornbluh (eds.), *The Cuban Missile Crisis (1962): A National Security Archive Documents Reader* (New York: New Press, 1992).

Philander D. Chase (ed.), *The Papers of George Washington. Revolutionary War Series* (Charlottesville: University Press of Virginia, 1985), vol. 1.

CIA, *The CIA Under Harry Truman*, ed. Michael Warner (Washington, D.C.: CIA, 1994).

CIA Documents on the Cuban Missile Crisis, 1962 (Washington, D.C.: CIA, 1992).

CIA: The Pike Report (Nottingham, England: Spokesman Books, 1977).

Commission on CIA Activities Within the United States, *Report to the President* (Washington, D.C.: U.S. Government Printing Office, 1975).

Documents on British Foreign Policy, 1919–1939 (London: HMSO).

Robert H. Ferrell (ed.), *Off the Record: The Private Papers of Harry S. Truman* (New York: Harper & Row, 1980).

John C. Fitzpatrick (ed.), *The Writings of George Washington* (Washington, D.C.: U.S. Government Printing Office, 1931–44).

Foreign Relations of the United States (Washington, D.C.: U.S. Government Printing Office).

G. Barry Golson (ed.), *The Playboy Interview* (New York: Wideview Books, 1981).

Stephen Gwynn (ed.), *The Letters and Friendships of Sir Cecil Spring Rice* (London: Constable, 1929).

H. R. Haldeman (with introduction and afterword by Stephen E. Ambrose), *The Haldeman Diaries: Inside the Nixon White House* (New York: Putnam, 1994).

David Jackson (ed.), *The Diaries of George Washington* (Charlottesville: University Press of Virginia, 1976), vol. 1.

Peter Kornbluh and Malcolm Byrne (eds.), *The Iran-Contra Scandal: The Declassified History* (New York: New Press, 1993).

Arthur S. Link (ed.), *The Papers of Woodrow Wilson* (Princeton, N.J.: Princeton University Press, 1966–92).

The "Magic" Background of Pearl Harbor (Washington, D.C.: Department of Defense, 1978)

Walter Millis (ed.), *The Forrestal Diaries* (London: Cassell, 1952).

Elting E. Morison (ed.), *The Letters of Theodore Roosevelt* (Cambridge, Mass.: Harvard University Press, 1951–54).

Operation ZAPATA: The "Ultrasensitive" Report and Testimony of the Board of Inquiry on the Bay of Pigs (Frederick, Md.: University Publications of America, 1981).

Drew Pearson, *Diaries 1949–1959*, ed. Tyla Abell (New York: Holt, Rinehart, 1974).

Public Papers of the Presidents (Washington, D.C.: U.S. Government Printing Office).

Milo M. Quaife (ed.), *The Diary of James K. Polk* (Chicago: A. C. McClurg & Co., 1910).

Elliott Roosevelt (ed.), *The Roosevelt Letters* (London: Harrap, 1950), vol. 2.

Samuel I. Rosenman (ed.), *The Public Papers and Addresses of Franklin D. Roosevelt, 1928–45* (New York: Random House/ Macmillan/ Harper & Brothers, 1938–50).

Donald B. Schewe (ed.), *Franklin D. Roosevelt and Foreign Affairs*, 2nd series (New York: Clearwater Publishing Co., 1980).

Charles Seymour (ed.), *The Intimate Papers of Colonel House* (Boston: Houghton Mifflin, 1926).

John Y. Simon (ed.), *The Papers of Ulysses S. Grant* (Carbondale and Edwardsville: Southern Illinois University Press, 1985), vol 14.

Athan Theoharis (ed.), *From the Secret Files of J. Edgar Hoover* (Chicago: Ivan R. Dee, 1991).

The Tower Commission Report (New York: Times Books, 1987).

United States Congress (documents cited in chronological order):

Joint Committee on the Investigation of the Pearl Harbor Attack, *Pearl Harbor Attack*, 79 Cong., 1 and 2 Sess. (Washington, D.C.: U.S. Government Printing Office, 1946).

Alleged Assassination Plots Involving Foreign Leaders: An Interim Report of the Select Committee to Study Governmental Operations with respect to Intelligence Activities [Church Committee]. U.S. Senate, 94 Cong., 1 Sess., Report no. 94-465 (Nov. 20, 1975).

Hearings before the Select Committee to Study Governmental Operations with Respect to Intelligence Activities of the United States Senate, 94 Cong., 1 Sess., pursuant to S. res. 21, vol. 7, Dec. 4 and 5, 1975.

Final Report of the Select Committee to Study Governmental Operations with Respect to Intelligence Activities [Church Committee]. U.S. Senate, 94 Cong., 2 Sess., Report no. 94-755 (April 26, 1976).

Senate Select Committee on Intelligence, *Annual Report to the Senate*, 95 Cong., 1 Sess. (Washington, D.C.: U.S. Government Printing Office, 1977).

The National Intelligence Estimates A-B Team Episode Concerning Soviet Strategic Capability and Objectives. Report of the Subcommittee on Collection, Production and Quality of the Senate Select Committee on Intelligence, 95 Cong. 2 Sess. (Washington, D.C.: U.S. Government Printing Office, 1978).

Senate Select Committee on Intelligence, *The Soviet Oil Situation: An Evaluation of CIA Analyses of Soviet Oil Production*, 95 Cong., 2 Sess (Washington, D.C.: U.S. Government Printing Office, 1978).

Senate Select Committee on Intelligence, *Report to the Senate Covering the Period May 16, 1977–December 31, 1978*, 96 Cong., 1 Sess. (Washington, D.C.: U.S. Government Printing Office, 1979).

National Intelligence Act of 1980. Hearings before the Senate Select Committee on Intelligence, 96 Cong., 2 Sess. (Washington, D.C.: U.S. Government Printing Office, 1980).

Nomination of William J. Casey: Hearing before the Select Committee on Intelligence of the United States Senate, 97 Cong., 1 Sess. (Washington, D.C.: U.S. Government Printing Office, 1981).

Nomination of Robert M. Gates: Hearing before the Select Committee on Intelligence of the United States Senate, 102 Cong., 1 Sess. (Washington, D.C.: U.S. Government Printing Office, 1992).

House of Representatives Committee on Armed Services, Subcommittee on Oversight and Investigations, *Intelligence Successes and Failures in Operations Desert Shield/Storm*, 103 Cong. 1 Sess., August 1993.

Lawrence E. Walsh, *Final Report of the Independent Counsel for Iran/Contra Matters* (Washington, D.C.: U.S. Court of Appeal for the District of Columbia Circuit, 1994).
Watergate: Chronology of a Crisis (Washington, D.C.: Congressional Quarterly, 1975).
Francis Wharton (ed.), *The Revolutionary Diplomatic Correspondence of the United States* (Washington, D.C.: U.S. Government Printing Office, 1889).

2. MEMOIRS

Dean Acheson, *Present at the Creation* (New York: W. W. Norton, 1969).
Sam Adams, "Vietnam Cover-Up: Playing War with Numbers," *Harper's*, May 1975.
Clinton P. Anderson, *Outsider in the Senate* (New York: World Publishing, 1970).
General Lafayette Charles Baker, *The History of the United States Secret Service* (Philadelphia: private printing, 1867).
George W. Ball, *The Past Has Another Pattern* (New York: W. W. Norton, 1982).
David Homer Bates, *Lincoln in the Telegraph Office* (New York: Century Co., 1907).
Charles E. Bohlen, *Witness to History, 1919–1969* (London: Weidenfeld and Nicolson, 1973).
Georgi Bolshakov, "The Hot Line," *New Times* [Moscow], 1989, nos. 4–6.
Zbigniew Brzezinski, *Power and Principle: Memoirs of the National Security Adviser* (London: Weidenfeld and Nicolson, 1983).
George Bush, *Looking Forward* (New York: Doubleday, 1987).
Jimmy Carter, *Keeping Faith* (London: Collins, 1982).

Anna Chennault, *The Education of Anna* (New York: Times Books, 1980).

William Clark, *From Three Worlds* (London: Sidgwick & Jackson, 1980).

Clark Clifford, *Counsel to the President* (New York: Doubleday, 1992).

William Colby, *Honorable Men: My Life in the CIA* (New York: Simon and Schuster, 1978).

William Colby, *Lost Victory* (Chicago: Contemporary Books, 1989).

Charles W. Colson, *Born Again* (London: Hodder and Stoughton, 1976).

Chester Cooper, *The Lion's Last Roar: Suez 1956* (New York: Harper & Row, 1978).

Brian Crozier, *Free Agent* (London: HarperCollins, 1993).

Josephus Daniels, *The Wilson Era: Years of War and After, 1917–1923* (Chapel Hill: University of North Carolina Press, 1946).

John W. Dean, *Blind Ambition* (New York: Simon and Schuster, 1976).

Charles de Gaulle, *Mémoires de Guerre*, paperback ed. (Paris: Plon, 1956).

Anthony Eden (Earl of Avon), *Full Circle: The Memoirs of Sir Anthony Eden* (London: Cassell, 1960).

John Ehrlichman, *Witness to Power: The Nixon Years* (New York: Simon and Schuster, 1982).

Dwight D. Eisenhower, *The White House Years: Mandate for Change, 1953–56* (London: Heinemann, 1963).

Dwight D. Eisenhower, *The White House Years: Waging Peace, 1956–61* (London: Heinemann, 1966).

Wilbur C. Eveland, *Ropes of Sand* (New York: W. W. Norton, 1980).

Judith Campbell Exner, *My Story* (New York: Grove, 1977).

Gerald R. Ford, *A Time to Heal* (London: W. H. Allen, 1979).

Admiral Sir Guy Gaunt, *The Yield of the Years* (London: Hutchinson, 1940).

Oleg Gordievsky, "Aldrich Ames, My Would-Be Killer," *The Spectator*, March 5, 1994

Mrs. [Rose] Greenhow, *My Imprisonment and the First Year of Abolition Rule at Washington* (London: Richard Bentley, 1867).

Edwin O. Guthman and Jeffrey Shulman (eds.)., *Robert Kennedy in His Own Words: The Unpublished Recollections of the Kennedy Years* (New York: Bantam Books, 1988).

Alexander M. Haig Jr., *Caveat* (London: Weidenfeld and Nicolson, 1984).

Alexander M. Haig Jr., *Inner Circles* (New York: Warner Books, 1992).

H. R. Haldeman, *The Ends of Power* (London: Sidgwick & Jackson, 1978).

Robert T. Hartmann, *Palace Politics: An Inside Account of the Ford Years* (New York: McGraw-Hill, 1980).

Roger Hilsman, *To Move a Nation* (New York: Doubleday, 1967).

Emmet Hughes, *The Ordeal of Power: A Political Memoir of the Eisenhower Administration* (London: Macmillan, 1963).

Cordell Hull, *Memoirs of Cordell Hull* (New York: Macmillan, 1948).

H. Montgomery Hyde, *Secret Intelligence Agent* (London: Constable, 1982).

Lyndon B. Johnson, *The Vantage Point* (London: Weidenfeld and Nicolson, 1972).

Hamilton Jordan, *Crisis: The Last Year of the Carter Presidency* (London: Michael Joseph, 1982).

Robert F. Kennedy, *Thirteen Days* (London: Macmillan, 1969).

James R. Killian, *Sputnik, Scientists and Eisenhower: A Memoir of the First Assistant to the President for Science and Technology* (Cambridge, Mass.: MIT Press, 1967).

Henry Kissinger, *White House Years* (Boston: Little, Brown & Co., 1979).

Henry Kissinger, *Years of Upheaval* (Boston: Little, Brown & Co., 1982).

Robert J. Lamphere and Tom Schachtman, *The FBI-KGB War*, paperback ed. (New York: Berkley, 1987).

Edwin T. Layton et al., *And I Was There* (New York: William Morrow, 1987).

G. Gordon Liddy, *Will* (London: Severn House, 1981).

Franklin Lindsay, *Beacons in the Night* (Stanford, Calif.: Stanford University Press, 1993).

Jeb Stuart Magruder, *An American Life* (New York: Atheneum, 1974).

W. Somerset Maugham, "Looking Back," *Sunday Express*, Sept. 30, Oct. 7, 1962.

William G. McAdoo, *Crowded Years* (New York: Houghton Mifflin, 1931).

Cord Meyer, *Facing Reality* (New York: Harper & Row, 1980).

Merle Miller, *Plain Speaking*, paperback ed. (New York: Berkley Medallion, 1974).

Robert Murphy, *Diplomat Among Warriors* (New York: Pyramid Books, 1965).

Arthur C. Murray, *At Close Quarters* (London: John Murray, 1946).

Paul H. Nitze, *From Hiroshima to Glasnost: At the Centre of Decision* (London: Weidenfeld and Nicolson, 1990).

Richard M. Nixon, *RN: The Memoirs of Richard Nixon*, paperback ed. (New York: Touchstone, 1990).

Oliver L. North, *Under Fire: An American Story* (London: Fontana, 1992).

David Atlee Phillips, *The Night Watch* (New York: Atheneum, 1977).

Allan Pinkerton, *The Spy of the Rebellion, Being a True Story of the Spy System of the United States Army During the Late Rebellion* (New York: G. W. Dillingham, 1888).

Ronald Reagan, *An American Life*, paperback ed. (New York: Pocket Books, 1992).

Donald T. Regan, *For the Record: From Wall Street to Washington*, paperback ed. (London: Arrow Books, 1988).

James Reston, *Deadline: A Memoir* (New York: Random House, 1991).

Captain Franz von Rintelen, *The Dark Invader* (London: Lovat Dickson, 1933).

Kermit Roosevelt, *Countercoup* (New York: McGraw-Hill, 1979).

Theodore Roosevelt, *An Autobiography* (New York: Charles Scribner's Sons, 1920).

Dean Rusk, *As I Saw It*, paperback ed. (New York: Penguin Books, 1991).

William Safire, *Before the Fall* (New York: Doubleday, 1975).

Daniel Schorr, *Clearing the Air* (Boston: Houghton Mifflin, 1977).

H. Norman Schwarzkopf, *It Doesn't Take a Hero* (New York: Bantam Press, 1992

Evelyn Shuckburgh, *Descent to Suez: Diaries, 1951–56* (London: Weidenfeld and Nicolson, 1986).

George P. Shultz, *Turmoil and Triumph: My Years as Secretary of State* (New York: Charles Scribner's Sons, 1993).

Russell Jack Smith, *The Unknown CIA* (New York: Berkley, 1992).

Frank Snepp, *Decent Interval* (New York: Random House, 1977).

Major Robert Stobo, *Memoirs of Major Robert Stobo of the Virginia Regiment* (Pittsburgh: John S. Davidson, 1854).

John Stockwell, *In Search of Enemies: A CIA Story* (New York: W. W. Norton, 1978).

Sir Kenneth Strong, *Intelligence at the Top* (London: Cassell, 1968).

Gwen Terasaki, *Bridge to the Sun* (London: Michael Joseph, 1957).

Margaret Thatcher, *The Downing Street Years* (London: HarperCollins, 1993).

Norman Thwaites, *Velvet and Vinegar* (London: Grayson & Grayson, 1932).

Harry S. Truman, *Memoirs*, paperback ed. (New York: Signet Books, 1965).

Margaret Truman, *Harry S. Truman* (New York: William Morrow, 1973).

Stansfield Turner, *Secrecy and Democracy: The CIA in Transition* (London: Sidgwick & Jackson, 1985).

Stansfield Turner, *Terrorism and Democracy* (Boston: Houghton Mifflin, 1991).

Cyrus Vance, *Hard Choices: Critical Years in America's Foreign Policy* (New York: Simon and Schuster, 1983).

Henry Julian Wadleigh, "Why I Spied for the Communists," part 7, New York *Post*, Home News, July 19, 1949.

Caspar Weinberger, *Fighting for Peace: Seven Critical Years in the Pentagon* (New York: Warner Books, 1990).

Sir Arthur Willert, *The Road to Safety* (London: Derek Verschoyle, 1952).

Edith Bolling Wilson, *Memoirs of Mrs Woodrow Wilson* (London: Putnam, 1939).

F. W. Winterbotham, *The Ultra Secret*, paperback ed. (London: Futura, 1975).

C. M. Woodhouse, *Something Ventured* (London: Granada, 1982).

Peter Wright, *Spycatcher* (New York: Viking, 1987).

Herbert O. Yardley, *The American Black Chamber* (London: Faber, 1931).

3. SECONDARY WORKS

James Adams, *The New Spies* (London: Hutchinson, 1994).

Jonathan Aitken, *Nixon: A Life* (London: Weidenfeld and Nicolson, 1992).

Stephen E. Ambrose, *Eisenhower* (New York: Simon and Schuster, 1984), vol 2.

Stephen E. Ambrose, *Ike's Spies: Eisenhower and the Espionage Establishment* (Garden City, N.Y.: Doubleday, 1981).

Stephen E. Ambrose, *Nixon* (New York: Simon and Schuster, 1987–91).

Jack Anderson, "CIA Eavesdrops on Kremlin Chiefs," Washington *Post*, Sept. 16, 1971.

Christopher Andrew, "Churchill and Intelligence," *Intelligence and National Security*, vol. 3 (1988), no. 2; reprinted in Michael Handel (ed.), *Leaders and Intelligence* (London: Frank Cass, 1988).

Christopher Andrew, "Codebreakers and Foreign Offices," in Christopher Andrew and David Dilks (eds.), *The Missing Dimension: Governments and Intelligence Communities in the Twentieth Century* (London: Macmillan, 1984).

Christopher Andrew, "France and the German Menace," in Ernest May (ed.), *Knowing One's Enemies: Intelligence Assessment Before the Two World Wars* (Princeton, N.J.: Princeton University Press, 1984).

Christopher Andrew, "The Growth of the Australian Intelligence Community and the Anglo-American Connection," *Intelligence and National Security*, vol. 4 (1989), no. 2.

Christopher Andrew, *Her Majesty's Secret Service*, paperback ed. (New York: Penguin Books, 1987).

Christopher Andrew, "KGB Foreign Intelligence from Brezhnev to the Coup," *Intelligence and National Security*, vol. 8 (1993), no. 3.

Christopher Andrew, "The Making of the Anglo-American Sigint Alliance," in Hayden B. Peake and Samuel Halpern (eds.), *In the Name of Intelligence: Essays in Honor of Walter Pforzheimer* (Washington, D.C.: NIBC Press, 1994).

Christopher Andrew, "The Nature of Military Intelligence," in Keith Neilson and B. J. C. McKercher (eds.), *Go Spy the Land: Military Intelligence in History* (Westport, Conn.: Praeger, 1992).

Christopher Andrew and Oleg Gordievsky, *KGB: The Inside Story of its Foreign Operations from Lenin to Gorbachev*, paperback ed. (New York: HarperPerennial, 1991).

Christopher Andrew and Oleg Gordievsky, *Le KGB dans le monde* (Paris: Fayard, 1990).

J. Cutler Andrews, *The North Reports the Civil War* (Pittsburgh: University of Pittsburgh Press, 1955).

J. Cutler Andrews, *The South Reports the Civil War* (Princeton, N.J.: Princeton University Press, 1970).

Robert G. Angevine, "Gentlemen Do Read Each Other's Mail: American Intelligence in the Interwar Era," *Intelligence and National Security*, vol. 7 (1992), no. 2.

Alan Axelrod, *The War Between the Spies: A History of Espionage During the American Civil War* (New York: Atlantic Monthly Press, 1992).

Ray Stannard Baker, *Woodrow Wilson, Life and Letters* (London: Heinemann, 1928–39).

Desmond Ball and Robert Windren, "Soviet Signals Intelligence (Sigint): Organization and Management," *Intelligence and National Security*, vol. 4 (1989).

James Bamford, *The Puzzle Palace* (Boston: Houghton Mifflin, 1982).

Patrick Beesly, *Room 40* (London: Hamish Hamilton, 1982).

Larry Berman, *Lyndon Johnson's War*, paperback ed. (New York: W. W. Norton, 1991).

Carl Bernstein, "The Holy Alliance," *Time*, Feb. 24, 1992.

Michael R. Beschloss, *Kennedy v. Khrushchev: The Crisis Years, 1960–63* (London: Faber, 1991).

Michael R. Beschloss, *Mayday: Eisenhower, Khrushchev and the U-2 Affair* (London: Faber, 1986).

Michael R. Beschloss and Strobe Talbott, *At the Highest Levels: The Inside Story of the End of the Cold War* (Boston: Little, Brown & Co., 1993).

Bruce W. Bidwell, *History of the Military Intelligence Division, Department of the Army General Staff: 1775–1941* (Frederick, Md.: University Publications of America, 1986).

Kai Bird, *The Chairman: John J. McCloy and the Making of the American Establishment* (New York: Simon and Schuster, 1992).

Ian Black and Benny Morris, *Israel's Secret Wars* (London: Hamish Hamilton, 1991).

Walter S. Bowen and Henry Edward Neal, *The United States Secret Service* (Philadelphia: Chilton, 1960).

Piers Brendon, *Ike: The Life and Times of Dwight D. Eisenhower* (London: Secker and Warburg, 1987).

Dino A. Brugioni, "Arlington and Fairfax Counties: Land of Many Reconnaissance Firsts," *Northern Virginia Heritage*, Feb. 1985

Dino A. Brugioni, *Eyeball to Eyeball: The Inside Story of the Cuban Missile Crisis* (New York: Random House, 1991).

Dino A. Brugioni, "The President, Khe Sanh, and the 26th Marines," *Leatherneck*, Sept. 1986.

Thomas H. Buckley, *The United States and the Washington Conference, 1921–1922* (Knoxville: University of Tennessee Press, 1970).

McGeorge Bundy, *Danger and Survival* (New York: Random House, 1988).

Kathleen Burk, *Britain, America and the Sinews of War, 1914–1918* (London: George Allen & Unwin, 1985).

William E. Burrows, *Deep Black* (New York: Berkley, 1988).

Larry Cable, *Unholy Grail: The U.S. and the Wars in Vietnam, 1965–8* (New York: Routledge, 1991).

Daniel Callaghan, *Dangerous Capabilities* (New York: HarperCollins, 1990).

Ted Galen Carpenter, "Closing the Nuclear Umbrella," *Foreign Affairs*, March-April 1994.

A. Brooke Caruso, *The Mexican Spy Company* (Jefferson, N.C.: McFarland, 1991).

Anthony Cave Brown, *The Last Hero: Wild Bill Donovan*, Vintage Books ed. (New York: Random House, 1984).

Anthony Cave Brown, *"C": The Secret Life of Sir Stewart Menzies, Spymaster to Winston Churchill* (New York: Macmillan, 1987).

Ray S. Cline, *Secrets, Spies and Scholars* (Washington, D.C.: Acropolis Books, 1976).

Mark Clodfelter, *The Limits of Airpower: The American Bombing of North Vietnam* (New York: Free Press, 1989).

Stanley Coben, *A. Mitchell Palmer: Politician* (New York: Columbia University Press, 1963).

Charles G. Cogan, "The In-Culture of the DO," *Intelligence and National Security*, vol. 8 (1993).

Charles G. Cogan, "The Response of the Strong to the Weak: The American Raid on Libya, 1986," *Intelligence and National Security*, vol. 6 (1991).

Len Colodny and Robert Gettlin, *Silent Coup*, paperback ed. (New York: St. Martin's Press, 1992).

A Consumer's Guide to Intelligence (Washington, D.C.: CIA, 1994).

William R. Corson, *The Armies of Ignorance* (New York: Dial Press, 1977).

Seth Cropsey, "The Only Credible Deterrent," *Foreign Affairs*, March-April 1994.

T. L. Cubbage II, "Westmoreland vs. CBS: Was Intelligence Corrupted by Policy Demands?," *Intelligence and National Security*, vol. 3 (1988)., no. 3.

Arthur Darling, *The Central Intelligence Agency: An Instrument of Government, to 1950* (University Park: Pennsylvania State University Press, 1990).

David Brion Davis (ed.)., *The Fear of Conspiracy* (Ithaca, N.Y.: Cornell University Press, 1971).

Nathaniel Davis, "The Angola Decision of 1975: A Personal Memoir," *Foreign Affairs*, Fall 1978.

David Dimbleby and David Reynolds, *An Ocean Apart* (London: BBC Books, 1988).

Reinhard R. Doerries, *Imperial Challenge: Ambassador Count Bernstorff and German-American Relations, 1908–1917* (Chapel Hill: University of North Carolina Press, 1989).

Does the Arms Control and Disarmament Agency Have a Future? (Washington, D.C.: Henry L. Stimson Center, 1992).

Robert J. Donovan, *Conflict and Crisis: The Presidency of Harry S. Truman, 1945–1948* (New York: W. W. Norton, 1977).

Robert J. Donovan, *Tumultuous Years: The Presidency of Harry S. Truman, 1949–1953* (New York: W. W. Norton, 1982).

Jeffrey M. Dorwart, *Conflict of Duty* (Annapolis, Md.: Naval Institute Press, 1983).

Jeffrey M. Dorwart, *The Office of Naval Intelligence* (Annapolis, Md.: Naval Institute Press, 1979).

Jeffrey M. Dorwart, "The Roosevelt-Astor Espionage Ring," *New York History*, vol. 62 (1981), no. 3.

John Dower, *War Without Mercy: Race and Power in the Pacific War* (New York: Pantheon Books, 1986).

Theodore Draper, *A Very Thin Line: The Iran-Contra Affairs*, paperback ed. (New York: Touchstone, 1992).

Theodore Draper, "Walsh's Last Stand," *New York Review of Books*, March 3, 1994.

Theodore Draper, "Nixon Redivivus," *New York Review of Books*, July 14, 1994.

Edward J. Drea, *MacArthur's ULTRA* (Lawrence: University of Kansas Press, 1992).

Fred Emery, *Watergate: The Corruption of American Politics and the Fall of Richard Nixon* (New York: Times Books, 1994).

Edward J. Epstein, *Legend: The Secret World of Lee Harvey Oswald* (New York: Reader's Digest Press, 1978).

"The Fall of the Shah of Iran," Case Study C16-88-794.0, Kennedy School of Government, Harvard University.

Ladislas Farago, *The Game of the Foxes* (London: Hodder and Stoughton, 1972).

Pierre Favier and Michel Martin-Roland, *La décennie Mitterrand* (Paris: Seuil, 1990), vol 1.

Thomas Fleming, "George Washington, General," in Robert Cowley (ed.), *Experience of War* (New York: W. W. Norton, 1992).

John E. Ferling, *The First of Men* (Knoxville: University of Tennessee Press, 1988).

John Ferris, "From Broadway House to Bletchley Park: The Diary of Captain Malcolm Kennedy, 1934–1946," *Intelligence and National Security*, vol. 4 (1989), no. 3.

Edwin C. Fishel, "The Mythology of Civil War Intelligence," *Civil War History*, vol. 10 (1964), no. 4.

James T. Flexner, *George Washington: The Forge of Experience (1732–1775)* (London: Leo Cooper, 1973).

Ronnie E. Ford, "Tet Revisited: The Strategy of the Communist Vietnamese," *Intelligence and National Security*, vol. 9 (1994), no. 1.

W. B. Fowler, *British-American Relations, 1917–1918: The Role of Sir William Wiseman* (Princeton, N.J.: Princeton University Press, 1969).

Lawrence Freedman, "Intelligence Operations in the Falklands," *Intelligence and National Security*, vol. 1 (1986), no. 3.

Lawrence Freedman and Virginia Gambia-Stonehouse, *Signals of War: The Falklands Conflict of 1982* (London: Faber, 1990).

Frank Freidel, *Franklin D. Roosevelt: The Ordeal* (Boston: Little, Brown & Co., 1954).

Frank Freidel, *Franklin D. Roosevelt: The Triumph* (Boston, Little, Brown & Co., 1956).

Richard M. Fried, *Nightmare in Red* (Oxford, England: Oxford University Press, 1990).

Michael Friendly and David Galen, *Martin Luther King, Jr.: The FBI File* (New York: Carroll & Graf, 1993).

Robert F. Futrell, "U.S. Air Force Intelligence in the Korean War," in Walter T. Hitchcock (ed.), *The Intelligence Revolution: A Historical Perspective* (Washington, D.C.: U.S. Air Force Academy, 1991).

John L. Gaddis, *Strategies of Containment* (Oxford, England: Oxford University Press, 1982).

Lloyd C. Gardiner and Warren F. Kimball, "The United States: Democratic Diplomacy," in David Reynolds, Warren F. Kimball, and A. O. Chubarian (eds.), *Allies at War* (London: Macmillan, 1994).

Raymond L. Garthoff, *Assessing the Adversary* (Washington, D.C.: Brookings Institution, 1991).

Raymond L. Garthoff, *Détente and Confrontation: American-Soviet Relations from Nixon to Reagan* (Washington, D.C.: Brookings Institution, 1985).

Mark J. Gasiorowski, "The 1953 Coup d'Etat in Iran," *International Journal of Middle East Studies*, no. 19 (Aug. 1987).

Robert M. Gates, "CIA and Openness": text of speech delivered Feb. 21, 1992.

Robert M. Gates, "CIA and the Collapse of the Soviet Union: Hit or Miss?": address to the Foreign Policy Association, New York, 20 May 1992.

Robert M. Gates, "Guarding Against Politicization," *Studies in Intelligence*, vol. 36 (1992), no. 5.

Robert M. Gates, "An Opportunity Unfulfilled: The Use and Perceptions of Intelligence at the White House," *Washington Quarterly*, Winter 1989.

Robert M. Gates, "Statement on Change in CIA and the Intelligence Community": text of speech delivered April 1, 1992.

Curt Gentry, *J. Edgar Hoover* (New York: W. W. Norton, 1991).

Martin Gilbert, *Winston S. Churchill* (London: Heinemann, 1966–88).

Sergei N. Goncharov, John W. Lewis, and Xue Litai, *Uncertain Partners: Stalin, Mao and the Korean War* (Stanford, Calif.: Stanford University Press, 1993).

Allan E. Goodman and Bruce D. Berkowitz, "Intelligence Without the Cold War," *Intelligence and National Security*, vol. 9 (1994), no. 1.

John Robert Greene, *The Limits of Power: The Nixon and Ford Administrations* (Bloomington and Indianapolis: Indiana University Press, 1992).

Fred I. Greenstein, *The Hidden-Hand Presidency* (New York: Basic Books, 1982).

John Gunther, *Roosevelt in Retrospect* (London: Hamish Hamilton, 1950).

David Halberstam, *The Best and the Brightest* (New York: Fawcett Crest, 1972).

Samuel Halpern, "Revisiting the Cuban Missile Crisis," *Society for Historians of American Foreign Relations Newsletter*, vol. 25 (1994), no. 1.

Nigel Hamilton, *JFK: Restless Youth* (London: Century Co., 1992).

William Hanchett, *The Lincoln Murder Conspiracies* (Urbana and Chicago: University of Illinois Press, 1983).

Philip Hanson, *Soviet Industrial Espionage: Some New Information* (London: Royal Institute of International Affairs, 1987).

Ruth R. Harris, "The 'Magic' Leak of 1941 and Japanese-American Relations," *Pacific Historical Review*, vol. 50 (1981), no. 1.

John L. Hart, "Popov: A Man Who Was Faithful," *Intelligence and National Security*, vol. 10 (1995), no. 1.

Robert McConnell Hatch, *Major John André: A Gallant in Spy's Clothing* (Boston: Houghton Mifflin, 1986).

Richard G. Head, Frisco W. Short, and Robert C. McFarlane, *Crisis Resolution: Presidential Decision Making in the Mayaguez and Korean Confrontations* (Boulder, Co.: Westview Press, 1978).

George C. Herring, *America's Longest War: The United States and Vietnam, 1950–1975*, 2nd ed. (New York: Knopf, 1986).

George C. Herring, *"Cold Blood": LBJ's Conduct of Limited War in Vietnam* (Washington, D.C.: U.S. Government Printing Office, 1990).

Seymour M. Hersh, *Kissinger: The Price of Power* (New York: Summit, 1983).

Seymour M. Hersh, *The Target Is Destroyed* (London: Faber, 1986).

Seymour M. Hersh, "Nixon's Last Cover-Up: The Tapes He Wants the Archives To Suppress," *New Yorker*, Dec. 14, 1992.

Seymour M. Hersh, "On the Nuclear Edge," *New Yorker*, March 29, 1993.

Seymour M. Hersh, "The Wild East," *Atlantic Monthly*, June 1994.

Richard G. Hewlett and Francis Duncan, *Atomic Shield 1947–1952* (University Park: Pennnsylvania University Press, 1969).

Donald R. Hickey, *The War of 1812* (Urbana and Chicago: University of Chicago Press, 1989).

Sir F. H. Hinsley et al., *British Intelligence in the Second World War* (London: HMSO, 1979–88).

Townsend Hoopes and Douglas Brinkley, *Driven Patriot: The Life and Times of James Forrestal* (New York: Knopf, 1992).

Alistair Horne, *Macmillan 1891–1956* (London: Macmillan, 1988).

Sir Michael Howard, *British Intelligence in the Second World War*, vol. 5: *Strategic Deception* (London: HMSO, 1990).

Henry Hurt, *Reasonable Doubt: An Investigation into the Assassination of John F. Kennedy* (New York: Henry Holt, 1985).

H. Montgomery Hyde, *The Quiet Canadian* (London: Hamish Hamilton, 1962).

Richard Immerman, *The CIA in Guatemala: The Foreign Policy of Intervention* (Austin: University of Texas Press, 1982).

Intelligence in the War of Independence (Washington, D.C.: CIA, 1976).

The Intelligence War in 1941: A 50th Anniversary Perspective (Washington, D.C.: CIA Center for the Study of Intelligence, 1992).

Walter Isaacson, *Kissinger: A Biography* (New York: Simon and Schuster, 1992).

Admiral Sir William James, *The Eyes of the Navy* (London: Methuen, 1955).

Rhodri Jeffreys-Jones, *The CIA and American Democracy* (New Haven: Yale University Press, 1989.

Joan M. Jensen, *The Price of Vigilance* (New York: Rand McNally, 1968).

Philip C. Jessup, *Elihu Root* (New York: Dodd, Mead & Co., 1938).

Loch K. Johnson, *America's Secret Power: The CIA in a Democratic Society* (Oxford, England: Oxford University Press, 1989).

Loch K. Johnson, *A Season of Inquiry: The Senate Intelligence Investigation* (Lexington: University Press of Kentucky, 1985).

David Kahn, "The Annotated 'The American Black Chamber,'" in Cipher A. Deavours et al. (eds.), *Cryptology Yesterday, Today and Tomorrow* (Norwood, Mass.: Artech House, 1987).

David Kahn, *The Codebreakers* (New York: Macmillan, 1967).

David Kahn, "The Intelligence Failure at Pearl Harbor," *Foreign Affairs*, Winter 1991–92.

David Kahn, "Pearl Harbor and the Inadequacy of Cryptanalysis," *Cryptologia*, vol. 15 (1991).

David Kahn, "Roosevelt, MAGIC, and ULTRA," *Cryptologia*, vol. 14 (1992).

David Kahn, *Seizing the Enigma* (Boston: Houghton Mifflin, 1991).

Zachary Karabell, " 'Inside the U.S. Espionage Den': The U.S. Embassy and the Fall of the Shah," *Intelligence and National Security*, vol. 8 (1993)., no. 1.

George F. Kennan, *Russia Leaves the War*, paperback ed. (Princeton, N.J.: Princeton University Press, 1989).

George F. Kennan, "The Sisson Documents," *Journal of Modern History*, vol. 28 (1956), no. 2.

Pamela Kessler, *Undercover Washington* (McLean, Va.: EPM Publications, 1992).

Warren F. Kimball, *The Juggler: Franklin Roosevelt as Wartime Statesman* (Princeton, N.J.: Princeton University Press, 1991).

Lyman B. Kirkpatrick, Jr., "Intelligence and Counterintelligence," in Alexander De Conde (ed.), *Encyclopedia of American Foreign Policy* (New York: Charles Scribner's Sons, 1978), vol. 2.

Peter Kornbluh, *Nicaragua: The Price of Intervention* (Washington, D.C.: Institute for Policy Studies, 1987).

Walter Lafeber, *The American Age: United States Foreign Policy at Home and Abroad since 1750* (New York: W. W. Norton, 1989).

William M. Leary (ed.), *The Central Intelligence Agency: History and Documents* (University: University of Alabama Press, 1984).

Melvyn P. Leffler, *A Preponderance of Power* (Stanford, Calif.: Stanford University Press, 1992).

Ronald Lewin, *The Other Ultra* (London: Hutchinson, 1982).

Thomas A. Lewis, *For King and Country* (New York: HarperCollins, 1992).

Arthur S. Link, *Campaigns for Progressivism and Peace, 1916–1917* (Princeton, N.J.: Princeton University Press, 1965).

Arthur S. Link, *Wilson: The Struggle for Neutrality, 1914–1915* (Princeton, N.J.: Princeton University Press, 1960).

Arthur S. Link, *Woodrow Wilson: Revolution, War and Peace* (Arlington Heights, Ill.: AMH Publishing Corporation, 1979).

John Bruce Lockhart, "Sir William Wiseman, Bart., Agent of Influence," unpublished talk to the British Study Group on Intelligence.

Milton Lomask, *Andrew Johnson: President on Trial* (New York: Octagon Books, 1973).

Mark M. Lowenthal, "Searching for National Intelligence: U.S. Intelligence and Policy Before the Second World War," *Intelligence and National Security*, vol. 6 (1991), no. 4.

W. Scott Lucas, *Divided We Stand: Britain, the United States and the Suez Crisis* (London: Hodder and Stoughton, 1991).

Jay Luvaas, "Lee at Gettysburg: A General Without Intelligence," *Intelligence and National Security*, vol. 5 (1990), no. 2.

Jay Luvaas, "The Role of Intelligence in the Chancellorsville Campaign, April-May, 1863," *Intelligence and National Security*, vol. 5 (1990), no. 2.

William Manchester, *Death of a President* (London: Michael Joseph, 1967).

Tom Mangold, *Cold Warrior: James Jesus Angleton, the CIA's Master Spy Hunter* (New York: Simon and Schuster, 1991).

Victor Marchetti and John D. Marks, *The CIA and the Cult of Intelligence*, revised ed. (New York: Dell, 1989).

David C. Martin, *Wilderness of Mirrors*, paperback ed. (New York: Ballantine Books, 1981).

David C. Martin and John Walcott, *Best Laid Plans: The Inside Story of America's War Against Terrorism* (New York: Harper & Row, 1988).

John B. Martin, *Overtaken by Events* (Garden City, N.Y.: Doubleday, 1966).

Peter Maslowski, "Military Intelligence Sources During the American Civil War: A Case Study," in Walter T. Hitchcock (ed.), *The Intelligence Revolution: A Historical Perspective* (Washington, D.C.: U.S. Air Force Academy, 1991).

Valery Masterov, "Spy Kuklinski: Traitor or Patriot?" *Moscow News*, 1992, no. 43.

W. Somerset Maugham, *Collected Short Stories* (London: Pan, 1976).

Ernest R. May (ed.), *American Cold War Strategy: Interpreting NSC 68* (Boston: Bedford Books, 1993).

Ernest R. May (ed.), *Knowing One's Enemies: Intelligence Assessment Before the Two World Wars* (Princeton, N.J.: Princeton University Press, 1984).

"The Mayaguez Incident," Case Study C14-82-443.0, Kennedy School of Government, Harvard University

Michael McClintock, *Instruments of Statecraft: U.S. Guerrilla Warfare, Counter-Insurgency, and Counter-Terrorism, 1940–1990* (New York: Pantheon Books, 1992).

David McCullough, *The Path Between the Seas* (New York: Simon and Schuster, 1977).

David McCullough, *Truman* (New York: Simon and Schuster, 1992).

Michael Medved, *The Shadow Presidents: The Secret History of the Chief Executives and Their Top Aides* (New York: Times Books, 1975).

Philip S. Meilinger, *Hoyt S. Vandenberg* (Bloomington and Indianapolis: Indiana University Press, 1989).

Patrick Mescall, "The Birth of the Defense Intelligence Agency," in Rhodri Jeffreys-Jones and Andrew Lownie (eds.), *North American Spies* (Edinburgh: Edinburgh University Press, 1991).

John C. Miller, *The Triumph of Freedom, 1775–1783* (Boston: Little, Brown & Co., 1948).

Ludwell Lee Montague, "General Walter Bedell Smith as Director of Central Intelligence," DCI Historical Series, DCI-1, DDRS, 1991, no. 60; also available in reprint (University Park: Pennsylvania State University Press, 1992).

Ted Morgan, *FDR: A Biography* (London: Grafton Books, 1986).

Samuel Eliot Morison, "The Henry-Crillon Affair of 1812," *Proceedings of the Massachusetts Historical Society*, 69 (1947–1950).

Samuel Eliot Morison, Henry Steele Comager, and William E. Leuchtenberg, *The Growth of the American Republic*, 7th ed. (New York: Oxford University Press, 1980).

Leonard Mosley, *Dulles: A Biography of Eleanor, Allen, and John Foster Dulles and Their Family Network* (New York: Dial Press, 1978).

Kerry Mullins and Aaron Wildavsky, "The Procedural Presidency of George Bush," *Political Science Quarterly*, vol. 107 (1992), no. 1.

Robert K. Murray, *Red Scare: A Study in National Hysteria, 1919–1920* (Minneapolis: University of Minnesota Press, 1955).

Timothy J. Naftali, "Intrepid's Last Deception: Documenting the Career of Sir William Stephenson," *Intelligence and National Security*, vol. 8 (1993), no. 3.

Timothy J. Naftali, "James Angleton and X-2 Operations in Italy," in George C. Chalou (ed.), *The Secrets War: The Office of Strategic Services in World War II* (Washington, D.C.: National Archives and Records Administration, 1992).

Richard G. Neustadt, "Truman in Action: A Retrospect," in Marc Landy (ed.), *Modern Presidents and the Presidency* (Lexington, Mass.: Lexington Books, 1985).

Richard G. Neustadt and Ernest May, *Thinking in Time: The Uses of History for Decision-Makers* (New York: Free Press, 1986).

Stephen B. Oates, *With Malice Toward None: The Life of Abraham Lincoln* (London: George Allen & Unwin, 1978).

Don Oberdorfer, *The Turn: How the Cold War Came to an End* (London: Jonathan Cape, 1992).

John M. Oseth, *Regulating U.S. Intelligence Operations* (Lexington: University Press of Kentucky, 1985).

The OSS Assessment of Men: Selection of Personnel for the Office of Strategic Services (New York: Rinehart & Co., 1948).

G. J. A. O'Toole, *The Encyclopedia of American Intelligence and Espionage* (New York: Facts on File, 1988).

G. J. A. O'Toole, *Honorable Treachery* (New York: Atlantic Monthly Press, 1991).

G. J. A. O'Toole, *The Spanish War: An American Epic* (New York: W. W. Norton, 1984).

A. Mitchell Palmer, "The Case Against the 'Reds,'" *Forum*, Feb. 1920.

Frederick D. Parker, "The Unsolved Messages of Pearl Harbor," *Cryptologia*, vol. 15 (1991), no. 4.

Thomas Parrish, *The Ultra Americans* (New York: Stein and Day, 1986).

Hayden B. Peake and Samuel Halpern (eds.), *In the Name of Intelligence: Essays in Honor of Walter Pforzheimer* (Washington, D.C.: NIBC Press, 1994).

Morton Pennypacker, *General Washington's Spies on Long Island and in New York* (Brooklyn, N.Y.: Long Island Historical Society, 1939).

Mark Perry, *Eclipse: The Last Days of the CIA* (New York: William Morrow, 1992).

Joseph E. Persico, *Casey: From the OSS to the CIA*, paperback ed. (New York: Penguin Books, 1991).

Ben Pimlott, *Wilson* (London: HarperCollins, 1992).

Gerald Posner, *Case Closed: Lee Harvey Oswald and the Assassination of John F. Kennedy* (New York: Random House, 1993).

Thomas Powers, *The Man Who Kept the Secrets* (London: Weidenfeld and Nicolson, 1979).

John Prados, *Keepers of the Keys: A History of the National Security Council from Truman to Bush* (New York: William Morrow, 1991).

John Prados, *Presidents' Secret Wars* (New York: William Morrow, 1986).

John Prados, *The Soviet Estimate*, revised ed. (Princeton, N.J.: Princeton University Press, 1986).

Gordon W. Prange, *At Dawn We Slept*, paperback ed. (New York: Penguin Books, 1982).

Gordon Prange, *Miracle at Midway* (New York: Penguin Books, 1983).

Stephen G. Rabe, "Vietnam: The War America Tried to Lose?," in T. G. Fraser and Keith Jeffery (eds.), *Men, Women and War* (Dublin: Lilliput Press, 1993).

John Ranelagh, *The Agency* (London: Weidenfeld and Nicolson, 1986).

John Ranelagh, *CIA: A History* (London: BBC Books, 1992).

Richard Reeves, *President Kennedy: Profile of Power* (New York: Simon and Schuster, 1993).

Thomas C. Reeves, *A Question of Character: A Life of John F. Kennedy* (Rocklin, Calif.: Prima Publishing, 1992).

David Reynolds, *The Creation of the Anglo-American Alliance 1937–41* (London: Europa Publications, 1981).

Jeffrey T. Richelson, *American Espionage and the Soviet Target* (New York: Quill, 1987).

Jeffrey T. Richelson and Desmond Ball, *The Ties That Bind*, 2nd ed. (Boston: Unwin Hyman, 1990).

Charles Roberts, *LBJ's Inner Circle* (New York: Delacorte, 1965).

Ishbel Ross, *Rebel Rose* (New York: Harper & Brothers, 1954).

Paul B. Ryan, *The Iranian Rescue Mission: Why It Failed* (Annapolis, Md.: Naval Institute Press, 1985).

Abbas W. Samii, "The Role of SAVAK in the 1978–79 Iranian Revolution," Ph.D. thesis (Cambridge Univeristy, 1994).

Edward F. Sayle, "The Historical Underpinning of the U.S. Intelligence Community," *International Journal of Intelligence and CounterIntelligence*, vol. 1 (1986), no. 1.

Arthur M. Schlesinger Jr., *Robert Kennedy and His Times* (New York: Ballantine Books, 1979).

Arthur M. Schlesinger Jr., *A Thousand Days* (London: André Deutsch, 1965).

Jerrold L. Schecter and Peter S. Deriabin, *The Spy Who Saved the World* (New York: Charles Scribner's Sons, 1992).

Eric Schmitt, "Spy-Satellite Unit Faces a New Life in Daylight," *New York Times*, Nov. 3, 1992.

Michael Schudson, *Watergate in American Memory* (New York: Basic Books, 1992).

Stephen W. Sears, *To the Gates of Richmond* (New York: Ticknor & Fields, 1992).

Deborah Shapley, *Promise and Power: The Life and Times of Robert McNamara* (Boston: Little, Brown & Co., 1993).

Robert E. Sherwood, *Roosevelt and Hopkins: An Intimate History* (New York: Harper, 1948).

Robert Shogan, *The Riddle of Power* (New York: Plume, 1992).

Mark Shulman, "The Rise and Fall of American Naval Intelligence," *Intelligence and National Security*, vol. 8 (1993), no. 2.

Gary Sick, *All Fall Down: America's Fateful Encounter with Iran* (London: Tauris, 1985).

Hugh Sidey, "L.B.J., Hoover and Domestic Spying," *Time*, Feb. 10, 1975.

Hugh Sidey, *A Very Personal Presidency* (New York: Atheneum, 1968).

Frank J. Smist Jr., *Congress Oversees the United States Intelligence Community, 1947–1989* (Knoxville: University of Tennessee Press, 1990).

Bradley F. Smith, *The Shadow Warriors* (London: André Deutsch, 1983).

Bradley F. Smith, *The Ultra-Magic Deals* (Novato, Calif.: Presidio, 1993).

Gaddis Smith, *Morality, Reason and Power: American Diplomacy in the Carter Years* (New York: Hill and Wang, 1986).

Jean Edward Smith, *George Bush's War* (New York: Henry Holt, 1992).

Richard Harris Smith, "The First Moscow Station: An Espionage Footnote to the Cold War," *International Journal of Intelligence and CounterIntelligence*, vol. 3 (1989), no. 3.

Theodore Sorensen, *Kennedy* (New York: Harper & Row, 1965).

Ronald H. Spector, *Eagle Against the Sun* (London: Viking, 1985).

"The SS-9 Controversy: Intelligence as Political Football," Case Study C16-89-884.0, Kennedy School of Government, Harvard University.

David Stafford, "'Intrepid': Myth and Reality," *Journal of Contemporary History*, vol. 22 (1987).

John W. Stepp and I. William Hill, *Mirror of War: The Washington Star Reports the Civil War* (Washington, D.C.: Castle Books, 1961).

William Stevenson, *A Man Called Intrepid*, paperback ed. (London: Sphere Books, 1977).

Mary E. Stuckey, *The President as Interpreter-in-Chief* (Chatham, N.J.: Chatham House Publishers, 1991).

Brian R. Sullivan, "'A Highly Commendable Action': William J. Donovan's Intelligence Mission for Mussolini and Roosevelt, December 1935—February 1936," *Intelligence and National Security*, vol. 7 (1991), no. 2.

Strobe Talbott, *The Master of the Game: Paul Nitze and the Nuclear Race*, paperback ed. (New York: Vintage Books, 1989).

Strobe Talbott, *The Russians and Reagan* (New York: Vintage Books, 1984).

Athan G. Theoharis and John Stuart Cox, *Boss: J. Edgar Hoover and the Great American Inquisition*, paperback ed. (New York: Bantam Books, 1990).

Edmund R. Thompson, "Intelligence at Yorktown," *Defense 81*, Sept. 1981.

Gregory F. Treverton, *Covert Action* (New York: Basic Books, 1987).

Thomas F. Troy, *Donovan and the CIA* (Washington, D.C.: CIA Center for the Study of Intelligence, 1981).

Stephen Vaughn, "Spies, National Security, and the 'Inertia Projector': The Secret Service Films of Ronald Reagan," *American Quarterly*, vol. 39 (1987), no. 3.

Douglas Waller, "The CIA's New Spies," *Newsweek*, April 12, 1993.

Geoffrey C. Ward, *Before the Trumpet: Young Franklin Roosevelt*, paperback ed. (New York: Harper & Row, 1986).

Geoffrey C. Ward, *A First-Class Temperament: The Emergence of Franklin Roosevelt*, paperback ed. (New York: HarperPerennial, 1990).

Wesley K. Wark, *The Ultimate Enemy: British Intelligence and Nazi Germany 1933–1939* (London: Tauris, 1985).

Kathryn Weathersby (ed.), "From the Russian Archives: New Findings on the Korean War," *Cold War International History Project Bulletin* (Washington, D.C.: Woodrow Wilson Center), Fall 1993.

Allen Weinstein, *Perjury: The Hiss-Chambers Case* (New York: Knopf, 1978).

Nigel West, *A Thread of Deceit: Espionage Myths of the Second World War*, paperback ed. (New York: Dell, 1986).

Theodore H. White, *Breach of Faith: The Fall of Richard Nixon* (London: Jonathan Cape, 1975).

Don Whitehead, *The FBI Story* (London: Frederic Muller, 1957).

Garry Wills, "Father Knows Best," *New York Review of Books*, Nov. 5, 1992.

Robin W. Winks, *Cloak and Gown* (New York: William Morrow, 1987).

James J. Wirtz, *The Tet Offensive* (Ithaca, N.Y.: Cornell University Press, 1991).

David Wise, *The American Police State* (New York: Random House, 1976).

David Wise, *Molehunt: The Secret Search for Traitors That Shattered the CIA* (New York: Random House, 1992).

Jules Witcover, *Sabotage at Black Tom: Imperial Germany's Secret War in America, 1914–1917* (Chapel Hill, N.C.: Algonquin Books, 1989).

Roberta Wohlstetter, *Pearl Harbor: Warning and Decision* (Stanford, Calif.: Stanford University Press, 1962).

Bob Woodward, *The Commanders*, paperback ed. (New York: Simon and Schuster, 1992).

Bob Woodward, *Veil: The Secret Wars of the CIA 1981–1987* (New York: Simon and Schuster, 1987).

R. James Woolsey, address to conference entitled "The Origins and Development of the CIA in the Administration of Harry S. Truman," March 17, 1994.

Peter Wyden, *Bay of Pigs* (London: Jonathan Cape, 1979).

Daniel Yergin, *Shattered Peace: The Origins of the Cold War and the National Security State* (Boston: Houghton Mifflin, 1977).

Mohammad Yousaf and Mark Adkin, *Bear Trap: Afghanistan's Untold Story* (London: Leo Cooper, 1992).

Philip Ziegler, *Wilson* (London: Weidenfeld and Nicolson, 1993).

INDEX